A-Z CARDIFF

CONTENTS

Key to Map Pages	2-3	Map Pages	6-120
Large Scale Cardiff City Centre	4-5	Index to Streets, Towns, Villages, Hospitals and selected Places of Interest	121-176

REFERENCE

Motorway M4

Proposed

A Road A48

Proposed

B Road B4562

Dual Carriageway

One-way Street
Traffic flow on A Roads is also indicated by a heavy line on the driver's left.

Restricted Access

Pedestrianized Road

Track / Footpath (selected)

Residential Walkway

Railway — Station, Level Crossing, Tunnel

Built-up Area — BRIAR CL.

Local Authority Boundary

National Boundary

National Park Boundary

Posttown Boundary

Postcode Boundary (within Posttown)

Map Continuation 15 — Large Scale City Centre 5

Airport

Car Park (selected)

Church or Chapel

Cycleway (selected)

Fire Station

Hospital

House Numbers (A & B Roads only) 13 8

Information Centre

National Grid Reference 320

Police Station

Post Office

Safety Camera with Speed Limit 30
Fixed cameras and long term road works cameras
Symbols do not indicate camera direction

Toilet: without facilities for the Disabled
with facilities for the Disabled

Viewpoint

Educational Establishment

Hospital or Healthcare Building

Industrial Building

Leisure or Recreational Facility

Place of Interest

Public Building

Shopping Centre or Market

Other Selected Buildings

SCALE

Map Pages 6-120 1:15,840

0 ¼ ½ Mile

0 250 500 750 Metres

4 inches (10.16 cm) to 1 mile 6.31 cm to 1 kilometre

Map Pages 4-5 1:7,920

0 ⅛ ¼ Mile

0 100 200 300 Metres

8 inches (20.32 cm) to 1 mile 12.63 cm to 1 kilometre

Copyright of Geographers' A-Z Map Company Limited

Fairfield Road, Borough Green, Sevenoaks, Kent TN15 8PP
Telephone: 01732 781000 (Enquiries & Trade Sales)
01732 783422 (Retail Sales)

www.a-zmaps.co.uk

Copyright © Geographers' A-Z Map Co. Ltd.

Edition 4 2009

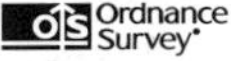

This product includes mapping data licensed from Ordnance Survey® with the permission of the Controller of Her Majesty's Stationery Office.

© Crown Copyright 2008. All rights reserved. Licence number 100017302

Safety camera information supplied by www.PocketGPSWorld.com
Speed Camera Location Database Copyright 2008 © PocketGPSWorld.com

2
BRECON BEACONS NATIONAL PARK
MERTHYR TYDFIL
(Merthyr Tudful)
TREDEGAR
ABERTILLERY
(Abertyleri)
Aberdare
(Aberdar)
Mountain Ash
(Aberpennar)
RHONDDA
St.Gwynno Forest
Abercynon
Blackwood
(Coed Duon)
Newbridge
(Cefn Bychan)
River Taff
Ebbw River
Rhymney River
Sirhowy River
A465
A470
A469
A4046
A467
B4246
B4276
A4059
B4275
A4233
A4054
A4048
B4263
B4471
B4251
A472
A4061
B4224
B4254
B4273
A4058
A4093
A4119
B4451
B4280
A473
M4
A4222
A48
B4270
A4226
B4268
B4265
Glyncoch
14
15
PONTYPRIDD
Crosskeys
16
17
Risca
Abertridwr
Bedwas
Machen
Rhydyfelin
24
25
26
27
28
29
30
31
32
33
Treforest
Penyrheol
CAERPHILLY
(Caerffili)
Lower Machen
Church Village
Nantgarw
Gwaun-y-bara
40
41
42
43
44
45
46
47
48
49
50
51
Beddau
Llantrisant
Taff's Well
Thornhill
CARDIFF GATE
64
65
66
67
68
69
70
71
72
73
74
75
Pencoed
INSET PAGE 78
Talbot Green
Creigiau
Pentyrch
Llanishen
Rhiwbina
Pentwyn
St. Mellons
35
34
32
30
29
29a
33
Llanharry
Pontyclun
CARDIFF WEST
Radyr
Whitchurch
Birchgrove
Cyncoed
Rumney
78
79
80
81
82
83
84
85
86
87
88
89
Llandaff
Roath
Tremorfa
Canton
COWBRIDGE
(Y Bont-Faen)
Ely River
92
93
94
95
96
97
Caerau
CARDIFF
(Caerdydd)
90
91
Llanblethian
(Llanfleiddan)
Grangetown
98
99
100
101
102
103
Wenvoe
Llandough
(Llandoch)
Dinas Powys
Penarth
104
105
106
107
108
109
Colcot
Palmerstown
Cosmeston
Llantwit Major
(Llanilltud Fawr)
St. Athan
(Sain Tathan)
CARDIFF INTERNATIONAL AIRPORT
BARRY (Barri)
Sully
110
111
112
113
114
115
116
117
118
119
120
Rhoose
(Y Rhws)
Barry Island
(Ynys y Barri)
BRISTOL CHANNEL
(MÔR HAFREN)

KEY TO MAP PAGES *Allwedd i Dudalennau'r Map*

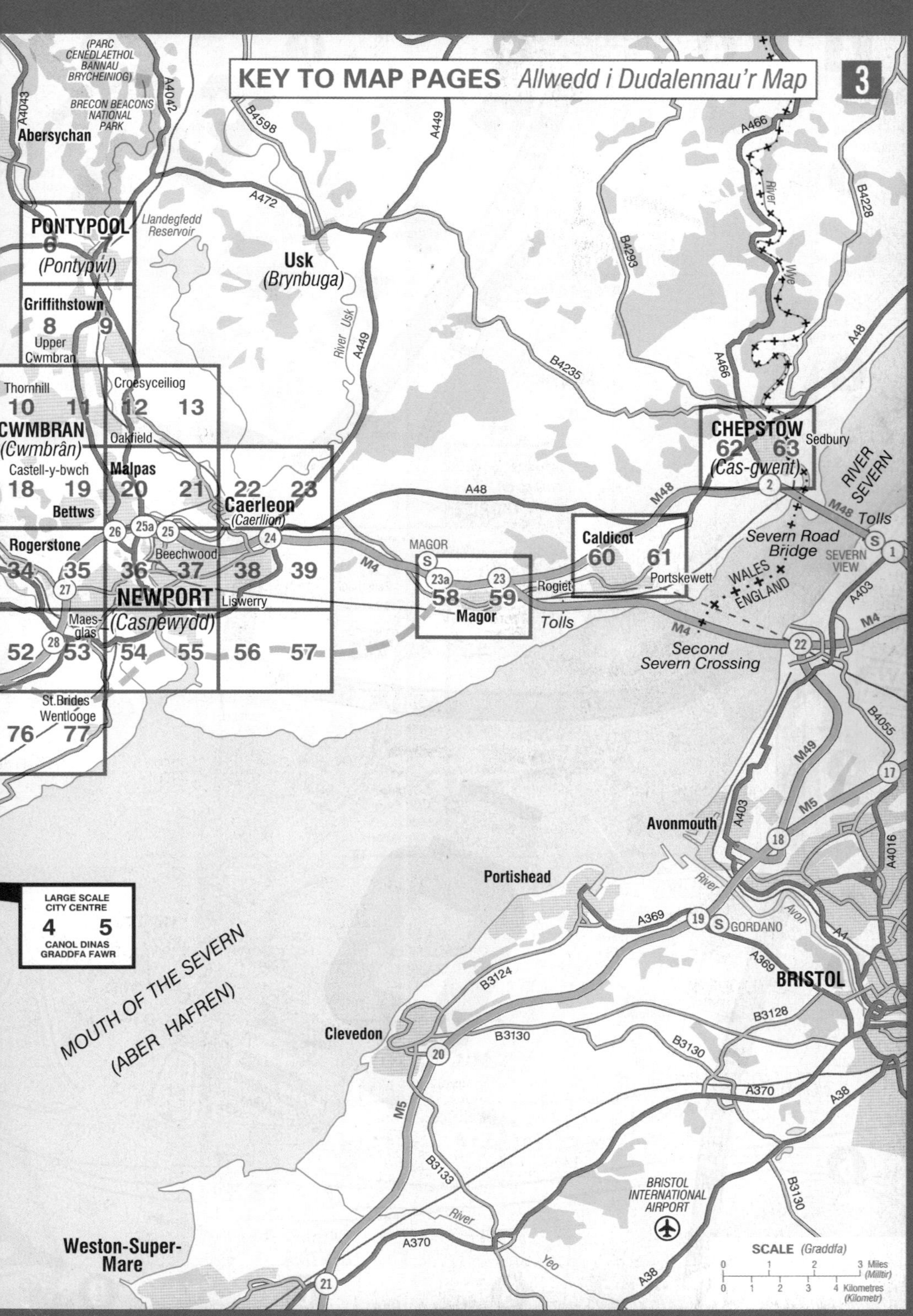

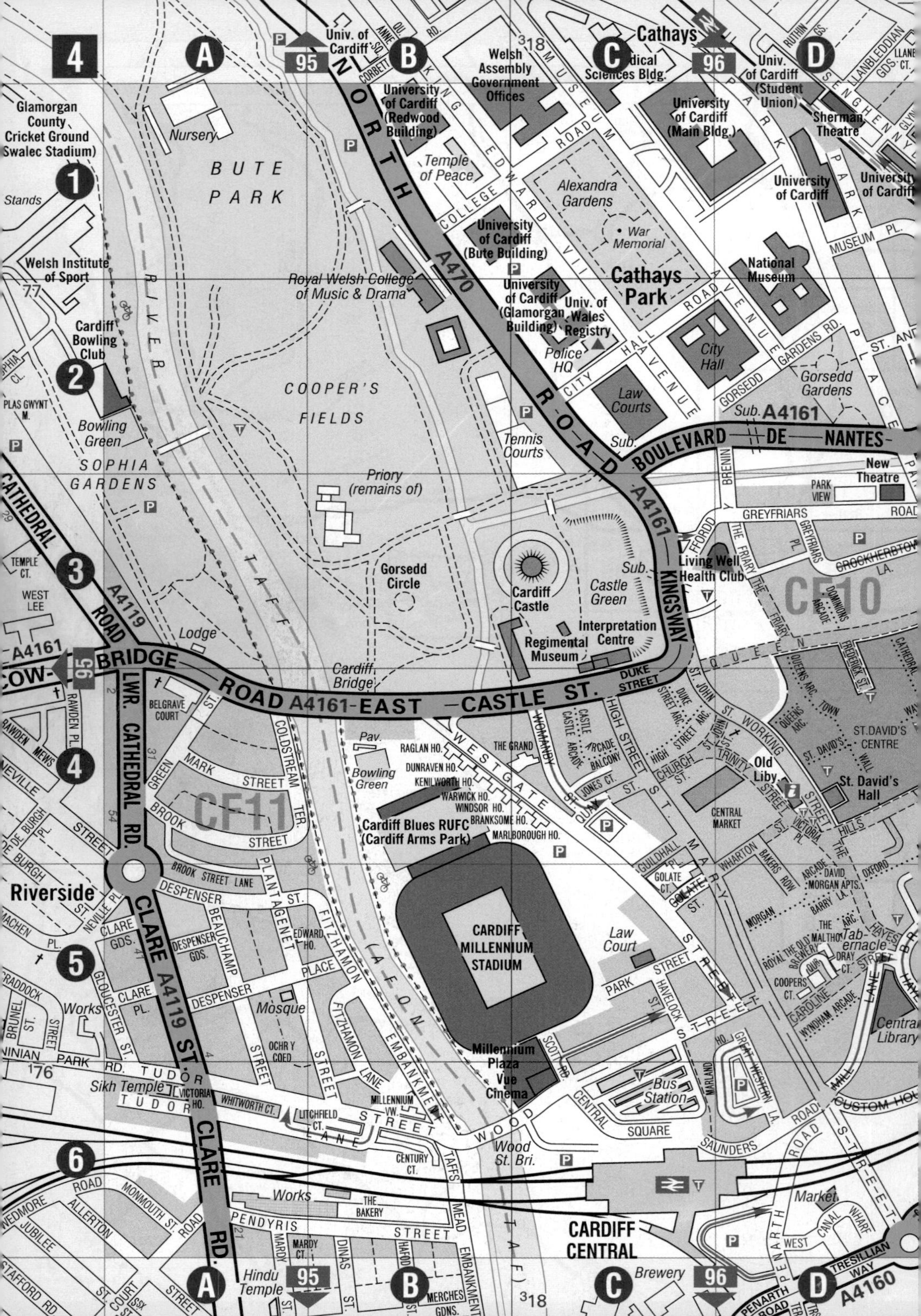
A
B
C
D
1
2
3
4
5
6
95
96
318
Univ. of Cardiff
Cathays
Medical Sciences Bldg.
Welsh Assembly Government Offices
Univ. of Cardiff (Student Union)
Glamorgan County Cricket Ground (Swalec Stadium)
Stands
Nursery
BUTE PARK
NORTH ROAD
A470
University of Cardiff (Redwood Building)
Temple of Peace
University of Cardiff (Main Bldg.)
Sherman Theatre
University of Cardiff
Alexandra Gardens
War Memorial
MUSEUM ROAD
KING EDWARD VII
COLLEGE
PARK PLACE
MUSEUM PL.
National Museum
University of Cardiff (Bute Building)
University of Cardiff (Glamorgan Building)
Univ. of Wales Registry
Cathays Park
Welsh Institute of Sport
Royal Welsh College of Music & Drama
RIVER TAFF
Cardiff Bowling Club
Police HQ
City Hall
CITY HALL ROAD
GORSEDD GARDENS RD.
Gorsedd Gardens
Law Courts
COOPER'S FIELDS
Bowling Green
SOPHIA GARDENS
PLAS GWYNT M.
Tennis Courts
A4161
BOULEVARD DE NANTES
New Theatre
PARK VIEW
GREYFRIARS ROAD
Priory (remains of)
CATHEDRAL ROAD
TEMPLE CT.
WEST LEE
Gorsedd Circle
Cardiff Castle
Castle Green
Living Well Health Club
KINGSWAY
CF10
Interpretation Centre
Regimental Museum
Lodge
A4119
COWBRIDGE ROAD
A4161 EAST
CASTLE ST.
DUKE STREET
QUEEN ST.
ST. DAVID'S CENTRE
St. David's Hall
Cardiff Bridge
BELGRAVE COURT
RAWDEN PL.
RAWDEN MEWS
NEVILLE ST.
LWR. CATHEDRAL RD.
MARK STREET
BROOK STREET
CF11
COLDSTREAM TER.
Pav.
Bowling Green
THE GRAND
WESTGATE STREET
WOMANBY
CASTLE ARCADE
HIGH STREET
CHURCH ST.
ST. JOHN ST.
WORKING STREET
Old Liby.
RAGLAN HO.
DUNRAVEN HO.
KENILWORTH HO.
WARWICK HO.
WINDSOR HO.
BRANKSOME HO.
MARLBOROUGH HO.
Cardiff Blues RUFC (Cardiff Arms Park)
JONES CT.
QUAY ST.
CENTRAL MARKET
DE BURGH ST.
Riverside
BROOK STREET LANE
DESPENSER ST.
PLANTAGENET
FITZHAMON EMBANKMENT
CARDIFF MILLENNIUM STADIUM
GUILDHALL PL.
GOLATE CT.
GOLATE ST.
ST. MARY STREET
WHARTON ST.
BAKERS ROW
MORGAN ARCADE
DAVID MORGAN APTS.
BARRY LA.
CLARE GDS.
CLARE RD.
A4119
EDWARD HO.
DESPENSER GDS.
BEAUCHAMP
PLACE
Law Court
PARK STREET
HAVELOCK ST.
ROYAL ARC.
THE OLD BREWERY
THE MALTHOUSE
Tabernacle
CAROLINE ST.
WYNDHAM ARCADE
MILL LANE
Central Library
MACHEN PL.
CLARE PL.
DESPENSER
Mosque
GLOUCESTER ST.
Works
BRUNEL ST.
CRADDOCK ST.
NINIAN PARK RD.
176
TUDOR
Sikh Temple
VICTORIA HO.
WHITWORTH CT.
OCHR Y COED
FITZHAMON LANE
MILLENNIUM VW.
LITCHFIELD CT.
TUDOR STREET
TUDOR LANE
Millennium Plaza Vue Cinema
SCOTT RD.
CENTRAL SQUARE
Bus Station
WOOD STREET
Wood St. Bri.
MARLAND HO.
GREAT WESTERN LA.
SAUNDERS ROAD
CUSTOM HOUSE ST.
CENTURY CT.
TAFFS MEAD EMBANKMENT
Works
THE BAKERY
PENDYRIS STREET
MARDY ST.
MARDY CT.
HAFOD ST.
DINAS ST.
CARDIFF CENTRAL
Market
CANAL WHARF
WEST CANAL
PENARTH ROAD
TRESILLIAN WAY
A4160
Brewery
MERCHES GDNS.
Hindu Temple
ALLERTON ST.
MONMOUTH ST.
JUBILEE
STAFFORD RD.
COURT
CLARE ST.

E
F
G
H
5
96
19
1
2
3
4
5
6
176
147
77
16
31
MISKIN
LOWTHER RD.
SALISBURY ST.
LOWTHER CT.
CRANBROOK STREET
GORDON ROAD
RICHMOND ROAD
RICHMOND CRES.
BEDFORD ST.
RUSSELL ST.
TAVISTOCK ST.
South Wales Baptist College
Mosque
LLANTWIT ST.
SENGHENYDD PL.
SENGHENYDD ROAD
SENGHENYDD HALL
SENGHENYDD COURT
GORDON HALL
PARK GROVE
PRINCES CT.
ST. ANDREW'S PLACE
ST. ANDREW'S CRESCENT
ST. ANDREW'S LA.
STUTTGARTER STRASSE
DUMFRIES PL.
PARK PLACE
WINDSOR PLACE
WINDSOR LA.
PARK LANE
CITY ROAD
B4261
PENLLINE ST.
PENFORD CT.
Buddhist Cen.
BEDFORD STREET
TALWORTH ST.
BYRON ST.
MILTON ST.
SHAKESPEARE CT.
SHAKESPEARE ST.
SHELLEY WALK
CLIVE PL.
DYLAN PL.
PLWYD RD.
HARDY PL.
CROFT ST.
QUAIL CT.
GROUSE ST.
ELM STREET LA.
ST. PARTRIDGE
ELM STREET
ELM STREET LANE
TEAL ST.
WILLOW CT.
LYNWOOD CT.
ELMWOOD CT.
ASHWOOD CT.
NORWOOD CT.
PARTRIDGE LA.
UPP. CLIFTON ST.
CLIFTON HO.
Lib.
FOUR ELMS ROAD
B4487
St. Peter's RC Prim. Sch.
WORDSWORTH AVENUE
COWPER PL.
Taibah Sch.
WOODLAND PL.
RODEN CT.
SOUTHEY STREET
VERE ST.
CASTLE LANE
OXFORD LANE
OXFORD ST.
PASCALL CT.
ST. PETER'S STREET
YMCA
RICHMOND CT.
School
Coleg Glan Hafren
WEST GROVE
EAST GROVE
WALK
PARADE
The Academy
Comm. Cen.
Hindu Temple
WEST GRO. CT.
TRINITY CT.
THE WALK
THE GROVE
BURGES HO.
STEPHENSON CT.
FOUR ELMS CT.
LONGCROSS CT.
A4161
NEWPORT ROAD
CF24
ORBIT STREET
GOLD ST.
PIERCEFIELD PL.
METAL ST.
SILVER ST.
SYSTEM ST.
STAR ST.
SUN ST.
Adamsdown Primary School
GLOSSOP RD.
LONGCROSS STREET
METEOR STREET
PLANET STREET
COMET STREET
ECLIPSE ST.
CONSTELLATION STREET
ORION CT.
KNIGHT CT.
GALSTON ST.
Prim. Sch.
ADMIRAL HO.
HOWARD PL.
HOWARD GDS.
HOWARD TER.
NEWPORT ROAD LANE
HOSP.
GLOSSOP TER.
TERRACE
University of Wales Institute Cardiff
WINDSOR CT.
AUGUSTA ST.
MOIRA ST.
MOIRA PLACE
STREET
University of Cardiff (Trevithick & Queen's Buildings)
FITZALAN COURT
FITZALAN RD.
FITZALAN PL.
A4160
KNOX ROAD
SANDON RD.
SANDON PL.
Mag. Court
Cemetery Gardens
MOIRA TERRACE
ADAMS COURT
NEWTON COURT
NORTH LUTON PL.
SOUTH LUTON PL.
W. LUTON PL.
TY'R YSGOL
WINDSOR MEWS
ADAMSDOWN SQ.
ADAMSDOWN SQUARE
ADAMSDOWN PLACE
KAMES PLACE
GARESFIELD ST.
CLYDE ST.
LEOPD ST.
CARDIFF QUEEN ST.
Offs.
CAPITOL
STATION TERRACE
CHURCHILL WAY
CHARLES ST.
DEN ROCHE PL.
WESLEY
NORTH EDWARD ST.
EDWARD ST.
LANDMARK PL.
Cardiff
WESLEY LANE
RC Cathedral
BARRACKS LA.
ST. DAVID'S LINK
FREDERICK ST.
DAVID ST.
LITTLE FREDERICK ST.
LOVE LA.
GUILDFORD ST.
GUILDFORD CR.
SANDON STREET
HMP CARDIFF
WINDSOR ROAD
Warehouses
ORIEL HOUSE
ADAMSCROFT PLACE
THARSIS CL.
DAVIS ST.
Adamsdown
CUMNOCK PL.
CUMNOCK ST.
KINGARTH ST.
ADAMSDOWN PL.
FFORDD OTTWY
SANQUAHAR ST.
SPRUCE CL.
APPLEWOOD CL.
E. TYNDALL ST.
KEEN RD.
Cardiff International Arena
MARY ANN STREET
MILLICENT ST.
Cineworld Cin.
TREDEGAR ST.
University of Glamorgan
TA Centre
MORGAN ST.
GARTH ST.
DUFFRYN ST.
TAFF ST.
PELLETT ST.
Depots
TY PONT HAEARN
ADAM ST.
CENTRAL LINK
A4234
Depot
BAY CLOSE
EAST BAY CLOSE
GUEST RD.
OCEAN WAY
TYNDALL STREET
ROSEMARY ST.
ELLEN STREET
Warehouses
BUTE TER.
ALTOLUSSO
TYNDALL STREET INDUSTRIAL ESTATE
ROLAND ST.
SCHOONER WAY
HOWARD CT.
KEYES CT.
CITY WHARF
NELSON CT.
ATLANTIC WHARF
JELLICOE CT.
ANSON CT.
BEAUFORT CT.
BLAKE CT.
BEATTY CT.
YORK CT.
Atlantic Wharf
EARL CUNNINGHAM CT.
Wks.
EAST WHARF RD.
PARKLANDS INDUSTRIAL ESTATE
TRIDENT CT.
EAST MOORS RD.
MOORS
Welsh National Ten. Cen.
Works
CENTRE TRADING ESTATE
SCHOOL ST.
JOHN ST.
ST. TYNDALL
COLUMBUS WALK
BRIGANTINE PL.
RALEIGH WALK
DRAKE WALK
SPILLERS & BAKERS
ANCHOR CT.
LANSANNOR DR.
MERVINIAN CL.
PLACE
BUTE ST.
HERBERT
LLOYD GEORGE AV.
CALLAGHAN SQUARE
HOPE ST.
EDWARD ENGLAND WHARF
SORRENTO HO.
MESSINA HO.
ROXBY CT.
THORNABY CT.
CANAL PDE.
Prim. Sch.
Atlantic Wharf (Disused)
TEMPLAR INDUSTRIAL

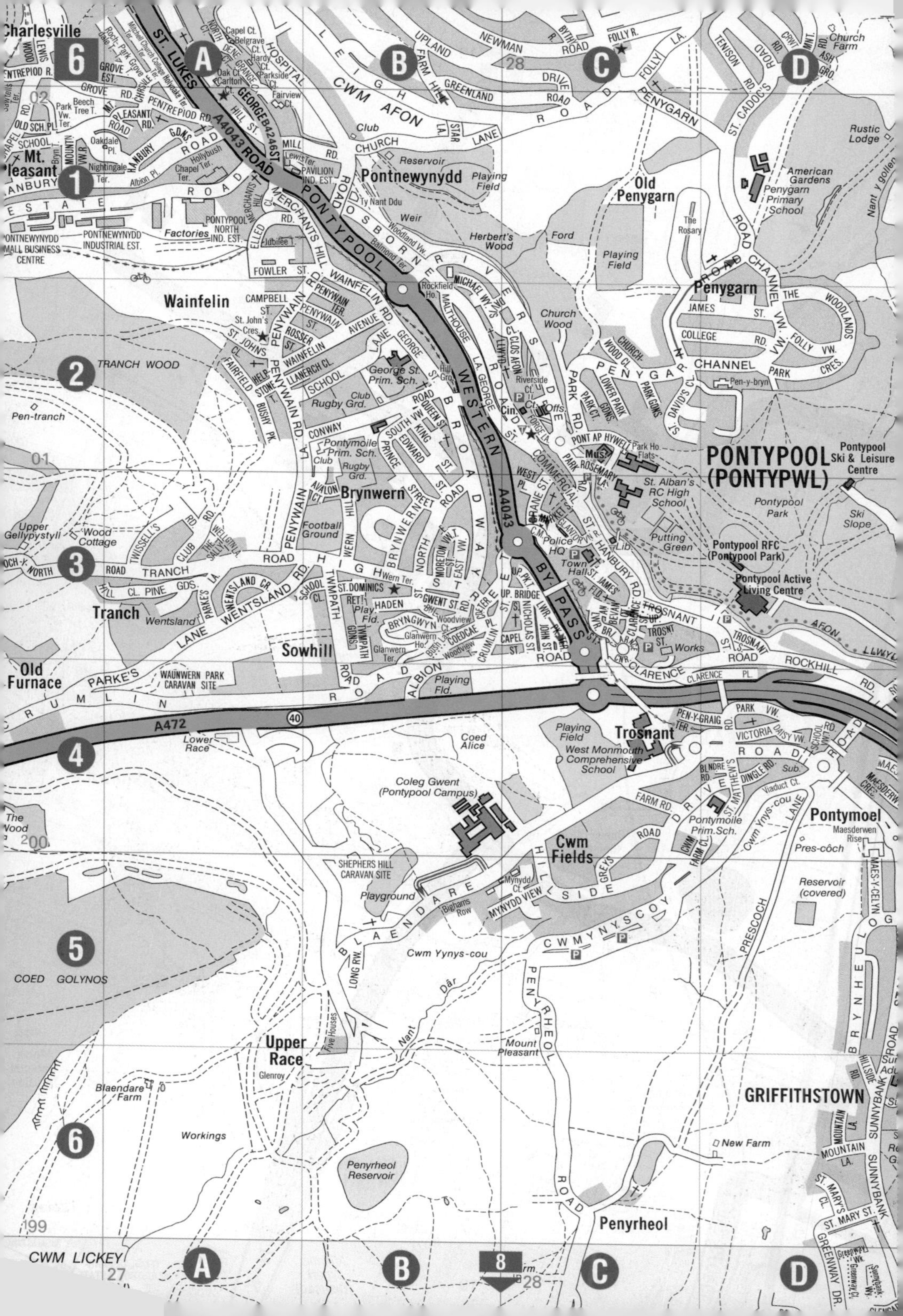
6
Charlesville
A
B
C
D
ST. LUKES
NORTH DENE CT.
Capel Ct.
Belgrave Ct.
Hardy Ct.
Parkside Ct.
Oak Ct.
Carlton Ct.
GRANGE
GEORGE HILL ST.
HOSPITAL
Fairview Ct.
LEIGH
UPLAND FARM HILL
NEWMAN ROAD
GREENLAND ROAD
BYTHY R.
FOLLY R.
FOLLY LA.
DRIVE
28
CWM AFON
PENYGARN
TENISON ROAD
CRWYS RD.
MNT. ASH GRO.
Church Farm
ST. CADOC'S
Rustic Lodge
LEWIS TER.
WOOD
ENTREPIOD R.
GROVE EST.
GROVE RD.
02
Park Vw. Ter.
Beech Tree T.
PENTREPIOD RD.
OLD SCH. PL.
SCHOOL
Mt. Pleasant
HANBURY
Oakdale Pl.
Nightingale Ter.
Hollybush Chapel Ter.
Albion Pl.
ROAD
A4043 ROAD
B4246 ST.
Club
CHURCH
MILL RD.
Lewis Ter.
PAVILION IND. EST.
STAR LA.
LANE
Reservoir
Pontnewynydd
Playing Field
Old Penygarn
American Gardens
Penygarn Primary School
1
ESTATE
PONTNEWYNYDD SMALL BUSINESS CENTRE
PONTNEWYNYDD INDUSTRIAL EST.
Factories
PONTYPOOL NORTH IND. EST.
MERCHANTS HILL
PONTYPOOL
OSBORNE RD.
Ty Nant Ddu
Weir
Woodland Vw.
Balmond Ter.
Herbert's Wood
Ford
The Rosary
Playing Field
ROAD CHANNEL
ELLED RD.
Jubilee T.
FOWLER ST.
WAINFELIN RD.
Rockfield Ho.
MICHAEL WY.
RIVERSIDE
Church Wood
Penygarn
THE WOODLANDS
JAMES ST.
COLLEGE RD.
FOLLY VW.
Wainfelin
CAMPBELL ST.
St. John's Cres.
PENYWAIN TER.
AVENUE
MALTHOUSE LA.
CLOS AFON
LLWYD CL.
CHURCH WOOD CL.
PENYGAR CHANNEL
PARK CRES.
Pen-y-bryn
2
TRANCH WOOD
ST. JOHNS CL.
FAIRFIELD
HELPSTONE
ROSSER ST.
WAINFELIN
LLANERCH CL.
SCHOOL
GEORGE ST.
George St. Prim. Sch.
Hill Gro.
WESTERN
BROADWAY
Riverside Ct.
PARK RD.
LOWER PARK GDNS.
PARK GDNS.
PARK CT.
ST. DAVID'S CL.
Pen-tranch
BUSHY PK.
PENYWAIN RD.
Club
Rugby Grd.
CONWAY
QUEEN ST.
SOUTH VW.
KING
EDWARD
PRINCE
Cin.
Offs.
FORGE LA.
PONT AP HYWEL
Park Ho. Flats
Mus.
PONTYPOOL (PONTYPWL)
Pontypool Ski & Leisure Centre
01
Pontymoile Prim. Sch.
Club
Rugby Grd.
A4043
COMMERCIAL
ROSEMARY LA.
PARK
WEST PL.
St. Alban's RC High School
Pontypool Park
AVALON CT.
Brynwern
STREET ROAD
Ski Slope
Upper Gellypystyll
Wood Cottage
TWISSELL'S
CLUB RD.
WELLINGTON LA.
THE SALLY
Football Ground
WERN HILL
BRYNWERN
NORTH ST.
MORETON VW. T.
EAST VW.
CRANE ST.
MARKET ST.
GLANTORVYN R.
C.M.
Police HQ
Town Hall
Lib.
Putting Green
Pontypool RFC (Pontypool Park)
3
NORTH
ROAD
TRANCH
HILL CL.
PINE GDS.
PARKE'S LA.
WENTSLAND CR.
WENTSLAND RD.
SCHOOL CL.
TWMPATH
ST. DOMINICS
HIGH STREET
Wern Ter.
RETT.
HADEN
GWENT ST. RD.
Play. Fld.
BRYNGWYN
Glanwern Ho.
Woodview Ct.
COEDCAE
CRUMLIN PL.
CATER ST.
UP. PKT.
UP. BRIDGE
NICHOLAS ST.
LWR.
JOHN ST.
BY-PASS
ST. JAMES' FLD.
HANBURY RD.
TROSNANT ST.
Pontypool Active Living Centre
Tranch
Wentsland
LANE
TWMPATH GDNS.
Glanwern Ter.
Woodview
CAPEL ST.
ROAD
BEVAN
CLARENCE ST.
TROSNT ST.
Works
TROSNANT
AFON LLWYD
Old Furnace
PARKE'S
WAUNWERN PARK CARAVAN SITE
Sowhill
ROAD
ALBION
Playing Fld.
CLARENCE
CLARENCE PL.
ROCKHILL RD.
CRUMLIN
ROAD
A472
40
Playing Field
Trosnant
PEN-Y-GRAIG TER.
PARK VW.
VICTORIA
DAISY VW.
SCHOOL RD.
ROAD
4
Lower Race
Coed Alice
West Monmouth Comprehensive School
ROAD
BLNDRE RD.
DRIVE
ST. MATTHEW'S
DINGLE RD.
Sub.
MAESDERWEN CRES.
Coleg Gwent (Pontypool Campus)
FARM RD.
Viaduct Ct.
Pontymoile Prim.Sch.
Pontymoel
Maesderwen Rise
The Wood
200
Cwm Fields
ROAD
Cwm Ynys-cou LANE
Pres-côch
SHEPHERS HILL CARAVAN SITE
CWM FARM CT.
GREYS
HILLSIDE
MAES-Y-CELYN
Playground
Mynydd Ct.
BLAENDARE
Bighams Row
MYNYDD VIEW
CWMYNYSCOY
PRESCOCH
Reservoir (covered)
5
COED GOLYNOS
LONG RW.
Cwm Ynys-cou
CWMYNYSCOY
PENYRHEOL
BRYNHEULOG
Dâr
Nant
Five Houses
Upper Race
Mount Pleasant
Glenroy
HILLSIDE RD.
SUNNYBANK
Blaendare Farm
GRIFFITHSTOWN
6
Workings
New Farm
MOUNTAIN LA.
MOUNTAIN
SUNNYBANK
Penyrheol Reservoir
ROAD
ST. MARY'S CL.
Penyrheol
ST. MARY ST.
199
GREENWAY DR.
Greenway Wk.
CWM LICKEY
27
8
28
Sunnybank Wy.

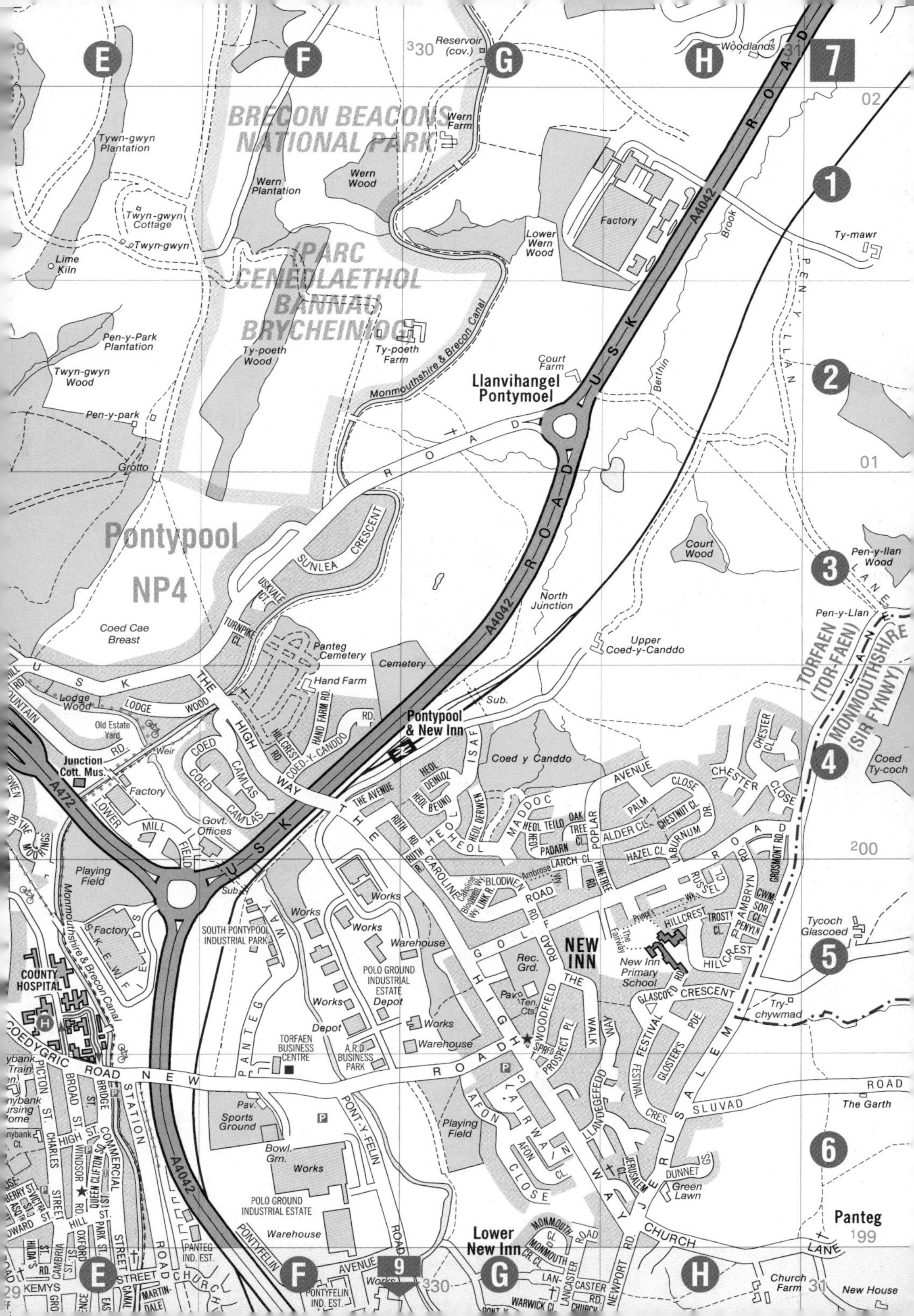

7
E
F
G
H
330
31
Reservoir (cov.)
Woodlands
02
BRECON BEACONS NATIONAL PARK
(PARC CENEDLAETHOL BANNAU BRYCHEINIOG)
Wern Farm
Tywn-gwyn Plantation
Wern Plantation
Wern Wood
Twyn-gwyn Cottage
Twyn-gwyn
Lime Kiln
Lower Wern Wood
Factory
A4042
USK ROAD
Brook
Ty-mawr
PEN-Y-LLAN
1
Pen-y-Park Plantation
Twyn-gwyn Wood
Ty-poeth Wood
Ty-poeth Farm
Monmouthshire & Brecon Canal
Court Farm
Llanvihangel Pontymoel
Berthin
2
Pen-y-park
ROAD
Grotto
01
Pontypool
NP4
SUNLEA CRESCENT
USKVALE CT.
TURNPIKE CL.
Coed Cae Breast
Court Wood
North Junction
Pen-y-llan Wood
3
LANE
Pen-y-Llan
Upper Coed-y-Canddo
TORFAEN (TOR-FAEN)
MONMOUTHSHIRE (SIR FYNWY)
Panteg Cemetery
Cemetery
Hand Farm
USK RD.
MOUNTAIN
Lodge Wood
LODGE
WOOD
THE HIGH WAY
HAND FARM RD.
HILLCREST RD.
COED-Y-CANDDO RD.
Sub.
Pontypool & New Inn
Old Estate Yard
Weir
RD.
Junction Cott. Mus.
A472
Factory
COED
CAMLAS
LOWER MILL FIELD
Govt. Offices
ISAF
Coed y Canddo
AVENUE
CHESTER CL.
CHESTER CLOSE
CLOSE
4
Coed Ty-coch
HEOL DEINIOL
HEOL BEUNO
THE AVENUE
HEOL DERWEN
MADDOC
PALM
CHESTNUT CL.
HEOL TEILO
OAK TREE CL.
POPLAR
ALDER CL.
LABURNUM DR.
PADARN
RUTH RD.
RUTH
CAROLINE
HEOL
ROAD
HAZEL CL.
LARCH CL.
PINETREE
CROSMONT RD.
200
THE MOORINGS
Playing Field
Sub.
Works
Caroline Bldwen Wy.
LINK R.
BLODWEN ROAD
Ambrose Wk.
RUSSEL CL.
AMBRYN RD.
CWM. SOR CL.
Prince's Wk.
The Fairway
HILLCREST
TROSTY CL.
PENYLIN
Tycoch Glascoed
Monmouthshire & Brecon Canal
Factory
SKEW FIELDS
SOUTH PONTYPOOL INDUSTRIAL PARK
PANTEG WAY
Warehouse
GOLF RD.
NEW INN
New Inn Primary School
HILLCREST
GLASCOED RD.
5
COUNTY HOSPITAL
POLO GROUND INDUSTRIAL ESTATE
Depot
Rec. Grd.
Pav.
Ten. Cts.
THE WALK
WOODFIELD ROAD
GLASCOED CRESCENT
Try-chywmad
COEDYGRIC ROAD
Depot
Works
Warehouse
TORFAEN BUSINESS CENTRE
A.R.D. BUSINESS PARK
HIGH
PROSPECT PL.
SPRFD.
WAY
FESTIVAL PDE
JERUSALEM
Picton St.
BROAD ST.
BRIDGE ST.
STATION
NEW ROAD
ROAD
CLAIRWAIN
FESTIVAL CRES
GLOSTER'S
SLUVAD
ROAD
The Garth
Pav. Sports Ground
PONT-Y-FELIN
Playing Field
AFON
AFON CL.
LLANDEGFEDD WAY
CHARLES STREET
HIGH ST.
COMMERCIAL
WINDSOR RD.
QUEEN CLIFTON
Bowl. Grn.
Works
CLOSE
CL.
JERUSALEM CL.
DUNNET GS.
Green Lawn
6
BERRY ST.
VICTRIA ST.
ASOLD
HOWARD
HILL
OXFORD ST.
PARK ST.
STREET
ROAD
A4042
POLO GROUND INDUSTRIAL ESTATE
PONTYFELIN
Warehouse
ROAD
Lower New Inn
MONMOUTH CL.
MONMOUTH CR. CL.
ROAD
NEWPORT RD.
CHURCH
LANE
Panteg
199
HILDA'S
CAMBRIA ST.
ST. RD.
PANTEG IND. EST.
AVENUE
9
Works
LAN-
LANCASTER
29
KEMYS
STREET
CANAL
MARTIN-DALE
CHURCH
PONTYFELIN IND. EST.
330
WARWICK CL.
CASTER RD.
CHURCH
Church Farm
31
New House

27
28
A
B
C
D
6
Penyrheol
Reservoir
Penyrheol
ROAD
ST. MARY'S CL.
ST. MARY ST.
SUNNYB.
99
CWM LICKEY
(CWM LLEUCU)
Hill Farm
GRIFFITHSTOWN
1
Cwm Lickey
Pond
CWRDY
ROAD
LANE
CWRDY
Cwrdy
Wood
ST. AUGUSTINE RD.
ST. ANTHONY'S CL.
ST. AUGUSTINE RD.
ST. BENEDICT CL.
GREENWAY
MAPLE
ROWAN
SPRING TER.
ASHGROVE
CLOSE
SYCAMORE RD.
ROAD
ROAD
SOUTH
WEST
AV.
AVENUE
2
White
House
Cefn-llwyd
The
Bungalow
Ysgubor-
goed
SPRINGFIELD
SYCAMORE
ROAD
SOUTH
MAPLE CRES.
KEMEYS
FAWR CL.
HAWTHORN
Kemys
Fawr
Inf. Sch.
Whitehall
MYNYDD TWYN - GLAS
Pontypool
NP4
198
Capel-llwyd
OAKLANDS
MAPLE
BEECH
WELLFIELD
RD.
LA.
SOUTH
Oaklands
Quarries
(dis.)
3
Uplands
Wain Hywel
Little
Greenmeadow
Farm
Mountain
Farm
Monmouthshire & Bre
Bryn
Tunnel
PONTNEWYDD
GOLF COURSE
Yewtree
Wren's Nest
Farm
COED GWAUN-Y-FFEIRIAD
4
Glyn Bran
Cottage
Maes-gwyn
MOUNTAIN
Blaen Bran
Reservoirs
Weir
Mine Slope
Cottages
FIVE
LOCKS
97
GREENFIELD
CL.
Upper Cwmbran
Pencoed
Cwm Bran
Five Locks
Club
House
Blaen
Bran
UPPER
CWMBRAN
ROAD
TY PWCA
ROAD
LOCKS
MAESGWYN
CL.
PENYPARC
Severn Vw.
TRAM
ROAD
BETHEL LA.
Coed
Gwern-Esgob
Works
5
The
Square
THORNHILL
CL.
Playing
Field
RHIW
MELIN
Heol
Newydd
MAENDY
PL.
YSGOL
PWCA
PL.
TY
MYNYDD
WENTWORTH
Weir
ROAD
FIVE
TY TRAPPA
MEADOWBROOK
BEECH CL.
PARC
CROWN AV.
Graig
Vw.
The
Hawthorns
LAUREL WLK.
MAENDY PL.
HEOL
CADOC R.
MAEN
WAUN HYWEL
DINGLE LA.
TRAPPA
GLENSIDE
CL.
Rec.
Grd.
Football
Ground
Lowlands
Penywaun
Farm
Resr.
(covered)
SYCAMORE
LAUREL GRN.
GREENWOOD AV.
Celyn Ct.
NANT
CELYN CL.
BARNFIELD PL.
RD.
MOUNT
GILWERN PL.
GOVILON PL.
PARFITT
PLEASANT
Rec. Grd.
Bellevue
Woodlands
Community
Primary
School
COED
Chestnut Grn.
Maendy Sq.
PWCA
MAENDY
WOOD
RISE
Gorse
House
OLDBRIDGE
CT.
HAFOD CT.
CEDAR
WALK
GREENWOOD
CENTRAL
CHANNEL
VIEW
ADIT WLK.
THE RISE
HILLTOP GRN.
BRYNCELYN
PL.
MAINDEE
TER.
PLEASANT
Gelli-gravog
BAGLEY
ARAN
CL.
GREENWOOD
THE LEAS
CELYN
Pontnewydd
Prim. Sch.
Pontnewydd
Prim. Sch.
The Graigs
HAFOD
CAM CT.
RD.
BANWLL
CT.
HAFOD
DORLEIGH
ROAD
ARAN
COURT
BROAD
VIEW
West
Pontnewydd
6
TAFF CT.
BERKELEY CT.
MARL COURT
WIMBORNE
RISE
THE BIRCHES
BRYN
COED
CAE
CHURCH
PADDOCK CL.
Garn-Wen
Park
House
Farm
TERN
THE
Football
Ground
Church Wood
CHURCH WOOD RD.
HILLSIDE CT.
BOX
96
RHYMNEY
CT.
HAFREN
DERFEL CT.
THORNHILL
CWMBRAN
(CWMBRÂN)
TRINITY
W
A
Y
TY
Church
Wood
Hillside
Cottage
Graig Fawr
Subway
Brook
10
11
TY BOX RD.
MAENDY
Thornhill
Works
Church Wood
Graig
CRAIG

9
Panteg
Lower New Inn
Pont-y-felin
Griffithstown
Griffithstown Railway Mus.
Sebastopol
Cwmbran NP44
Pontrhydyrun
Pontnewydd
Northville
Cwmbran
Croesyceiliog
A4042
A4051
CROESYCEILIOG BY-PASS
CWMBRAN DRIVE
NEWPORT ROAD
CHAPEL LANE
AVONDALE RD.
AVONDALE ROAD
PONTRHYDYRUN RD.
CHURCH LANE
TRE-HERBERT ROAD
NORTH ROAD
EDLOGAN WAY
GREENHILL ROAD
SOUTH STREET
LANSDOWNE ROAD
CHURCH WOOD ROAD
STATION STREET
COMMERCIAL ST.
ST. DAVID'S RD.
RD. AFON
POLO GROUND INDUSTRIAL ESTATE
PONTYFELIN IND. EST.
PANTEG IND. EST.
AVONDALE BUSINESS PARK
LYN PAC TRADING EST.
Panteg Steel Works
Chemical Disposal Works
Butcher's Wood
Craig-y-felin Wood
Coed y Gwaelod
Coed Tre-Herbert
Garw Wood
Greater Gwent Crematorium
GREENMEADOW GOLF COURSE
TORFEAN (TOR-FAEN)
MONMOUTHSHIRE (SIR FYNWY)
Race Farm
Club House
Driving Range
Ty-Cadno
Coed-y-gwaelod
Ty-côch
Church Farm
New House
Coed-Llwyd Farm
Coed Llwyd Bungalow
Hen Eglwys Farm
Cwm-heron Wood
Pontrhydyrun House
Wren's Nest
Tir-brychiad
Weir
Playing Field
Football Ground
Rugby Football Grd.
Esporta Health & Fitness
St. David's RC Jun & Inf. Sch.
Croesyceiliog North Road Inf. Sch.
Edlogan Sq.
Timber Yard
Works
Depot
School
Panteg House
George Lansbury Home
Tennis Courts
Bowling Green
Canal
E
F
G
H
1
2
3
4
5
6
7
11
12
29
330
31
96
97
198
99

10
Garn-Wen
Hillside Cottage
Thornhill
Graig Fawr
Greenmeadow Community Farm
Greenmeadow Wood
Pen-llan-gwyn
Greenmeadow
Llanderfel Farm
Dowlais
EBBW FOREST
Greenmeadow Primary Sch.
Maes-y-Rhiw Resr. (covered)
Tranch Wood
Fairwater High School
Fairwater Leisure Centre
Craig-Llywarch
Upper House Farm
Pen-y-wyrlod Farm
Tunley
Old Row
New Row
Four Houses
Penheol-y-badd-fach
Penheol-y-badd-fawr
Henllys C in W Sch.
Incline Farm
Fairwater
Fairwater Sports & Social Club
Football Ground
Coed Eva Jun. & Inf. Schs.
Coed Eva
Coed Meyrick-moel
Sports Grd.
Nant y Milwr
Henllys
Blaen-y-cwm
Pant-yr-heol
Coed y Tranch
Ty-trappau
Pensarn Farm
Pen-y-werlod
Cock-y-north
Green Court Farm
Pentrefield Cott.
Cefn Perthy
Coed Caeau-duon
Springfield Hall
Gelli-fach
Coed Mary-David
8
18

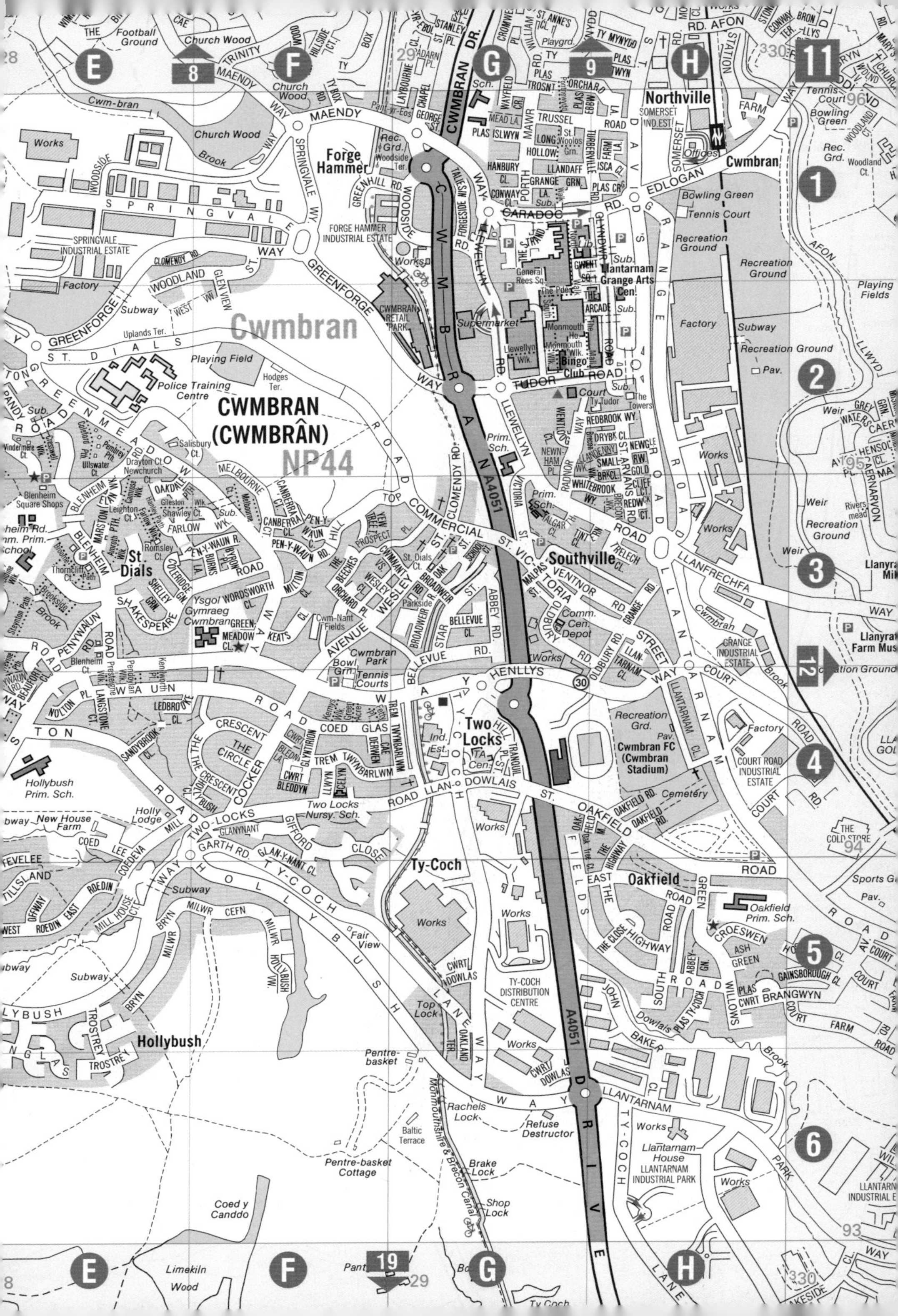

11
Cwmbran
CWMBRAN (CWMBRÂN)
NP44
Northville
Forge Hammer
Southville
St. Dials
Two Locks
Ty-Coch
Oakfield
Hollybush
Llantarnam Grange Arts Cen.
Cwmbran FC (Cwmbran Stadium)
Police Training Centre
Cwmbran Retail Park
Forge Hammer Industrial Estate
Springvale Industrial Estate
Court Road Industrial Estate
Grange Industrial Estate
Llantarnam Industrial Park
Ty-Coch Distribution Centre
Llantarnam House
Monmouthshire & Brecon Canal
Church Wood
Coed y Canddo
Limekiln Wood
Pentre-basket Cottage
Refuse Destructor
Hollybush Prim. Sch.
Oakfield Prim. Sch.
Cwmbran Park
Playing Field
Recreation Ground
Factory
Works
A4051
CWMBRAN DRIVE
8
9
12
19

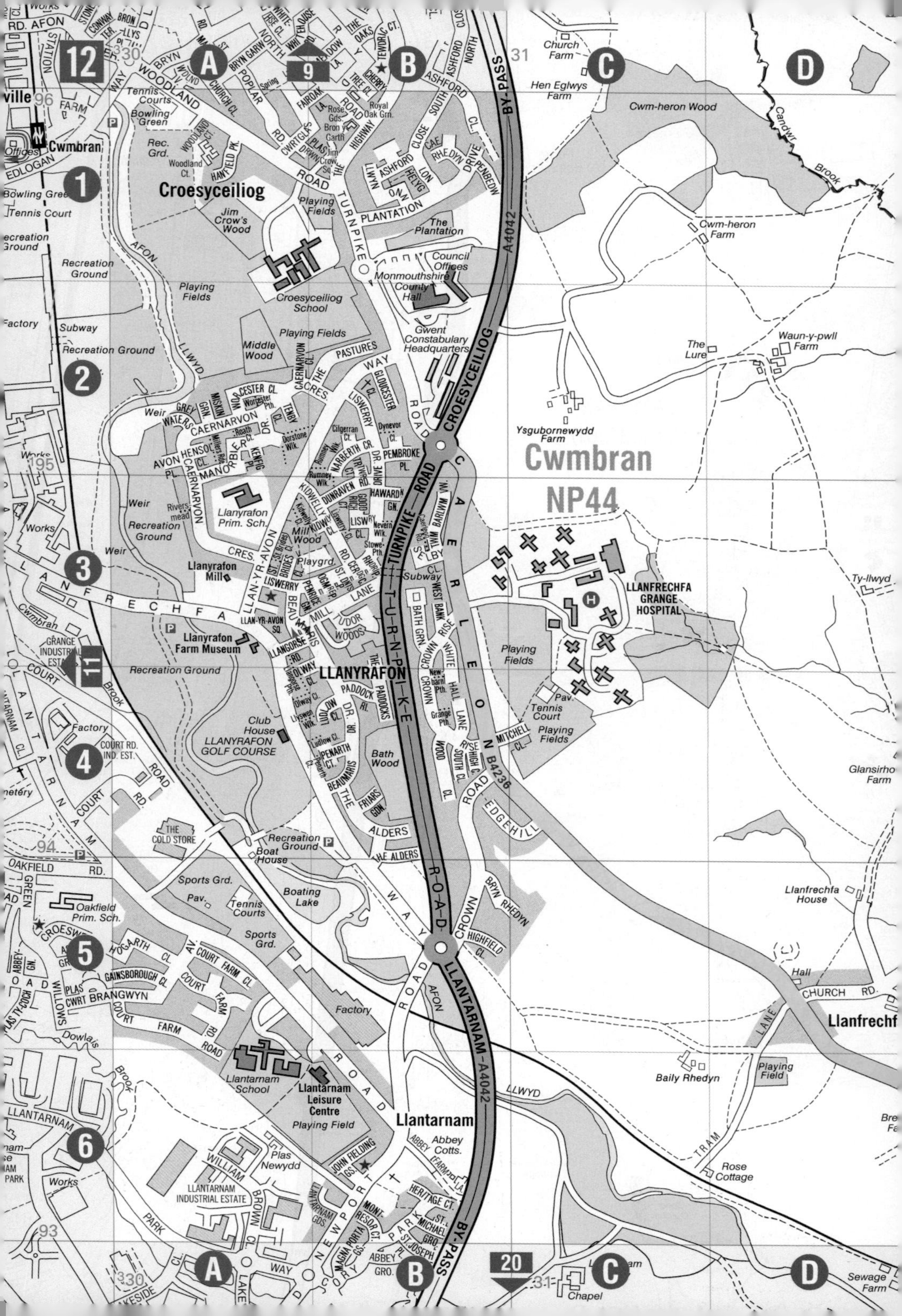
12
A
B
C
D
1
2
3
4
5
6
9
11
20
31
330
93
94
95
96
Cwmbran
NP44
Croesyceiliog
LLANYRAFON
Llantarnam
Llanfrechf
LLANFRECHFA GRANGE HOSPITAL
Croesyceiliog School
Monmouthshire County Hall
Council Offices
Gwent Constabulary Headquarters
Llanyrafon Prim. Sch.
Llanyrafon Mill
Llanyrafon Farm Museum
LLANYRAFON GOLF COURSE
Club House
Llantarnam School
Llantarnam Leisure Centre
Playing Field
LLANTARNAM INDUSTRIAL ESTATE
Oakfield Prim. Sch.
THE COLD STORE
Boating Lake
Boat House
Recreation Ground
Playing Fields
Sports Grd.
Tennis Courts
Factory
Works
Jim Crow's Wood
Middle Wood
Bath Wood
Mill Wood
Cwm-heron Wood
Cwm-heron Farm
Hen Eglwys Farm
Church Farm
Waun-y-pwll Farm
The Lure
Ysguborneywdd Farm
Ty-llwyd
Glansirho Farm
Llanfrechfa House
Baily Rhedyn
Rose Cottage
Sewage Farm
Chapel
Hall
The Plantation
CROESYCEILIOG BY-PASS
A4042
LLANTARNAM ROAD
TURNPIKE ROAD
CAERLEON ROAD
B4236
LLANFRECHFA WAY
NEWPORT ROAD
WOODLAND ROAD
AFON LLWYD
Brook
Candwr Brook
CHURCH RD.
TRAM LANE
COURT FARM ROAD
OAKFIELD RD.
EDGEHILL
CROWN ROAD
BRYN RHEDYN
HIGHFIELD CL.
PLANTATION
PASTURES
GLOUCESTER
PEMBROKE PL.
CAERNARVON
HAWARDEN
DUNRAVEN RD.
KIDWELLY
LISWERRY
LLANGORSE
PADDOCKS
BEAUMARIS
PENARTH
FRIARS
ALDERS
THE ALDERS
MITCHELL CL.
WHITE HALL LANE
BATH GRN.
WEST BANK RISE
Subway
Weir
EDLOGAN
STATION
RD. AFON
COURT RD. IND. EST.
GRANGE INDUSTRIAL ESTATE
LLANTARNAM
WILLIAM
Plas Newydd
Abbey Cotts.
JOHN FIELDING

E
F
G
H
32
33
34
96
95
94
93
1
2
3
4
5
6
The Old Rectory
Perthellic Farm
Celynen
TRE-HERBERT
Llanthewy Vach
Sor Brook
Court Perrott
Llandegveth
Court Perrott Cottages
Weir
PENYGLOG
ROAD
Cefn-tila
Cefn-tila-bach
White House
TRE-HERBERT ROAD
NANTSOR ROAD
Pont Waun-y-pwll
Lan-y-nant
Ty-Capten Farm
Sor Brook
Gwern Dywyll
Candwr Brook
Pont Lan Sor
Pen-y-wain Farm
Berth-llwyd
Little Creigydd Farm
Roughton Farm
Lan-Sor Wood
Roughton House
Creigydd Farm
The Hollies
Cefn Llwyn
Newport
NP18
Pen-y-banc
Sarelle Cottage
MONMOUTHSHIRE
TORFAEN
(SIR FYNWY)
(TOR-FAEN)
Lindens
GATLAS
Pentopyn
Candwr Farm
Reservoir
Pant-yr-eos Farm
Church Farm
Gilwern Brake
Shaftesbury Farm
Candwr Brook
CANDWR LANE
Waterworks
B4236
Sunny Pl.
LANE
LAMB
BADGERS MDW.
CANDWR
BRECHFA CL.
GILWERN FM. CL.
Gilwern Farm
Ponthir Church of Wales School
SCHOOL CL.
PARK
PONTHIR
21
Brook Farm
Cassandra
ROAD
OAKLANDS
LANE

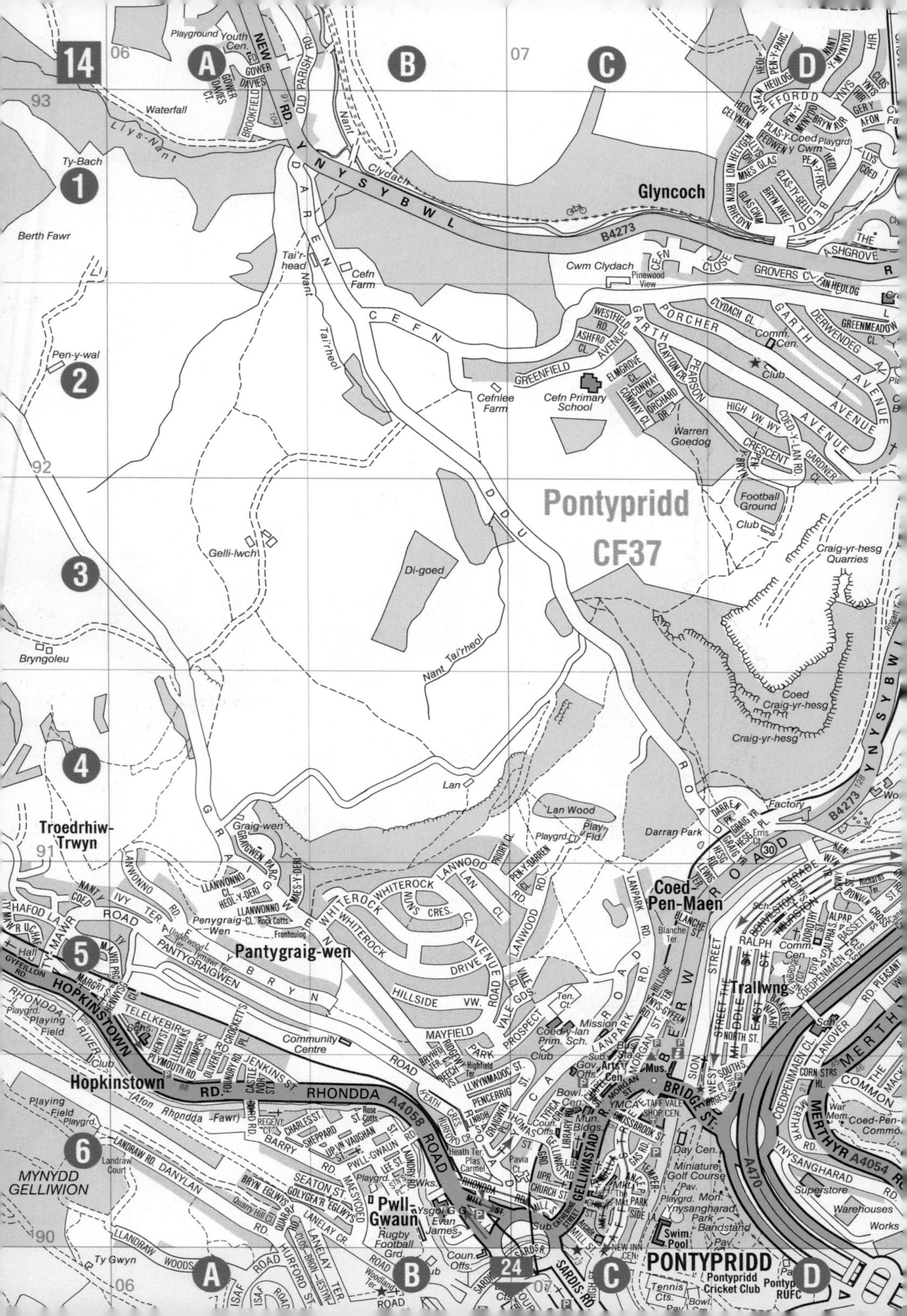

Pontypridd
CF37
Glyncoch
Hopkinstown
Pantygraig-wen
Troedrhiw-Trwyn
Coed-Pen-Maen
Trallwng
Pwll-Gwaun
PONTYPRIDD
MYNYDD GELLIWION
YNYSYBWL
B4273
RHONDDA RD.
A4058 ROAD
HOPKINSTOWN
MERTHYR A4054 RD.
A470
CEFN DDU
DAREN
ROAD
GRAIGWEN
BRYN Y
NEW RD.
OLD PARISH RD.
Playground Youth Cen.
Waterfall
Lllys-Nant
Ty-Bach
Berth Fawr
Pen-y-wal
Gelli-lwch
Di-goed
Bryngoleu
Nant Tai'rheol
Tai'r-head
Cefn Farm
Cefnlee Farm
Cefn Primary School
Warren Goedog
Football Ground
Club
Craig-yr-hesg Quarries
Coed Craig-yr-hesg
Craig-yr-hesg
Lan
Lan Wood
Darran Park
Factory
Cwm Clydach
Pinewood View
Comm. Cen.
Community Centre
Rugby Football Grd.
Swim. Pool
Pontypridd Cricket Club
Pontypridd RUFC
Miniature Golf Course
Ynysangharad Park
Bandstand
Superstore
Warehouses
Works
Playing Field
Landraw Court
Ty Gwyn
24

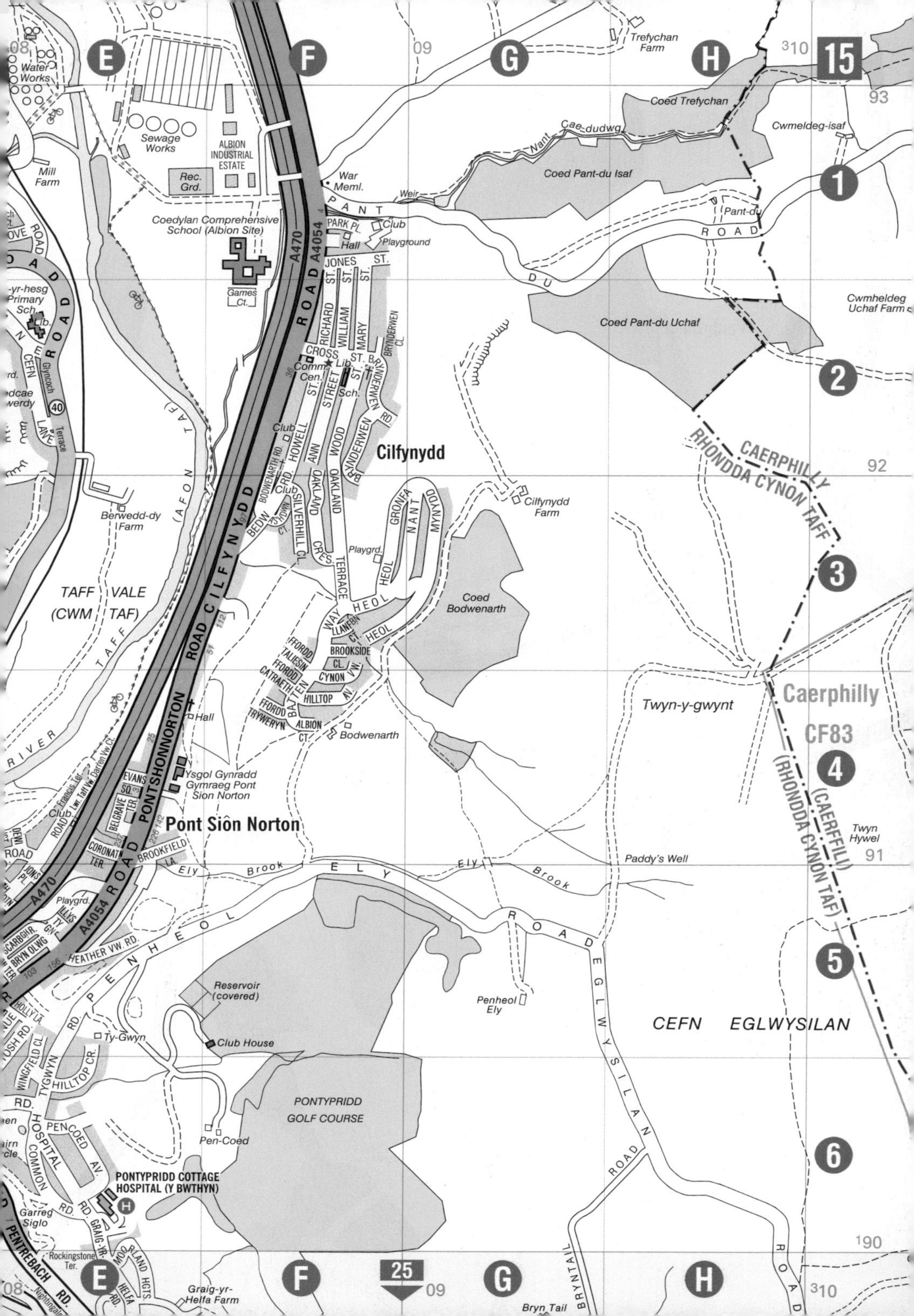

15
Cilfynydd
Pont Siôn Norton
Caerphilly
CF83
CAERPHILLY
RHONDDA CYNON TAFF
(CAERFFILI)
(RHONDDA CYNON TAF)
TAFF VALE
(CWM TAF)
RIVER TAFF
(AFON TAF)
CEFN EGLWYSILAN
PONTYPRIDD GOLF COURSE
PONTYPRIDD COTTAGE HOSPITAL (Y BWTHYN)
Coed Trefychan
Coed Pant-du Isaf
Coed Pant-du Uchaf
Coed Bodwenarth
Trefychan Farm
Cwmeldeg-isaf
Cwmheldeg Uchaf Farm
Cae-dudwg
Nant
Pant-du
PANT DU ROAD
War Meml.
Weir
Sewage Works
ALBION INDUSTRIAL ESTATE
Rec. Grd.
Water Works
Mill Farm
Coedylan Comprehensive School (Albion Site)
Games Ct.
Primary Sch.
Lib.
Glyncoch
Terrace
Berwedd-dy Farm
Cilfynydd Farm
Twyn-y-gwynt
Twyn Hywel
Paddy's Well
Ely Brook
PENHEOL ELY ROAD
EGLWYSILAN ROAD
Penheol Ely
Reservoir (covered)
Club House
Ty-Gwyn
Pen-Coed
Bodwenarth
Ysgol Gynradd Gymraeg Pont Sion Norton
Hall
Club
Playground
Playgrd.
Comm. Cen.
Sch.
A470
A4054
CILFYNYDD ROAD
PONTSHONNORTON ROAD
PARK PL.
JONES ST.
RICHARD ST.
WILLIAM ST.
MARY ST.
CROSS ST.
BRYNDERWEN CL.
BRYNDERWEN RD.
HOWELL ST.
ANN ST.
WOOD ST.
OAKLAND ST.
OAKLAND CRES.
SILVERHILL CL.
BODWENARTH RD.
BEDW
TERRACE
GRONFA
NANT
MYNYDD
HEOL
WAY
LLANFABON
BROOKSIDE
CYNON VW.
HILLTOP AV.
FFORDD TALIESIN
FFORDD CATRAETH
FFORDD TRYWERYN
BATTEN
ALBION CT.
EVANS SQ.
BELGRAVE TER.
CORONATION TER.
BROOKFIELD LA.
HEATHER VW. RD.
BRYN OLWG
HILLTOP CR.
WINGFIELD CL.
TYGWYN RD.
HOSPITAL RD.
COMMON
PENCOED AV.
GRAIG-YR-HELFA RD.
MOORLAND HGTS.
Rockingstone Ter.
Garreg Siglo
PENTREBACH RD.
Graig-yr-Helfa Farm
Bryn Tail
BRYNTAIL
Francis Ter.
Lwr. Taff Vw.
Darren Vw. Ct.
DEWI
ROAD
25

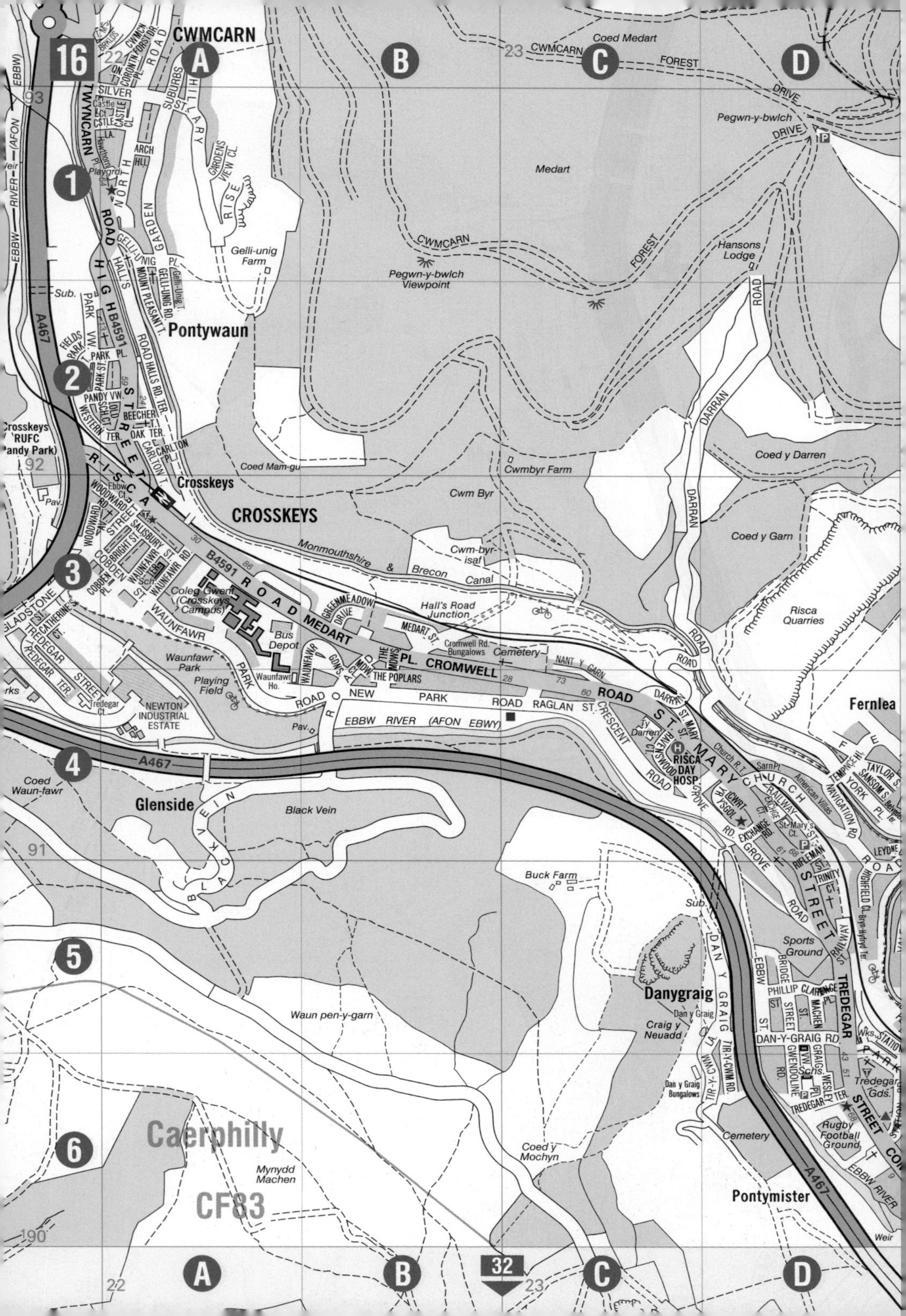

16
CWMCARN
Coed Medart
CWMCARN FOREST DRIVE
Pegwn-y-bwlch
Medart
Gelli-unig Farm
Pegwn-y-bwlch Viewpoint
Hansons Lodge
Pontywaun
Crosskeys RUFC (Pandy Park)
Coed Mam-gu
Cwmbyr Farm
Coed y Darren
Cwm Byr
Crosskeys
CROSSKEYS
Coed y Garn
Cwm-byr-isaf
Monmouthshire & Brecon Canal
Risca Quarries
Coleg Gwent (Crosskeys Campus)
Hall's Road Junction
Bus Depot
Cromwell Rd. Bungalows
Cemetery
Waunfawr Park
Playing Field
THE POPLARS
NEWTON INDUSTRIAL ESTATE
EBBW RIVER (AFON EBWY)
Fernlea
RISCA DAY HOSP.
A467
Coed Waun-fawr
Glenside
Black Vein
Buck Farm
Sports Ground
Danygraig
Waun pen-y-garn
Craig y Neuadd
Dan y Graig Bungalows
Tredegar Gds.
Rugby Football Ground
Caerphilly
Cemetery
Coed y Mochyn
Mynydd Machen
CF83
Pontymister
32

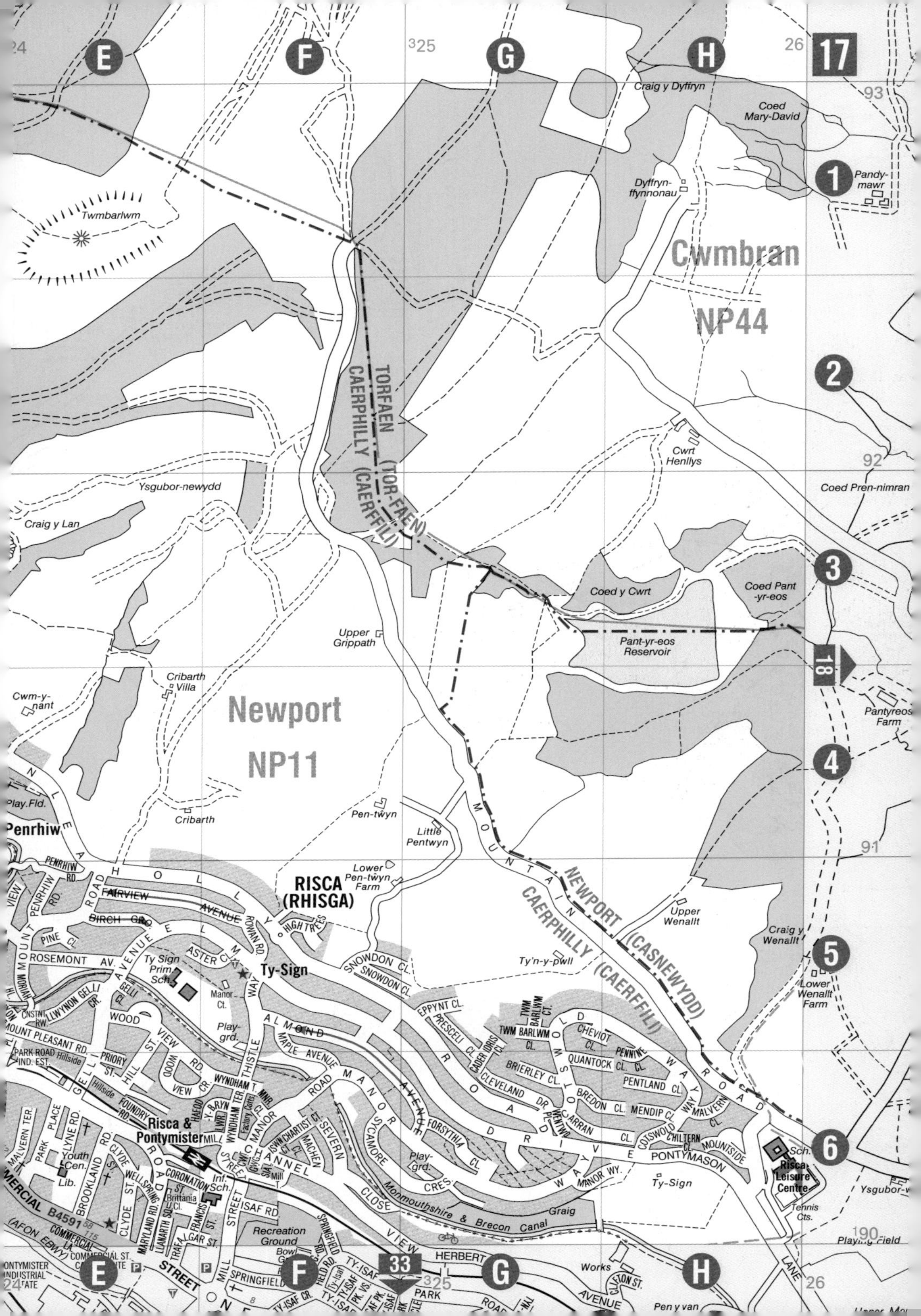

E
F
G
H
325
26
24
93
92
91
190
1
2
3
4
5
6
18
33
Twmbarlwm
Craig y Dyffryn
Coed Mary-David
Pandy-mawr
Dyffryn-ffynnonau
Cwmbran
NP44
TORFAEN
CAERPHILLY
(TOR-FAEN)
(CAERFFILI)
Cwrt Henllys
Coed Pren-nimran
Ysgubor-newydd
Craig y Lan
Coed y Cwrt
Coed Pant-yr-eos
Pant-yr-eos Reservoir
Upper Grippath
Cribarth Villa
Cwm-y-nant
Newport
NP11
Pantyreos Farm
Cribarth
Pen-twyn
Little Pentwyn
Lower Pen-twyn Farm
Play.Fld.
Penrhiw
RISCA
(RHISGA)
NEWPORT
(CASNEWYDD)
CAERPHILLY
(CAERFFILI)
MOUNTAIN ROAD
Upper Wenallt
Craig y Wenallt
Lower Wenallt Farm
Ty'n-y-pwll
Ty-Sign
Ty Sign Prim. Sch.
Manor Ct.
Play-grd.
HOLLY ROAD
PENRHIW RD.
FAIRVIEW AVENUE
BIRCH GRO.
ROWAN RD.
HIGH TREES
PINE CL.
ROSEMONT AV.
ASTER CL.
SNOWDON CL.
MOUNT MORIAH
VIEW
GELLI CL.
GELLI CR.
LLWYNON
CNSTNT. RW.
WOOD
MOUNT PLEASANT RD.
PARK ROAD Hillside IND. EST.
PRIORY ST.
HILL ST.
VIEW RD.
WOOD VIEW CR.
THISTLE WAY
ALMOND AVENUE
MAPLE AVENUE
MANOR ROAD
MANOR AVENUE
WYNDHAM T.
MNR.
WYNDHAM TER.
Factory Cotts.
HAFOD
Y-BRYN
LWR.
Hillside
FOUNDRY RD.
Risca & Pontymister
MILL STREET
CHANNEL
CHARTIST CT.
SEVERN
MACHEN
SYCAMORE CRES.
FORSYTHIA CL.
EPPYNT CL.
PRESCELI CL.
CADER IDRIS CL.
TWM BARLWM CL.
TWM BARLWM CT.
CHEVIOT CL.
PENNINE CL.
QUANTOCK CL.
BRIERLEY CL.
CLEVELAND DR.
PENTLAND CL.
BREDON CL.
MENDIP CL.
CARRAN CL.
WENTWO.
COTSWOLD DRIVE
COTSWOLD CL.
CHILTERN CL.
MALVERN CL.
WAY ROAD
PONTYMASON
MOUNTSIDE
MANOR WY.
Sch.
Risca Leisure Centre
Tennis Cts.
Playing Field
Ysgubor-y
Monmouthshire & Brecon Canal
Graig
VIEW
HERBERT
Works
CLIFTON ST.
AVENUE
Pen y van
LANE
MALVERN TER.
PARK PLACE
LYNE RD.
Youth Cen.
Lib.
BROOKLAND RD.
CLYDE RD.
CLYDE ST.
WELLSPRING ST.
MARYLAND RD.
LLANARTH SQ.
CORONATION ST.
Brittania Cl.
Inf. Sch.
FRANCIS ST.
TRAFALGAR ST.
ISAF RD.
Recreation Ground
Bowl. Gr.
SPRINGFIELD RD.
SPRINGFIELD
COMMERCIAL B4591
(AFON EBWY)
COMMERCIAL LA.
COMMERCIAL ST.
PONTYMISTER INDUSTRIAL ESTATE
STREET
TY-ISAF
TY-ISAF CR.
PARK
ROAD

18
26
A
B
C
D
Coed Caeau-duon
10
27
Springfield Hall
93
Coed Mary-David
Gelli-fach
1
Pandy-mawr
Pandy-bach
LANE
Coed y Bedw
Castell Farm
Greenmeadow
PENTRE
Cwm Farm
Castell-y-Bŵch
Henllys Vale House
Henllys Vale
Primrose Cottage
2
Ffynnon Erw-wen
COED Y TWRCH
Nant-y-Pandy
Henllys
Ffynnon-dwyn
(TOR-FAEN)
(CASNEWYDD)
92
Coed Shon Uchaf
Coed Pren-nimran
Nant
TORFAEN
NEWPORT
Cefn Adam
Lan-is-haul
CRAIG-CEILIOG
3
Coed Pant-yr-eos
Mill Cottage
17
Tynewydd
Pantyreos Farm
MILL WOOD
4
Pantyreos
Brook
Church Farm
COED
CRAIG Y
CEILOG
91
Tregwillym House
Park Farm
Craig y Wenallt
Coed Bedw
5
Lower Wenallt Farm
Garth
Maes-y-coed
HENLLYS LANE
COED BALD
Garth Fach
Golynos
NP10
MOUNTAIN
Golynos Fach Farm
Golynos Fawr Farm
Bettws
Brook
6
Sch.
Risca Leisure Centre
Heol-fawr
Golynos Cottage
GROES ROAD
MOUNTSIDE
PONTYMASON
Ysgubor-wen
Mescoed Bach
Tennis Cts.
MESCOED MAWR
190
Playing Field
NEWPORT GOLF COURSE
34
LANE
Gwern-y-C

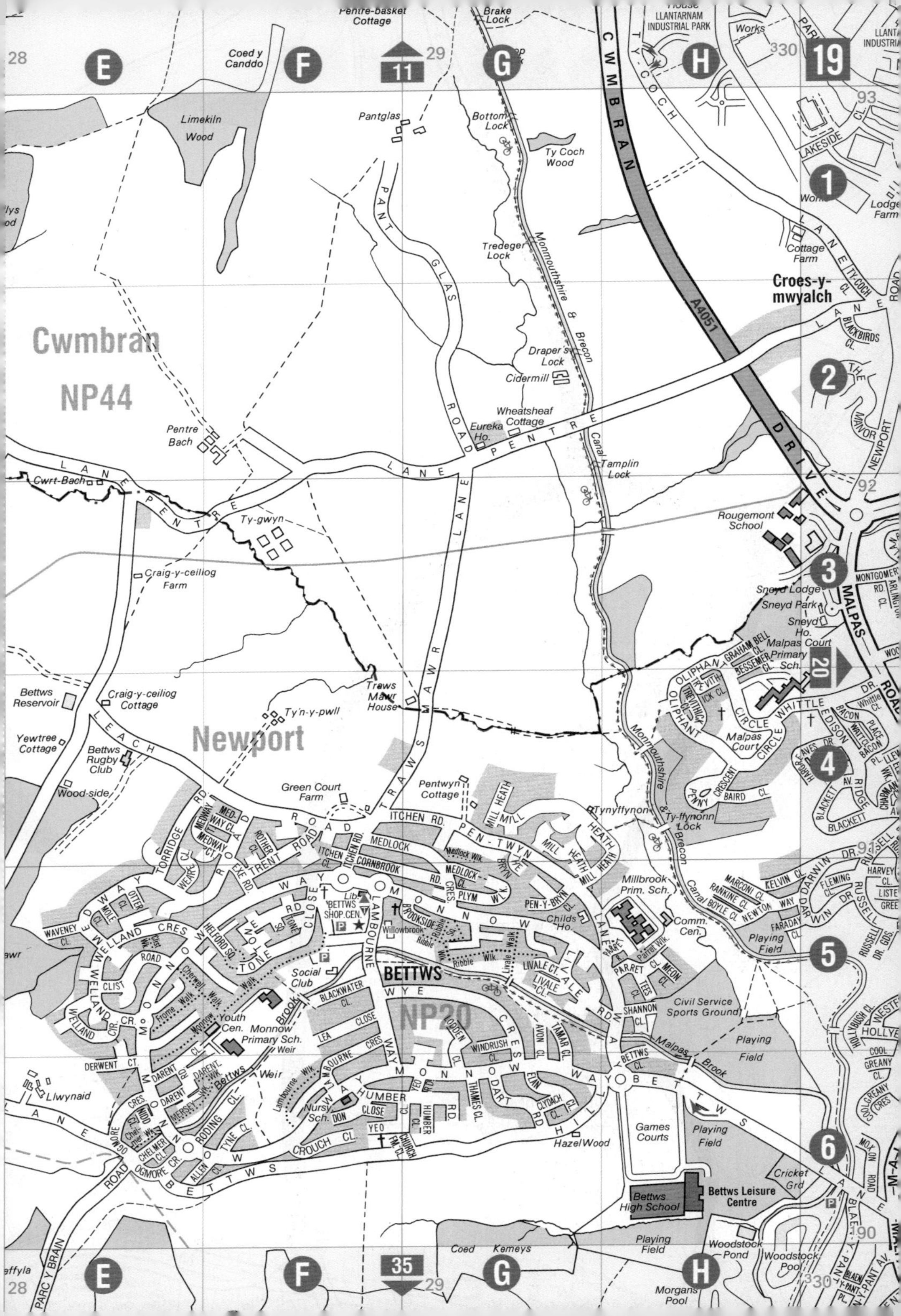
Pentre-basket Cottage
Brake Lock
LLANTARNAM INDUSTRIAL PARK
Works
19
11
Coed y Canddo
Limekiln Wood
Pantglas
Bottom Lock
Ty Coch Wood
CWMBRAN
TY-COCH
LAKESIDE
Tredeger Lock
Monmouthshire & Brecon Canal
Cottage Farm
Croes-y-mwyalch
A4051
DRIVE
BLACKBIRDS CL.
THE MANOR
NEWPORT
Cwmbran
NP44
Draper's Lock
Cidermill
PANT GLAS ROAD
Wheatsheaf Cottage
Eureka Ho.
PENTRE LANE
Pentre Bach
Cwrt-Bach
Tamplin Lock
Ty-gwyn
Rougemont School
Craig-y-ceiliog Farm
MALPAS
MONTGOMERY RD.
ARLINGTON CL.
Sneyd Lodge
Sneyd Park
Sneyd Ho.
Malpas Court Primary Sch.
20
Bettws Reservoir
Craig-y-ceiliog Cottage
Trews Mawr House
Ty'n-y-pwll
TRAWS MAWR LANE
Newport
Yewtree Cottage
Bettws Rugby Club
LEACH ROAD
Wood-side
Green Court Farm
Pentwyn Cottage
Tynyffynon
Ty-ffynonn Lock
CIRCLE
WHITTLE
EDISON
BACON
Malpas Court
CRESCENT
BAIRD CL.
PENNY
BLACKETT AV.
RIDGE
ITCHEN RD.
PEN-TWYN
MILL HEATH
MEDLOCK
CORNBROOK
TORRIDGE
MEDWAY
TRENT ROAD
EXE RD.
Millbrook Prim. Sch.
KELVIN CL.
DARWIN DR.
RUSSELL
FLEMING
MARCONI CL.
RANKINE CL.
BOYLE CL.
NEWTON WAY
FARADAY
Playing Field
Comm. Cen.
Childs Ho.
PEN-Y-BRYN
BROOKSIDE
PLYM WK.
Lib.
BETTWS SHOP.CEN.
LAMBOURNE
CLOSE
TONE
HELFORD SQ.
WAVENEY CL.
WELLAND CRES
CLIST
Cherwell Walk
Frome Walk
Youth Cen.
Monnow Primary Sch.
Weir
Social Club
BLACKWATER CL.
BETTWS
WYE CRES
NP20
LIVALE CT.
PARRET CL.
MEON
TEES
SHANNON CL.
Civil Service Sports Ground
Malpas Brook
LODDEN CL.
WINDRUSH CL.
AVON CL.
TAMAR CL.
DERWENT CT.
DARENT
Betws
LEA CLOSE
MONNOW WAY
Lambourne Wlk.
HUMBER
YEO
THAMES CL.
DART
ELAN
CLYDACH CL.
Llwynaid
OGMORE CR.
CHELMER CL.
RODING CL.
TYNE CL.
Nursy. Sch.
CROUCH CL.
CHURCH FM. CL.
HILL
HazelWood
Games Courts
Playing Field
BETTWS LANE
Cricket Grd
Bettws Leisure Centre
Bettws High School
Coed Kemeys
Woodstock Pond
Woodstock Pool
Morgans Pool
BLAEN-Y-PANT AV.
PARC Y BRAIN
35
E
F
G
H
1
2
3
4
5
6
28
29
330
92
93
90

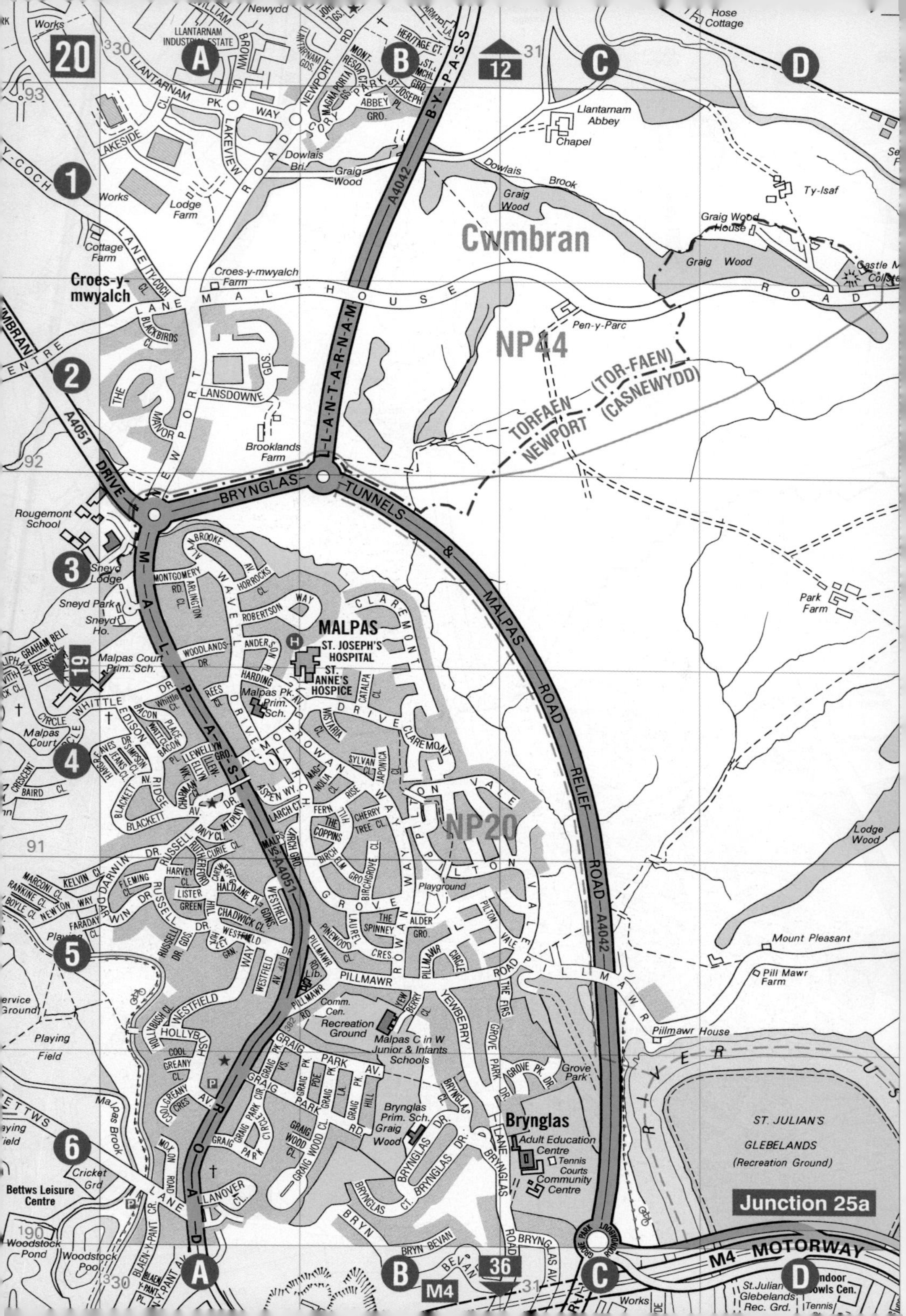
20
12
36
19
Cwmbran
Croes-y-mwyalch
MALPAS
Bryngias
NP44
NP20
TORFAEN (TOR-FAEN)
NEWPORT (CASNEWYDD)
Junction 25a
M4 MOTORWAY
LLANTARNAM INDUSTRIAL ESTATE
Llantarnam Abbey
Chapel
Ty-Isaf
Graig Wood House
Graig Wood
Castle M. Collste
Pen-y-Parc
Brooklands Farm
Rougemont School
Sneyd Lodge
Sneyd Park
Sneyd Ho.
ST. JOSEPH'S HOSPITAL
ST. ANNE'S HOSPICE
Malpas Pk. Prim. Sch.
Malpas Court Prim. Sch.
Malpas Court
Park Farm
Lodge Wood
Mount Pleasant
Pill Mawr Farm
Pillmawr House
ST. JULIAN'S GLEBELANDS (Recreation Ground)
Adult Education Centre
Tennis Courts
Community Centre
Grove Park
Bryngias Prim. Sch.
Graig Wood
Malpas C in W Junior & Infants Schools
Recreation Ground
Comm. Cen.
Playground
Playing Field
Bettws Leisure Centre
Cricket Grd
Woodstock Pond
Woodstock Pool
Malpas Brook
Cottage Farm
Lodge Farm
Croes-y-mwyalch Farm
Rose Cottage
Dowlais Brook
Indoor Bowls Cen.
St.Julian Glebelands Rec. Grd.
TUNNELS & MALPAS ROAD RELIEF ROAD A4042
LLANTARNAM BY-PASS
MALPAS ROAD A4051
BRYNGLAS
MALTHOUSE LANE
RIVER USK

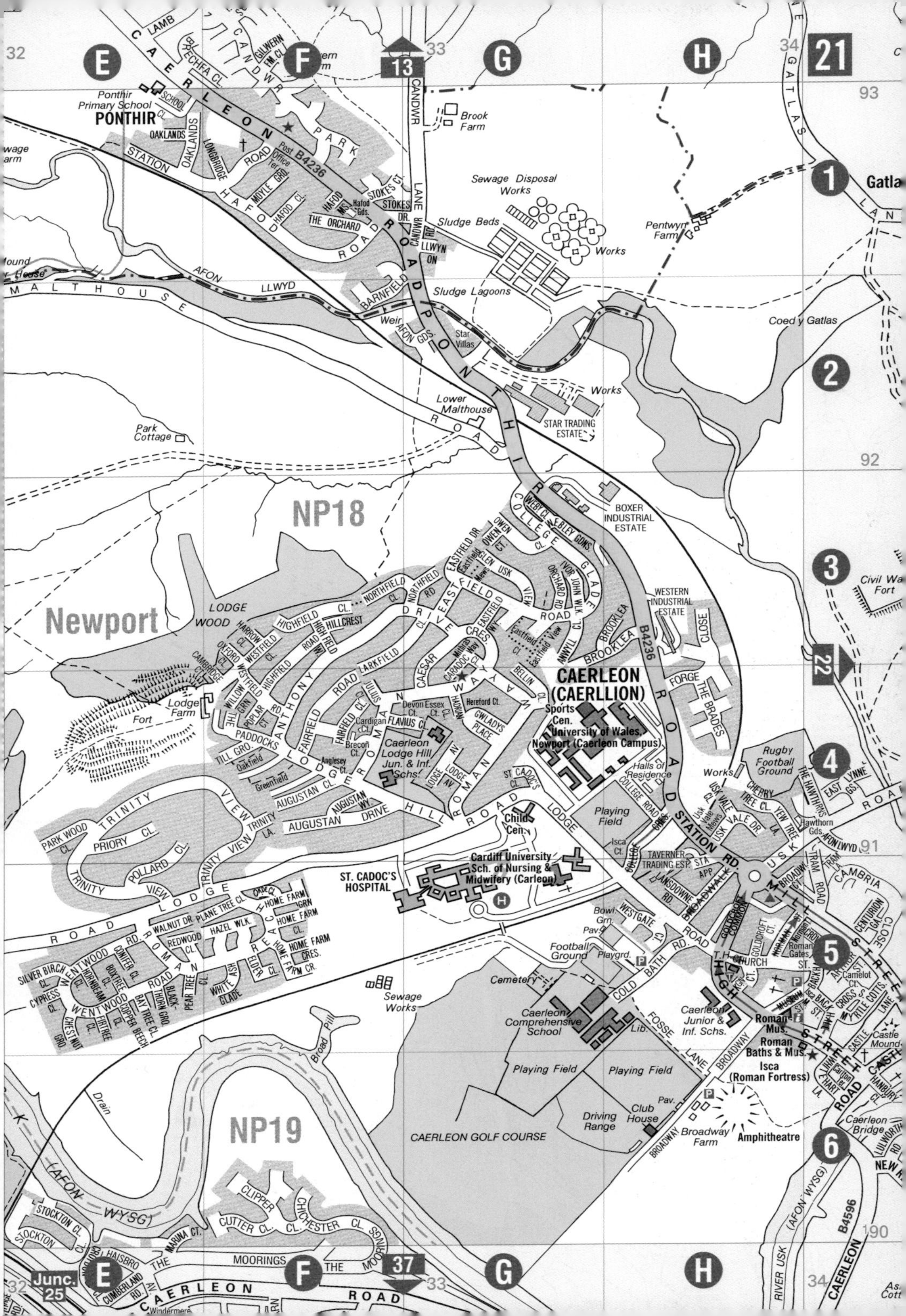
21
CAERLEON
(CAERLLION)
PONTHIR
Newport
NP18
NP19
Ponthir Primary School
Brook Farm
Sewage Disposal Works
Sludge Beds
Sludge Lagoons
Works
Pentwyn Farm
Coed y Gatlas
Lower Malthouse
Park Cottage
STAR TRADING ESTATE
BOXER INDUSTRIAL ESTATE
WESTERN INDUSTRIAL ESTATE
Civil War Fort
LODGE WOOD
Lodge Farm
Fort
Caerleon Lodge Hill Jun. & Inf. Schs.
Sports Cen.
University of Wales, Newport (Caerleon Campus)
Halls of Residence
Rugby Football Ground
Playing Field
Child. Cen.
Cardiff University Sch. of Nursing & Midwifery (Carleon)
ST. CADOC'S HOSPITAL
TAVERNER TRADING EST.
Football Ground
Cemetery
Sewage Works
Caerleon Comprehensive School
Caerleon Junior & Inf. Schs.
Roman Mus.
Roman Baths & Mus.
Isca (Roman Fortress)
Castle Mound
Amphitheatre
Broadway Farm
Club House
Driving Range
CAERLEON GOLF COURSE
Caerleon Bridge
RIVER USK
(AFON WYSG)
AFON LLWYD
Broad Pill
Drain
B4236
B4596
CAERLEON ROAD
PONTHIR ROAD
STATION RD.
HIGH STREET
MALTHOUSE ROAD
LODGE ROAD
CANDWR LANE
Junc. 25
13
22
37

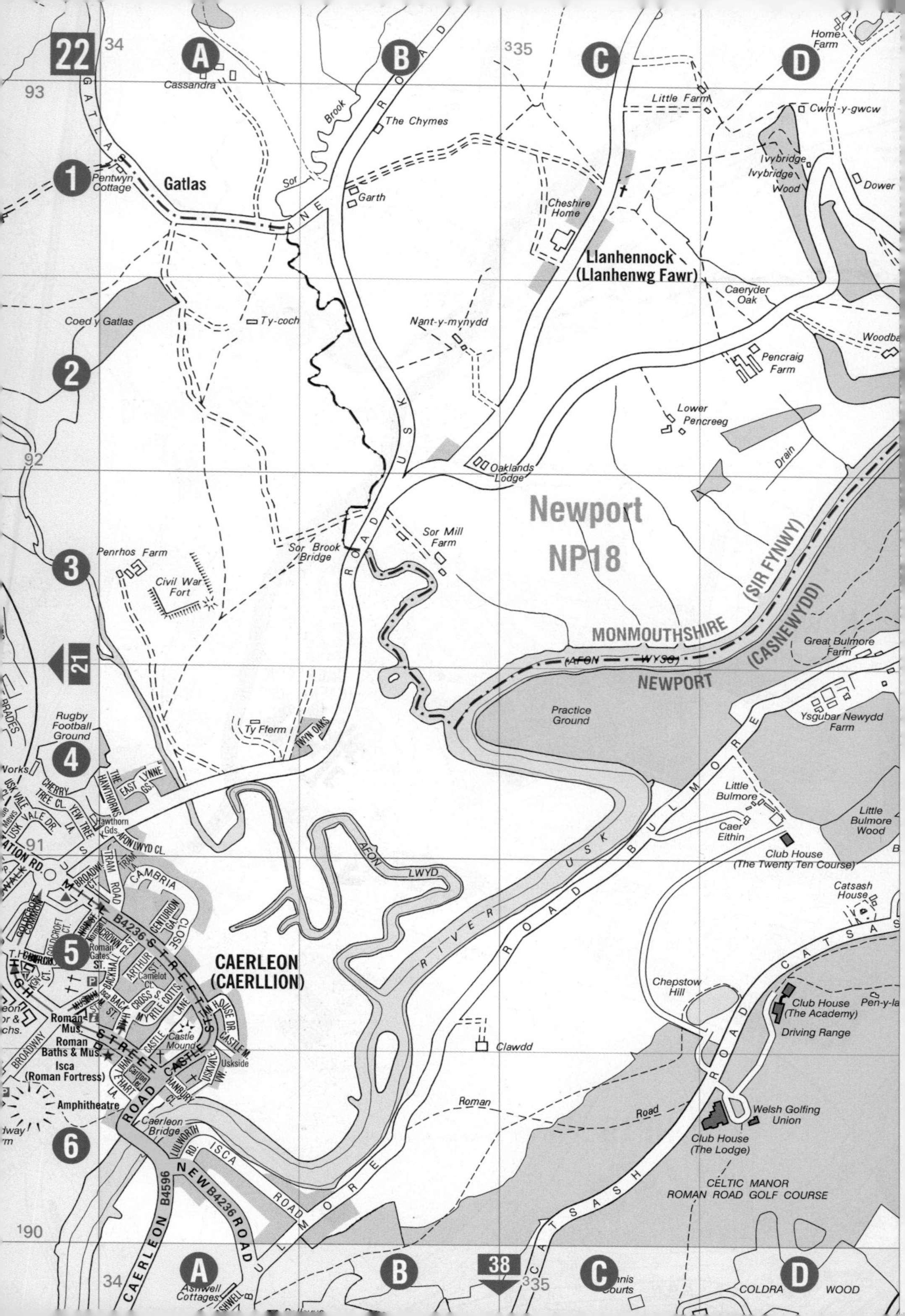

Gatlas
Pentwyn Cottage
Cassandra
The Chymes
Garth
Sor Brook
Coed y Gatlas
Ty-coch
Penrhos Farm
Civil War Fort
Sor Brook Bridge
Sor Mill Farm
Ty Fferm
Twyn Oaks
Rugby Football Ground
Llanhennock (Llanhenwg Fawr)
Cheshire Home
Little Farm
Cwm-y-gwcw
Ivybridge
Ivybridge Wood
Dower
Caeryder Oak
Nant-y-mynydd
Pencraig Farm
Lower Pencreeg
Drain
Oaklands Lodge
Newport NP18
MONMOUTHSHIRE (SIR FYNWY)
NEWPORT (CASNEWYDD)
AFON WYSG
Great Bulmore Farm
Ysgubar Newydd Farm
Practice Ground
Little Bulmore
Little Bulmore Wood
Caer Eithin
Club House (The Twenty Ten Course)
Catsash House
Chepstow Hill
Club House (The Academy)
Driving Range
Welsh Golfing Union
Club House (The Lodge)
CELTIC MANOR ROMAN ROAD GOLF COURSE
Roman Road
Clawdd
CAERLEON (CAERLLION)
Afon Lwyd
RIVER USK
BULMORE ROAD
CATSASH ROAD
Castle Mound
Roman Mus.
Roman Baths & Mus.
Isca (Roman Fortress)
Amphitheatre
Caerleon Bridge
Uskside
CAERLEON B4596
NEW B4236 ROAD
ISCA ROAD
Ashwell Cottages
Tennis Courts
COLDRA WOOD
34
335
93
92
91
190
21
38

23
36
37
38
93
92
91
190
E
F
G
H
1
2
3
4
5
6
39
Garn-fawr
Garn-fach
Glen Usk
Pant-gwyn
Castle Mill
RIVER USK
(AFON WYSG)
A449
Underpass
Kemeys Farm
Kemeys House
Redland Pool
Depot
KEMEYS GRAIG
Abernant Farm
CELTIC MANOR
THE TWENTY TEN GOLF COURSE
ROAD
Woodward's Farm
LANE
Coed-y-cearau
Pen-toppen-ash
Oak Tree
Great Bulmore
NEW WOOD
NEW WOOD
Crows Ridge
The Bluebirds
Pen-y-Bryn
Sleepyhollow
Mount Tudor
CELTIC MANOR
THE MONTGOMERIE GOLF COURSE
Chapel Cottage
COED-Y-CAERAU
Treclover
Reservoir (covered)
Woodville Bungalow
Cat's Ash
Draenllwyn
ROAD
OLD
ROMAN
ROAD
Windy Ridge
Langstone Prim. Sch.
Cat's Ash Farm
CATSASH
CELTIC MANOR
THE MONTGOMERIE GOLF COURSE
Caeffynnon
The Gorelands
The Headlands
TREGARN RD.
MAGOR RD.
B4245
ROAD
Priory Wood
Priory Farm
A48
Langstone
Langstone Park
Columbus House
PRIORY
PRIORY GRO.
PRIORY VW.
LANGSTONE BUS. VILLAGE
DR.
WALK
CRES.
STOCKWOOD
SILURE
CL.
STOCKWOOD VIEW
Garden Centre
WY.
ROSECROFT
DRIVE
SPARTAN
SPARTAN CL.
GRENADIER
Rec. Grd.
Park End Ct.
PARK END
CHEPSTOW
ROAD
THE GLEN
Delbury
THE PADDOCK
CHEPSTOW
OLD
THE NURSERIES

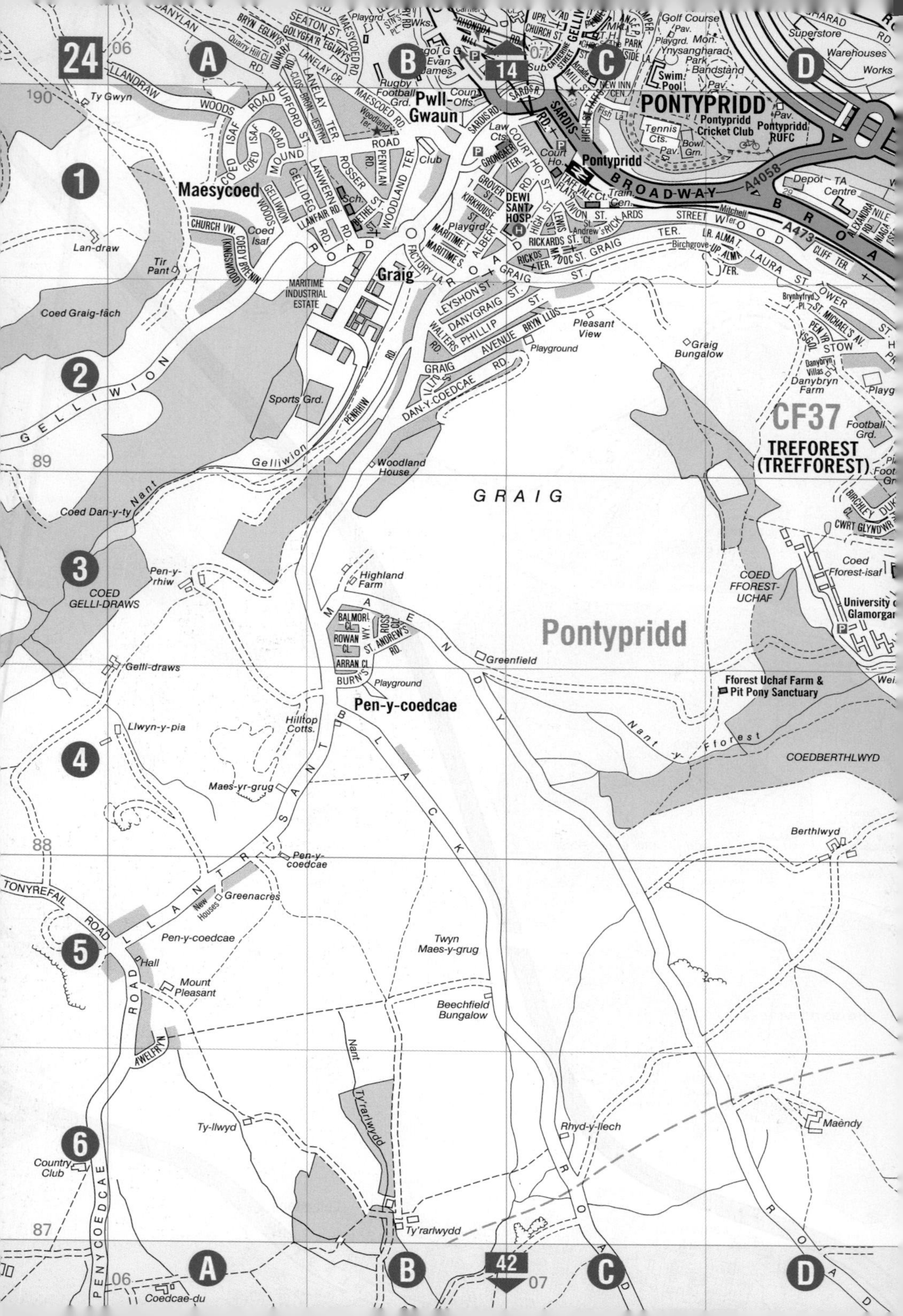

24
Maesycoed
Pwll-Gwaun
PONTYPRIDD
Pontypridd
Pontypridd Cricket Club
Pontypridd RUFC
BROADWAY
A4058
A473
Graig
MARITIME INDUSTRIAL ESTATE
DEWI SANT HOSP
Coed Graig-fâch
Lan-draw
Tir Pant
Ty Gwyn
LLANDRAW
WOODS
Sports Grd.
GELLIWION
Gelliwion
GRAIG
Woodland House
Coed Dan-y-ty
Nant
COED GELLI-DRAWS
Pen-y-rhiw
Highland Farm
Pontypridd
Greenfield
Pen-y-coedcae
Playground
Gelli-draws
Llwyn-y-pia
Hilltop Cotts.
Maes-yr-grug
Pen-y-coedcae
Greenacres
New Houses
TONYREFAIL ROAD
LLANTRISANT
Pen-y-coedcae
Hall
Mount Pleasant
Twyn Maes-y-grug
Beechfield Bungalow
AWELFRYN
Nant
Ty'rarlwydd
Ty-llwyd
Rhyd-y-llech
Country Club
PENYCOEDCAE
Ty'rarlwydd
Coedcae-du
Maendy
Berthlwyd
COEDBERTHLWYD
Nant-y-Fforest
Fforest Uchaf Farm & Pit Pony Sanctuary
COED FFOREST-UCHAF
Coed Fforest-isaf
CF37
TREFOREST (TREFFOREST)
Danybryn Farm
Graig Bungalow
Pleasant View
Superstore
Warehouses
Works
Golf Course
Ynysangharad Park
Swim. Pool

PONTYPRIDD COTTAGE HOSPITAL (Y BWTHYN)
E
F
15
G
H
Pentrebach
Graig-yr-Helfa Farm
Bryn Tail
Hillside View
Hendre-Prosse
Tir Cae-mawr
Craig-fach
Coleg Morgannwg (Centre for Art & Design Technology)
Cemetery
Coed Glyn-Taf
Glyntaff Crematorium
Ffynnon-Rhingyll
GLYNTAFF
Glyn-Taf
Treforest
Coed Craig-lwyd
RHYDYFELIN
Heol-y-Celyn Prim. & Rhydyfelin Nursy. Schs.
Newman RC Comp. Sch.
Ysgol Gyfun Garth Olwg
Coleg Morgannwg
Michael's RC Prim. Sch.
Govt. Offices
Works
DYNEA CARAVAN SITE
Hawthorn
Hawthorn Leisure Cen.
Hawthorn Primary & High Schools
Factory
Glen Afon
Caeglas
Recreation Ground
Graig y Fforest Farm
Heol-y-Cawl Bungalow
Heol-y-cawl
CF38
Coed Tir-isaf
Tavern-y-Coed
Lowlands
MELIN CORRWG BUS. PARC
TAFF BUSINESS CEN.
Kidz Playgrd.
TONTEG INDUSTRIAL ESTATE
Fardre-uchaf
Olcote Ho.
43
PENTREBACH
A4054
A470
A473
CARDIFF ROAD
CARDIFF (COLLEGE WAY)
LLANTWIT ST.
GRAIG Y FFOREST
EGLWYSILAN ROAD
BRYNTAIL
DYNEA ROAD
26
1
2
3
4
5
6

A
B
C
D
1
2
3
4
5
6
310
11
190
89
88
87
Coed Caeorrwg
Nant Corrwg
EGLWYSILAN ROAD
Cae-nawr
Ffynnon-Rhingyll
Ffynnon Llan
The Old Rectory
Gleneagles
Pant-drain
Coed Craig-lwyd
Garth
ABERTRIDWR
Coed Ty'n-y-parc
Ty'n-y-parc
Rugby Field
Ckt. Grd.
TY'N Y PARC
FFORDD
GARTH ESTATE
Garth Villas
WINDSOR PL.
HILLSIDE AV.
WOODLAND TER.
CHURCH RD.
MORGAN
TRIDWR RD.
HENDRE RD.
Greenfield Pl.
Pumping Station
EGLWYSILAN FRANCIS WY.
FRANCIS ST.
DAN-Y-MEIO
Nant Ilan
Aber-Fawr
Senghenrydd Dyke
Mynydd Meio
CAERPHILLY
RHONDDA CYNON TAFF
Pontypridd
25
DYNEA CT.
DYNEA CL.
Playgrd.
DYNEA CARAVAN SITE
DAN-YR-ALLT CL.
ELM ST.
HEOL-Y-BRYN
CF37
Taff Valley Quad Bike & Activity Centre
RHYDYFELIN
PINEWOOD CR.
CORRWG
FFORESTNEWYDD
BRYNFAB R.
ARFONFAB CR.
CLOS ANEURIN
Gelli Hirion
MAES YR AWEL
GLAN Y NANT
MAES GAVOL
MAES UCHAF
Gelli Deg
MAES Y FELIN
GELLI HIRION INDUSTRIAL ESTATE
Depot
Superstore
Lonydd
Country Vw.
CRWYS
CRWYS CR.
GWILI RD.
Midway Park
FFYNNONBWLA
Ffynnonbwla
Mynydd-mayo
Ffynnon-isaf
CARDIFF ROAD
A470
A4054
THE RISE
WILLIAMS CL.
Williams Pl.
UPPER BOAT IND. PK.
MELIN CORRWG BUS. PARC
HIRAETHOG RD.
HEOL-Y-BWNSI
Llwyn Onn Farm
Pen-y-groes
Upper Boat
West Winds
Tai'r Level
Ffynnonwen
Pav.
RIVER TAFF
Upper Boat
Diabetic Service
TAFF BUSINESS CEN.
Kidz Playgrd.
TONTEG INDUSTRIAL ESTATE
TREFOREST IND. EST.
SEVERN RD.
Factories
Works
GWAELOD-Y-GARTH RD.
TAFFS
AFON
TAF
MAIN AV.
HEOL GROESWEN
HEOL TY MAEN
44
Heol-y-bwnsy
Nant

27
Caerphilly CF83
Cardiff CF15
Craigyfedw
Penyrheol
Hendredenny Park
Groes-wen
(CAERFFILI)
(RHONDDA CYNON TAF)
HIGH STREET
B4263
THOMAS ST.
GRAIG-Y-FEDW
DAN-Y-GRAIG
CAERPHILLY BY-PASS
A468
CENYDD RD.
STATION TER.
HENDREDENNY DRIVE
GROESWEN ROAD
GYPSY LANE
BOWLS LANE
Cwm yr Aber
Cae'r-llwyn
Waterfall
Cwmceffy
Cwmaber Infants School
Cwmaber Junior Sch.
YMCA
Library
Rec. Grd.
Pont y Felin
Coed Cae pica
Hendredenny-uchaf Farm
Plymouth House
Hendredenny-ganol
Graig-wen
Cwm-Ifor
Pen yr Heol Las Farm
Cwarrau-mawr
CWM FFOR
Cwn Ifor Primary Sch.
Aneurin Park
Bowls Terrace
Orchards Poultry Farm
St. Cenydd Comprehensive School
Hendre Jun. Sch.
St. Cenydd Leisure Cen.
Hendredenny Park Primary Sch.
Playing Fields
Ty-newydd
Tai Cae bryn
Ty-llwyd
Cartref
Bryngolau
Groes-wen Farm
Pantyrefin Cottage
Ty-isaf
Ty Isaf Bungalows
28
45
190
13
14
88
89
87

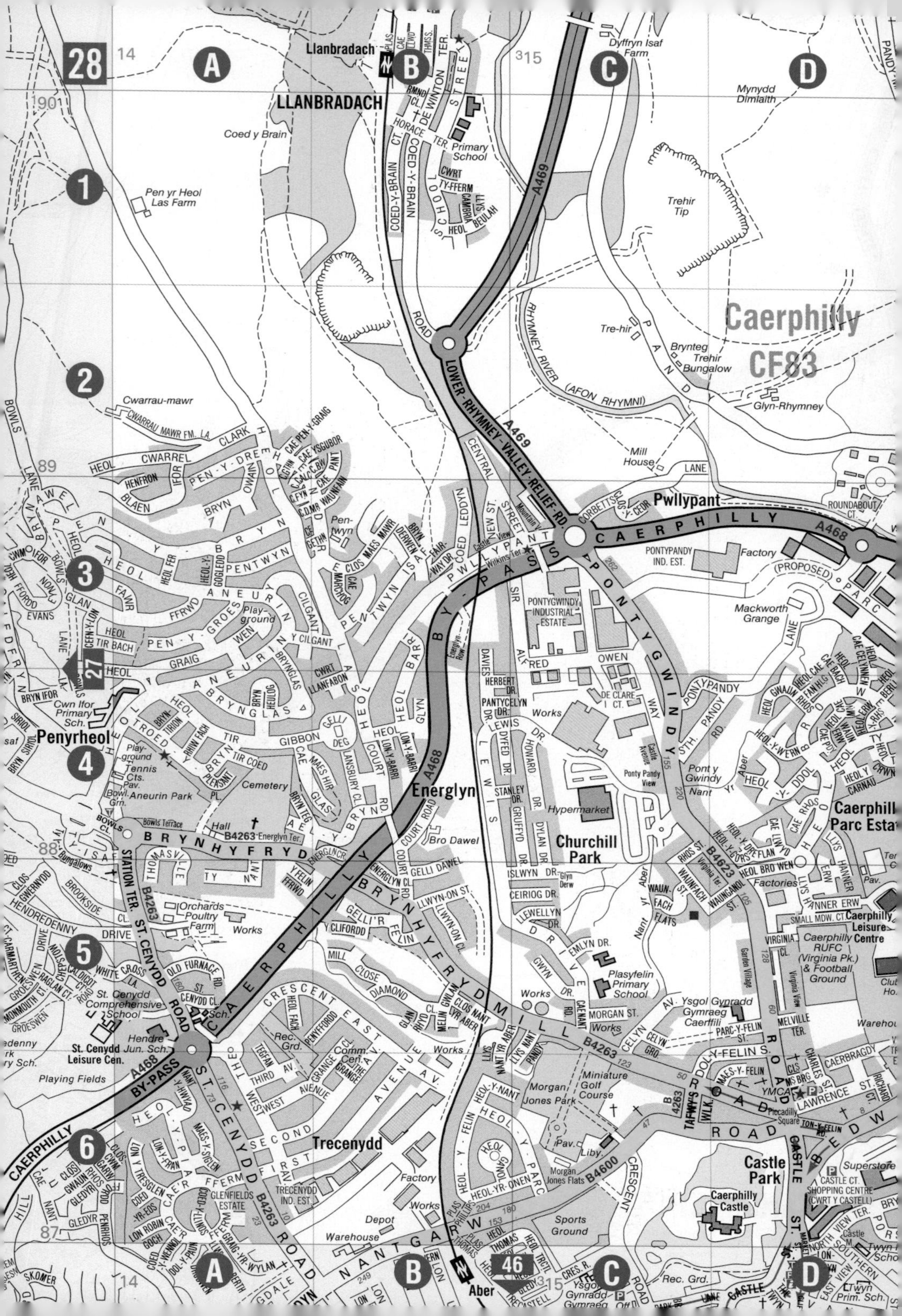
LLANBRADACH
Llanbradach
Coed y Brain
Pen yr Heol Las Farm
Dyffryn Isaf Farm
Mynydd Dimlaith
Trehir Tip
Caerphilly
CF83
Tre-hir
Brynteg
Trehir Bungalow
Glyn-Rhymney
RHYMNEY RIVER (AFON RHYMNI)
Cwarrau-mawr
Mill House
Pwllypant
CAERPHILLY
A468
A469
LOWER RHYMNEY VALLEY RELIEF RD.
PONTYPANDY IND. EST.
Factory
Mackworth Grange
PONTYGWINDY INDUSTRIAL ESTATE
BY-PASS
Penyrheol
Cwn Ifor Primary Sch.
Aneurin Park
Cemetery
Energlyn
BRYNHYFRYD
Orchards Poultry Farm
Hypermarket
Churchill Park
Ponty Pandy View
Caerphilly Parc Estate
Plasyfelin Primary School
St. Cenydd Comprehensive School
Hendre Jun. Sch.
St. Cenydd Leisure Cen.
Playing Fields
Trecenydd
Miniature Golf Course
Morgan Jones Park
Castle Park
Caerphilly Castle
Sports Ground
Depot
Warehouse
CASTLE CT. SHOPPING CENTRE (CWRT Y CASTELL)
Superstore
Caerphilly Leisure Centre
Caerphilly RUFC (Virginia Pk.) & Football Ground
Factories
Aber
46
27
A
B
C
D
1
2
3
4
5
6
14
315
190
89
88
87

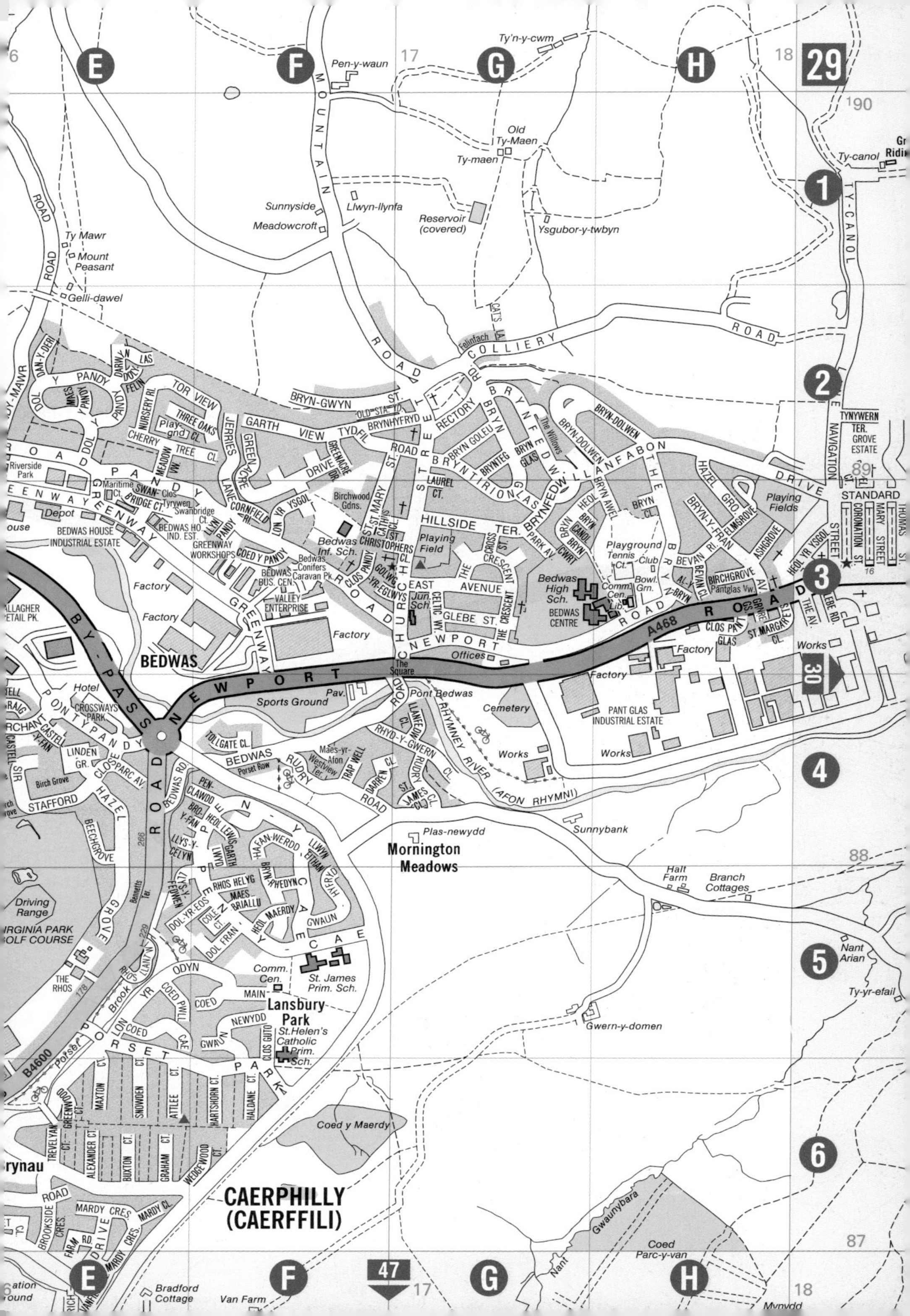

29
30
47
BEDWAS
CAERPHILLY
(CAERFFILI)
Mornington
Meadows
Lansbury
Park
NEWPORT ROAD
A468 ROAD
BY-PASS ROAD
B4600
MOUNTAIN ROAD
COLLIERY ROAD
TY-CANOL
NAVIGATION
STANDARD
PANT GLAS
INDUSTRIAL ESTATE
BEDWAS HOUSE
INDUSTRIAL ESTATE
Bedwas
High
Sch.
BEDWAS
CENTRE
Sports Ground
Cemetery
RHYMNEY RIVER
(AFON RHYMNI)
Coed y Maerdy
Gwaunybara
Coed
Parc-y-van
Reservoir
(covered)
Ty-maen
Old
Ty-Maen
Pen-y-waun
Ty'n-y-cwm
Meadowcroft
Sunnyside
Llwyn-llynfa
Ysgubor-y-twbyn
Ty Mawr
Mount
Peasant
Gelli-dawel
Plas-newydd
Sunnybank
Halt
Farm
Branch
Cottages
Nant
Arian
Ty-yr-efail
Gwern-y-domen
Ty-canol
Driving
Range
Bradford
Cottage
Van Farm
St. James
Prim. Sch.
St.Helen's
Catholic
Prim.
Sch.
The
Square
Pont Bedwas
Playing
Field
Playing
Fields
Bedwas
Inf. Sch.
Factory
Works
Offices

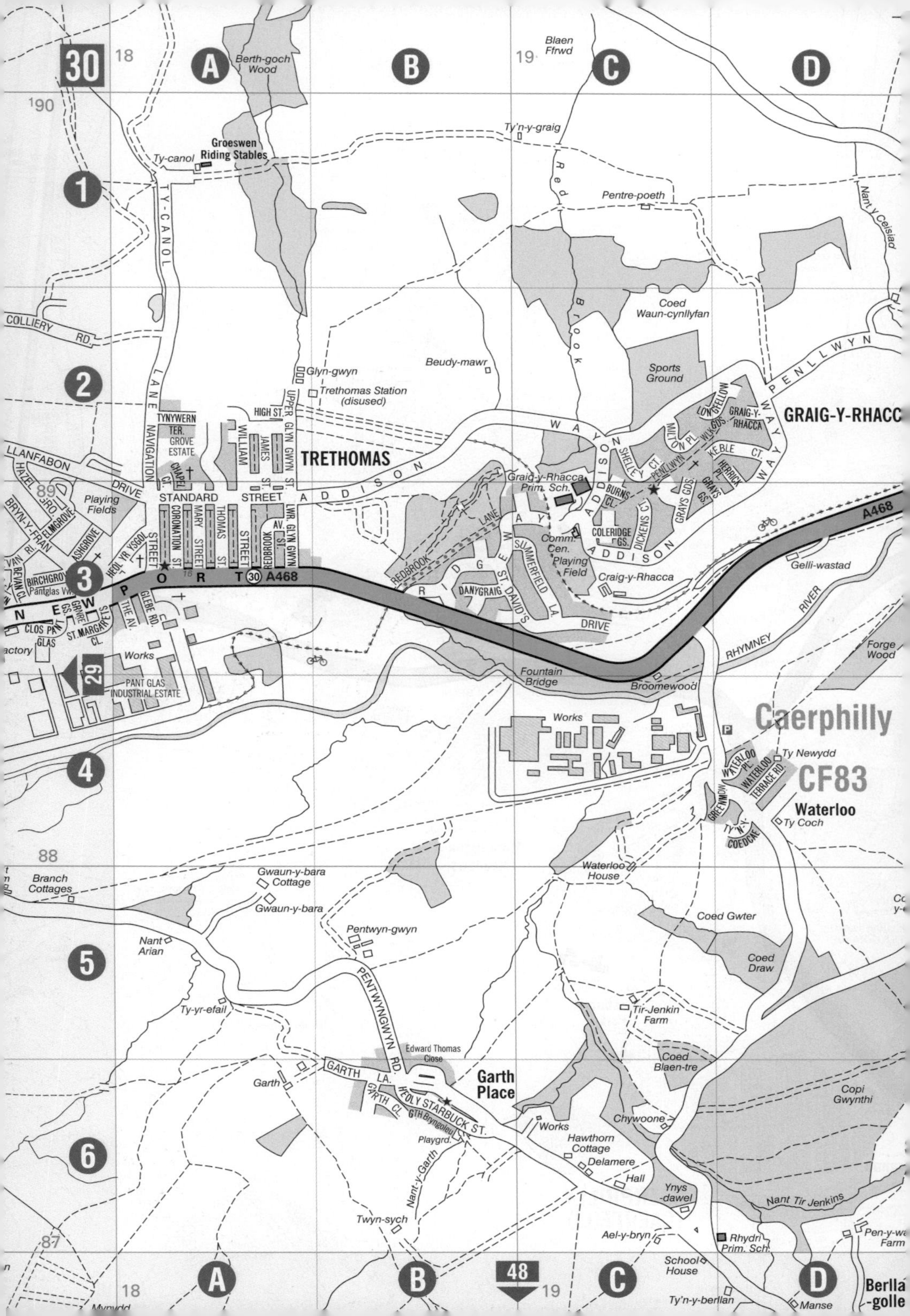

30
A
B
C
D
1
2
3
4
5
6
18
19
190
89
88
87
Berth-goch Wood
Blaen Ffrwd
Ty'n-y-graig
Groeswen Riding Stables
Ty-canol
TY-CANOL LANE
Red Brook
Pentre-poeth
Nant y Ceisiad
Coed Waun-cynllyfan
COLLIERY RD.
Beudy-mawr
Glyn-gwyn
Trethomas Station (disused)
Sports Ground
PENLLWYN WAY
GRAIG-Y-RHACC
TYNYWERN TER.
GROVE ESTATE
HIGH ST.
WILLIAM
JAMES ST.
UPPER GLYN GWYN ST.
TRETHOMAS
ADDISON WAY
LLANFABON DRIVE
HAZEL GRO.
BRYN-Y-FRAN
ELMGROVE
ASHGROVE
Playing Fields
CHAPEL CT.
STANDARD STREET
CORONATION ST.
MARY STREET
THOMAS ST.
STREET
REDBROOK AV.
LWR. GLYN GWYN ST.
HEOL YR YSGOL
STREET
BIRCHGROVE
BEVAN CL.
Pantglas Vw.
NEW PORT RD.
A468
GLEBE RD.
THE AV.
GRANGE GS.
ST. MARGARET'S CL.
CLOS PANT GLAS
Factory
Works
29
PANT GLAS INDUSTRIAL ESTATE
Graig-y-Rhacca Prim. Sch.
LANE
REDBROOK
RIDGEWAY
DANYGRAIG
ST. DAVID'S
SUMMERFIELD LA.
DRIVE
Comm. Cen.
Playing Field
Craig-y-Rhacca
COLERIDGE GS.
DICKENS CT.
BURNS CL.
SHELLEY CT.
PENLLWYN
MILTON PL.
WYE GDS.
LONGFELLOW
GRAIG-Y-RHACCA
KEBLE CT.
HERRICK PL.
GRAYS GDS.
GRAYS GS.
Gelli-wastad
RHYMNEY RIVER
Forge Wood
Fountain Bridge
Broomewood
Works
Caerphilly
CF83
Ty Newydd
WATERLOO PL.
WATERLOO TERRACE RD.
GREENMOW
TY-N-Y-COEDCAE
Waterloo
Ty Coch
Waterloo House
Branch Cottages
Gwaun-y-bara Cottage
Gwaun-y-bara
Pentwyn-gwyn
Coed Gwter
Coed Draw
Nant Arian
PENTWYNGWYN RD.
Ty-yr-efail
Tir-Jenkin Farm
Edward Thomas Close
Coed Blaen-tre
GARTH LA.
Garth
GARTH CL.
HEOLY STARBUCK ST.
GTH Bryngoleu
Garth Place
Copi Gwynthi
Works
Chywoone
Hawthorn Cottage
Playgrd.
Delamere
Hall
Nant-y-Garth
Ynys-dawel
Nant Tir Jenkins
Twyn-sych
Ael-y-bryn
Rhydri Prim. Sch.
Pen-y-wa Farm
School House
48
Ty'n-y-berllan
Manse
Berlla -golle
Mynydd

MACHEN
Chatham
Draethen
COMMERCIAL ROAD
HILL
WESLEY ROAD
CHATHAM
COMMERCIAL A468 RD.
RHYD-Y-GWERN LANE
LANE GREEN ROW
THE CRESCENT
CWMNOFYDD LANE
(AFON RHYMNI)
Pen-rhiw
Pen-rhiw Warren
Ty'r-ffynnon Farm
Ty-draw
PENRHIW
Cwm Fedw
Ty-canol Farm
TY CANOL LA.
Coed y Fedw
Bovil-uchaf
Coed Pen-llwyn
Shake Holes
Rec. Grd.
Forge Bridge
Plas Newydd
Forge Wood
Birchgrove Cottage
Glynwendron
Cwmnofydd Farm
Cwm-diffrwyth
Ty Ffern
Greenwood
Machen Mill
Rhyd y Gwern
Generals Well
Rhyd-y-Gwern Farm
Woodland Cottage
Cats Haven
Mynydd y Bwlch
Coed Cefn-pwll-du
Copi Gwynthi
Penhow Farm
Coed Llwyn-hir
Dan-y-Graig
Cwm Leyshon
Cwm-Leyshon Quarry
Yew Tree
Nant y Draethen
The Row
Coed Craig-Ruperr
32
49

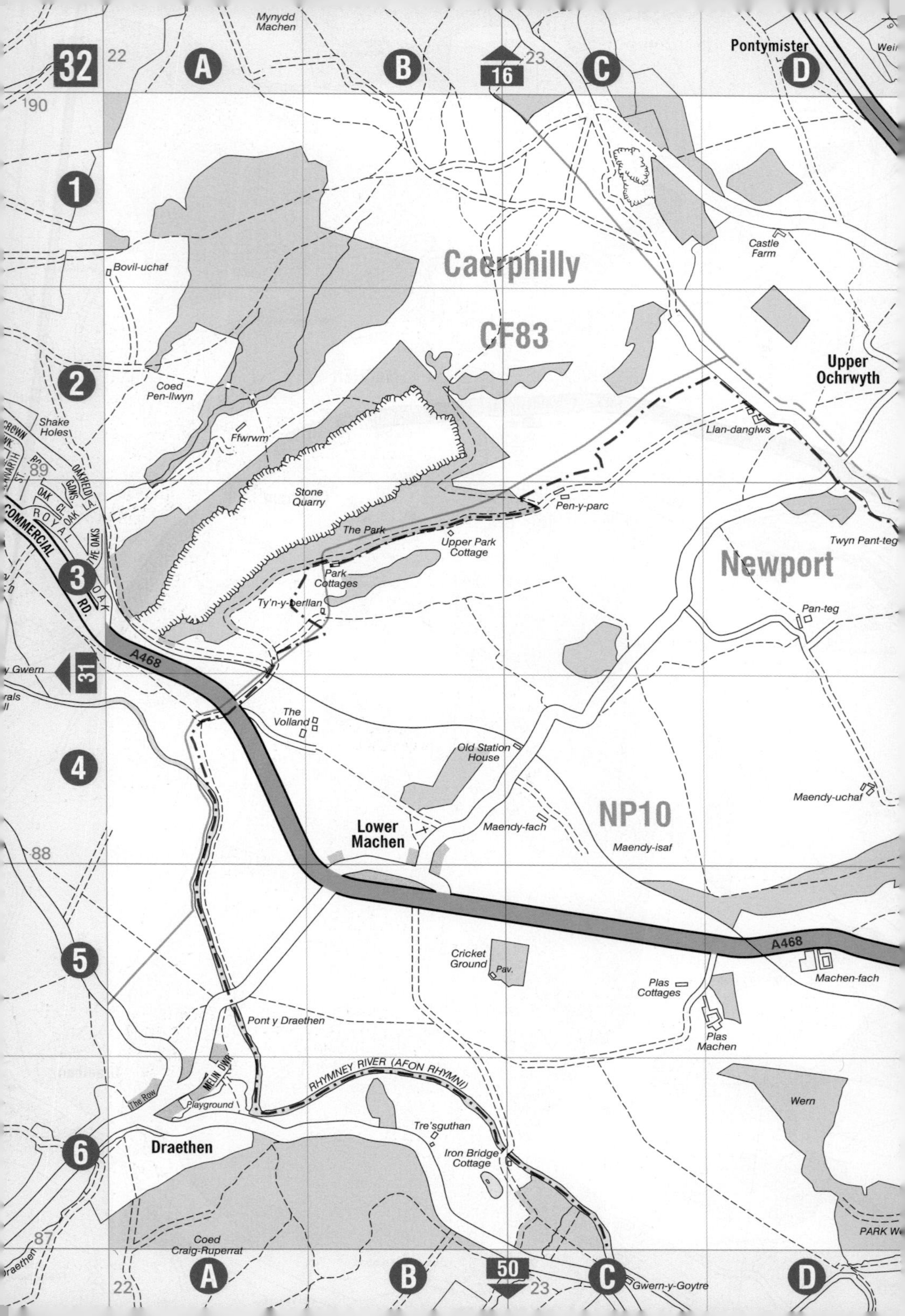
Mynydd Machen
22
A
B
16
23
C
Pontymister
D
190
1
Caerphilly
Castle Farm
Bovil-uchaf
CF83
Upper Ochrwyth
2
Coed Pen-llwyn
Shake Holes
Ffwrwm
Llan-danglws
89
Stone Quarry
Pen-y-parc
OAKFIELD
GDNS.
OAK CL.
OAK LA.
ROYAL
COMMERCIAL
THE OAKS
The Park
Upper Park Cottage
Twyn Pant-teg
Newport
3
OAK RD.
Park Cottages
Ty'n-y-berllan
Pan-teg
A468
31
The Volland
Old Station House
4
NP10
Maendy-uchaf
Lower Machen
Maendy-fach
Maendy-isaf
88
A468
Cricket Ground
Pav.
5
Machen-fach
Plas Cottages
Pont y Draethen
Plas Machen
RHYMNEY RIVER (AFON RHYMNI)
MELIN DWR
The Row
Playground
Wern
Tre'sguthan
6
Draethen
Iron Bridge Cottage
87
Coed Craig-Ruperrat
PARK W
A
50
B
C
Gwern-y-Goytre
D
22
23

33
RISCA (RHISGA)
Lower Ochrwyth
NP11
Fox Hill (Twyn y Cadno)
Rhiwderin (Rhiwderyn)
Rogerstone
CAERPHILLY (CAERFFILI)
NEWPORT (CASNEWYDD)
A467
A468
B4591
RISCA ROAD
NEWPORT ROAD
PENTRE TAI ROAD
PONTYMASON LANE
CAERPHILLY RD.
VIEW HERBERT
Monmouthshire & Brecon Canal
Coed Mawr
Coed y Squire
Coed Pwll-neidr
Coed y Meirch
Coed Bedw
Graig Wyllt
Park Wood
Penrhiw-gwiail
Heollas Farm
Hedda Farm
Cwmcaddon
Tam-y-coed
Cwm-y-Nant
Old Pontymister Farm
Factory
Superstore
Coed-mawr Cottage
Llwyn-deri
Rhyd-lydan
Five Lanes Farm
Pump-heol Farm
Pant-glâs
Foxhill
Twyn-y-cadno
Pentre Tai
Pentwyn
Sunnybank
Ty-côch
Maypole
Park Cottage
The Carpenters
Ty'n-y-ffynnon
Oakfield House
Neuadda
Coc-y-north
Cwm Dyllu
Park House
Pen y van
Upper Mount Pleasant
Lower Pleasant
Oaktree Cottage
Playing Field
Risca Leisure Centre
Ysgubor-w
Ty-Sign
Graig
Works
Recreation Ground
Islwyn Workshops
Birds Ind. Est.
Pontymister Industrial Estate
Commercial St. Caravan Site
Lib.
Inf. Sch.
17
51
34
E F G H
1 2 3 4 5 6
324 325 26
87 88 89 190

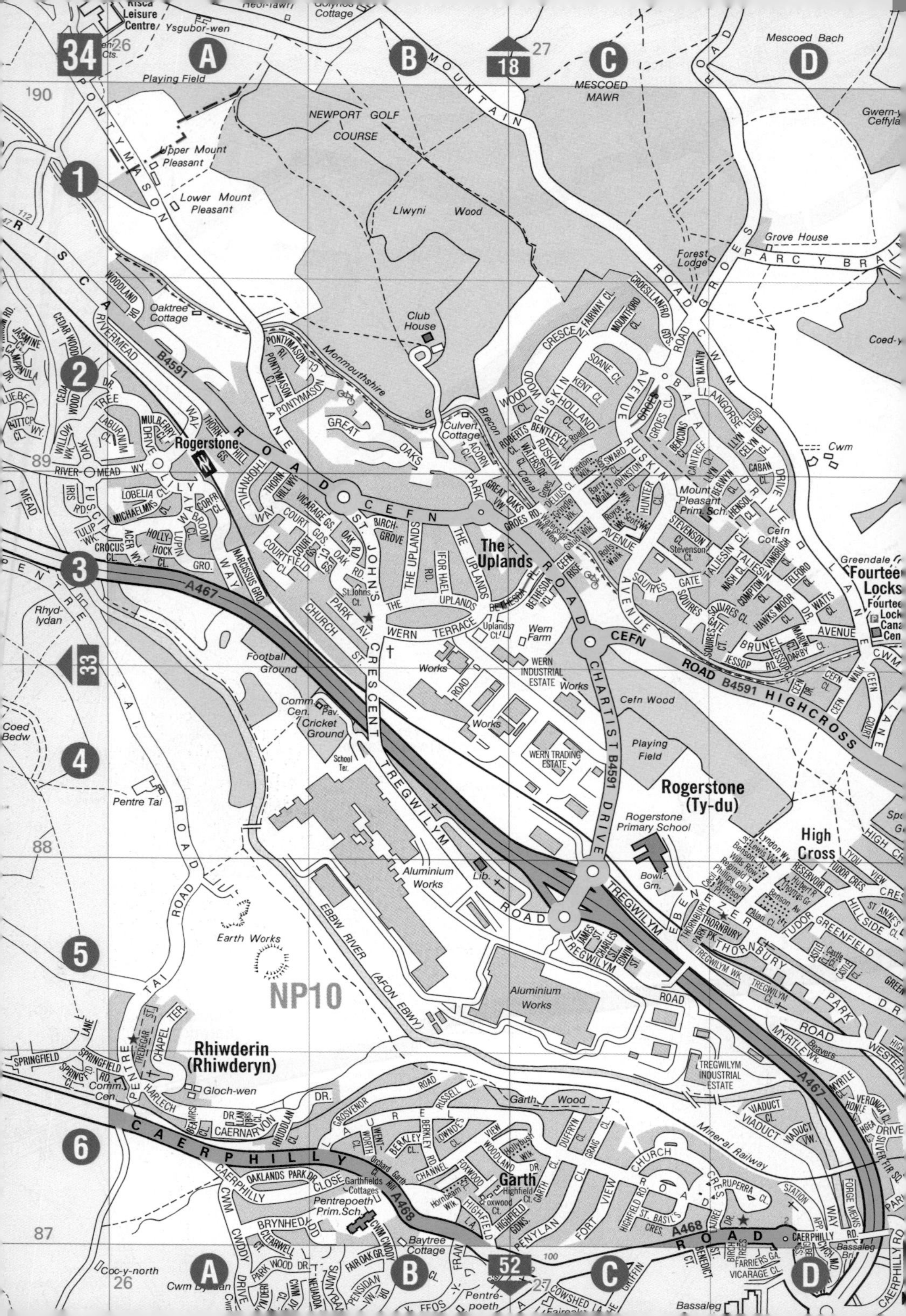
34
A
B
C
D
18
27
26
190
Kisca Leisure Centre
Ysgubor-wen
Playing Field
Mescoed Bach
MESCOED MAWR
NEWPORT GOLF COURSE
Upper Mount Pleasant
Lower Mount Pleasant
Llwyni Wood
Grove House
Forest Lodge
PARC Y BRAIN
Club House
Monmouthshire
Brecon
Canal
Culvert Cottage
Oaktree Cottage
RIVERMEAD
B4591
Rogerstone
89
RISCA
PONTYMASON
1
2
3
4
5
6
33
Cwm
Mount Pleasant Prim. Sch.
Greendale
Fourteen Locks
Canal Cen.
The Uplands
CEFN ROAD
WERN TERRACE
ST. JOHN'S CRESCENT
Football Ground
Comm. Cen.
Pav.
Cricket Ground
Rhyd-lydan
Coed Bedw
Wern Farm
WERN INDUSTRIAL ESTATE
Works
Cefn Wood
Playing Field
WERN TRADING ESTATE
CHARTIST DRIVE B4591
ROAD B4591 HIGHCROSS
Rogerstone (Ty-du)
Rogerstone Primary School
High Cross
Bowl. Grn.
School Ter.
Pentre Tai
88
TREGWILYM
Aluminium Works
Lib.
EBBW RIVER (AFON EBWY)
Earth Works
NP10
TREGWILYM INDUSTRIAL ESTATE
Rhiwderin (Rhiwderyn)
Gloch-wen
Garth Wood
Mineral Railway
A467
CAERPHILLY ROAD
A468
Garth
Pentrepoeth Prim. Sch.
Garthfields Cottages
Baytree Cottage
87
Coc-y-north
Cwm Dyffran
52
100
Pentre-poeth
Bassaleg

35
19
53
36
Junction 26
Junction 27
M4 MOTORWAY
M4
NP20
Newport
Coed Garw
Coed Kemeys
Bettws High School
Bettws Leisure Centre
Playing Field
Woodstock Pond
Woodstock Pool
Morgans Pool
Malpas Brook
Canal Bank
Gwastad Mawr
Club Ho.
Wern-ddu Wood
Wern-ddu
Ynysyfro
Ynysyfro Reservoir
Tredegar Park Golf Course
Barrack Hill
Bottom Lock
Waen Lock
Well Wood
Grove Farm
Strawberry Farm
Alteryn
Allt-yr-yn Nature Reserve
Alteryn Wood
Monmouthshire & Brecon Canal
Cwrt-y-mwnws Lock
Cwrt-y-mwnws
Fourteen Locks
Pensarn Farm
Recreation Ground
Ridgeway
Allt-yr-yn
University of Wales Newport (Allt-yr-yn Campus)
Cwrt-y-mwns Farm
Stud & Riding School
Coed y Glasllwych
The Woodlands
High Cross Prim. Sch.
Glasllwych
Glasllwych Prim. Sch.
Glasllwych B4591 Cres.
Risca Road
B4591
B4241
Fields Park
Coed-melyn Park
Chapel
Cemetery
St. Woolos
Playing Fields
Nant Coch
Clytha Park
Stow Park
Bassaleg Road
Tredegar Fort
Deer Park House
Sports Ground
Tennis Courts
Stratford Ho.
Gaer Inf. & Jun. Schools
Comm. Cen. & Youth Cen.
Play. Fld.
Hillview
Monmouth Ct.
The Beeches
Grange Ct.
Lib.
Bassaleg

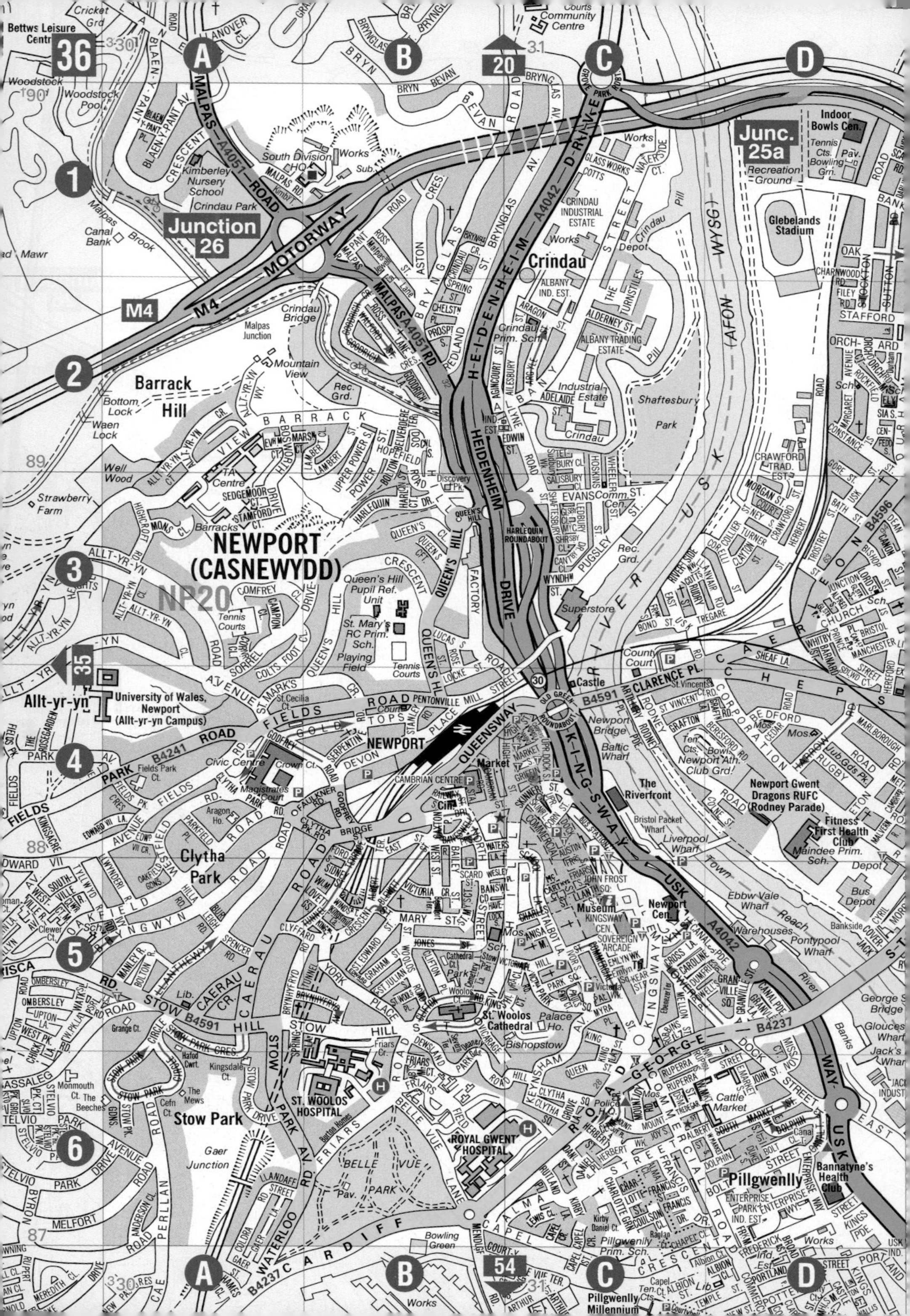

36
20
54
35
A
B
C
D
1
2
3
4
5
6
Junction 26
Junc. 25a
M4
MOTORWAY
NEWPORT (CASNEWYDD)
NP20
Crindau
Barrack Hill
Clytha Park
Stow Park
Pillgwenlly
Allt-yr-yn
University of Wales, Newport (Allt-yr-yn Campus)
Glebelands Stadium
Shaftesbury Park
Crindau Industrial Estate
Albany Trading Estate
Royal Gwent Hospital
St. Woolos Hospital
St. Woolos Cathedral
Newport Gwent Dragons RUFC (Rodney Parade)
The Riverfront
Museum
Newport Cen.
Castle
Market
Superstore
Harlequin Roundabout
Old Green Roundabout
Heidenheim Drive
Kingsway
Queensway
Usk Way
River Usk (Afon Wysg)
Malpas Road A4051
B4591
B4237
A4042
B4241
B4596
Bettws Leisure Centre
Kimberley Nursery School
Crindau Park
Queen's Hill Pupil Ref. Unit
St. Mary's RC Prim. Sch.
Civic Centre
Magistrates Court
Bannatyne's Health Club
Fitness First Health Club
Maindee Prim. Sch.
Indoor Bowls Cen.
Recreation Ground
Gaer Junction
Belle Vue Park
Bishopstow
Cattle Market
County Court
Newport Bridge
Mountain View
Malpas Junction
Strawberry Farm
Well Wood

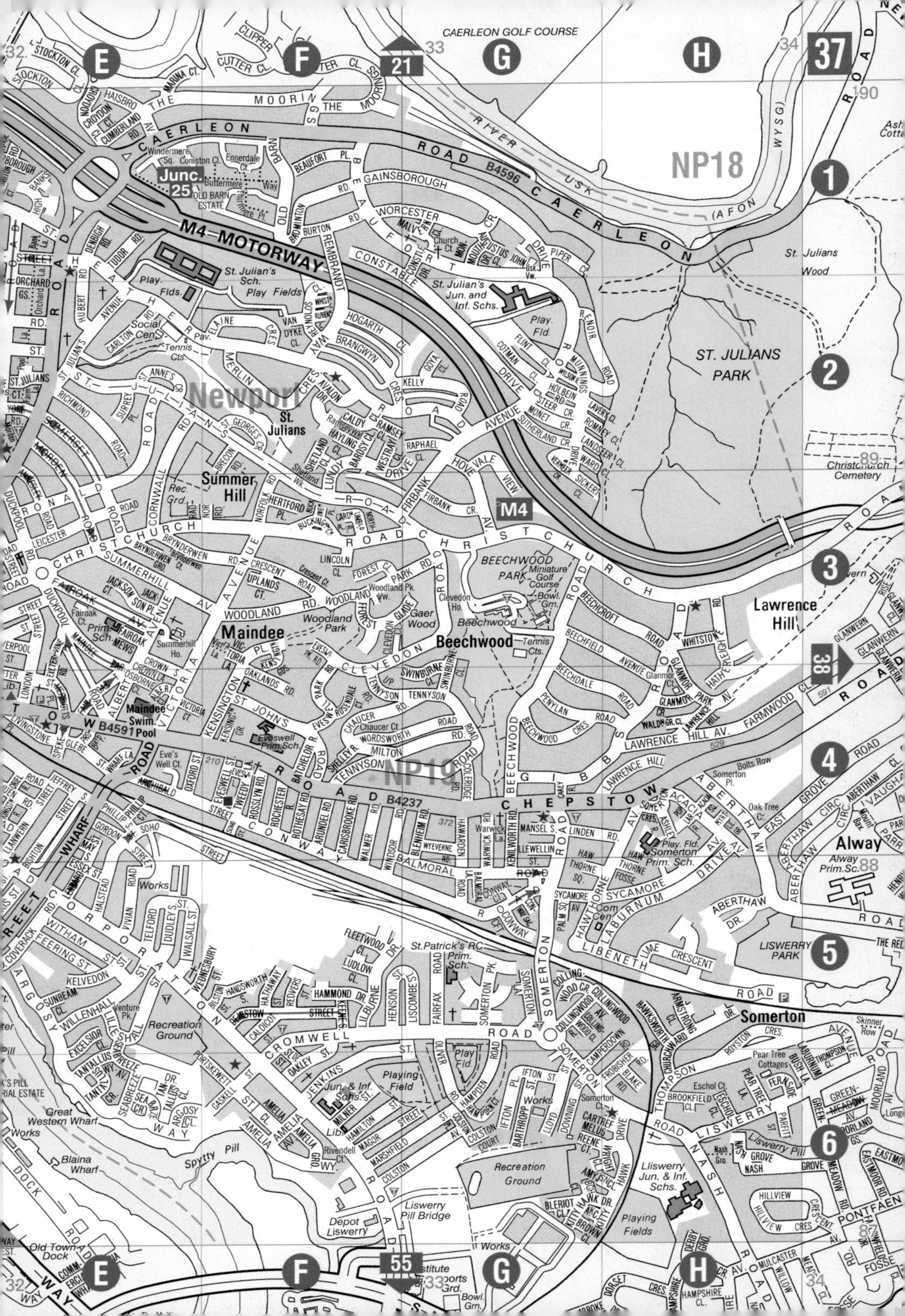

37
21
55
38
E
F
G
H
1
2
3
4
5
6
NP18
NP19
Newport
CAERLEON GOLF COURSE
RIVER USK (AFON WYSG)
CAERLEON ROAD B4596
M4 MOTORWAY
M4
Junc. 25
OLD BARN ESTATE
ST. JULIANS PARK
St. Julians Wood
Christchurch Cemetery
St. Julians
Summer Hill
Maindee
Beechwood
BEECHWOOD PARK
Miniature Golf Course
Lawrence Hill
Alway
Alway Prim.Sc.
LISWERRY PARK
Somerton
CHEPSTOW ROAD B4237
CHRISTCHURCH ROAD
CORPORATION ROAD
WHARF ROAD
Maindee Swim. Pool
W B4591
St. Julian's Sch.
St. Julian's Jun. and Inf. Schs.
Eveswell Prim.Sch.
Somerton Prim. Sch.
St.Patrick's RC Prim. Sch.
Lliswerry Jun. & Inf. Schs.
Recreation Ground
Playing Fields
Great Western Wharf
Blaina Wharf
Spytty Pill
Lisweryy Pill
Lisweryy Pill Bridge
Old Town Dock
Playing Field
Woodland Park
Gaer Wood

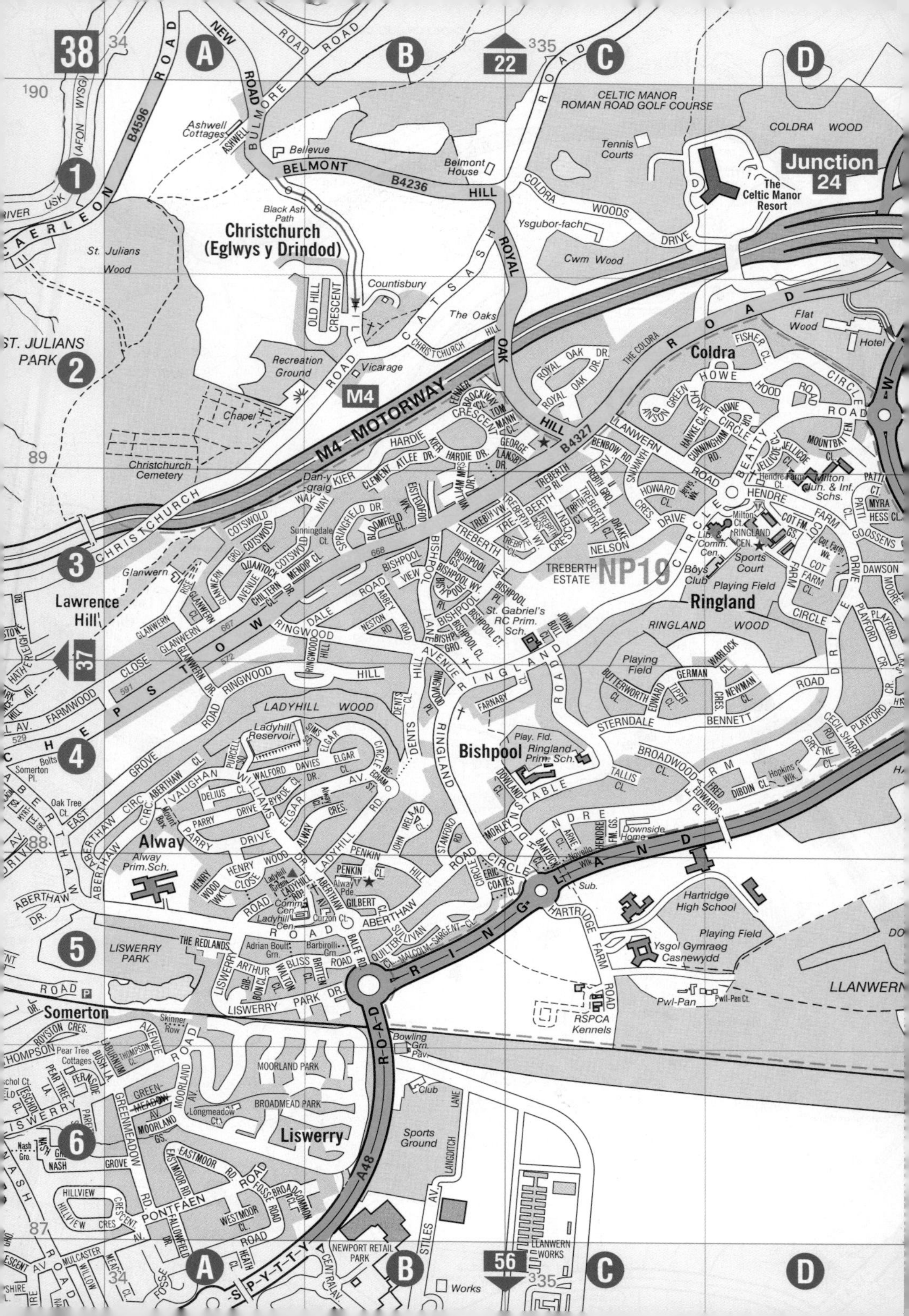

38
22
56
37
Junction 24
The Celtic Manor Resort
CELTIC MANOR ROMAN ROAD GOLF COURSE
COLDRA WOOD
Christchurch (Eglwys y Drindod)
St. Julians Wood
ST. JULIANS PARK
Lawrence Hill
Christchurch Cemetery
Chapel
Recreation Ground
Vicarage
M4 MOTORWAY
M4
Coldra
Flat Wood
Hotel
Cwm Wood
Ysgubor-fach
Tennis Courts
Belmont House
Bellevue
Ashwell Cottages
Black Ash Path
Countisbury
The Oaks
NP19
TREBERTH ESTATE
Ringland
RINGLAND WOOD
Playing Field
Sports Court
Boys Club
Milton Jun. & Inf. Schs.
St. Gabriel's RC Prim. Sch.
Bishpool
Ringland Prim. Sch.
Play. Fld.
LADYHILL WOOD
Ladyhill Reservoir
Alway
Alway Prim. Sch.
Hartridge High School
Ysgol Gymraeg Casnewydd
RSPCA Kennels
Pwl-Pan
LLANWERN
Somerton
LISWERRY PARK
Lisweerry
Liswerry
Sports Ground
MOORLAND PARK
BROADMEAD PARK
NEWPORT RETAIL PARK
LLANWERN WORKS
Works
Glanwern
Sunningdale Ct.
Dan-y-graig
Downside Home
CHEPSTOW ROAD
RINGLAND CIRCLE
HENDRE FARM DRIVE
ROYAL OAK HILL
COLDRA WOODS DRIVE
BELMONT HILL B4236
B4327
B4596
A48
CHRISTCHURCH ROAD
CAERLEON ROAD
BULMORE ROAD
NEW ROAD

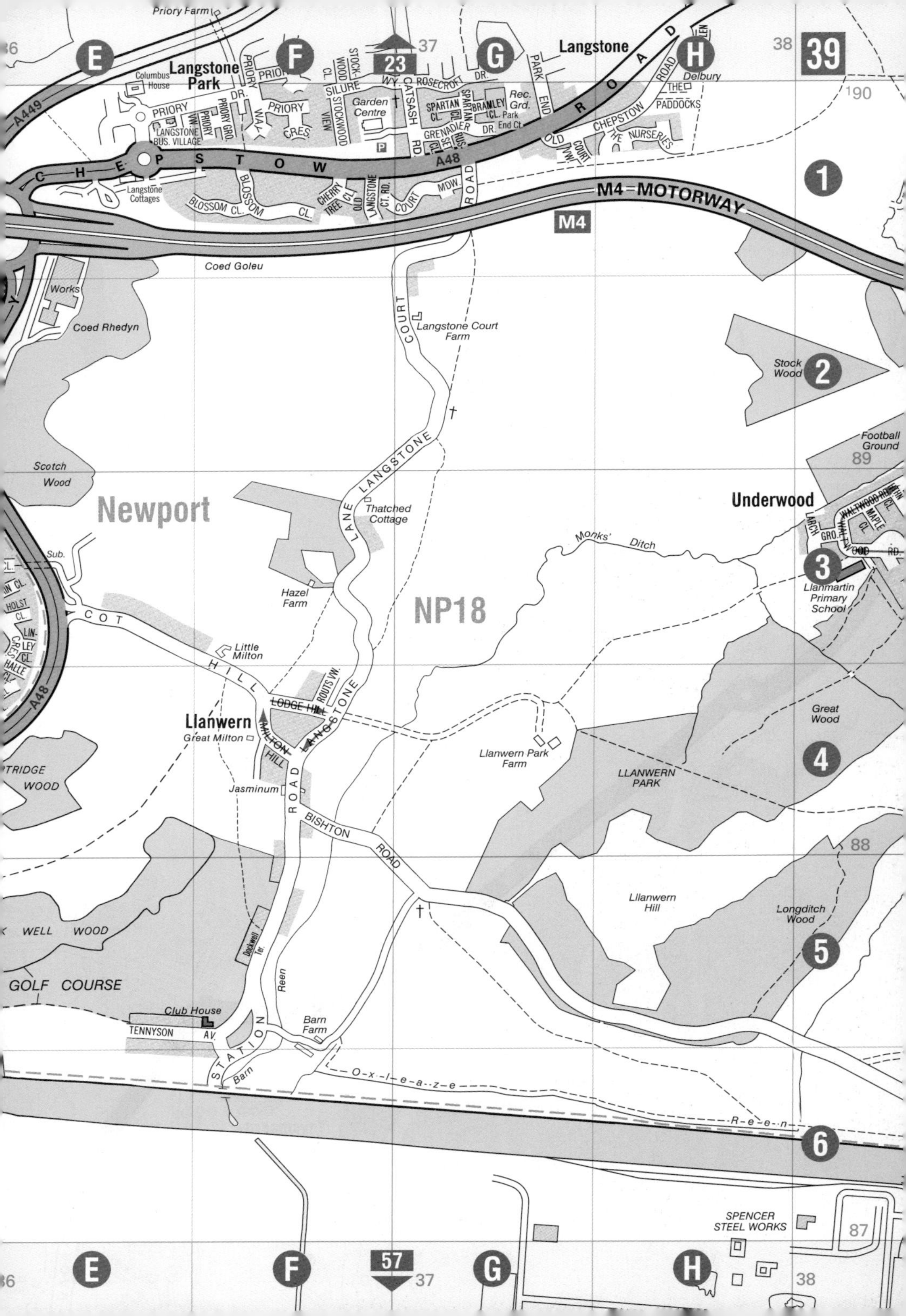

Priory Farm
Langstone Park
Columbus House
Langstone
Delbury
PRIORY
LANGSTONE BUS. VILLAGE
PRIORY GRO.
PRIORY WAY
PRIORY CRES.
SILURE
STOCKWOOD VIEW
Garden Centre
CATSASH RD.
ROSECROFT DR.
GRENADIER DR.
SPARTAN CL.
BRAMLEY CL.
Rec. Grd.
Park End Ct.
PARK END
CHEPSTOW ROAD
A48
THE PADDOCKS
THE NURSERIES
OLD COURT VW.
A449
Langstone Cottages
BLOSSOM CL.
CHERRY TREE CL.
OLD LANGSTONE CT. RD.
COURT MDW.
M4 MOTORWAY
M4
Coed Goleu
Works
Coed Rhedyn
LANGSTONE COURT
Langstone Court Farm
Stock Wood
Football Ground
Scotch Wood
Newport
LANGSTONE LANE
Thatched Cottage
Underwood
LARCH GRO.
WALTWOOD RD.
MAPLE CL.
Monks' Ditch
Sub.
Hazel Farm
NP18
Llanmartin Primary School
COT HILL
HOLST CL.
LINLEY CL.
HALLE CRES.
Little Milton
LODGE HILL
ROUTS VW.
Llanwern
Great Milton
MILTON HILL
Great Wood
Llanwern Park Farm
LLANWERN PARK
TRIDGE WOOD
Jasminum
BISHTON ROAD
Llanwern Hill
Longditch Wood
WELL WOOD
Dockwell Ter.
Reen
GOLF COURSE
Club House
TENNYSON AV.
STATION
Barn Farm
Barn
O-x-l-e-a-z-e
R-e-e-n
SPENCER STEEL WORKS
E F G H
1 2 3 4 5 6
36 37 38
190 89 88 87

23

57

02
03
A
B
C
D
87
86
185
84
1
2
3
4
5
6
Pantyddrainan
Nant Muchudd
Ty-cwr
THE MEADOWS
GWERN HEULOG
TYLCHA FACH CL.
Nant Melyn
Porth
CF39
TONYREFAIL
Craig Afon
ELY VALLEY ROAD
HEOL
Playgrd.
Comm. Cen.
The Chestnuts
Garth-grabban Bungalow
Garth-grabban
Rhiwfelin Fawr
ELWYN ST.
COLLWYN ST.
Garth Hall
Coedely
(Coed-elái)
Bedw
Pontyclun
CF72
STREET
VALLEY RD.
ELY VALLEY ROAD
A4119
ELY RIVER
Mynydd Garthmaelwg
Pentglas
(AFON ELAI)
Works
Dyffryn-uchaf
Royal Mint
Dyffryn-isaf
Factory
STIRLING DR.
LLANTRISANT INDUSTRIAL ESTATE
Nant Cwm-du
MYNYDD GARTHMAELWG
YNYSMAERDY TER.
PEMBROKE CR.
GLAN-YR-ELY
Hall
Ellis
ANSARI CT.
Ynysmaerdy
Mardy
Hafod
Ty-Maelwg
Forest View
ROYAL GLAMORGAN HOSPITAL
64
RHODFA MARICS
Nant

64

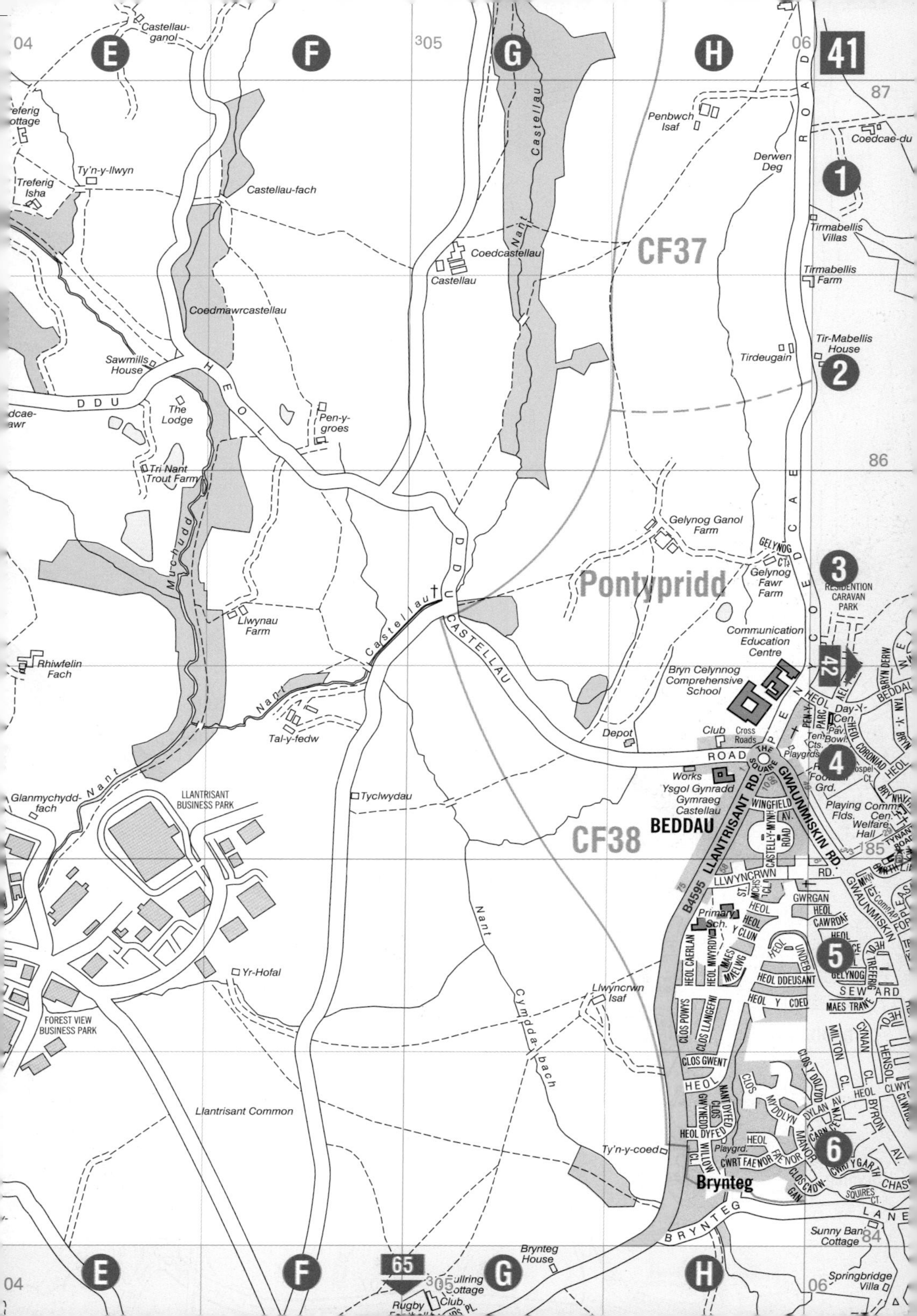
E
F
G
H
04
305
06
87
86
185
84
1
2
3
4
5
6
42
65
Castellau-ganol
Treferig Cottage
Ty'n-y-llwyn
Treferig Isha
Castellau-fach
Castellau
Nant
Coedcastellau
Castellau
CF37
Penbwch Isaf
Derwen Deg
Coedcae-du
Tirmabellis Villas
Tirmabellis Farm
Tir-Mabellis House
Tirdeugain
Coedmawrcastellau
Sawmills House
DDU
HEOL
The Lodge
Pen-y-groes
Tri Nant Trout Farm
Gelynog Ganol Farm
GELYNOG CT.
Gelynog Fawr Farm
Pontypridd
RESIDENTION CARAVAN PARK
Communication Education Centre
Murchudd
Llwynau Farm
Castellau
CASTELLAU
Rhiwfelin Fach
Bryn Celynnog Comprehensive School
Nant
Tal-y-fedw
Depot
Club
Cross Roads
ROAD
THE SQUARE
Works
Ysgol Gynradd Gymraeg Castellau
LLANTRISANT RD.
GWAUNMISKIN RD.
B4595
WINGFIELD AV.
CASTELL-Y-MYNYDD ROAD
BEDDAU
CF38
Glanmychydd-fach
LLANTRISANT BUSINESS PARK
Tyclwydau
Playing Fields
Cen.
Welfare Hall
LLWYNCRWN RD.
GWRGAN
HEOL CAWRDAF
Primary Sch.
HEOL Y CLUN
HEOL CAERLAN
HEOL MWYRDY
MAES MAELWG
HEOL UNDEB
HEOL DDEUSANT
GELYNOG
HEOL TREFERIG
SEWARD
MAES TRANE
HEOL Y COED
CLOS POWYS
CLOS LLANGEFNI
CLOS GWENT
MILTON CL.
CYNAN
HENSOL CL.
CLOS Y DOLYDD
HEOL CLWYD
BYRON AV.
DYLAN AV.
MYDDOLYN
GWYNEDD
CLOS NANT DYFED
HEOL DYFED
WILLOW CL.
CWRT FAENOR
FAENOR
MANOR
CARN CELYN
CWM Y GARTH
CLOS CADWGAN
SQUIRES CT.
Playgrd.
Nant
Cymdda-bach
Llwyncrwn Isaf
Yr-Hofal
FOREST VIEW BUSINESS PARK
Llantrisant Common
Ty'n-y-coed
Brynteg
BRYNTEG
LANE
Sunny Bank Cottage
Springbridge Villa
Brynteg House
Bullring Cottage
Rugby Club
PEN-Y-COEDCAE ROAD
HEOL PEN-Y-PARC
Day-Y-Cen.
Pav.
Bowl.
Ten. Cts.
Playgrds.
HEOL CORONIAD
Football Grd.
Gospel Ct.
BRYN DERW
BEDDAU
TAN-Y-BRYN
GWAUNMISKIN
Comm. Ap.

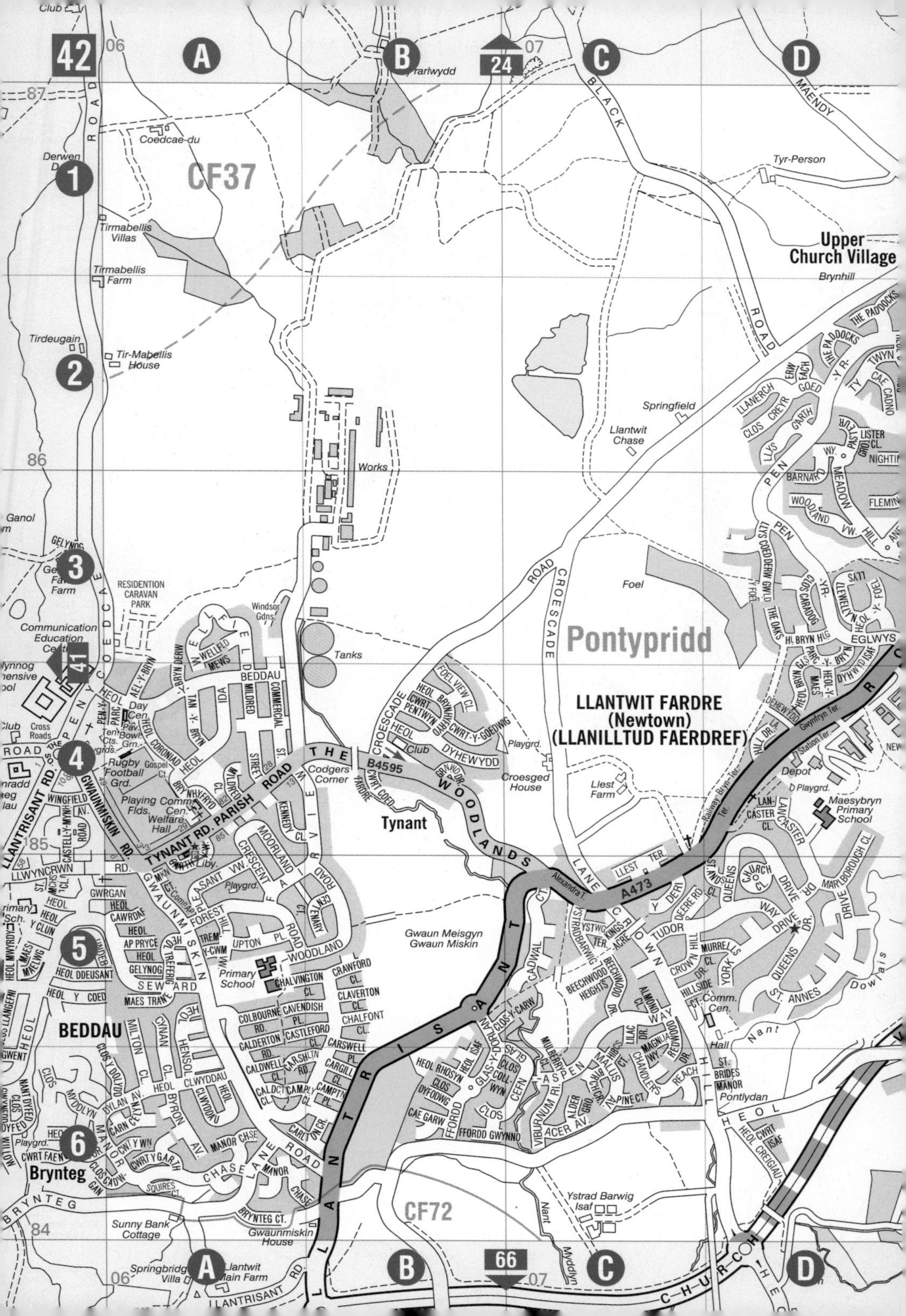
A
B
C
D
24
06
07
87
86
84
185
1
2
3
4
5
6
CF37
CF72
Coedcae-du
Derwen
Tirmabellis Villas
Tirmabellis Farm
Tirdeugain
Tir-Mabellis House
Tyr-Person
Upper Church Village
Brynhill
BLACK ROAD
MAENDY
Springfield
Llantwit Chase
Works
Ganol
GELYNOG
RESIDENTION CARAVAN PARK
Communication Education Centre
Windsor Gdns.
Tanks
Foel
Pontypridd
CROESCADE ROAD
LLANTWIT FARDRE
(Newtown)
(LLANILLTUD FAERDREF)
Playgrd.
Croesged House
Llest Farm
Codgers Corner
B4595
THE WOODLANDS
Tynant
TYNANT RD.
PARISH ROAD
Rugby Football Grd.
Playing Flds.
Welfare Hall
Liby.
LLANTRISANT RD.
GWAUNMISKIN RD.
COEDCAE ROAD
Gwaun Meisgyn
Gwaun Miskin
Primary School
BEDDAU
Brynteg
BRYNTEG
Sunny Bank Cottage
Gwaunmiskin House
Springbridge Villa
Llantwit Main Farm
LLANTRISANT
LLANTRISANT RD.
CHURCH
Ystrad Barwig Isaf
Nant Myddlyn
66
A473
Alexandra T.
LLEST TER.
Maesybryn Primary School
Depot
Station Ter.
Gwynfryn Ter.
Railway Bryn Ter.
Comm. Cen.
Hall
Nant
Dowlais
Pontlydan
HEOL
ST. BRIDES MANOR
QUEENS DRIVE
MARLBOROUGH CL.
ST. ANNES
YORK
CROWN HILL
TUDOR
HILLSIDE CT.
BEECHWOOD HEIGHTS
CADWAL
VIBURNUM RI.
ACER AV.
FFORDD GWYNNO
HEOL RHOSYN
HEOL ISAF
CAE GARW
MALLUS
CHANDLERS
REACH
EGLWYS
THE PADDOCKS
PEN
LLYS
HEOL CRWT ISAF
HEOL CREIGIAU
CHALVINGTON CL.
CRAWFORD CL.
CLAVERTON CL.
CHALFONT CL.
CARSWELL PL.
CARGILL CL.
CAMPTN PL.
CASTLEFORD CL.
CAVENDISH PL.
COLBOURNE RD.
CALDERTON RD.
CALDWELL CL.
WOODLAND ROAD
UPTON PL.
FOREST HILL
PLEASANT VW.
MOORLAND CRESCENT
KENNEDY CL.
CENTENARY CT.
RIVERVIEW
BEDDAU
MILDRED
COMMERCIAL ST.
STREET
IDA
TAN-Y-BRYN
HEOL CORONIAD
SEWARD
MAES TRANE
HEOL Y COED
HEOL DDEUSANT
GELYNOG
HEOL AP PRYCE
HEOL CAWRDAF
GWRGAN
LLWYNCRWN
MILTON CL.
CYNAN CL.
HENSOL
CLWYDDAU
HEOL BYRON AV.
DYLAN AV.
CARN CEIYN
MANOR CHSE
CHASE LANE
MANOR ROAD
SQUIRES CT.
BRYNTEG CT.
WINGFIELD
CASTELL-Y-MYNYDD
HEOL DYHEWYDD
CROESCADE
FOELVIEW CL.
CWRT PENTWYN
CWRT-Y-GOEDWIG
Club
Cross Roads

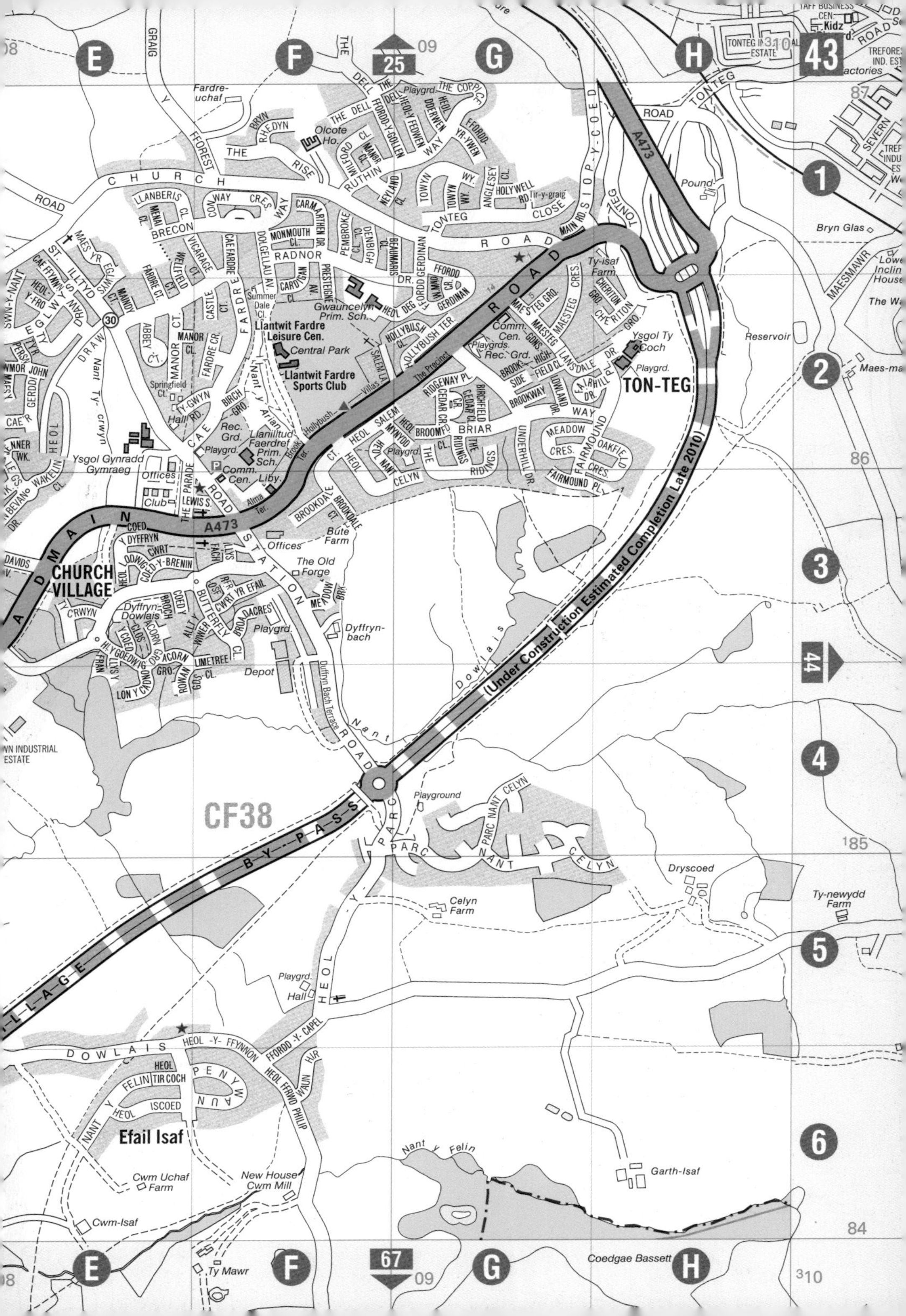

CHURCH VILLAGE
TON-TEG
Efail Isaf
CF38
A473
MAIN ROAD
CHURCH VILLAGE BY-PASS
(Under Construction Estimated Completion Late 2010)
Llantwit Fardre Leisure Cen.
Central Park
Llantwit Fardre Sports Club
Gwauncelyn Prim. Sch.
Ysgol Ty Coch
Ysgol Gynradd Gymraeg
Llanilltud Faerdref Prim. Sch.
Comm. Cen.
Liby.
Offices
Club
Playgrd.
Playground
Rec. Grd.
Bute Farm
The Old Forge
Dyffryn-bach
Depot
Duffryn Bach Terrace
STATION ROAD
TONTEG ROAD
CHURCH ROAD
HEOL-Y-PARC
DOWLAIS
HEOL-Y-FFYNNON
FFORDD-Y-CAPEL
Celyn Farm
Dryscoed
Ty-newydd Farm
Garth-Isaf
Nant y Felin
Cwm Uchaf Farm
New House Cwm Mill
Cwm-Isaf
Ty Mawr
Coedgae Bassett
Fardre-uchaf
Olcote Ho.
Ty-isaf Farm
Pound
Bryn Glas
Reservoir
Maes-mawr
TONTEG IND. ESTATE
TREFOREST IND. EST.
TAFF BUSINESS CEN.
Kidz
25
67
44
E
F
G
H
1
2
3
4
5
6
08
09
310
84
185
86
87
30

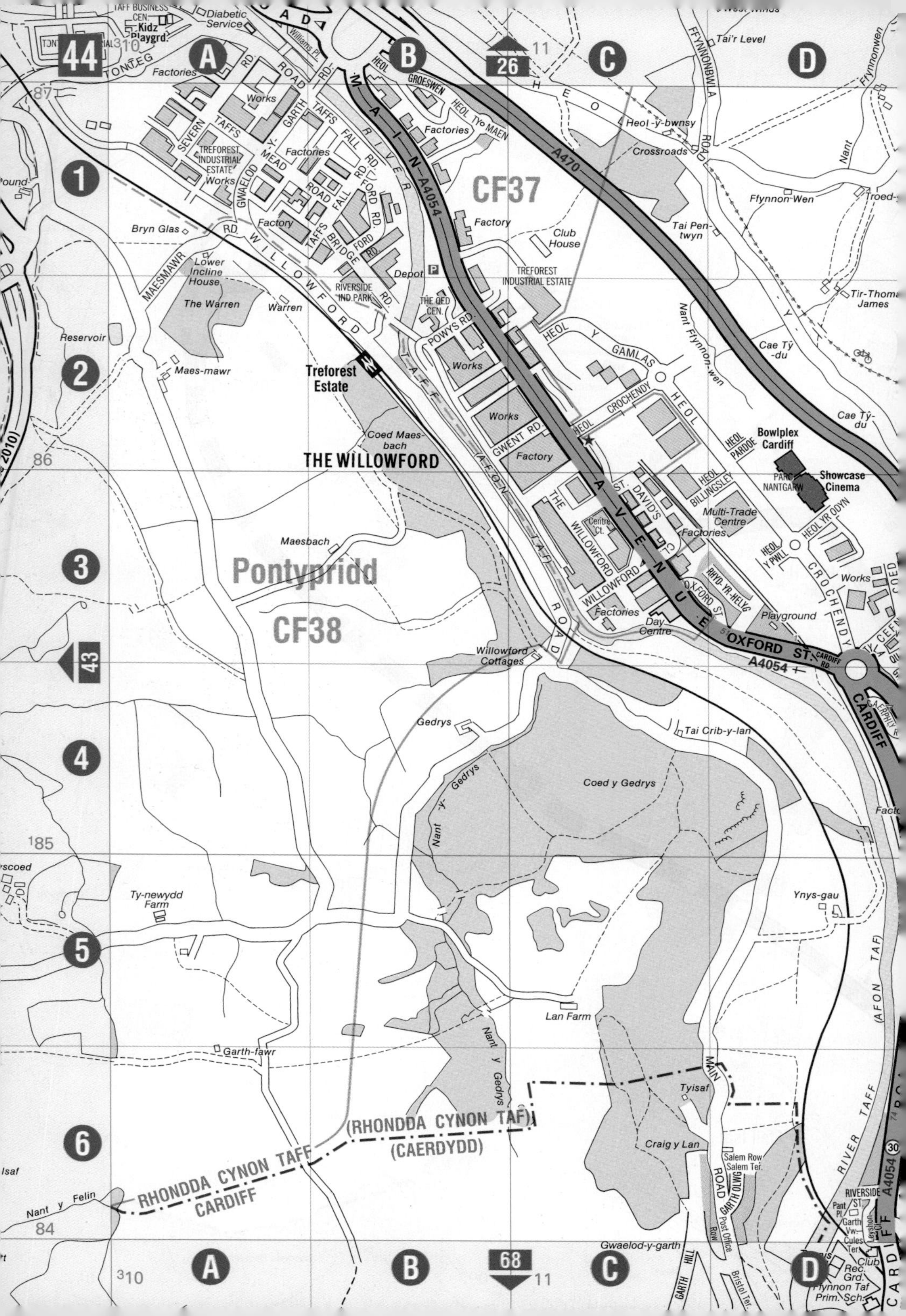

44
A
B
C
D
26
11
68
43
1
2
3
4
5
6
310
87
86
185
84
Taff Business Cen.
Diabetic Service
Kidz Playgrd.
Tonteg
Factories
Works
Severn
Taffs
Garth
Treforest Industrial Estate
Gwaelod-y-Mead
Taffs Fall Rd.
Ford Rd.
Taffs Bridge Rd.
Factory
Bryn Glas
Maesmawr Rd.
Lower Incline House
The Warren
Warren
Willowford Rd.
Riverside Ind. Park
Depot
Reservoir
Maes-mawr
Treforest Estate
Coed Maes-bach
THE WILLOWFORD
Main Avenue
A4054
Heol Groeswen
Heol Tŷ Maen
CF37
Club House
A470
Heol-y-bwnsy
Crossroads
Ffynnonbwla Road
Ffynnon-Wen
Tai Pen-twyn
Tai'r Level
Nant Ffynnon-wen
Tir-Thomas James
Cae Tŷ-du
Heol y Gamlas
Heol Crochendy
Heol Pardoe
Bowlplex Cardiff
Parc Nantgarw
Showcase Cinema
Heol Billingsley
Multi-Trade Centre
Heol yr Odyn
Heol y Pwll
Crochendy
Works
Playground
Powys Rd.
The Qed Cen.
Gwent Rd.
St. David's Cl.
The Willowford
Centre Ct.
Rhyd-yr-Helyg
Oxford St.
Day Centre
Afon Taf
Pontypridd
CF38
Maesbach
Willowford Cottages
Gedrys
Tai Crib-y-lan
Nant-y-Gedrys
Coed y Gedrys
Ynys-gau
Ty-newydd Farm
Lan Farm
Garth-fawr
Nant y Gedrys
Tyisaf
Main Road
Craig y Lan
(Rhondda Cynon Taf)
(Caerdydd)
Rhondda Cynon Taf
Cardiff
Nant y Felin
Salem Row
Salem Ter.
Garth Olwg
Post Office Row
Gwaelod-y-garth
Garth Hill
Bristol Ter.
River Taff
Riverside
Pant St.
Garth Vw.
Cules Ter.
Club
Rec. Grd.
Ffynnon Taf Prim. Sch.
Cardiff Rd.

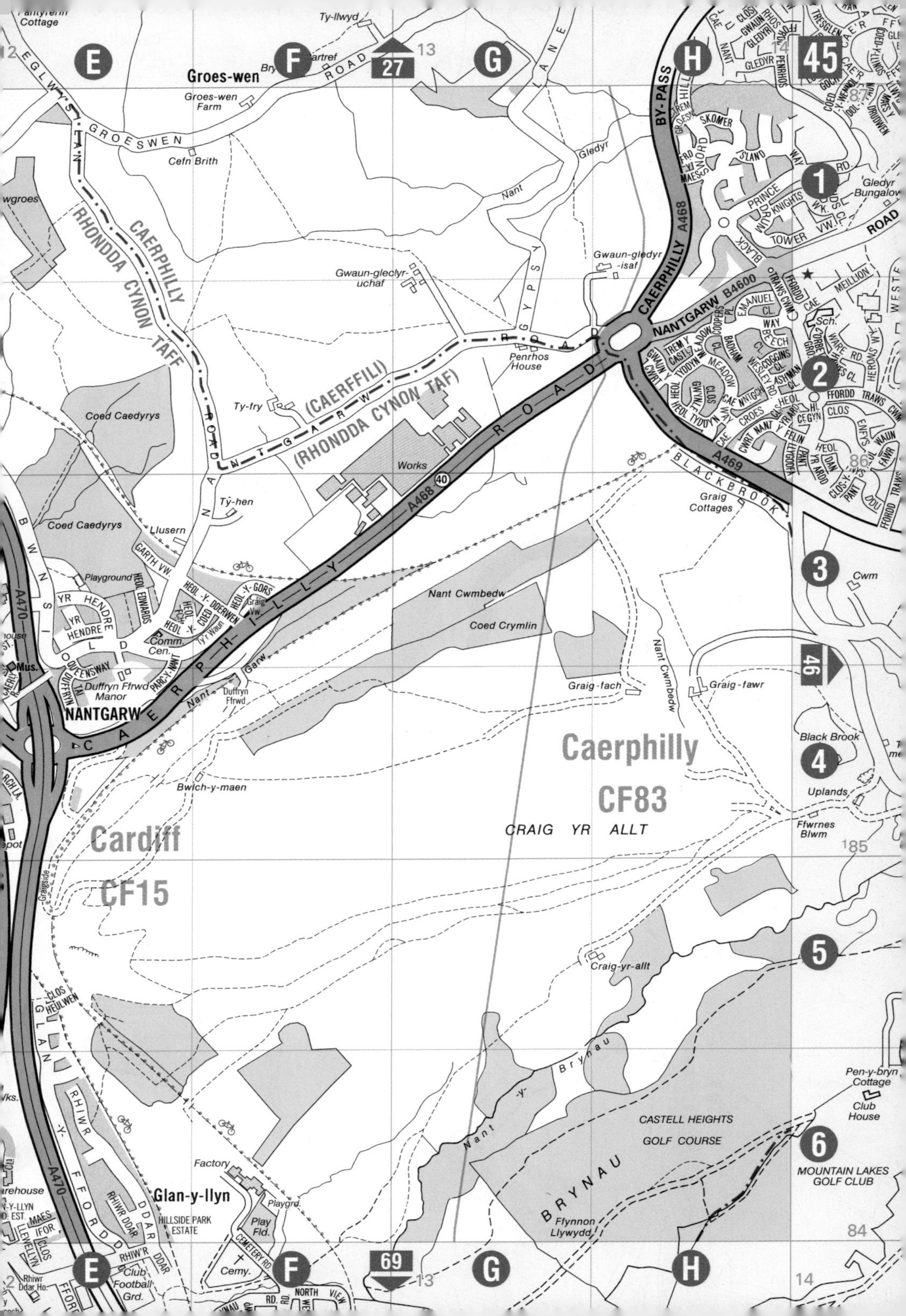
Groes-wen
Groes-wen Farm
GROESWEN
Cefn Brith
Ty-llwyd
ROAD
27
69
CAERPHILLY
RHONDDA CYNON TAFF
(CAERFFILI)
(RHONDDA CYNON TAF)
Coed Caedyrys
Ty-fry
Works
A468
40
Tŷ-hen
Llusern
Playground
Penrhos House
Gwaun-gleclyr-uchaf
Gwaun-gledyr-isaf
GYPSY LANE
Gledyr
Nant
BY-PASS
Gledyr Bungalow
NANTGARW B4600
CAERPHILLY A468
A469
BLACKBROOK
Graig Cottages
Cwm
Nant Cwmbedw
Coed Crymlin
Graig-fach
Graig-fawr
46
Black Brook
Uplands
Ffwrnes Blwm
Caerphilly
CF83
CRAIG YR ALLT
Cardiff
CF15
Bwlch-y-maen
NANTGARW
Duffryn Ffrwd Manor
Duffryn Ffrwd
Nant Garw
Comm. Cen.
Mus.
A470
Craig-yr-allt
Brynau
Nant-y-Brynau
CASTELL HEIGHTS GOLF COURSE
BRYNAU
Ffynnon Llywydd
Pen-y-bryn Cottage
Club House
MOUNTAIN LAKES GOLF CLUB
Factory
Glan-y-llyn
Playgrd.
Play Fld.
HILLSIDE PARK ESTATE
Cemy.
CEMETERY RD.
Club Football Grd.
Rhiwr Ddar Ho.
NORTH VIEW
E
F
G
H
1
2
3
4
5
6
13
14
84
185
86
87

Caerphilly
CAERPHILLY COMMON
CF83
TWYN GARWA
WATFORD ROAD
A469 ROAD
THORNHILL ROAD
THORNHILL
MOUNTAIN ROAD
B4623
NANTGARW ROAD
LON-Y-RHEDYN
B4600
B4263
ST. CENYDD RD.
ST. MARTIN'S ROAD
St. Martins
Denscombe
Watford Park
Bryngwyn
CAERPHILLY GOLF COURSE
CAERPHILLY DISTRICT MINERS HOSPITAL
WESTERN INDUSTRIAL ESTATE
St. Martin Comp. Sch.
Magistrates Court
Club House
Caerphilly Castle
Castle Park
CASTLE CT. SHOPPING CENTRE (CWRT Y CASTELL)
Caerphilly
Aber
Sports Ground
Ysgol Gymraeg Y Castell
Rec. Grd.
Factory
Depot
Warehouse
TRECENYDD IND. EST.
GLENFIELDS ESTATE
Morgan Jones Flats
Plas Watford
Cwm
Graig Cottages
Graig-fawr
Black Brook
Tymelyn
Uplands
Ffwrnes Blwm
Bryn-yr-haul
Mount Pleasant
Fern Bank
Waun-waelod
Ty-nant
Garn Lwyd
Twyn-y-Gwow Cotts.
Cwmwbwb
Glyn Glas
Ty'n-y-coedcae
RHONDDA CYNON TAFF
CAERPHILLY
RHONDDA CYNON TAF
(CAERFFILI)
BRYN-Y-PEN
WAUNWAELOD WAY
HEOL-Y-FFOREST
RHIWBINA HILL
CASTELL HEIGHTS GOLF COURSE
Pen-y-bryn Cottage
MOUNTAIN LAKES GOLF COURSE
Blaengwynlais
Graig-goch
Blaengwynlais Quarries
Wenallt
WENALLT
COED-Y-BRIWANT
Cwm Nofydd
Cwmnofydd
Cefncarnau-fawr
Cefncarnau-fach
RIDGEWAY GOLF COURSE
Driving Range
Nant
Felen
BLACKBROOK
28
45
70
A
B
C
D
1
2
3
4
5
6

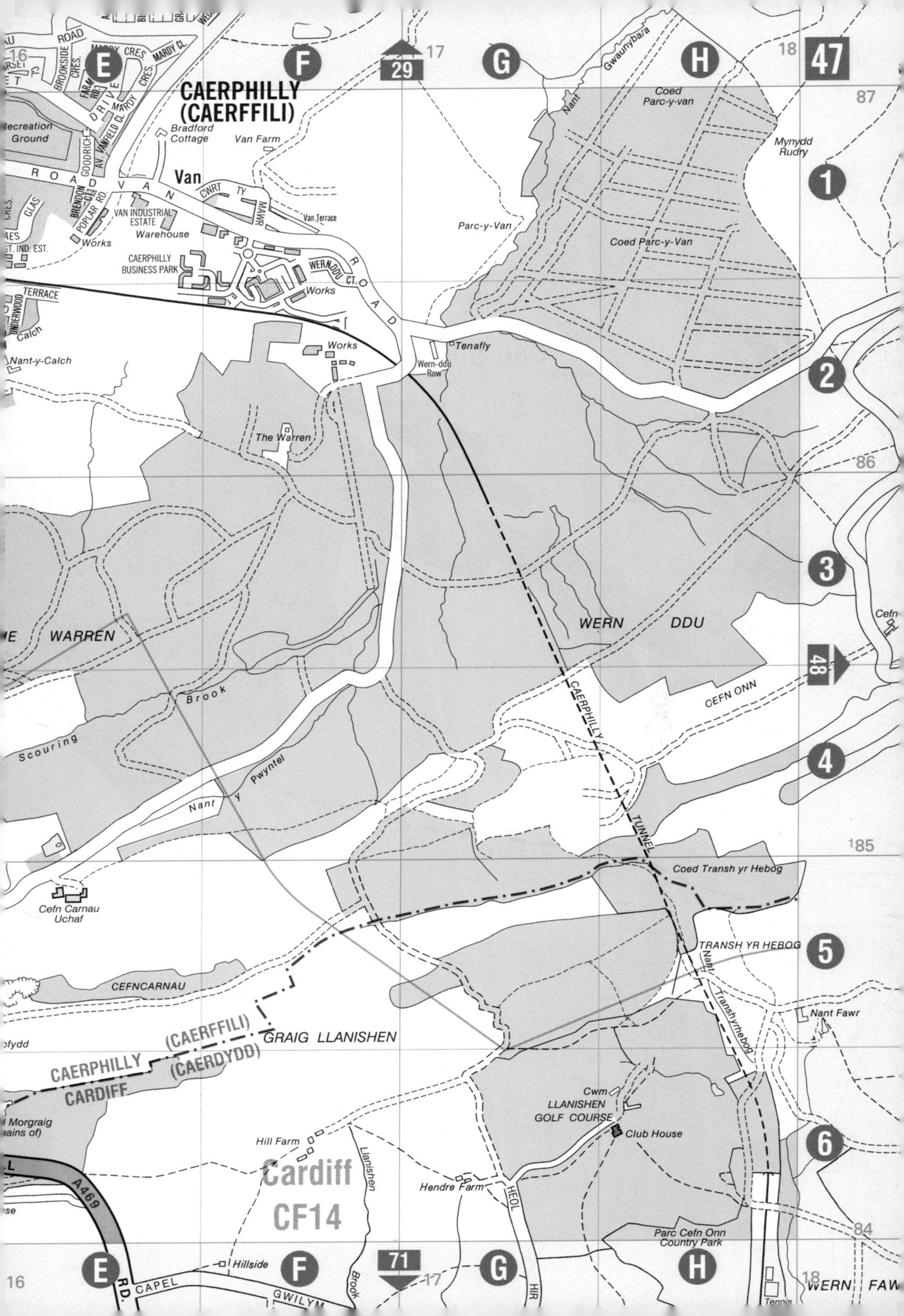

CAERPHILLY
(CAERFFILI)
Van
Bradford Cottage
Van Farm
Recreation Ground
GOODRICH AV.
VANFIELD CL.
MARDY DRIVE
FARM RD.
BROOKSIDE CRES.
BROOKSIDE ROAD
MARDY CRES.
MARDY CL.
BRENDON CT.
POPLAR RD.
VAN ROAD
CWRT TY MAWR
Van Terrace
VAN INDUSTRIAL ESTATE
Warehouse
Works
CAERPHILLY BUSINESS PARK
WERNDDU CT.
TERRACE
UNDERWOOD
Calch
Nant-y-Calch
Tenafly
Wern-ddu Row
The Warren
WARREN
Brook
Scouring
Nant y Pwyntel
Cefn Carnau Uchaf
CEFNCARNAU
GRAIG LLANISHEN
(CAERFFILI)
(CAERDYDD)
CAERPHILLY
CARDIFF
Morgraig
Hill Farm
Cardiff
CF14
Llanishen
Hendre Farm
HEOL HIR
A469
Hillside
CAPEL GWILYM RD.
Brook
Cwm LLANISHEN GOLF COURSE
Club House
Parc Cefn Onn Country Park
Tennis
WERN FAW
Nant Fawr
Nant Transhyrhebog
TRANSH YR HEBOG
Coed Transh yr Hebog
CAERPHILLY TUNNEL
CEFN ONN
WERN DDU
Cefn-
Parc-y-Van
Coed Parc-y-Van
Coed Parc-y-van
Mynydd Rudry
Nant Gwaunybara
E F G H
1 2 3 4 5 6
16 17 18
84 185 86 87
29
71
48

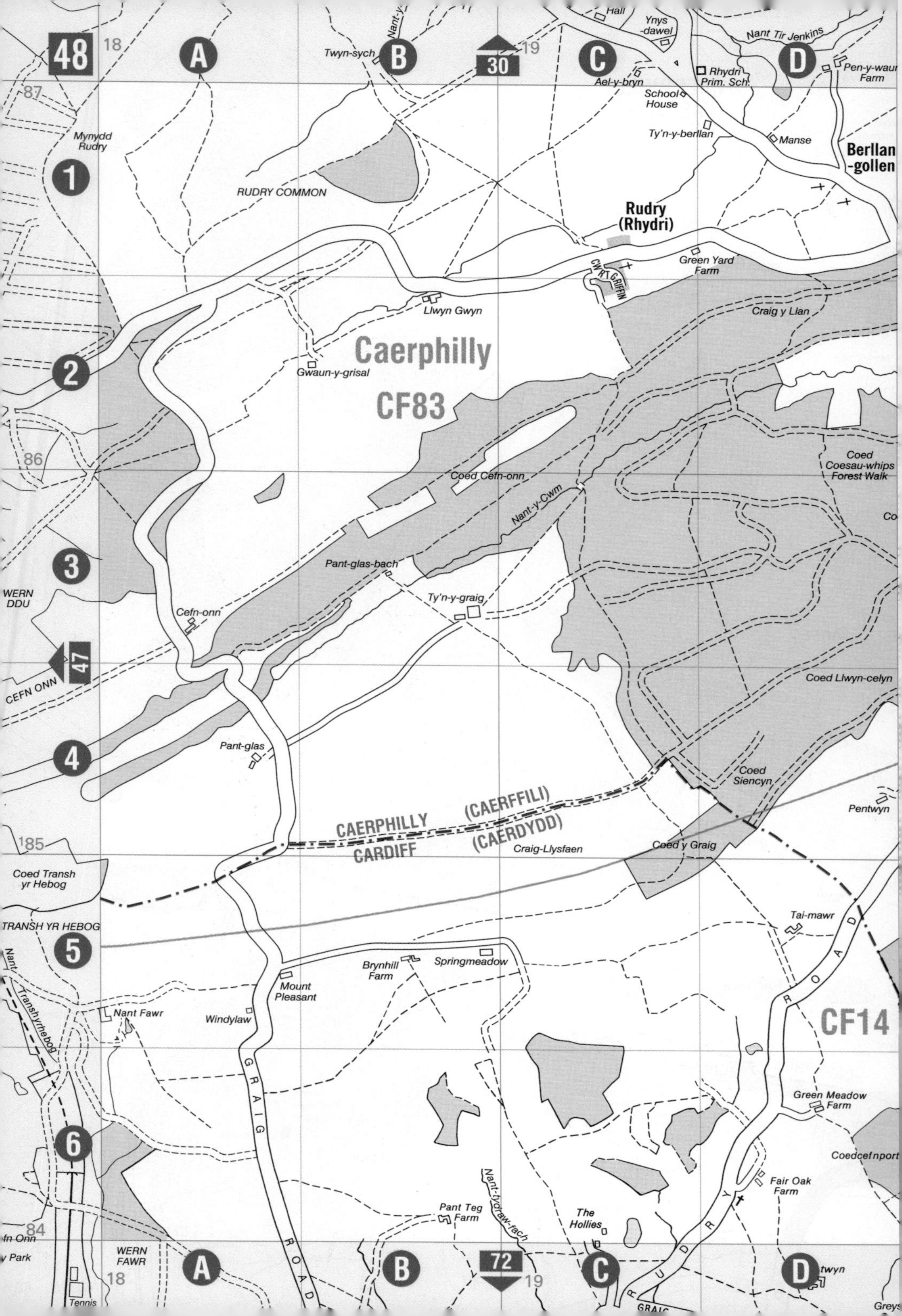
18
A
Twyn-sych
Nant-y-
B
30
19
C
Hall
Ynys
-dawel
Ael-y-bryn
Rhydri
Prim. Sch.
School
House
Nant Tir Jenkins
D
Pen-y-waun
Farm
87
Mynydd
Rudry
1
Ty'n-y-berllan
Manse
Berllan
-gollen
RUDRY COMMON
Rudry
(Rhydri)
Green Yard
Farm
CWRT GRIFFIN
Llwyn Gwyn
Craig y Llan
2
Caerphilly
Gwaun-y-grisal
CF83
86
Coed
Coesau-whips
Forest Walk
Coed Cefn-onn
Nant-y-Cwm
3
Pant-glas-bach
WERN
DDU
Ty'n-y-graig
Cefn-onn
47
CEFN ONN
Coed Llwyn-celyn
4
Pant-glas
Coed
Siencyn
CAERPHILLY
(CAERFFILI)
(CAERDYDD)
CARDIFF
Pentwyn
185
Craig-Llysfaen
Coed y Graig
Coed Transh
yr Hebog
TRANSH YR HEBOG
Tai-mawr
5
Nant
Transhyrhebog
Brynhill
Farm
Springmeadow
Mount
Pleasant
Nant Fawr
Windylaw
ROAD
CF14
GRAIG
Green Meadow
Farm
6
Coedcefnport
Nant-tydraw-fach
Fair Oak
Farm
Pant Teg
Farm
The
Hollies
RUDRY
84
WERN
FAWR
A
B
72
19
C
D
twyn
18
Tennis
GRAIG
Greys

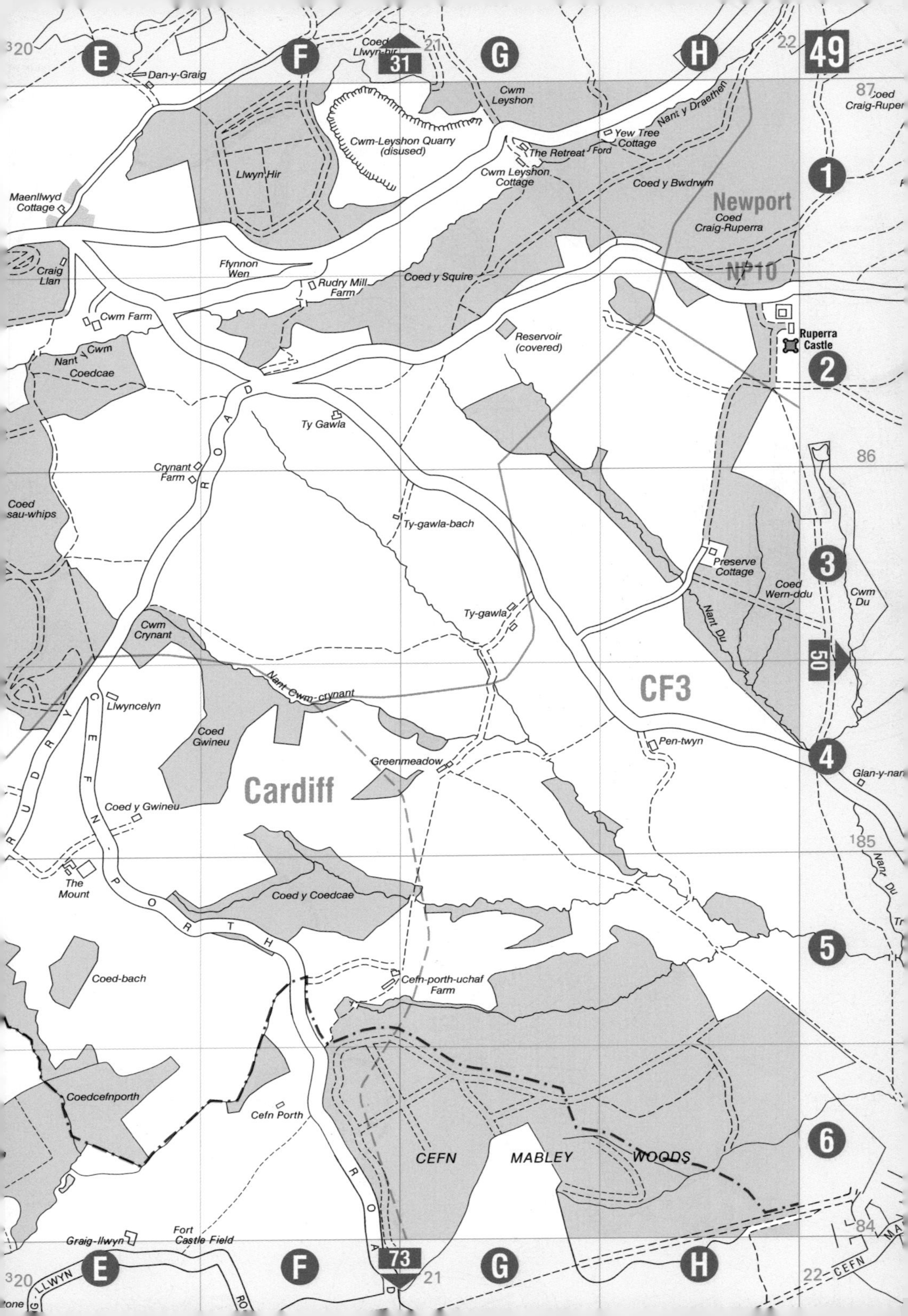

31
73
50
Cardiff
CF3
Newport
NP10
Coed Llwyn-hir
Dan-y-Graig
Cwm Leyshon
Cwm-Leyshon Quarry (disused)
Llwyn Hir
Nant y Draethen
Yew Tree Cottage
The Retreat
Ford
Cwm Leyshon Cottage
Coed y Bwdrwm
Coed Craig-Ruperra
Coed Craig-Ruper
Maenllwyd Cottage
Craig Llan
Ffynnon Wen
Rudry Mill Farm
Coed y Squire
Cwm Farm
Nant y Cwm
Coedcae
Reservoir (covered)
Ruperra Castle
Ty Gawla
Crynant Farm
Coed sau-whips
Ty-gawla-bach
Preserve Cottage
Coed Wern-ddu
Cwm Du
Nant Du
Ty-gawla
Cwm Crynant
Nant Cwm-crynant
Llwyncelyn
Coed Gwineu
Greenmeadow
Pen-twyn
Glan-y-nan
Coed y Gwineu
The Mount
Coed y Coedcae
Coed-bach
Cefn-porth-uchaf Farm
Coedcefnporth
Cefn Porth
CEFN MABLEY WOODS
Graig-llwyn
Fort Castle Field
RUDRY ROAD
CEFN PORTH ROAD
LLWYN
CEFN

A
B
C
D
32
22
23
87
Coed Craig-Ruperrat
Coed y Goitre
Gwern-y-Goytre
RHYMNEY RIVER (AFON RHYMNI)
PARK WO
1
Craig Ruperra
Coed Craig-Ruperra
Gwern-Leyshon Wood
NP10
Gwernleyshon Farm
Ruperra Castle
2
Coed Llanvedw
Ruperra Home Farm
Ruperra House
86
Coed Brain
Mill Wood
Bridge Farm
3
Preserve Cottage
Coed Wern-ddu
Cwm Du
Y Graig
Nant Du
49
Coed y Tranch
The Mill House
Nant y Cor
Nant y Cor Fach
Nant y Cor Fawr
4
Glan-y-nant
Cardiff
CF3
185
Cefn Llwyd Farm
Cefn Fawr Farm
(AFON RHYMNI)
Nant Du
Trwyn-yr-hwch
Chur
5
Nant Fawr
RHYMNEY RIVER
Ty-Treherne
Daintree House
Fairoak Cottage
Tai Derwen
Home Farm
Cefn Mably Lodge
Ty-hir Farm
CEFN MABLEY WOODS
6
Cefn Mably Farm
ROAD
PARK
Pentreporth
Fairwater Bungalow
Fairwater Farm
84
BEGAN
CEFN MABLY
74
Wern Uchaf
Reservoirs
AFON CL.

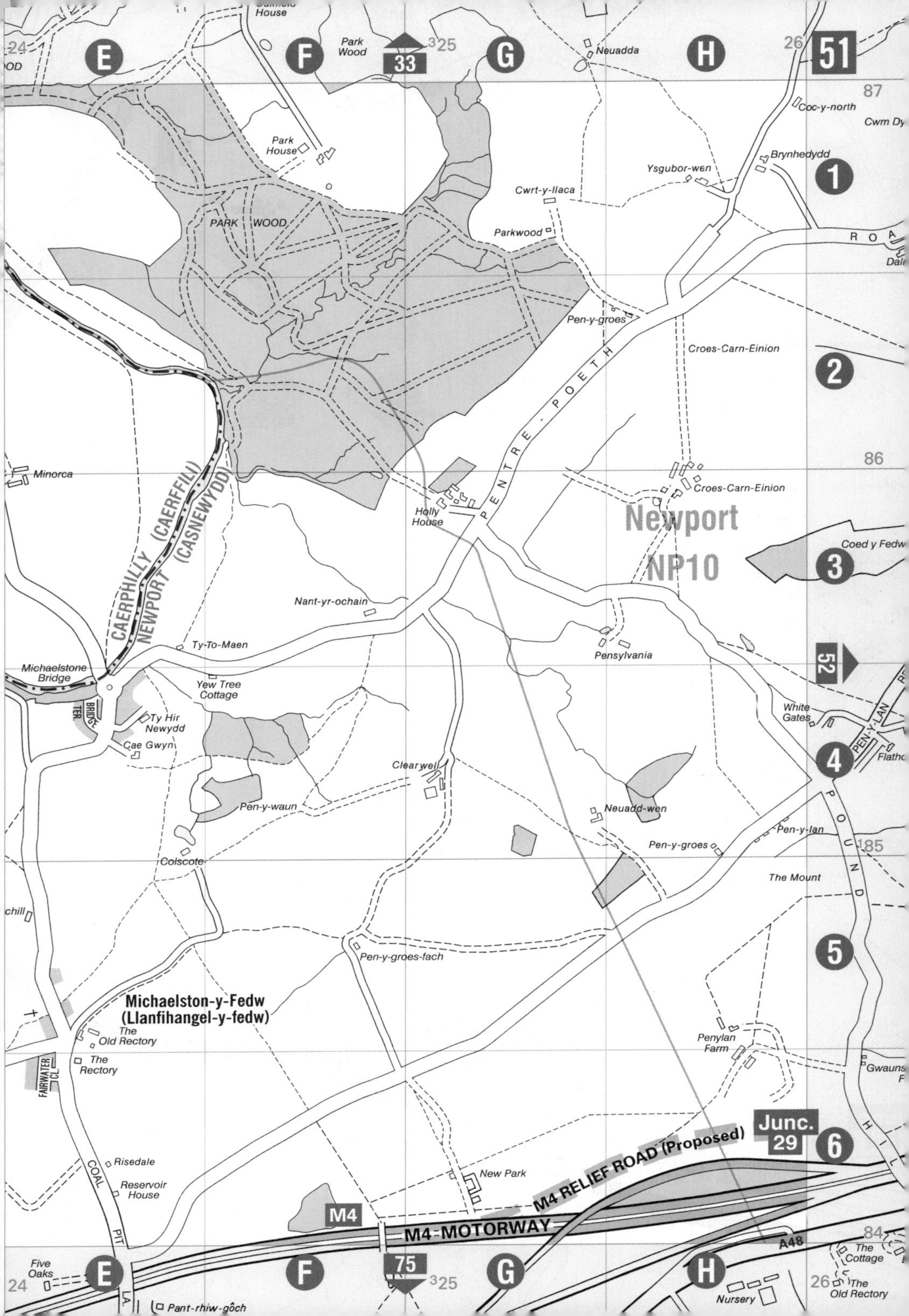

51
E
F
G
H
33
325
26
24
87
86
185
84
1
2
3
4
5
6
52
75
Park Wood
Neuadda
Coc-y-north
Cwm Dy
Brynhedydd
Ysgubor-wen
Cwrt-y-llaca
Park House
PARK WOOD
Parkwood
ROA
Pen-y-groes
Croes-Carn-Einion
PENTRE - POETH
Minorca
CAERPHILLY (CAERFFILI)
NEWPORT (CASNEWYDD)
Holly House
Newport
NP10
Coed y Fedw
Nant-yr-ochain
Ty-To-Maen
Pensylvania
Michaelstone Bridge
BRIDGE TER.
Yew Tree Cottage
Ty Hir Newydd
Cae Gwyn
White Gates
PEN-Y-LAN
Clearwell
Pen-y-waun
Neuadd-wen
Pen-y-lan
POUND
Colscote
The Mount
Pen-y-groes-fach
Michaelston-y-Fedw
(Llanfihangel-y-fedw)
The Old Rectory
The Rectory
FAIRWATER CL.
Penylan Farm
Gwauns
Junc. 29
M4 RELIEF ROAD (Proposed)
HILL
COAL PIT LA.
Risedale
Reservoir House
New Park
M4
M4-MOTORWAY
A48
Five Oaks
The Cottage
Pant-rhiw-gôch
Nursery

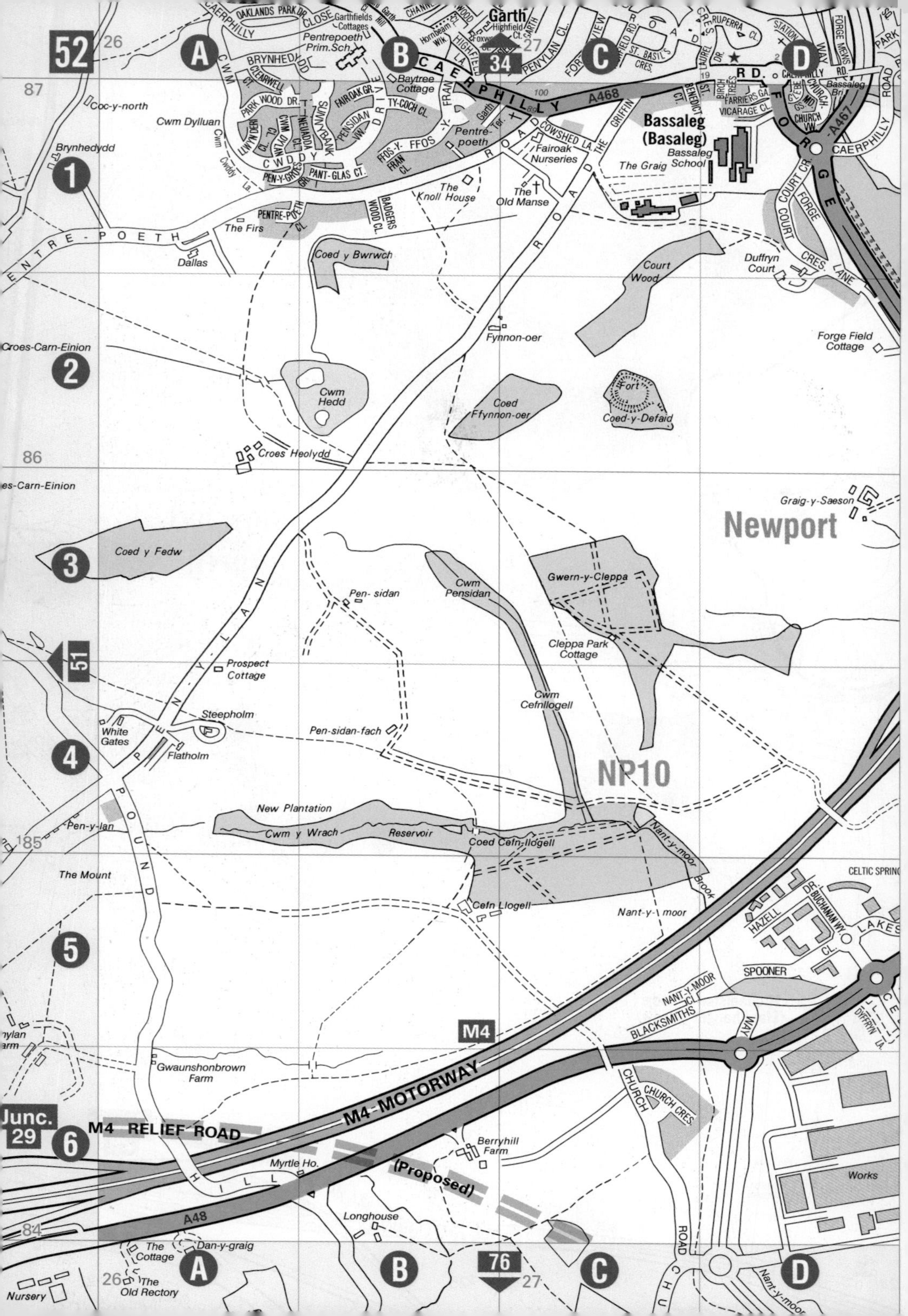
52
Garth
34
76
Bassaleg
(Basaleg)
Bassaleg School
The Graig
Newport
NP10
M4-MOTORWAY
M4
M4 RELIEF ROAD
(Proposed)
Junc. 29
A468
A467
A48
CAERPHILLY RD.
FORGE RD.
PENYLAN RD.
POUND HILL
PENTRE-POETH
Pentrepoeth Prim.Sch.
Baytree Cottage
Pentre-poeth
Fairoak Nurseries
The Old Manse
The Knoll House
The Firs
Dallas
Brynhedydd
Coc-y-north
Cwm Dylluan
Croes-Carn-Einion
Coed y Bwrwch
Fynnon-oer
Cwm Hedd
Coed Ffynnon-oer
Fort
Coed-y-Defaid
Court Wood
Duffryn Court
Forge Field Cottage
Croes Heolydd
Coed y Fedw
Graig-y-Saeson
Gwern-y-Cleppa
Cwm Pensidan
Pen- sidan
Cleppa Park Cottage
Cwm Cefnllogell
Prospect Cottage
Steepholm
White Gates
Flatholm
Pen-sidan-fach
New Plantation
Cwm y Wrach
Reservoir
Coed Cefn-llogell
Nant-y-moor Brook
Pen-y-lan
The Mount
Cefn Llogell
Nant-y- moor
CELTIC SPRING
Gwaunshonbrown Farm
Berryhill Farm
Myrtle Ho.
Longhouse
The Cottage
Dan-y-graig
The Old Rectory
Nursery
Works
SPOONER
NANT-Y-MOOR CL.
BLACKSMITHS WAY
CHURCH RD.
CHURCH CRES.
HAZELL DR.
BUCHANAN WY.
LAKES
DUFFRYN LA.
Nant-y-moor
COURT CRES.
FORGE LANE
COWSHED LA.
THE GRIFFIN
BENEDICT CT.
BIRCH TREES
FARRIERS GA.
VICARAGE CL.
GLEBE
CHURCH VW.
Bassaleg Bri.
CAERPHILLY RD.
PARK
STATION
FORGE MEWS
RUPERRA CL.
LAUREL DR.
ST. BASIL'S CRES.
PENYLAN CL.
FOREST VIEW
HIGHFIELD LA.
Hornbeam Wk.
Highfield
Garthfields Cottages
OAKLANDS PARK DR.
CLOSE
BRYNHEDYDD
CWM CWDDY DRIVE
CLEARWELL CT.
PARK WOOD DR.
LLWYN DERI CL.
CWM DYLAN CL.
NEUADDA CT.
SUNNYBANK
FAIR OAK GR.
PENSIDAN VW.
TY-COCH CL.
FFOS-Y-FRAN
FFOS-Y-FRAN CL.
PANT-GLAS CT.
PEN-Y-GROES GR.
BADGERS WOOD CL.
Garth Ter.
A
B
C
D
1
2
3
4
5
6
26
27
84
86
87
185
51

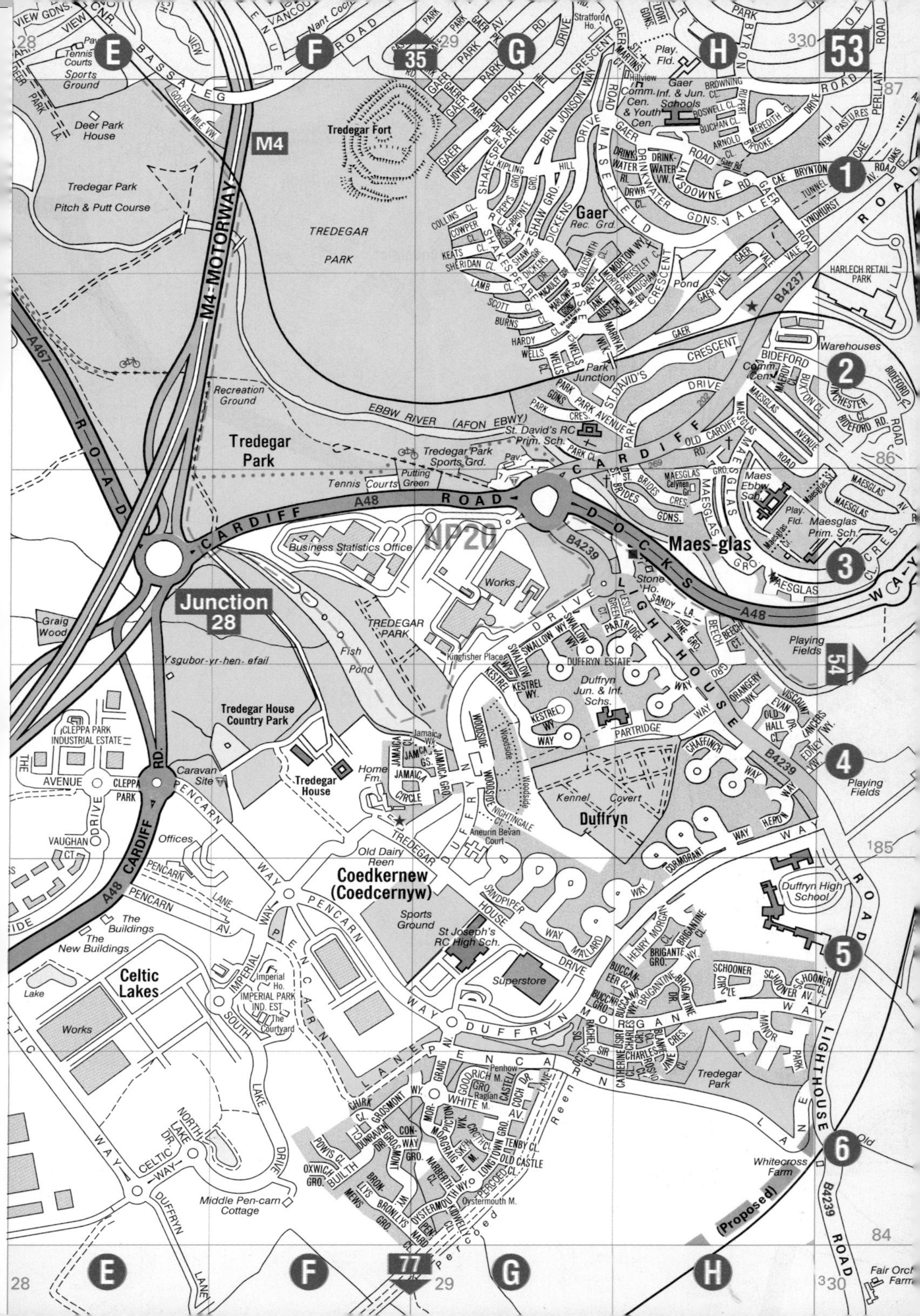
53
35
77
54
Tredegar Fort
M4
M4-MOTORWAY
Tredegar Park
Pitch & Putt Course
Deer Park House
Tennis Courts
Sports Ground
TREDEGAR PARK
Gaer
Rec. Grd.
Gaer Inf. & Jun. Schools
Comm. Cen. & Youth Cen.
HARLECH RETAIL PARK
Warehouses
Comm. Cen.
EBBW RIVER (AFON EBWY)
Recreation Ground
Tredegar Park
St. David's RC Prim. Sch.
Tredegar Park Sports Grd.
Tennis Courts
Putting Green
CARDIFF ROAD
A48
Maes-glas
Maes Ebbw Sch.
Maesglas Prim. Sch.
Business Statistics Office
NP20
Works
Junction 28
Graig Wood
Ysgubor-yr-hen-efail
Fish Pond
TREDEGAR PARK
Kingfisher Place
DUFFRYN ESTATE
Duffryn Jun. & Inf. Schs.
Playing Fields
Tredegar House Country Park
Tredegar House
Home Fm.
CLEPPA PARK INDUSTRIAL ESTATE
Caravan Site
Offices
Duffryn
Kennel Covert
Aneurin Bevan Court
Old Dairy
Reen
Coedkernew (Coedcernyw)
Sports Ground
St Joseph's RC High Sch.
Superstore
Duffryn High School
The Buildings
The New Buildings
Celtic Lakes
Lake
Works
Imperial Ho.
IMPERIAL PARK IND. EST
The Courtyard
Tredegar Park
Whitecross Farm
(Proposed)
Middle Pen-carn Cottage
Oystermouth M.
LIGHTHOUSE ROAD
B4239
B4237
DOCKS WAY
DUFFRYN WAY
PENCARN WAY
Fair Orch Farm

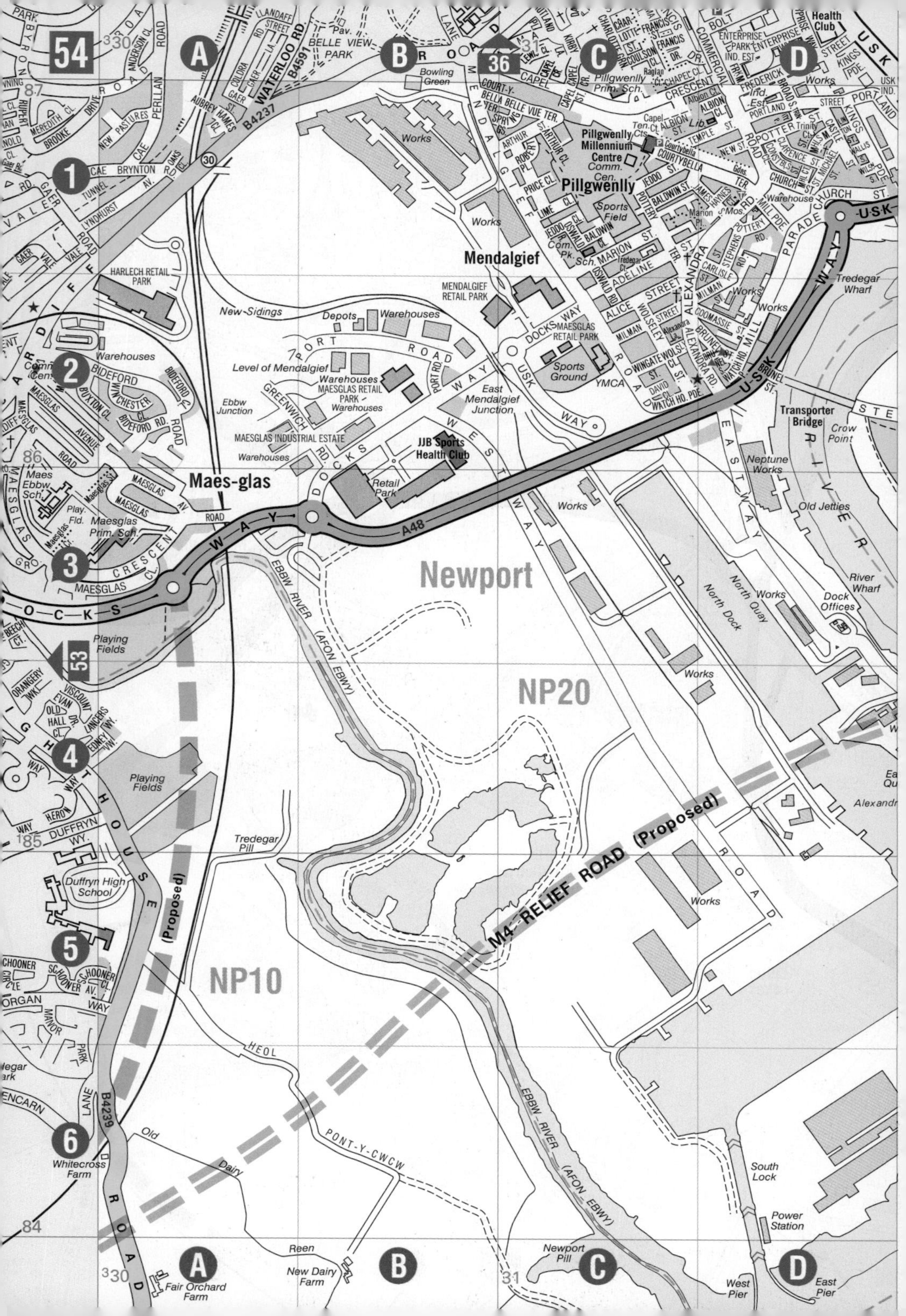

Newport
NP20
NP10
Pillgwenlly
Mendalgief
Maes-glas
Pillgwenlly Millennium Centre
Comm. Cen.
Pillgwenlly Prim. Sch.
Sports Field
Sports Ground
YMCA
MENDALGIEF RETAIL PARK
MAESGLAS RETAIL PARK
HARLECH RETAIL PARK
MAESGLAS INDUSTRIAL ESTATE
JJB Sports Health Club
Retail Park
Level of Mendalgief
East Mendalgief Junction
Ebbw Junction
New Sidings
Depots
Warehouses
Works
Bowling Green
Belle View Park
Transporter Bridge
Crow Point
Neptune Works
Old Jetties
River Wharf
Dock Offices
North Quay
North Dock
Tredegar Wharf
Tredegar Pill
Newport Pill
South Lock
Power Station
West Pier
East Pier
Playing Fields
Duffryn High School
Maesglas Prim. Sch.
Maes Ebbw Sch.
Whitecross Farm
Fair Orchard Farm
New Dairy Farm
Reen
Old Dairy
HEOL PONT-Y-CWCW
EBBW RIVER (AFON EBWY)
M4 RELIEF ROAD (Proposed)
(Proposed)
A48
B4237
B4591
B4239
WATERLOO RD.
CARDIFF ROAD
DOCKS WAY
USK WAY
WEST WAY
EAST WAY ROAD
PORT ROAD
ALEXANDRA ROAD
COMMERCIAL ROAD
DUFFRYN WY.
LIGHTHOUSE ROAD
ENTERPRISE PARK IND. EST.
36
53

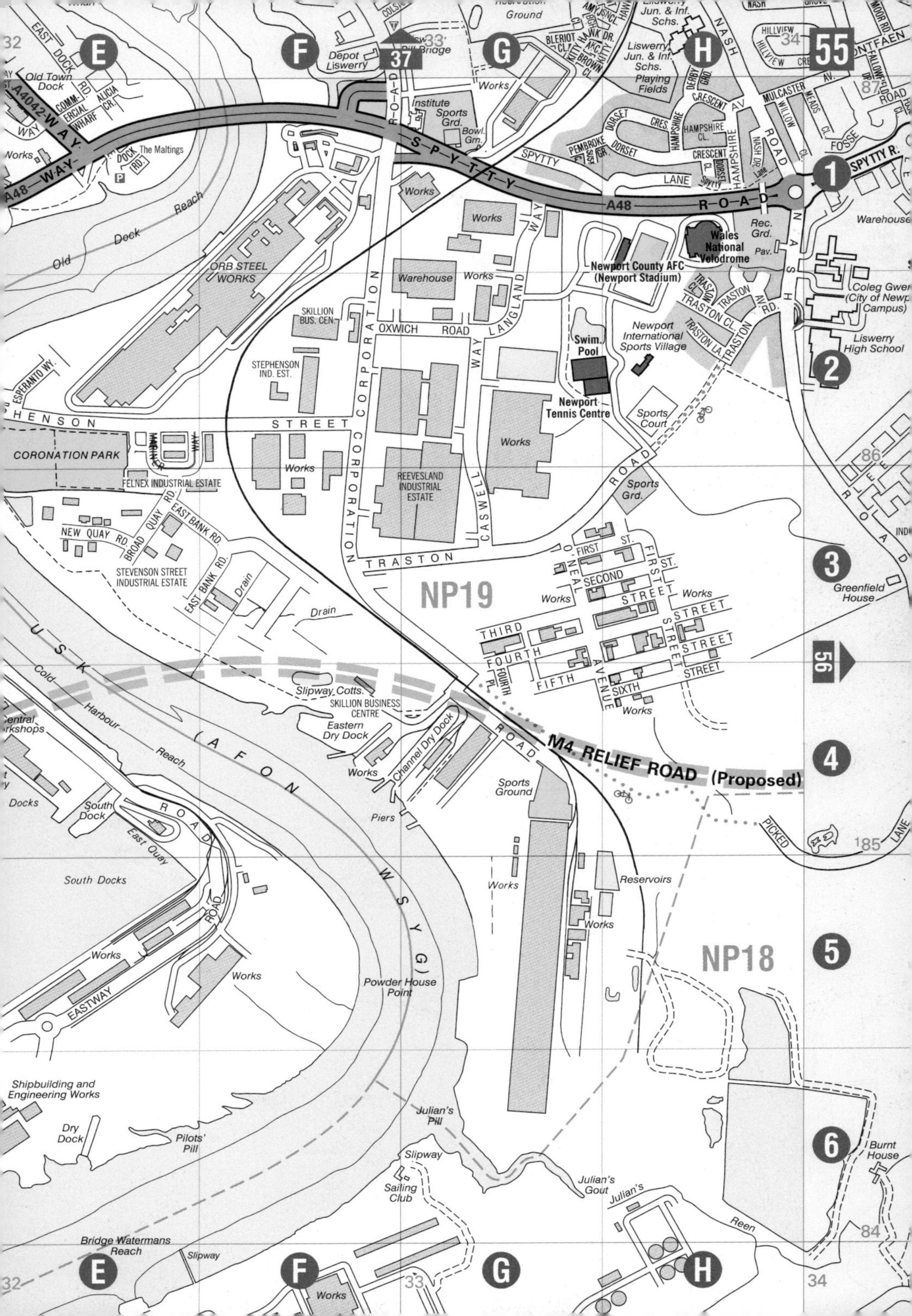

55
37
56
NP19
NP18
A48 ROAD
SPYTTY ROAD
A4042 WAY
M4 RELIEF ROAD (Proposed)
ORB STEEL WORKS
Wales National Velodrome
Newport County AFC (Newport Stadium)
Newport International Sports Village
Swim. Pool
Newport Tennis Centre
Coleg Gwent (City of Newport Campus)
Liswerry High School
REEVESLAND INDUSTRIAL ESTATE
STEPHENSON IND. EST.
SKILLION BUS. CEN.
FELNEX INDUSTRIAL ESTATE
STEVENSON STREET INDUSTRIAL ESTATE
SKILLION BUSINESS CENTRE
CORONATION PARK
CORPORATION ROAD
TRASTON ROAD
STEPHENSON STREET
OXWICH ROAD
CASWELL WAY
LANGLAND WAY
NASH ROAD
USK (AFON WYSG)
Cold Harbour Reach
Old Dock Reach
South Docks
South Dock
East Quay
Eastern Dry Dock
Channel Dry Dock
Powder House Point
Julian's Pill
Pilots' Pill
Shipbuilding and Engineering Works
Dry Dock
Sailing Club
Bridge Watermans Reach
Slipway
Julian's Gout
Reen
Burnt House
Greenfield House
Reservoirs
Sports Ground
Works
Warehouse
The Maltings
Old Town Dock
Depot Liswerry
Pill Bridge
Institute Sports Grd.
Liswerry Jun. & Inf. Schs.
Playing Fields
PICKED LANE
Slipway Cotts.
Piers
Drain
EASTWAY

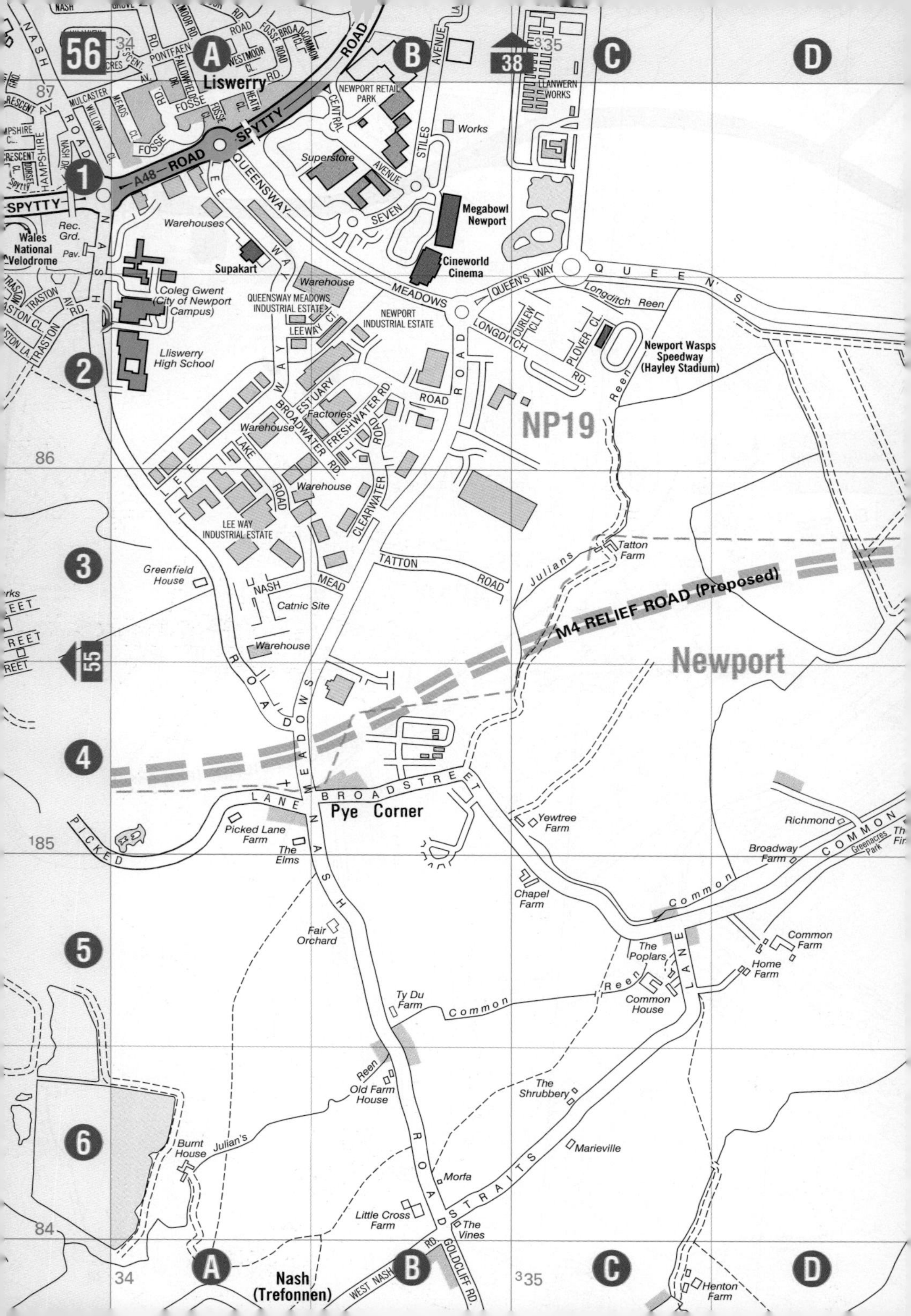
56
Lliswerry
Newport Retail Park
Superstore
Works
Llanwern Works
Megabowl Newport
Cineworld Cinema
Supakart
Warehouses
Wales National Velodrome
Rec. Grd.
Coleg Gwent (City of Newport Campus)
Lliswerry High School
Queensway Meadows Industrial Estate
Newport Industrial Estate
Newport Wasps Speedway (Hayley Stadium)
NP19
Lee Way Industrial Estate
Factories
Warehouse
Greenfield House
Catnic Site
Tatton Farm
M4 RELIEF ROAD (Proposed)
Newport
Pye Corner
Picked Lane Farm
The Elms
Yewtree Farm
Richmond
Broadway Farm
Chapel Farm
Fair Orchard
The Poplars
Common Farm
Home Farm
Common House
Ty Du Farm
Old Farm House
The Shrubbery
Burnt House
Marieville
Morfa
Little Cross Farm
The Vines
Nash (Trefonnen)
Henton Farm
A48 ROAD
SPYTTY ROAD
QUEENSWAY
MEADOWS
QUEEN'S WAY
LONGDITCH ROAD
NASH ROAD
NASH MEADOWS
BROADSTREET COMMON
STRAITS LANE
GOLDCLIFF RD.
WEST NASH RD.
PICKED LANE
55
38

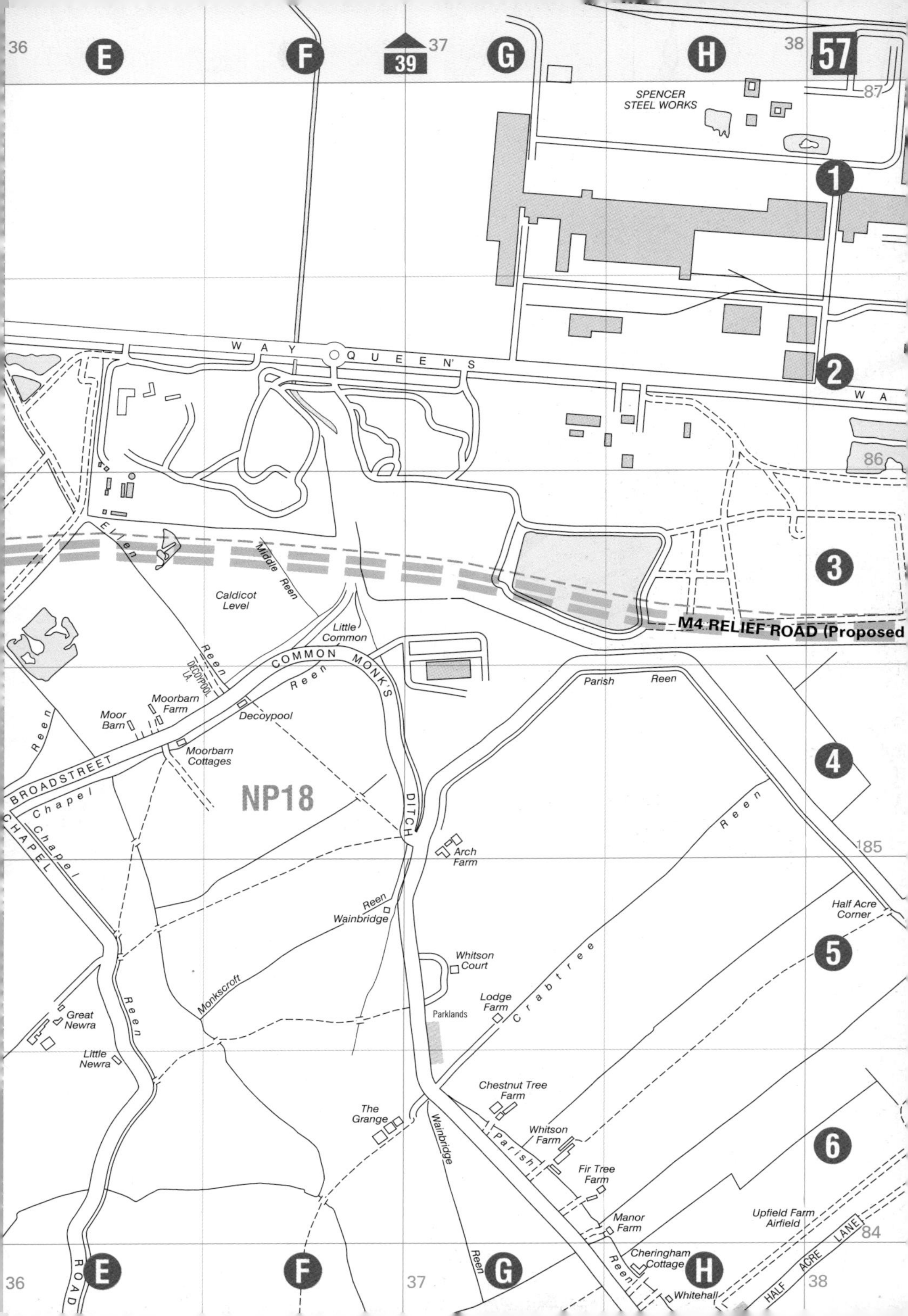

36
E
F
37
39
G
H
38
57
87
SPENCER STEEL WORKS
1
2
W A Y
Q U E E N ' S
W A
86
3
Caldicot Level
Middle Reen
Ellen
M4 RELIEF ROAD (Proposed
Little Common
COMMON
MONK'S
Reen
DECOYPOOL LA.
Moorbarn Farm
Moor Barn
Decoypool
Moorbarn Cottages
BROADSTREET
Chapel
CHAPEL
NP18
DITCH
Parish
4
185
Arch Farm
Reen
Wainbridge
Half Acre Corner
5
Whitson Court
Monkscroft
Great Newra
Little Newra
Lodge Farm
Crabtree
Parklands
Chestnut Tree Farm
The Grange
Wainbridge
Whitson Farm
Parish
6
Fir Tree Farm
Manor Farm
Upfield Farm Airfield
84
HALF ACRE LANE
ROAD
Cheringham Cottage
Whitehall

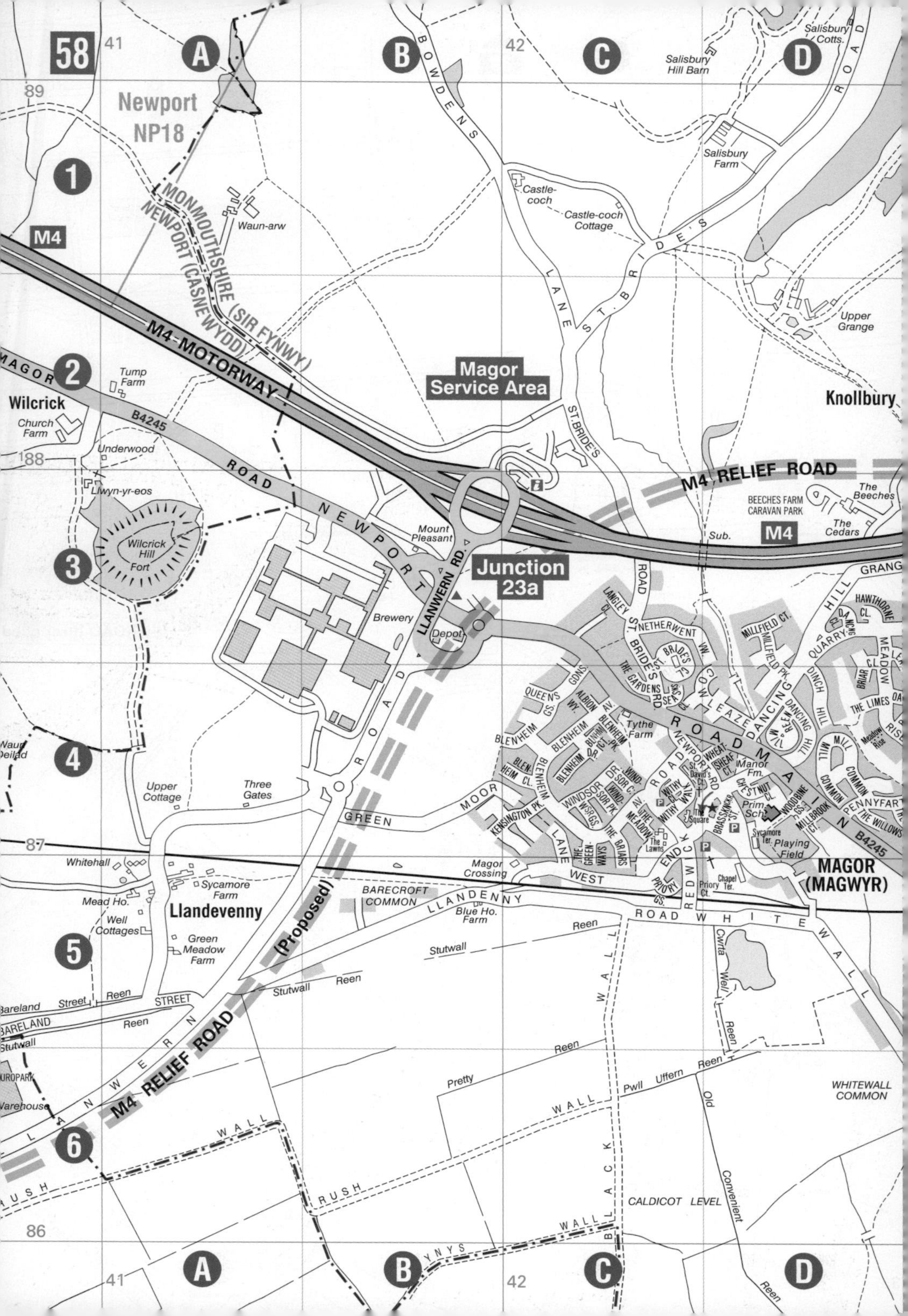
Newport
NP18
MONMOUTHSHIRE
NEWPORT (CASNEWYDD)
(SIR FYNWY)
Waun-arw
M4
M4-MOTORWAY
Castle-coch
Castle-coch Cottage
Salisbury Hill Barn
Salisbury Cotts.
Salisbury Farm
BOWDENS
ST. BRIDE'S
LANE
Upper Grange
Knollbury
Magor Service Area
MAGOR
Tump Farm
Wilcrick
Church Farm
B4245
Underwood
ROAD
NEWPORT
Llwyn-yr-eos
Wilcrick Hill Fort
M4 RELIEF ROAD
The Beeches
BEECHES FARM CARAVAN PARK
The Cedars
Sub.
Mount Pleasant
LLANWERN RD.
Junction 23a
Brewery
Depot
GRANGE
HILL
HAWTHORNE CL.
MILLFIELD CT.
MILLFIELD PK.
QUARRY
MEADOW
DINCH HILL
BRIAR CL.
THE LIMES
DANCING HILL
RISE
Meadow Rise
MILL COMMON
PENNYFARTHING
THE WILLOWS
WOODBINE GS.
MILLBROOK CT.
B4245
LANGLEY CL.
NETHERWENT
ST. BRIDES RD.
ST. BRIDES CL.
THE GARDENS
COW LEAZE
QUEENS GS.
ALBION WY.
BLENHEIM
Tythe Farm
NEWPORT RD.
WHEAT-SHEAF CT.
Manor Fm.
ROAD
MAIN
KENSINGTON PK.
WINDSOR DR.
WINDSOR PK.
WITHY CL.
WITHY WALK
St. David's Ct.
The Square
BRASSKNOCKER ST.
CHESTNUT CL.
Prim. Sch.
Sycamore Ter.
Playing Field
MAGOR (MAGWYR)
Upper Cottage
Three Gates
MOOR
GREEN
THE GREENWAYS
THE BRIARS
THE MEADOW
The Lawns
ENDICK
REDWICK
Chapel Ter.
Priory Ct.
PRIORY GS.
WEST
LANE
Whitehall
Magor Crossing
Sycamore Farm
Mead Ho.
Llandevenny
BARECROFT COMMON
LLANDENNY
Blue Ho. Farm
ROAD WHITE WALL
Well Cottages
Green Meadow Farm
(Proposed)
Stutwall
Reen
Cwrta Well
Bareland Street
STREET
BARELAND
Stutwall
EUROPARK
Warehouse
LLANWERN
Pretty
Pwll Uffern
Old
Convenient
WHITEWALL COMMON
WALL
RUSH
CALDICOT LEVEL
BLACK WALL
YNYS
41
42
89
88
87
86
A
B
C
D
1
2
3
4
5
6

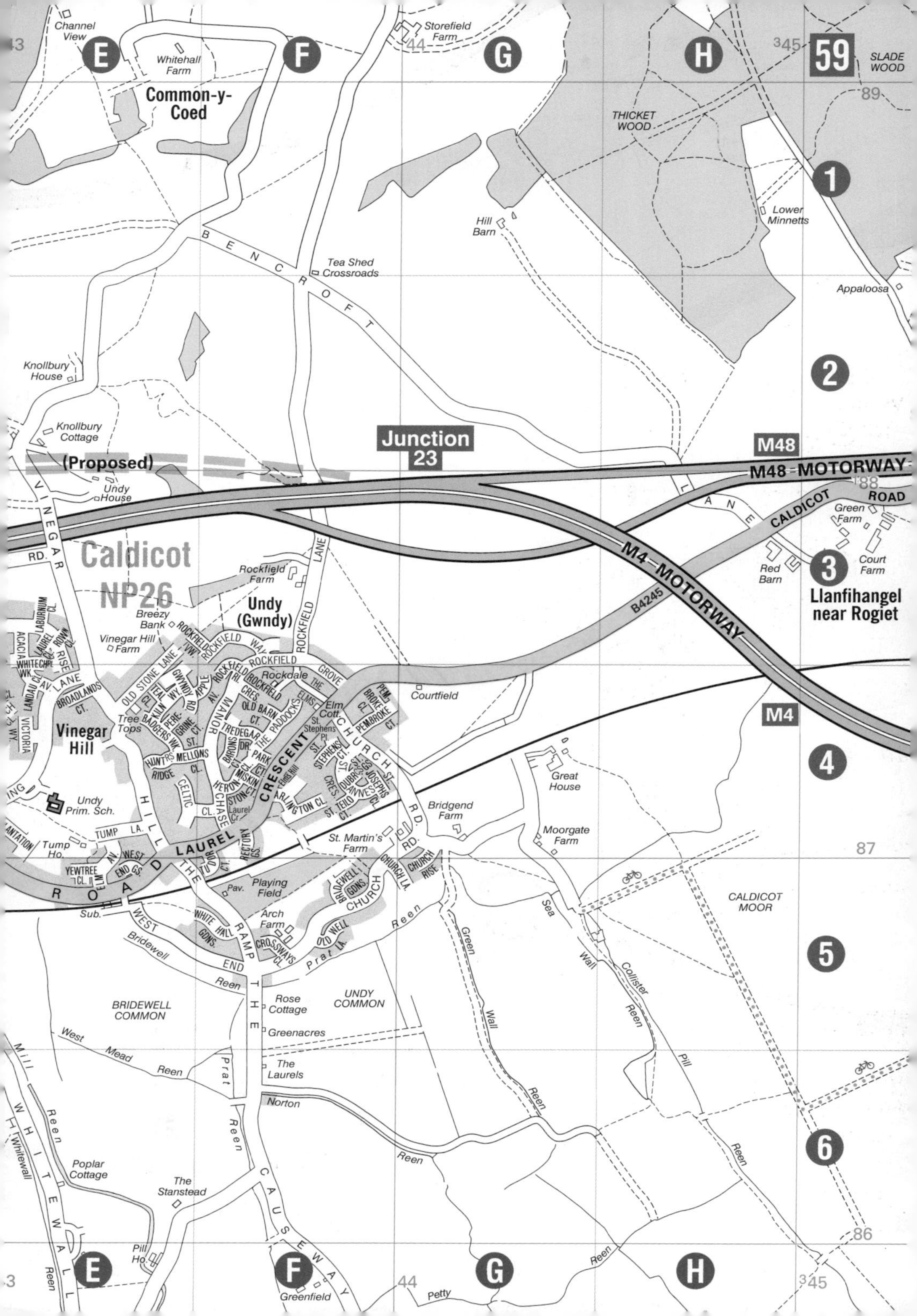

Channel View
Whitehall Farm
Common-y-Coed
Storefield Farm
SLADE WOOD
THICKET WOOD
Lower Minnetts
Hill Barn
Tea Shed Crossroads
BENCROFT
Appaloosa
Knollbury House
Knollbury Cottage
Junction 23
M48
M48 MOTORWAY
(Proposed)
Undy House
CALDICOT ROAD
Green Farm
LANE
Caldicot NP26
Rockfield Farm
Red Barn
Court Farm
Llanfihangel near Rogiet
M4 MOTORWAY
B4245
Undy (Gwndy)
Breezy Bank
Vinegar Hill Farm
ROCKFIELD LANE
ROCKFIELD WAY
Rockdale
THE GROVE
Courtfield
Vinegar Hill
Tree Tops
CRESCENT
M4
Great House
Undy Prim. Sch.
Bridgend Farm
Moorgate Farm
Tump Ho.
TUMP LA.
LAUREL ROAD
St. Martin's Farm
Playing Field
Pav.
Arch Farm
CALDICOT MOOR
Sub.
WEST END
Bridewell
THE RAMP
Prat La.
Reen
Rose Cottage
UNDY COMMON
BRIDEWELL COMMON
Greenacres
West Mead Reen
The Laurels
Prat
Norton
Green Wall
Collister Reen
Sea Wall
Pill
Whitewall
WHITEWALL
Mill
Poplar Cottage
The Stanstead
CAUSEWAY
Pill Ho.
Greenfield
Petty
87
86
88
89
43
44
345
E
F
G
H
1
2
3
4
5
6

Caldicot
NP26
CALDICOT
Caer-went
VENTA SILVRVM
(Roman Town)
Rogiet
Severn Tunnel
Junction
Caldicot
M48 MOTORWAY
M48
A48
50
NEWPORT ROAD
ROGIET RD.
B4245
CHEPSTOW ROAD
CHURCH ROAD
DEWSTOW ROAD
CALDICOT ROAD
SANDY LANE
DEWSTOW GOLF COURSE
Driving Range
Club House
Little Dewstow
Dewstow Farm
Rustic Lodge
Gate Ho.
Dewstow House
Dewstow Lodge
Keepers Lodge
Ifton Quarries
Ifton Crest
Ifton Manor
IFTON INDUSTRIAL PARK
CHEESEMAN'S TRAD. EST.
IFTON QUARRY IND. EST.
Works
Reservoir
(covered)
Llantwinatt
Brockwells Farm
The Woodlands
Caerwent Quarries
(stone)
Woodland Valley
Rock House
The Elms
East View
The Grange
Mayfield
Caerwent Brook Cottages
Upper Rodge Wood
Sea View
Rodge Farm
Nedern Brook
Westgate Farm
Ten Elms
St. Stephen's Church
Great House Farm
Elms Farm
New House Farm
Slough Farm
Highfield
Play Area
Playing Field
Rugby Ground
Playground
Depot
Sewage Works
Summerway Reen
Ifton Bank Reen
Caldicot Comprehensive School
Caldicot Community College & Leisure Centre
Durand Prim. Sch.
Caldicot St. Mary's Jun. Sch.
Caldicot West End Inf. Sch.
Inf. Sch.
King George's Field
Bowl Grn.
Wesley Bldgs.
Albion Ho.
Lib.
Hall
Church Farm
Court Ho.
Brookside
Cemy.
Playing Field
WOODSTOCK WAY
LONGCROFT ROAD
WESTFIELD
GOLDFINCH CLOSE
STATION
GARTHALAN DRIVE
BETJEMAN AV.
SHAKESPEARE DR.
TENNYSON
KEATS
LONGFELLOW CL.
MASEFIELD RD.
BYRON PL.
KIPLING
FERNEY CROSS
SHELLY
WOODLAND VW.
FERNLEIGH RD.
PARK RD.
DEWSTON GDNS.
BIRBECK
OAKLEY CLOSE
SYCAMORE AV.
FIRS
HERBERT RD.
ASH GROVE
WILLOW CL.
TROGGI
BUDDEN CR.
CHURCH FIELD AV.
MONKS CRES.
DANCARGA DR.
GREENFIELD
CAE MAWR RD.
JUBILEE WY.
DURAND RD.
LINNET RD.
MALLARD AV.
CURLEW AV.
KINGFISHER
FALCON CL.
PLOVER CR.
KESTREL CL.
SWALLOW DR.
BLACKBIRD
STAFFORD R.
FITZWALTER RD.
COBB CR.
ELAN WAY
TAFF RD.
WENTWOOD VW.
CASTLE LEA
PROSPECT CR.
COURT HOUSE CL.
LLANTHONY CL.
HEOL TEIFI
ST. TATHAN'S PL.
BISHOP CL.
CANNON CADOC CL.
MARTINS RD.
VERNON GRO.
HIGHFIELD LANE
CENTURIONS CT.
CWRT MORGAN
VICARAGE GDNS.
ST. STEPHEN'S
POUND LA.
IFTON TER.
GRENVILLE TER.
YEW TREE RI.
CHESTNUT
POPLAR CL.
A
B
C
D
1
2
3
4
5
6
47
48
88
89
190

61
E
F
G
H
49
350
190
89
88
1
2
3
4
5
6
Traskney
Slidyhill Wood
Verlands Wood
Hawthorn
Little Peterstow Farm
Parkwall Farm
Parkwall Lodge
Lorna Doone
A48
Bentley Green
Woodside
Sunny Bank
M48
Crick
Depot
Wks.
OLD SHIRENEWTON RD.
M48 MOTORWAY
Uplands
The Croft
West View
Bradbury's Farm
Crick Ho.
CRICK
WALNUT GRO.
Killcrow Hill
Severn Farm
ROAD
B4245
Oak Grove
Hill Barn
Ballan Wood
CRICK RD.
MOUNT
Central Farm
Little Ballan
Crown Hill Nurseries
Coltshay Hill
LLAN
OOR
The Berries
Motte & Bailey
Cartref
Crown Hill Farm
Rectory Farm
Crown Hill
Leechpool
Harpson Barn
Leechpool House
The Bungalow
Mount Ballan
Nedern
Crossways
BALLAN
Ruffets
Farthing Hill
CALDICOT
Brook
Red Gates
Lower Leechpool Farm
Withy Beds
CALDICOT CASTLE COUNTRY PARK
PORTSKEWETT HILL
Caldicot Castle
STOW BALL HILL
Archbishop Rowan Williams C in W Prim. Sch.
Lodge
CASTLEGATE BUS. PARK
PORTSKEWETT (PORTH YSGEWIN)
Hall
CASTLE LEA
CASTLE
LODGE CR.
CASTLE LODGE CL.
Arthurs Ct.
TREETOPS
OAKLANDS PK.
CRICK RD.
KING HAROLD'S
Manor VW. Farm
BLACK ROCK RD.
LABRNM GR.
HODGES CL.
HESTN
CROFT
LABURNUM T.
STATION
HILL BARN VW.
SUNNY-
CASTLE CT.
GRAY HILL VW.
CASTLE WAY
PILL WAY
CALDICOT ROAD
MAIN
Nedern Bri.
LODGE WAY
WEDGE WOOD DR.
HILL BARN VW.
Station Bungalows
ROAD
DEEPWEIR DR.
DEEPWEIR
PILL
PASS
BEACON BUS. PARK
WAY
GDS.
ORCHARD
St. Mary's Pl.
ST. MARY'S PL.
CLOSE MANOR WY.
CANTERBURY WAY
SUDBROOK
Hillhouse Barn
Castertown Pill
Ebley Gdns.
CASTLE COURT
NORMAN WAY
THE SOUTH BROOK VIEW
Rec. Grd.
Deepweir
DEEPWEIR GDS.
REDMEADOW CR.
MOORLANDS VW.
DENNY VW.
RAILWAY VW.
ESTUARY VW.
SEVERN BRIDGE INDUSTRIAL ESTATE
ROW
SYMONDSCLIFF
Southbrook
Electricity Sub Station
NG AV
ORCHID DRIVE
OLD PILL FARM IND. EST.
Severn
Tunnel
The Terrace Marine Sea Ter.
View
Sudbrook
The Pill
Ysgol Gymraeg y Ffin
The Villas
Church Row
Factory
PILL FARM IND. ESTATE
Paper Mill
CAMP
ROAD
Stone Cotts.
Post Office Row
Fort
Walker Flats
Old Row
RD.
M4

Chepstow
NP16
Crossway Green
Mounton
Pwllmeyric
(Pwllmeurig)
Newton Green
Hayes Gate
USK ROAD
B4235
ST. LAWRENCE ROAD
WYE ROAD
A466
WELSH ST.
B4293
ITTON RD.
To Chepstow Race Course 1km
NEWPORT ROAD
A48
NEWPORT A48 RD.
FAIR VIEW
VALLEY
MOUNTON ROAD
ST. LAWRENCE LANE
STONES
SMOOTH
CHAPEL LANE
MATHERN ROAD
M48
Mounton Brook
Mill Race
GREAT BARNETS WOOD
Bishop's Barnets Wood
Reservoir (covered)
Cockshoot
Uplands
Forest Lodge
Cophill
St. Anne's
Chepstow School
Castle Wood
Chepstow and Dist. Leis. Cen.
Barnetts Farm
The Grange
Traphill Wood
Ticken Hill
Trap Hill
Wallwern Wood
Mounton House School
Bigs Wood
Brynderwin
Bigwood
Woodlands Grove
Mounton House Park
Trelenny
St. Lawrence House
CHEPSTOW COMM. HOSP.
Playing Field
Wyelands Lodge
Oak Bluff
St. Tewdric
Home Farm
Wyelands
Lodge
East Wood
Eastwood Cottage
Rose Cottages
Newton Meadows
Sunnyside
New Hall
Alpha Bungalow
The Buftons
Langstone
Community Centre
Hayes Gate Farm
Playing Field

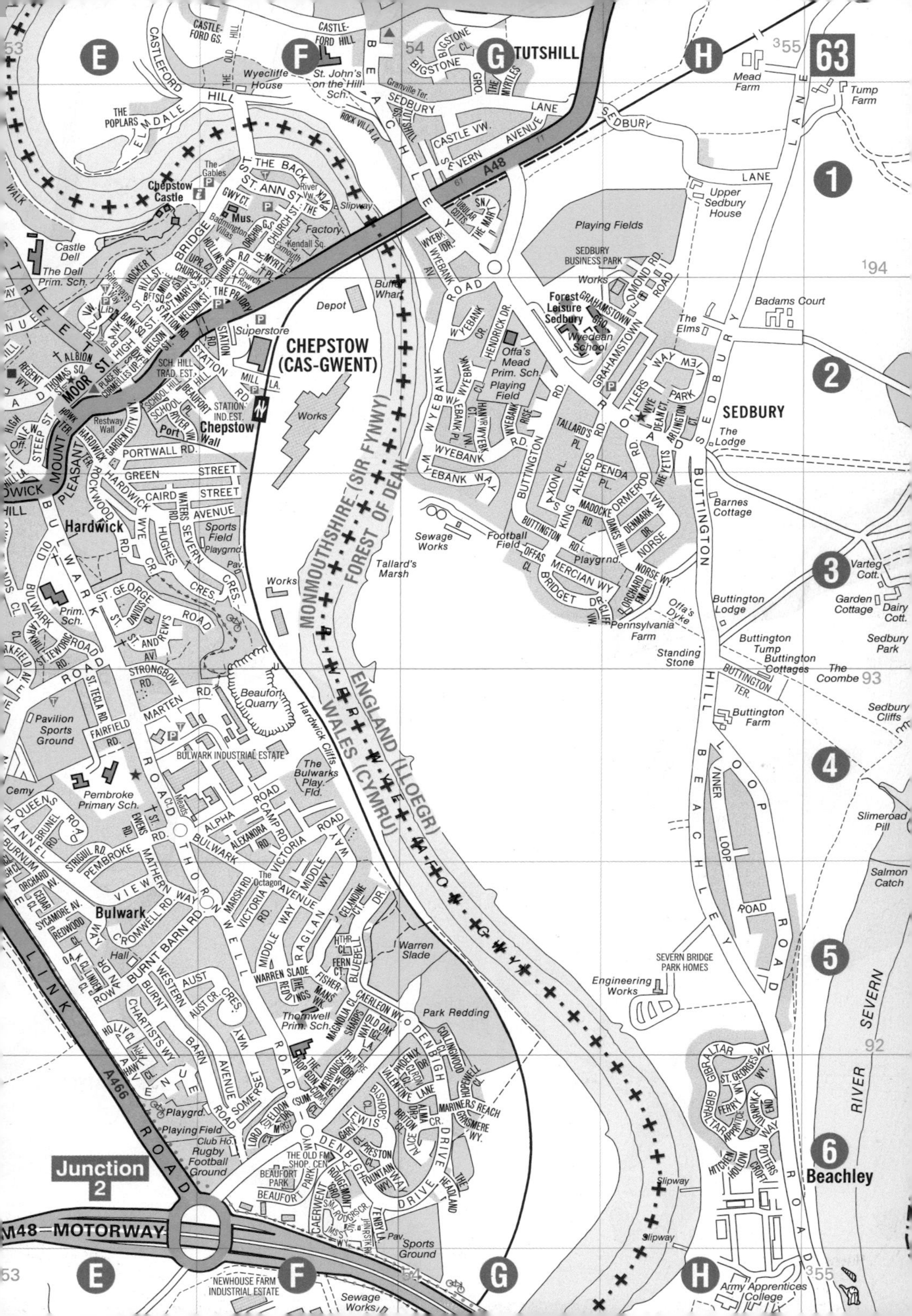
CHEPSTOW
(CAS-GWENT)
SEDBURY
TUTSHILL
Beachley
Bulwark
Hardwick
Junction
2
M48—MOTORWAY
A48
A466
LINK ROAD
ENGLAND (LLOEGR)
WALES (CYMRU)
MONMOUTHSHIRE (SIR FYNWY)
FOREST OF DEAN
RIVER SEVERN
Chepstow Castle
Chepstow Wall
Port Wall
St. John's on the Hill Sch.
Wyecliffe House
Castle Dell
The Dell Prim. Sch.
Offa's Mead Prim. Sch.
Playing Field
Forest Leisure Sedbury
Wyedean School
SEDBURY BUSINESS PARK
Playing Fields
Upper Sedbury House
Badams Court
Mead Farm
Tump Farm
Barnes Cottage
Varteg Cott.
Garden Cottage
Dairy Cott.
Buttington Lodge
Buttington Tump
Buttington Cottages
Buttington Farm
Sedbury Park
The Coombe
Sedbury Cliffs
Slimeroad Pill
Salmon Catch
Standing Stone
Pennsylvania Farm
Offa's Dyke
Tallard's Marsh
Sewage Works
Football Field
Engineering Works
SEVERN BRIDGE PARK HOMES
Army Apprentices College
Beaufort Quarry
BULWARK INDUSTRIAL ESTATE
The Bulwarks Play. Fld.
Hardwick Cliffs
Pembroke Primary Sch.
Pavilion Sports Ground
Thornwell Prim. Sch.
Park Redding
Warren Slade
Rugby Football Ground
Playing Field
Sports Ground
NEWHOUSE FARM INDUSTRIAL ESTATE
THE OLD FM. SHOP. CEN.
Superstore
Depot
Works
STATION IND. EST.
SCH. HILL TRAD. EST.
Sports Field
Restway Wall
Mus.
Factory
Buffs Wharf
Slipway
Cemy
Hall
Club Ho.
The Gables
The Elms
The Lodge
BUTTINGTON ROAD
SEDBURY LANE
BEACHLEY ROAD
INNER LOOP ROAD
HILL
MOOR ST.
HIGH ST.
BRIDGE ST.
PORTWALL RD.
BULWARK ROAD
THORNWELL ROAD
BURNT BARN RD.
DENBIGH DRIVE
WYEBANK ROAD
MOUNT PLEASANT
E
F
G
H
1
2
3
4
5
6
53
54
355
92
93
94

MYNYDD GARTHMAELWG
Coed-Cae Farm
Graig-lwyd
Coedynysmaerdy
Ynysmaerdy
Forest View
ROYAL GLAMORGAN HOSPITAL
RHODFA MARICS
Welsh Blood Service
Ely Meadow (Gwaun Eli)
Muchudd
Nant
Graig House
Graig Ilan
A4119
ELY
Weirs
Works
(AFON ELAI)
ELY RIVER
LLANTRISANT & PONTYCLUN GOLF COURSE
Talbot Green
Club Ho.
MAES-Y-RHEDYN
TALBOT SQUARE
ROAD
HEOL
Prim. Sch.
Halls
Hall
Garth Maelwg
Comm. Cen.
Play. Fld.
COWBRIDGE
FANHEULOG
SPRINGFIELD
CLOS
PINE COURT ROAD
FIRBANKS WY.
FAIRWAYS VW.
PINEWOOD HILL
WOODFIELD
FOREST WLK.
FOREST HILLS DR.
DUNRAVEN CRES.
LANELAY CL.
LANELAY PK.
LANELAY GRO.
LANELAY
Lanelay Farm
LANELAY CT.
Fire Service HQ
Lanelay Hall
Playing Fields
Factory
Garth-uchaf
Garth-isaf Farm
The Kennels
TWYN
HEOL
Works
A473
GREEN
Sewage Works
COEDCAE LANE INDUSTRIAL ESTATE
PARK
LANE
LANELAY INDUSTRIAL ESTATE
THE BEECHES INDUSTRIAL ESTATE
Mwyndy Junction
Factory
Hypermarket
Factory
COWBRIDGE A4222 RD.
Hendre Owen
Nant Melyn
COED TRECASTELL
WOODLANDS WORKSHOPS
CAMBRIAN IND. EST. (WEST SIDE)
CAMBRIAN IND. EST. (EAST SIDE)
Woodland Terrace
ASH GRO.
COEDCAE
GARW
Coed Trecastle
Tyle-garw
LLWYN ONN
COED MERI CT.
TYLAGARW
Works
Tylagarw Terrace
TYLE
Trecastle
PANT Y DDERWEN
School House
YNYSDDU
CLOS YNYSDDU
ELY VALLEY IND. ESTATE
MAELOG CT.
MERTHYR ST.
LEWIS ST.
ELY ST.
LON ELAI
SCHOOL ST.
STATION APP.
Railway Ter.
Pontyclun
JUNCTION INDUSTRIAL ESTATE
Playgrd.
STATION T.
STUART ST.
CERDIN
CASTAN
PALALWYF
ORSAF
HEOL YR
RIVERS EDGE
Hall
LLANTRISANT ROAD
David's Ct.
HEOL
CLUN CRES.
CLUN AVENUE
WINDSOR CT.
PONTYCLUN
Club
Playgrd.
Rugby Ground
FAIR VIEW CL.
RHYD Y NANT
TIR-AFON
LLWYNFEN RD.
DERWEN AV.
Club
Bowl. Grn.
Prim. Sch.
Lib.
Heol Dafydd
Pontyclun Prim. Sch.
FFORDD GLAN
TALYGARN
YR AFON
Bro-Dawel Cl.
MAES-YR-AFON
TEGEAN
HEOL GLAN ELAI
HEOL-Y-FELIN
MAESYFELIN CR.
PARK CR.
War Meml.
Playgrd.
Pav.
Sports Ground
MILLFIELD
ELY RIVER
(AFON ELAI)
COWBRIDGE A4222 ROAD
CLOS BRENIN
Ty-draw
Ty-du
Depot
Football Ground
DANYBRYN
Nant Felin-fach
Tynal Cottage
THE
A B C D
1 2 3 4 5 6
02 03
84 83 182 81
30
5
38
40
50
79
81
14

40

78

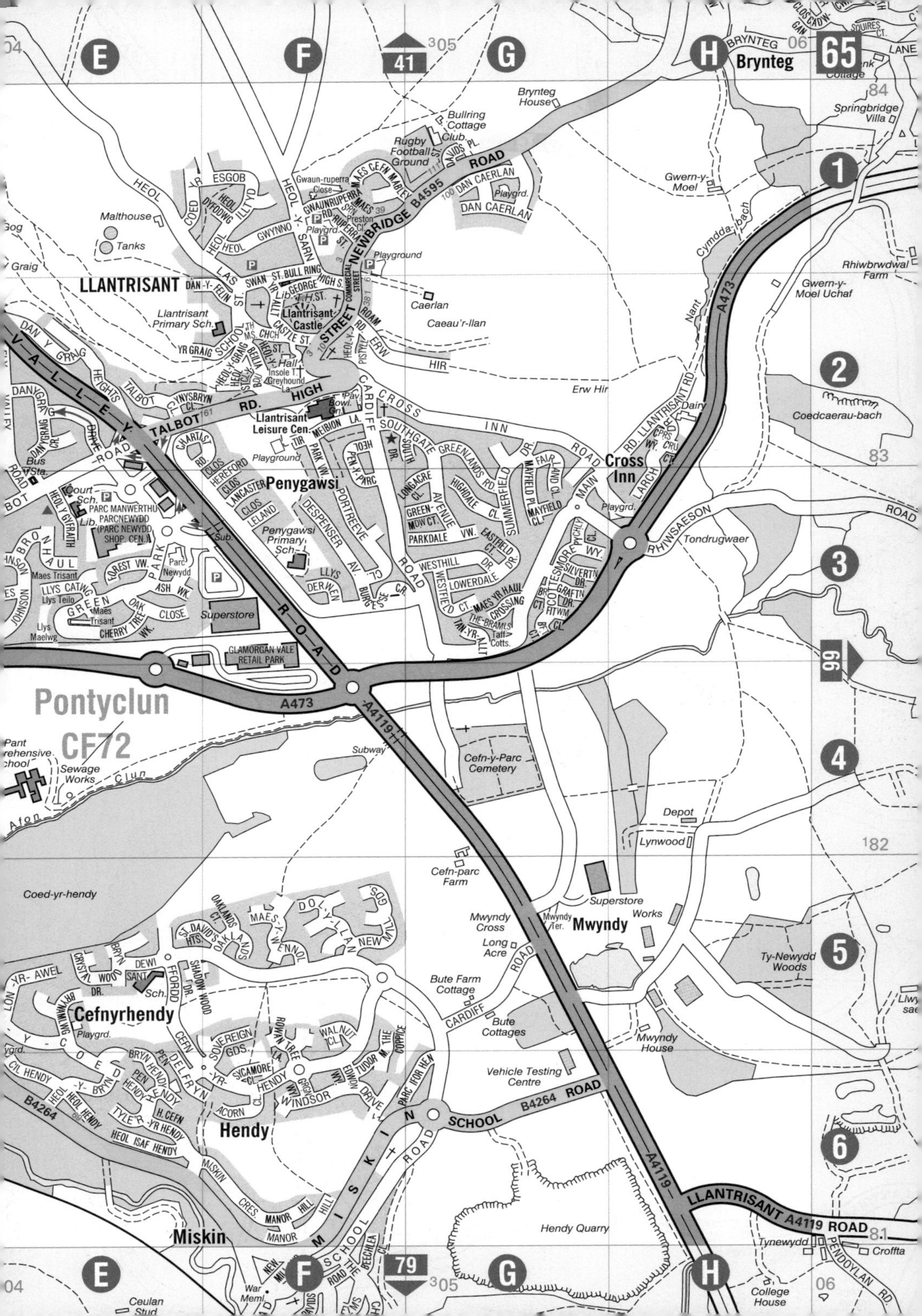
65
Brynteg
LLANTRISANT
Llantrisant Castle
Llantrisant Leisure Cen.
Llantrisant Primary Sch.
Penygawsi
Penygawsi Primary Sch.
Cross Inn
Pontyclun
CF72
Mwyndy
Cefnyrhendy
Hendy
Miskin
Hendy Quarry
Coed-yr-hendy
Cefn-y-Parc Cemetery
Glamorgan Vale Retail Park
Superstore
Parc Manwerthu Parcnewydd (Parc Newydd Shop. Cen.)
Vehicle Testing Centre
Bute Cottages
Bute Farm Cottage
Mwyndy House
Mwyndy Cross
Long Acre
Cefn-parc Farm
Lynwood
Depot
Works
Ty-Newydd Woods
Tondrugwaer
Erw Hir
Coedcaerau-bach
Gwern-y-Moel
Gwern-y-Moel Uchaf
Rhiwbrwdwal Farm
Springbridge Villa
Brynteg House
Bullring Cottage
Rugby Football Ground
Malthouse
Tanks
Caerlan
Caeau'r-llan
Sewage Works
Afon Clun
Subway
Playground
Tynewydd
Croffta
College House
War Meml.
Ceulan Stud
A473
A4119
B4595
B4264
Newbridge Road
Llantrisant A4119 Road
School Road
Cardiff Road
Cross Inn Road
Rhiwsaeson Road
Talbot Rd.
High Street
Commercial Street
Valley Road
Miskin Road
41
79
99
E
F
G
H
1
2
3
4
5
6

Brynteg
BRYNTEG
06
CHASE
SQUIRES CT.
MANOR
LANE
CHASE
BRYNTEG CT.
LLANTRISANT RD.
Sunny Bank Cottage
Gwaunmiskin House
Ystrad Barwig Isaf
07
42
A
B
C
D
BY-PASS
84
Springbridge Villa
Llantwit Main Farm
LLANTRISANT
RD.
Nant
Brook Farm
Westmoor
CHURCH
VILLAGE
(Under Construction Est. Comp. Late 2010)
Pontypridd
1
A473
Rhiwbrwdwal Farm
Myddlyn
Disgwylfa
Gwern-y-Moel Uchaf
Ty uchaf
Hendrescythan
2
Fort
The Lodge
Coedcaerau-bach
83
Ty-Mawr Farm
Coed-y-Graig
Pontyclun
CF72
RHIWSAESON
Hillcroft
Rhiwsaeson
Tondrugwaer
3
ROAD
RHONDDA CYNON TAFF
CARDIFF
Sports Ground
Ty'n y Cae Farm
Pav.
Tor-y-coed Farm
Afon
Sewage Works
Clun
65
Llwyn-y-brain-mawr
Llwyn-y-brain-bach
HEOL
TY
CREIGIAU
Llwynmilwas Farm
Smithy
Llwynmilwas
4
182
Porthandro
(CAERDYDD)
(RHONDDA CYNON TAF)
5
Ty-Newydd Woods
CREIGIAU GOLF COURSE
PARC-Y-BR
Ford
Club House
Llwyn-saer
Brofiscin Farm
TRE GARTH CL.
TRE GARTH CT.
Maendy Farm
Creigiau Primary School
ROAD
CREIGIAU
PARC
6
PARC-Y-FELIN
GLAN CREIGIAU
BRYN CREIGIAU
HEOL-YR-HAUL
HEOL BROFISCIN
LLYS CARADOG
Groes-faen
PEN Y GROES
PARK
FFORDD DOL-Y-FELIN
MAES
LLANTRISANT
Llwyn yr Eos
LA.
PARC
ROAD MAIN A4119 RD. 30
81
Tynewydd
PENDOYLAN RD.
Croffta
Redgate Ter.
The Smithy
Maes Mawr
80
Playg
LLYS DYFF
06
College House
07
Cottages
Hill Cottage

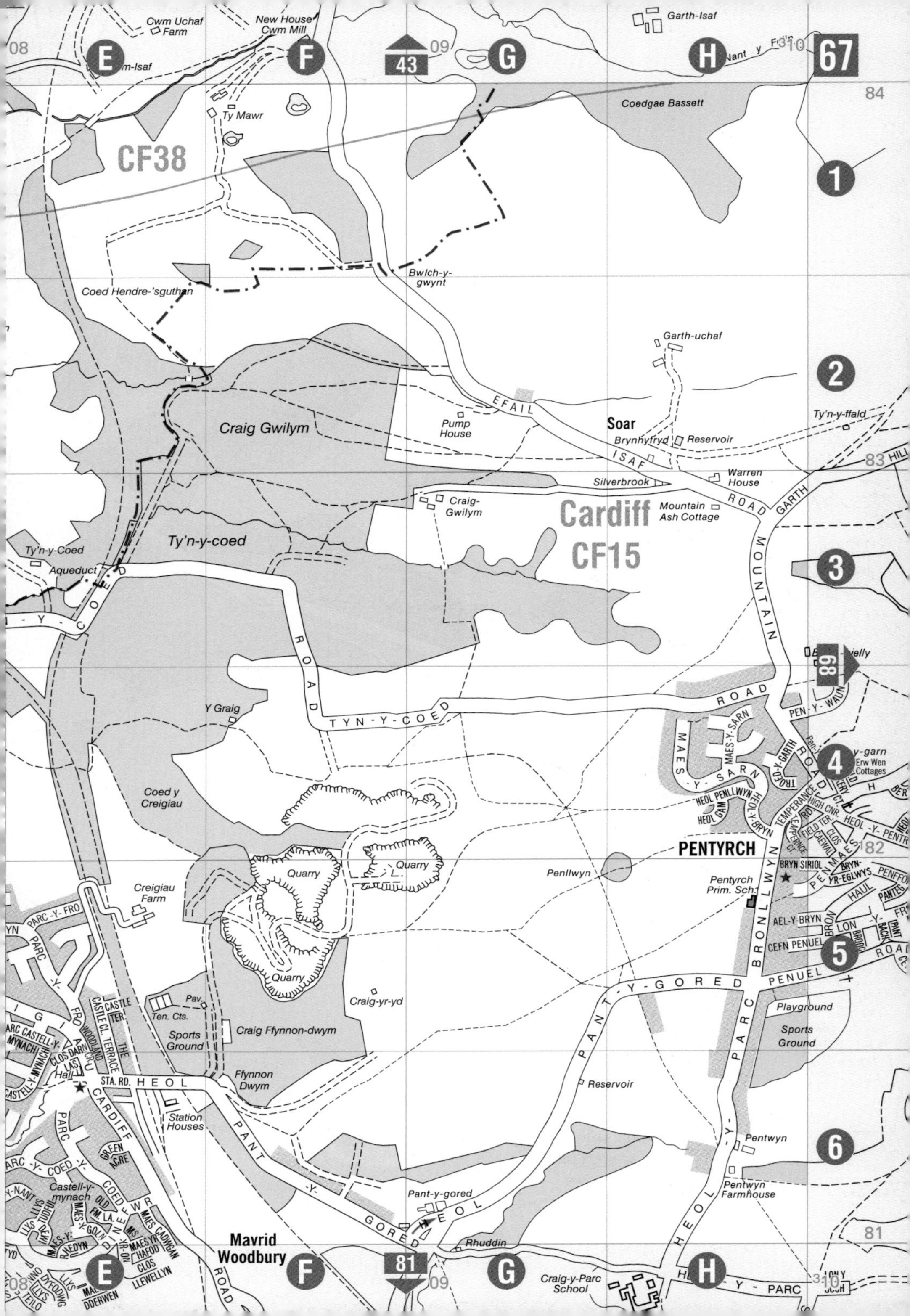
Cwm Uchaf Farm
New House
Cwm Mill
Garth-Isaf
Nant y Fid
43
81
68
Ty Mawr
CF38
Coedgae Bassett
Bwlch-y-gwynt
Coed Hendre-'sguthan
Garth-uchaf
Ty'n-y-ffald
Soar
Brynhyfryd
Reservoir
Pump House
EFAIL
ISAF
Craig Gwilym
Silverbrook
Warren House
Craig-Gwilym
Mountain Ash Cottage
Cardiff
CF15
GARTH
ROAD
MOUNTAIN
Ty'n-y-coed
Ty'n-y-Coed
Aqueduct
TYN-Y-COED ROAD
Y Graig
PEN-Y-WAUN
MAES-Y-SARN
TROED-Y-GARTH
Erw Wen Cottages
HEOL PENLLWYN
HEOL GAM
HEOL-Y-BRYN
TEMPERANCE CT.
HIGH CNR.
FIELD TER.
CAEWAL CLOS
HEOL-Y-PENTRE
Coed y Creigiau
PENTYRCH
Quarry
Penllwyn
Pentyrch Prim. Sch.
BRYN SIRIOL
PENMAES
BRYN-YR-EGLWYS
HAUL
PANTEG
AEL-Y-BRYN
BRON LON
CEFN PENUEL
PENUEL ROAD
BRONLLWYN
Creigiau Farm
PARC-Y-FRO
PANT-Y-GORED
Playground
Sports Ground
Craig-yr-yd
Pav.
Ten. Cts.
Craig Ffynnon-dwym
CASTLE TER.
CASTLE CL.
TERRACE
THE
WOODLAND
CLOS DARN-Y-CRU
LAST Hall
STA. RD.
HEOL
Ffynnon Dwym
Reservoir
Station Houses
PANT
CARDIFF ROAD
PARC
GREEN ACRE
PARC-Y-COED
Castell-y-mynach
Pentwyn
Pentwyn Farmhouse
HEOL-Y-PARC
Pant-y-gored
HEOL GORED
Rhuddin
Mavrid Woodbury
Craig-y-Parc School
MAES CADWGAN
MAES-YR-HAFOD
CLOS LLEWELLYN
DERWEN
LLYS DYFODWG
LLYS TEILO
LLYS TUDFUL
MAES-Y-GOLAU
FM. LA.
OLD
DINEFWR
CASTELL-Y-MYNACH
PARC CASTELL-Y-MYNACH
HILL

44
82
67
GARTH HILL
Gwaelod-y-garth
PENTYRCH
CF15
CARDIFF RD.
MAIN ROAD
GARTH ROAD
MOUNTAIN ROAD
HEOL GOCH
CHURCH ROAD
CAERAU LANE
HEOL-Y-PARC
Gwaelod-y-garth
Bristol T.
Post Office Row
GARTH OLWG
Salem Ter.
RIVERSIDE
Pant Pl.
ST.
Garth Vw.
Leyshon Ct.
Cules Ter.
Tennis Courts
Club
Rec. Grd.
Ffynnon Taf Prim. Sch.
PARK LA.
Bowl. Grn.
Pav.
Ten.Cts
Glanyrafon
SCHOOL
Ysgol Gynradd Gwaelod y Garth Prim. Sch.
PATMORE CL.
LANE
Coed Rhiw'r Ceiliog
HEOL-Y-NANT
Georgetown
NANT Y GARTH
Mount Pleasant
Caerwen
Ty'n-y-ffald
Warren House
Mountain Ash Cott.
Nant Cwmllwydrew
Coed-y-bedw
Blaen-bielly
Ton-mawr
PEN-Y-WAUN
Pen-y-garn
Erw Wen Cottages
Pen-Y-Cwm
OLD BAKERY CT.
HEOL
CEFN BYCHAN
CLOS CEFN BYCHAN
BERTHLWYD
HEOL DANYRODYN
FAIR MEADOW
CHARTWELL CT.
PENTRE-Y-FRO
HEOL PENLIN
HEOL GAM
MAES-Y-SARN
TEMPERANCE RD.
HIGH CNR.
FIELD TER.
CLOS CAEWAL
TEMPERANCE CT.
PENMAES
BRYN SIRIOL
BRYN-YR-EGLWYS
PENFFORDD
PANTEG
PANTGLAS
HAUL
LON
BRON
BRODIG
PANT BACH
AEL-Y-BRYN
CEFN PENUEL
BRONLLWYN
Pentyrch Prim. Sch.
HEOL PANT-Y-GORED
PENUEL
CEFN LLAN
Playground
Sports Ground
Old Trial Pit
Cefn Colstyn
Ash Grove
Graig-hir
Cwm-y-fuwch
Pant-y-caeau
Pentwyn
Pentwyn Farmhouse
Llwynda'-ddu
Coedcae Fawr
Coed Pant-tawel
MAES
HEO
GOCH
PARC
WILLOW

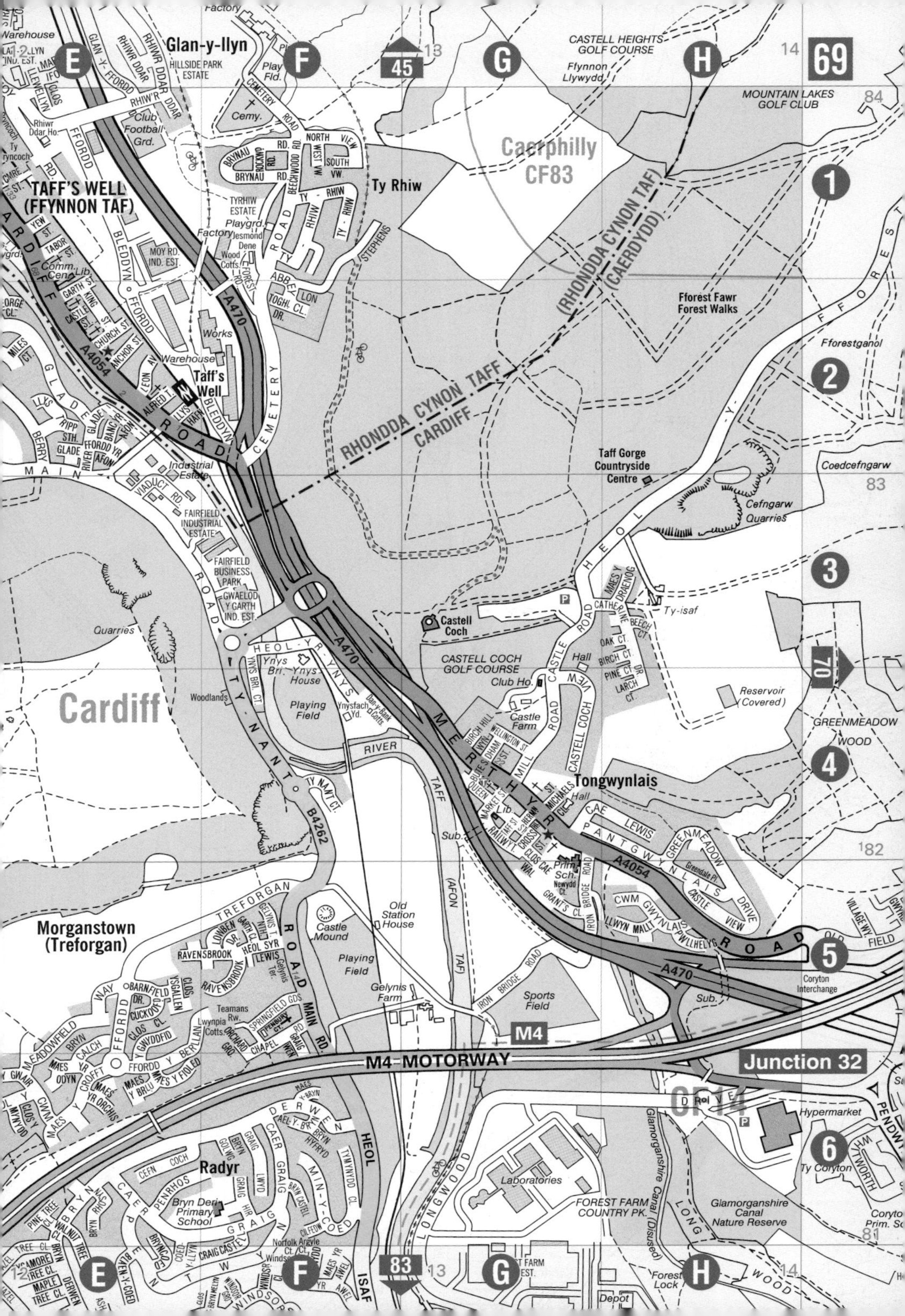

TAFF'S WELL (FFYNNON TAF)
Glan-y-llyn
Ty Rhiw
Caerphilly CF83
Cardiff
Morganstown (Treforgan)
Radyr
Tongwynlais
RHONDDA CYNON TAFF
CARDIFF
(RHONDDA CYNON TAF) (CAERDYDD)
Fforest Fawr Forest Walks
Fforestganol
Coedcefngarw
Cefngarw Quarries
Taff Gorge Countryside Centre
Castell Coch
CASTELL COCH GOLF COURSE
CASTELL HEIGHTS GOLF COURSE
Ffynnon Llywydd
MOUNTAIN LAKES GOLF CLUB
GREENMEADOW WOOD
Reservoir (Covered)
Ty-isaf
M4 MOTORWAY
Junction 32
Coryton Interchange
Hypermarket
Ty Coryton
Glamorganshire Canal Nature Reserve
Glamorganshire Canal (Disused)
FOREST FARM COUNTRY PK.
Laboratories
Forest Lock
Depot
Bryn Deri Primary School
Old Station House
Castle Mound
Gelynis Farm
Playing Field
Sports Field
Quarries
Woodlands
FAIRFIELD INDUSTRIAL ESTATE
FAIRFIELD BUSINESS PARK
GWAELOD Y GARTH IND. EST.
MOY RD. IND. EST.
TYRHIW ESTATE
HILLSIDE PARK ESTATE
A470
A4054
B4262
45
83
70

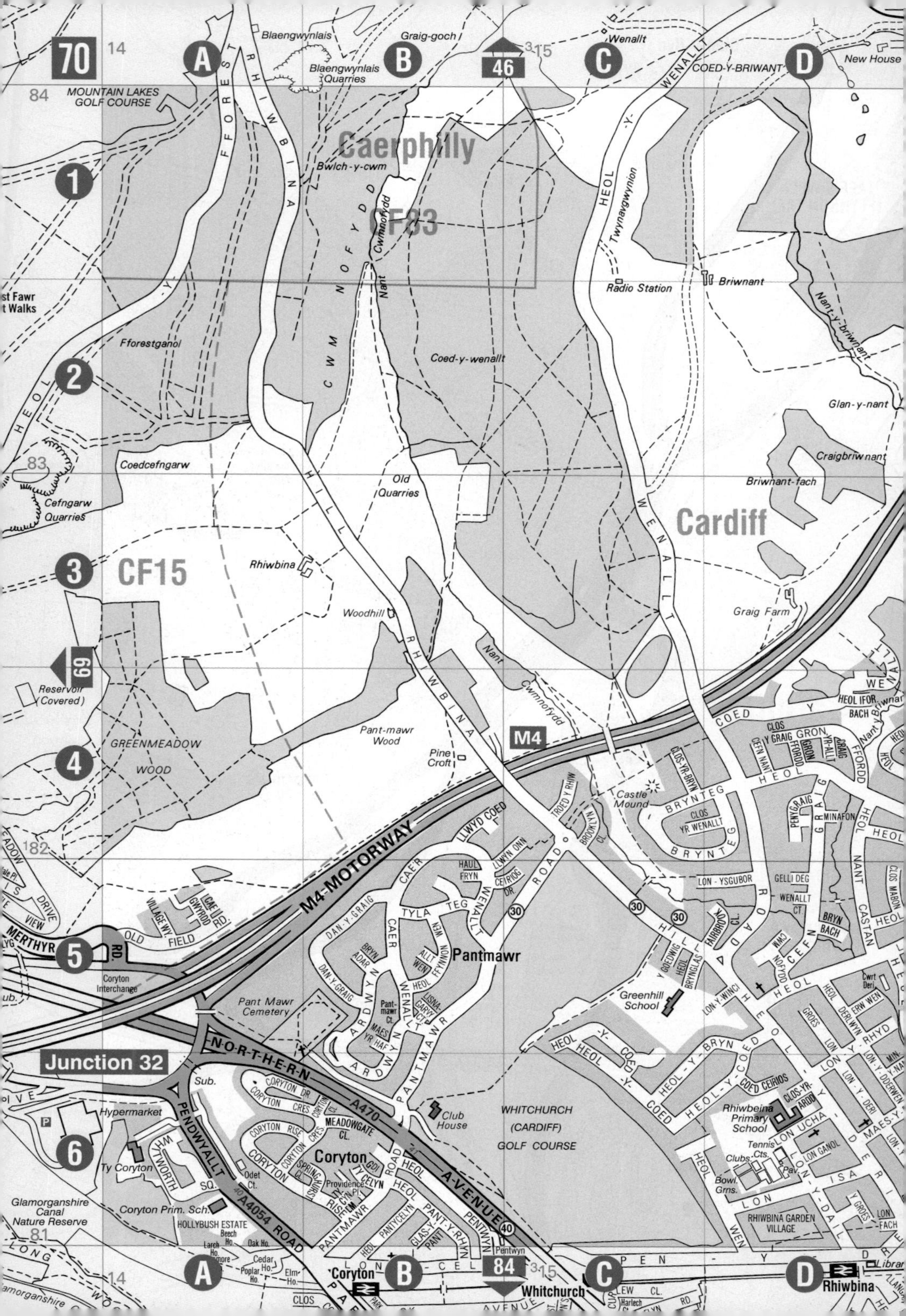
Blaengwynlais
Graig-goch
Wenallt
New House
COED-Y-BRIWANT
Blaengwynlais Quarries
MOUNTAIN LAKES GOLF COURSE
Caerphilly
Bwlch-y-cwm
CF83
Cwmnofydd
Nant
Radio Station
Briwnant
Nant-y-briwnant
Fforestganol
Coed-y-wenallt
Glan-y-nant
Coedcefngarw
Old Quarries
Craigbriwnant
Briwnant-fach
Cefngarw Quarries
Cardiff
CF15
Rhiwbina
Woodhill
Graig Farm
Reservoir (Covered)
GREENMEADOW WOOD
Pant-mawr Wood
Pine Croft
M4
M4-MOTORWAY
Castle Mound
Pantmawr
Coryton Interchange
Pant Mawr Cemetery
Junction 32
NORTHERN AVENUE
A470
Greenhill School
Hypermarket
Ty Coryton
Coryton
Club House
WHITCHURCH (CARDIFF) GOLF COURSE
Rhiwbeina Primary School
Glamorganshire Canal Nature Reserve
Coryton Prim. Sch.
HOLLYBUSH ESTATE
A4054 ROAD
PENDWYALLT
RHIWBINA GARDEN VILLAGE
Coryton
Whitchurch
Rhiwbina
HEOL-Y-WENALLT
RHIWBINA HILL
CWM NOFYDD
FFOREST
MERTHYR RD.
OLD FIELD
HEOL-Y-BRYN
HEOL-Y-COED
PEN-Y-DRE

46
69
84

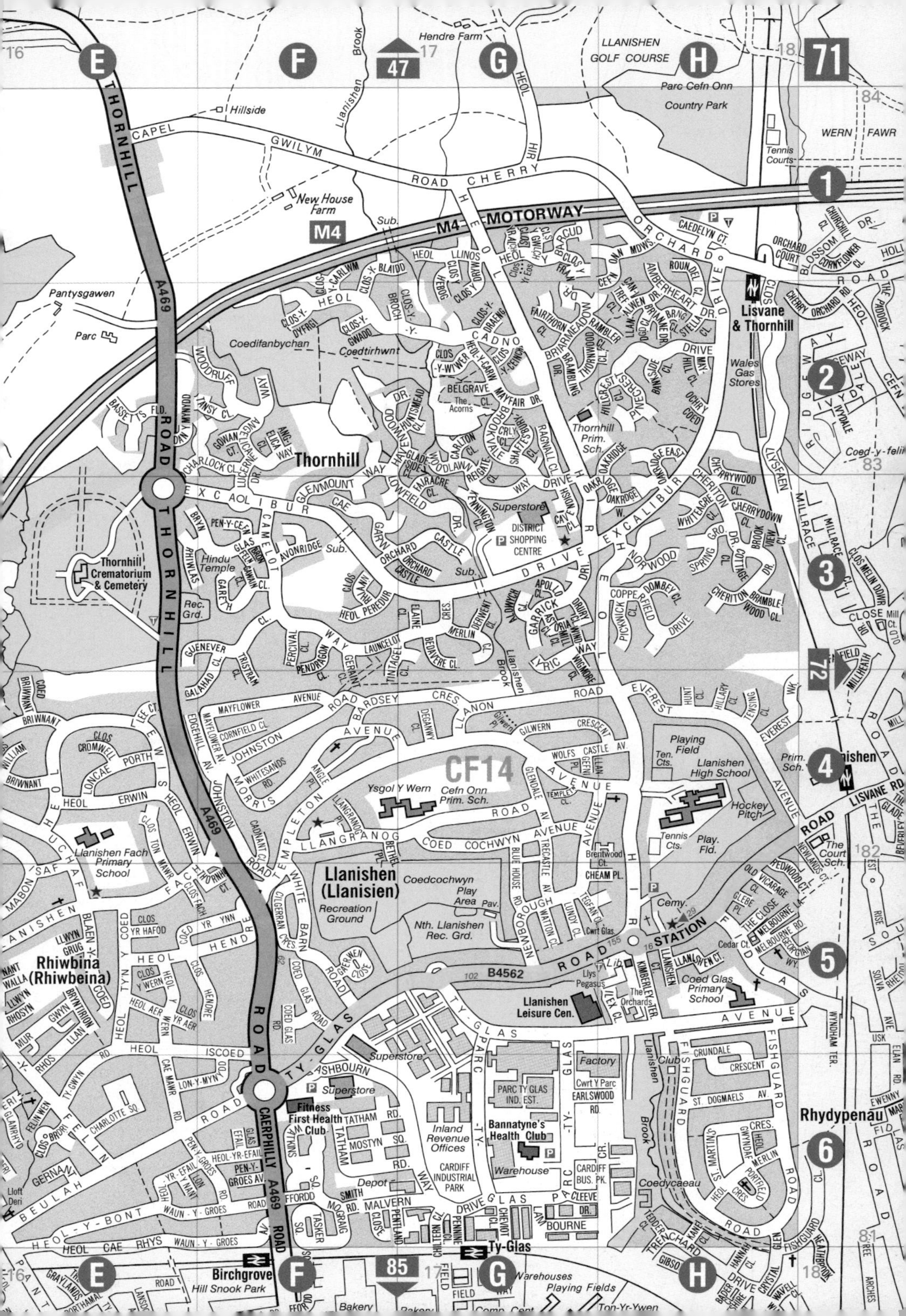
71
47
85
72
M4
CF14
Thornhill
Llanishen (Llanisien)
Rhiwbina (Rhiwbeina)
Rhydypenau
Ty-Glas
Birchgrove
Lisvane & Thornhill
Llanishen
Hendre Farm
Llanishen Golf Course
Parc Cefn Onn Country Park
Wern Fawr
Hillside
New House Farm
Pantysgawen
Parc
Coedifanbychan
Coedtirhwnt
Thornhill Crematorium & Cemetery
Hindu Temple
Thornhill Prim. Sch.
District Shopping Centre
Superstore
Ysgol Y Wern
Cefn Onn Prim. Sch.
Llanishen High School
Llanishen Fach Primary School
Coed Glas Primary School
Llanishen Leisure Cen.
Bannatyne's Health Club
Fitness First Health Club
Inland Revenue Offices
Cardiff Industrial Park
Parc Ty Glas Ind. Est.
Cardiff Bus. Pk.
Coedcochwyn Play Area
Recreation Ground
Nth. Llanishen Rec. Grd.
Wales Gas Stores
Playing Field
Hockey Pitch
Tennis Courts
M4 Motorway
Thornhill Road
Caerphilly Road
A469
B4562
Station Road
Excalibur Drive
Heol Hir
Cherry Orchard Road
Capel Gwilym Road
Llanon Road
Everest Avenue
Fishguard Road
Ty-Glas Avenue
Ty-Glas Road
Heol Erwin
Heol Uchaf
Templeton Avenue
Coed Cochwyn Avenue
Millrace
Ridgeway
Lisvane Rd.
Heol-y-Bont
Heol Cae Rhys
Waun-y-Groes
Beulah Road
Camelot Way
Glenmount Way
Hill Snook Park
Warehouses
Playing Fields
Ton-Yr-Ywen

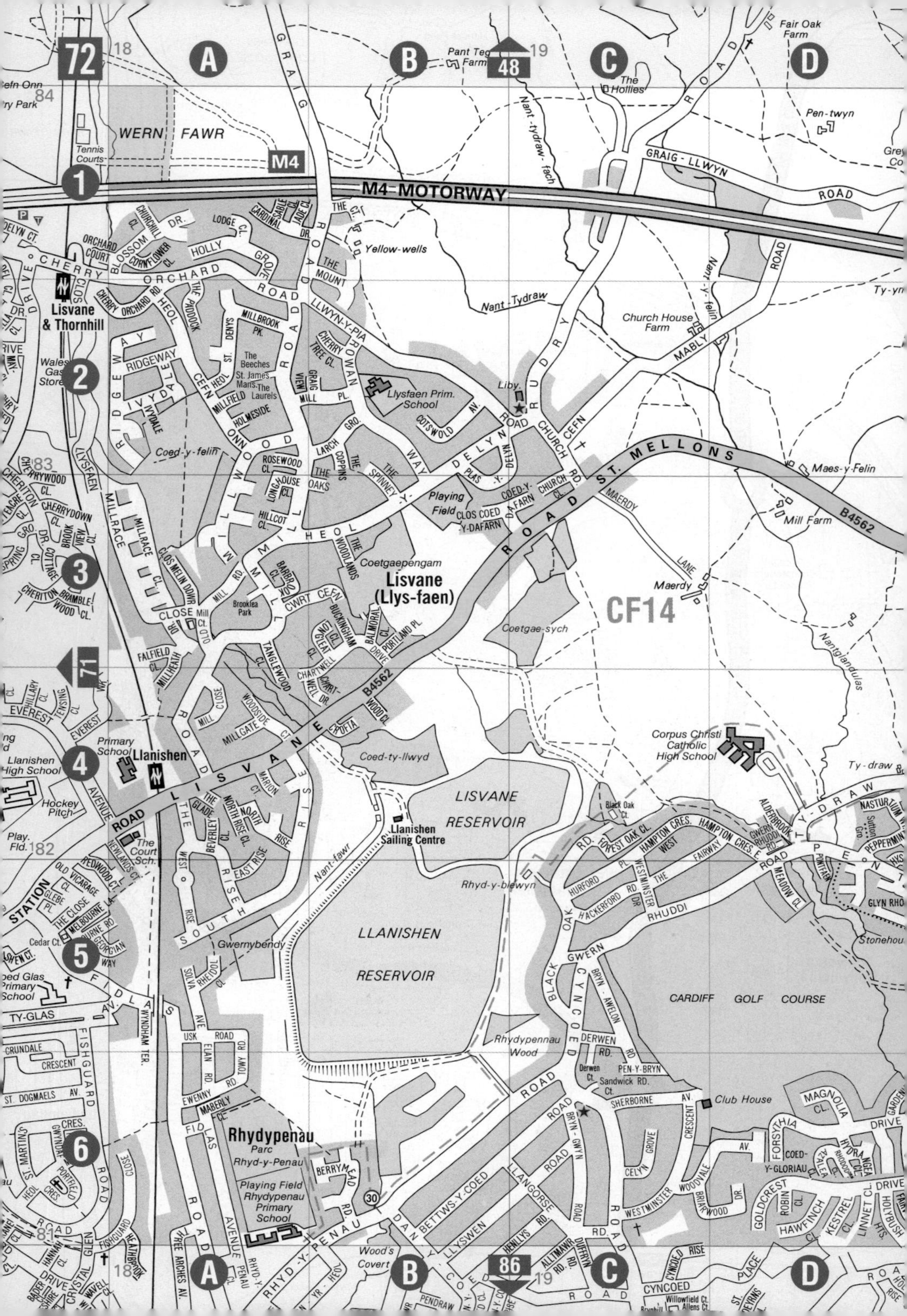

72
A
B
C
D
1
2
3
4
5
6
18
19
84
83
182
81
48
86
71
M4
M4 MOTORWAY
CF14
WERN FAWR
Tennis Courts
Pant Teg Farm
The Hollies
Fair Oak Farm
Pen-twyn
GRAIG-LLWYN ROAD
GRAIG ROAD
Nant-tydraw-fach
Yellow-wells
Nant-Tydraw
Church House Farm
Nant-y-felin
MABLY ROAD
RUDRY ROAD
CHURCH RD.
CEFN
Liby.
Llysfaen Prim. School
Lisvane & Thornhill
Wales Gas Store
CHERRY ORCHARD RD.
ORCHARD ROAD
CHERRY CLOS
ORCHARD COURT
BLOSSOM DR.
CHURCHILL CL.
CORNFLOWER CL.
HOLLY GROVE
LODGE CL.
CARDINAL DR.
SABLE CL.
JADE CL.
THE CT.
THE MOUNT
LLWYN-Y-PIA ROAD
ROWAN PL.
CHERRY TREE CL.
GRAIG VIEW
MILL PL.
COTSWOLD AV.
DELYN ROAD
DELYN WAY
PLAS-Y-DELYN
THE SPINNEY
THE COPPINS
THE OAKS
LARCH GRO.
ROSEWOOD CL.
LONGHOUSE CL.
HILLCOT CL.
HEOL-Y-MILL
MILLWOOD
CEFN ONN ROAD
HEOL ST. DENYS
MILLBROOK PK.
The Beeches
St. James Mans.
The Laurels
MILLFIELD
HOLMESIDE
THE PADDOCK
HEOL
RIDGEWAY
IVYDALE
Coed-y-felin
LLYSFAEN
MILLRACE
MILLRACE CL.
CLOS MELIN DWR
MILL RD.
MILL CLOSE
Mill Ct.
OLD MILL DR.
Brooklea Park
BARBROOK CL.
CWRT CEFN
BUCKINGHAM CL.
NOT CL.
GLEAT CL.
BALMORAL CL.
PORTLAND PL.
DRIVE
TANGLEWOOD CL.
CHARTWELL
CHARTWELL DR.
WOOD CL.
CROFTA
Coetgaepengam
Lisvane (Llys-faen)
Coetgae-sych
Maerdy
MAERDY
LANE
ST. MELLONS ROAD
B4562
Maes-y-Felin
Mill Farm
Nantglandulas
PLAYING FIELD
CLOS COED-Y-DAFARN
COED-Y-DAFARN
CHURCH CL.
FALFIELD
MILLHEATH
WOODSIDE CT.
MILLGATE
LISVANE ROAD
Llanishen
Primary School
Llanishen High School
Hockey Pitch
Play. Fld.
AVENUE
EVEREST
EVEREST
TENSING CL.
HILLARY CL.
THE GLADE
THE WEST RISE
NORTH RISE CL.
NORTH CL.
MARION CT.
EAST RISE
BEVERLEY CL.
SOUTH RISE
RISE
Coed-ty-llwyd
LISVANE RESERVOIR
Llanishen Sailing Centre
Nant-fawr
Rhyd-y-blewyn
LLANISHEN RESERVOIR
Gwernybendy
RHEIDOL CL.
SOLVA AVE
The Court Sch.
NEWLANDS CT.
REDWOOD CT.
OLD VICARAGE
GLEBE PL.
THE CLOSE
MELBOURNE
MELBOURNE RD
GEORGIAN WAY
STATION
Cedar Ct.
Coed Glas Primary School
FIDLAS AV.
TY-GLAS
FISHGUARD ROAD
WYNDHAM TER.
CRUNDALE CRESCENT
ST. DOGMAELS AV.
GWYNDAF CRES.
ST. MARTIN'S CRES.
PORTFIELD CRES.
HEOL
CLOSE
CRYSTAL GLEN
HANNAH CL.
BADER DRIVE
WAVELL
HEATHBROOK
FISHGUARD
USK ROAD
ELAN RD.
TOWY RD.
EWENNY RD.
MABERLY CT.
FIDLAS ROAD
AVENUE
THREE ARCHES AV.
RHYD-Y-PENAU
Rhydypenau
Parc Rhyd-y-Penau
Playing Field
Rhydypenau Primary School
BERRYMEAD RD.
RHYD-Y-PENAU ROAD
RHYD-Y-HEOL
Wood's Covert
DAN-Y-COED
LLYSWEN
BETTWS-Y-COED ROAD
LLANGORSE ROAD
HENLLYS RD.
ALLTMAWR RD.
DUFFRYN RD.
BRYN-GWYN ROAD
PENDRAW
CYNCOED ROAD
CYNCOED RISE
CYNCOED PLACE
Willowfield Ct.
Allens Ct.
Rhydypennau Wood
DERWEN RD.
Derwen Ct.
Sandwick RD.
PEN-Y-BRYN Ct.
SHERBORNE AV.
CRESCENT
CELYN GROVE
WESTMINSTER
WOODVALE
BRIARWOOD DR.
Club House
BLACK OAK
GWERN RHUDDI
BRYN-AWELON
HURFORD PL
HACKERFORD RD
WESTMINSTER DR
THE WEST FAIRWAY
HAMPTON CRES.
HAMPTON CRES. E.
FOREST OAK CL.
Black Oak Ct.
GWERN RHUDDI RD.
ALDERBROOK
MEADOW CL.
PONTFAEN
TY-DRAW ROAD
PENTWYN
Corpus Christi Catholic High School
Ty-draw
CARDIFF GOLF COURSE
Stonehou
GLYN RHO
NASTURTIUM
PEPPERMINT
Sutton Gro.
MAGNOLIA CL.
FORSYTHIA AV.
COED-Y-GLORIAU
AZALEA
HYDRANGEA
GOLDCREST
ROBIN CL.
HAWFINCH CL.
KESTREL CL.
LINNET CL.
HOLYBUSH
DRIVE
GARDENS
Ty-yn

73
E
F
G
H
49
87
74
1
2
3
4
5
6
CEFN MABLEY WOODS
Fort Castle Field
Graig-llwyn
GRAIG-LLWYN ROAD
CEFN-PORTH ROAD
HEOL MAES-Y-BRYN
PARC-Y-PARC
CF3
Llan
Berllan
Parkwall
M4
M4 MOTORWAY
Junction 30
Nant Glandulas
Malthouse Wood
Malthouse Farm
Mandalay
PARKWALL ROAD
Ash Tree Court
Cardiff Gate Service Area
CARDIFF GATE BUSINESS PARK
Prennau House
Regus Ho.
Rhymney Ho.
ST. MELLONS ROAD
B4562
Cardiff
CARDIFF GATE RETAIL PARK
Superstore
BRIDGE ROAD
LINK ROAD
A4232
PENTWYN-NORTH
Llangattock
Bryngolau
Comm. Cen.
Pontprennau
PONTPRENNAU
CARDIFF SPIRE HOSP
THE AVENUE INDUSTRIAL PARK
Glebe
St. Edeyrn's Church
Church Farm
CHURCH ROAD
AVENUE
New Mill Farm
MILL LANE
PENTWYN ROAD
Factory
CF23
St. Bernadette's R C Primary Sch.
Pentwyn
The Hollies School
Comm. Cen.
Glyncoed Jun. & Inf. Schools
Bryn Celyn Prim. Sch.
Prim. Sch.
A48
EASTERN
St. Cadoc's Catholic Primary School
Glan-Yr-Afon Primary School
Llanrumney (Llanrhymni)
Rhymney River
Playing Fields
Pentwyn Interchange
Lower Rookery
20
21
22
83
84
81

74
50
88
73
Junction 30
Junction 29a
M4 MOTORWAY
M4
A48(M) MOTORWAY
A48(M)
EASTERN AVENUE
A48
B4562
B4487
NEWPORT
CARDIFF
(CASNEWYDD)
(CAERDYDD)
Cardiff
CF3
Began
Old St. Mellons
St. Mellons
Rhymney Valley Nurseries
Reservoir
Reservoirs
Wern Uchaf
Pentreporth
Fairwater Bungalow
Fairwater Farm
Began Farm
Maes-y-crochan Farm
St. Julian's Farm
Brook House
Pistyll-yr-achddu
Began House
Bridge Farm
Llanedern Bridge
Marleigh Lodge
Pwll-coch
Goitre Farm
St. Mellons Interchange
Recreation Ground
Tennis Court
Ty'r-bont
Glebe
St. Edeyrn's Church
Church Farm
New Mill Farm
Superstore
CARDIFF GATE RETAIL PARK
St. Cadoc's Catholic Primary School
St. John's College
THE EASTERN BUSINESS PARK
Offices
Oakfield Jun. & Inf. Sch.
Pen-Y-Bryn Prim. Sch.
St. Mellons C in W Primary Sch.
DISTRICT SHOPPING CENTRE
Broadlands Ho.
WILLOWBROOK LAB. UNITS
Cath-Cobb Wood
Playing Field
Faendre Gardens
Lower Rookery
Ty Coch
RIVER RHYMNEY
(AFON RHYMNI)
BEGAN ROAD
DRUIDSTONE ROAD
BRIDGE ROAD
PENTWYN LINK ROAD
NORTH A4232
TYR WINCH ROAD
NEWPORT ROAD
WILLOWBROOK
WERN FAWR LANE
HERITAGE PARK
CHURCH RD.
MILL LANE
BURNHAM AVENUE
HONITON ROAD
SEDGEMOOR ROAD
ELGAR AVENUE
COUNTISBURY AVENUE
CRICKHOWELL RD.
HASTINGS CRES.
Llyn y Corwydd

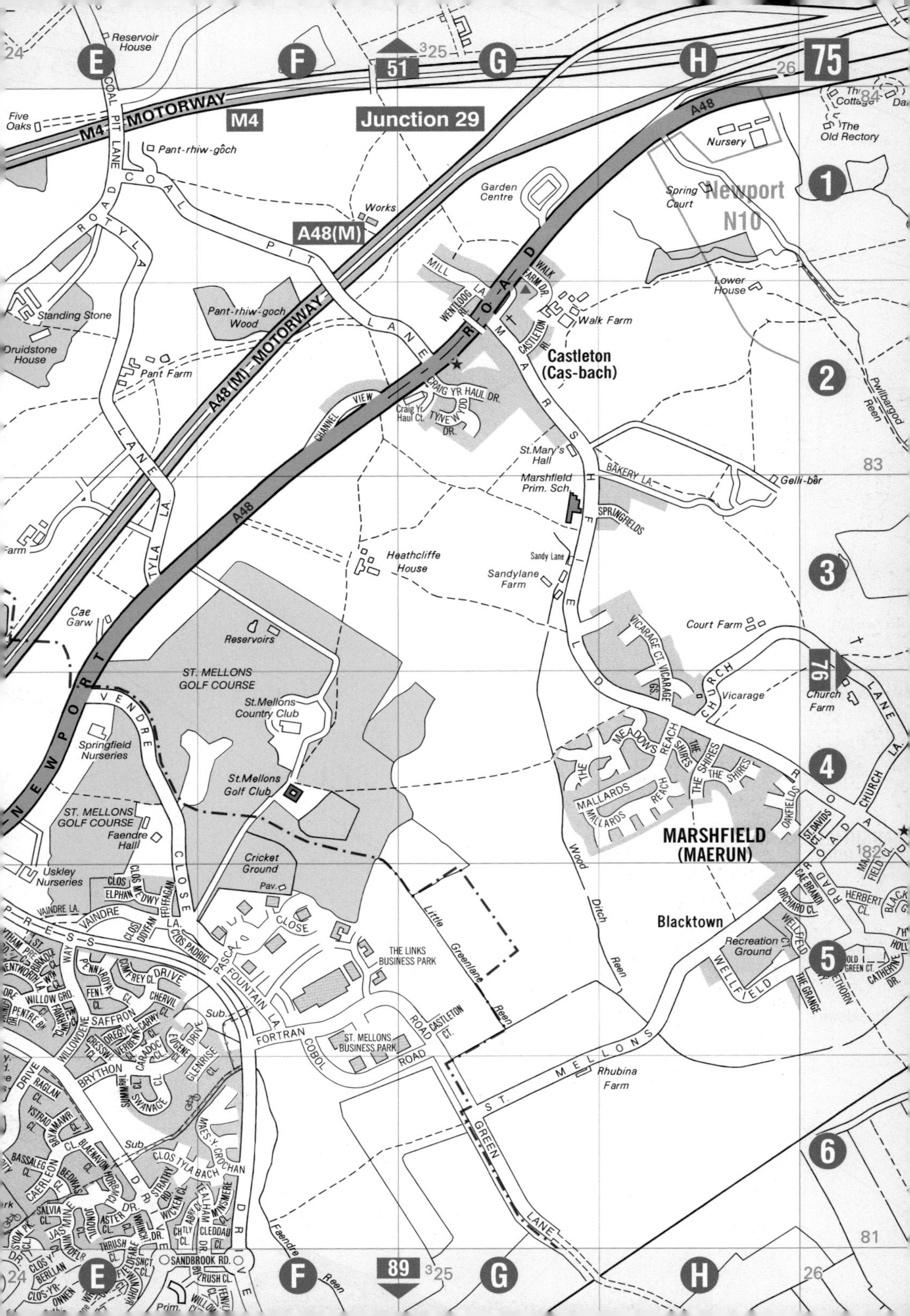
MARSHFIELD
(MAERUN)
Castleton
(Cas-bach)
Blacktown
Newport
N10
Junction 29
M4
M4 MOTORWAY
A48(M) MOTORWAY
A48(M)
A48
NEWPORT ROAD
ST. MELLONS ROAD
MARSHFIELD ROAD
CHURCH LANE
COAL PIT LANE
TYLA LANE
PIT LANE
GREEN LANE
ST. MELLONS GOLF COURSE
St.Mellons Golf Club
St.Mellons Country Club
Springfield Nurseries
Uskley Nurseries
Faendre Hall
Cricket Ground
THE LINKS BUSINESS PARK
ST. MELLONS BUSINESS PARK
Reservoirs
Heathcliffe House
Sandylane Farm
Sandy Lane
Marshfield Prim. Sch
St.Mary's Hall
Court Farm
Vicarage
Church Farm
Recreation Ground
Rhubina Farm
Walk Farm
Lower House
Spring Court
Nursery
The Old Rectory
The Cottage
Garden Centre
Works
Pant-rhiw-gôch
Pant-rhiw-goch Wood
Standing Stone
Druidstone House
Pant Farm
Cae Garw
Five Oaks
Reservoir House
Gelli-bêr
Wood Ditch Reen
Little Greenlane Reen
Pwllbargod Reen
Faendre Reen
51
89
76
75
E
F
G
H
1
2
3
4
5
6
24
3 25
26
81
83
84
182

52
75
A
B
C
D
1
2
3
4
5
6
26
27
84
83
182
81
A48
B4239
Myrtle Ho.
HILL
Works
The Cottage
Dan-y-graig
The Old Rectory
Nursery
Longhouse
Ty'n-y-brwyn
Tyn-y-brwyr Reen
Nant y Selsig
CHURCH RD.
CHURCH
Nant-y-moor
Club House
The Stud Farm
Maerdy Farm
Cowleaze Reen
Coedkernew
PARC GOLF RANGE
Lower House
Pwllbargod
PERCOED
LANE
HAWSE LANE
Reen
Gelli-bêr
Drenewydd
TYMAWR LANE
Court Farm
CHURCH LANE
CHURCH LA.
Vicarage
Church Farm
Tymawr Farm
Cardiff CF3
Penning
MARSH-FIELD ROAD
THE SHIRES
OAKFIELDS
ST. DAVIDS CT.
MARSHFIELD (MAERUN)
CAMBRIAN DR.
CAMBRIAN GS.
CAMBRIAN CL.
CAMBRIAN GRO.
WOODFIELD CL.
Glandwr Fm.
MARYSFIELD CL.
CAE BRANDI
ORCHARD CL.
HERBERT CL.
BLACKTOWN GDNS.
PENTWYN TER.
BAKERS CT.
ST. MELLONS ROAD
WELLFIELD CT.
Rec. Grd.
WELLFIELD
THE HOLLIES
OLD GREEN CT.
CATHERINE DR.
WHITETHORN WY.
THE GRANGE
Blacktown
Horsecroft
WENTLOOGE LEVEL
Station Ho.
BROADWAY ROAD
Broadway
Blackwater
Summerway
Greenacre Farm
Drains
Gout Farm
Club Ho.
PETERSTONE GOLF & COUNTRY CLUB
Gout Fawr
PETERSTONE GOLF COURSE

77
53
E
F
G
H
1
2
3
4
5
6
84
83
182
81
28
29
330
Newport
NP10
St. Bride's Wentlooge
(Llansanffraid Gwynllwg)
M4 RELIEF ROAD (Proposed)
(Proposed)
MOUTH OF THE SEVERN
(ABER HAFREN)
LIGHTHOUSE RD.
B4239
LIGHTHOUSE ROAD
BEACH ROAD
LIGHTHOUSE PARK
CHURCH RD
NEVILLE PARK
Church House Park
GREEN LANE
PERCOED LANE
Percoed
WHEEL LANE
OUTFALL LANE
Hawse LANE
Sealand
Reen
Wharf
Hawse
Morfa-Gronw
DUFFRYN
Oystermouth
Fair Orchard Farm
Ty-hir
Dulce Domum
Pear Tree Cottage
Pound Farm House
New House Farm
New Farm
Ty-mawr Farm
Sea View
Sutton Cottage
Ty-llwyd
Sunnybank Lodge
Glan-y-mor
Old House
Fox Covert
Great Pen-carn
Pont-estyll
Middle Pen-carn Cottage
Maerdy Farm
Hawse Farm
Red House
Nursery
Greenmoor Farm
Cherry Orchard
Walnut Tree Farm
Springfield
Orchard Farm
Bryn Glas Farm
Farm

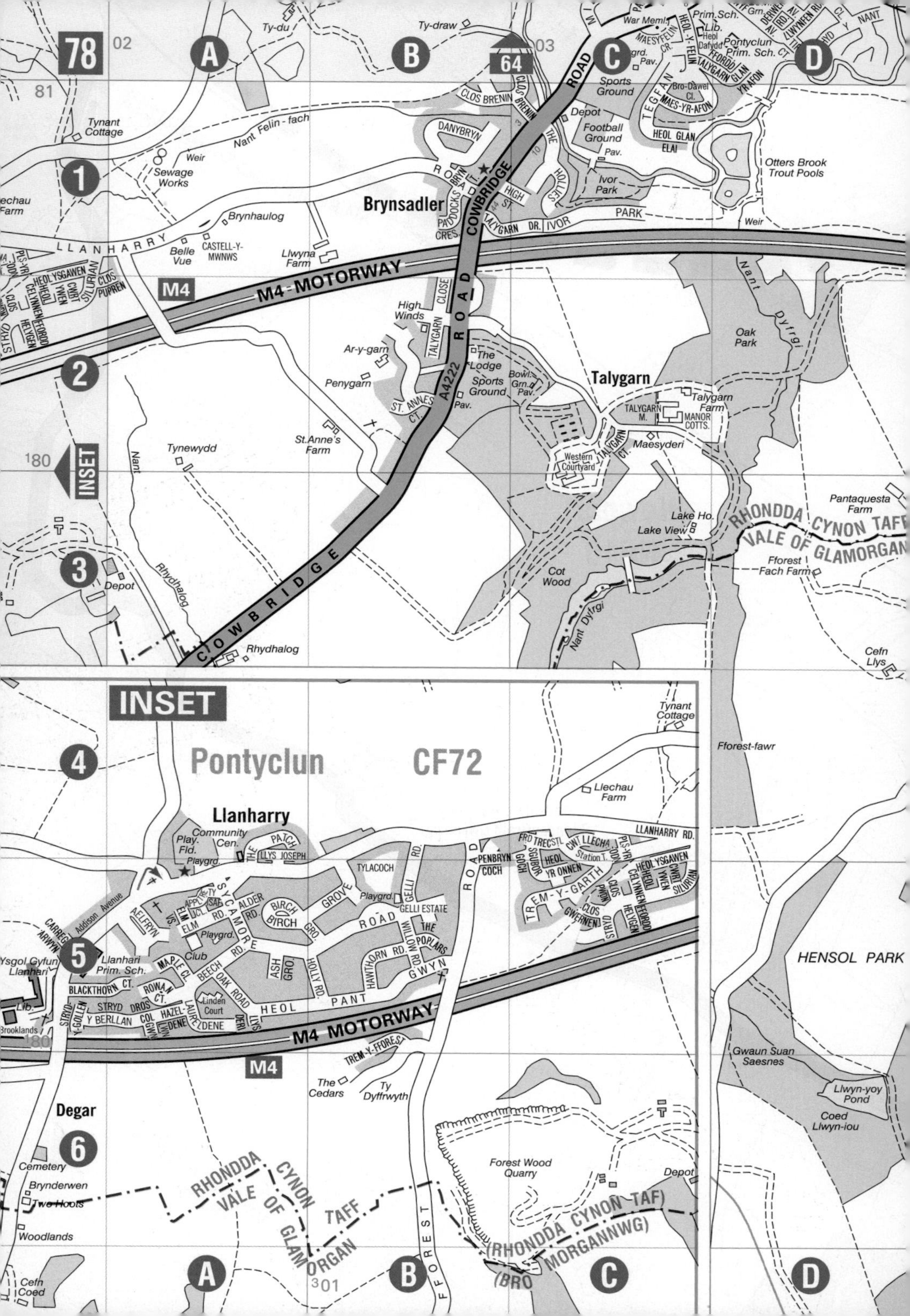
02
03
81
64
A
B
C
D
1
2
3
4
5
6
Ty-du
Ty-draw
War Meml.
Prim.Sch.
Lib.
Pontyclun Prim. Sch.
Sports Ground
CLOS BRENIN
Tynant Cottage
Nant Felin - fach
Weir
Sewage Works
DANYBRYN
Depot
Football Ground
Pav.
HEOL GLAN ELAI
Otters Brook Trout Pools
Ivor Park
Brynsadler
COWBRIDGE ROAD
HIGH ST.
PADDOCKS CRES.
TALYGARN DR.
IVOR PARK
Weir
Brynhaulog
LLANHARRY
Belle Vue
CASTELL-Y-MWNWS
Llwyna Farm
M4
M4 MOTORWAY
High Winds
TALYGARN CLOSE
A4222
Ar-y-garn
Penygarn
The Lodge
Sports Ground
Bowl. Grn.
ST. ANNES CT.
Talygarn
Talygarn Farm
TALYGARN M.
MANOR COTTS.
Oak Park
Nant Dyfrgi
St.Anne's Farm
Tynewydd
Nant
180
INSET
Maesyderi
Western Courtyard
Depot
Rhydhalog
Lake Ho.
Lake View
RHONDDA CYNON TAFF
VALE OF GLAMORGAN
Pantaquesta Farm
Fforest Fach Farm
Cot Wood
Nant Dyfrgi
Cefn Llys
Pontyclun
CF72
Llanharry
Community Cen.
Play. Fld.
Playgrd.
LLYS JOSEPH
THE PATCH
TYLACOCH
GELLI ESTATE
PENBRYN COCH
LLANHARRY RD.
Station T.
TREM-Y-GARTH
Tynant Cottage
Llechau Farm
Fforest-fawr
HENSOL PARK
SYCAMORE
BIRCH GRO.
GROVE ROAD
WILLOW RD.
THE POPLARS
HAWTHORN RD.
HOLLY RD.
ASH GRO.
BEECH RD.
OAK ROAD
HEOL PANT GWYN
Club
Llanhari Prim. Sch.
Ysgol Gyfun Llanhari
Addison Avenue
BLACKTHORN CT.
ROWAN CT.
MAPLE CL.
Linden Court
STRYD DROS Y BERLLAN
Lib.
Brooklands
M4 MOTORWAY
TREM-Y-FFOREST
The Cedars
Ty Dyffrwyth
Degar
Cemetery
Brynderwen
Two Hoots
Woodlands
Cefn Coed
RHONDDA CYNON TAFF
VALE OF GLAMORGAN
Forest Wood Quarry
Depot
(RHONDDA CYNON TAF)
(BRO MORGANNWG)
FFOREST
Gwaun Suan Saesnes
Llwyn-yoy Pond
Coed Llwyn-iou
301

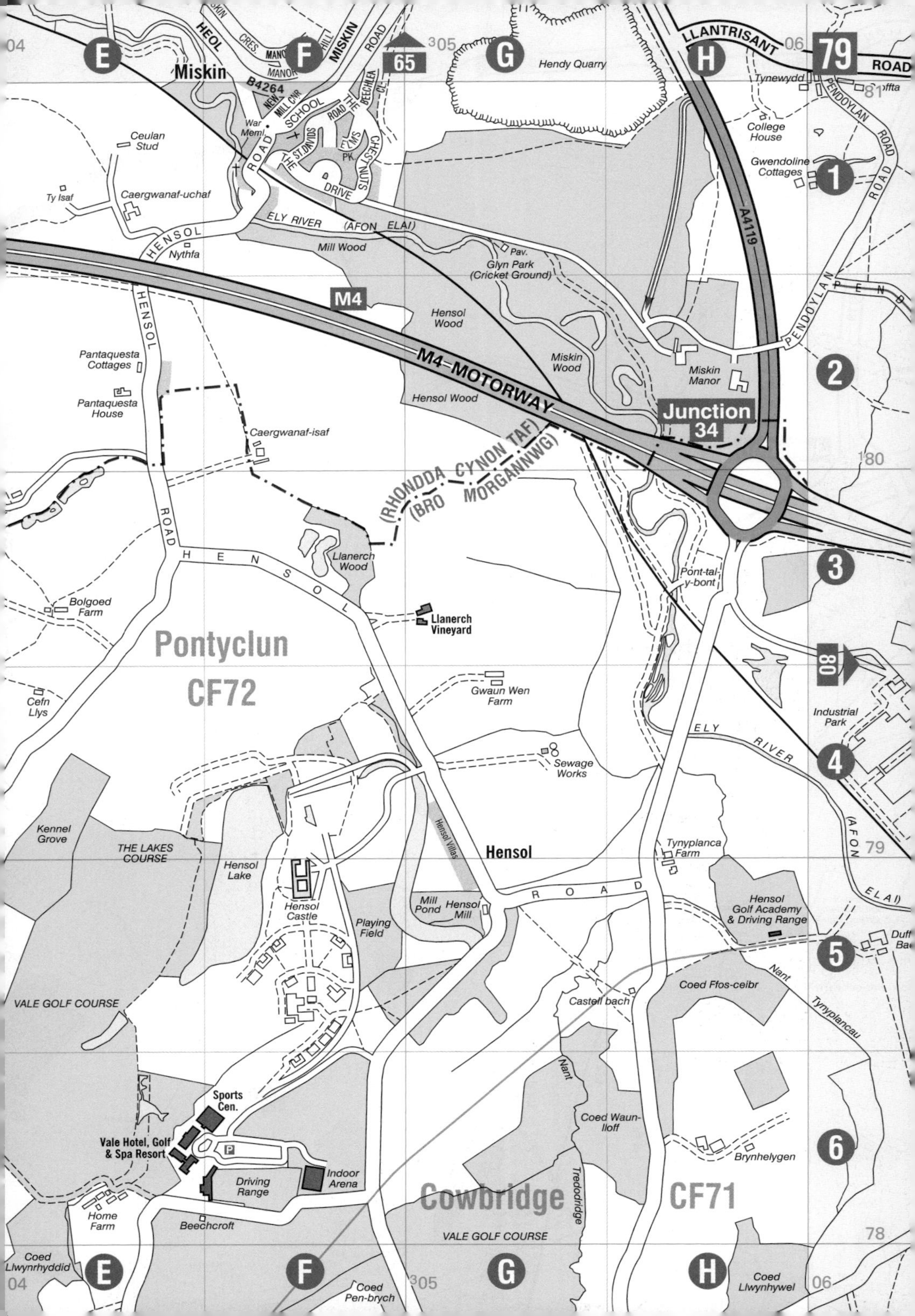
Miskin
HEOL MISKIN
CRES
MANOR
HILL
MISKIN ROAD
65
305
Hendy Quarry
LLANTRISANT ROAD
06
B4264
NEW MILL CNR
SCHOOL ROAD
THE BEECHLEA CL.
War Meml.
THE ST. DAVIDS
ELMS PK.
CHESTNUTS DRIVE
Ceulan Stud
Ty Isaf
Caergwanaf-uchaf
Tynewydd
Coffta
81
PENDOYLAN ROAD
College House
Gwendoline Cottages
A4119
ELY RIVER (AFON ELAI)
HENSOL
Nythfa
Mill Wood
Pav.
Glyn Park (Cricket Ground)
M4
Hensol Wood
Miskin Wood
Miskin Manor
PENDOYLAN PEN
HENSOL ROAD
Pantaquesta Cottages
Pantaquesta House
M4 MOTORWAY
Hensol Wood
Junction 34
Caergwanaf-isaf
180
(RHONDDA CYNON TAF)
(BRO MORGANNWG)
HENSOL
Llanerch Wood
Pont-tal-y-bont
Bolgoed Farm
Llanerch Vineyard
Pontyclun
CF72
80
Cefn Llys
Gwaun Wen Farm
Industrial Park
ELY RIVER
Sewage Works
(AFON ELAI)
Kennel Grove
THE LAKES COURSE
Hensol Lake
Hensol Villas
Hensol
Tynyplanca Farm
79
ROAD
Hensol Castle
Mill Pond
Hensol Mill
Hensol Golf Academy & Driving Range
Playing Field
Duff Ba
VALE GOLF COURSE
Castell bach
Coed Ffos-ceibr
Nant Tynyplancau
Nant
Coed Waun-lloff
Sports Cen.
Vale Hotel, Golf & Spa Resort
P
Driving Range
Indoor Arena
Brynhelygen
Tredodridge
Cowbridge
CF71
Home Farm
Beechcroft
VALE GOLF COURSE
78
Coed Llwynrhyddid
04
305
Coed Pen-brych
Coed Llwynhywel
06
E
F
G
H
1
2
3
4
5
6

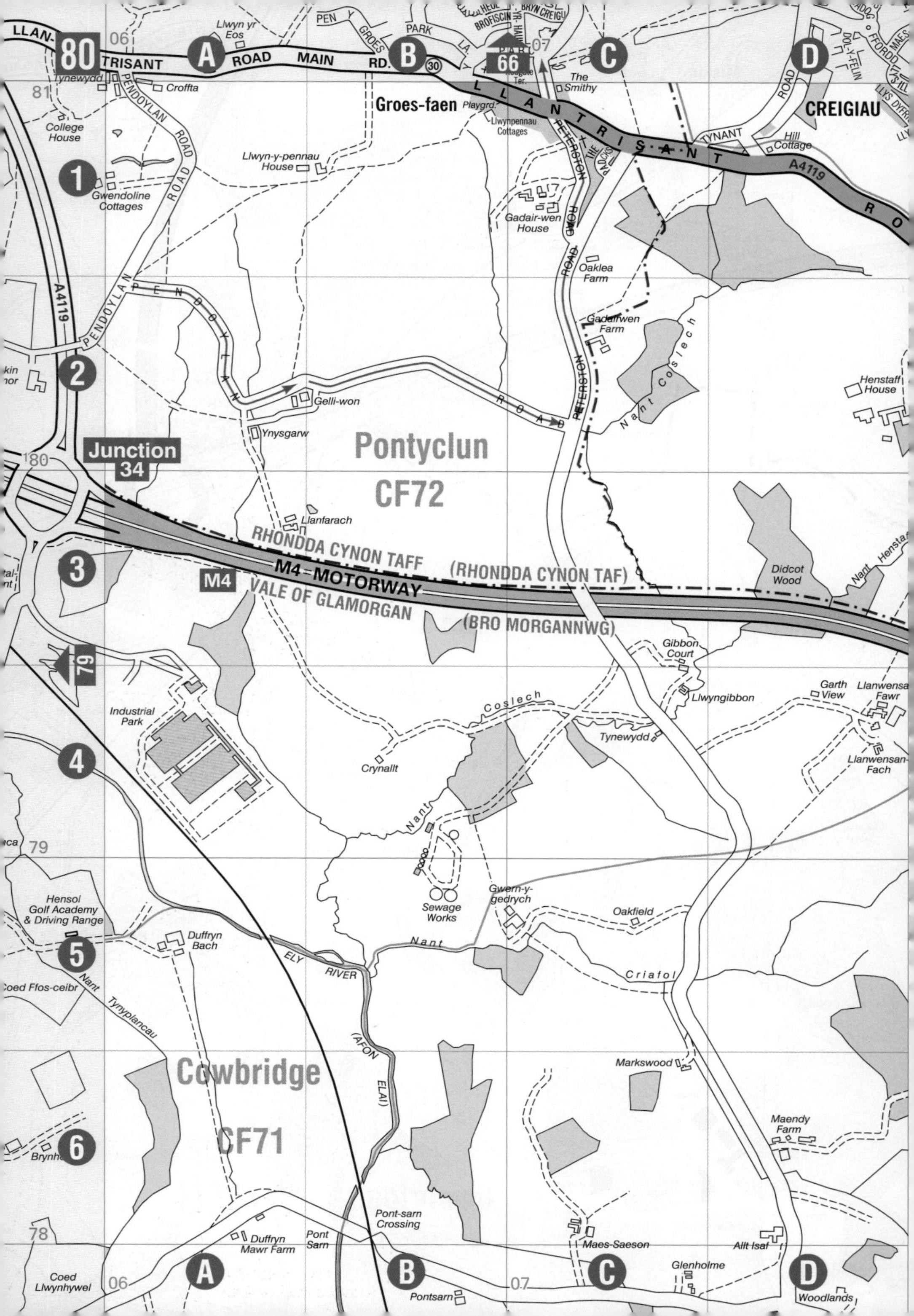
LLAN-
TRISANT ROAD
MAIN RD.
Llwyn yr Eos
PEN Y GROES
PARK LA.
66
The Smithy
Groes-faen
Playgrd.
Llwynpennau Cottages
LLANTRISANT RO
A4119
CREIGIAU
TYNANT
Hill Cottage
DOLY-FELIN
Tynewydd
Croffta
College House
PENDOYLAN ROAD
Llwyn-y-pennau House
Gwendoline Cottages
Gadair-wen House
PETERSTON ROAD
THE PADDOCKS
Oaklea Farm
Gadairwen Farm
Nant Coslech
Henstaff House
Gelli-won
Ynysgarw
Junction 34
Pontyclun
CF72
Llanfarach
RHONDDA CYNON TAFF
(RHONDDA CYNON TAF)
M4
M4-MOTORWAY
VALE OF GLAMORGAN
(BRO MORGANNWG)
Didcot Wood
Nant Henstaff
Gibbon Court
Llwyngibbon
Garth View
Llanwensan Fawr
Llanwensan-Fach
79
Industrial Park
Coslech
Tynewydd
Crynallt
Nant
Sewage Works
Gwern-y-gedrych
Oakfield
Hensol Golf Academy & Driving Range
Duffryn Bach
ELY RIVER
Nant
Criafol
Coed Ffos-ceibr
Nant Tynyplancau
(AFON ELAI)
Cowbridge
CF71
Markswood
Maendy Farm
Brynhe
Pont-sarn Crossing
Pont Sarn
Duffryn Mawr Farm
Maes-Saeson
Allt Isaf
Glenholme
Coed Llwynhywel
Pontsarn
Woodlands
A B C D
1 2 3 4 5 6
06 07 78 79 80 81

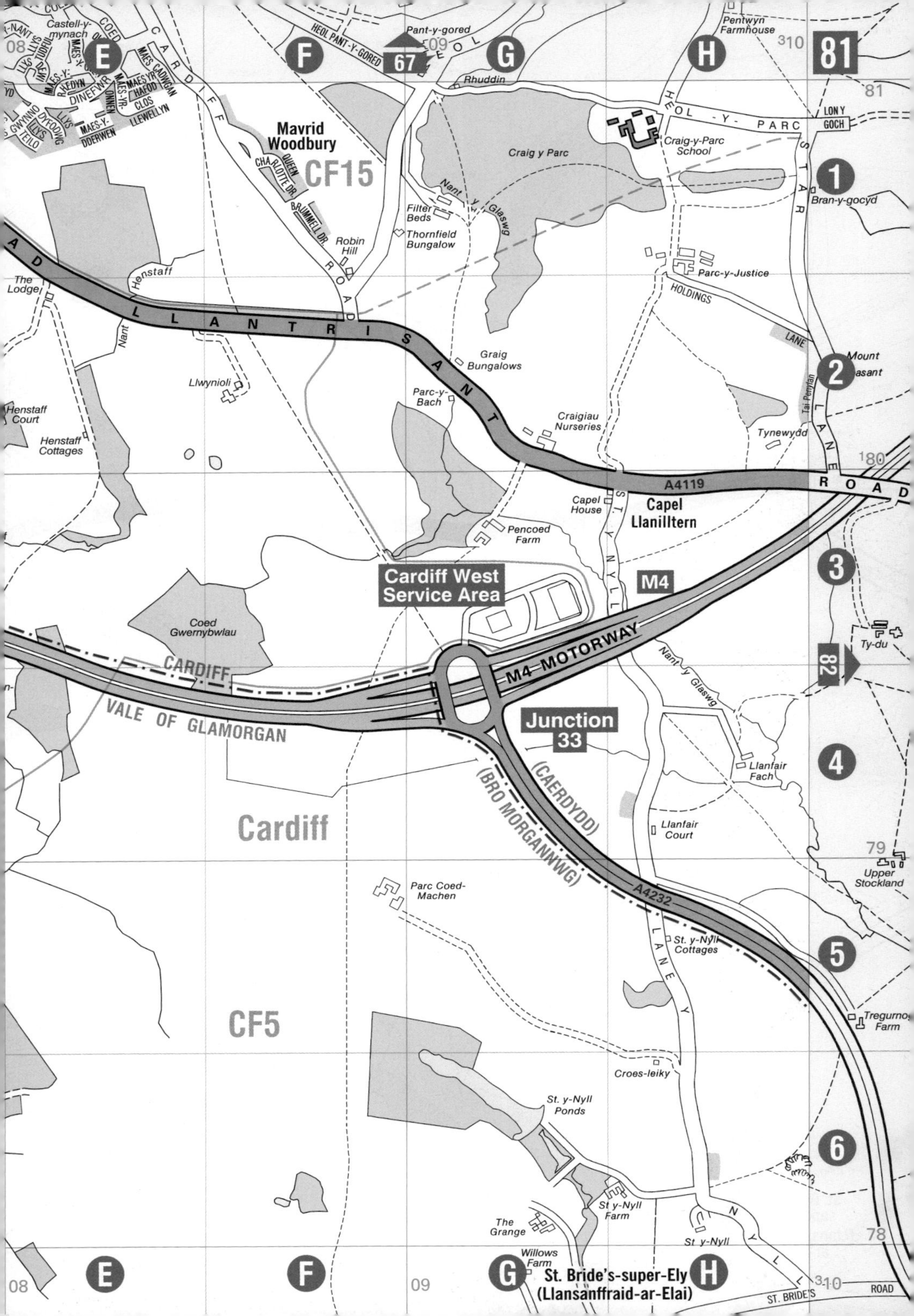

Castell-y-mynach
Pant-y-gored
HEOL PANT-Y-GORED
67
HEOL
Rhuddin
Pentwyn Farmhouse
310
81
E
F
G
H
HEOL -Y- PARC
LON Y GOCH
Craig-y-Parc School
Craig y Parc
Mavrid Woodbury
CF15
QUEEN CHARLOTTE DR.
BRUMMELL DR.
CARDIFF
MAES CADWGAN
MAES-YR-HAFOD
CLOS LLEWELLYN
MAES-YR-ONNEN
DINEFWR
RHEDYN
MAES-Y-DDERWEN
DYFODWG
GWYNNO
TEILO
LLYS
1
Bran-y-gocyd
STAR
Nant y Glasswg
Filter Beds
Thornfield Bungalow
Robin Hill
ROAD
Parc-y-Justice
HOLDINGS
LANE
Henstaff
The Lodge
LLANTRISANT
Nant
Graig Bungalows
2
Mount Pleasant
Tai-Penylan
Llwynioli
Parc-y-Bach
Henstaff Court
Henstaff Cottages
Craigiau Nurseries
Tynewydd
180
A4119
ROAD
Capel House
Capel Llanilltern
ST. Y NYLL
Pencoed Farm
3
Cardiff West Service Area
M4
Coed Gwernybwlau
M4 MOTORWAY
Ty-du
82
CARDIFF
VALE OF GLAMORGAN
Nant y Glaswg
Junction 33
4
(CAERDYDD)
(BRO MORGANNWG)
Llanfair Fach
Cardiff
Llanfair Court
79
Upper Stockland
Parc Coed-Machen
A4232
St. y-Nyll Cottages
LANE
5
CF5
Tregurnog Farm
Croes-leiky
St. y-Nyll Ponds
6
St y-Nyll Farm
The Grange
St y-Nyll
78
Willows Farm
St. Bride's-super-Ely
(Llansanffraid-ar-Elai)
08
09
ST. BRIDE'S ROAD

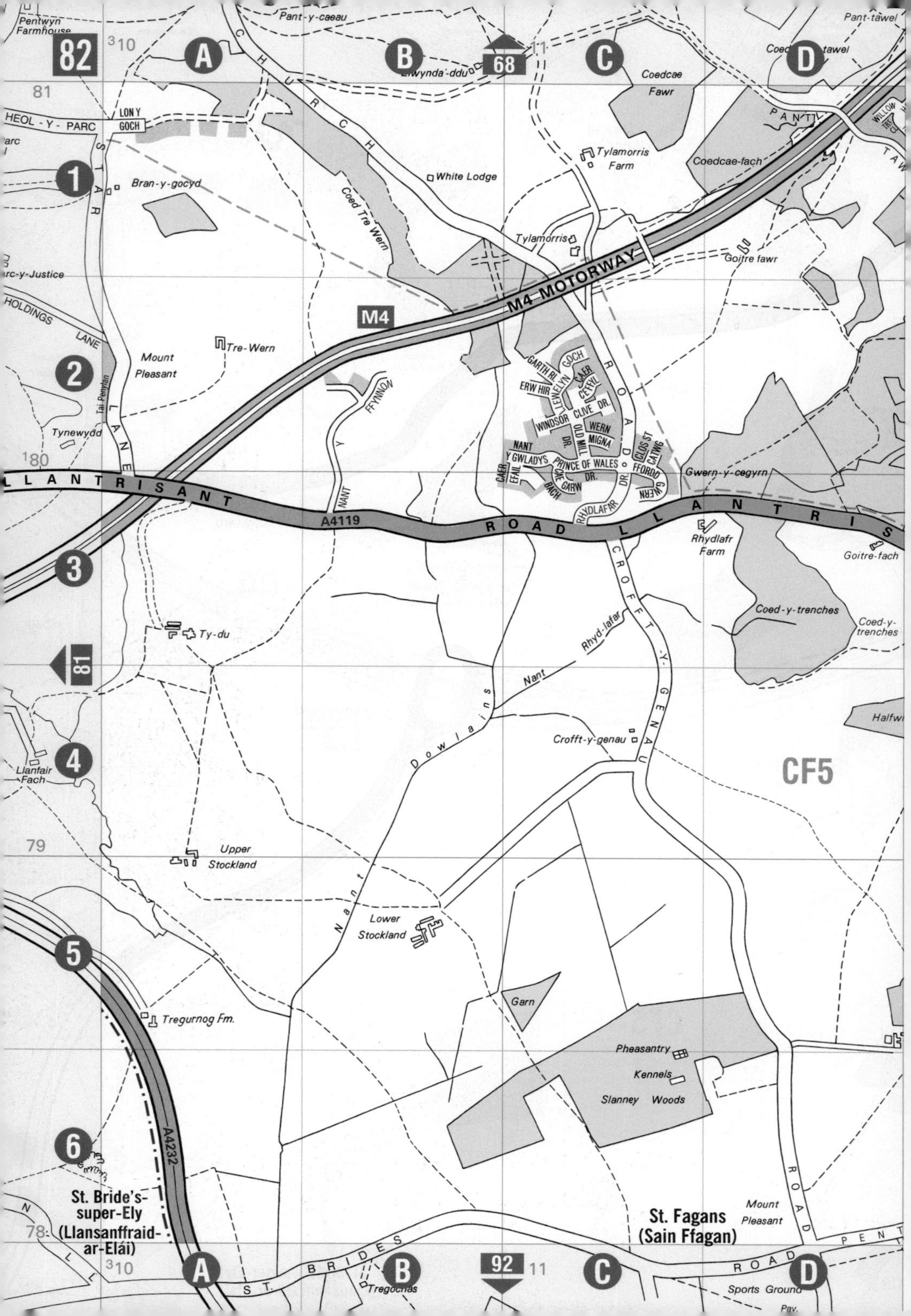
Pentwyn Farmhouse
Pant-y-caeau
Pant-tawel
Coedcae-tawel
Llwynda-ddu
68
Coedcae Fawr
HEOL - Y - PARC
LON Y GOCH
PANT
WILLOW
TAW
Bran-y-gocyd
White Lodge
Coed Tre Wern
Tylamorris Farm
Coedcae-fach
Tylamorris
Goitre fawr
Parc-y-Justice
HOLDINGS LANE
M4 MOTORWAY
M4
Tre-Wern
Mount Pleasant
Tai Penylan
Tynewydd
STAR LANE
FFYNNON
NANT Y FFYNNON
GARTH RI.
GOCH
CAER CEFFYL
ERW HIR
LEWELYN
CLIVE DR.
WINDSOR DR.
OLD MILL
WERN MIGNA
NANT Y GWLADYS
PRINCE OF WALES DR.
CLOS ST CATWG
CAER EFAIL
CAE GARW
BACH
FFORDD GWERN
Gwern-y-cegyrn
RHYDLAFAR DR.
LLANTRISANT ROAD
A4119
LLANTRIS
Rhydlafr Farm
Goitre-fach
CROFFT-Y-GENAU ROAD
Ty-du
81
Coed-y-trenches
Rhyd-lafar
Nant
Halfwi
Dowlais Nant
Crofft-y-genau
Llanfair Fach
CF5
Upper Stockland
Lower Stockland
Garn
Tregurnog Fm.
Pheasantry
Kennels
Slanney Woods
A4232
St. Bride's-super-Ely (Llansanffraid-ar-Elái)
St. Fagans (Sain Ffagan)
Mount Pleasant
ST. BRIDES ROAD
PENT
Tregochas
Sports Ground
Pav.
92
A
B
C
D
1
2
3
4
5
6
310
311
81
180
79
78

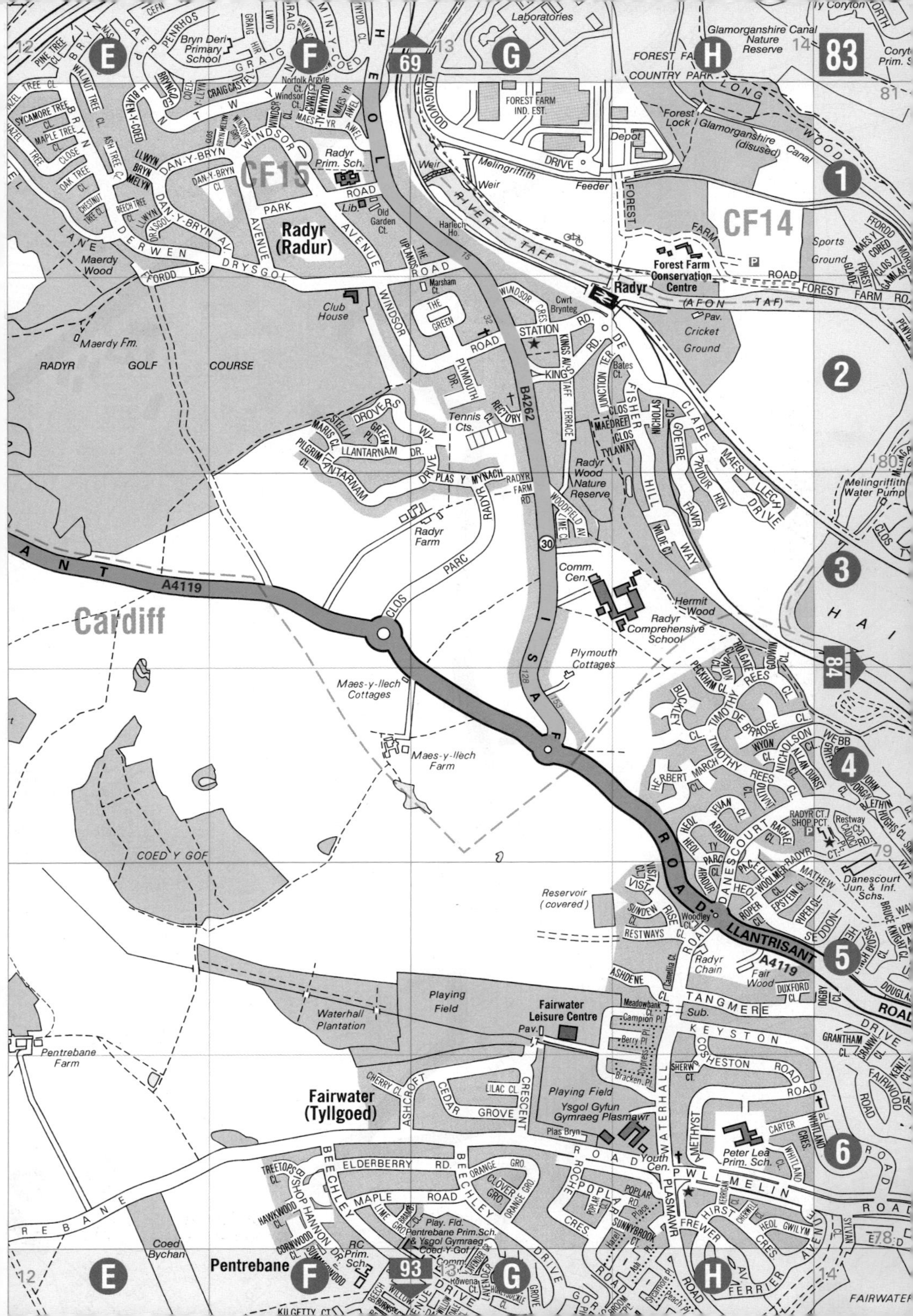
83
69
84
93
E
F
G
H
1
2
3
4
5
6
12
13
14
78
79
80
81
Laboratories
Bryn Deri Primary School
Glamorganshire Canal Nature Reserve
FOREST FARM COUNTRY PARK
FOREST FARM IND. EST.
Depot
Forest Lock
Glamorganshire Canal (disused)
LONG WOOD
LONGWOOD DRIVE
Melingriffith Feeder
Weir
RIVER TAFF
CF15
CF14
Radyr Prim. Sch.
Lib.
Old Garden Ct.
Harlech Ho.
Radyr (Radur)
PARK AVENUE
WINDSOR
DAN-Y-BRYN
DERWEN
FFORDD LAS
DRYSGOL ROAD
Maerdy Wood
Maerdy Fm.
Club House
RADYR GOLF COURSE
THE GREEN
PLYMOUTH DR.
STATION ROAD
Cwrt Brynteg
Radyr
Forest Farm Conservation Centre
FOREST FARM ROAD
(AFON TAF)
Pav.
Cricket Ground
Sports Ground
B4262
HEOL ISAF
Tennis Cts.
RECTORY CL.
TAFF TERRACE
JUNCTION TER.
FISHER
CLARE
GOETRE
MAES Y LLECH DRIVE
Radyr Wood Nature Reserve
Melingriffith Water Pump
LLANTARNAM DR.
PLAS Y MYNACH
RADYR FARM RD.
Radyr Farm
PARC
CLOS
A4119
Cardiff
Comm. Cen.
Radyr Comprehensive School
Hermit Wood
Plymouth Cottages
Maes-y-llech Cottages
Maes-y-llech Farm
COED Y GOF
DANESCOURT
Danescourt Jun. & Inf. Schs.
RADYR CT. SHOP PCT.
LLANTRISANT ROAD
Reservoir (covered)
Radyr Chain
Fair Wood
TANGMERE
Sub.
KEYSTON
COSHESTON ROAD
Playing Field
Waterhall Plantation
Fairwater Leisure Centre
Ysgol Gyfun Gymraeg Plasmawr
Plas Bryn
Youth Cen.
Peter Lea Prim. Sch.
Pentrebane Farm
Fairwater (Tyllgoed)
ASHCROFT
CEDAR GROVE
CRESCENT
WATERHALL ROAD
PWLLMELIN ROAD
PLASMAWR ROAD
ELDERBERRY RD.
BEECHLEY DRIVE
MAPLE ROAD
PENTREBANE
Coed Bychan
Pentrebane
RC Prim. Sch.
Play. Fld. Pentrebane Prim. Sch. & Ysgol Gymraeg Coed-Y-Gof
FERRIER AVENUE
FAIRWATER

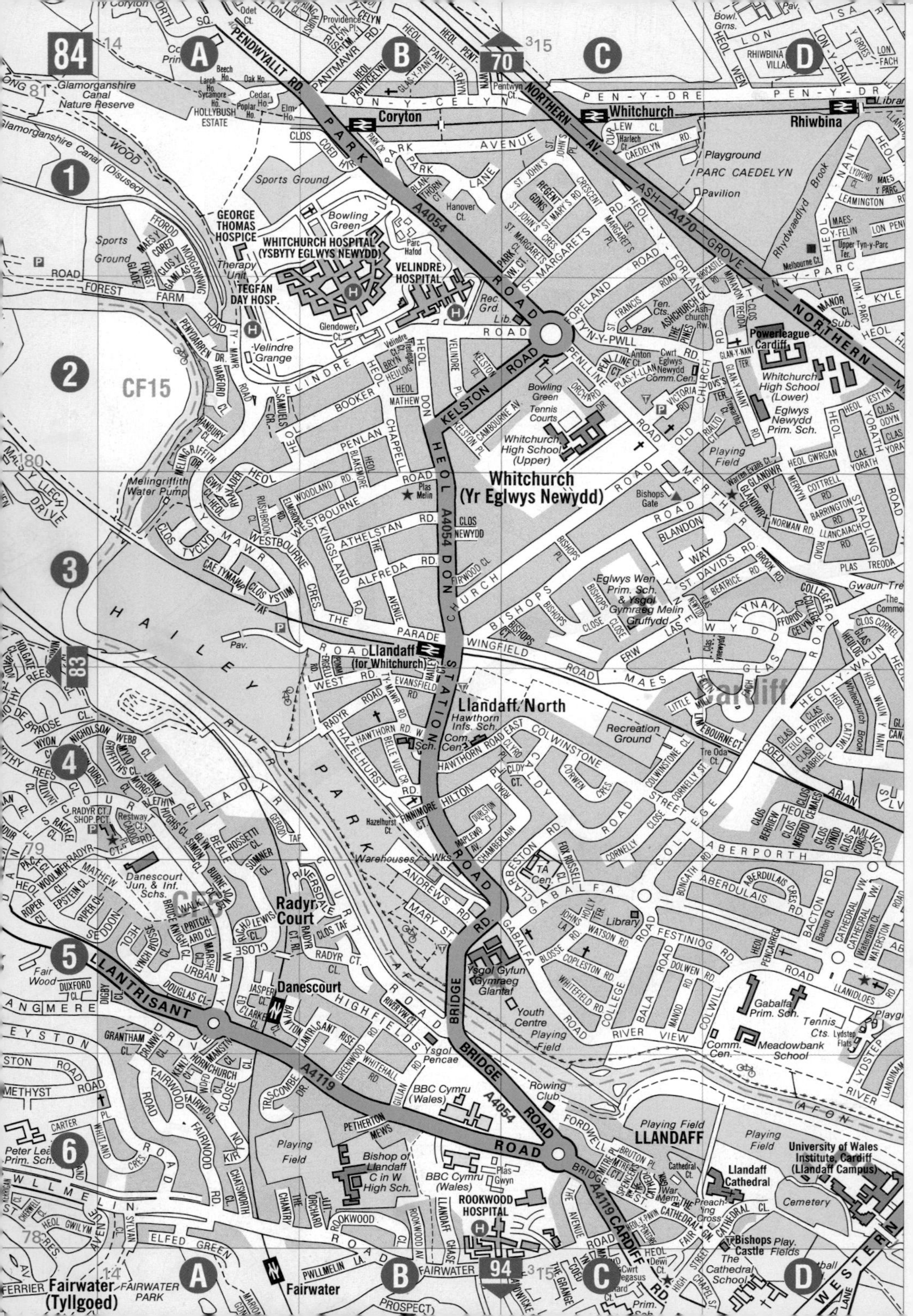

84
70
83
94
A
B
C
D
1
2
3
4
5
6
Glamorganshire Canal Nature Reserve
Glamorganshire Canal (Disused)
HOLLYBUSH ESTATE
PENDWYALLT RD.
LON-Y-CELYN
Coryton
Whitchurch
Rhiwbina
PEN-Y-DRE
RHIWBINA VILLAGE
NORTHERN AV.
PARK ROAD
A4054
A470
ASH GROVE
PARC CAEDELYN
Playground
Pavilion
Sports Ground
GEORGE THOMAS HOSPICE
WHITCHURCH HOSPITAL (YSBYTY EGLWYS NEWYDD)
VELINDRE HOSPITAL
TEGFAN DAY HOSP.
Therapy Unit
Velindre Grange
Bowling Green
FOREST FARM ROAD
CF15
KELSTON ROAD
HEOL Y FORLAN
TY-N-Y-PWLL ROAD
Powerleague Cardiff
Whitchurch High School (Lower)
Eglwys Newydd Prim. Sch.
Whitchurch High School (Upper)
Whitchurch (Yr Eglwys Newydd)
MERTHYR ROAD
Bishops Gate
Melingriffith Water Pump
HEOL A4054 DON
CHURCH ROAD
Eglwys Wen Prim. Sch. & Ysgol Gymraeg Melin Gruffydd
HAILEY PARK
RIVER TAFF
Llandaff (for Whitchurch)
STATION ROAD
WINGFIELD ROAD
Llandaff North
Hawthorn Infs. Sch.
Recreation Ground
Cardiff
Warehouses
Radyr Court
RADYR COURT ROAD
Danescourt Jun. & Inf. Schs.
CF5
LLANTRISANT ROAD
Danescourt
A4119
BRIDGE ROAD
Ysgol Gyfun Gymraeg Glantaf
Youth Centre
Playing Field
Library
GABALFA
COLLEGE ROAD
ABERPORTH
Gabalfa Prim. Sch.
Meadowbank School
Comm. Cen.
Ysgol Pencae
BBC Cymru (Wales)
Rowing Club
AFON
LLANDAFF
Bishop of Llandaff C in W High Sch.
ROOKWOOD HOSPITAL
Llandaff Cathedral
University of Wales Institute, Cardiff (Llandaff Campus)
Cemetery
Bishops Castle
Bishops Play. Fields
The Cathedral School
CARDIFF RD.
WESTERN
Peter Lea Prim. Sch.
Fairwater (Tyllgoed)
FAIRWATER PARK
Fairwater

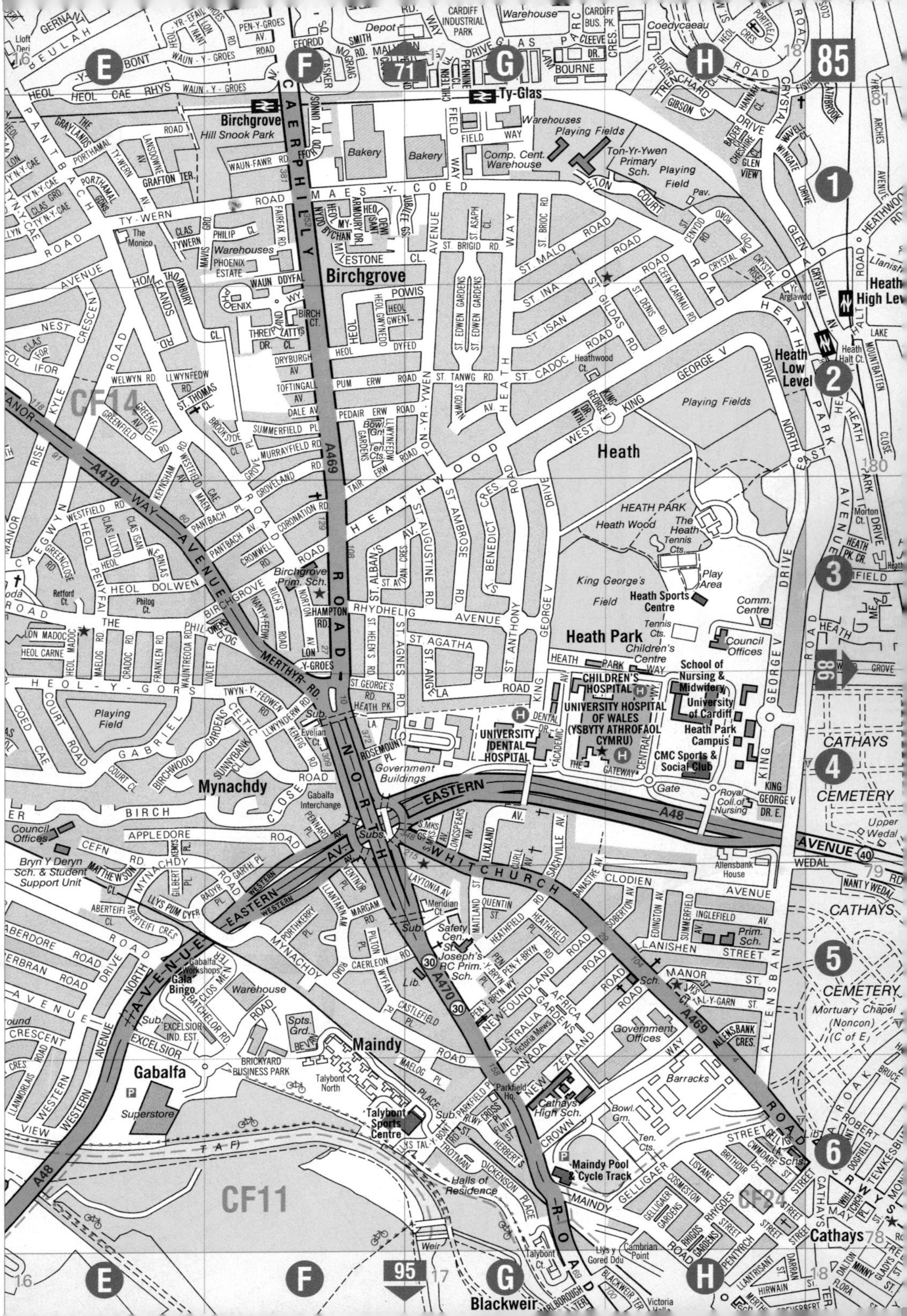

E
F
G
H
71
95
86
1
2
3
4
5
6
16
17
18
78
79
80
81
Birchgrove
Ty-Glas
Hill Snook Park
Bakery
Warehouses
Playing Fields
Ton-Yr-Ywen Primary Sch.
Playing Field
Comp. Cent. Warehouse
Cardiff Industrial Park
Cardiff Bus. Pk.
Coedycaeau
Depot
Heath High Level
Heath Low Level
Heath
Heath Park
Heath Wood
The Heath
King George's Field
Heath Sports Centre
Play Area
Comm. Centre
Council Offices
Children's Centre
School of Nursing & Midwifery
University of Cardiff
Heath Park Campus
CHILDREN'S HOSPITAL
UNIVERSITY HOSPITAL OF WALES (YSBYTY ATHROFAOL CYMRU)
UNIVERSITY DENTAL HOSPITAL
CMC Sports & Social Club
Royal Coll. of Nursing
Government Buildings
Gabalfa Interchange
CATHAYS
CEMETERY
Mortuary Chapel
(Noncon)
(C of E)
Upper Wedal
Allensbank House
Mynachdy
Council Offices
Bryn Y Deryn Sch. & Student Support Unit
Gabalfa
Superstore
Gala Bingo
Gabalfa Workshops
Excelsior Ind. Est.
Brickyard Business Park
Maindy
Talybont North
Talybont Sports Centre
Halls of Residence
Maindy Pool & Cycle Track
Cathays High Sch.
Barracks
Government Offices
St. Joseph's RC Prim. Sch.
Safety Cen.
Birchgrove Prim. Sch.
The Monico
Phoenix Estate
Cathays
Blackweir
CF11
CF14
CF24
A469
A470
A48
CAERPHILLY ROAD
NORTH ROAD
EASTERN AVENUE
WHITCHURCH ROAD
MERTHYR RD.
HEATH HALT RD.
KING GEORGE V DRIVE
HEATHWOOD ROAD
ALLENSBANK ROAD
MAES-Y-COED
TY-WERN ROAD
WESTERN AVENUE
TAF
Weir

72
85
96
A
B
C
D
1
2
3
4
5
6
Cyncoed
Cardiff
Pen-y-Lan
Roath Park
Cathays
CF14
CF23
CF24
Heath High Level
Heath Low Level
Cardiff High School
Playing Field
Rhydypenau Primary School
Springwood Primary School
Lakeside Primary Sch.
All Saints C in W Prim. Sch.
St. Teilo's C in W High Sch.
St. David's Catholic College
Ty Gwyn Special Sch.
University of Wales Institute Cardiff (Cyncoed Campus)
UWIC Inter Cardiff FC
Indoor Athletics Stadium
Athletics Track
Halls of Residence
Multisports Centre
Tennis Centre
Spts.Cen. for the Disabled
Astro Turf
Rugby Grd.
ROATH PARK LAKE
Landing Stage
Boathouse
Scott Memorial
ROATH PARK
Recreation Ground
CATHAYS CEMETERY
Mortuary Chapel (Noncon) (C of E)
Council Offices
Comm. Centre
Royal Coll. of Nursing
Synagogue
Observatory
Playing Field
University Court
Heath Junction
Wood's Covert
Nant Fawr Ct.
Rec. Grd.
Roy Jenkins Hall
Mosque
AVENUE
CELYN
LAKE ROAD NORTH
LAKESIDE DRIVE
CYNCOED ROAD
HEATH PARK AVENUE
KING GEORGE V DRIVE
ALLENSBANK ROAD
WHITCHURCH RD.
CRWYS RD.
A48
A469
WEDAL
WESTERN AVENUE
PEN-Y-LAN ROAD
MARLBOROUGH
WATERLOO
MELROSE
BLENHEIM ROAD

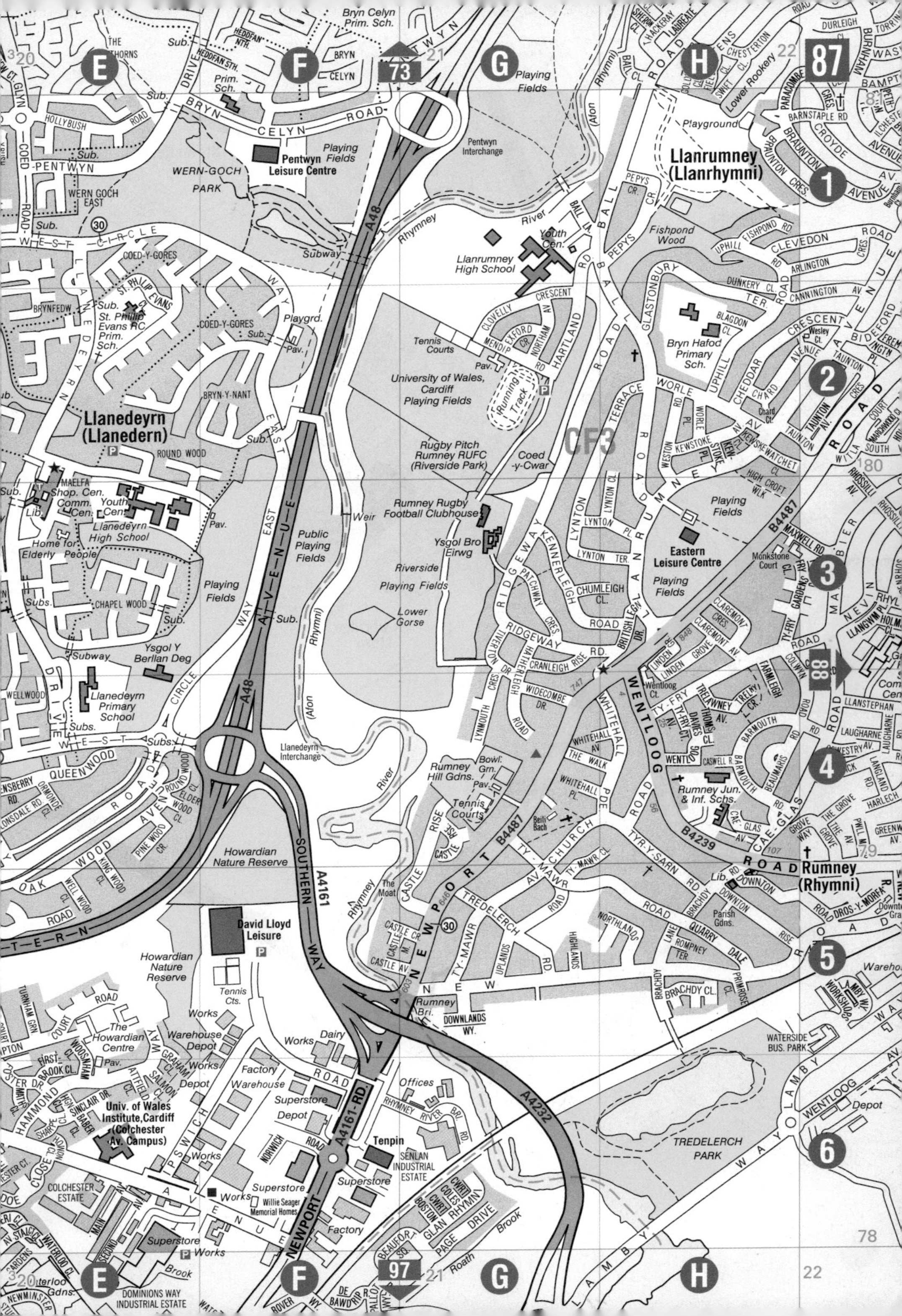

Llanrumney
(Llanrhymni)
Llanedeyrn
(Llanedern)
Rumney
(Rhymni)
CF3
Pentwyn Leisure Centre
Playing Fields
WERN-GOCH PARK
WERN GOCH EAST
Pentwyn Interchange
Llanrumney High School
Youth Cen.
Fishpond Wood
Bryn Hafod Primary Sch.
University of Wales, Cardiff Playing Fields
Tennis Courts
Running Track
Rugby Pitch Rumney RUFC (Riverside Park)
Coed -y-Cwar
Rumney Rugby Football Clubhouse
Ysgol Bro Eirwg
Riverside Playing Fields
Lower Gorse
Public Playing Fields
Eastern Leisure Centre
Monkstone Court
Rumney Hill Gdns.
Rumney Jun. & Inf. Schs.
Parish Gdns.
Howardian Nature Reserve
David Lloyd Leisure
The Howardian Centre
Univ. of Wales Institute, Cardiff (Colchester Av. Campus)
Tenpin
SENLAN INDUSTRIAL ESTATE
COLCHESTER ESTATE
DOMINIONS WAY INDUSTRIAL ESTATE
Willie Seager Memorial Homes
TREDELERCH PARK
WATERSIDE BUS. PARK
St. Philip Evans RC Prim. Sch.
Llanedeyrn High School
Home for Elderly People
Ysgol Y Berllan Deg
Llanedeyrn Primary School
MAELFA Shop. Cen.
Comm. Cen.
Llanedeyrn Interchange
Bryn Celyn Prim. Sch.
Rhymney River
Afon Rhymni
A48
A4161
A4232
B4487
B4239
A4161 RD.
SOUTHERN WAY
NEWPORT ROAD
EASTERN AVENUE
WENTLOOG ROAD
LLANRUMNEY AVENUE
BALL ROAD
RIDGEWAY
EAST WAY
CIRCLE WAY WEST
LLANEDEYRN DRIVE
BRYN CELYN ROAD
COED-Y-GORES
TY-MAWR AV.
TY-MAWR RD.
TREDELERCH RD.
CHURCH RD.
TYR-Y-SARN RD.
LAMBY WAY
IPSWICH ROAD
73
97
88

A
B
C
D
1
2
3
4
5
6
74
87
Llanrumney
Trowbridge
St. Mellons
Trowbridge Mawr
Rumney (Rhymni)
Wentloog
Newton
St. Illtyd's Catholic High School
Rumney High Sch.
Greenway Primary School
Trowbridge Jun. Sch.
St. John Lloyd RC Primary School
Coleg Glan Hafren (Trowbridge Campus)
Recreation Ground
Playing Field
Playing Fields
CAPITAL BUSINESS PARK
SPRING MEADOW BUSINESS PARK
ALEXANDRA INDUSTRIAL ESTATE
WENTLOOG CORPORATE PARK
LAMBY INDUSTRIAL PARK
WATERSIDE BUS. PARK
EASTGATE BUS. PK.
MELLYN MAIR BUS. CEN.
THE LAURELS BUS. PARK
RINGSIDE BUS. CEN.
CAPITAL POINT
Warehouse
Depot
Longcross Farm
Sea Bank Farm
Maerdy Farm
Newton Willows Farm
Ty-to-maen
Newlands
Pen-pill
Cath-Cobb Wood
Oakfield Prim. Sch.
B4487
B4239
NEWPORT ROAD
WENTLOOG AVENUE
WENTLOOG ROAD
MARDY ROAD
GREENWAY ROAD
TROWBRIDGE ROAD
HENDRE ROAD
WILLOWBROOK DRIVE
CRICKHOWELL ROAD
COUNTISBURY AVENUE
LAMBY WAY
PARKWAY
NEWTON ROAD
NEWLANDS ROAD
22
23
78
79
80
81

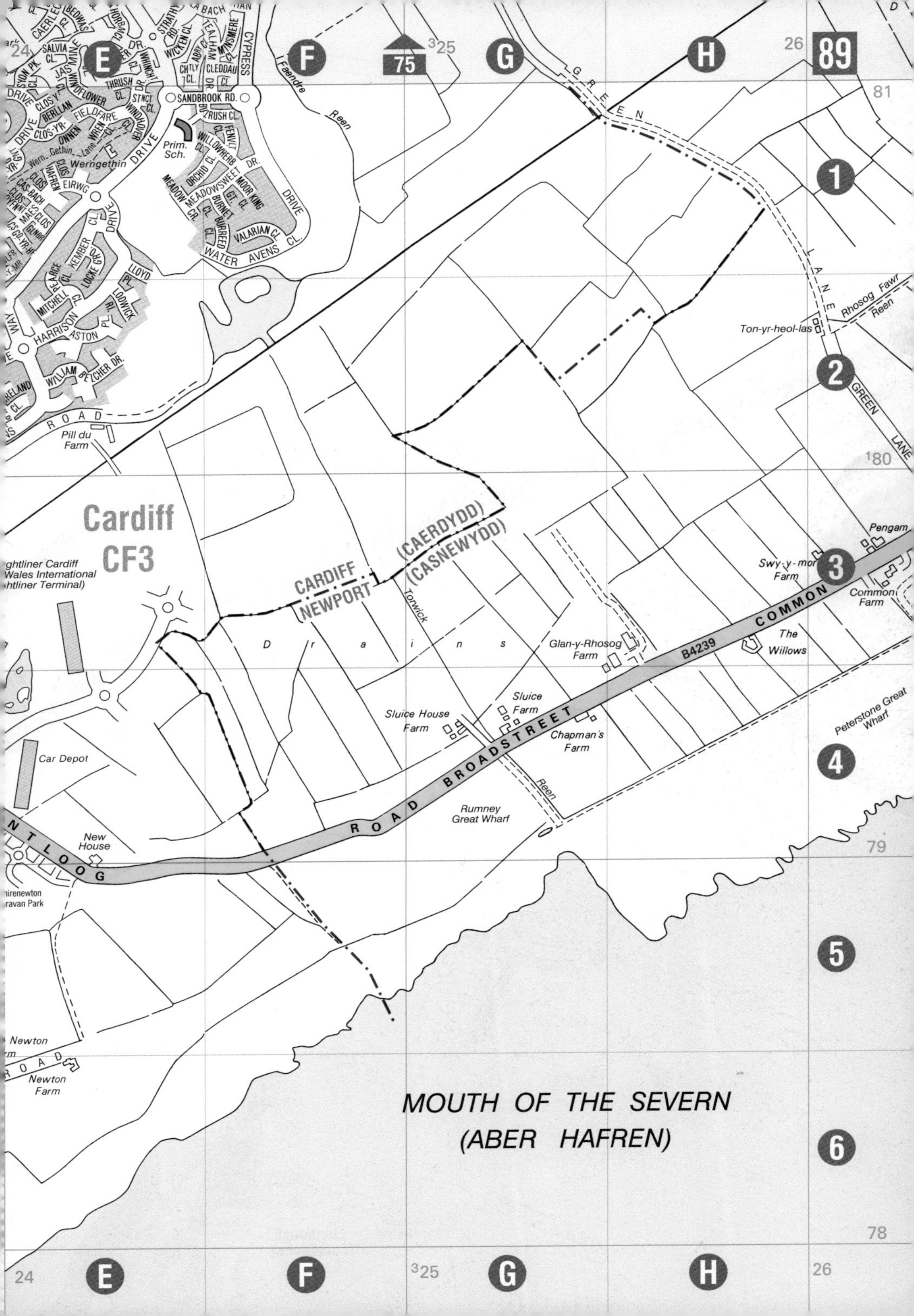

75
E
F
G
H
24
325
26
81
80
79
78
1
2
3
4
5
6
Cardiff
CF3
CARDIFF
NEWPORT
(CAERDYDD)
(CASNEWYDD)
MOUTH OF THE SEVERN
(ABER HAFREN)
B4239
COMMON
BROADSTREET
ROAD
NTLOOG
GREEN LANE
Ton-yr-heol-las
Rhosog Fawr Reen
Pengam
Swy-y-mor Farm
Common Farm
The Willows
Glan-y-Rhosog Farm
Sluice Farm
Sluice House Farm
Chapman's Farm
Peterstone Great Wharf
Rumney Great Wharf
Reen
Torwick
D r a i n s
Car Depot
New House
Pill du Farm
Newton Farm
Faendre Reen
Prim. Sch.
SANDBROOK RD.
Wherngethin DRIVE
WATER AVENS CL.
VALARIAN CL.
MOOR KING CL.
MEADOWSWEET DR.
MEADOW CR.
ORCHID CL.
WILLOWHERB CL.
BURNET CL.
BURREED CL.
THRUSH CL.
WINDHOVER CL.
FIELDFARE CL.
WINDFLOWER
JASMINE CL.
SALVIA CL.
SYON PK.
BERLLAN
ONNEN
WREN
EIRWG
HAFREN
CAS BACH
LLOYD PL.
LODWICK RI.
KEMBER CL.
LOCKE GRO.
PEARCE CL.
MITCHELL CL.
HARRISON
ASTON PL.
WILLIAM BELCHER DR.
CYPRESS
CLEDDAU
TEALHAM DR.
WICKEN CL.
MINSMERE CL.

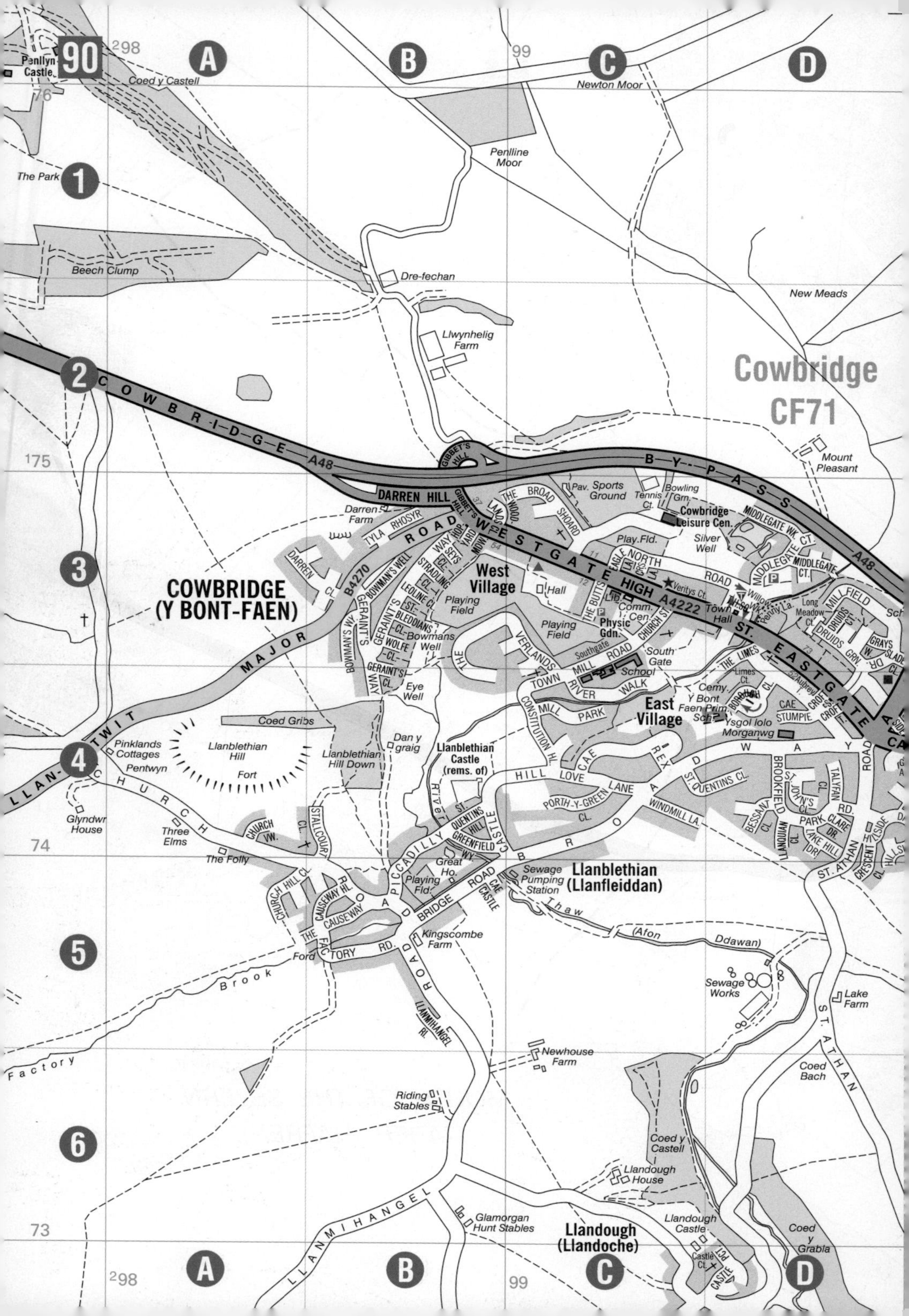
90
Cowbridge
CF71
COWBRIDGE
(Y BONT-FAEN)
West Village
East Village
Llanblethian
(Llanfleiddan)
Llandough
(Llandoche)
Penllyn Castle
Coed y Castell
Newton Moor
Penlline Moor
The Park
Beech Clump
Dre-fechan
New Meads
Llwynhelig Farm
COWBRIDGE BY-PASS
A48
GIBBET'S HILL
DARREN HILL
Mount Pleasant
Darren Farm
Pav. Sports Ground
Tennis Ct.
Bowling Grn.
Cowbridge Leisure Cen.
Play.Fld.
Silver Well
WESTGATE
HIGH ST. A4222
EASTGATE
NORTH ROAD
MIDDLEGATE
MILLFIELD
Town Hall
Playing Field
Hall
Physic Gdn.
Comm. Cen.
Lib.
South Gate
School
Cemy.
Y Bont Faen Prim. Sch.
Ysgol Iolo Morganwg
Bowmans Well
Eye Well
MAJOR ROAD
B4270
LLAN-TWIT
Coed Gribs
Llanblethian Hill
Fort
Llanblethian Hill Down
Dan y graig
Llanblethian Castle (rems. of)
Pinklands Cottages
Pentwyn
Glyndwr House
Three Elms
The Folly
CHURCH
PICCADILLY
Great Ho.
Playing Fld.
Sewage Pumping Station
BRIDGE ROAD
Thaw
(Afon Ddawan)
Ford
Brook
Factory
Kingscombe Farm
LLANMIHANGEL RD.
Newhouse Farm
Riding Stables
Sewage Works
Lake Farm
ST. ATHAN
Coed Bach
Coed y Castell
Llandough House
Glamorgan Hunt Stables
LLANMIHANGEL
Llandough Castle
Castle Ct.
CASTLE PCT.
Coed y Grabla
A B C D
1 2 3 4 5 6
298
99
175
74
73
76

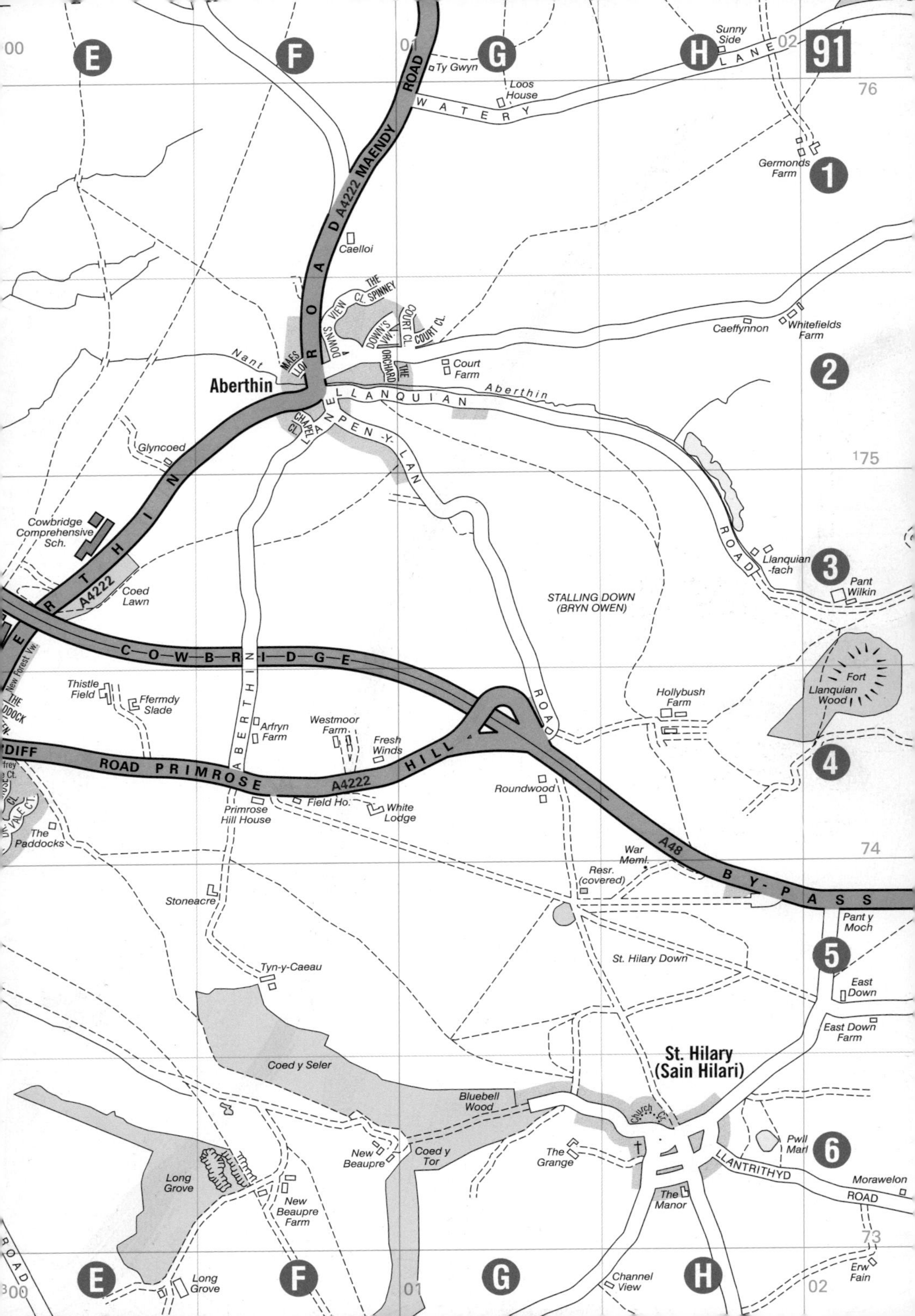

Ty Gwyn
Loos House
WATERY LANE
Sunny Side
MAENDY ROAD A4222
Germonds Farm
Caelloi
THE SPINNEY
VIEW CL.
DOWN'S VIEW
DOWN'S VW.
COURT CL.
ORCHARD THE
MAES LLOI
Caeffynnon
Whitefields Farm
Nant
Court Farm
Aberthin
LLANQUIAN
Aberthin
CHAPEL CL.
PEN-Y-LAN
Glyncoed
Cowbridge Comprehensive Sch.
A4222
Coed Lawn
ROAD
Llanquian -fach
Pant Wilkin
STALLING DOWN (BRYN OWEN)
COWBRIDGE
ABERTHIN
Thistle Field
Fferndy Slade
Arfryn Farm
Westmoor Farm
Fresh Winds
HILL
PRIMROSE
ROAD
A4222
Hollybush Farm
Fort
Llanquian Wood
Roundwood
Field Ho.
White Lodge
Primrose Hill House
The Paddocks
New Forest Vw.
THE PADDOCK
A48
BY-PASS
War Meml.
Resr. (covered)
Stoneacre
Pant y Moch
St. Hilary Down
Tyn-y-Caeau
East Down
East Down Farm
St. Hilary (Sain Hilari)
Coed y Seler
Bluebell Wood
Church Ct.
New Beaupre
Coed y Tor
The Grange
Pwll Marl
LLANTRITHYD ROAD
Morawelon
Long Grove
New Beaupre Farm
The Manor
Channel View
Erw Fain
Long Grove

82
98
A
B
C
D
1
2
3
4
5
6
310
11
78
77
76
75
ST. BRIDE'S ROAD
ST. BRIDES ROAD
NYLL
y-Nyll
Tregochas
Mount Pleasant
PENTREBANE
CROFFT-Y-GENAU
Sports Ground
Pav.
Tynewydd
The Rock
Pen-hefyd
Pwll Arthur
St. Brides Place
Nant Rhych
Nant Dowlais
A4232
VALE OF GLAMORGAN
CARDIFF
(BRO MORGANNWG)
(CAERDYDD)
Tabernacle
MAES-Y-GAD
St. Fagans: National History Museum
St. Fagans Castle
Llwyn-yr-eos
ELY RIVER (AFON ELAI)
Tyn-y-Caeau
Castle Farm
Tydraw
CASTLE
Pentwyn
St. George's (Sain Siorys)
Ty-fry
LANE
Gilfach Glyd
PERSONDY
MICHAELSTON ROAD
Nant y Ffordd
Ffordd-isaf
Ffordd Cottages
Weirs
CLOS-Y-CWARRA
FFORDD-Y-BARCER
CRSTA
CLOS GRO.
Y-GOF
DENISON WY.
DEEPDENE
DEEPWOOD CL.
DEEPFD CL.
CWRT
FALCONWOOD DR.
NANT-Y-DROPE
LONGREACH CL.
SWALLOWHRST CL.
HAMPSTEAD WLK.
Drope Farm
COED NANT-Y-DOWLAIS
ARHYD
NANT-YR-ARTHUR
NANT-Y-RHOS
NANT-Y-PERPA
NANT-YR-ELY
Drope Gds.
NANT-Y-PLAC
MANSELL
GOODWOOD CL.
BARNWOOD CRES.
AV.
Michaelston Cl.
Drope
DROPE ROAD
Drope Ter.
Nant y Drope
ROYDE CL.
COEDRIGLAN
JESTYN CL.
TRAHERNE DR.
Prim. Sch.
Children's Cen.
Michaelston Comm. Coll.
CL.
PANTEG
ROAD
Penmaen
PONTRILAS CL.
CAENEWYDD CL.
LLANOVER
Caebach Cl.
Rhiwderyn Cl.
Llangybi Cl.
LLANOVER RD.
DRIVE
PATREANE
WAY
Fish Pond
COEDARHYD-Y-GLYN PARK
Coedarhyd-y-glyn
Haelfaes
Superstores
COPTHORNE WY.
VALEGATE RETAIL PARK
P

Fairwater (Tyllgoed)
Cardiff Ski Centre
Fairwater Park
Pentrebane
St. Fagans (Sain Ffagan)
Fairwater Primary School
Community Centre
Herbert Thompson Primary School
Recreation Ground
Plymouth Great Wood
Llanmaes House
Llanmaes Farm
Community Hall
Cardiff
CF5
Michaelston-super-Ely
Ely (Trelái)
Western Leisure Centre
Superstore
Fitness First
Caerau
Hywel Dda Jun. & Infs. Schs.
Cwrt-Yr-Ala Jun. Sch.
Caerau Infant Sch.
Caerau Nursery Sch.
Windsor Clive Jun. & Inf. Schs.
St. Francis RC Prim. Sch.
Caerau Wood
Castle Ring
St. Mary's Church
Caerau Fort
Western Cemetery
Glamorgan Wanderers RUFC
Curling Pond
A48
A4232
Cardiff Road
St. Fagans Road
Cowbridge Road West
Heol Trelai
River Ely

83
94
99

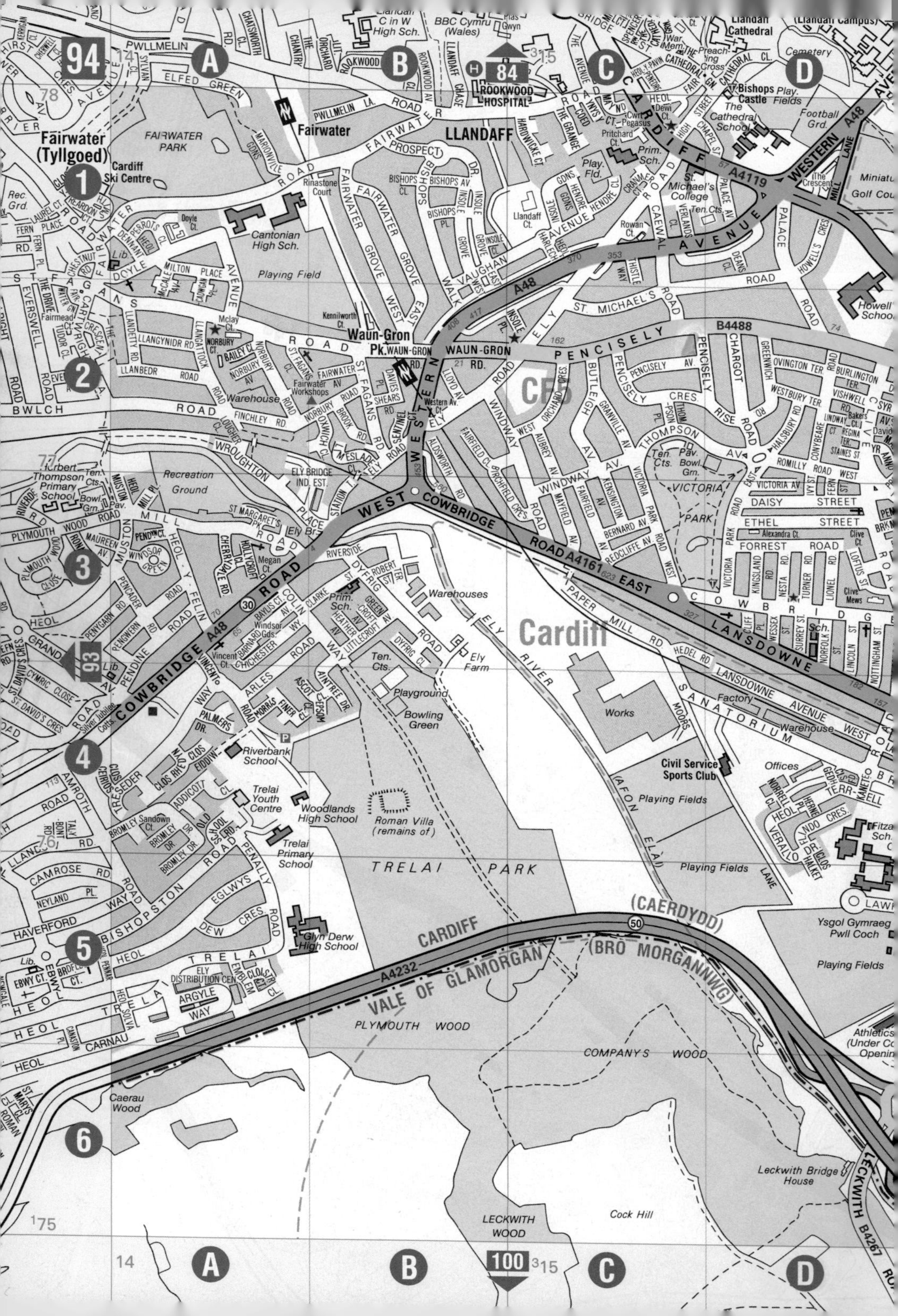
94
A
B
C
D
84
100
93
1
2
3
4
5
6
Fairwater (Tyllgoed)
Cardiff Ski Centre
FAIRWATER PARK
Fairwater
LLANDAFF
ROOKWOOD HOSPITAL
Llandaff Cathedral
BBC Cymru (Wales)
C in W High Sch.
Bishops Castle
The Cathedral School
Bishops Play. Fields
Football Grd.
Cemetery
St. Michael's College
Cantonian High Sch.
Playing Field
Waun-Gron Pk.
Fairwater Workshops
Warehouse
Recreation Ground
Herbert Thompson Primary School
ELY BRIDGE IND. EST.
Warehouses
Ely Farm
Cardiff
Works
Civil Service Sports Club
Playing Fields
Playground
Bowling Green
Riverbank School
Trelai Youth Centre
Woodlands High School
Roman Villa (remains of)
Trelai Primary School
TRELAI PARK
Glyn Derw High School
CARDIFF (CAERDYDD)
VALE OF GLAMORGAN (BRO MORGANNWG)
PLYMOUTH WOOD
COMPANY'S WOOD
Caerau Wood
LECKWITH WOOD
Cock Hill
Leckwith Bridge House
Ysgol Gymraeg Pwll Coch
Howell's School
Miniature Golf Course
WESTERN AVENUE
COWBRIDGE ROAD
COWBRIDGE ROAD EAST
COWBRIDGE ROAD WEST
LANSDOWNE AVENUE
SANATORIUM ROAD
PAPER MILL RD
ELY RIVER
PENCISELY ROAD
ST. MICHAEL'S ROAD
FAIRWATER ROAD
HEOL TRELAI
BISHOPSTON ROAD
MILL ROAD
WROUGHTON PL.
BWLCH ROAD
ST. FAGANS ROAD
VICTORIA PARK
LECKWITH B4267
A48
A4119
A4161
A4232
B4488
CF5

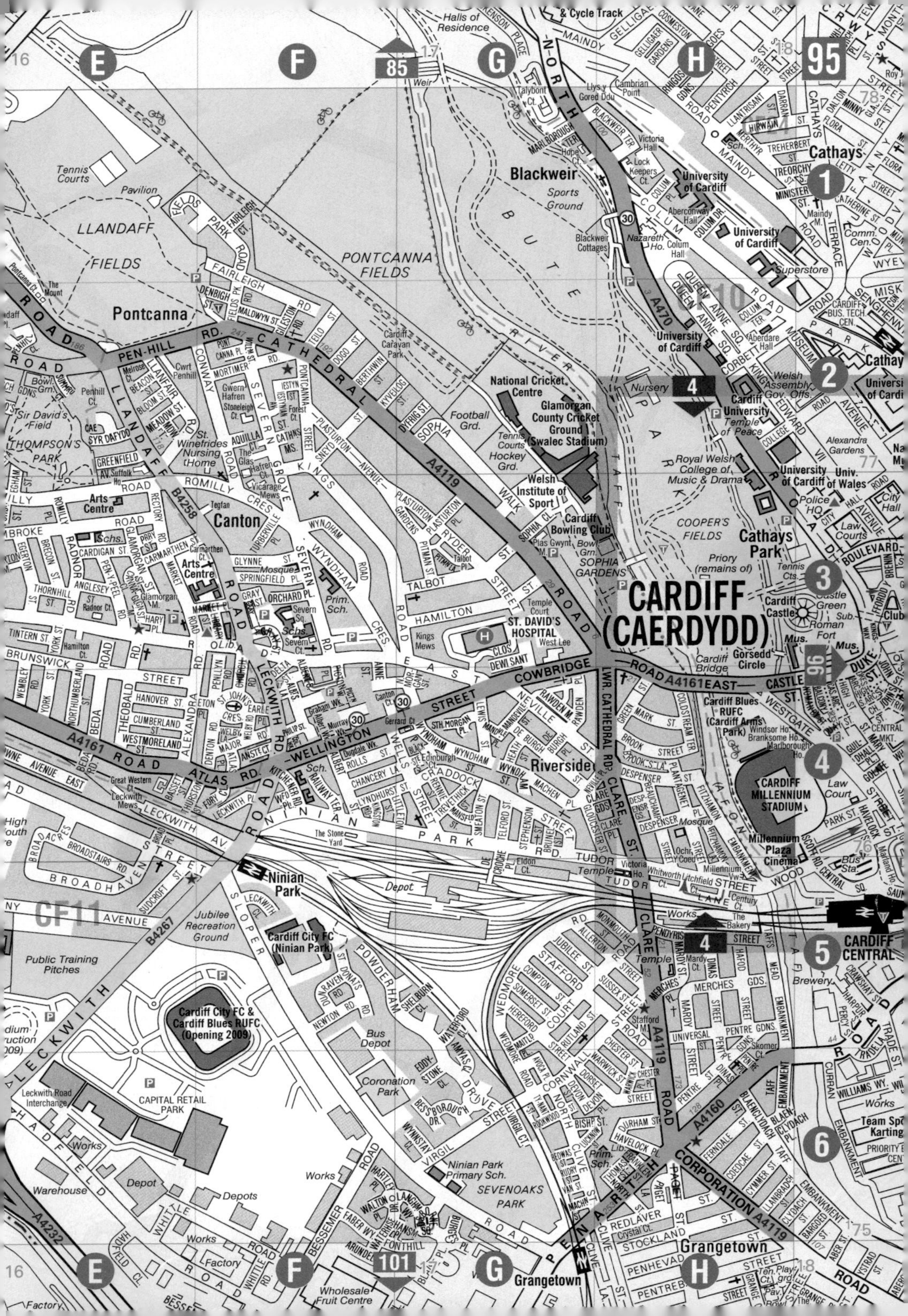
CARDIFF
(CAERDYDD)
Cathays Park
Cardiff Castle
Canton
Riverside
Pontcanna
Blackweir
Grangetown
Cathays
LLANDAFF FIELDS
PONTCANNA FIELDS
COOPER'S FIELDS
SOPHIA GARDENS
CARDIFF MILLENNIUM STADIUM
Cardiff City FC (Ninian Park)
Cardiff City FC & Cardiff Blues RUFC (Opening 2009)
Ninian Park
CARDIFF CENTRAL
Grangetown
National Cricket Centre
Glamorgan County Cricket Ground (Swalec Stadium)
Welsh Institute of Sport
Cardiff Bowling Club
ST. DAVID'S HOSPITAL
Royal Welsh College of Music & Drama
University of Cardiff
Cardiff University
Univ. of Wales
Welsh Assembly Gov. Offs.
Temple of Peace
Cardiff Blues RUFC (Cardiff Arms Park)
Millennium Plaza Cinema
CAPITAL RETAIL PARK
Leckwith Road Interchange
Jubilee Recreation Ground
Public Training Pitches
Sevenoaks Park
Coronation Park
Bus Depot
Ninian Park Primary Sch.
Wholesale Fruit Centre
Halls of Residence
& Cycle Track
CATHEDRAL ROAD
COWBRIDGE ROAD EAST
CASTLE ST.
CORPORATION ROAD
CLARE ROAD
LWR. CATHEDRAL RD.
LECKWITH ROAD
NINIAN PARK ROAD
WELLINGTON STREET
LLANDAFF ROAD
PEN-HILL RD.
NORTH ROAD
PENARTH ROAD
SLOPER ROAD
BOULEVARD
A4119
A4161
A4160
A470
A4232
B4258
B4267
CF10
CF11
85
101
96
4
E
F
G
H
1
2
3
4
5
6
16
17
18
75
76
77
78

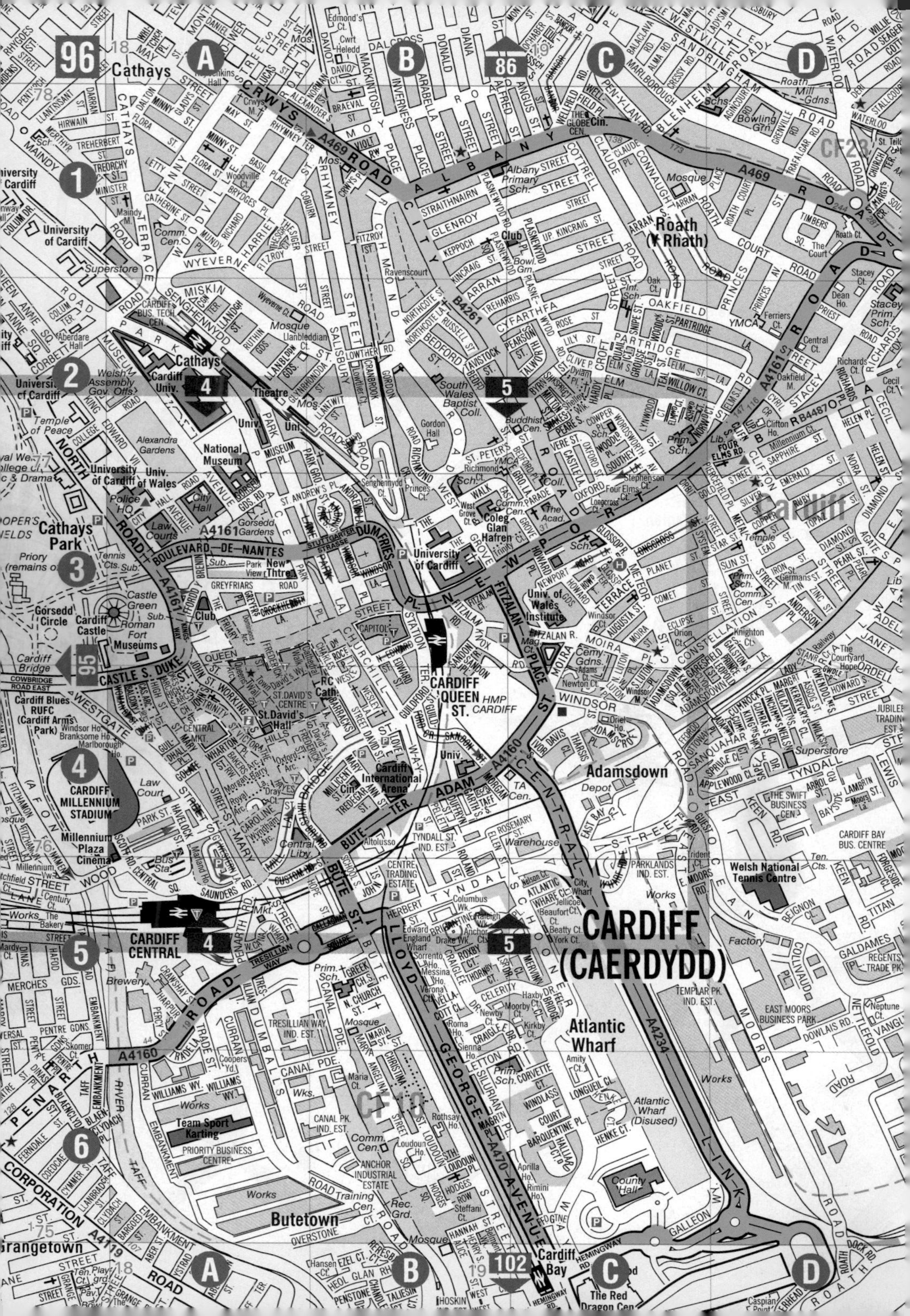

CARDIFF
(CAERDYDD)
Cathays
Cathays Park
Roath
(Y Rhath)
Adamsdown
Atlantic Wharf
Butetown
Grangetown
Cardiff Castle
Gorsedd Circle
CARDIFF MILLENNIUM STADIUM
Millennium Plaza Cinema
National Museum
City Hall
Law Courts
University of Cardiff
Univ. of Wales
Cardiff International Arena
St.David's Hall
ST. DAVID'S CENTRE
CARDIFF QUEEN ST.
HMP CARDIFF
CARDIFF CENTRAL
Cardiff Bay
The Red Dragon Cen.
County Hall
Welsh National Tennis Centre
CARDIFF BAY BUS. CENTRE
Team Sport Karting
PRIORITY BUSINESS CENTRE
ANCHOR INDUSTRIAL ESTATE
TEMPLAR PK. IND. EST.
EAST MOORS BUSINESS PARK
Atlantic Wharf (Disused)
Cardiff Blues RUFC (Cardiff Arms Park)
Coleg Glan Hafren
Univ. of Wales Institute
South Wales Baptist Coll.
Welsh Assembly Gov. Offs.
Temple of Peace
BOULEVARD-DE-NANTES
CRWYS ROAD
CITY ROAD
NEWPORT ROAD
NORTH ROAD
LLOYD GEORGE AVENUE
CENTRAL LINK
CORPORATION ROAD
PENARTH ROAD
A469
A4161
A4160
A4234
A4119
A470
B4261
B4487
CF10
CF23
86
102
95

97
87
103
CF3
CF24
Pengam
Fitness First Cardiff East
Tremorfa
Tremorfa Park
Tremorfa Nursery Sch.
St. Alban's RC Prim. Sch.
Splott
Splott Swim. Pool
Splott Park
Recreation Ground
Baden Powell Prim. Sch.
Willows High School
Pengam Green
Superstore
Seawall Road Industrial Estate
Pengam Industrial Estate
Caravan Site
Welsh Water Pumping Station
(Proposed)
Rhymney River Sailing & Angling Club
Rhymney River (Afon Rhymni)
Little Wharf Saltings
Tremorfa Foreshore
Welsh Water Treatment Works
Waste Water Treatment Works
Tremorfa Industrial Estate
Allied Industrial Park
Mineral Railway
Tidal Sidings
Pacific Business Park
Portmanmoor Road Industrial Estate
Seaview Industrial Estate
Moorland Park
Guardian Industrial Estate
Clydesmuir Industrial Estate
Pengam Junction
St. Catherine's Park
Dominions Way Industrial Estate
Colchester Factory Estate
Waterloo Gdns.
Mouth of the Severn (Aber Hafren)
Cardiff Heliport
Cardiff Docks
Roath Dock
South Point
Charnwood Park
East Bay Link Road (proposed)
Rover Way
Lamby Way
Newport Road A4161
A4232
Ocean Way
Tide Fields Road
Seawall Road
Willows Avenue
Muirton Road
Moorland Road
Clipper Road
Works
Depot

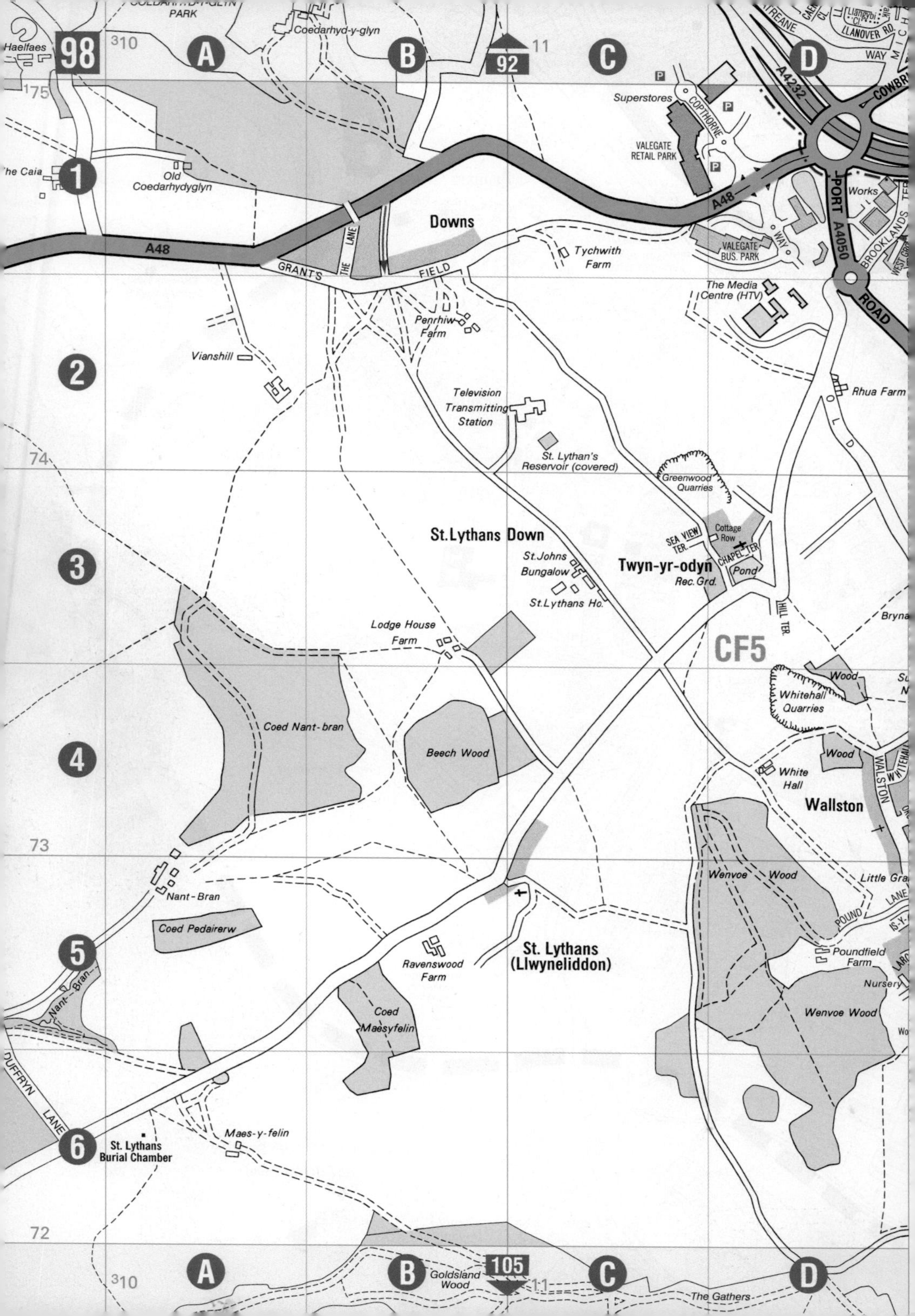

98
92
105
CF5
Haelfaes
Coedarhyd-y-glyn
PARK
The Caia
Old Coedarhydyglyn
A48
Downs
GRANTS
THE LANE
FIELD
Tychwith Farm
Superstores
COPTHORNE
VALEGATE RETAIL PARK
A4232
COWBRI
LLANOVER RD.
PORT A4050
ROAD
Works
BROOKLANDS
WAY
VALEGATE BUS. PARK
The Media Centre (HTV)
Penrhiw Farm
Vianshill
Rhua Farm
OLD
Television Transmitting Station
St. Lythan's Reservoir (covered)
Greenwood Quarries
St.Lythans Down
SEA VIEW TER.
Cottage Row
CHAPEL TER.
Twyn-yr-odyn
Pond
Rec. Grd.
St.Johns Bungalow
St.Lythans Ho.
HILL TER.
Lodge House Farm
Wood
Whitehall Quarries
Coed Nant-bran
Beech Wood
White Hall
Wallston
WALSTON
Wenvoe Wood
Little Gra
POUND LANE
Nant-Bran
Coed Pedairerw
St. Lythans (Llwyneliddon)
Ravenswood Farm
Poundfield Farm
Nursery
Wenvoe Wood
Coed Maesyfelin
DUFFRYN LANE
Maes-y-felin
St. Lythans Burial Chamber
Goldsland Wood
The Gathers

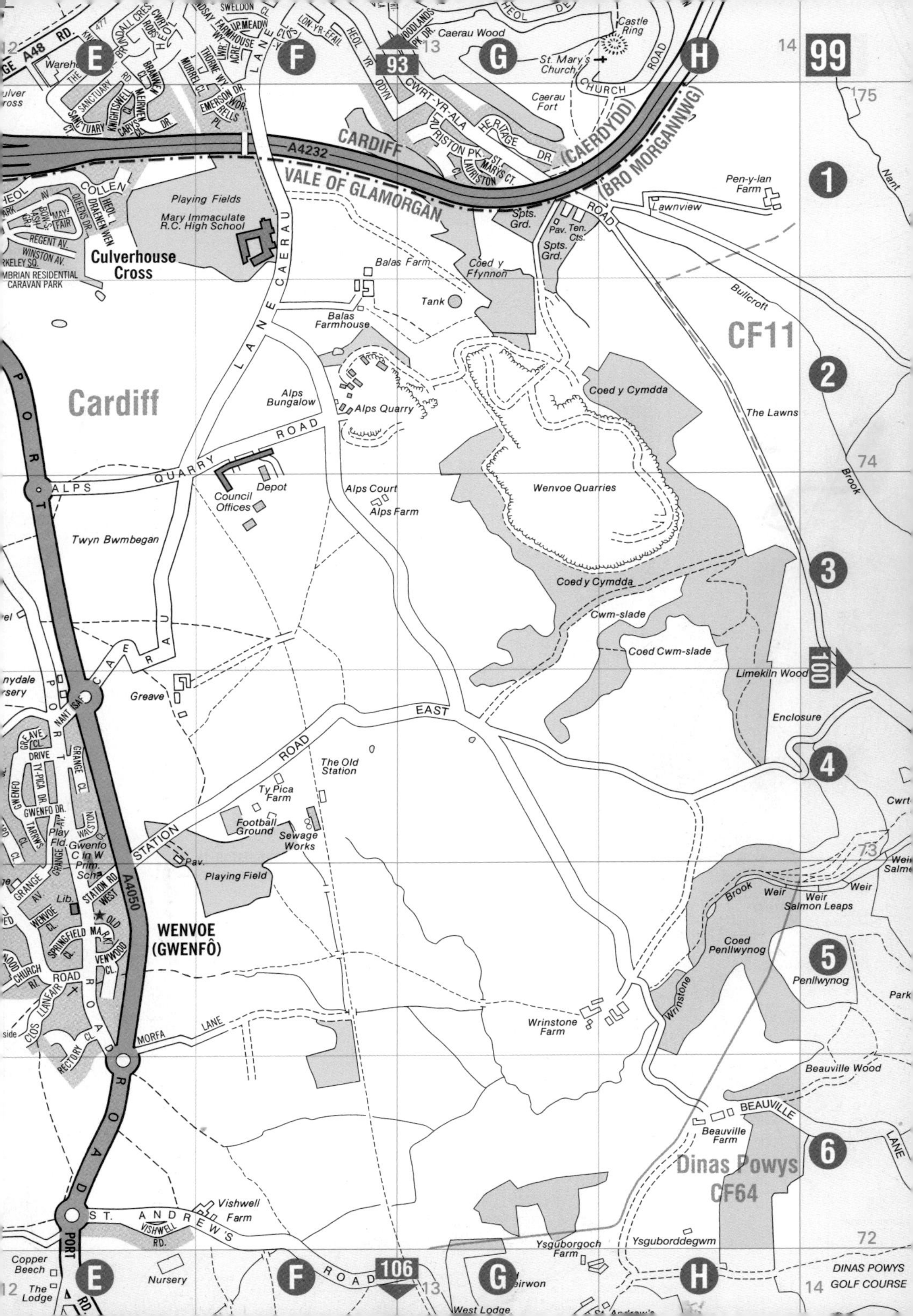

99
93
106
100
CF11
Dinas Powys
CF64
Cardiff
Culverhouse Cross
WENVOE
(GWENFÔ)
CARDIFF
(CAERDYDD)
VALE OF GLAMORGAN
(BRO MORGANNWG)
A4232
A4050
A48
Caerau Wood
Castle Ring
St. Mary's Church
Caerau Fort
Pen-y-lan Farm
Lawnview
Playing Fields
Mary Immaculate R.C. High School
Balas Farm
Coed y Ffynnon
Tank
Balas Farmhouse
Bullcroft
Alps Bungalow
Alps Quarry
Coed y Cymdda
The Lawns
Council Offices
Depot
Alps Court
Alps Farm
Wenvoe Quarries
Twyn Bwmbegan
Cwm-slade
Coed Cwm-slade
Limekiln Wood
Enclosure
Greave
The Old Station
Ty Pica Farm
Football Ground
Sewage Works
Playing Field
Salmon Leaps
Coed Penllwynog
Penllwynog
Wrinstone Farm
Beauville Wood
Beauville Farm
Vishwell Farm
Ysguborgoch Farm
Ysguborddegwm
Nursery
Copper Beech
The Lodge
West Lodge
DINAS POWYS GOLF COURSE

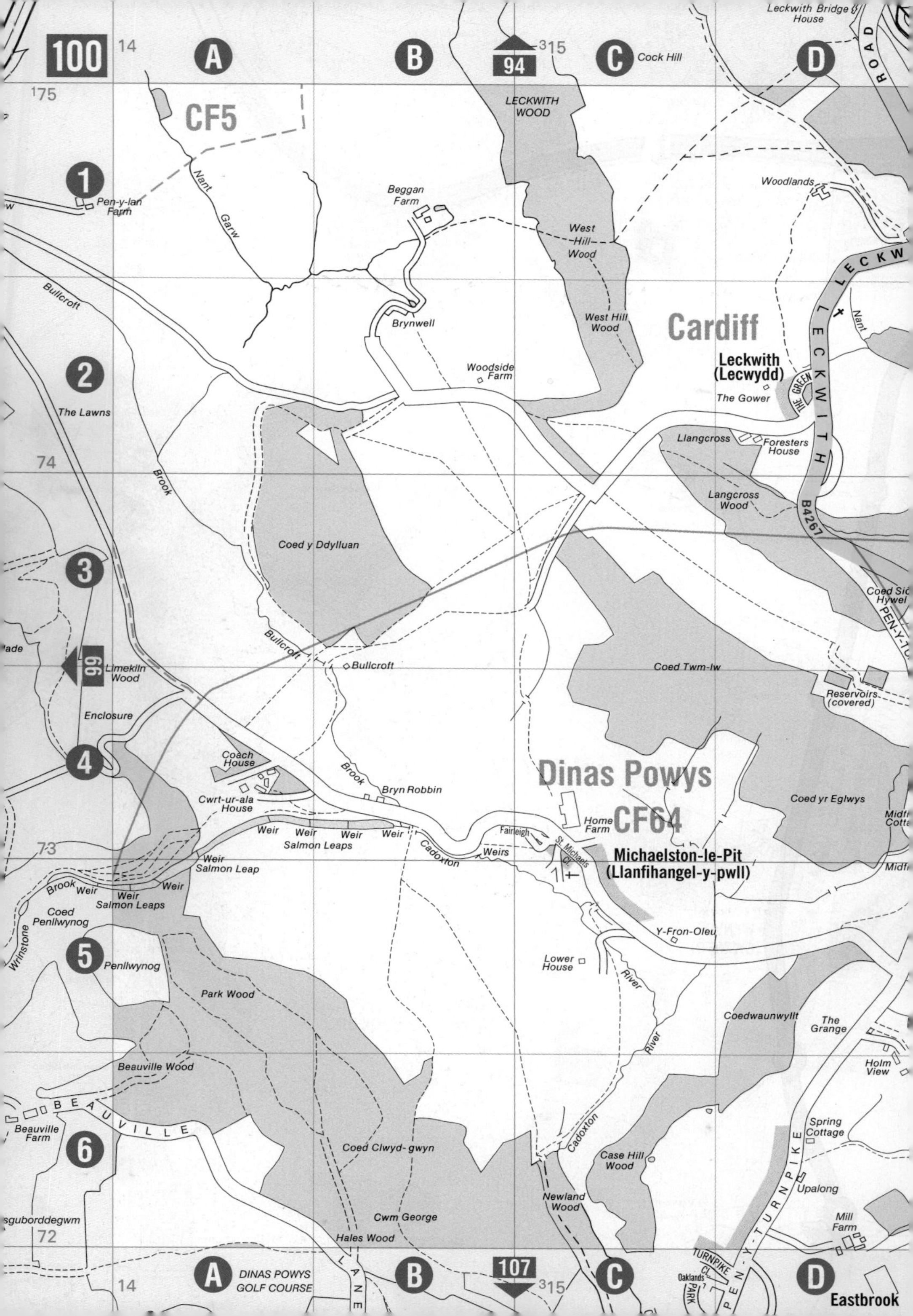

14
A
B
94
315
C
Cock Hill
D
Leckwith Bridge House
ROAD
175
CF5
LECKWITH WOOD
1
Pen-y-lan Farm
Nant Garw
Beggan Farm
West Hill Wood
Woodlands
LECKW
Bullcroft
Brynwell
West Hill Wood
Cardiff
Nant
2
The Lawns
Woodside Farm
Leckwith (Lecwydd)
The Gower
THE GREEN
LECKWITH
Llangcross
Foresters House
74
Brook
Langcross Wood
B4267
Coed y Ddylluan
3
Coed Hywel
99
Limekiln Wood
Bullcroft
Bullcroft
Coed Twm-lw
Reservoirs (covered)
Enclosure
4
Coach House
Brook
Bryn Robbin
Dinas Powys
Coed yr Eglwys
Cwrt-ur-ala House
Weir
Weir
Weir
Weir
Salmon Leaps
Home Farm
CF64
Faireigh
St. Michaels Cl.
73
Weir
Salmon Leap
Cadoxton
Weirs
Michaelston-le-Pit (Llanfihangel-y-pwll)
Brook
Weir
Weir
Weir
Salmon Leaps
Coed Penllwynog
Y-Fron-Oleu
Wrinstone
5
Penllwynog
Lower House
River
Park Wood
Coedwaunwyllt
River
The Grange
Beauville Wood
Holm View
BEAUVILLE
Beauville Farm
6
Coed Clwyd-gwyn
Cadoxton
Spring Cottage
Case Hill Wood
PEN-Y-TURNPIKE
Upalong
sguborddegwm
Newland Wood
Cwm George
Mill Farm
72
Hales Wood
A
DINAS POWYS GOLF COURSE
LANE
B
107
315
C
TURNPIKE CL.
Oaklands
PARK
D
Eastbrook

E
F
G
H
95
108
102
1
2
3
4
5
6
16
17
18
72
73
74
175
CF11
CF64
Grangetown
Penarth
Llandough
(Landochau)
Cogan
Windsor Quay
Llandough Hospital
(Ysbyty Landochau)
Cardiff International Sports Village
Cardiff International Pool
Cardiff Arena
(Ice Rink)
Cardiff Bay Retail Park
Leckwith Industrial Estate
Gulf Industrial Area
West Point Industrial Estate
Penarth Road Retail Park
Llandough Trading Estate
Celtic Gateway Bus. Park
Wholesale Fruit Centre
Sorting Office
Gas Works
Sewage Works
Superstore
Warehouse
Warehouses
Works
Depot
Factory
Brick Works
Channel View Leisure Cen.
White Water Centre
Playing Fields
Play Area
The Marl
Leisure Centre
Playing Field
Cogan Prim. Sch.
Cogan Nursy. Sch.
Llandough Primary Sch.
Ninian Park Primary Sch.
Ysgol Pen y Garth
Llanfair Unit
Ferry Road Interchange
Cogan Junc.
Cardiff
Vale of Glamorgan
(Caerdydd)
(Bro Morgannwg)
Grangetown
Butetown Link
Link A4232
Spur
Cogan Spur
Windsor Road
Penarth Road
Barry Road
Andrew Road
Redlands Road
Penlan Road
Leckwith Road
Cardiff Road
Corporation Road
Ferry Road
Clive Street
Hadfield Road
Bessemer Road
Sloper Road
Sevenoaks Park
Marconi Avenue
Terra Nova Way
Empire Way
International Dr.
Olympian Drive
Dunleavy Dr.
Watkiss Way
Llandough Hill
Lewis Road
Greenway Cl.
Corbett Road
Sully Road
Coleridge Road
Brindley Road
Holden Rd.
Leckwith Road
Fleet Way
Stuart Cl.
Stadium Cl.
Tollgate Cl.
Lyon Cl.
A4232
A4160
A4055
A4119
B4267
50
Afon Elai
Ely
Tidal Harbour
Landing Stage
Wharf
Factory Wood
Factory Cottage
Ynyston Farm
Coed-y-stover
Coed reigiaidd
Cydfin
Clip-coch
Cwm Cydfin
Llandough Rectory
Lodge
Reservoir Wood
Lewis Road Play. Flds.
Croft Mawr
Holms Farm
East Brook
Cogan Tunnel
Hazelhurst
Sunnybank
Dingle Rd.

Butetown
Grangetown
CORPORATION A4119 RD.
CLARENCE ROAD
JAMES ST.
EMBANKMENT
Clarence Bridge
Mosque
Cardiff Bay
Hollywood Bowl
The Red Dragon Centre
Odeon Cinema
Arts Cen.
Cardiff Bays
Wales Millennium Centre
Roald Dahl Plass
The National Assembly for Wales
The Assembly at the Pierhead
Pier Head
Techniquest
Graving Docks
INNER HARBOUR
Norwegian Church Arts Centre
Cardiff Bay Visitors Centre
Waterfront Park
ROATH BASIN
Cardiff
Junction Lock
Swing Bridge
Adventurer's Quay
Channel View Leisure Cen.
Play Area
Playing Fields
THE MARL
Tennis Courts
Hamadryad Park
Wetlands Nature Reserve
RIVER TAF
Windsor Quay
BUTETOWN A4232
Transit Sheds
QUEEN ALEXANDRA DOCK
Entrance Channel
CARGO ROAD
Customs Waterguard
Channel Oil Works
BARRAGE
PENARTH FLATS
Ferry Road Interchange
CARDIFF INTERNATIONAL SPORTS VILLAGE
Cardiff International Pool
Cardiff Arena (Ice Rink)
Cardiff Bay Yacht Club
COGAN SPUR A4055
ELY
TIDAL HARBOUR
CARDIFF
VALE OF GLAMORGAN
Weir
Cefn-y-wrach
Breakwaters
Portway Marina
Penarth
Marine Bldgs.
Headlands School
PENARTH
(CAERDYDD)
(BRO MORGANNWG)
Penarth Head
Dingle Road
WINDSOR
A4160
CF11
CF64
96
101
109

E
F
G
H
320
21
22
97
175
ROAD
Depot
OLD CLIPPER ROAD
CLIPPER RD.
FORESHORE
CLOS
South Point
Boom
ROATH DOCK
OLD CLIPPER RD.
WAY
VIKING
Works
ROAD
Cardiff Heliport
South Point
Waste Recycling Centre
CARDIFF DOCKS
ROVER
Fletcher's Wharf
Oil Storage Terminal
PLACE
ROAD
LONGSHIPS
ROAD
COLDSTORES
Works
Warehouses
CF10
King's Wharf
ROAD
Timber Depot
ROAD
CARDIFF FLATS
MOUTH OF THE SEVERN
(ABER HAFREN)
1
2
3
4
5
6
74
73
72

08
A
Coed y Graig
B
09
DYFFRYN GOLWCH
C
Dyffryn Gardens
D
72
Whitton Mawr
Doghill Farm
Moat
Home Farm
Dyffryn
1
Treoda
Ffynnon Whitton-mawr
Little Hamston Farm
Little Hamston
Whitton Lodge
Dyffryn Mill
A4226
2
River Waycock
Goldsland
Great Hamston
71
Old Wallace
Brook
Moulton
3
Northcliff Farm
Northcliff Cottage
Grovelands
A4226
Lidmore
Lidmore Mill
4
Coed Garw
Ffynnon y Coed
Brynhill
40
Nant
170
Lidmore Wood
BRYNHIL
Sutton
Coed y Capel
5
Highlight
Coed Bach
Suddon Mawr
Sutton Wood
SHERBOU CL
Sewage Works
Barry
CF62
BEAU
ANDOVER
Welsh Hawking Centre
Ffynnon yr Hofel
6
A4226
Coed Mawr
Middleton Plantation
WAYCOCK
Coed yr Ychen
69
ROAD
A
B
116
C
D
08
09
Walters Farm

98
117
106
Cardiff
CF5
Goldsland Wood
Cwmlatter
THE GATHERS
WENVOE CASTLE GOLF COURSE
Goldsland
Goldsland Brook
Club House
Wenvoe Castle
Front Lawn
WENVOE CASTLE GOLF COURSE
New Wallace
Bears Wood
Driving Range
Nant Brynhill
Coed Brynhill-fawr
Great Brynhill Farm
Bryn Hafren Comprehensive School
Little Brynhill Farm
GOLF COURSE
PORT ROAD EAST
A4050
Colcot
Colcot Prim. Sch.
Reservoirs (covered)
Club House
Merthyr Dyfan Recreation Ground
Merthyr Dyfan
Holm Vw. Leisure Cen.
PORT ROAD WEST
A4226
COLCOT ROAD
White Farm
Cold Brook
Playing Fields
Colcot Leisure Centre
Barry Comprehensive School
BARRY HOSP.
Recreation Ground
Oakfield Prim. Sch. & Ysgol Gwaun y Nant
Gibbonsdown
Ysgol Maes Dyfan
Playing Fields
Ysgol Bro Morgannwg
Cemetery
Community Centre
Highlight Farm
Superstore
Copper Beech
The Lodge
Lawn
Fairways

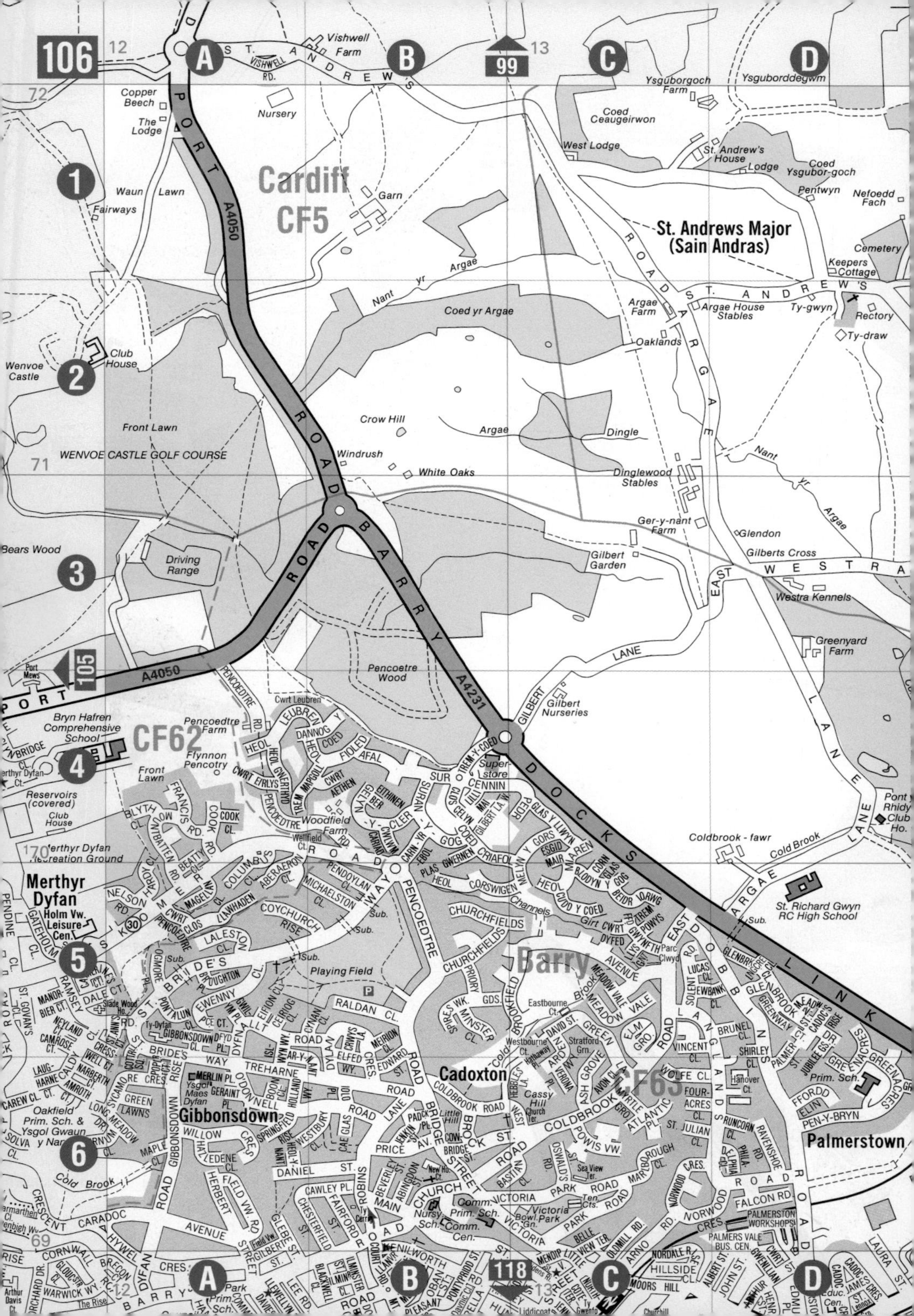
A
B
C
D
99
12
13
72
71
69
170
1
2
3
4
5
6
105
118
Cardiff
CF5
CF62
CF63
St. Andrews Major
(Sain Andras)
Vishwell Farm
Vishwell Rd.
St. Andrew's
Port Road
A4050
Barry Road
A4231
Docks Link
Copper Beech
The Lodge
Nursery
Ysguborgoch Farm
Ysguborddegwm
Coed Ceaugeirwon
West Lodge
St. Andrew's House
Lodge
Coed Ysgubor-goch
Pentwyn
Nefoedd Fach
Waun
Lawn
Fairways
Garn
Cemetery
Keepers Cottage
Nant yr Argae
Coed yr Argae
Argae Farm
Argae House Stables
Ty-gwyn
Rectory
Ty-draw
Oaklands
Club House
Wenvoe Castle
Front Lawn
Crow Hill
Argae
Dingle
Wenvoe Castle Golf Course
Windrush
White Oaks
Dinglewood Stables
Ger-y-nant Farm
Glendon
Gilberts Cross
Bears Wood
Driving Range
Gilbert Garden
East Westra
Westra Kennels
Greenyard Farm
Port Mews
Pencoetre Wood
Lane
Gilbert Nurseries
Argae Lane
Bryn Hafren Comprehensive School
Pencoedtre Farm
Flynnon Pencotry
Reservoirs (covered)
Club House
Merthyr Dyfan Recreation Ground
Pont y Rhidy Club Ho.
Coldbrook - fawr
Cold Brook
Merthyr Dyfan
Holm Vw. Leisure Cen.
St. Richard Gwyn RC High School
Super-store
Playing Field
Barry
Cadoxton
Gibbonsdown
Palmerstown
Oakfield Prim. Sch. & Ysgol Gwaun y Nant
Pencoedtre
Churchfields
Coldbrook Road
Victoria Park
Caradoc Avenue
Main Road
Church Street
Brock St.
Bridge Street
Norwood Cres.
Falcon Rd
Palmerston Workshops
Palmers Vale Bus. Cen.
Moors Hill
Barry Rd.

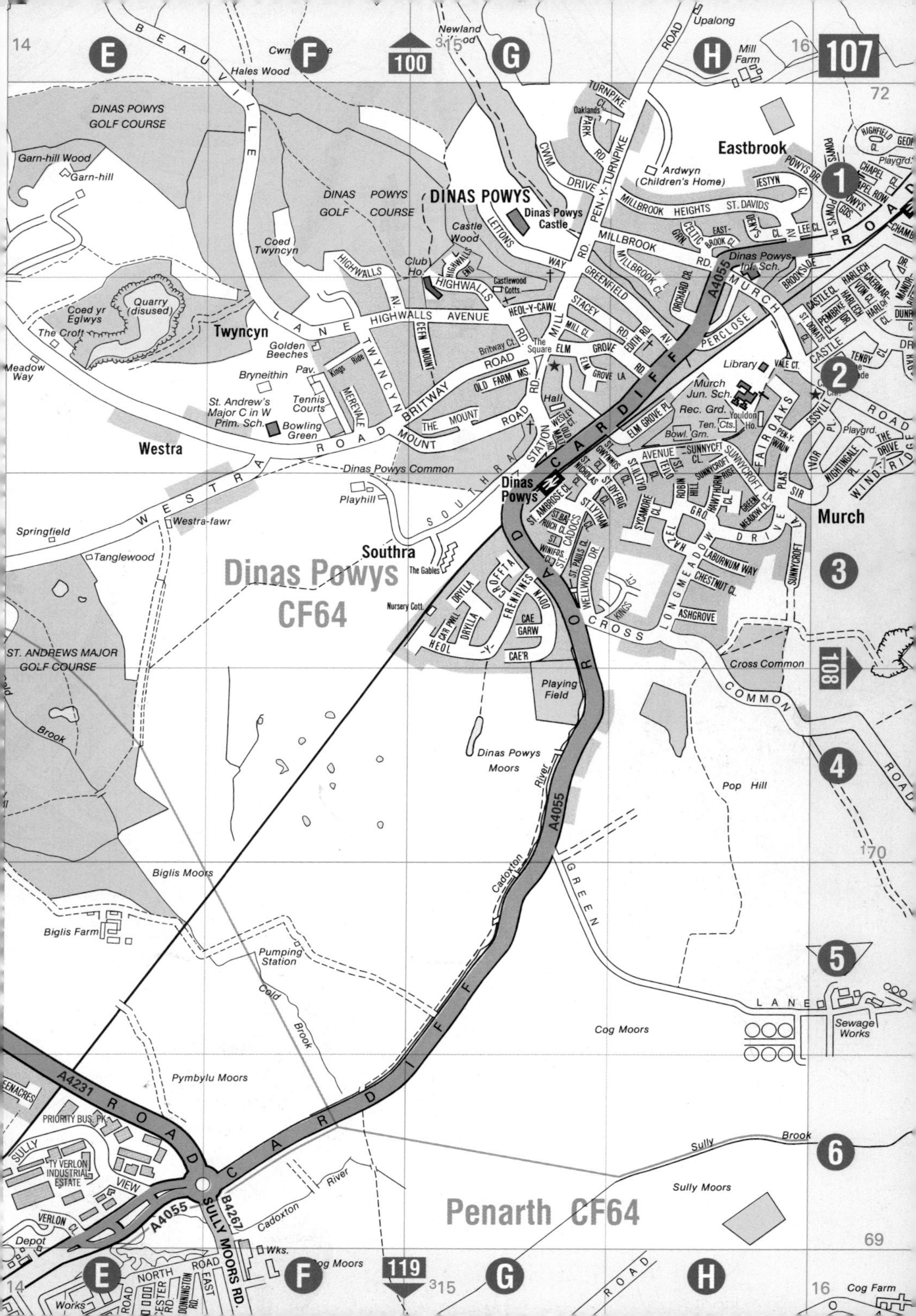
Dinas Powys
CF64
Penarth CF64
DINAS POWYS
Eastbrook
Murch
Twyncyn
Westra
Southra
Dinas Powys Castle
DINAS POWYS GOLF COURSE
ST. ANDREWS MAJOR GOLF COURSE
Garn-hill Wood
Garn-hill
Coed yr Eglwys
Quarry (disused)
The Croft
Meadow Way
Coed Twyncyn
Castle Wood
Club Ho.
Golden Beeches
Bryneithin
Pav.
Tennis Courts
St. Andrew's Major C in W Prim. Sch.
Bowling Green
Springfield
Westra-fawr
Tanglewood
Playhill
The Gables
Nursery Cott.
Dinas Powys Common
Playing Field
Dinas Powys Moors
Cross Common
Pop Hill
Biglis Moors
Biglis Farm
Pumping Station
Cold Brook
Cog Moors
Sewage Works
Pymbylu Moors
Sully Brook
Sully Moors
PRIORITY BUS. PK.
TY VERLON INDUSTRIAL ESTATE
Depot
Wks.
Works
Cog Farm
Hales Wood
Newland Wood
Upalong
Mill Farm
Ardwyn (Children's Home)
Dinas Powys Inf. Sch.
Library
Murch Jun. Sch.
Rec. Grd.
Ten. Cts.
Bowl. Grn.
Youldon Ho.
Hall
The Square
Castlewood Cotts.
Oaklands
Playgrd.
A4055
A4231
B4267
CARDIFF ROAD
SULLY MOORS RD.
BEAUVILLE LANE
WESTRA ROAD
MOUNT ROAD
BRITWAY ROAD
TWYNCYN
HIGHWALLS AVENUE
MILLBROOK RD.
PEN-Y-TURNPIKE RD.
CROSS COMMON ROAD
LONGMEADOW DRIVE
GREEN LANE
SOUTHRA
MURCH RD.
14
15
16
72
71
170
69
E
F
G
H
1
2
3
4
5
6
100
108
119

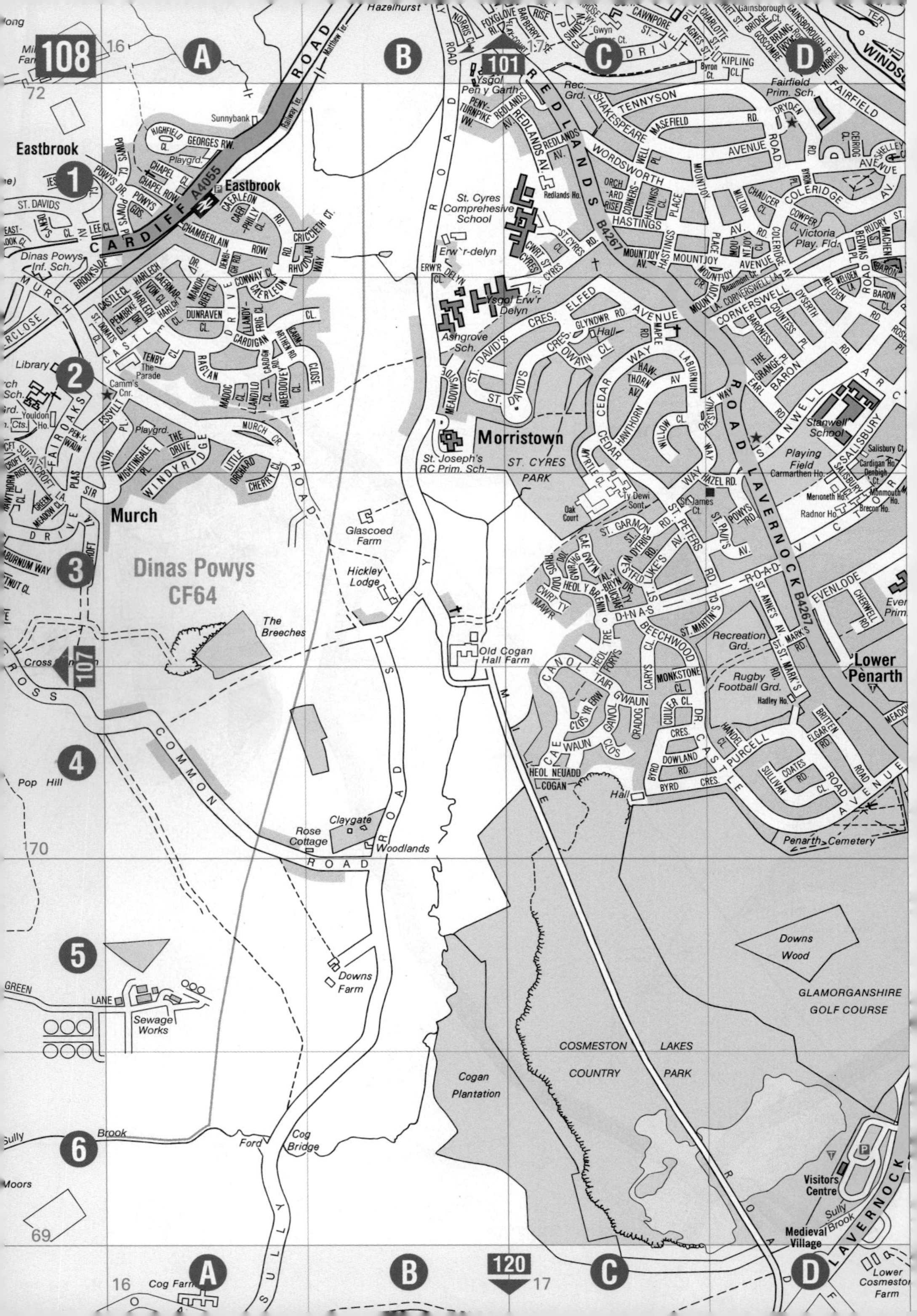
Eastbrook
Murch
Dinas Powys
CF64
Morristown
Lower Penarth
The Breeches
Glascoed Farm
Hickley Lodge
Old Cogan Hall Farm
Rose Cottage
Claygate
Woodlands
Downs Farm
Sewage Works
Cog Bridge
Ford
Sully Brook
Pop Hill
Moors
Cog Farm
Hazelhurst
Sunnybank
Library
Camm's Cnr.
The Parade
Dinas Powys Inf. Sch.
St. Cyres Comprehesive School
Erw'r-delyn
Ysgol Erw'r Delyn
Ashgrove Sch.
St. Joseph's RC Prim. Sch.
ST. CYRES PARK
Ty Dewi Sont.
Oak Court
St. James Ct.
Stanwell School
Playing Field
Victoria Play. Fld.
Recreation Grd.
Rugby Football Grd.
Hadley Ho.
Hall
Penarth Cemetery
Fairfield Prim. Sch.
Ysgol Pen y Garth
Rec. Grd.
Redlands Ho.
Downs Wood
GLAMORGANSHIRE GOLF COURSE
COSMESTON LAKES COUNTRY PARK
Cogan Plantation
Visitors Centre
Medieval Village
Lower Cosmeston Farm
CARDIFF ROAD A4055
SULLY ROAD
CROSS COMMON ROAD
REDLANDS ROAD B4267
LAVERNOCK ROAD B4267
DINAS ROAD
STANWELL ROAD
VICTORIA ROAD
CASTLE AVENUE
MURCH ROAD
WINDYRIDGE
GREEN LANE
Cross Common 107
101
120
A B C D
1 2 3 4 5 6
16 17 69 70 72

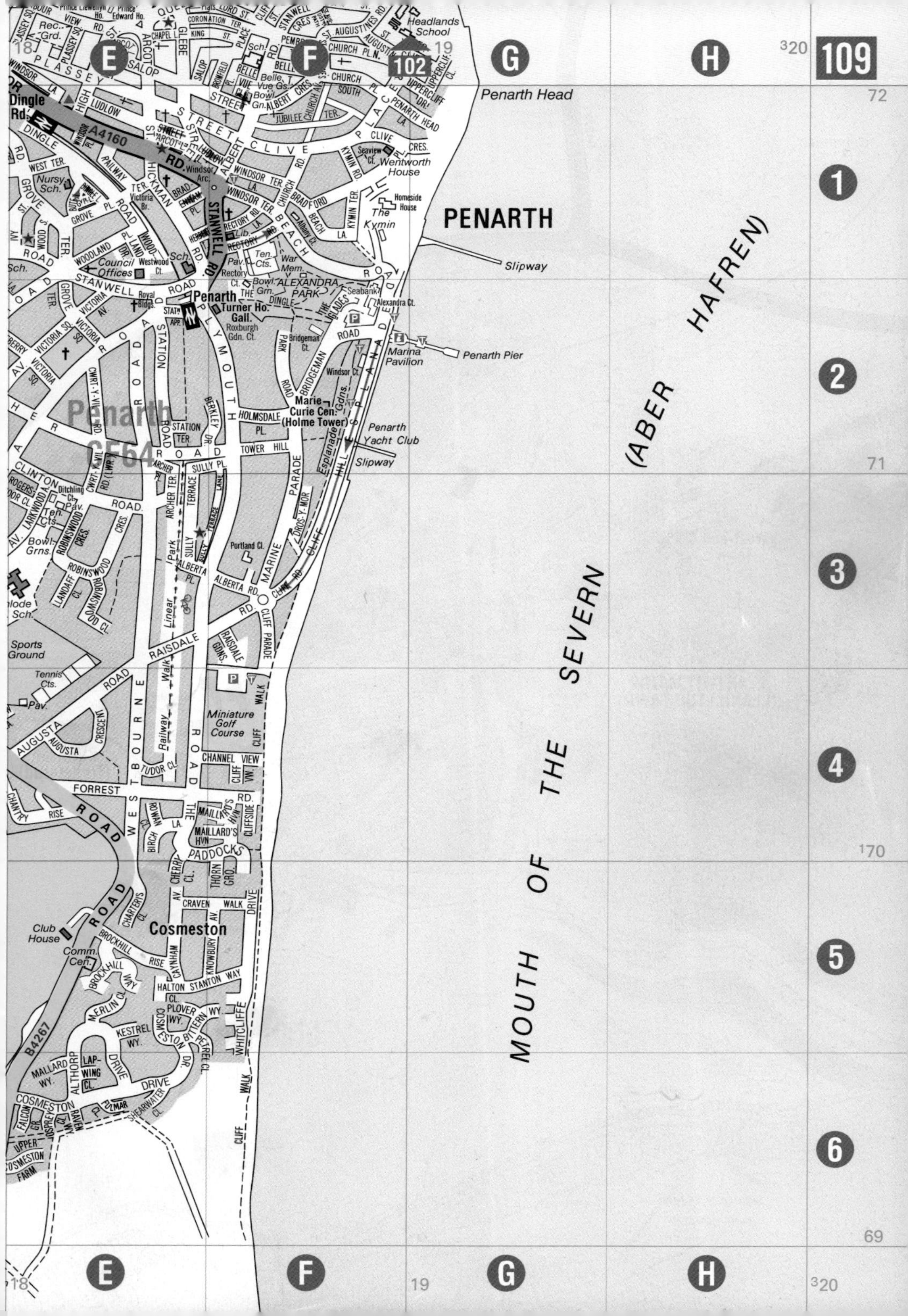
PENARTH
MOUTH OF THE SEVERN
(ABER HAFREN)
Penarth Head
Penarth Pier
Marina Pavilion
Penarth Yacht Club
Slipway
Slipway
Penarth
CF64
Cosmeston
Headlands School
Turner Ho. Gall.
Marie Curie Cen. (Holme Tower)
Miniature Golf Course
Sports Ground
Club House
Comm. Cen.
Council Offices
The Kymin
Homeside House
Wentworth House
Alexandra Park
A4160
B4267
Dingle Rd.
Stanwell Rd.
Plymouth Road
Station Road
Westbourne Road
Raisdale Road
Forrest Road
Clive Place
Esplanade
Marine Parade
Cliff Parade
Cliff Walk
Linear Park
Railway Walk
Holmsdale Pl.
Tower Hill
Cosmeston Drive
Upper Cosmeston Farm
E
F
G
H
1
2
3
4
5
6
18
19
320
69
170
71
72
102

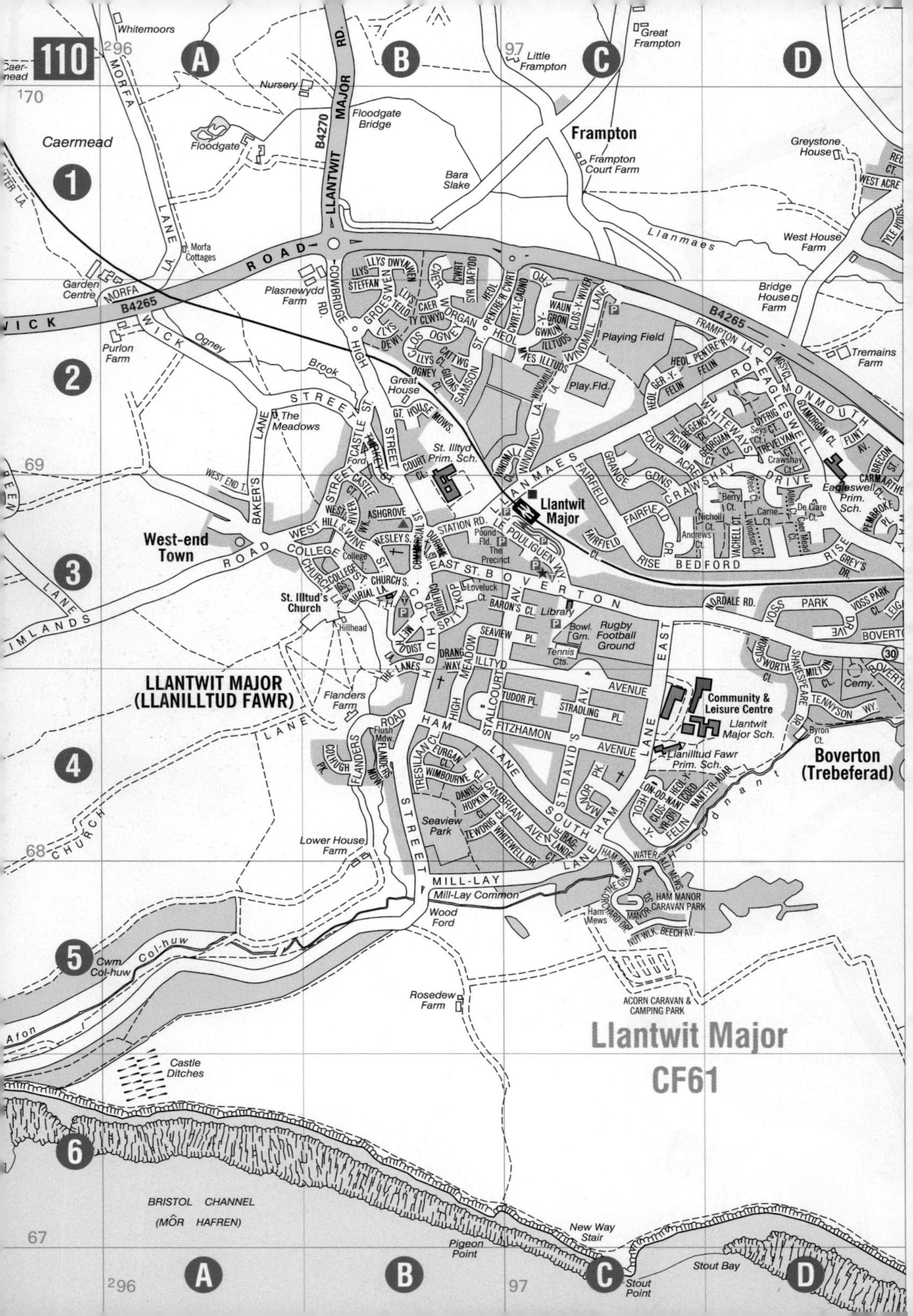
Llantwit Major
CF61
LLANTWIT MAJOR
(LLANILLTUD FAWR)
Llantwit Major
Boverton
(Trebeferad)
West-end Town
Frampton
Caermead
Whitemoors
Nursery
Floodgate Bridge
Floodgate
Little Frampton
Great Frampton
Frampton Court Farm
Greystone House
Bara Slake
Morfa Cottages
Garden Centre
Plasnewydd Farm
Purlon Farm
West House Farm
Bridge House Farm
Tremains Farm
Great House
The Meadows
St. Illtyd Prim. Sch.
St. Illtud's Church
Hillhead
Flanders Farm
Flush Mdw.
Playing Field
Play.Fld.
Pound Fld.
The Precinct
Library
Bowl. Grn.
Rugby Football Ground
Tennis Cts.
Community & Leisure Centre
Llantwit Major Sch.
Llanilltud Fawr Prim. Sch.
Eagleswell Prim. Sch.
Cemy.
Seaview Park
Lower House Farm
Mill-Lay Common
Wood Ford
Ham Mews
HAM MANOR CARAVAN PARK
ACORN CARAVAN & CAMPING PARK
Rosedew Farm
Cwm Col-huw
Afon
Castle Ditches
BRISTOL CHANNEL
(MÔR HAFREN)
New Way Stair
Pigeon Point
Stout Point
Stout Bay
LLANTWIT MAJOR RD.
B4270
B4265
WICK ROAD
MORFA LANE
WICK
Ogney
Brook
STREET
BAKER'S LANE
WEST END T.
COLLEGE ROAD
CHURCH LANE
IMLANDS
COWBRIDGE RD.
HIGH STREET
CASTLE ST.
TURKEY ST.
COURT CL.
GT. HOUSE MDWS.
ASHGROVE
WESLEY S.
COMMERCIAL ST.
STATION RD.
LE POULIGUEN WY.
EAST ST.
BOVERTON
LLANMAES
FAIRFIELD
GRANGE
FOUR ACRE
GDNS.
CRAWSHAY DRIVE
WHITEWAYS
PICTON
REGENCY
GEORGIAN CT.
DYFRIG
TREVELYAN CT.
Seys Ct.
Crawshay Ct.
Berry Ct.
Rees Cl.
Nicholl Ct.
Andrews Ct.
VACHELL CT.
Windsor Cl.
Carne Ct.
Allen Ct.
De Clare Ct.
Caer Mead Cl.
RISE BEDFORD
GREY'S DR.
MONMOUTH
EAGLESWELL ROAD
GLAMORGAN CL.
FLINT AV.
BRECON
CARMARTHEN
PEMBROKE PL.
FRAMPTON LA.
HEOL PENTRE'R FELIN
HEOL GER-Y-FELIN
WINDMILL LANE
WINDMILL LA.
WINDMILL CL.
MAES ILLTUDS
CLOS-Y-WIVER
WAUN-Y-GRON
GWAUN ILLTUDS
CWRT-Y-CADNO
HEOL PENTRE'R CWRT
HEOL WORGAN ST.
SYR DAFYDD
CWRT CAER
LLYS DWYNWEN
LLYS STEFFAN
GROESWEN
LLYS TEILO
CAER TY CLWYD
CLOS OGNEY
OGNEY CL.
LLYS CL.
CATTWG
GILDAS
SAMSON
LLYS DEWI
WEST ST.
RIVER WK.
WINE ST.
HILL S.
CASTLE CT.
CHURCH S.
COLLEGE T.
BURIAL LA.
COLHUGH ST.
COLHUGH
SPITZKOP
METHODIST LA.
Loveluck Ct.
BARON'S CL.
SEAVIEW PL.
DRANGWAY
MEADOW
ILLTYD
HIGH
STALLCOURT AV.
TUDOR PL.
STRADLING PL.
AVENUE
FITZHAMON
ST. DAVID'S AV.
HAM LANE
EAST LANE
THE LANES
ROAD
FLANDERS
FLANDERS MDW.
COLHUGH PK.
TRESILIAN CL.
FURGAN CL.
WIMBOURNE CL.
DANIEL
HOPKIN CL.
CAMBRIAN AVENUE
TEWDRIG CL.
WHITEWELL DR.
BAGLANDE CT.
SOUTH HAM LANE
MANOR PK.
LON-OD-NANT
HEOL-Y-COED
CLOS-YR-ON
HEOL-Y-FELIN
NANT-YR-ADAR
Hoddnant
WATERHALL MEWS
HAM MNR.
ORCHARD DR.
MANOR
NUT WLK.
BEECH AV.
MILL-LAY
NORDALE RD.
VOSS PARK
PARK DRIVE
BOVERTON
WORDSWORTH CL.
SHAKESPEARE DR.
MILTON CL.
TENNYSON WY.
Byron Ct.
WEST ACRE
TYLE HOUSE
CHURCH LANE
296
97
170
69
68
67
A
B
C
D
1
2
3
4
5
6
30

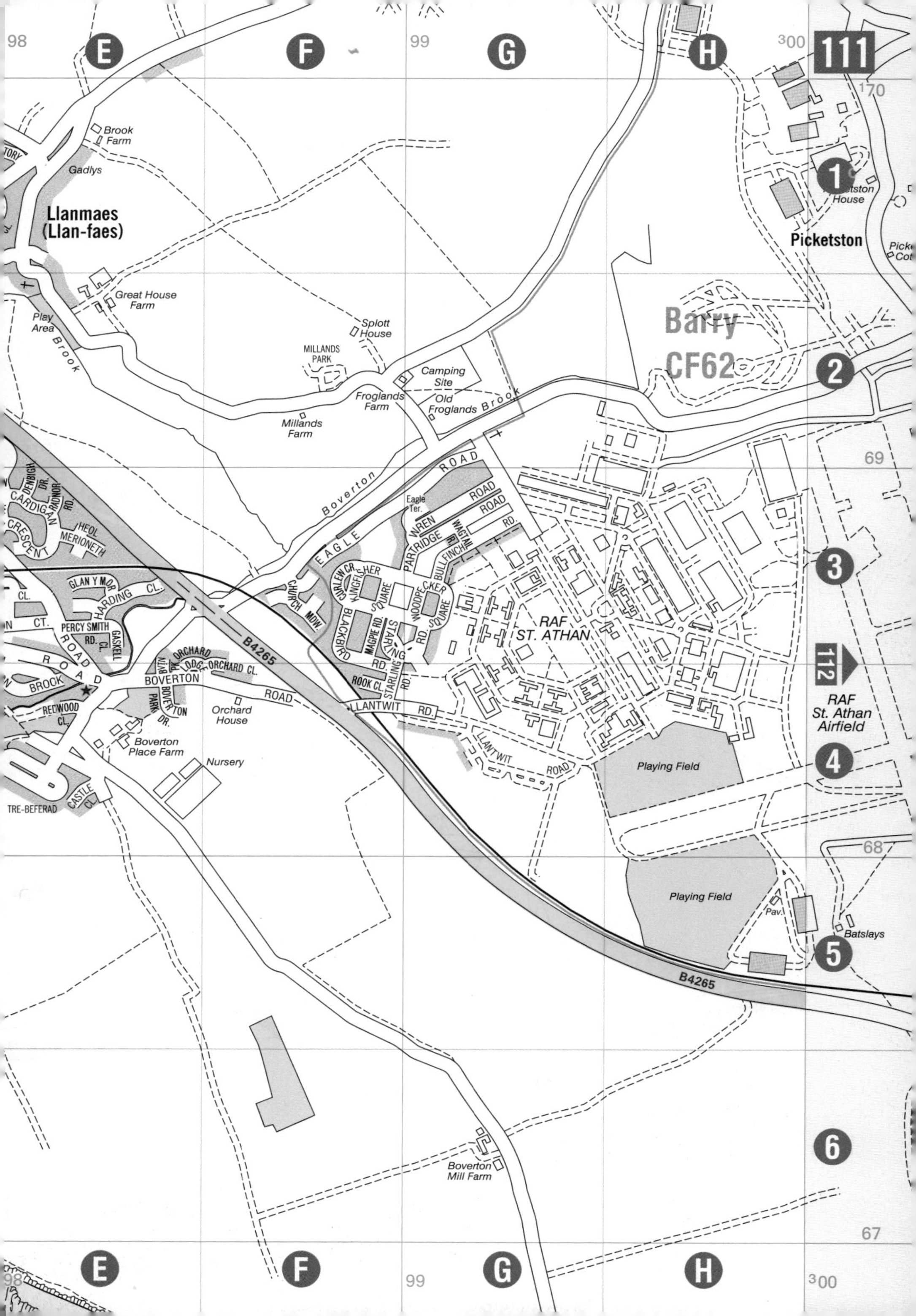
Llanmaes
(Llan-faes)
Picketston
Barry
CF62
RAF
ST. ATHAN
RAF
St. Athan
Airfield
112
B4265
Brook Farm
Gadlys
Great House Farm
Play Area
Brook
Splott House
MILLANDS PARK
Camping Site
Froglands Farm
Old Froglands
Millands Farm
Boverton
ROAD
EAGLE
Eagle Ter.
WREN
PARTRIDGE
WAGTAIL
BULLFINCH
WOODPECKER
SQUARE
KINGFISHER
SQUARE
CURLEW CR.
BLACKBIRD
MAGPIE RD.
STARLING
ROOK CL.
CHURCH MDW.
LLANTWIT RD.
LLANTWIT ROAD
Playing Field
Playing Field
Pav.
Batslays
DENBIGH DR.
RADNOR RD.
CARDIGAN CRESCENT
HEOL MERIONETH
GLAN Y MOR
HARDING CL.
PERCY SMITH RD.
GASKELL CL.
BROCK
REDWOOD CL.
BOVERTON
ORCHARD CL.
BOVERTON PARK DR.
Orchard House
Boverton Place Farm
Nursery
CASTLE CL.
TRE-BEFERAD
Boverton Mill Farm
E
F
G
H
1
2
3
4
5
6
98
99
300
170
69
68
67

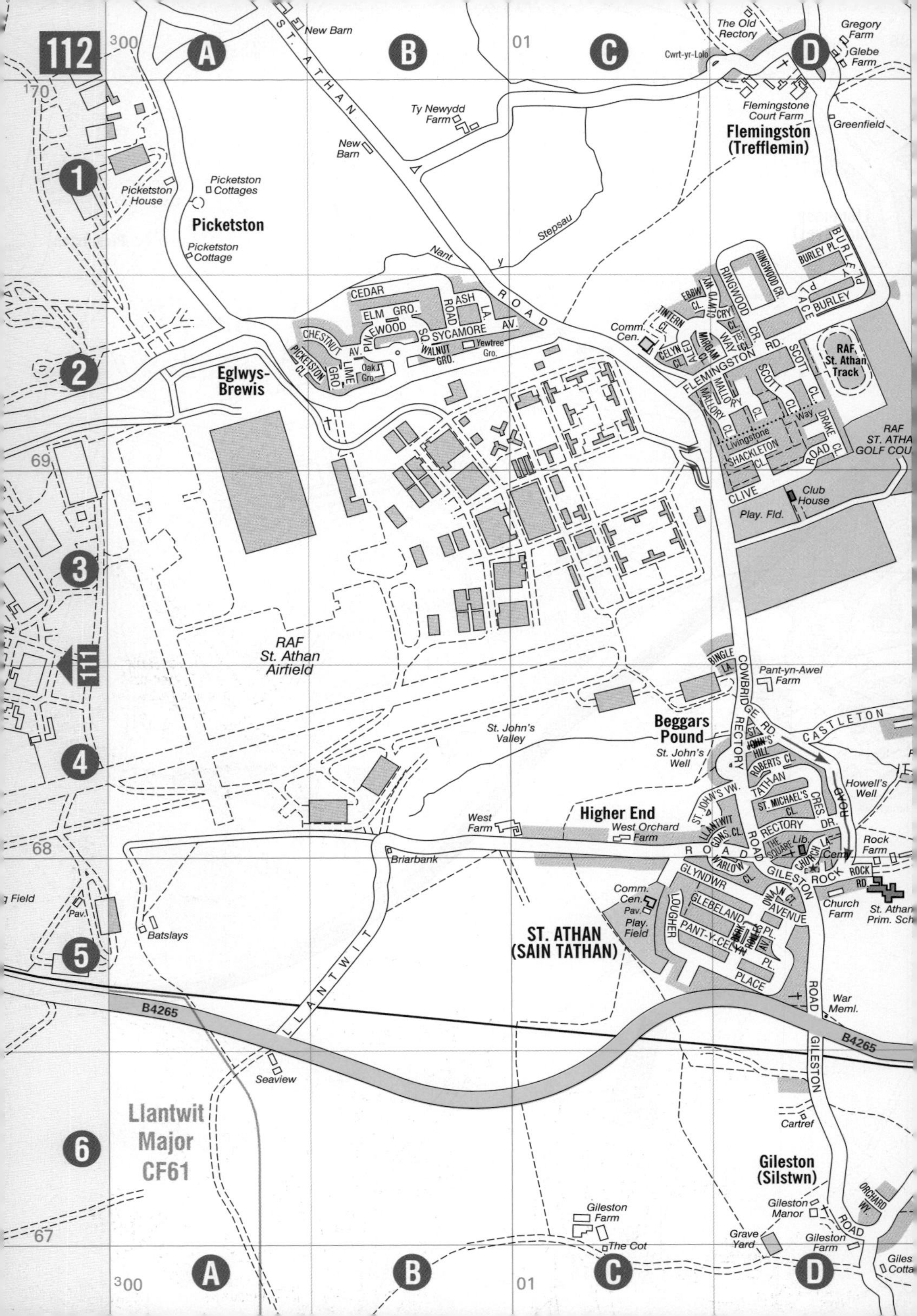

Picketston
Picketston Cottages
Picketston House
Picketston Cottage
New Barn
Ty Newydd Farm
The Old Rectory
Cwrt-yr-Lolo
Gregory Farm
Glebe Farm
Flemingstone Court Farm
Greenfield
Flemingston (Trefflemin)
Stepsau
Nant y
ROAD
ST. ATHAN
CEDAR
ELM GRO.
ASH ROAD
LA.
PINEWOOD SQ.
SYCAMORE AV.
CHESTNUT AV.
WALNUT GRO.
Yewtree Gro.
PICKETSTON CL.
LIME GRO.
Oak Gro.
Eglwys-Brewis
BURLEY PL.
BURLEY PLACE
RINGWOOD CR.
RINGWOOD
EBBW CL.
CWRT Y VA
CRYI CL.
TINTERN CL.
CELYN CL.
ALED CL.
MARGAM WAY
TEIFI CL.
Comm. Cen.
FLEMINGSTON RD.
SCOTT
SCOTT CL.
CR.
MALLORY
MALLORY CL.
Livingstone Way
DRAKE CL.
SHACKLETON CL.
ROAD
CLIVE
RAF St. Athan Track
RAF ST. ATHAN GOLF COU
Club House
Play. Fld.
RAF St. Athan Airfield
BINGLE LA.
Pant-yn-Awel Farm
COWBRIDGE RD.
RECTORY
CASTLETON
Beggars Pound
St. John's Valley
St. John's Well
ST. JOHN'S HILL
ROBERTS CL.
TATHAN
Howell's Well
ST. MICHAEL'S CL.
CRES.
DR.
ST. JOHN'S VW.
LLANTWIT GDNS. CL.
Higher End
West Farm
West Orchard Farm
RECTORY
THE SQUARE
Lib.
CHURCH LA.
Cemy.
Rock Farm
ROCK RD.
ROAD
Briarbank
WARLOW CL.
GLYNDWR
GILESTON ROCK
OWAIN CT.
AVENUE
GLEBELAND
LOUGHER
PANT-Y-CELYN
PL.
PLACE
Church Farm
St. Athan Prim. Sch
Comm. Cen.
Pav.
Play. Field
ST. ATHAN (SAIN TATHAN)
Batslays
Pav.
Field
LLANTWIT
B4265
War Meml.
GILESTON ROAD
Seaview
Llantwit Major CF61
Cartref
Gileston (Silstwn)
ORCHARD WY.
Gileston Manor
ROAD
Gileston Farm
The Cot
Grave Yard
Gileston Farm
Giles Cotta
111
A
B
C
D
1
2
3
4
5
6
300
01
170
69
68
67

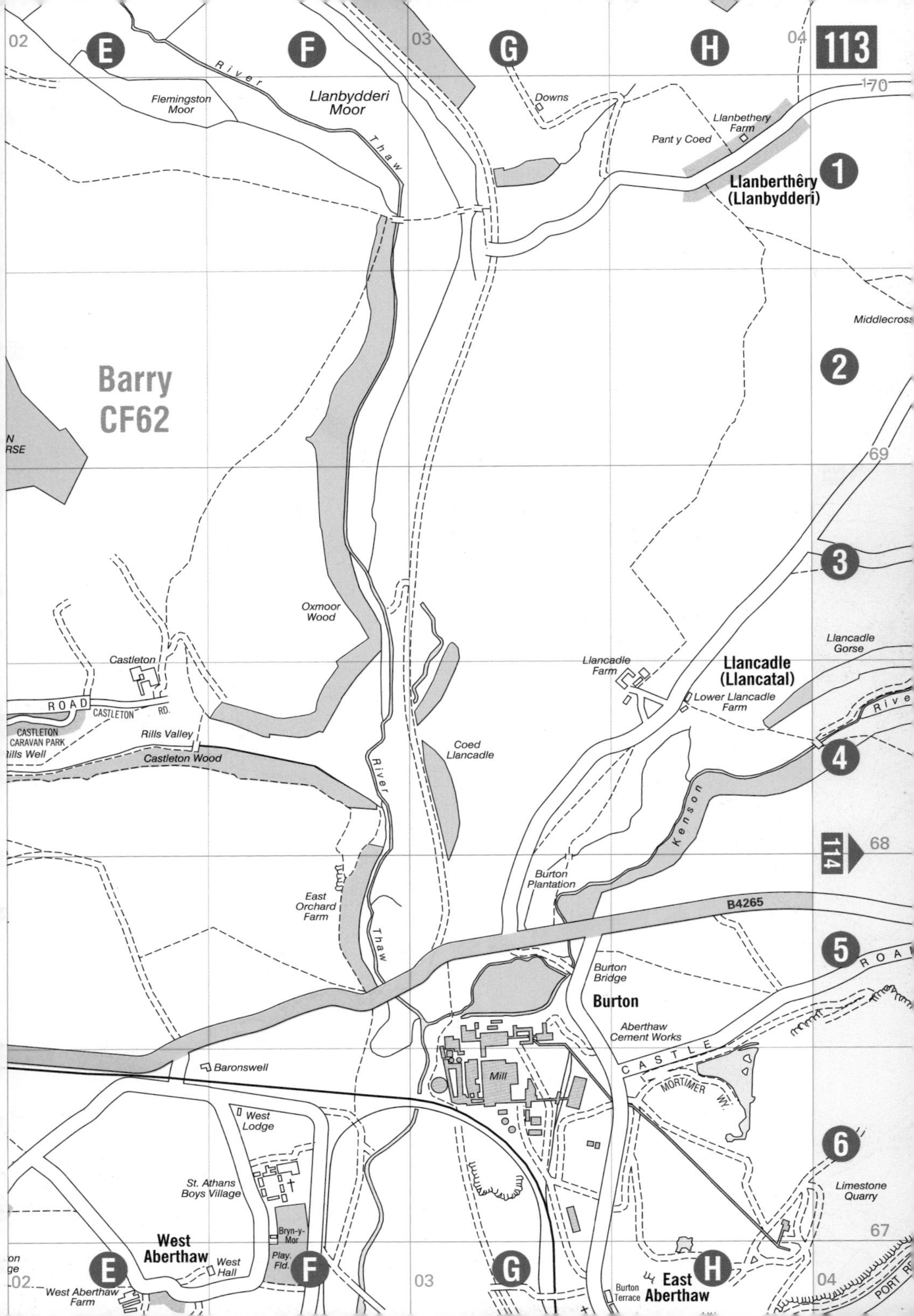
02
E
F
03
G
H
04
River
Flemingston Moor
Llanbydderi Moor
Thaw
Downs
Llanbethery Farm
Pant y Coed
170
1
Llanberthêry (Llanbydderi)
Middlecross
2
Barry CF62
69
3
Oxmoor Wood
Castleton
Llancadle Farm
Llancadle Gorse
Llancadle (Llancatal)
Lower Llancadle Farm
ROAD
CASTLETON
RD.
CASTLETON CARAVAN PARK
Rills Valley
Rills Well
Castleton Wood
Coed Llancadle
River
4
Kenson
114
68
Burton Plantation
East Orchard Farm
B4265
Thaw
5
Burton Bridge
Burton
Aberthaw Cement Works
CASTLE
Baronswell
Mill
MORTIMER WY.
West Lodge
6
St. Athans Boys Village
Limestone Quarry
Bryn-y-Mor
West Aberthaw
West Hall
Play. Fld.
67
E
F
G
H
02
03
04
West Aberthaw Farm
Burton Terrace
East Aberthaw
PORT

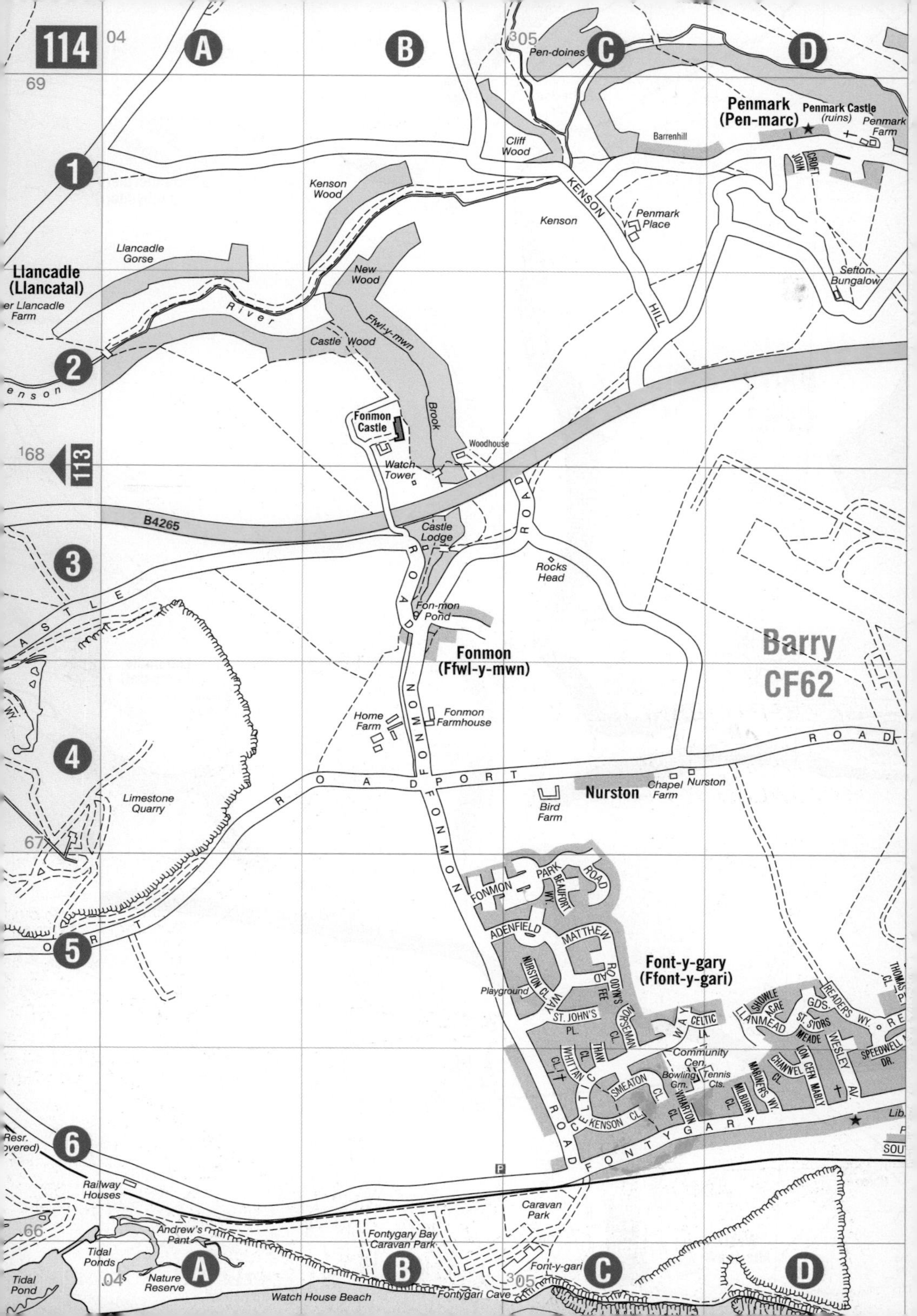
04
A
B
C
D
69
305
Pen-doines
Penmark
(Pen-marc)
Penmark Castle
(ruins)
Penmark
Farm
Barrenhill
JOHN
CROFT
Cliff
Wood
1
KENSON
Kenson
Wood
Kenson
Penmark
Place
Llancadle
Gorse
Llancadle
(Llancatal)
er Llancadle
Farm
New
Wood
River
Ffwl-y-mwn
Castle Wood
HILL
Sefton
Bungalow
2
enson
Fonmon
Castle
Brook
Woodhouse
168
113
Watch
Tower
B4265
Castle
Lodge
ROAD
3
Rocks
Head
ASTLE
Fon-mon
Pond
Fonmon
(Ffwl-y-mwn)
Barry
CF62
FONMON
Home
Farm
Fonmon
Farmhouse
4
ROAD
PORT
Limestone
Quarry
Nurston
Chapel
Farm
Nurston
Bird
Farm
67
FONMON
PARK
ROAD
BEAUFORT
WY.
ADENFIELD
MATTHEW
5
Font-y-gary
(Ffont-y-gari)
NURSTON CL.
ODYN'S
FEE
Playground
WAY
ST. JOHN'S
PL.
NORSEMAN
CL.
WAY
CELTIC
LA.
SHOWLE
ACRE
LLANMEAD
GDS.
ST. SYORS
MEADE
READERS WY.
THOMAS
CL.
WESLEY
AV.
SPEEDWELL
DR.
Community
Cen.
Bowling
Grn.
Tennis
Cts.
THAW
CL.
WHITTAN
CL.
CELTIC
SMEATON
CL.
KENSON CL.
WHARTON
CL.
MILBURN
CL.
MARINERS WY.
CHANNEL
CL.
LON CEFN MABLY
FONTYGARY
ROAD
Lib.
SOU
6
Resr.
(covered)
Railway
Houses
Caravan
Park
66
Andrew's
Pant
Fontygary Bay
Caravan Park
Tidal
Ponds
Tidal
Pond
Nature
Reserve
04
305
Font-y-gari
Watch House Beach
Fontygari Cave

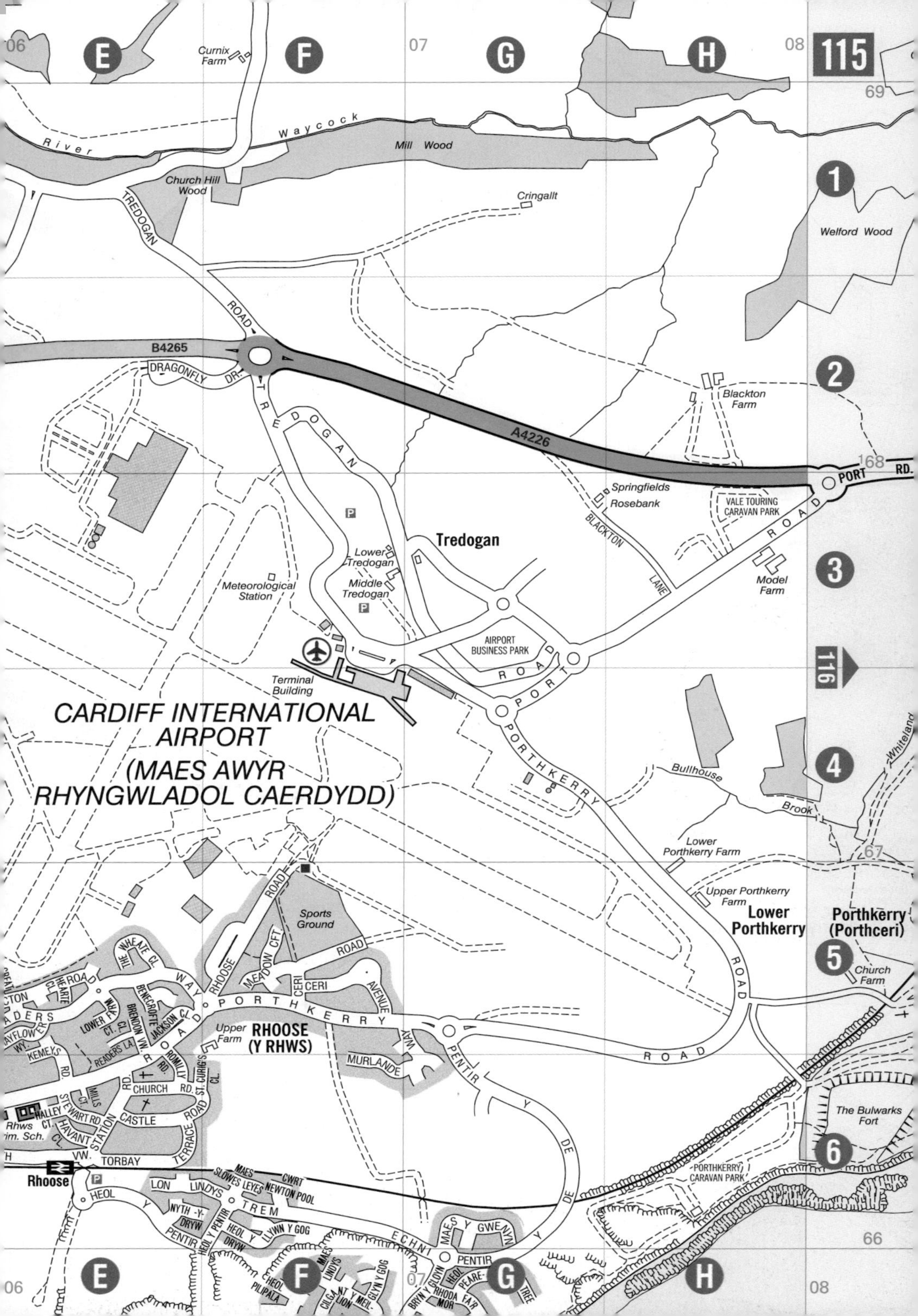

E
F
G
H
06
07
08
69
168
67
66
1
2
3
4
5
6
Curnix Farm
River Waycock
Mill Wood
Church Hill Wood
TREDOGAN ROAD
Cringallt
Welford Wood
B4265
DRAGONFLY DR.
A4226
Blackton Farm
PORT RD.
Springfields
Rosebank
VALE TOURING CARAVAN PARK
BLACKTON LANE
PORT ROAD
Model Farm
Tredogan
Lower Tredogan
Middle Tredogan
Meteorological Station
AIRPORT BUSINESS PARK
Terminal Building
CARDIFF INTERNATIONAL AIRPORT
(MAES AWYR RHYNGWLADOL CAERDYDD)
116
PORTHKERRY
Bullhouse
Brook
Whiteland
Lower Porthkerry Farm
Upper Porthkerry Farm
Lower Porthkerry
Porthkerry (Porthceri)
Church Farm
Sports Ground
MEADOW CFT.
CERI AVENUE
CERI ROAD
RHOOSE ROAD
RHOOSE WAY
PORTHKERRY ROAD
Upper Farm
RHOOSE (Y RHWS)
MURLANDE WAY
PENTIR Y DE
The Bulwarks Fort
PORTHKERRY CARAVAN PARK
THE WHEATE CL.
HEARTE CL.
BENECROFTE
BRENDON VW.
LOWER FRY CT. CL.
JACKSON CL.
ROMILLY RD.
READERS LA.
KEMEYS RD.
MAYFLOWER WY.
CHURCH RD.
ST. CURIG'S CL.
MILLS CT.
STEWART RD.
CASTLE
TERRACE ROAD
HALLEY CT.
HAVANT CL.
STATION
Rhws Prim. Sch.
TORBAY VW.
Rhoose
HEOL Y
LON LINDYS
SLOWES LEYES
MAES CWRT
NEWTON POOL
TREM ECHNI
NYTH -Y- DRYW
HEOL Y PENTIR
HEOL Y DRYW
PENTIR
LLWYN Y GOG
MAES Y GWENYN
PENTIR
HEOL PILIPALA
MAES LINDYS
CILGANT Y MEILLION
GLYN Y GOG
BRYN Y GLOYN
HEOL PEARE-TREE
RHODA FAR MOR

Coed yr Ychen
104
Middleton Plantation
WAYCOCK A4226
Walters Farm
Welford Wood
Middleton Wood
ROAD
WAYCOCK CROSS
PORT
New Farm
Green Farm
Ty-newydd Farm
STRADLING CL.
RHEIDOL
CLEDWEN CL.
PONTYPR
ST. JAMES CRES.
WAY
TALWG
Broad Cl.
NANT
Bowl. Grn.
Ten. Cts.
Blackton Farm
Welford
PORT A4226
Cwm-cidy Farm
CWM-CIDY LANE
Mill Wood
FFORDD
FOREST DR.
CLOS CWM BARRI
FOREST VW.
HEOL MR. FOREST
VALE TOURING CARAVAN PARK
PORT ROAD
Farm
Cwm Cidi
PARK
Barry
Cwm-cidy Cotts.
COUNTRY
Nant Talwg
115
CF62
West Ridge
Whitelands Brook
Barry Brook
Cwm Barri
Coed yr Odyn
Coed Yr. Odyn
PARK
Bullhouse
Brook
Knock-man-down Wood
PORTHKERRY
RISE
AWELON
BRON
TAN-Y-FRON
PORTH-Y-CASTE
WESTWARD
WLK. BULL CLIFF
CLIFF WOOD VW.
SW-Y-MOR
Cliff Wood
DINGLE CL.
Upper Porthkerry Farm
Lower Porthkerry
Porthkerry Viaduct
Westward Corner
MARINE
TREM-Y-DON
MIN-Y-MOR
MARINE DR.
PEN-Y-BRYN
ROAD
Porthkerry (Porthceri)
Pitch & Putt Course
Golden Stairs
Bull Cliff
Devil's Church
DRIVE
Birch Grove Wood
Church Farm
KNAP
PORTHKERRY
Porthkerry House
Bullcliff Rocks
CAR
Glan Hafren
Pebble Beach
TERRACE
The Bulwarks Fort
PORTHKERRY CARAVAN PARK
BRISTOL CHANNEL
(MÔR HAFREN)
A
B
C
D
1
2
3
4
5
6
08
09
66
67
168
69

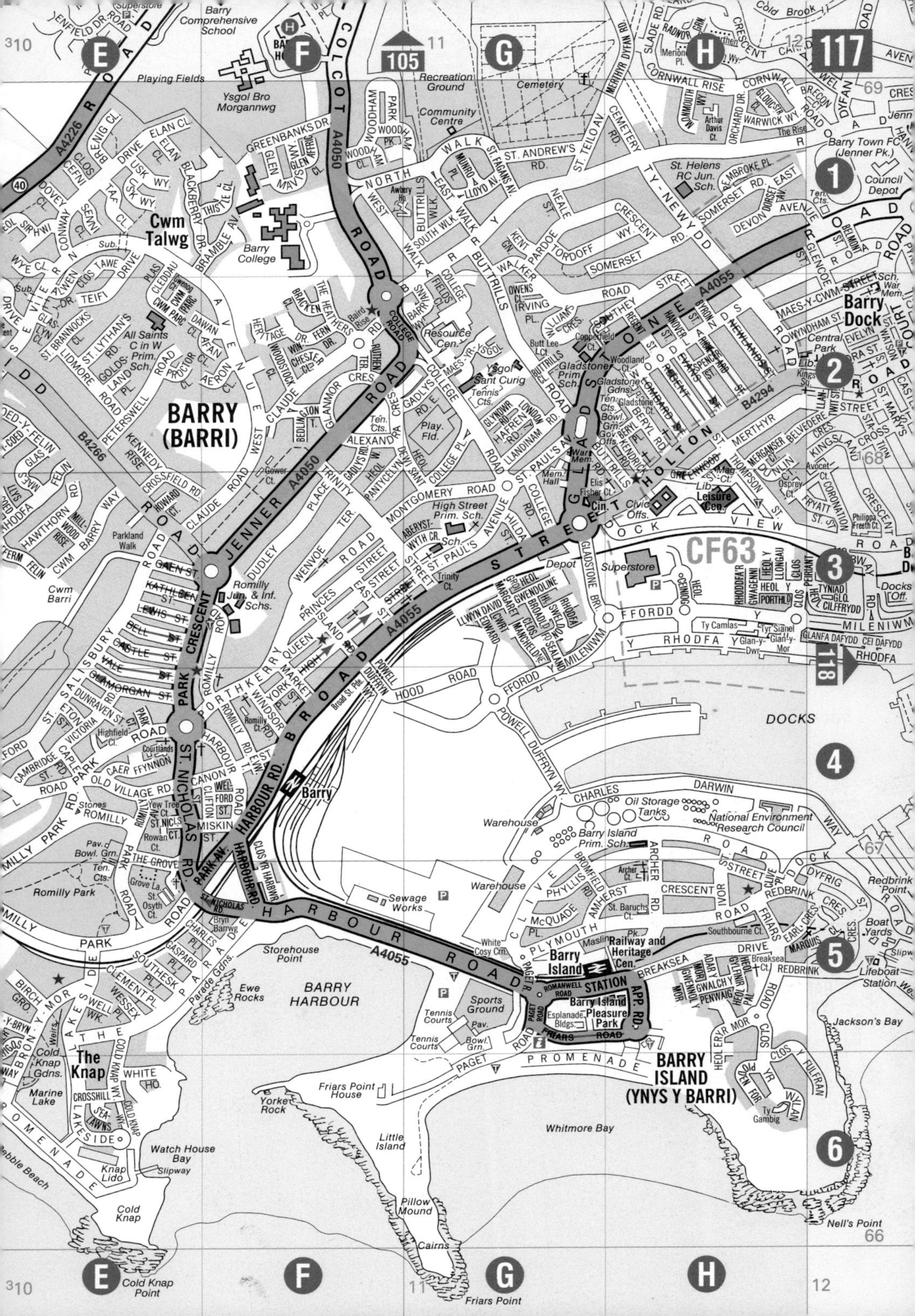

BARRY (BARRI)
BARRY ISLAND (YNYS Y BARRI)
CF63
105
118
Barry Dock
Barry Island
Barry
Cwm Talwg
The Knap
Cwm Barri
Romilly Park
BARRY HARBOUR
DOCKS
Whitmore Bay
Jackson's Bay
Nell's Point
Friars Point
Friars Point House
Little Island
Pillow Mound
Cairns
Yorke Rock
Cold Knap
Cold Knap Point
Watch House Bay
Knap Lido
Slipway
Marine Lake
Ewe Rocks
Storehouse Point
Redbrink Point
Boat Yards
Lifeboat Station
Barry Comprehensive School
Playing Fields
Ysgol Bro Morgannwg
Recreation Ground
Cemetery
Community Centre
Barry College
All Saints C in W Prim. Sch.
Barry Town FC (Jenner Pk.)
Council Depot
St. Helens RC Jun. Sch.
Romilly Jun. & Inf. Schs.
High Street Prim. Sch.
Gladstone Prim. Sch.
Ysgol Sant Curig
Resource Cen.
Superstore
Leisure Cen.
Civic Offs.
Oil Storage Tanks
National Environment Research Council
Barry Island Prim. Sch.
Warehouse
Sewage Works
Sports Ground
Tennis Courts
Railway and Heritage Cen.
Barry Island Pleasure Park
Esplanade Bldgs.
COLCOT ROAD
A4050
JENNER ROAD
BROAD STREET
A4055
HARBOUR ROAD
HOLTON ROAD
B4294
B4266
A4226
PARK CRESCENT
ST. NICHOLAS RD.
HARBOUR RD.
PARK AV.
GLADSTONE RD.
DOCK VIEW ROAD
PROMENADE
PAGET ROAD
FRIARS ROAD
APP. RD.
STATION
BREAKSEA DRIVE
PLYMOUTH RD.
CLIVE ROAD
DOCK ROAD
CHARLES DARWIN WAY
POWELL DUFFRYN WY.
FFORDD Y MILENIWM
Y RHODFA
MONTGOMERY ROAD
ST. PAUL'S AVENUE
COLLEGE ROAD
NORTH WALK
WEST WALK
BUTTRILLS ROAD
TY-NEWYDD ROAD
SOMERSET RD.
ST. ANDREW'S RD.
GREENBANKS DR.
CLAUDE ROAD
AVENUE
PETERSWELL ROAD
ROMILLY PARK RD.
ST. SALISBURY ROAD
PORTHKERRY RD.
THE GROVE

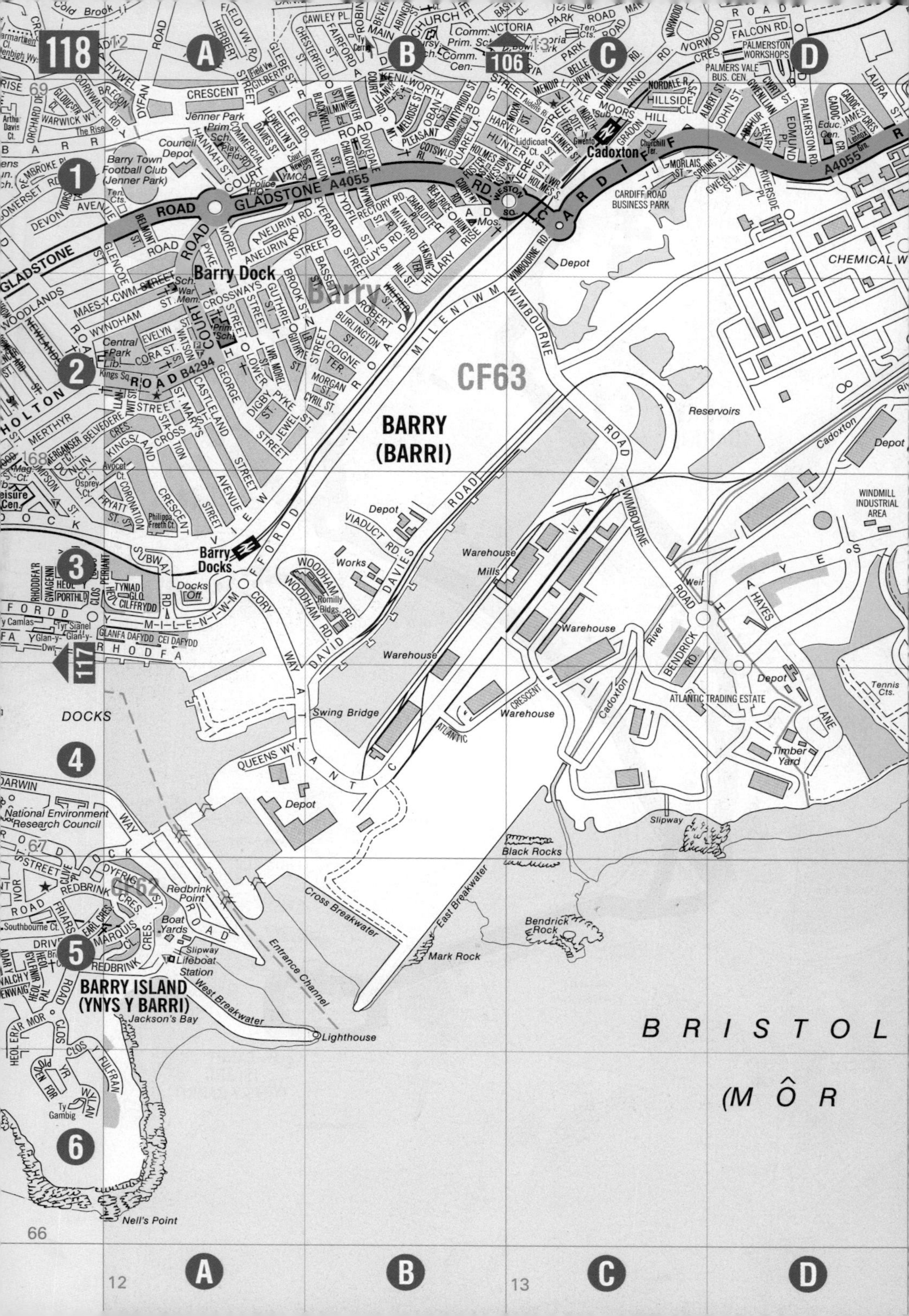
BARRY
(BARRI)
CF63
CF62
BARRY ISLAND
(YNYS Y BARRI)
Barry Dock
Barry Docks
Cadoxton
B R I S T O L
(M Ô R
DOCKS
GLADSTONE ROAD A4055
CARDIFF ROAD A4055
HOLTON ROAD B4294
MILENIWM
FFORDD Y MILENIWM
RHODFA
ATLANTIC WAY
WIMBOURNE ROAD
DAVIES ROAD
DAVID DAVIES ROAD
DOCK VIEW
COURT ROAD
QUEENS WY.
DARWIN WAY
HAYES ROAD
BENDRICK RD.
WOODHAM RD.
VIADUCT RD.
CHEMICAL W
Jenner Park
Barry Town Football Club (Jenner Park)
Council Depot
Central Park
Kings Sq.
Swing Bridge
Warehouse
Mills
Works
Depot
Reservoirs
ATLANTIC TRADING ESTATE
WINDMILL INDUSTRIAL AREA
CARDIFF ROAD BUSINESS PARK
PALMERSTON WORKSHOPS
PALMERS VALE BUS. CEN.
Timber Yard
Tennis Cts.
Slipway
Black Rocks
Bendrick Rock
Mark Rock
East Breakwater
Cross Breakwater
West Breakwater
Entrance Channel
Lighthouse
Jackson's Bay
Nell's Point
Redbrink Point
Boat Yards
Lifeboat Station
National Environment Research Council
Ty Gambig
Romilly Bldgs.
Docks Off.
Leisure Cen.
Philippa Freeth Ct.
106
117
A
B
C
D
1
2
3
4
5
6
12
13
66
67
69
168

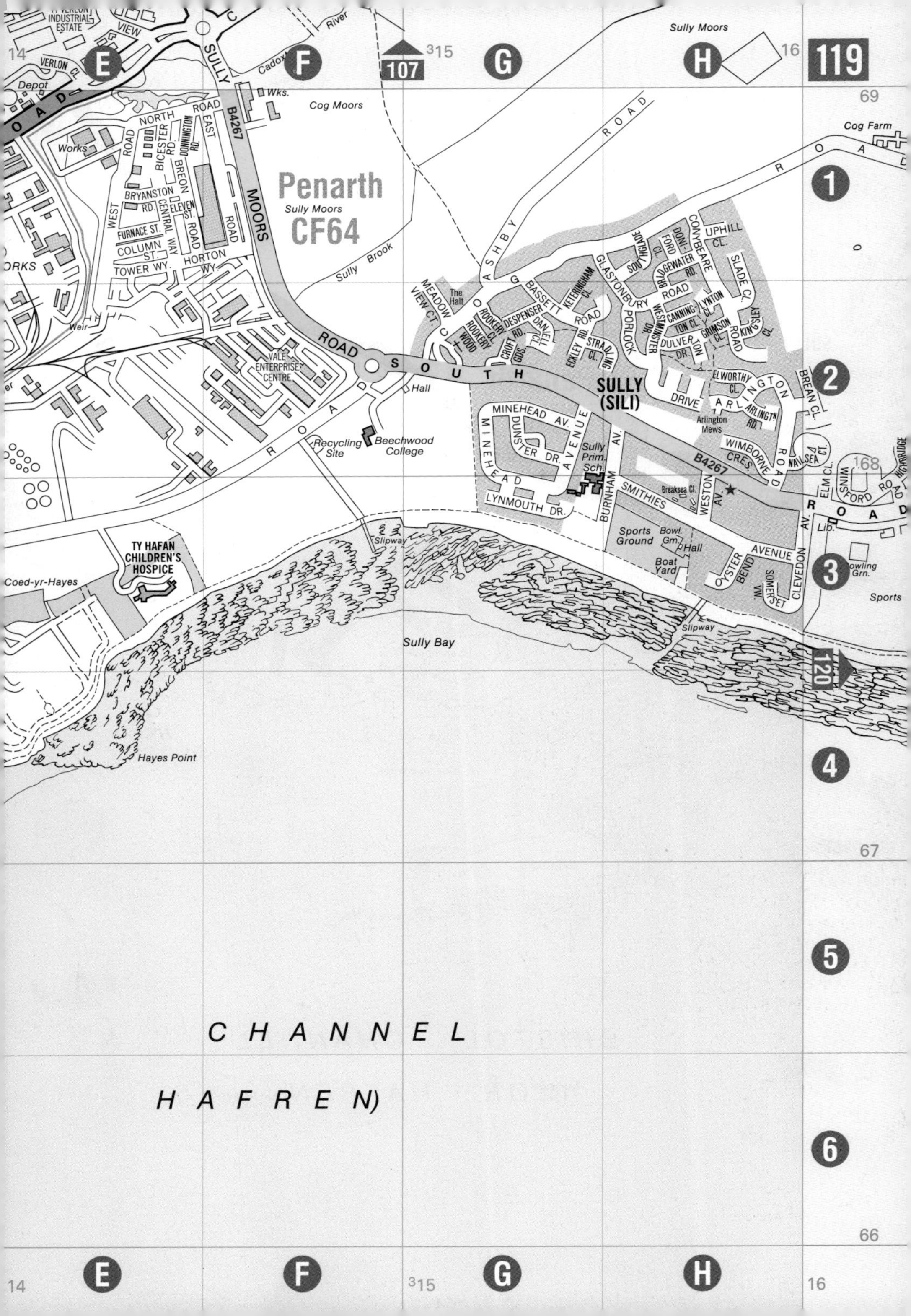
Penarth
CF64
Sully Moors
SULLY
(SILI)
CHANNEL
HAFREN)
Sully Bay
Hayes Point
Cog Moors
Cog Farm
TY HAFAN
CHILDREN'S
HOSPICE
Coed-yr-Hayes
VALE
ENTERPRISE
CENTRE
Recycling
Site
Beechwood
College
Sully
Prim.
Sch.
Sports
Ground
Bowl.
Grn.
Boat
Yard
Hall
Slipway
Works
Wks.
Depot
VERLON CL.
INDUSTRIAL
ESTATE
VIEW
SULLY MOORS ROAD
B4267
SOUTH ROAD
ASHBY ROAD
NORTH ROAD
EAST ROAD
BICESTER RD.
DONNINGTON RD.
BREON
BRYANSTON RD.
ELEVEN ST.
WEST ROAD
FURNACE ST.
CENTRAL WAY
COLUMN ST.
TOWER WY.
HORTON WY.
Sully Brook
Weir
Cadoxton River
MEADOW VIEW CT.
The Halt
ROOKERY CL.
ROOKERY WOOD
CROFT GDS.
DESPENSER RD.
DANVELL CL.
BASSETT ROAD
KETERINGHAM CL.
ECKLEY RD.
STRADLING CL.
GLASTONBURY ROAD
SOUTHGATE
BRIDGEWATER RD.
DONI-FORD CL.
CONYBEARE
UPHILL CL.
SLADE CL.
KINGSLEY CL.
PORLOCK
WESTMINSTER DR.
CANNING-TON CL.
LYNTON CL.
GRIMSON CL.
DULVER-TON DR.
ELWORTHY CL.
ARLINGTON DRIVE
ARLINGTON RD.
Arlington Mews
BREAN CL.
WIMBORNE CRES.
NAILSEA CT.
ELM CL.
WINSFORD RD.
HIGHBRIDGE
MINEHEAD AV.
MINEHEAD AVENUE
DUNSTER DR.
LYNMOUTH DR.
BURNHAM AV.
SMITHIES
Breaksea Cl.
WESTON AV.
CLEVEDON AV.
AVENUE
OYSTER BEND
SOMERSET VW.
Lib.
Bowling Grn.
Sports
107
120
14
315
16
66
67
68
69

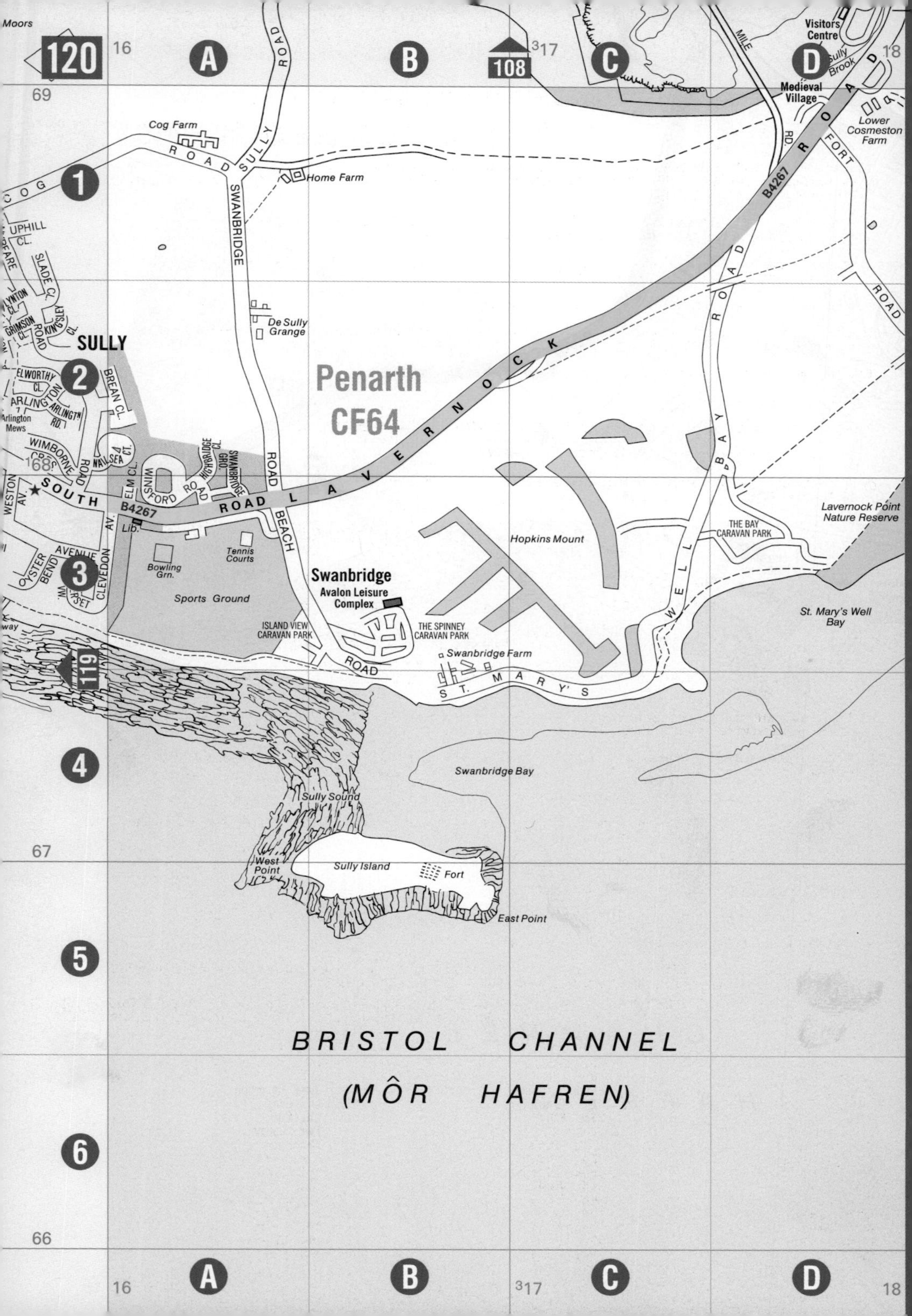
Moors
16
A
B
108
317
C
D
18
69
Cog Farm
ROAD SULLY ROAD
Home Farm
Visitors Centre
Sully Brook
Medieval Village
Lower Cosmeston Farm
FORT RD.
B4267 ROAD
COG
1
UPHILL CL.
SLADE CL.
SWANBRIDGE
De Sully Grange
ROAD
SULLY
2
ELWORTHY CL.
ARLINGTON
ARLINGTN RD.
Arlington Mews
BREAN CL.
Penarth
CF64
LAVERNOCK ROAD
BAY ROAD
WIMBORNE CRES.
NAILSEA CT.
ELM CL.
WINSFORD RO AD
HIGHBRIDGE CL.
SWANBRIDGE GRO.
168
WESTON AV.
SOUTH
B4267
Lib.
BEACH
Tennis Courts
Bowling Grn.
Hopkins Mount
Lavernock Point Nature Reserve
THE BAY CARAVAN PARK
AVENUE
OYSTER BEND
3
CLEVEDON AV.
Sports Ground
Swanbridge
Avalon Leisure Complex
WELL
St. Mary's Well Bay
ISLAND VIEW CARAVAN PARK
THE SPINNEY CARAVAN PARK
Swanbridge Farm
119
ROAD
ST. MARY'S
4
Swanbridge Bay
Sully Sound
67
West Point
Sully Island
Fort
East Point
5
BRISTOL CHANNEL
(MÔR HAFREN)
6
66

INDEX

Including Streets, Places & Areas, Hospitals etc., Industrial Estates,
Selected Flats & Walkways, Service Areas, Stations and Selected Places of Interest.

HOW TO USE THIS INDEX

1. Each street name is followed by its Postcode District, then by its Locality abbreviation(s) and then by its map reference; e.g. **Aberdaron Rd.** CF3: Rum . . . .2B **88** is in the CF3 Postcode District and the Rumney Locality and is to be found in square 2B on page **88**. The page number is shown in bold type.

2. A strict alphabetical order is followed in which Av., Rd., St., etc. (though abbreviated) are read in full and as part of the street name; e.g. **Ash Cl.** appears after **Ashchurch Row** but before **Ashcroft Cres.**

3. Streets and a selection of flats and walkways too small to be shown on the maps, appear in the index with the thoroughfare to which it is connected shown in brackets; e.g. **Alton Ter.** *NP4: P'pool . . . .2B **6** (off Osborne Rd.)*

4. Addresses that are in more than one part are referred to as not continuous.

5. Places and areas are shown in the index in **BLUE TYPE** and the map reference is to the actual map square in which the town centre or area is located and not to the place name shown on the map; e.g. **ABERTRIDWR 2E 27**

6. An example of a selected place of interest is **Amgueddfa Pontypool Mus. 2C 6**

7. An example of a station is **Aber Station (Rail) 1B 46**

8. Service Areas are shown in the index in **BOLD CAPITAL TYPE**; e.g. **CARDIFF GATE SERVICE AREA 3H 73**

9. An example of a hospital or hospice is **BARRY HOSPITAL 6F 105**

10. Map references for entries that appear on large scale pages **4** & **5** are shown first, with small scale references shown in brackets; e.g. **Adams Ct.** CF24: Card 4G **5** (4C **96**)

MYNEGAI

Yn cynnwys Strydoedd, Lleoedd ac Ardaloedd, Ysbytai ac ati., Stadau Diwydiannol,
Fflatiau a Llwybrau Troed dethol, Ardaloedd Gwasanaeth, Gorsafoedd a Detholiad o Fannau Diddorol.

SUD I DDEFNYDDIOR'R MYNEGAI HWN

1. Dilynir pob enw stryd gan ei Ardal Cod Post, wedyn gan fyrfodd(au) ei Leoliad ac wedyn gan ei gyfeirnod map; e.e. mae **Aberdaron Rd.** CF3: Rum . . . .2B **88** yn Ardal Cod Post CF3 a Lleoliad Rumney a gellir dod o hyd iddi yn sgwâr 2B ar dudalen **88**. Dangosir Rhif y Dudalen mewn teip trwm.

2. Glynir yn gaeth wrth drefn y wyddor, gyda Av., Rd., St., ayb (er eu bod wedi eu talfyrru) yn cael eu darllen yn llawn ac fel rhan o enw'r stryd; e.e. mae **Ash Cl.** yn ymddangos ar ôl **Ashchurch Row** ond cyn **Ashcroft Cres.**

3. Mae strydoedd a detholiad o fflatiau a llwybrau troed sy'n rhy fychan i'w dangos ar y mapiau, yn ymddangos yn y mynegai gyda'r dramwyfa y mae'n gysylltiedig â hi wedi'i dangos mewn cromfachau; e.e. **Alton Ter.** *NP4: P'pool . . . .2B **6** (off Osborne Rd.)*

4. Cyfeirir at gyfeiriadau sydd mewn mwy nag un rhan fel cyfeiriadau nan ydynt yn barhaus.

5. Dangosir ardaloedd a lleoedd yn y mynegai mewn **TEIP GLAS** ac mae'r cyfeirnod map yn cyfeirio at y sgwâr ar y map lle mae lleoliad canol y dref neu'r ardal ac nid at yr enw lle a ddangosir ar y map; e.e. **ABERTRIDWR 2E 27**

6. Enghraifft o fan diddorol dethol yw **Amgueddfa Pontypool Mus. 2C 6**

7. Enghraifft o gorsaf yw **Aber Station (Rail) 1B 46**

8. Ardaloedd Gwasanaeth yn y mynegai mewn **PRIFLYTHYRENNAU TEIP BRAS**; e.e. **CARDIFF GATE SERVICE AREA 3H 73**

9. Enghraifft o Ysbyty neu Hosbis yw **BARRY HOSPITAL 6F 105**

10. Mae cyfeirnodau map ar gyfer cofnodion sy'n ymddangos ar dudalennau ar raddfa fawr **4** & **5** yn cael eu dangos gyntaf, gyda chyfeirnodau map ar raddfa fechan yn cael eu dangos mewn cromfachau; e.e. **Adams Ct.** CF24: Card 4G **5** (4C **96**)

GENERAL ABBREVIATIONS *Talfyriadau Cyffredinol*

App. : Approach
Arc. : Arcade
Av. : Avenue
Bri. : Bridge
Bldg. : Building
Bldgs. : Buildings
Bungs. : Bungalows
Bus. : Business
Cvn. : Caravan
Cen. : Centre
Chu. : Church
Circ. : Circle
Cl. : Close
Comn. : Common
Cnr. : Corner
Cotts. : Cottages
Ct. : Court
Cres. : Crescent
Cft. : Croft
Dr. : Drive
E. : East
Emb. : Embankment
Ent. : Enterprise
Est. : Estate
Fld. : Field
Flds. : Fields
Gdn. : Garden
Gdns. : Gardens
Gth. : Garth
Ga. : Gate
Gt. : Great
Grn. : Green
Gro. : Grove
Hgts. : Heights
Ho. : House
Ho's. : Houses
Ind. : Industrial
Info. : Information
Junc. : Junction
La. : Lane
Lit. : Little
Lwr. : Lower
Mnr. : Manor
Mans. : Mansions
Mkt. : Market
Mdw. : Meadow
Mdws. : Meadows
M. : Mews
Mt. : Mount
Mus. : Museum
Nth. : North

General Abbreviations *Talfyriadau Cyffredinol*

Pde. : Parade
Pk. : Park
Pas. : Passage
Pl. : Place
Pct. : Precinct
Res. : Residential
Ri. : Rise
Rd. : Road
Rdbt. : Roundabout
Shop. : Shopping
Sth. : South
Sq. : Square
St. : Street
Ter. : Terrace
Trad. : Trading
Up. : Upper
Va. : Vale
Vw. : View
Vs. : Villas
Vis. : Visitors
Wlk. : Walk
W. : West
Yd. : Yard

LOCALITY ABBREVIATIONS *Byrfoddau Lleoliadau*

Abers : **Abersychan**
A'thin : **Aberthin**
Abert : **Abertridwr**
Barry : **Barry**
Bass : **Bassaleg**
B'ly : **Beachley**
Bed : **Beddau**
B'ws : **Bedwas**
Bet : **Bettws**
Bov : **Boverton**
Bryng : **Brynglas**
Bryns : **Brynsadler**
Brynt : **Brynteg**
Bul : **Bulwark**
C'ln : **Caerleon**
Caer : **Caerphilly**
C'ent : **Caerwent**
Cald : **Caldicot**
Cap L : **Capel Llanilltern**
Card : **Cardiff**
Cas : **Castleton**
Cat A : **Cat's Ash**
Cefn M : **Cefn Mably**
Chep : **Chepstow**
Chris : **Christchurch**
Chu V : **Church Village**
C'fydd : **Cilfynydd**
Coed : **Coedely**
Coed E : **Coed Eva**
Coedk : **Coedkernew**
C'bri : **Cowbridge**
Cre : **Creigiau**
Cri : **Crick**
C'iog : **Croesyceiliog**
C Inn : **Cross Inn**
Cros K : **Cross Keys**
Cul C : **Culverhouse Cross**
C'avn : **Cwmavon**
C'brn : **Cwmbran**
C'crn : **Cwmcarn**
Cyn : **Cyncoed**
Din P : **Dinas Powys**
Drae : **Draethen**
Duf : **Duffryn**
E Abe : **East Aberthaw**
E Isaf : **Efail Isaf**
E Bre : **Eglwys-Brewis**
Ely : **Ely**
F'wtr : **Fairwater**
F'ton : **Flemingston**
Fon : **Fonmon**
Gile : **Gileston**
Glas : **Glascoed**
Glync : **Glyncoch**
Glynt : **Glyntaff**
Gold : **Goldcliff**
G'mdw : **Greenmeadow**
Grif : **Griffithstown**
Groes F : **Groes-Faen**
Gro-w : **Groes-wen**
Gwae G : **Gwaelod-y-garth**
Heath : **Heath**
H'lys : **Henllys**
Hens : **Hensol**
H'bush : **Hollybush**
Kem I : **Kemeys Inferior**
L'stne : **Langstone**
Lave : **Lavernock**
Leck : **Leckwith**
L'vne : **Lisvane**
Lit M : **Little Mill**
L'thian : **Llanblethian**
L'brad : **Llanbradach**
L'dff : **Llandaff**
Llan N : **Llandaff North**
L'veth : **Llandegveth**
L'nny : **Llandevenny**
L'dgh : **Llandough**
L'dyrn : **Llanedeyrn**
Llanf : **Llanfrechfa**
L'harry : **Llanharry**
L'shn : **Llanishen**
L'maes : **Llanmaes**
L'rmy : **Llanrumney**
L'tnam : **Llantarnam**
L'sant : **Llantrisant**
Llan F : **Llantwit Fardre**
Llan M : **Llantwit Major**
L'wrn : **Llanwern**
L'rfn : **Llanyrafon**
Mac : **Machen**
Maen : **Maendy**
Magor : **Magor**
Malp : **Malpas**
M'fld : **Marshfield**
Math : **Mathern**
Mic P : **Michaelston-le-Pit**
Mic F : **Michaelston-y-Fedw**
Mis : **Miskin**
Morg : **Morganstown**
Moun : **Mounton**
Mwy : **Mwyndy**
N'grw : **Nantgarw**
Nash : **Nash**
New I : **New Inn**
Newp : **Newport**
Oakf : **Oakfield**
Old M : **Old St Mellons**
P'seg : **Pantygasseg**
P'rth : **Penarth**
P'ark : **Penmark**
Pent : **Pentwyn**
P'rch : **Pentyrch**
Pen c : **Pen-y-coedcae**
P'garn : **Penygarn**
Pen L : **Pen-y-Lan**
P'rheol : **Penyrheol**
Pet W : **Peterstone Wentlooge**
P'hir : **Ponthir**
Pnwd : **Pontnewydd**
P'nydd : **Pontnewynydd**
Pontp : **Pontprennau**
Pon'run : **Pontrhydyrun**
P'clun : **Pontyclun**
P'pool : **Pontypool**
P'prdd : **Pontypridd**
P'waun : **Pontywaun**
Pskwt : **Portskewett**
Pwllm : **Pwllmeyric**
Rad : **Radyr**
Red : **Redwick**
R'ina : **Rhiwbina**
R'drn : **Rhiwderin**
R'son : **Rhiwsaeson**
Rho : **Rhoose**
R'fln : **Rhydyfelin**
Ris : **Risca**
Roger : **Rogerstone**
Rog : **Rogiet**
Rud : **Rudry**
Rum : **Rumney**
St And : **St Andrews Major**
St Ath : **St Athan**
St Bri E : **St Bride's-super-Ely**
St Bri W : **St Bride's Wentlooge**
St D : **St Dials**
St F : **St Fagans**
St G : **St George's**
St H : **St Hilary**
St M : **St Mellons**
St N : **St Nicholas**
Seba : **Sebastopol**
Sed : **Sedbury**
Sen : **Senghenydd**
Sud : **Sudbrook**
Sul : **Sully**
S'dge : **Swanbridge**
Taff W : **Taff's Well**
T Grn : **Talbot Green**
Taly : **Talygarn**
Thorn : **Thornhill**
Tong : **Tongwynlais**
Tont : **Tonteg**
T'fail : **Tonyrefail**
T'gan : **Tredogan**
T'rest : **Treforest**
Treh : **Trehafod**
Tret : **Trethomas**
Trev : **Trevethin**
Tut : **Tutshill**
Two L : **Two Locks**
Twyn : **Twyn-yr-odyn**
Ty C : **Ty Canol**
T Coch : **Ty Coch**
Tyle : **Tyle-garw**
Under : **Underwood**
Undy : **Undy**
Up Bo : **Upper Boat**
Up Chu : **Upper Church Village**
Up Cwm : **Upper Cwmbran**
Up R : **Upper Race**
Wel : **Welsh St Donats**
Wen : **Wenvoe**
W Abe : **West Aberthaw**
Whit : **Whitchurch**
W'son : **Whitson**
Wilc : **Wilcrick**
Y'erdy : **Ynysmaerdy**
Y'bwl : **Ynysybwl**

1st The Queen's Dragoon Guards
Regimental Mus. . . . . .3C **4 (3A 96)**

A

Abbey Cl. CF15: Taff W 1F **69**
Abbey Ct. CF38: Chu V 2E **43**
Abbey Farm La. NP44: L'tnam 6B **12**
Abbey Grn. NP44: Oakf 5H **11**
Abbey Gro. NP44: L'tnam 1B **20**
Abbey Rd. NP19: Newp 3B **38**
NP44: C'brn 3G **11**
Abbots M. NP20: Newp 6B **36**
Aberaeron Cl. CF62: Barry 5A **106**
Aberbran Rd. CF14: Llan N 5E **85**
Aberconway Hall CF10: Card 1H **95**
Abercynon St. CF11: Card 1A **102**
Aberdare Hall CF10: Card 2H **95**
Aberdaron Rd. CF3: Rum 2B **88**
Aberdore Rd. CF14: Llan N 5E **85**
Aberdovey Cl. CF64: Din P 2A **108**
Aberdovey St. CF24: Card 4E **97**
Aberdulais Cres. CF14: Llan N 5D **84**
Aberdulais Rd. CF14: Llan N 5D **84**
Aberfawr Rd. CF83: Abert 2E **27**
Aberfawr Ter. CF83: Abert 2E **27**
Abergele Cl. CF3: Rum 1C **88**
Abergele Rd. CF3: Rum 2B **88**
Abernethy Cl. CF3: St M 6E **75**

Aberporth Rd. CF14: Llan N 4D **84**
Aber Station (Rail) 1B **46**
Aber St. CF11: Card 1A **102**
Aberteifi Cl. CF14: Llan N 5E **85**
Aberteifi Cres. CF14: Llan N 5E **85**
Aberthaw Av. NP19: Newp 5B **38**
Aberthaw Circ. NP19: Newp 5H **37**
Aberthaw Cl. NP19: Newp 4A **38**
Aberthaw Dr. NP19: Newp 5H **37**
Aberthaw Rd. CF5: Ely 4G **93**
NP19: Newp 4H **37**
ABERTHIN 2F **91**
Aberthin La. CF71: A'thin, C'bri 4F **91**
Aberthin Rd. CF71: A'thin, C'bri 4D **90**
ABERTRIDWR 2E **27**
Aberystwyth Cres. CF62: Barry 3G **117**
Aberystwyth St. CF24: Card 4E **97**
Abingdon St. CF63: Barry 6B **106**
Acacia Av. NP19: Newp 4H **37**
NP26: Undy 3E **59**
Acacia Sq. NP19: Newp 4H **37**
Acacia St. CF37: R'fln 4G **25**
Academic Av. CF14: Heath 4G **85**
Acer Av. CF38: Llan F 6C **42**
Acer Way NP10: Roger 3A **34**
Acorn Cvn. & Camping Pk.
CF61: Llan M 5C **110**
Acorn Cl. CF72: Mis 6F **65**
NP10: Roger 2B **34**
Acorn Gro. CF23: Pontp 4G **73**
CF38: Chu V 3E **43**
Acorns, The CF14: Thorn 2G **71**
Adams Ct. CF24: Card 4G **5** (4C **96**)
Adamscroft Pl. CF10: Card 4G **5** (4C **96**)
ADAMSDOWN 4H **5** (4C **96**)
Adamsdown La. CF24: Card 4H **5** (4C **96**)
Adamsdown Pl. CF24: Card 4H **5** (4D **96**)
Adamsdown Sq. CF24: Card 4H **5** (4C **96**)
Adam St. CF24: Card 5F **5** (4B **96**)
Adar y Mor CF62: Barry 5H **117**
Addicott Cl. CF5: Ely 4A **94**
Addison Av. CF72: L'harry 5A **78**
Addison Cres. CF5: Ely 4G **93**
Addison Way CF83: Tret, Mac 3B **30**
Adelaide Pl. CF10: Card 1B **102**
Adelaide St. CF10: Card 1B **102**
NP20: Newp 2C **36**
Adeline St. CF24: Card 3D **96**
NP20: Newp 1C **54**
Adenfield Way CF62: Rho 5B **114**
Adit Wlk. NP44: Pnwd 6C **8**
(not continuous)
Admiral Ho. CF24: Card 2G **5**
Adrian Boult Grn. NP19: Newp 5A **38**
Adventurer's Quay
CF10: Card 1D **102**
Aelfryn CF72: L'harry 5A **78**
Aelybryn CF37: P'prdd 5A **14**
Ael-y-Bryn CF15: P'rch 5H **67**
CF15: Rad 6F **69**
CF23: L'dyrn 3D **86**
CF38: Bed 4A **42**
CF83: Caer 4A **28**
CF83: Tret 3H **29**
Ael-y-Coed CF62: Barry 2D **116**
Aeron Cl. CF62: Barry 2F **117**
Afal Sur CF63: Barry 4B **106**
Afan Cl. CF62: Barry 2F **117**
Afon Cl. CF3: Old M 1B **74**
NP4: New I 6G **7**
Afon Ebbw Rd. NP10: Roger 2G **33**
Afon Gdns. NP18: P'hir 2G **21**
Afon Lwyd Cl. NP18: C'ln 4A **22**
Afon Mead NP10: Roger 3H **33**
Afon Ter. NP44: Pon'run 6F **9**
Africa Gdns. CF14: Card 5G **85**
Agate St. CF24: Card 3D **96**
Agincourt Rd. CF23: Pen L 1D **96**
Agincourt St. NP20: Newp 2B **36**
Agnes St. CF64: P'rth 6G **101**
Ailesbury St. NP20: Newp 2C **36**
Ainon Ct. CF24: Card 4E **97**
Aintree Dr. CF5: Ely 4B **94**
Airport Bus. Pk. CF62: T'gan 3G **115**
Alanbrooke Av. NP20: Malp 3A **20**
Alan Cl. NP10: Roger 5D **34**

Albany Ct. CF64: P'rth 1F **109**
Albany Ind. Est. NP20: Newp 2C **36**
Albany Rd. CF24: Card 1B **96**
Albany St. NP20: Newp 2C **36**
Albany Trad. Est. NP20: Newp 2C **36**
Alberta Pl. CF64: P'rth 3E **109**
Alberta Rd. CF64: P'rth 3F **109**
Albert Av. NP19: Newp 4E **37**
Albert Ct. NP19: Newp 4E **37**
Albert Cres. CF64: P'rth 1F **109**
Albert Rd. CF37: P'prdd 1B **24**
CF64: P'rth 1F **109**
Albert St. CF11: Card 3F **95**
(Delta St.)
CF11: Card 4F **95**
(Wellington St.)
CF63: Barry 1C **118**
NP20: Newp 6C **36**
Albert St. La. CF11: Card 4F **95**
Albert Ter. NP20: Newp 5B **36**
Albert Wlk. CF11: Card 4F **95**
Albion Cl. NP20: Newp 1D **54**
Albion Ct. CF37: C'fydd 4F **15**
NP20: Newp 1C **54**
Albion Ho. NP26: Cald 5C **60**
Albion Ind. Est. CF37: C'fydd 1F **15**
Albion Pl. NP4: P'nydd 1A **6**
Albion Rd. NP4: P'pool 4B **6**
Albion Sq. NP16: Chep 2E **63**
Albion St. NP20: Newp 1C **54**
Albion Way NP26: Magor 4C **58**
Alcock Cl. NP19: Newp 6G **37**
Alcove Wood NP16: Chep 2C **62**
Alderbrook CF23: Cyn 4D **72**
Alder Cl. NP4: New I 4H **7**
Alder Gro. CF38: Llan F 6C **42**
NP20: Malp 5B **20**
Alderney Ho. CF11: Card 4A **102**
Alderney St. NP20: Newp 2C **36**
Alder Rd. CF23: Card 5B **86**
CF72: L'harry 5A **78**
Alders, The NP44: L'rfn 4B **12**
Alderwood Cl. CF3: St M 6C **74**
Aldsworth Rd. CF5: Card, F'wtr 2B **94**
Aldwych Cl. CF14: Thorn 3G **71**
Aled Way CF62: St Ath 2C **112**
Alexander Ct. CF83: Caer 6E **29**
Alexander St. CF24: Card 1A **96**
Alexandra Ct. CF5: Card 3D **94**
CF64: P'rth 2F **109**
*NP20: Newp 1D **54***
(off Alexandra Rd.)
Alexandra Cres. CF62: Barry 2F **117**
Alexandra Ind. Est.
CF3: Rum 4B **88**
Alexandra La. NP20: Newp 2C **54**
Alexandra Rd. CF5: Card 4E **95**
CF37: T'rest 1D **24**
NP4: Seba 2E **9**
NP16: Bul 4F **63**
NP20: Newp 2C **54**
Alexandra Ter. CF38: Llan F 5C **42**
Alexandria CF11: Card 5H **101**
Alfreda Rd. CF14: Whit 3B **84**
Alfred St. CF24: Card 6B **86**
NP19: Newp 3D **36**
Alfred Ter. CF15: Taff W 2E **69**
Alianore Rd. NP26: Cald 6C **60**
Alice Cres. NP16: Bul 6G **63**
Alice St. CF10: Card 1B **102**
NP20: Newp 2C **54**
Alicia Cres. NP20: Newp 1E **55**
Allan Durst Cl. CF5: L'dff 4H **83**
Allen Cl. CF3: Old M 5C **74**
NP20: Bet 6E **19**
Allen Ct. CF61: Bov 3D **110**
Allensbank Cres. CF14: Card 5H **85**
Allensbank Ho. CF14: Card 5H **85**
Allensbank Rd. CF14: Card, Heath 5H **85**
Allens Ct. CF23: Cyn 1C **86**
Allerton St. CF11: Card 6A **4** (5G **95**)
Allied Ind. Pk. CF24: Card 4F **97**
Alltmawr Rd. CF23: Cyn 1C **86**
Allt Wen CF14: R'ina 5B **70**
ALLT-YR-YN 4H **35**
Allt-yr-yn Av. NP20: Newp 4G **35**

Allt-yr-yn Cl. NP20: Newp 3A **36**
Allt-yr-yn Ct. NP20: Newp 3A **36**
Allt-yr-yn Cres. NP20: Newp 2A **36**
Allt-yr-yn Hgts. NP20: Newp 3H **35**
Allt-yr-yn Nature Reserve 3H **35**
Allt-yr-yn Rd. NP20: Newp 3H **35**
Allt-yr-yn Vw. NP20: Newp 4G **35**
Allt-yr-yn Way NP20: Newp 2A **36**
Allt y Wennol CF23: Pontp 4F **73**
Allt y Wiwer CF38: Chu V 3E **43**
Alma Cl. NP20: Newp 6C **36**
Alma Dr. NP16: Bul 6G **63**
Alma Pl. NP4: Seba 2E **9**
Alma Rd. CF23: Pen L 6C **86**
Alma St. CF83: Mac 2G **31**
NP20: Newp 6C **36**
Alma Ter. CF38: Chu V 3F **43**
Almond Av. NP11: Ris 5F **17**
Almond Cl. CF38: Llan F 5C **42**
Almond Dr. CF23: Pent 4F **73**
NP20: Malp 4A **20**
Alpha Pl. CF37: P'prdd 5D **14**
Alpha Rd. NP16: Bul 4F **63**
Alpha St. CF37: P'prdd 5D **14**
Alps Quarry Rd.
CF5: Wen 3E **99**
Altair Ho. CF10: Card 1D **102**
Althorp Dr. CF64: P'rth 6E **109**
Altolusso CF10: Card 5E **5** (4B **96**)
Alton Ter. *NP4: P'pool 2B **6***
(off Osborne Rd.)
ALWAY 5B **38**
Alway Cl. NP19: Newp 4B **38**
Alway Cres. NP19: Newp 4A **38**
Alway Pde. NP19: Newp 5B **38**
Alwen Dr. CF14: Thorn 2H **71**
CF62: Barry 2E **117**
Alwyn Cl. NP10: Roger 2C **34**
Amalfi Ho. *CF10: Card 6C **96***
(off Ffordd Garthorne)
Amber Cl. CF23: Pent 4F **73**
Ambergate Dr. CF23: Pent 5F **73**
Amberheart Dr. CF14: Thorn 1H **71**
Amberley Cl. CF23: Pent 5F **73**
Amberwood Cl. CF23: Pent 4F **73**
Amblecote Cl. CF23: Pent 4F **73**
Ambleside Av. CF23: Cyn 5A **86**
Ambrooke Cl. CF23: Pent 4F **73**
Ambrose Way NP4: New I 5G **7**
Ambryn Rd. NP4: New I 5H **7**
Amelia Av. NP19: Newp 6F **37**
Amelia Cl. NP19: Newp 6F **37**
Amelia Gro. NP19: Newp 6F **37**
Amelia Way NP19: Newp 6F **37**
American Vs. NP11: Ris 4D **16**
Amesbury Rd. CF23: Pen L 6D **86**
Amethyst Rd. CF5: F'wtr 6H **83**
Amgueddfa Pontypool Mus. 2C **6**
Amherst Cres. CF62: Barry 5G **117**
Amherst St. CF11: Card 1H **101**
Amity Ct. CF10: Card 6C **96**
Amroth Ct. CF62: Barry 6H **105**
Amroth Rd. CF5: Ely 4H **93**
Amroth Wlk. NP44: St D 3E **11**
Amyas Cl. CF11: Card 6G **95**
Amy Johnson Cl. NP19: Newp 6G **37**
Anchorage, The CF64: P'rth 5H **101**
Anchor Ct. CF10: Card 6F **5** (5B **96**)
Anchor Ind. Est. CF10: Card 6B **96**
Anchor Rd. CF64: P'rth 5A **102**
Anchor St. CF15: Taff W 2E **69**
Anderson Cl. NP20: Newp 6A **36**
Anderson Pl. CF24: Card 3D **96**
NP20: Malp 3A **20**
Andover Cl. CF62: Barry 6D **104**
Andrew Rd. CF64: P'rth 6F **101**
Andrews Ct. CF61: Llan M 3C **110**
Andrew's Rd. CF14: Llan N 5B **84**
Aneurin Bevan Ct. NP4: P'pool 3C **6**
NP10: Duf 4G **53**
Aneurin Bevan Dr. CF38: Chu V 3D **42**
Aneurin Rd. CF63: Barry 1A **118**
Angelica Way CF14: Thorn 2F **71**
Angelina St. CF10: Card 6B **96**
Angiddy Cl. NP26: Cald 4D **60**
Angle Cl. CF62: Barry 5H **105**

Angle Pl. CF14: L'shn 4F **71**
Anglesey Cl. CF38: Tont 1G **43**
CF61: Bov 2D **110**
Anglesey Ct. NP18: C'ln 4F **21**
Anglesey St. CF5: Card 3E **95**
Angus St. CF24: Card 6C **86**
Anisa M. NP20: Newp 5C **36**
Annesley Rd. NP19: Newp 3E **37**
Anne St. CF11: Card 4F **95**
Ann St. CF37: C'fydd 2F **15**
Ansari Ct. CF72: Y'erdy 6D **40**
Anson Ct. CF10: Card 6G **5**
Anson Grn. NP19: Newp 2C **38**
Anstee Ct. CF11: Card 4F **95**
Anthony Dr. NP18: C'ln 4F **21**
Anton Ct. CF14: Whit 2C **84**
Anwyll Cl. NP18: C'ln 3G **21**
Apollo Cl. CF14: Thorn 3G **71**
Apple Av. NP26: Undy 4F **59**
Appledore Rd. CF14: Llan N 4E **85**
Appletree Cl. CF72: L'harry 5A **78**
Applewood Cl.
CF24: Card 5H **5** (4D **96**)
Apprentice Cl. NP16: B'ly 6H **63**
Aprilla Ho. CF10: Card 6C **96**
Aquila Ho. CF10: Card 1D **102**
Aquilla Ct. CF11: Card 2F **95**
Arabella St. CF24: Card 6B **86**
Aragon Ho. NP20: Newp 4A **36**
Aragon St. NP20: Newp 2C **36**
Aran Ct. NP44: Thorn 6B **8**
Arbroath Ct. CF24: Card 2F **97**
Arcade CF37: P'prdd 6C **14**
Arcade, The NP44: C'brn 2H **11**
Archer Ct. CF62: Barry 5H **117**
Archer Cres. CF5: Ely 3H **93**
Archer Pl. CF5: Ely 3G **93**
CF64: P'rth 2E **109**
Archer Rd. CF5: Ely 3F **93**
CF62: Barry 4H **117**
CF64: P'rth 2D **108**
NP44: G'mdw 2D **10**
Archer Ter. CF5: Ely 3H **93**
CF64: P'rth 3E **109**
Arch Hill NP11: P'waun 1A **16**
Archibald St. NP19: Newp 4E **37**
Arcot La. CF64: P'rth 1E **109**
Arcot La. Nth. CF64: P'rth 6A **102**
Arcot St. CF64: P'rth 6A **102**
ARD Bus. Pk. NP4: New I 5F **7**
Arden Way CF63: Barry 6C **106**
Ardwyn CF14: R'ina 5B **70**
Arfonfab Cres. CF37: R'fln 5H **25**
Argae La. CF63: Barry 5D **106**
CF64: St And 2C **106**
Argosy Cl. NP19: Newp 6E **37**
Argosy Way NP19: Newp 5E **37**
Argyle Ct. CF15: Rad 6F **69**
Argyle St. NP20: Newp 2C **36**
Argyle Way CF5: Ely 5A **94**
Arles Rd. CF5: Ely 4A **94**
Arlington Cl. NP20: Malp 3A **20**
NP26: Undy 4F **59**
Arlington Ct. NP16: Sed 2H **63**
Arlington Cres. CF3: L'rmy 1A **88**
Arlington M. CF64: Sul 2H **119**
Arlington Rd. CF64: Sul 2H **119**
Armoury Dr. CF14: Heath 1F **85**
Armstrong Cl. NP19: Newp 5H **37**
Arne Cl. NP19: Newp 4C **38**
Arnold Av. CF3: L'rmy 5A **74**
Arnold Cl. NP20: Newp 1H **53**
Arno Rd. CF63: Barry 1C **118**
Arnside Rd. CF23: Pen L 5C **86**
Arran Cl. CF37: Pen c 3B **24**
NP11: Ris 6G **17**
Arran Pl. CF24: Card 1C **96**
Arran St. CF24: Card 2B **96**
(not continuous)
Arrol St. CF24: Card 4D **96**
Arthur Bliss Rd.
NP19: Newp 5A **38**
Arthur Cl. NP20: Newp 1C **54**
Arthur Davis Ct.
CF62: Barry 1H **117**
Arthurs Ct. NP26: Pskwt 5F **61**
Arthur St. CF24: Card 2E **97**
CF63: Barry 1D **118**
NP18: C'ln 5A **22**
NP20: Newp 1C **54**
Artillery Pl. NP19: Newp 4C **36**
Arudur Hen CF15: Rad 2H **83**
Arundel Cl. NP44: G'mdw 2C **10**
Arundel Pl. CF11: Card 1F **101**
Arundel Rd. NP19: Newp 4F **37**
Ar-y-Nant CF63: Barry 5A **106**
Ascot Cl. CF5: Ely 4A **94**
Asgog St. CF24: Card 4D **96**
Ashbourn Way CF14: L'shn 6F **71**
Ashburton Av. CF3: L'rmy 6A **74**
Ashby Rd. CF64: Sul 1G **119**
Ashchurch Cl. CF14: Whit 2C **84**
Ashchurch Row CF14: Whit 2C **84**
Ash Cl. NP16: Bul 5E **63**
Ashcroft Cres. CF5: F'wtr 6F **83**
Ashdene Cl. CF5: F'wtr 5H **83**
Ashdown Cl. CF3: St M 6D **74**
Ashdown Ct. CF37: C'fydd 3F **15**
Ashfield Ct. CF3: St M 6C **74**
Ashford Cl. CF37: Glync 2C **14**
NP44: C'iog 6H **9**
Ashford Cl. Nth. NP44: C'iog 6H **9**
Ashford Cl. Sth. NP44: C'iog 1B **12**
Ash Grn. NP44: Oakf 5H **11**
Ash Gro. CF5: Cul C 1E **99**
CF14: Whit 1C **84**
CF63: Barry 6C **106**
CF64: L'dgh 5G **101**
CF72: L'harry 5A **78**
CF72: Tyle 5B **64**
NP4: Trev 1D **6**
NP26: Cald 4C **60**
Ashgrove CF37: Glync 1D **14**
CF61: Llan M 3B **110**
CF64: Din P 3H **107**
CF83: Tret 3H **29**
Ashgrove Cl. NP4: Seba 2D **8**
Ash La. CF62: E Bre 2B **112**
Ashleigh Ct. NP44: H'lys 4B **10**
Ashley Rd. NP19: Newp 4H **37**
Ashman Cl. CF83: Caer 2H **45**
Ash Pl. CF5: F'wtr 1H **93**
Ash Sq. CF37: R'fln 4G **25**
Ash Tree Cl. CF15: Rad 1E **83**
Ash Tree Ct. CF23: Pontp 2G **73**
Ash Wlk. CF72: T Grn 3E **65**
Ashwell NP18: C'ln 1A **38**
Ashwood Ct. CF24: Card 1H **5** (2C **96**)
Aspen Cl. CF3: St M 6C **74**
Aspen Way CF38: Llan F 6C **42**
NP20: Malp 4A **20**
(not continuous)
Asquith St. NP4: Grif 6E **7**
Assembly at the Pierhead, The 2C **102**
Aster Cl. CF3: St M 6E **75**
NP11: Ris 5F **17**
Aston Cres. NP20: Bryng 1B **36**
Aston Pl. CF3: St M 2E **89**
Astoria Cl. CF14: Thorn 3G **71**
Athelstan Rd. CF14: Whit 3B **84**
Atlantic Cres. CF63: Barry 4B **118**
Atlantic Pl. CF63: Barry 6C **106**
Atlantic Trad. Est. CF63: Barry 4C **118**
Atlantic Way CF63: Barry 4A **118**
ATLANTIC WHARF 6G **5** (5C **96**)
Atlantic Wharf Cl. CF10: Card 6G **5** (5C **96**)
Atlas Ho. CF10: Card 1D **102**
Atlas Pl. CF5: Card 4F **95**
Atlas Rd. CF5: Card 4F **95**
Attfield Cl. CF23: Pen L 6E **87**
Attlee Ct. CF83: Caer 6E **29**
Aubrey Av. CF5: Card 2C **94**
Aubrey Hames Cl. NP20: Newp 1A **54**
Aubrey Ter. CF71: C'bri 4D **90**
Auckland Rd. NP20: Newp 6F **35**
Augusta Cres. CF64: P'rth 4E **109**
Augustan Cl. NP18: C'ln 4F **21**
Augustan Dr. NP18: C'ln 4F **21**
Augustan Way NP18: C'ln 4F **21**
Augusta Rd. CF64: P'rth 4E **109**
Augusta St. CF24: Card 3H **5** (3C **96**)
Augustus John Cl. NP19: Newp 1G **37**
Aust Cres. NP16: Bul 5E **63**
Austen Cl. CF3: L'rmy 5B **74**
Austin Friars NP20: Newp 4C **36**
Austin Rd. NP4: Seba 2E **9**
Australia Rd. CF14: Card 5G **85**
Avalon Ct. NP4: P'pool 3B **6**
Avalon Dr. NP19: Newp 2F **37**
Avalon Leisure Complex 3B **120**
Avenue, The CF3: Rum 5A **88**
CF5: L'dff 6C **84**
CF14: Whit 3B **84**
CF37: P'prdd 6D **14**
CF83: Tret 3A **30**
NP4: Grif 1E **9**
NP4: New I 4F **7**
NP10: Coedk 4E **53**
NP20: Newp 6C 36
(off Clytha Sq.)
NP26: Cald 6B **60**
Avenue Ind. Pk., The CF23: Pent 5G **73**
Avoca Pl. CF11: Card 6G **95**
Avocet Ct. CF63: Barry 2A **118**
Avon Cl. CF63: Barry 6C **106**
NP20: Bet 5G **19**
NP26: Cald 4C **60**
Avondale Bus. Pk.
NP44: Pon'run 5E **9**
Avondale Cl. NP44: Pon'run 5F **9**
Avondale Cres. CF11: Card 1A **102**
NP44: Pon'run 4F **9**
Avondale Gdns. CF11: Card 1A **102**
Avondale Gdns. Sth. CF11: Card 1A **102**
Avondale Rd. CF11: Card 1A **102**
NP4: Seba 3F **9**
NP44: Pon'run 3F **9**
Avondale Way NP44: Pon'run 4F **9**
Avonmuir Rd. CF24: Card 1F **97**
Avon Pl. NP44: L'rfn 2A **12**
Avonridge CF14: Thorn 3F **71**
Awbery Ho. CF62: Barry 1F **117**
Awelfryn CF37: Pen c 6A **24**
Awel Mor CF23: L'dyrn 4D **86**
Axbridge Cres. CF3: L'rmy 1B **88**
Axminster Rd. CF23: Pen L 1E **97**
Azalea Cl. CF23: Pent 6D **72**
Azalea Rd. NP10: Roger 2G **33**

B

Baber Cl. CF23: Pen L 6E **87**
Back, The NP16: Chep 1F **63**
(not continuous)
Backhall St. NP18: C'ln 5A **22**
Bacon Pl. NP20: Malp 4A **20**
Bacton Ct. CF14: Llan N 5D **84**
Bacton Rd. CF14: Llan N 5D **84**
Baden Rd. CF24: Card 3G **97**
Bader Cl. CF14: L'shn 1H **85**
Badgers Dene NP16: Chep 2D **62**
Badgers Mdw. NP16: Pwllm 4B **62**
NP18: P'hir 6F **13**
Badgers Mede NP44: G'mdw 2D **10**
Badgers Wlk. NP26: Undy 4E **59**
Badgers Wood Cl. NP10: Bass 1B **52**
Badham Cl. CF83: Caer 2H **45**
Badminton Rd. NP19: Newp 1F **37**
Badminton Vs. NP16: Chep 1F **63**
Bagley Ct. NP44: Thorn 6B **8**
Bailey Cl. CF5: F'wtr 2A **94**
Bailey's Hay NP16: Math 6B **62**
Baileys Ter. *NP4: P'nydd 1A 6*
(off Hanbury Rd.)
Bailey St. NP20: Newp 4B **36**
Baird Cl. NP20: Malp 4H **19**
Baird Ri. CF62: Barry 2F **117**
Bakers Ct. CF3: M'fld 5A **76**
CF5: Card 2D **94**
Baker's La. CF61: Llan M 3A **110**
Bakers Row CF10: Card 4D **4** (4A **96**)
Bakers Wharf CF37: P'prdd 5D **14**
Bakery, The CF11: Card 6B **4** (5H **95**)
Bakery La. CF3: Cas 2H **75**
Balaclava Rd. CF23: Pen L 6C **86**
Bala Dr. NP10: Roger 2C **34**
Bala Rd. CF14: Llan N 5C **84**

Baldwin Cl. CF5: L'dff 3H 83
NP20: Newp 1C 54
Baldwin St. NP20: Newp 1C 54
Balfe Rd. NP19: Newp 5B 38
Ball Cl. CF3: L'rmy 6H 73
Ball La. CF3: L'rmy 1G 87
Ball Rd. CF3: L'rmy 1H 87
Balmond Ter. NP4: P'pool 1B 6
Balmoral Cl. CF14: L'vne 3B 72
CF37: Pen c 3B 24
Balmoral Ct. CF62: Barry 5E 105
Balmoral La. NP19: Newp 5G 37
Balmoral Rd. NP19: Newp 5G 37
Baltic Ter. NP44: T Coch 6G 11
Baltimore Cl. CF23: Pontp 3G 73
Bampton Rd. CF3: L'rmy 6A 74
Banastre Av. CF14: Card 5G 85
Banc yr Afon CF15: Gwae G 2E 69
Baneswell Courtyard
NP20: Newp 5B 36
Baneswell Rd. NP20: Newp 4B 36
Bangor Ct. *CF24: Card 6C 86*
(off Bangor La.)
Bangor La. CF24: Card 6C 86
Bangor St. CF24: Card 6C 86
Bank La. NP19: Newp 1E 37
Bankside NP19: Newp 5D 36
Bankside Cl. CF14: Thorn 2H 71
Bank Sq. NP16: Chep 2E 63
Bank St. NP16: Chep 2E 63
NP19: Newp 1D 36
Bannatyne's Health Club
Cardiff 6G 71
Newport 6D 36
Bantock Cl. NP19: Newp 4C 38
Banwell Ct. NP44: Thorn 6B 8
Banwell Pl. CF3: L'rmy 1A 88
Barberry Ri. CF64: P'rth 6G 101
Barbirolli Grn. NP19: Newp 5B 38
Barbrook Cl. CF14: L'vne 3A 72
Bardsey Cres. CF14: L'shn 4F 71
Bardsy Cl. NP19: Newp 2F 37
Bareland St. NP26: L'nny 5A 58
Bargoed St. CF11: Card 6A 96
Barletta Ho. *CF10: Card 6B 96*
(off Vellacott Cl.)
Barmouth Rd. CF3: Rum 4H 87
Barnard Av. CF5: Ely 3A 94
Barnard St. NP19: Newp 3D 36
Barnard Way CF38: Chu V 3D 42
Barnets NP44: G'mdw 2D 10
Barnets Wood NP16: Chep 2C 62
Barnfield NP18: P'hir 2F 21
Barnfield Cl. CF23: Pontp 4H 73
Barnfield Dr. CF15: Morg 5E 69
Barnfield Pl. NP44: Pnwd 5C 8
Barnstaple Rd. CF3: L'rmy 1A 88
Barnwood Cres. CF5: Ely 5D 92
Baron Cl. CF64: P'rth 2D 108
Baroness Pl. CF64: P'rth 2D 108
Baron La. CF64: P'rth 1D 108
Baron Rd. CF64: P'rth 2D 108
Baron's Cl. CF61: Llan M 3B 110
Barons Ct. NP26: Undy 4F 59
Baron's Ct. Rd. CF23: Pen L 5D 86
Barquentine Pl.
CF10: Card 6C 96
BARRACK HILL 2B 36
Barrack Hill NP20: Newp 2A 36
Barracks La. CF10: Card 4E 5 (4B 96)
Barrenhill CF62: P'ark 1C 114
BARRI 3F 117
Barrians Way CF62: Barry 2G 117
Barrie Gdns. NP20: Newp 1G 53
Barrington Rd. CF14: Whit 3D 84
BARRY 3F 117
BARRY DOCK 1A 118
Barry Docks Link Rd.
CF63: Barry 3B 106
Barry Docks Station (Rail) 3A 118
BARRY HOSPITAL 6F 105
BARRY ISLAND 5G 117
Barry Island Pleasure Pk. 5G 117
Barry Island Station (Rail) 5G 117
Barry La. CF10: Card 5D 4 (4A 96)
Barry Leisure Cen. 3H 117
Barry Rd. CF37: P'prdd 6A 14
CF62: Barry 1G 117
CF63: Barry 1G 117
CF64: L'dgh 6F 101
Barry Station (Rail) 4F 117
Barry Wlk. NP10: Roger 3C 34
Barthropp St. NP19: Newp 6G 37
Bartlett St. CF83: Caer 1D 46
Bartlett St. Ind. Est. CF83: Caer 1D 46
BASALEG 1D 52
Basil Pl. CF24: Card 1A 96
BASSALEG 1D 52
Bassaleg Cl. CF3: St M 6E 75
Bassaleg Rd. NP20: Newp 6E 35
Bassett Rd. CF64: Sul 2G 119
Bassetts Fld. CF14: R'ina, Thorn 2E 71
Bassett St. CF5: Card 4E 95
CF37: P'prdd 5D 14
CF63: Barry 1B 118
Bastian Cl. CF63: Barry 6B 106
Batchelor Rd. CF14: Card 5E 85
NP19: Newp 4F 37
Bates Ct. CF15: Rad 2H 83
Bath Grn. NP44: Llanf 3B 12
Bath St. NP19: Newp 3D 36
Batten Way CF37: C'fydd 4F 15
Bay Cvn. Pk., The CF64: S'dge 3D 120
Baylis Ct. CF5: Ely 3A 94
Baynton Cl. CF5: L'dff 5A 84
Bayside Rd. CF24: Card 4D 96
Bay Tree Cl. NP18: C'ln 5E 21
Beach La. CF64: P'rth 1F 109
BEACHLEY 6H 63
Beachley Rd. NP16: B'ly 4H 63
NP16: Tut 1F 63
Beach Rd. CF64: P'rth 1F 109
CF64: S'dge 3A 120
NP10: St Bri W 4H 77
Beachway CF62: Barry 6D 116
Beacon Bus. Pk. NP26: Pskwt 5F 61
Beacons Cl. NP10: Roger 2C 34
Beacon St. CF11: Card 2E 95
Beale Cl. CF5: L'dff 4A 84
Beatrice Rd. CF14: Whit 3D 84
CF63: Barry 1B 118
Beatrix CF11: Card 5H 101
Beatty Av. CF23: Cyn 2A 86
Beatty Cl. CF62: Barry 4A 106
Beatty Ct. CF10: Card 6G 5 (5C 96)
Beatty Rd. NP19: Newp 2D 38
Beauchamp St. CF11: Card 5A 4 (4H 95)
(not continuous)
Beaufort Cl. NP44: F'wtr 4E 11
Beaufort Ct. CF10: Card 6G 5 (5C 96)
CF72: C Inn 3G 65
Beaufort Pk. NP16: Bul 6F 63
Beaufort Pk. Way NP16: Bul 6F 63
Beaufort Pl. NP16: Chep 2E 63
NP19: Newp 1F 37
Beaufort Rd. NP19: Newp 1F 37
Beaufort Sq. CF24: Card 6F 87
NP16: Chep 2E 63
Beaufort Ter. NP20: Newp 5B 36
Beaufort Way CF62: Rho 5C 114
Beaumaris Cl. CF38: Tont 1F 43
NP10: R'drn 6A 34
Beaumaris Dr. NP44: L'rfn 3A 12
Beaumaris Rd. CF3: Rum 4H 87
Beaumont Cl. CF62: Barry 6D 104
Beaumont Ct. CF64: P'rth 2D 108
Beauville La. CF64: Din P 6H 99
Beavers Wlk. NP10: Roger 5D 34
Beck Ct. CF23: Pontp 3H 73
Beckgrove Cl. CF24: Card 1G 97
Beda Rd. CF5: Card 4E 95
Bedavere Cl. CF14: Thorn 3G 71
BEDDAU 4H 41
Beddick NP44: G'mdw 2C 10
Bedford Cl. NP44: G'mdw 2C 10
Bedford Pl. CF24: Card 1G 5 (2C 96)
Bedford Ri. CF61: Bov 3C 110
Bedford Rd. NP19: Newp 4D 36
Bedford St. CF24: Card 1F 5 (2B 96)
(not continuous)
Bedlington Ter. CF62: Barry 2F 117
BEDWAS 3G 29
Bedwas Bus. Cen. CF83: B'ws 3F 29
Bedwas Cen. CF83: B'ws 3G 29
Bedwas Cl. CF3: St M 6E 75
Bedwas Conifers Cvn. Pk. CF83: B'ws 3F 29
Bedwas Ho. Ind. Est. CF83: B'ws 3E 29
(not continuous)
Bedwas Pl. CF64: P'rth 1D 108
Bedwas Rd. CF83: Caer 6D 28
(not continuous)
Bedwas St. CF11: Card 6G 95
Bedw Rd. CF37: C'fydd 3F 15
Beecham St. NP19: Newp 4B 38
Beech Av. CF61: Llan M 5C 110
Beech Cl. CF83: Caer 2H 45
NP44: Pnwd 5D 8
Beech Ct. CF15: Tong 3H 69
Beechcroft Rd. NP19: Newp 3G 37
Beechdale Rd. NP19: Newp 4G 37
Beecher Av. CF11: Card 2H 101
Beecher Ter. NP11: Cros K 2A 16
Beeches, The CF14: L'vne 2A 72
NP20: Newp 6H 35
NP44: C'brn 3F 11
Beeches Farm Cvn. Pk. NP26: Magor 3D 58
Beeches Ind. Est., The CF72: P'clun 4C 64
Beechfield Av. NP19: Newp 3G 37
Beech Gro. NP10: Duf 3H 53
NP16: Bul 3D 62
Beechgrove CF83: Caer 4E 29
Beech Ho. CF14: Whit 6A 70
Beeching Way *CF38: Chu V 1E 43*
(off Brecon Way)
Beechlea Cl. CF72: Mis 1F 79
Beechleigh Cl. NP44: G'mdw 2B 10
Beechley Dr. CF5: F'wtr 6F 83
Beech Rd. CF5: F'wtr 1F 93
CF72: L'harry 5A 78
NP4: Seba 2D 8
NP26: Cald 4B 60
Beech Tree Cl. CF15: Rad 1E 83
Beech Tree Ter. NP4: P'nydd 1A 6
Beech Vs. CF37: P'prdd 6B 14
BEECHWOOD 4G 37
Beech Wood NP16: Chep 2C 62
Beechwood Cres. NP19: Newp 4G 37
Beechwood Dr. CF38: Llan F 5C 42
CF64: P'rth 3C 108
Beechwood Hgts. CF38: Llan F 5C 42
Beechwood Rd. CF15: Taff W 1F 69
NP19: Newp 4G 37
Beechwood St. CF37: R'fln 4H 25
BEGAN 2B 74
Began Rd. CF3: Old M 2B 74
BEGGARS POUND 4C 112
Beidr Iorwg CF63: Barry 5C 106
Beignon Cl. CF24: Card 5D 96
Beili Bach CF3: Rum 4G 87
Belgrave Cl. CF14: Thorn 2G 71
Belgrave Ct. CF11: Card 4A 4
NP4: P'nydd 1A 6
Belgrave Ter. CF37: P'prdd 4E 15
Belle Vw. Ter. CF63: Barry 6C 106
Belle Vue Cl. CF64: P'rth 6B 102
Bellevue Cl. NP44: C'brn 3G 11
Belle Vue Cres. CF14: Llan N 4B 84
Belle Vue La. NP20: Newp 6B 36
Bellevue Rd. NP44: C'brn 4G 11
Belle Vue Ter. CF37: T'rest 2E 25
CF64: P'rth 6B 102
NP20: Newp 1C 54
Bellevue Ter. NP44: H'lys 4A 10
Bellin Cl. NP18: C'ln 4G 21
Bell St. CF62: Barry 3E 117
Belmont Hill NP18: Chris 1A 38
Belmont St. CF63: Barry 1A 118
Belmont Wlk. CF10: Card 6B 96
Belvedere Cres. CF63: Barry 2H 117
Belvedere Ter. NP11: Ris 4D 16
NP20: Newp 2B 36
Belvoir Ct. CF72: C Inn 3G 65
Benbow Rd. NP19: Newp 2C 38
Bencroft La. NP26: Rog, Undy 1F 59
Bendrick Rd. CF63: Barry 3C 118
Benecrofte CF62: Rho 5E 115
Ben Jonson Way NP20: Newp 1G 53
Bennetts Ter. CF83: Caer 5E 29

Benson Av. NP10: Roger 4D **34**
(not continuous)
Bentley Cl. NP10: Roger 2C **34**
Beresford Ct. CF24: Card 1E **97**
Beresford Rd. CF24: Card 1E **97**
NP19: Newp 4D **36**
Beresford Rd. La. CF24: Card 1E **97**
Berkeley Ct. NP44: Thorn 6B **8**
Berkeley Cres. NP4: Seba 3E **9**
Berkeley Sq. CF5: Cul C 1E **99**
Berkley Cl. NP10: Bass 6B **34**
Berkley Dr. CF64: P'rth 2F **109**
Berkley Rd. NP10: Bass 6B **34**
Berkrolles Av. CF62: St Ath 5D **112**
BERLLAN-GOLLEN 1D **48**
Bernard Av. CF5: Card 3C **94**
Berry Ct. CF61: Bov 3D **110**
Berrymead Rd. CF23: Cyn 6B **72**
Berry Pl. CF5: F'wtr 5H **83**
Bertha St. CF37: T'rest 4E **25**
Berthin NP44: G'mdw 2D **10**
Berthlwyd CF15: P'rch 4A **68**
Berthwin St. CF11: Card 2F **95**
Bertram St. CF24: Card 2D **96**
Berw Rd. CF37: P'prdd 5C **14**
Beryl Pl. CF62: Barry 2H **117**
Beryl Rd. CF62: Barry 2H **117**
Bessant Cl. CF71: C'bri, L'thian 4D **90**
Bessborough Dr. CF11: Card 6G **95**
Bessemer Cl. CF11: Card 1E **101**
NP20: Malp 3H **19**
Bessemer Rd. CF11: Card 1F **101**
Bethania Row CF3: Old M 1B **88**
Bethany Cl. *NP11: P'waun* *1A* ***16***
(off Silver St.)
Bethel La. NP44: Up Cwm 5B **8**
Bethel Pl. CF14: L'shn 4F **71**
Bethel St. CF37: P'prdd 1B **24**
Bethesda Cl. NP10: Roger 3C **34**
Bethesda Pl. NP10: Roger 3B **34**
Betjeman Av. NP26: Cald 6B **60**
BETTWS 5F **19**
Bettws Cl. NP20: Bet 6H **19**
Bettws Hill NP20: Bet 6E **19**
Bettws La. NP20: Bet, Malp 6H **19**
Bettws Leisure Cen. 6H **19**
Bettws Shop. Cen. NP20: Bet 5F **19**
Bettws-y-Coed Rd. CF23: Cyn 6B **72**
Betwyns *NP44: F'wtr* *4E* ***11***
(off Henllys Way)
Beulah Rd. CF14: R'ina 6E **71**
Bevan Cl. CF83: Tret 3H **29**
Bevan Pl. CF14: Card 5F **85**
Bevan Ri. CF83: Tret 3H **29**
Bevans' La. NP44: Pnwd 3D **8**
Beverley Cl. CF14: L'shn 4A **72**
Beverley St. CF63: Barry 6B **106**
Bicester Rd. CF64: Sul 1E **119**
Bideford Cl. NP20: Newp 2A **54**
Bideford Rd. CF3: L'rmy 2A **88**
NP20: Newp 2H **53**
Bighams Row NP4: P'pool 5B **6**
Bigstone Cl. NP16: Tut 1G **63**
Bigstone Gro. NP16: Tut 1G **63**
Bilston St. NP19: Newp 5F **37**
Bingle La. CF62: St Ath 3D **112**
Birbeck Rd. NP26: Cald 5B **60**
Birch Cl. NP26: Undy 4E **59**
Birch Ct. CF14: Heath 2F **85**
CF15: Tong 3H **69**
Birch Cres. CF38: Llan F 6C **42**
Birches, The NP44: Pnwd 6C **8**
Birchfield Cl. CF38: Tont 2G **43**
Birchfield Cres. CF5: Card 2B **94**
BIRCHGROVE 1F **85**
Birch Gro. CF38: Chu V 2F **43**
CF62: Barry 5E **117**
CF72: L'harry 5A **78**
CF83: Caer 4E **29**
NP11: Ris 5E **17**
NP44: H'lys 5C **10**
Birchgrove CF37: P'prdd 1C **24**
CF83: Tret 3H **29**
NP10: Roger 3B **34**
Birchgrove Cl. NP20: Malp 5B **20**
Birchgrove Rd. CF14: Heath, Whit 3F **85**
Birchgrove Station (Rail) 1F **85**
Birch Hill CF15: Tong 4G **69**
NP20: Malp 4B **20**
Birch La. CF64: P'rth 4E **109**
Birchley Cl. CF37: T'rest 3D **24**
Birch Rd. CF5: F'wtr 1H **93**
Birch Trees NP10: Bass 1D **52**
Birch Wlk. CF5: F'wtr 1H **93**
Birchwood Av. CF37: T'rest 4E **25**
Birchwood Gdns. CF14: Whit 4E **85**
CF83: B'ws 3F **29**
Birchwood La. CF23: Pen L 4B **86**
Birchwood Rd. CF23: Pen L 4B **86**
Birdsfield Cotts. *CF37: P'prdd* *1B* ***24***
(off Grover St.)
Birds Ind. Est. NP11: Ris 1E **33**
Birdwood Gdns. NP16: Math 6C **62**
Birkdale Cl. CF3: St M 5E **75**
Bishop Cl. NP26: C'ent 1B **60**
Bishop Hannon Dr. CF5: F'wtr 6F **83**
Bishops Av. CF5: L'dff 1B **94**
Bishops Castle 6D **84**
Bishops Cl. CF5: L'dff 1B **94**
CF14: Whit 3C **84**
NP16: Bul 6F **63**
Bishops Ct. CF14: Whit 3C **84**
Bishops Ga. CF14: Whit 3C **84**
Bishops Mead NP16: Math 6B **62**
Bishops Pl. CF5: L'dff 1B **94**
CF14: Whit 3C **84**
Bishops Rd. CF14: Whit 3C **84**
Bishopston Rd. CF5: Ely 5H **93**
Bishop St. CF11: Card 6G **95**
NP19: Newp 3D **36**
Bishops Wlk. CF5: L'dff 1B **94**
BISHPOOL 4B **38**
Bishpool Av. NP19: Newp 3B **38**
Bishpool Cl. NP19: Newp 3B **38**
Bishpool Ct. NP19: Newp 3B **38**
Bishpool Gdns. NP19: Newp 3B **38**
Bishpool Gro. NP19: Newp 3B **38**
Bishpool La. NP19: Newp 3B **38**
Bishpool Pl. NP19: Newp 3B **38**
Bishpool Ri. NP19: Newp 3B **38**
Bishpool Vw. NP19: Newp 3B **38**
Bishpool Way NP19: Newp 3B **38**
Bishton Rd. NP18: L'wrn 4F **39**
Bishton St. NP19: Newp 4E **37**
Bisley Cl. CF24: Card 2H **97**
Bittern Way CF64: P'rth 5E **109**
Blackberry Dr. CF62: Barry 1E **117**
Blackberry Way CF23: Pontp 4G **73**
Black Bird Cl. NP10: Roger 6E **35**
Blackbird Rd. CF62: St Ath 3F **111**
NP26: Cald 6D **60**
Blackbirds Cl. NP44: L'tnam 2A **20**
Blackbirds Way CF3: Old M 5B **74**
Blackbrook CF83: Caer 2H **45**
Blackett Av. NP20: Malp 4A **20**
Blackmoor Pl. CF3: L'rmy 1A **88**
Black Oak Ct. CF23: Cyn 4C **72**
Black Oak Rd. CF23: Cyn 5C **72**
Black Prince Rd. CF83: Caer 1H **45**
Black Rd. CF37: Pen c 4B **24**
CF38: Up Chu 4B **24**
Black Rock Rd. NP26: Pskwt 5H **61**
Blacksmiths Way NP10: Coedk 5C **52**
Blackstone St. CF11: Card 4G **95**
Blackthorn Ct. CF72: L'harry 5A **78**
Blackthorn Gro. NP18: C'ln 5E **21**
Blackton La. CF62: P'ark 3G **115**
BLACKTOWN 5H **75**
Blacktown Gdns. CF3: M'fld 5A **76**
Blackvein Rd. NP11: Cros K 5A **16**
Black Wall NP26: Magor 6C **58**
BLACKWATER 1G **95**
Blackwater Cl. NP20: Bet 5F **19**
Blackweir Cotts. CF10: Card 1G **95**
Blackweir Ter. CF10: Card 1H **95**
Blackwell Cl. CF63: Barry 1B **118**
Blaenavon Cl. CF3: St M 6E **75**
Blaenclydach Pl. CF11: Card 6H **95**
Blaenclydach St. CF11: Card 6H **95**
Blaendare Rd. NP4: P'pool 4D **6**
NP4: P'pool, Up R 5B **6**
(not continuous)
Blaen Ifor CF83: Caer 3A **28**
Blaenwern NP44: Pon'run 5F **9**
Blaen-y-Coed CF14: R'ina 5E **71**
CF15: Rad 1E **83**
Blaen-y-Cwm Vw. NP44: H'lys 4B **10**
Blaen-y-Pant Av. NP20: Malp 1A **36**
Blaen-y-Pant Cres. NP20: Malp 6A **20**
Blaen-y-Pant Pl. NP20: Malp 1A **36**
Blagdon Cl. CF3: L'rmy 2H **87**
Blaina Cl. CF3: St M 6D **74**
Blaise Pl. CF11: Card 1G **101**
Blake Ct. CF10: Card 6G **5**
Blake Rd. NP19: Newp 6H **37**
Blanche Cl. NP10: Duf 5H **53**
Blanche St. CF24: Card 2E **97**
CF37: P'prdd 5C **14**
Blanche Ter. CF37: P'prdd 5C **14**
Blandings Ct. CF23: Cyn 1C **86**
Blandon Way CF14: Whit 3C **84**
Blanthorn Ct. CF14: Whit 1B **84**
Blenheim Av. NP26: Magor 4C **58**
Blenheim Cl. CF62: Barry 6E **105**
NP26: Magor 4C **58**
Blenheim Ct. NP26: Magor 4C **58**
NP44: St D 3E **11**
Blenheim Dr. NP26: Magor 4C **58**
Blenheim Gdns. NP26: Magor 4C **58**
Blenheim Pk. NP26: Magor 4C **58**
Blenheim Rd. CF23: Pen L 1C **96**
NP19: Newp 4G **37**
NP44: St D 3E **11**
Blenheim Sq. Shops NP44: St D 3E **11**
Bleriot Cl. NP19: Newp 6G **37**
Blethin Cl. CF5: L'dff 4A **84**
Blewitt St. NP20: Newp 5B **36**
Blodwen Rd. NP4: New I 5G **7**
Blodwen Way NP4: New I 5G **7**
Blodyn y Gog CF63: Barry 5C **106**
Bloomfield Cl. NP19: Newp 3B **38**
Bloom St. CF11: Card 2E **95**
Blosse Rd. CF14: Llan N 5C **84**
Blossom Cl. NP18: L'stne 1F **39**
Blossom Dr. CF14: L'vne 1A **72**
Bluebell Ct. NP44: Ty C 3B **10**
Bluebell Dr. CF3: Old M 5B **74**
NP16: Bul 5F **63**
Bluebell Way NP10: Roger 2H **33**
Blue Ho. Rd. CF14: L'shn 4G **71**
Blyth Cl. CF62: Barry 4A **106**
Boddington Ter. *NP18: C'ln* *5A* ***22***
(off Cross St.)
Bodnant Cl. CF3: St M 1D **88**
Bodwenarth Rd. CF37: C'fydd 3F **15**
Boleyn Wlk. CF23: Pen L 5C **86**
Bolt Cl. NP20: Newp 6D **36**
Bolton Rd. NP20: Newp 5A **36**
Bolton St. NP20: Newp 3B **36**
Bolts Row NP19: Newp 4H **37**
Bolt St. NP20: Newp 6D **36**
Boncath Rd. CF14: Llan N 5C **84**
Bond St. NP19: Newp 3C **36**
Bonvilston Rd. CF37: P'prdd 5D **14**
Bonvilston Ter. CF37: P'prdd 5D **14**
Booker St. CF24: Card 2E **97**
Boon Cl. CF63: Barry 6A **106**
Borage Cl. CF23: Pontp 4E **73**
Borough Av. CF62: Barry 5F **105**
Borough Cl. CF71: C'bri 4D **90**
Borrowdale Cl. CF23: Pen L 5C **86**
Borth Rd. CF3: Rum 2B **88**
Boswell Cl. CF3: L'rmy 5H **73**
NP20: Newp 1H **53**
Bosworth Dr. NP20: Newp 2A **36**
Boulevard de Nantes
CF10: Card 2C **4** (3A **96**)
BOVERTON 4E **111**
Boverton Brook CF61: Bov 4D **110**
Boverton Brook Shops *CF61: Bov* *4E* ***111***
(off Boverton Rd.)
Boverton Ct. CF61: Bov 3D **110**
Boverton Pk. CF61: Bov 4E **111**
Boverton Pk. Dr. CF61: Bov 4E **111**
Boverton Rd. CF61: Bov, Llan M 3C **110**
Boverton St. CF23: Card 6B **86**
Bovil Vw. CF83: Mac 2G **31**
Bowdens La. NP26: Magor 1B **58**

Bowen Pl. *NP20: Newp* 6C **36**
(off Francis Dr.)
Bowleaze NP44: G'mdw 2D **10**
Bowley Ct. CF24: Card 4E **97**
Bowlplex
Cardiff 2D **44**
Bowls Cl. CF83: Caer 4H **27**
Bowls La. CF83: Caer 2H **27**
(not continuous)
Bowls Ter. CF83: Caer 4A **28**
Bowman's Way CF71: C'bri 3B **90**
Bowmans Well CF71: C'bri 3B **90**
Bow St. CF5: Cul C 1E **99**
Boxer Ind. Est. NP18: C'ln 3H **21**
Boxtree Cl. NP18: C'ln 5E **21**
Boyle Cl. NP20: Malp 5H **19**
Brachdy Cl. CF3: Rum 5H **87**
Brachdy La. CF3: Rum 5H **87**
Brachdy Rd. CF3: Rum 5H **87**
Bracken Pl. CF5: F'wtr 6H **83**
Bradacres CF38: Chu V 3F **43**
Bradenham Pl. CF64: P'rth 1E **109**
Brades, The NP18: C'ln 4H **21**
Bradford Pl. CF64: P'rth 1F **109**
Bradford St. CF11: Card 1H **101**
CF83: Caer 1C **46**
Bradley St. CF24: Card 2E **97**
Braeval St. CF24: Card 1B **96**
Brain Cl. NP19: Newp 3E **39**
Bramble Av. CF62: Barry 1F **117**
Bramble Cl. CF5: F'wtr 6F **83**
Bramble Ri. CF64: P'rth 6G **101**
Brambles, The CF72: C Inn 3G **65**
Bramblewood Cl. CF14: Thorn 3H **71**
Brambling Dr. CF14: Thorn 2G **71**
Bramley Cl. NP18: L'stne 1G **39**
Bramshill Dr. CF23: Pontp 4H **73**
Brandreth Gdns. CF23: Pen L 5C **86**
Brandreth Rd. CF23: Pen L 4B **86**
Brangwyn Av. NP44: L'tnam 5H **11**
Brangwyn Cl. CF64: P'rth 6H **101**
Brangwyn Cres. NP19: Newp 2F **37**
Branksome Ho. CF10: Card 4B **4** (4H **95**)
Branwen Cl. CF5: Ely 6E **93**
Brassknocker St. NP26: Magor 4D **58**
Braunton Av. CF3: L'rmy 1H **87**
Braunton Cres. CF3: L'rmy 1H **87**
Brayford Pl. CF3: L'rmy 5A **74**
Breaksea Cl. CF64: Sul 3H **119**
Breaksea Ct. CF62: Barry 5H **117**
Breaksea Dr. CF62: Barry 5H **117**
Breakwater Ho. CF11: Card 4A **102**
Brean Cl. CF64: Sul 2A **120**
Brechfa Cl. NP18: P'hir 6E **13**
Brecon Beacons National Pk. 1F **7**
Brecon Ct. CF62: Barry 1A **118**
NP18: C'ln 4F **21**
Brecon Ho. CF64: P'rth 3D **108**
Brecon Rd. NP19: Newp 2F **37**
Brecon St. CF5: Card 3E **95**
CF61: Bov 2D **110**
Brecon Wlk. NP44: C'brn 2G **11**
Brecon Way CF38: Tont 1E **43**
Bredon Cl. NP11: Ris 6G **17**
Brendon Cl. CF3: L'rmy 1A **88**
Brendon Ct. CF83: Caer 1E **47**
Brendon Vw. Cl. CF62: Rho 5E **115**
Brenig Cl. CF14: Thorn 2H **71**
CF62: Barry 1E **117**
Brentwood Ct. CF14: L'shn 4G **71**
Breon Rd. CF64: Sul 1E **119**
Brianne Dr. CF14: Thorn 2H **71**
Briar Cl. CF5: F'wtr 1G **93**
NP26: Undy 4D **58**
Briarmeadow Dr. CF14: Thorn 2G **71**
Briars, The NP26: Magor 4C **58**
Briartree Mnr. *CF24: Card* 2D **96**
(off Newport Rd.)
Briar Way CF38: Tont 2G **43**
Briarwood Dr. CF23: Cyn 6C **72**
Brickyard Bus. Pk. CF14: Card 6F **85**
Brickyard La. NP20: Newp 5F **35**
Bridewell Gdns. NP26: Undy 5F **59**
Bridgefield St. CF83: Abert 1E **27**
Bridgeman Ct. CF64: P'rth 2F **109**
Bridgeman Rd. CF64: P'rth 2F **109**
Bridge Rd. CF3: Old M 2H **73**
CF5: L'dff 5B **84**
CF14: Llan N 5B **84**
CF37: T'rest 1B **44**
CF71: L'thian 5B **90**
Bridge St. CF5: L'dff 6C **84**
CF10: Card 5D **4** (4B **96**)
CF37: P'prdd 6C **14**
CF37: T'rest 2E **25**
CF63: Barry 6B **106**
CF64: P'rth 6H **101**
NP4: Grif 6E **7**
NP11: Ris 5D **16**
NP16: Chep 1E **63**
NP20: Newp 4B **36**
Bridget Dr. NP16: Sed 3G **63**
Bridge Ter. CF3: Mic F 4E **51**
Bridgewater Rd. CF64: Sul 1H **119**
Bridgwater Rd. CF3: L'rmy 1A **88**
Brierley Cl. NP11: Ris 6G **17**
Briers Ga. NP44: H'lys 5A **10**
Brigantine Cl. NP10: Duf 5H **53**
Brigantine Dr. NP10: Duf 5H **53**
Brigantine Gro. NP10: Duf 5H **53**
Brigantine Pl. CF10: Card 6F **5** (5B **96**)
Brigantine Way NP10: Duf 5H **53**
Brigham Ct. CF83: Caer 5G **27**
Bright St. NP11: Cros K 3A **16**
Brindley Rd. CF11: Card 1F **101**
Bristol Packet Wharf NP20: Newp 4C **36**
Bristol St. NP19: Newp 3D **36**
Bristol Ter. CF15: Gwae G 1D **68**
Bristol Vw. Cl. NP44: G'mdw 1C **10**
Britannia Quay CF10: Card 2C **102**
Brithdir St. CF24: Card 6H **85**
British Legion Dr. CF3: Rum 3H **87**
Briton Cl. NP16: Bul 6G **63**
Brittania Cl. NP11: Ris 6E **17**
Britten Cl. NP19: Newp 5B **38**
Britten Rd. CF64: P'rth 4D **108**
Britway Ct. CF64: Din P 2G **107**
Britway Rd. CF64: Din P 2G **107**
Broadacres CF11: Card 4E **95**
Broad Cl. CF62: Barry 2D **116**
Broadcommon Cl. NP19: Newp 6A **38**
Broadfield Ct. CF5: Ely 5H **93**
Broadhaven CF11: Card 5E **95**
Broadlands Ct. CF3: St M 6C **74**
NP26: Undy 4E **59**
Broadlands Ho. CF3: St M 6C **74**
Broadmead Pk. NP19: Newp 6A **38**
Broad Pl. CF11: Card 4E **95**
Broad Quay Rd. NP19: Newp 3E **55**
Broad Shoard, The CF71: C'bri 3C **90**
Broadstairs Rd. CF11: Card 4E **95**
Broad St. CF11: Card 4D **94**
CF62: Barry 4F **117**
NP4: Grif 6E **7**
NP20: Newp 1D **54**
Broad St. Comn. NP18: Nash 4B **56**
Broadstreet Comn. CF3: Pet W 4G **89**
Broad St. Pde. CF62: Barry 4F **117**
Broad Vw. NP44: Pnwd 6C **8**
Broadwalk NP18: C'ln 5H **21**
Broadwater Rd. NP19: Newp 2A **56**
Broadway CF3: Pet W 5B **76**
CF24: Card 2D **96**
CF37: P'prdd, T'rest 1C **24**
CF71: C'bri, L'thian 4C **90**
NP4: P'pool 2B **6**
NP18: C'ln 6H **21**
Broadweir Rd. NP44: C'brn 3G **11**
Broadwell Cl. CF3: St M 1D **88**
Broadwell Ct. NP18: C'ln 5H **21**
Broadwood Cl. NP19: Newp 4C **38**
Bro Athro CF3: Rum 3B **88**
Brocastle Rd. CF14: Whit 1D **84**
Brockhampton Rd. CF3: St M 6D **74**
Brockhill Ri. CF64: P'rth 5E **109**
Brockhill Way CF64: P'rth 5E **109**
Brock St. CF63: Barry 6B **106**
Bro-Dawel Cl. CF72: P'clun 1C **78**
Brodeg CF15: P'rch 5A **68**
Bromfield Pl. CF64: P'rth 6B **102**
Bromfield Rd. CF62: Barry 5G **117**
Bromfield St. CF11: Card 1H **101**
Bromley Dr. CF5: Ely 4A **94**
Bromsgrove St. CF11: Card 1H **101**
Bron Awelon CF62: Barry 4D **116**
Bron Felen CF14: Thorn 3F **71**
Bron Haul CF15: P'rch 5A **68**
Bronhaul CF72: T Grn 3E **65**
Bronllwyn CF15: P'rch 5H **67**
Bronllys Gro. NP10: Duf 6F **53**
Bronllys M. NP10: Duf 6F **53**
Bronllys Pl. NP44: C'iog 6G **9**
Bronmynydd CF83: Abert 3E **27**
Bron Rhiw CF83: Mac 2F **31**
Bronrhiw Av. CF83: Caer 2D **46**
Bronrhiw Fach CF83: Caer 2D **46**
Bronte Cl. CF3: L'rmy 5A **74**
Bronte Cres. CF3: L'rmy 5A **74**
Bronte Gro. NP20: Newp 1G **53**
Bronwydd Av. CF23: Pen L 5C **86**
Bronwydd Cl. CF23: Pen L 5C **86**
Bronwydd Rd. CF24: Card 1G **97**
Bron y Garth NP44: C'iog 1B **12**
Bron-y-Mor CF62: Barry 5E **117**
Brook Ct. *CF5: F'wtr* 2B **94**
(off St Fagans Rd.)
Brookdale Ct. CF38: Chu V 3F **43**
Brookfield CF37: Y'bwl 1A **14**
Brookfield Av. CF63: Barry 5C **106**
Brookfield Cl. NP19: Newp 6H **37**
Brookfield Dr. CF3: St M 1C **88**
Brookfield La. CF37: P'prdd 4E **15**
Brookfield Pk. Rd. CF71: C'bri 4D **90**
Brookland Ho. NP44: Pnwd 6E **9**
Brookland Rd. NP11: Ris 6E **17**
Brooklands CF72: L'harry 5A **78**
NP11: C'crn 1A **16**
Brooklands Ter. CF5: Cul C 1D **98**
Brookland Ter. NP44: Pnwd 5E **9**
Brooklea NP18: C'ln 3G **21**
Brooklea Pk. CF14: L'vne 3A **72**
Brooklyn Cl. CF14: R'ina 4C **70**
Brook Rd. CF5: F'wtr 2B **94**
CF14: Whit 3D **84**
Brookside CF38: Tont 2G **43**
CF64: Din P 2H **107**
NP20: Bet 5G **19**
NP26: Cald 3C **60**
NP44: St D 3E **11**
Brookside Cl. CF14: Heath 2F **85**
CF37: C'fydd 3F **15**
CF83: Caer 5H **27**
Brookside Cres. CF83: Caer 6E **29**
Brook St. CF11: Card 4A **4** (4H **95**)
CF37: T'rest 3E **25**
CF63: Barry 2A **118**
CF83: Abert 1E **27**
NP44: Pon'run 4E **9**
Brook St. La. CF11: Card 5A **4** (4H **95**)
Brook Ter. CF38: Chu V 2F **43**
Brookvale Dr. CF14: Thorn 2G **71**
Brookview Cl. CF14: Thorn 3H **71**
Brookway CF38: Tont 2G **43**
Broom Cl. NP10: Roger 3A **34**
Broome Path NP44: St D 3E **11**
Broomfield Cl. CF38: Tont 2G **43**
Broomfield St. CF83: Caer 1D **46**
Broom Pl. CF5: F'wtr 1H **93**
Broughton Pl. CF63: Barry 5A **106**
Brown Cl. NP19: Newp 6G **37**
Brown Ct. CF3: St M 2D **88**
Browning Cl. CF3: L'rmy 6H **73**
NP20: Newp 1H **53**
Bro-y-Fan CF83: Caer 4E **29**
Bruce Knight Cl. CF5: L'dff 5A **84**
Bruce St. CF24: Card 6A **86**
Brummell Dr. CF15: Cre 1F **81**
Brundall Cres. CF5: Ely 6E **93**
Brunel Av. NP10: Roger 3D **34**
Brunel Cl. CF63: Barry 5D **106**
Brunel Rd. NP16: Bul 4E **63**
NP44: F'wtr 3C **10**
Brunel St. CF11: Card 5A **4** (4G **95**)
NP20: Newp 2D **54**
(not continuous)
Brunswick St. CF5: Card 3E **95**
Bruton Pl. CF5: L'dff 6C **84**
Bryanston Rd. CF64: Sul 1E **119**

Brydges Pl. CF24: Card . . . 1A **96**
Bryn, The CF83: Tret . . . 2H **29**
NP20: Bet . . . 5G **19**
Bryn Aber CF83: Abert . . . 1E **27**
Bryn Aber Ter. CF83: Abert . . . 1E **27**
Bryn Adar CF14: R'ina . . . 5B **70**
Brynamlwg CF72: P'clun . . . 5E **65**
BRYNAU . . . 6E **29**
Bryn Aur CF37: Glync . . . 1D **14**
Brynau Rd. CF15: Taff W . . . 1F **69**
CF83: Caer . . . 6D **28**
Bryn Awel CF37: Glync . . . 1D **14**
CF83: B'ws . . . 3H **29**
Brynawel CF83: Caer . . . 3H **27**
Bryn-Awelon Rd. CF23: Cyn . . . 5C **72**
Bryn Bach CF14: R'ina . . . 5D **70**
Brynbala Way CF3: Rum . . . 2C **88**
Bryn Barrwg CF62: Barry . . . 5F **117**
Bryn Bevan NP20: Bryng . . . 6B **20**
Bryn Calch CF15: Morg . . . 5E **69**
Bryn Canol CF83: B'ws . . . 3G **29**
Bryn Castell CF15: Rad . . . 6F **69**
Bryn Celyn CF23: Pent . . . 6F **73**
Bryncelyn Pl. NP44: Pnwd . . . 6D **8**
Bryn Celyn Rd. CF23: Pent . . . 1F **87**
NP44: Pnwd . . . 6C **8**
Bryn Cl. CF83: Tret . . . 3H **29**
Bryncoch CF15: Taff W . . . 1E **69**
Bryncoed CF15: Rad . . . 6E **69**
Bryncoed Ter. CF83: Abert . . . 1E **27**
Bryn Creigiau CF72: Groes F . . . 6C **66**
Bryncyn CF23: Pent . . . 5F **73**
Bryn Derw CF38: Bed . . . 4A **42**
Bryn Derwen CF15: Rad . . . 6E **69**
CF83: Caer . . . 3B **28**
Brynderwen CF37: C'fydd . . . 2F **15**
Brynderwen Cl. CF23: Cyn . . . 3C **86**
CF37: C'fydd . . . 2F **15**
Brynderwen Ct. NP19: Newp . . . 3E **37**
Brynderwen Gro. NP19: Newp . . . 3E **37**
Brynderwen Rd. CF37: C'fydd . . . 2F **15**
NP19: Newp . . . 3E **37**
Bryn Dewi Sant CF72: Mis . . . 5E **65**
Bryn-Dolwen CF83: B'ws . . . 2G **29**
Bryn Eglwys CF37: P'prdd . . . 6A **14**
NP44: C'iog . . . 6G **9**
Brynfab Rd. CF37: R'fln . . . 5H **25**
Brynfedw CF23: L'dyrn . . . 2E **87**
CF83: B'ws . . . 2G **29**
Bryn Garw NP44: C'iog . . . 6G **9**
Bryngelli Ter. CF83: Abert . . . 1E **27**
BRYNGLAS . . . 6A **20**
Bryn Glas CF14: Thorn . . . 3E **71**
CF83: B'ws . . . 2G **29**
Brynglas CF83: Caer . . . 3A **28**
NP44: H'bush . . . 5E **11**
Brynglas Av. NP20: Bryng . . . 6C **20**
Brynglas Cl. NP20: Bryng . . . 6B **20**
Brynglas Ct. NP20: Bryng . . . 6B **20**
Brynglas Cres. NP20: Bryng . . . 1B **36**
Brynglas Dr. NP20: Bryng . . . 6B **20**
Brynglas Rd. NP20: Bryng . . . 2B **36**
Brynglas Tunnels & Malpas Rd.
NP18: L'tnam . . . 3A **20**
NP20: L'tnam, Malp . . . 3A **20**
Bryn Goleu CF83: B'ws . . . 2G **29**
Bryngoleu CF83: Rud . . . 6B **30**
Bryn Golwg CF15: Rad . . . 6F **69**
Bryn Gomer NP44: C'iog . . . 5G **9**
BRYNGWYN . . . 2C **46**
Bryngwyn CF83: Caer . . . 2B **46**
Bryngwyn Rd. NP4: P'pool . . . 3B **6**
NP20: Newp . . . 5H **35**
Bryn-Gwyn Rd. CF23: Cyn . . . 6C **72**
Bryn-Gwyn St. CF83: B'ws . . . 2F **29**
Brynhafod Rd. CF83: Abert . . . 1E **27**
Bryn Haidd CF23: Pent . . . 6F **73**
Brynhedydd NP10: Bass, R'drn . . . 6A **34**
Bryn Heol CF83: B'ws . . . 3G **29**
Bryn Heulog CF14: Whit . . . 2B **84**
CF83: Caer . . . 4A **28**
Brynheulog CF23: Pent . . . 6F **73**
NP4: Grif, P'pool . . . 5D **6**
Bryn Heulog Ter. CF83: Mac . . . 1F **31**
Brynhill CF23: Cyn . . . 1C **86**
Brynhill Cl. CF62: Barry . . . 5F **105**
Bryn Hyfryd CF15: Rad . . . 6F **69**
Brynhyfryd CF38: Bed . . . 4A **42**
CF83: B'ws . . . 2F **29**
CF83: Caer . . . 4A **28**
NP44: C'iog . . . 5G **9**
Brynhyfryd Av. NP20: Newp . . . 5B **36**
Brynhyfryd Pl. CF37: T'rest . . . 2D **24**
Brynhyfryd Rd. NP20: Newp . . . 5A **36**
Brynhyfryd Ter. CF37: P'prdd . . . 6B **14**
CF83: Mac . . . 2F **31**
Bryn-Hyfryd Ter. NP11: Ris . . . 5D **16**
Bryn Ifor CF83: Caer . . . 4H **27**
Bryn Ilan CF37: Glynt . . . 1F **25**
Bryn Llus CF37: P'prdd . . . 2C **24**
Brynmawr Cl. CF3: St M . . . 6E **75**
Bryn Milwr NP44: H'bush . . . 5E **11**
Bryn Nant CF83: Caer . . . 3H **27**
Bryn Olwg CF37: P'prdd . . . 5E **15**
Brynonnen Ct. NP44: H'lys . . . 5B **10**
Bryn Owain CF83: Caer . . . 3A **28**
Bryn Pinwydden CF23: Pent . . . 5E **73**
Bryn Rhedyn CF37: Glync . . . 1D **14**
CF38: Tont . . . 1F **43**
NP44: Llanf . . . 5B **12**
Bryn-Rhedyn CF83: Caer . . . 5F **29**
Bryn Rhosyn CF15: Rad . . . 6E **69**
BRYNSADLER . . . 1B **78**
Bryn Siriol CF15: P'rch . . . 5H **67**
CF83: Caer . . . 4H **27**
Bryntail Rd. CF37: P'prdd, R'fln . . . 1G **25**
BRYNTEG . . . 6H **41**
Bryn Teg CF83: Caer . . . 4A **28**
Brynteg CF14: R'ina . . . 4C **70**
CF83: B'ws . . . 2G **29**
Brynteg Cl. CF23: Cyn . . . 3C **86**
Brynteg Ct. CF38: Bed . . . 6A **42**
Brynteg La. CF38: Bed . . . 6A **42**
CF72: Brynt . . . 6H **41**
Bryn Ter. CF38: Llan F . . . 4D **42**
CF72: Bryns . . . 1B **78**
NP4: P'nydd . . . 1A **6**
Bryntirion CF14: R'ina . . . 5E **71**
CF83: B'ws . . . 2G **29**
CF83: Caer . . . 4A **28**
BRYNWERN . . . 3B **6**
Brynwern NP4: P'pool . . . 3B **6**
Bryn-y-Fran Av. CF83: Tret . . . 3H **29**
Bryn y Gloyn CF62: Rho . . . 6G **115**
Bryn-y-Mor CF62: W Abe . . . 6F **113**
Bryn-y-Nant CF23: L'dyrn . . . 2F **87**
Bryn-yr-Eglwys CF15: P'rch . . . 5A **68**
Bryn-yr-Ysgol CF83: Caer . . . 3H **27**
Brython Dr. CF3: St M . . . 6E **75**
Buccaneer Cl. NP10: Duf . . . 5H **53**
Buccaneer Gro. NP10: Duf . . . 5G **53**
Buccaneer Way NP10: Duf . . . 5H **53**
Buchanan Way NP10: Coedk . . . 5D **52**
Buchan Cl. NP20: Newp . . . 1H **53**
Buckingham Cl. CF14: L'vne . . . 3B **72**
Buckingham Cres. NP19: Newp . . . 3F **37**
Buckingham Pl. CF62: Barry . . . 5E **105**
NP19: Newp . . . 3F **37**
Buckle Wood NP16: Chep . . . 2C **62**
Buckley Cl. CF5: L'dff . . . 4H **83**
Budden Cres. NP26: Cald . . . 4C **60**
Builth Cl. NP10: Duf . . . 6F **53**
Bull Cliff Wlk. CF62: Barry . . . 5C **116**
Bullfinch Rd. CF62: St Ath . . . 3G **111**
Bull Ring CF72: L'sant . . . 1F **65**
Bulmore Rd. NP18: C'ln . . . 1A **38**
Bulrush Cl. CF3: St M . . . 1F **89**
BULWARK . . . 4E **63**
Bulwark Av. NP16: Bul . . . 4F **63**
Bulwark Ind. Est. NP16: Bul . . . 4E **63**
Bulwark Rd. NP16: Bul . . . 3E **63**
Bunyan Cl. CF3: L'rmy . . . 5B **74**
Burberry Cl. NP10: Roger . . . 2H **33**
Burford Gdns. CF11: Card . . . 4H **101**
Burges Ho. CF24: Card . . . 1H **5**
Burges Pl. CF11: Card . . . 6G **95**
Burgesse Cres. CF72: L'sant . . . 3F **65**
Burial La. CF61: Llan M . . . 3B **110**
Burleigh Rd. NP20: Newp . . . 5A **36**
Burley Pl. CF62: St Ath . . . 1D **112**
Burlington St. CF63: Barry . . . 2B **118**
Burlington Ter. CF5: Card . . . 2D **94**
Burnaby St. CF24: Card . . . 3E **97**
Burne Jones Cl. CF5: L'dff . . . 5A **84**
Burnfort Rd. NP20: Newp . . . 6G **35**
Burnham Av. CF3: L'rmy . . . 6A **74**
CF64: Sul . . . 3H **119**
Burnham Ct. CF3: L'rmy . . . 1A **88**
Burns Cl. CF83: Mac . . . 3C **30**
NP20: Newp . . . 2G **53**
Burns Cres. CF62: Barry . . . 5H **105**
NP26: Cald . . . 6B **60**
Burnside Ct. CF5: F'wtr . . . 1F **93**
Burns La. NP44: St D . . . 3F **11**
Burn's Way CF37: Pen c . . . 4B **24**
Burnt Barn Rd. NP16: Bul . . . 5E **63**
Burreed Cl. CF3: St M . . . 1F **89**
BURTON . . . 5G **113**
Burton Homes NP20: Newp . . . 6B **36**
NP26: C'ent . . . 1B **60**
Burton Rd. NP19: Newp . . . 1F **37**
Burton Ter. CF62: E Abe . . . 6H **113**
Burt Pl. CF10: Card . . . 1B **102**
Burt St. CF10: Card . . . 2B **102**
Burwell Cl. CF23: Pontp . . . 4H **73**
Bush La. NP4: P'pool . . . 3B **6**
(not continuous)
Bushy Pk. NP4: P'pool . . . 2A **6**
Bute Cres. CF10: Card . . . 1C **102**
Bute Esplanade CF10: Card . . . 2B **102**
Bute La. CF64: P'rth . . . 1E **109**
Bute Pl. CF10: Card . . . 1C **102**
Bute St. CF10: Card . . . 6E **5** (5B **96**)
(not continuous)
CF15: Tong . . . 4G **69**
Bute Ter. CF10: Card . . . 5E **5** (4B **96**)
BUTETOWN . . . 6B **96**
Butetown History & Arts Cen. . . . 1C **102**
Butetown Link CF10: Card . . . 3A **102**
CF11: Card . . . 3A **102**
Butetown Link Rd. CF10: Card . . . 1C **102**
Butleigh Av. CF5: Card . . . 2C **94**
Butterbur Pl. CF5: Ely . . . 4E **93**
Buttercup Cl. NP10: Roger . . . 2H **33**
Buttercup Ct. NP44: Ty C . . . 4B **10**
Butterfield Dr. CF23: Pontp . . . 4E **73**
Butterfly Cl. CF38: Chu V . . . 3F **43**
Buttermere Way NP19: Newp . . . 1F **37**
Butterworth Cl. NP19: Newp . . . 4C **38**
Buttington Hill NP16: Sed, B'ly . . . 3H **63**
Buttington Rd. NP16: Sed . . . 3G **63**
Buttington Ter. NP16: B'ly . . . 4H **63**
Butt Lee Ct. CF62: Barry . . . 2G **117**
Buttrills Cl. CF62: Barry . . . 2G **117**
Buttrills Rd. CF62: Barry . . . 1G **117**
Buttrills Wlk. CF62: Barry . . . 1G **117**
Butts, The CF71: C'bri . . . 3C **90**
Buxton Cl. NP20: Newp . . . 2H **53**
Buxton Ct. CF83: Caer . . . 6E **29**
Bwlch Rd. CF5: F'wtr . . . 2H **93**
Byrd Cres. CF64: P'rth . . . 4C **108**
Byrde Cl. NP19: Newp . . . 4A **38**
Byron Av. CF38: Bed . . . 6A **42**
Byron Ct. CF61: Llan M . . . 4D **110**
CF64: P'rth . . . 6H **101**
Byron Pl. CF64: P'rth . . . 1D **108**
NP26: Cald . . . 6B **60**
NP44: St D . . . 3F **11**
Byron Rd. NP20: Newp . . . 6H **35**
Byron St. CF24: Card . . . 1G **5** (2C **96**)
CF62: Barry . . . 2H **117**
Bythway Rd. NP4: Trev . . . 1C **6**
Byways NP44: G'mdw . . . 2D **10**

C

Caban Cl. NP10: Roger . . . 2D **34**
Cader Idris Cl. NP11: Ris . . . 6G **17**
Cadman Cl. CF24: Card . . . 2G **97**
Cadnant Cl. CF14: L'shn . . . 4F **71**
Cadoc Cl. NP26: C'ent . . . 1B **60**
Cadoc Cres. CF63: Barry . . . 1D **118**
Cadoc Pl. CF5: L'dff . . . 4A **84**
Cadoc Rd. NP44: Pnwd . . . 5C **8**
Cadoxton Station (Rail) . . . 1C **118**
Cadvan Rd. CF5: Ely . . . 3F **93**
Cadwal Ct. CF38: Llan F . . . 5C **42**

Cadwgan Pl. CF5: F'wtr 2A **94**
Cae Bach CF83: Mac 2E **31**
Caebach Cl. CF5: Ely 6D **92**
Cae Bedw CF83: Caer 2B **28**
Cae Brandi CF3: M'fld 5A **76**
Cae-Bryn CF83: Abert 1E **27**
Cae Brynton Rd. NP20: Newp 1H **53**
Cae Cadno CF38: Chu V 2D **42**
Cae Calch CF83: Caer 3A **28**
Cae Canol CF64: P'rth 4C **108**
Cae Caradog CF83: Caer 3G **27**
Cae Castle CF71: L'thian 5B **90**
Cae Croes Heol CF83: Caer 2H **45**
Caedel Ct. CF14: Thorn 1H **71**
Caedelyn Rd. CF14: Whit 1C **84**
Cae Derwen NP44: Two L 4F **11**
Cae Du Mawr CF83: Caer 3A **28**
Cae Fardre CF38: Chu V, Tont 1F **43**
Cae Ffynnon CF38: Chu V 1E **43**
CF83: Caer 3A **28**
Cae Garw CF14: Thorn 3F **71**
CF38: Llan F 6B **42**
CF64: Din P 3G **107**
Cae Garw Bach CF5: St F 3C **82**
Cae Gethin CF83: Caer 2A **28**
Cae Glas CF63: Barry 6B **106**
CF83: Caer 4A **28**
Cae-Glas Av. CF3: Rum 4H **87**
Cae-Glas Rd. CF3: Rum 4H **87**
Cae Gwyn CF64: P'rth 3C **108**
Caegwyn Rd. CF14: Heath, Whit 3E **85**
Cae Gwyrdd CF15: Tong 5A **70**
Cae Leon CF62: Barry 4H **105**
Cae Lewis CF15: Tong 4H **69**
Cae Llwyd CF83: Caer 4D **28**
Cae Maen CF14: Heath 3F **85**
Cae Marchog CF83: Caer 3B **28**
Cae Mawr Av. NP26: Cald 5C **60**
Cae Mawr Gro. NP26: Cald 5C **60**
Cae Mawr Rd. CF14: R'ina 6E **71**
NP26: Cald 5C **60**
Cae Meillion CF83: Caer 2A **46**
Caenant CF37: R'fln 3F **25**
Cae Nant Gledyr CF83: Caer 6H **27**
Cae Nant Goch CF83: Caer 2H **45**
Caenant Rd. CF83: Caer 5C **28**
Caenewydd Cl. CF5: Ely 6D **92**
Caepalish *NP4: P'nydd* *1A* ***6***
(off Pentrepiod Rd.)
Caepalish Pl. *NP4: P'nydd* *1A* ***6***
(off Pentrepiod Rd.)
Cae Pandy CF83: Caer 4D **28**
Cae Pant CF83: Caer 3B **28**
Cae Pen-y-Graig CF83: Caer 2A **28**
Cae Perllan Rd.
NP20: Newp 1A **54**
CAERAU 5G **93**
Caerau Ct. CF5: Ely 5G **93**
CF72: C Inn 2H **65**
Caerau Ct. Rd. CF5: Ely 5G **93**
Caerau Cres. NP20: Newp 5A **36**
Caerau La. CF5: Ely 6F **93**
CF5: Ely, Wen 3E **99**
CF15: P'rch 5B **68**
Caerau Pk. Cres. CF5: Ely 5G **93**
Caerau Pk. Pl. CF5: Ely 5G **93**
Caerau Pk. Rd. CF5: Ely 5G **93**
Caerau Rd. CF5: Ely 5G **93**
NP20: Newp 5A **36**
Caerbragdy CF83: Caer 6D **28**
Caer Cady Cl. CF23: Cyn 3C **86**
Caer Castell Pl. CF3: Rum 2A **88**
Caer Ceffyl CF5: St F 2C **82**
CAERDYDD 3E **5** (4A **96**)
Caer Efail CF5: St F 3C **82**
Cae Rex CF71: L'thian 4C **90**
Cae'r Fferm CF83: Caer 6A **28**
CAERFFILI 1D **46**
Caer Ffynnon CF62: Barry 4E **117**
Cae'r Gerddi CF38: Chu V 2E **43**
Caer Graig CF15: Rad 6E **69**
Cae Rhedyn NP44: C'iog 1B **12**
Cae Rhos CF83: Caer 4D **28**
CAERLEON 5H **21**
Caerleon Cl. CF3: St M 6E **75**
Caerleon Ct. CF83: Caer 5G **27**
Caerleon Rd. CF14: Card 5F **85**
CF64: Din P 2A **108**
NP18: C'ln 3D **36**
NP18: P'hir 3B **12**
NP19: Newp 3D **36**
NP44: Llanf 3B **12**
(not continuous)
Caerleon Roman Baths & Mus. 5H **21**
Caerleon Way NP16: Bul 5F **63**
CAERLLION 5H **21**
Caer Mead Cl. CF61: Bov 3D **110**
Caernarvon Cl. CF64: Din P 2A **108**
NP44: L'rfn 2A **12**
Caernarvon Ct. CF83: Caer 5H **27**
Caernarvon Cres. NP44: L'rfn 2A **12**
Caernarvon Dr. NP10: R'drn 6A **34**
Caernarvon Gdns. CF62: Barry 5G **105**
Caernarvon Way CF3: Rum 2B **88**
Cae'r Odyn CF64: Din P 3G **107**
CAERPHILLY 1D **46**
Caerphilly Bus. Pk. CF83: Caer 1E **47**
Caerphilly By-Pass CF83: Caer 2H **45**
Caerphilly Castle 6D **28**
Caerphilly Cl. CF64: Din P 1A **108**
NP10: R'drn 6A **34**
CAERPHILLY DISTRICT MINERS HOSPITAL 2B **46**
Caerphilly Leisure Cen. 5D **28**
CAERPHILLY PARC ESTATE 4D **28**
Caerphilly Rd.
CF14: Heath, L'shn, R'ina 6F **71**
CF15: N'grw 4D **44**
(not continuous)
CF83: Sen 1D **26**
NP10: Bass, R'drn 6A **34**
(not continuous)
Caerphilly Station (Rail) 1D **46**
Caerphilly Vis. Cen. *1D* ***46***
(off Castle St.)
Caer ty Clwyd CF61: Llan M 2B **110**
Caer Wenallt CF14: R'ina 5B **70**
CAER-WENT 1A **60**
Caerwent Gdns. NP26: C'ent 1B **60**
Caerwent La. NP16: Bul 6F **63**
Caerwent Rd. CF5: Ely 4E **93**
NP4: Trev 1D **6**
NP44: C'iog 4F **9**
Caer Worgan CF61: Llan M 1B **110**
Cae Samson CF5: Ely 5G **93**
Caesar Cres. NP18: C'ln 4G **21**
Cae Stumpie CF71: C'bri 4D **90**
Cae Syr Dafydd CF11: Card 2E **95**
Cae Tymawr CF14: Whit 3A **84**
Cae Uwchllyn CF83: Caer 2A **46**
Caewal Rd. CF5: L'dff 1C **94**
Cae Yorath CF14: Whit 2D **84**
Cae-yr-Ebol NP44: Pnwd 6E **9**
Cae Ysgubor CF83: Caer 2A **28**
Caird St. NP16: Chep 3E **63**
Cairnmuir Rd. CF24: Card 2F **97**
Calderton Rd. CF38: Bed 5A **42**
Caldey Island Ho. CF11: Card 4A **102**
CALDICOT 5D **60**
Caldicot By-Pass NP26: Cald 6C **60**
Caldicot Castle 4E **61**
Caldicot Castle Country Pk. 4E **61**
Caldicot Ct. CF83: Caer 5H **27**
Caldicot Rd. CF5: Ely 5H **93**
NP26: C'ent 2B **60**
NP26: Cri, Pskwt 5E **61**
NP26: Rog 5A **60**
Caldicot Station (Rail) 6B **60**
Caldicot St. NP19: Newp 5F **37**
Caldicott Cl. CF38: Bed 6A **42**
Caldicot Way NP44: Pon'run 5F **9**
Caldwell Cl. CF38: Bed 6A **42**
Caldy Cl. CF62: Barry 6H **105**
NP19: Newp 2F **37**
Caldy Ct. CF14: Llan N 4C **84**
Caldy Rd. CF14: Llan N 4C **84**
Caledfryn Way CF83: Caer 3H **27**
Callaghan Ct. CF24: Card 3E **97**
Callaghan Sq. CF10: Card 6E **5** (5B **96**)
Cambourne Av. CF14: Whit 2B **84**
Cambourne Cl. CF62: Barry 6E **105**
Cambria CF11: Card 5H **101**
Cambria Cl. NP18: C'ln 5A **22**
Cambrian Av. CF61: Llan M 4B **110**
Cambrian Cen. NP20: Newp 4B **36**
Cambrian Cl. CF3: M'fld 4A **76**
Cambrian Cres. *CF3: M'fld* *4A* ***76***
(off Cambrian Way)
Cambrian Dr. CF3: M'fld 4A **76**
Cambrian Gdns. CF3: M'fld 4A **76**
Cambrian Gro. CF3: M'fld 4A **76**
Cambrian Ind. Est. (East Side)
CF72: P'clun 5C **64**
Cambrian Ind. Est. (West Side)
CF72: P'clun 5C **64**
Cambrian Pl. CF37: T'rest 2E **25**
Cambrian Point CF24: Card 6H **85**
Cambrian Res. Cvn. Pk. CF5: Cul C 1E **99**
Cambrian Rd. NP20: Newp 4B **36**
Cambrian Way CF3: M'fld 4A **76**
Cambria Rd. CF5: Ely 6F **93**
Cambria St. NP4: Grif 1E **9**
Cambridge Ct. NP18: C'ln 3E **21**
Cambridge Rd. NP19: Newp 4D **36**
Cambridge St. CF11: Card 1A **102**
CF62: Barry 4E **117**
Cam Ct. NP44: Thorn 6A **8**
Camellia Av. NP10: Roger 2H **33**
Camellia Ct. CF5: F'wtr 5H **83**
Camelot Ct. NP18: C'ln 5A **22**
Camelot Pl. NP19: Newp 3D **36**
Camelot Way CF14: Thorn 3F **71**
Cameron St. CF24: Card 2E **97**
Camm's Cnr. CF64: Din P 2A **108**
Campanula Dr. NP10: Roger 2H **33**
Campbell Dr. CF11: Card 3H **101**
Campbell St. NP4: P'pool 2A **6**
Camperdown Rd. NP19: Newp 6G **37**
Camperly Cl. CF38: Bed 6A **42**
Campion Cl. NP20: Newp 3A **36**
NP44: H'lys 5C **10**
Campion Pl. CF5: F'wtr 5H **83**
Camp Rd. NP16: Bul 4F **63**
NP26: Sud 6H **61**
Campton Pl. CF38: Bed 6B **42**
Camrose Ct. CF62: Barry 5H **105**
Camrose Rd. CF5: Ely 5H **93**
Camrose Wlk. NP44: St D 3E **11**
Canada Rd. CF14: Card 6G **85**
Canal Cl. NP4: Grif 1E **9**
Canal Cotts. CF37: P'prdd 5D **14**
Canal Pde. CF10: Card 6E **5** (5B **96**)
NP20: Newp 5C **36**
(not continuous)
Canal Pk. Ind. Est. CF10: Card 6B **96**
Canal St. NP20: Newp 2B **36**
Canal Ter. NP20: Newp 6D **36**
Canaston Pl. CF5: Ely 5H **93**
Canberra Cl. NP44: C'brn, G'mdw 3F **11**
Canberra Cres. NP20: Newp 5F **35**
Candwr La. NP18: P'hir 5G **13**
Candwr Pk. NP18: P'hir 6F **13**
Candwr Rd. NP18: P'hir 1G **21**
Cannington Av. CF3: L'rmy 2A **88**
Cannington Cl. CF64: Sul 2H **119**
Cannon La. NP26: C'ent 1B **60**
Canon St. CF62: Barry 4F **117**
NP19: Newp 3D **36**
Canopus Cl. CF3: St M 1B **88**
Canterbury Cl. NP20: Newp 3C **36**
Canterbury Way NP26: Pskwt 5G **61**
CANTON 3E **95**
Canton Ct. CF11: Card 4F **95**
Cantref Cl. CF14: Thorn 2H **71**
NP10: Roger 2C **34**
Capel Ct. NP4: P'nydd 1A **6**
NP20: Newp 1C **54**
(Albion St.)
NP20: Newp *6C* ***36***
(off Capel Cres.)
Capel Cres. NP20: Newp 6B **36**
Capel Edeyrn CF23: Pontp 5H **73**
Capel Gwilym Rd. CF14: Thorn 1E **71**
Capella Ho. CF10: Card 1D **102**
CAPEL LLANILLTERN 3H **81**
Capel St. NP4: P'pool 3C **6**
NP20: Newp 1C **54**
Capital Bus. Pk. CF3: Rum 5B **88**

Capital Point CF3: Rum 5B 88
Capital Retail Pk. CF11: Card 6E 95
Capitol CF10: Card 3E 5 (3B 96)
Caple Rd. CF62: Barry 4E 117
Caradoc Av. CF63: Barry 6H 105
Caradoc Cl. CF3: St M 6E 75
NP18: C'ln 4G 21
Caradoc Rd. NP44: C'brn 1G 11
Caraway Cl. CF3: St M 5E 75
CARDIFF 3E 5 (4A 96)
Cardiff Arena Ice Rink 4A 102
Cardiff Arms Pk. 4B 4 (4H 95)
Cardiff Athletics Stadium 5F 95
Cardiff Bay Bus. Cen. CF24: Card 4D 96
Cardiff Bay Retail Pk. CF11: Card 3H 101
CARDIFF BAYS 1C 102
Cardiff Bay Station (Rail) 1C 102
Cardiff Bay Vis. Cen. 2C 102
Cardiff Bay Yacht Club 5A 102
Cardiff Blues RUFC 4B 4 (4H 95)
Cardiff Bowling Club 2A 4 (3G 95)
Cardiff Bus. Pk. CF14: L'shn 6G 71
Cardiff Bus. Technology Cen.
CF10: Card 2A 96
Cardiff Cvn. Pk. CF11: Card 2F 95
Cardiff Castle 3C 4 (3H 95)
Cardiff Central Station (Rail) 6C 4 (5A 96)
Cardiff City FC 5F 95
Cardiff Ga. Bus. Pk. CF23: Pontp 3G 73
Cardiff Ga. Retail Pk. CF23: Pontp 3H 73
CARDIFF GATE SERVICE AREA 3H 73
CARDIFF HELIPORT 6F 97
Cardiff Heliport 1G 103
Cardiff Ind. Pk. CF14: L'shn 6G 71
CARDIFF INTERNATIONAL AIRPORT 3F 115
Cardiff International Arena 5E 5 (4B 96)
Cardiff International Pool 4H 101
Cardiff International Sports Village 4H 101
Cardiff Millennium Stadium 5B 4 (4H 95)
Cardiff Queen Street Station (Rail)
3F 5 (3B 96)
Cardiff RC Cathedral 4E 5 (4B 96)
Cardiff Rd. CF5: L'dff 6C 84
CF5: St F 2E 93
CF15: Cre 6E 67
CF15: N'grw, Taff W 3D 44
CF37: R'fln, T'rest 2E 25
CF63: Barry, Din P 1C 118
CF64: Din P, P'rth 6F 107
CF71: C'bri 4D 90
CF72: L'sant 2F 65
CF72: Mwy 5G 65
CF83: Caer 1D 46
NP10: Coedk 5E 53
NP20: Newp 3F 53
Cardiff Rd. Bus. Pk. CF63: Barry 1C 118
CARDIFF ROYAL INFIRMARY WEST WING
2H 5 (3C 96)
Cardiff Ski Cen. 1A 94
CARDIFF SPIRE HOSPITAL 4F 73
Cardiff University
Colum Rd. 1H 95
Cardiff University Sports Hall 6F 85
CARDIFF WEST SERVICE AREA 3G 81
Cardigan Cl. CF38: Tont 2F 43
CF64: Din P 2A 108
NP44: C'iog 5F 9
Cardigan Ct. NP18: C'ln 4F 21
Cardigan Cres. CF61: Bov 3E 111
NP44: C'iog 5F 9
Cardigan Ho. CF64: P'rth 2D 108
Cardigan Pl. NP19: Newp 3F 37
Cardigan Rd. CF64: Din P 2A 108
Cardigan St. CF5: Card 3E 95
Cardinal Dr. CF14: L'vne 1A 72
Carew Cl. CF62: Barry 6H 105
Carey Rd. NP19: Newp 4G 37
Carfax Path NP44: F'wtr 4D 10
Cargill Cl. CF38: Bed 6B 42
Cargo Rd. CF10: Card 3C 102
Carisbrooke Rd. NP19: Newp 4F 37
Carisbrooke Way CF23: Pen L 4C 86
Carling Pl. CF5: Ely 6E 93
Carlisle St. CF24: Card 3E 97
NP20: Newp 1D 54
Carlotta Way CF10: Card 1B 102
Carlton Cl. CF14: Thorn 2G 71
Carlton Ct. NP4: P'nydd 1A 6
Carlton Cres. CF38: Bed 6A 42
Carlton Pl. NP11: Cros K 2A 16
Carlton Rd. NP19: Newp 2E 37
Carlton Ter. NP11: Cros K 2A 16
NP18: C'ln 6A 22
Carmarthen Cl. CF61: Bov 3D 110
CF62: Barry 6H 105
Carmarthen Ct. CF5: Card 3F 95
CF83: Caer 5H 27
Carmarthen Dr. CF38: Tont 1F 43
Carmarthen Ho. CF64: P'rth 3D 108
Carmarthen Rd. CF64: Din P 2A 108
Carmarthen St. CF5: Card 3E 95
Carmel Ct. CF23: Pen L 5C 86
Carn Celyn CF38: Bed 6A 42
Carne Ct. CF61: Bov 3D 110
Carnegie Dr. CF23: Cyn 2B 86
Carn-yr-Ebol CF63: Barry 4B 106
Caroline Rd. NP4: New I 5G 7
Caroline St. CF10: Card 5D 4 (4A 96)
NP20: Newp 5C 36
Caroline Way NP4: New I 5G 7
Carpenters Arms La. NP20: Newp 4C 36
Ca'r Pwll CF64: Din P 3G 107
Carreg Arwyn CF72: L'harry 5A 78
Carshalton Rd. CF38: Bed 6A 42
Carswell Pl. CF38: Bed 5B 42
Carter Pl. CF5: F'wtr 6H 83
Cartref Melus NP19: Newp 6G 37
Cartwright Ct. CF24: Card 6B 86
Cartwright Grn. NP20: Malp 5A 20
Cartwright La. CF5: F'wtr 2H 93
Carys Cl. CF5: Ely 1E 99
CF64: P'rth 4C 108
CAS-BACH 2G 75
CAS-GWENT 2E 63
CASNEWYDD 4C 36
Caspian Cl. CF3: St M 1D 88
Caspian Point CF10: Card 1D 102
Castan Rd. CF72: P'clun 6D 64
Castellau Rd. CF38: Bed 3G 41
Castell Coch 3G 69
Castell Coch Dr. NP10: Duf 6G 53
Castell Coch Vw. CF15: Tong 4G 69
Castell Meredith CF83: Caer 4E 29
Castell Morgraig CF83: Caer 4E 29
Castell Morgraig (remains of) 6D 46
CASTELL-Y-BWCH 2C 18
Castell-y-Fan CF83: Caer 4E 29
Castell-y-Mwnws CF72: L'harry 1A 78
Castell-y-Mynach Rd. CF38: Bed 4H 41
Castertown Pill NP26: Cald 6E 61
Castle Arc. CF10: Card 4C 4
Castle Arc. Balcony
CF10: Card 4C 4 (4A 96)
Castle Av. CF3: Rum 5F 87
CF64: P'rth 4D 108
CF83: Caer 4C 28
Castle Cl. CF15: Cre 5E 67
CF61: Bov 4E 111
CF64: Din P 2A 108
NP10: Roger 5D 34
(not continuous)
NP11: P'waun 1A 16
Castle Ct. CF38: Chu V 2F 43
CF61: Llan M 3B 110
CF71: L'dgh 6C 90
NP11: P'waun 1A 16
NP26: Pskwt 6E 61
(Castertown Pill)
NP26: Pskwt 5F 61
(Gray Hill Vw.)
NP44: H'lys 5B 10
Castle Ct. Shop. Cen. CF83: Caer 6D 28
Castle Cres. CF3: Rum 5F 87
Castle Dr. CF64: Din P 2A 108
Castlefield Pl. CF14: Card 5G 85
Castleford Cl. CF38: Bed 5A 42
Castleford Gdns. NP16: Tut 1F 63
Castleford Hill NP16: Tut 1E 63
Castle Gdns. NP16: Chep 1D 62
NP26: Cald 4C 60
Castlegate Bus. Pk. NP26: Pskwt 5F 61
Castle Grn. CF5: St G 3A 92
Castle Hill CF5: St F 2D 92
CF71: L'thian 4B 90
Castle Ivor St. CF37: P'prdd 6A 14
Castleland St. CF63: Barry 2A 118
Castle La. CF24: Card 1G 5 (2C 96)
NP11: P'waun 1A 16
NP18: C'ln 5A 22
Castle Lea NP26: Cald 5D 60
Castle Lodge Cl. NP26: Cald 5E 61
Castle Lodge Cres. NP26: Cald 5E 61
Castle M. *CF71: L'thian 5C 90*
(off Bridge St.)
CF83: Caer 6D 28
NP18: C'ln 5A 22
Castle Mound 5A 22
CASTLE PARK 6D 28
Castle Pk. Cl. NP20: Newp 6F 35
Castle Pk. Rd. NP20: Newp 6F 35
Castle Pct. CF71: L'dgh 6D 90
Castle Ri. CF3: Rum 5G 87
Castle Rd. CF15: Tong 3G 69
CF62: Fon 6H 113
CF62: Rho 6E 115
Castle St. CF10: Card 4B 4 (4H 95)
CF15: Taff W 2E 69
CF37: T'rest 2E 25
CF61: Llan M 2B 110
CF62: Barry 3E 117
CF72: L'sant 2F 65
CF83: Caer 6D 28
NP18: C'ln 6A 22
NP20: Newp 1D 54
CASTLETON 2G 75
Castleton Cvn. Pk. CF62: St Ath 4E 113
Castleton Ct. CF3: St M 5G 75
Castleton Ri. CF3: Cas 2G 75
Castleton Rd. CF62: St Ath 4D 112
Castle Vw. CF15: Tong 5H 69
CF83: Caer 3B 28
NP16: Tut 1G 63
Castle Way NP26: Pskwt 5E 61
Castle Wood NP16: Chep 2C 62
Castlewood Cotts. CF64: Din P 2G 107
Cas Troggi NP26: Cald 4C 60
Caswell Rd. CF3: Rum 4H 87
Caswell Way NP19: Newp 3G 55
Catalpa Cl. NP20: Malp 4B 20
CATHAYS 6A 86
CATHAYS PARK 1C 4 (3A 96)
Cathays Station (Rail) 1C 4 (2A 96)
Cathays Ter. CF24: Card 6A 86
Cath Cob Cl. CF3: St M 1C 88
Cathedral Cl. CF5: L'dff 6D 84
Cathedral Ct. CF5: L'dff 6C 84
NP20: Newp 5B 36
Cathedral Grn., The CF5: L'dff 6C 84
Cathedral Rd. CF11: Card 3A 4 (2F 95)
Cathedral Vw. CF14: Llan N 5D 84
Cathedral Wlk. CF10: Card 3D 4 (3A 96)
Catherine Cl. NP10: Duf 6H 53
Catherine Dr. CF3: M'fld 5A 76
CF15: Tong 3H 69
Catherine Meazy Flats CF64: P'rth 6B 102
Catherine St. CF24: Card 1A 96
CF37: P'prdd 6C 14
Catkin Dr. CF64: P'rth 6G 101
Catrine CF11: Card 5H 101
CAT'S ASH 5G 23
Catsash Rd. NP18: Cat A, Chris, L'stne 2B 38
Cat's La. CF83: B'ws 2G 29
Cattwg Cl. CF61: Llan M 2B 110
Causeway, The CF71: L'thian 5B 90
NP26: Undy 5F 59
Causeway Hill CF71: L'thian 5B 90
Cavendish Cl. CF14: Thorn 3G 71
Cavendish Pl. CF38: Bed 5A 42
Cawley Pl. CF63: Barry 6B 106
Cawnpore St. CF64: P'rth 6G 101
CAXDOXTON 6B 106
Caxton Pl. CF23: Pent 5G 73
NP20: Newp 4B 36
Caynham Av. CF64: P'rth 5E 109
Cecil Ct. CF24: Card 2D 96
Cecil La. NP10: Roger 5D 34
Cecil Sharp Rd. NP19: Newp 4D 38
Cecil St. CF24: Card 2D 96

Cedar Cl. NP16: Bul .5E **63**
Cedar Ct. CF14: L'shn .5H **71**
Cedar Cres. CF38: Tont .2G **43**
Cedar Gro. CF5: F'wtr .6G **83**
Cedar Ho. CF14: Whit .1A **84**
Cedar La. CF37: R'fln .4H **25**
Cedar Rd. CF62: E Bre .2B **112**
NP19: Newp .4D **36**
Cedar Wlk. NP44: Up Cwm .6B **8**
Cedar Way CF64: P'rth .2C **108**
Cedar Wood Cl. NP10: Roger .2H **33**
Cedar Wood Dr. NP10: Roger .2H **33**
Cefn Bychan CF15: P'rch .4A **68**
Cefn Carnau Rd. CF14: Heath .1H **85**
Cefn Cl. CF37: Glync .1C **14**
NP10: Roger .4D **34**
NP44: C'iog .5G **9**
Cefn Coch CF15: Rad .6E **69**
Cefn Coed CF15: N'grw .3D **44**
Cefn-Coed Av. CF23: Cyn .3B **86**
Cefn-Coed Cres. CF23: Cyn .4C **86**
Cefn-Coed Gdns. CF23: Cyn .4B **86**
Cefn-Coed Rd. CF23: Cyn .4B **86**
Cefn Ct. NP10: Roger .4D **34**
NP20: Newp .6A **36**
Cefn Dr. NP10: Roger .4D **34**
Cefn Graig CF14: R'ina .5D **70**
Cefn Ilan CF83: Abert .2D **26**
Cefn La. CF37: Glync .2B **14**
Cefn Llan CF15: P'rch .5A **68**
Cefn Mably Farm .6C **50**
Cefn Mably Pk. CF3: Cefn M .1A **74**
Cefn Mably Rd. CF14: L'vne .2C **72**
Cefn Milwr NP44: H'bush .5F **11**
Cefn Mt. CF64: Din P .2G **107**
Cefn Nant CF14: R'ina .4D **70**
Cefn Onn Mdws. CF14: Thorn .1H **71**
Cefn Penuel CF15: P'rch .5H **67**
Cefn-Porth Rd. CF14: L'vne .4E **49**
Cefn Ri. NP10: Roger .3C **34**
Cefn Rd. CF14: Llan N .4E **85**
NP10: Roger .3B **34**
Cefn Wlk. NP10: Roger .4D **34**
Cefn-y-Lon CF83: Caer .3H **27**
CEFNYRHENDY .5E **65**
Cei Dafydd CF63: Barry .3A **118**
Ceiriog Cl. CF63: Barry .5A **106**
CF64: P'rth .1D **108**
Ceiriog Cres. CF37: R'fln .3F **25**
Ceiriog Dr. CF14: R'ina .5C **70**
CF83: Caer .5C **28**
Celandine Ct. NP16: Bul .5F **63**
NP44: Ty C .3B **10**
Celandine Rd. CF5: Ely .4E **93**
Celerity Dr. CF10: Card .5B **96**
Celtic Cl. NP26: Undy .4E **59**
Celtic Gateway Bus. Pk. CF11: Card .4G **101**
Celtic Grn. CF64: Din P .1H **107**
CELTIC LAKES .5E **53**
Celtic Manor
The Twenty Ten Course .3E **23**
Celtic Manor Golf Courses .4F **23**
Celtic Manor Resort, The .1D **38**
Celtic Rd. CF14: Whit .4F **85**
Celtic Springs NP10: Coedk .5D **52**
Celtic Way CF62: Rho .6C **114**
CF83: B'ws .3G **29**
NP10: Coedk .5D **52**
Celyn Av. CF23: Cyn .2B **86**
CF83: Caer .5C **28**
Celyn Cl. CF62: St Ath .2C **112**
Celyn Ct. NP44: Pnwd .5C **8**
Celynen Gro. NP20: Newp .3H **53**
Celyn Gro. CF23: Cyn .6C **72**
CF83: Caer .5C **28**
Cemaes Cres. CF3: Rum .2C **88**
Cemetery La. NP20: Newp .5B **36**
Cemetery Rd. CF15: Taff W .2F **69**
CF37: Glynt .2F **25**
CF62: Barry .1H **117**
Cenfedd St. NP19: Newp .2D **36**
Cennin Pedr CF63: Barry .4B **106**
Centenary Ct. CF38: Bed .5B **42**
Central Av. NP19: Newp .1B **56**
Central Bldgs. *CF83: Tret* .*3A* ***30***
(off Newport Rd.)
Central Ct. CF24: Card .2D **96**
Central Link CF10: Card .5G **5** (4C **96**)
Central Mkt. CF10: Card .4D **4** (4A **96**)
Central M. NP4: P'pool .3C **6**
Central Sq. CF10: Card .6C **4** (5A **96**)
CF37: P'prdd .*5D* ***14***
(off Ralph St.)
Central St. CF83: Caer, L'brad .2B **28**
Central Way CF14: Heath .4H **85**
CF64: Sul .1E **119**
NP44: Pnwd .6C **8**
Centre Ct. CF37: T'rest .3C **44**
Centre Trad. Est. CF10: Card .6F **5** (5B **96**)
Centurion Cl. CF5: Ely .6H **93**
Centurion Ga. NP18: C'ln .5A **22**
Centurions Ct. NP26: C'ent .1C **60**
Century Ct. CF11: Card .6B **4** (5H **95**)
Cerdin Av. CF72: P'clun .6D **64**
Ceredig Ct. NP44: L'rfn .3B **12**
Ceri Av. CF62: Rho .5F **115**
Ceridwen Ter. *CF37: P'prdd* .*6C* ***14***
(off Bridge St.)
CF72: L'sant .*2F* ***65***
(off Heol-y-Beila)
Ceri Rd. CF62: Rho .5F **115**
Chadwick Cl. NP20: Malp .5A **20**
Chaffinch Way NP10: Duf .4H **53**
Chalfont Cl. CF38: Bed .5B **42**
Chalvington Cl. CF38: Bed .5A **42**
Chamberlain Rd. CF14: Llan N .4B **84**
Chamberlain Row CF64: Din P .1A **108**
Chamomile Cl. CF23: Pontp .4E **73**
Chancery La. CF11: Card .4F **95**
Chandlers Reach CF38: Llan F .6C **42**
Chandlers Way CF64: P'rth .5A **102**
Chandlery Way CF10: Card .1B **102**
Channel Cl. CF62: Rho .6D **114**
Channel Vw. CF3: Cas .2F **75**
CF64: P'rth .4F **109**
NP4: P'garn .1D **6**
NP10: Bass .6B **34**
NP11: Ris .6F **17**
NP16: Bul .4E **63**
NP44: Pnwd .6C **8**
Channel Vw. Flats CF11: Card .3H **101**
Channel View Recreation Cen. .2A **102**
Channel Vw. Rd. CF11: Card .2H **101**
Chantry, The CF5: L'dff .6A **84**
Chantry Ri. CF64: P'rth .4E **109**
Chapel Cl. CF64: Din P .1A **108**
CF71: A'thin .2F **91**
NP16: Pwllm .5B **62**
NP20: Newp .6C **36**
Chapel Ct. CF83: Tret .2A **30**
Chapel La. CF64: P'rth .6A **102**
NP16: Math, Pwllm .6B **62**
NP44: C'iog, Pnwd .4F **9**
Chapel M. *CF15: Tong* .*4G* ***69***
(off Railway Ter.)
Chapel Rd. CF15: Morg .5F **69**
NP4: P'nydd .1A **6**
NP18: Gold .4E **57**
Chapel Row CF3: Old M .6B **74**
CF64: Din P .1A **108**
Chapel Row La. CF3: Old M .6B **74**
Chapel St. CF5: L'dff .1C **94**
CF37: P'prdd .6C **14**
CF37: R'fln .4F **25**
NP44: Pnwd .1G **11**
Chapel Ter. CF5: Twyn .3D **98**
NP4: P'nydd .1A **6**
NP10: R'drn .5A **34**
NP26: Magor .5D **58**
Chapel Wood CF23: L'dyrn .3E **87**
Chapman Cl. NP20: Malp .4A **20**
Chapman Ct. NP20: Newp .5H **35**
Chapter Art Cen. .3E **95**
Chard Av. CF3: L'rmy .2H **87**
Chard Ct. CF3: L'rmy .2H **87**
Chargot Rd. CF5: L'dff .2D **94**
Charles Darwin Way CF62: Barry .4G **117**
Charles Pl. CF62: Barry .5E **117**
Charles St. CF10: Card .3E **5** (3B **96**)
CF37: P'prdd .6A **14**
CF83: Caer .6D **28**
NP4: Grif .6E **7**
Charles St. NP10: Roger .5C **34**
NP20: Newp .5C **36**
(not continuous)
NP44: Pnwd .5E **9**
CHARLESVILLE .1A **6**
Charlesville NP4: P'nydd .1A **6**
Charlock Cl. CF14: Thorn .2E **71**
Charlotte Grn. NP20: Newp .6C **36**
Charlotte Pl. CF63: Barry .1B **118**
Charlotte Sq. CF14: R'ina .6E **71**
Charlotte St. CF64: P'rth .6H **101**
NP20: Newp .6C **36**
Charlotte Wlk. *NP20: Newp* .*6C* ***36***
(off Alma St.)
Charnwood Dr. CF23: Pontp .4G **73**
Charnwood Pk. CF10: Card .6F **97**
Charnwood Rd. NP19: Newp .1D **36**
Charston NP44: G'mdw .2D **10**
Charter Av. CF62: Barry .5F **105**
Charteris Cl. CF64: P'rth .5E **109**
Charteris Cres. CF5: Ely .3H **93**
Charteris Rd. CF5: Ely .3H **93**
Chartist Ct. NP11: Ris .6F **17**
Chartist Dr. NP10: Roger .4C **34**
Chartist Rd. CF72: L'sant .2E **65**
Chartists Way NP16: Bul .5E **63**
Chartley Cl. CF3: St M .6E **75**
Chartwell Ct. CF15: P'rch .4A **68**
Chartwell Dr. CF14: L'vne .4B **72**
CHATHAM .2G **31**
Chatham CF83: Mac .2G **31**
Chatham Pl. *CF83: Mac* .*2H* ***31***
(off Chatham St.)
Chatham St. CF83: Mac .2H **31**
Chatsworth Cl. CF5: F'wtr .6A **84**
Chatterton Sq. CF11: Card .3H **101**
Chaucer Cl. CF3: L'rmy .5A **74**
CF64: P'rth .1D **108**
NP26: Cald .6B **60**
Chaucer Ct. NP19: Newp .4F **37**
Chaucer Rd. CF62: Barry .5H **105**
NP19: Newp .4F **37**
Cheam Pl. CF14: L'shn .5H **71**
Cheddar Cres. CF3: L'rmy .2H **87**
Cheeseman's Trad. Est. NP26: Rog .5A **60**
Chelmer Cl. NP20: Bet .6E **19**
Chelmer Wlk. NP20: Bet .6E **19**
Chelston Pl. NP20: Newp .2B **36**
CHEPSTOW .2E **63**
Chepstow & District Leisure Cen. .1D **62**
Chepstow Castle .1E **63**
Chepstow Cl. CF5: Ely .5H **93**
NP44: C'iog .5G **9**
CHEPSTOW COMMUNITY HOSPITAL .2D **62**
Chepstow Ct. CF83: Caer .5H **27**
Chepstow Mus. .1F **63**
Chepstow Ri. NP44: C'iog .5G **9**
Chepstow Rd. NP18: L'stne .1E **39**
NP18: Newp .2C **38**
NP19: Newp .4D **36**
NP26: Cald .5D **60**
Chepstow Station (Rail) .2F **63**
Cheriton Dr. CF14: Thorn .3H **71**
Cheriton Gro. CF38: Tont .2H **43**
Cheriton Path NP44: F'wtr .3D **10**
Cherry Cl. CF5: F'wtr .6F **83**
CF64: Din P .3A **108**
CF64: P'rth .5E **109**
Cherrydale Rd. CF5: Ely .3A **94**
Cherrydown Cl. CF14: Thorn .3H **71**
Cherry Orchard Rd. CF14: L'vne, Thorn .1G **71**
Cherry Tree Cl. CF14: L'vne .2B **72**
CF83: B'ws .2E **29**
NP18: C'ln .4H **21**
NP18: L'stne .1F **39**
NP20: Malp .4B **20**
NP44: C'iog .6H **9**
Cherry Tree Wlk. CF72: T Grn .3E **65**
Cherrywood Cl. CF14: Thorn .2H **71**
Chervil Cl. CF3: St M .5E **75**
Cherwell Cl. CF5: F'wtr .6H **83**
Cherwell Rd. CF64: P'rth .3D **108**
Cherwell Wlk. NP20: Bet .5E **19**
Cheshire Cl. CF14: L'shn .1H **85**
Chester Cl. CF3: St M .1D **88**
NP4: New I .4H **7**

Chester Ct. CF83: Caer 4H **27**
Chesterfield St. CF63: Barry 6A **106**
Chester Pl. CF11: Card 6H **95**
Chester St. CF11: Card 5H **95**
Chesterton Rd. CF3: L'rmy 6H **73**
Chestnut Av. CF62: E Bre 2B **112**
Chestnut Cl. CF64: Din P 3H **107**
CF83: Mac 2G **31**
NP4: New I 4H **7**
NP26: Magor 4D **58**
Chestnut Dr. NP26: Rog 5A **60**
Chestnut Grn. NP44: Up Cwm 6B **8**
Chestnut Gro. NP18: C'ln 5E **21**
Chestnut Rd. CF5: F'wtr 1H **93**
Chestnuts, The CF72: Mis 1F **79**
Chestnut St. CF37: R'fln 4G **25**
Chestnut Tree Cl. CF15: Rad 1E **83**
Chestnut Way CF64: P'rth 2D **108**
Cheviot Cl. CF14: L'shn 6G **71**
NP11: Ris 5G **17**
Chichester Cl. NP19: Newp 6F **21**
Chichester Rd. CF64: P'rth 6H **101**
Chichester Way CF5: Ely 3A **94**
Chick La. NP20: Newp 6H **35**
Chilcote St. CF63: Barry 1B **118**
CHILDREN'S HOSPITAL FOR WALES 4H **85**
Chiltern Cl. CF14: L'shn 6G **71**
NP11: Ris 6H **17**
NP19: Newp 3A **38**
Chirk Cl. NP10: Duf 6F **53**
Chorley Cl. CF5: F'wtr 2G **93**
CHRISTCHURCH 2B **38**
Christchurch Hill NP18: Chris 2B **38**
Christchurch Rd. NP18: Chris 3A **38**
NP19: Newp 3E **37**
Christina Cres. NP10: Roger 5E **35**
Christina St. CF10: Card 6B **96**
(not continuous)
Chumleigh Cl. CF3: Rum 3G **87**
Church Av. CF64: P'rth 1F **109**
Church Cl. CF14: L'vne 3C **72**
CF38: Llan F 5D **42**
NP4: New I 1G **9**
NP4: Trev 1C **6**
NP10: Newp 5E **35**
NP26: Cald 4D **60**
NP44: C'iog 6G **9**
Church Ct. NP19: Newp 1G **37**
Church Cres. CF71: St H 6H **91**
NP10: Bass 6C **34**
NP10: Coedk 6C **52**
Church Farm Cl. NP20: Bet 6G **19**
Churchfield Av. NP26: Cald 4C **60**
Churchfields CF63: Barry 5B **106**
Church Hill Cl. CF71: L'thian 5A **90**
Church Ho. Pk. NP10: St Bri W 4G **77**
Churchill Cl. CF14: L'vne 1A **72**
CHURCHILL PARK 4C **28**
Churchill Ter. CF63: Barry 1C **118**
Churchill Way CF10: Card 3E **5** (3B **96**)
Church La. CF3: M'fld 4H **75**
CF3: Old M 6B **74**
(not continuous)
CF15: N'grw 4E **45**
CF61: Llan M 4A **110**
(Colhugh Pk.)
CF61: Llan M 3B **110**
(College St.)
CF62: St Ath 5D **112**
(not continuous)
NP4: New I 6H **7**
NP4: Trev 1B **6**
NP10: Coedk 1C **76**
NP26: Undy 5F **59**
Churchmead NP10: Bass 1D **52**
Church Mdw. CF61: Bov 3F **111**
Church Pl. Nth. CF64: P'rth 6B **102**
Church Pl. Sth. CF64: P'rth 6B **102**
Church Ri. CF5: Wen 5E **99**
NP26: Undy 5G **59**
Church Rd. CF3: Old M 5H **73**
CF3: Rum 4G **87**
CF5: Card 4F **95**
CF5: Ely 6G **93**
CF5: St F 5A **68**
CF14: L'vne 2C **72**
Church Rd. CF14: Whit 3B **84**
CF15: P'rch 5A **68**
CF23: L'dyrn, Pontp 5G **73**
CF37: P'prdd 5D **14**
CF38: Tont 1E **43**
CF62: Rho 6E **115**
CF63: Barry 6B **106**
CF64: P'rth 1F **109**
CF71: L'thian 4A **90**
CF83: Abert 2D **26**
NP10: Coedk 6C **52**
NP10: St Bri W 4G **77**
NP11: Ris 4D **16**
NP16: Chep 1F **63**
NP19: Newp 3D **36**
NP26: Cald 3D **60**
NP26: Undy 4F **59**
NP44: Llanf 5D **12**
NP44: Pnwd 6D **8**
Church Rd. Ter. NP11: Ris 4D **16**
Church Row NP16: Chep 1F **63**
NP26: Sud 6H **61**
Church St. CF10: Card 4C **4** (4A **96**)
CF15: Taff W 2E **69**
CF37: P'prdd 6C **14**
CF61: Llan M 3B **110**
CF71: C'bri 3C **90**
CF72: L'sant 2F **65**
CF83: B'ws 3G **29**
CF83: Mac 2G **31**
NP10: Roger 3B **34**
NP18: C'ln 5H **21**
NP20: Newp 1D **54**
(not continuous)
Church Ter. CF23: Pen L 1D **96**
CF63: Barry 6C **106**
NP4: P'nydd 1A **6**
Church Vw. CF37: P'prdd 1A **24**
CF71: L'thian 4A **90**
NP10: Bass 1D **52**
Church Vw. Cl. CF64: L'dgh 4F **101**
CHURCH VILLAGE 3E **43**
Church Village By-Pass
CF38: E Isaf, Llan F 1B **66**
CF72: C Inn, R'son 1B **66**
Churchward Dr. NP19: Newp 6H **37**
Churchwood NP4: Grif 1E **9**
Churchwood Cl. NP4: P'garn 2C **6**
Church Wood Rd.
NP44: Pnwd 6D **8**
Cidermill Cl. NP16: Bul 6F **63**
Cilfedw CF15: Rad 6F **69**
CILFYNYDD 2F **15**
Cilfynydd Rd. CF37: C'fydd 3F **15**
Cilgant y Meillion CF62: Rho 6F **115**
Cilgerran Ct. NP44: L'rfn 2B **12**
Cilgerran Cres. CF14: L'shn 5F **71**
Cil Hendy CF72: P'clun 6E **65**
Cineworld Cinema
Cardiff 5E **5** (4B **96**)
Newport 1B **56**
Circle, The NP44: C'brn 4F **11**
Circle Way E. CF23: L'dyrn 1E **87**
Circle Way W.
CF23: Cyn, L'dyrn, Pen L 3D **86**
CF23: L'dyrn 2D **86**
City Hall Rd. CF10: Card 2C **4** (3A **96**)
City Link CF24: Card 1E **97**
City Lofts *CF24: Card 1B 96*
(off Crwys Rd.)
City Rd. CF24: Card 1B **96**
City Wharf CF10: Card 6G **5** (5C **96**)
Civil Service Sports Club 4C **94**
Claerwen Dr. CF23: Cyn 2B **86**
Clairwain NP4: New I 6G **7**
Clarbeston Rd. CF14: Llan N 5C **84**
Clare Drew Way
NP44: C'iog 6H **9**
Clare Dr. CF71: C'bri 4D **90**
Clare Gdns. CF11: Card 5A **4** (4H **95**)
Claremont NP20: Malp 3B **20**
Claremont Av. CF3: Rum 3H **87**
Claremont Cres.
CF3: Rum 3H **87**
Clarence Cnr. NP4: P'pool 3C **6**
Clarence Emb. CF10: Card 2A **102**
Clarence Pl. CF10: Card 1B **102**
NP4: P'pool 4C **6**
NP11: Ris 5D **16**
NP19: Newp 4C **36**
Clarence Rd. CF10: Card 1A **102**
CF11: Card 1A **102**
NP4: P'pool 4C **6**
Clarence St. NP4: P'pool 3C **6**
NP20: Newp 1D **54**
Clarendon CF23: Cyn 1D **86**
Clarendon Cl. NP16: Bul 6G **63**
Clarendon Rd. CF23: Pen L 4D **86**
Clare Pl. CF11: Card 5A **4** (4H **95**)
Clare Rd. CF11: Card 6A **4** (5H **95**)
Clare St. CF11: Card 5A **4** (4H **95**)
Clark Av. NP44: Pnwd 5D **8**
Clarke St. CF5: Ely 3B **94**
Clas Dyfrig CF14: Whit 4D **84**
Clas Gabriel CF14: Whit 4D **84**
Clas Ifor CF14: Whit 2E **85**
Clas Illtyd CF14: Whit 3E **85**
Clas Isan CF14: Whit 3E **85**
Clas Odyn CF14: Whit 2D **84**
Clas Teilo CF14: Whit 4D **84**
Clas-ty-Gelli CF37: Glync 1D **14**
Clas Tynewydd CF14: Whit 3D **84**
Clas Ty'n-y-Cae CF14: R'ina 1E **85**
Clas Tywern CF14: Heath 1E **85**
Clas Yorath CF14: Whit 2D **84**
Claude Pl. CF24: Card 1C **96**
Claude Rd. CF24: Card 1C **96**
CF62: Barry 2F **117**
CF83: Caer 1C **46**
Claude Rd. W. CF62: Barry 3E **117**
Claverton Cl. CF38: Bed 5B **42**
Claverton Way CF23: Pontp 4E **73**
Claymore Pl. CF11: Card 3A **102**
Clayton Cres. CF37: Glync 2C **14**
Clayton St. NP19: Newp 3D **36**
Clearwater Rd. NP19: Newp 3B **56**
Clearwater Way CF23: Cyn 2B **86**
Clearwell Ct. NP10: Bass 6A **34**
Cleddau Cl. CF3: St M 6F **75**
Cledwen Cl. CF62: Barry 2D **116**
Cleeve Dr. CF14: L'shn 6G **71**
Clement Atlee Dr. NP19: Newp 3B **38**
Clement Pl. CF62: Barry 5E **117**
Cleppa Pk. NP10: Coedk 4E **53**
Cleppa Pk. Ind. Est.
NP10: Coedk 4E **53**
Clevedon Av. CF64: Sul 3H **119**
Clevedon Cl. NP19: Newp 3F **37**
Clevedon Ho. NP19: Newp 3G **37**
Clevedon Rd. CF3: L'rmy 1H **87**
NP19: Newp 4F **37**
Cleveland Dr. NP11: Ris 6G **17**
Clewer Ct. NP20: Newp 5H **35**
Clewer Ct. M. NP20: Newp 5H **35**
Cliff Ct. CF10: Card 1C **102**
Cliff Hill CF64: P'rth 3F **109**
Cliff Pde. CF64: P'rth 3F **109**
Cliff Pl. CF5: Card 3D **94**
Cliff Rd. CF64: P'rth 3F **109**
Cliffside CF64: P'rth 4F **109**
Cliff St. CF64: P'rth 6B **102**
Cliff Ter. CF37: T'rest 1D **24**
Cliff Vw. NP16: Sed 3H **63**
Cliff Wlk. CF64: P'rth 6F **109**
(not continuous)
Cliff Wood Vw.
CF62: Barry 5C **116**
Clifton Ho. CF24: Card 1H **5** (2D **96**)
Clifton Pl. NP20: Newp 5B **36**
Clifton Rd. NP20: Newp 5B **36**
Clifton Sq. NP4: Grif 6E **7**
Clifton St. CF24: Card 1H **5** (2D **96**)
CF62: Barry 4F **117**
CF83: Caer 1D **46**
NP10: Roger 1H **33**
Clinton Rd. CF64: P'rth 2E **109**
Clipper Cl. NP19: Newp 6F **21**
Clipper Rd. CF10: Card 6F **97**
Clist Rd. NP20: Bet 5E **19**
Clist Wlk. NP20: Bet 5E **19**
Clive Ct. CF5: Card 3D **94**
Clive Cres. CF64: P'rth 1F **109**

Clive Hall Ct. *CF5: Card* . . . *2D* ***94***
(off Clive Rd.)
Clive La. CF11: Card . . . 1G **101**
CF64: P'rth . . . 6H **101**
Clive M. CF5: Card . . . 3D **94**
Clive Pl. CF24: Card . . . 1G **5** (2C **96**)
CF62: Barry . . . 5H **117**
CF64: P'rth . . . 1F **109**
Clive Rd. CF5: Card . . . 2D **94**
CF62: Barry . . . 5G **117**
CF62: St Ath . . . 3D **112**
Clive St. CF11: Card . . . 6H **95**
CF83: Caer . . . 1C **46**
Clodien Av. CF14: Card . . . 5H **85**
Cloister Ct. CF5: Ely . . . 5A **94**
Cloisters, The NP16: Chep . . . 1D **62**
Clomendy Rd. NP44: C'brn . . . 3G **11**
(Commercial St.)
NP44: C'brn . . . 1E **11**
(Woodland St.)
Clonakilty Way CF23: Pontp . . . 3G **73**
Clos Afon Llwyd NP4: P'pool . . . 2C **6**
Clos Aled NP26: Cald . . . 4D **60**
Clos Alwen NP26: Cald . . . 3D **60**
Clos Alyn CF23: Pontp . . . 4F **73**
Clos Aneurin CF37: R'fln . . . 5H **25**
Clos Avro CF24: Card . . . 2H **97**
Clos Berriew CF14: Llan N . . . 4D **84**
Clos Brenin CF72: Bryns . . . 6C **64**
Clos Bron Iestyn CF37: P'prdd . . . 6A **14**
Clos Brynderi CF14: R'ina . . . 6E **71**
Clos Bryn Melyn CF15: Rad . . . 1F **83**
Clos Cadwgan CF38: Bed . . . 6H **41**
Clos Cae'r Wern CF83: Caer . . . 3A **46**
Clos Cae Wal CF15: Tong . . . 4G **69**
Clos Caewal CF15: P'rch . . . 4A **68**
Clos Camlas CF37: P'prdd . . . 5D **14**
Clos Caradog CF38: Llan F . . . 3D **42**
Clos Cas-Bach CF3: St M . . . 1E **89**
Clos Cefn Bychan CF15: P'rch . . . 4B **68**
Clos Cefn Glas CF38: Llan F . . . 6B **42**
Clos Cefni CF62: Barry . . . 1E **117**
Clos Ceirios CF5: Ely . . . 4H **93**
Clos Celyn CF63: Barry . . . 4B **106**
Clos Cemaes CF14: Llan N . . . 4D **84**
Clos Chappell CF3: St M . . . 2D **88**
Clos Coed Hir CF14: Whit . . . 1B **84**
Clos Coed-y-Dafarn CF14: L'vne . . . 3B **72**
Clos Collwyn CF38: Llan F . . . 6B **42**
Clos Cornel CF14: Whit . . . 3D **84**
Clos Corris CF14: Llan N . . . 4D **84**
Clos Cradog CF64: P'rth . . . 4C **108**
(not continuous)
Clos Creyr CF38: Chu V, Llan F . . . 2D **42**
Clos Cromwell CF14: R'ina . . . 4E **71**
Clos Culver CF5: Ely . . . 6F **93**
Clos Cwm Barri CF62: Barry . . . 3D **116**
Clos Cwm Creunant CF23: Pontp . . . 4F **73**
Clos Cwm Du CF23: Pontp . . . 4F **73**
Clos Cwm Garw CF83: Caer . . . 6H **27**
Clos Cyncoed CF83: Caer . . . 3H **27**
Clos Darren Las CF15: Cre . . . 6E **67**
Clos Ddyfan CF3: St M . . . 5E **75**
Clos Derwen CF23: Pen L . . . 5B **86**
Clos Dewi Sant CF11: Card . . . 3G **95**
Clos Dol Heulog CF23: Pontp . . . 4F **73**
Clos Dwyerw CF83: Caer . . . 2A **46**
Clos Dyfnaint CF3: St M . . . 1E **89**
Clos Dyfodwg CF38: Llan F . . . 6B **42**
Close, The CF14: L'shn . . . 5H **71**
NP26: Cald . . . 5B **60**
NP26: Pskwt . . . 5F **61**
NP44: Oakf . . . 5H **11**
Clos Edno CF23: Cyn . . . 4C **86**
Clos Eiddiw CF5: Ely . . . 4A **94**
Clos Elphan CF3: St M . . . 5E **75**
Clos Enfys CF83: Caer . . . 2A **46**
Clos Fach CF14: R'ina . . . 5E **71**
Clos Gedrych CF11: Card . . . 4D **94**
Clos Glanaber CF3: St M . . . 1E **89**
Clos Glas Llwch CF3: St M . . . 2D **88**
Clos Guto CF83: Caer . . . 5F **29**
Clos Gwastir CF83: Caer . . . 2A **46**
Clos Gwaun Gledyr CF83: Caer . . . 6H **27**
Clos Gwent CF38: Bed . . . 6H **41**
Clos Gwernen CF72: L'harry . . . 5C **78**
Clos Gwernydd CF83: Caer . . . 5H **27**
Clos Gwlad-yr-Haf CF3: St M . . . 1E **89**
Clos Gwy CF23: Pontp . . . 4F **73**
Clos Gwynedd CF38: Bed . . . 6H **41**
Clos Gwynle CF83: Caer . . . 2H **45**
Clos Hafodyrynys CF3: St M . . . 1D **88**
Clos Hafren CF3: St M . . . 1E **89**
Clos Halket CF11: Card . . . 4D **94**
Clos Hector CF24: Card . . . 2H **97**
Clos Hendre CF14: R'ina . . . 5F **71**
Clos Hereford CF72: L'sant . . . 2F **65**
Clos Heulwen CF15: Taff W . . . 5E **45**
Clos Lancaster CF72: L'sant . . . 3F **65**
Clos Leland CF72: L'sant . . . 3F **65**
Clos Lindsay CF5: Ely . . . 6F **93**
Clos Llanfair CF5: Wen . . . 5E **99**
Clos Llangefni CF38: Bed . . . 5H **41**
Clos Llawhaden CF62: Barry . . . 5A **106**
Clos Llewellyn CF15: Cre . . . 1E **81**
CF15: Taff W . . . 6E **45**
Clos Llysfaen CF14: L'vne . . . 2H **71**
Clos Mabon CF14: R'ina . . . 5D **70**
Clos Maedref CF15: Rad . . . 2H **83**
Clos Maerun CF3: St M . . . 1D **88**
Clos Maes Brag CF83: Caer . . . 6D **28**
Clos Maes Mawr CF83: Caer . . . 3B **28**
Clos Maes-y-Mor CF3: St M . . . 2D **88**
Clos Mair CF23: Pen L . . . 4B **86**
Clos Mancheldowne CF62: Barry . . . 3G **117**
Clos Manmoel CF3: St M . . . 1D **88**
Clos Marion CF10: Card . . . 6F **97**
Clos Medwy CF3: St M . . . 5E **75**
Clos Meifod CF14: Llan N . . . 4D **84**
Clos Melin Ddwr CF14: L'vne . . . 3A **72**
Clos Menter CF14: Card . . . 5F **85**
Clos Morgan Gruffydd CF83: Abert . . . 2D **26**
Clos Myddlyn CF38: Bed . . . 6H **41**
Clos Nant Coslech CF23: Pontp . . . 4E **73**
Clos Nant Ddu CF23: Pontp . . . 4F **73**
Clos Nanteos CF23: Pontp . . . 5H **73**
Clos Nant Glaswg CF23: Pontp . . . 4E **73**
Clos Nant Mwlan CF23: Pontp . . . 3F **73**
Clos Nant y Cor CF23: Pontp . . . 4F **73**
Clos Nant y Cwm CF23: Pontp . . . 4F **73**
Clos Nant yr Aber CF83: Caer . . . 5B **28**
Clos Newydd CF14: Whit . . . 3B **84**
Clos Ogney CF61: Llan M . . . 2B **110**
Clos Padrig CF3: St M . . . 5E **75**
Clos Pandy CF83: B'ws . . . 3F **29**
Clos Pant Glas CF83: Tret . . . 3H **29**
Clos Pantycosyn CF3: St M . . . 1D **88**
Clos Parc Radyr CF15: Rad . . . 3F **83**
Clos Peiriant CF63: Barry . . . 3H **117**
Clos Pen y Clawdd CF3: St M . . . 1D **88**
Clos Pinwydden CF72: L'harry . . . 5C **78**
Clos Powys CF38: Bed . . . 5H **41**
Clos Pupren CF72: L'harry . . . 5C **78**
Clos Rhedyn CF5: Ely . . . 4A **94**
Clos Rheidol NP26: Cald . . . 3D **60**
Clos Rhiannon CF14: Thorn . . . 3F **71**
Clos St Catwg CF5: St F . . . 2C **82**
Clos Springfield CF72: T Grn . . . 3D **64**
Clos Synod CF14: Llan N . . . 4D **84**
Clos Taf CF5: L'dff . . . 5B **84**
Clos Tawe CF62: Barry . . . 1E **117**
Clos Tecwyn CF23: Pen L . . . 4B **86**
Clos Ton Mawr CF14: R'ina . . . 4E **71**
Clos Trefeddyg CF83: Mac . . . 3F **31**
Clos Tregare CF3: St M . . . 1D **88**
Clos Treoda CF14: Whit . . . 2D **84**
Clos-tr-Onnen CF3: St M . . . 1E **89**
Clos ty Bronna CF5: F'wtr . . . 2G **93**
Clos Tyclyd CF14: Whit . . . 3A **84**
Clos Tyla Bach CF3: St M . . . 6E **75**
Clos Tylaway CF15: Rad . . . 2H **83**
Clos ty-Melin CF37: R'fln . . . 3F **25**
Clos Tyniad Glo CF63: Barry . . . 3H **117**
Clos Tyrywen CF83: B'ws . . . 3E **29**
Clos Waun Fach *CF83: Caer* . . . *2H* ***45***
(off Heol Tyddyn)
Clos William CF14: R'ina . . . 4E **71**
Clos William Price CF37: Glynt . . . 1F **25**
Clos y Berllan CF3: St M . . . 1E **89**
Clos y Betws CF3: St M . . . 1D **88**
Clos-y-Blaidd CF14: Thorn . . . 2F **71**
Clos-y-Broch CF14: Thorn . . . 2G **71**
Clos-y-Carlwm CF14: Thorn . . . 2F **71**
Clos-y-Carw CF38: Llan F . . . 5B **42**
Clos-y-Cedr CF83: Caer . . . 3C **28**
Clos-y-Ceinach CF14: Thorn . . . 2G **71**
Clos y Coed CF38: Chu V . . . 3E **43**
Clos-y-Culfor CF3: St M . . . 1D **88**
Clos-y-Cwarra CF5: Ely . . . 4C **92**
Clos y Dolydd CF38: Bed . . . 6A **42**
Clos-y-Draenog CF14: Thorn . . . 2G **71**
Clos y Dryw CF14: Thorn . . . 2G **71**
Clos-y-Dyfrgi CF14: Thorn . . . 2F **71**
Clos-y-Ffynnon CF23: Pent . . . 4F **73**
Clos y Fran CF14: Thorn . . . 1G **71**
Clos y Fulfran CF62: Barry . . . 6H **117**
Clos y Gamlas CF14: Whit . . . 1A **84**
Clos y Gelyn CF23: Pent . . . 6F **73**
Clos-y-Gof CF5: Ely . . . 4D **92**
Clos y Graig CF14: R'ina . . . 4D **70**
Clos-y-Gwadd CF14: Thorn . . . 2F **71**
Clos y Gwalch CF14: Thorn . . . 1G **71**
Clos y Gwyddfid CF15: Morg . . . 5E **69**
Clos y Hebog CF14: Thorn . . . 1G **71**
Clos y Mynydd CF15: Morg . . . 6E **69**
Clos-y-Nant CF5: F'wtr . . . 1H **93**
Clos Ynysddu CF72: P'clun . . . 5C **64**
Clos-y-Pant CF83: Caer . . . 3A **46**
Clos yr Aer CF14: R'ina . . . 5E **71**
Clos yr Alarch CF14: Thorn . . . 1G **71**
Clos yr Arad CF83: Caer . . . 2H **45**
Clos-yr-Ardd CF14: R'ina . . . 6D **70**
Clos-yr-Bryn CF14: R'ina . . . 4C **70**
Clos yr Eos CF14: Thorn . . . 1G **71**
Clos yr Ewr CF64: P'rth . . . 4C **108**
Clos-yr-Gornant CF3: St M . . . 1E **89**
Clos yr Hafod CF14: R'ina . . . 5E **71**
Clos yr Harbwr CF62: Barry . . . 5F **117**
Clos-y-Rhiw CF5: Ely . . . 6F **93**
Clos-yr-Onnen CF61: Llan M . . . 4C **110**
Clos yr Wenallt CF14: R'ina . . . 4C **70**
Clos yr Wylan CF62: Barry . . . 5H **117**
Clos Ysbyty CF83: Caer . . . 2B **46**
Clos Ysgallen CF15: Morg . . . 5E **69**
Clos Ystum Taf CF14: Whit . . . 3A **84**
Clos y Wern CF14: R'ina . . . 5E **71**
Clos-y-Wiver CF61: Llan M . . . 2C **110**
Clos-y-Wiwer CF14: Thorn . . . 2G **71**
Clovelly Cres. CF3: L'rmy . . . 2G **87**
Clover Ct. NP44: Ty C . . . 4B **10**
Clover Gro. CF5: F'wtr . . . 6G **83**
Club Rd. NP4: P'pool . . . 3A **6**
Clun Av. CF72: P'clun . . . 5D **64**
Clun Cres. CF72: P'clun . . . 5D **64**
Clun Ter. CF24: Card . . . 5A **86**
Clwyd CF64: P'rth . . . 6C **102**
Clwyd Way CF62: St Ath . . . 2D **112**
Clydach Cl. CF37: Glync . . . 2D **14**
NP20: Bet . . . 6G **19**
Clydach Ct. CF37: Glync . . . 1D **14**
Clydach St. CF11: Card . . . 6H **95**
Clydesmuir Ind. Est. CF24: Card . . . 1F **97**
Clydesmuir Rd. CF24: Card . . . 2F **97**
Clyde St. CF24: Card . . . 4H **5** (4C **96**)
NP11: Ris . . . 6E **17**
Clyffard Cres. NP20: Newp . . . 5A **36**
Clyffes NP44: G'mdw . . . 2D **10**
Clyro Pl. CF14: Llan N . . . 4C **84**
Clytha Cres. NP20: Newp . . . 6C **36**
CLYTHA PARK . . . 5A **36**
Clytha Pk. Rd. NP20: Newp . . . 4A **36**
Clytha Sq. NP20: Newp . . . 6C **36**
CMC Sports & Social Club . . . **4H 85**
Coal Pit La. CF3: Cas, Mic F, Old M . . . 6E **51**
Coaster Pl. CF10: Card . . . 6F **97**
Coates Pl. CF3: L'rmy . . . 6B **74**
Coates Rd. CF64: P'rth . . . 4D **108**
Cobb Cres. NP26: Cald . . . 6C **60**
Cobden Pl. NP11: Cros K . . . 3A **16**
Cobden St. NP11: Cros K . . . 3A **16**
Cobol Rd. CF3: St M . . . 5F **75**
Coburn St. CF24: Card . . . 1B **96**
Coch-y-North Rd.
NP4: P'seg, P'nydd, P'pool . . . 3A **6**
Cocker Av. NP44: C'brn . . . 4F **11**
Coed Arhyd CF5: Ely . . . 5C **92**
Coed Arian CF14: Whit . . . 4D **84**
Coed Bach CF62: Barry . . . 6E **105**

Coed Briwnant CF14: R'ina 4E **71**
Coed Cae CF83: Caer 5E **29**
NP44: Pnwd 6C **8**
Coedcae La. CF72: Tyle 5B **64**
Coedcae La. Ind. Est. CF72: P'clun 4B **64**
Coedcae Pl. NP4: P'pool 3B **6**
Coedcae Rd. CF83: Abert 2E **27**
Coedcae St. CF11: Card 6H **95**
Coedcae Ter. NP4: P'pool 3B **6**
Coed Camlas NP4: New I 4F **7**
Coed Ceirios CF14: R'ina 6D **70**
COEDCERNYW 4F **53**
Coed Cochwyn Av. CF14: L'shn 4G **71**
Coed Criafol CF63: Barry 4B **106**
Coed Edeyrn CF23: L'dyrn 3D **86**
COED-ELÁI 3A **40**
COEDELY 3A **40**
Coeden Dal CF23: Pent 5E **73**
COED EVA 5D **10**
Coedeva Mill NP44: Coed E 5E **11**
Coed Garw NP44: C'iog 5G **9**
Coed Gethin CF83: Caer 3B **28**
Coed Glas NP44: Two L 4F **11**
Coed Glas Rd. CF14: L'shn 5F **71**
Coed Isaf Rd. CF37: P'prdd 1A **24**
COEDKERNEW 4F **53**
Coed Leddyn CF83: Caer 3B **28**
Coed Lee NP44: Coed E 4E **11**
Coed Main CF83: Caer 5F **29**
Coed Mawr CF62: Barry 6E **105**
Coed Mieri CF72: Tyle 5C **64**
COED-PEN-MAEN 5C **14**
Coedpenmaen Cl. CF37: P'prdd 6D **14**
Coedpenmaen Rd. CF37: P'prdd 5D **14**
Coed Pwll CF83: Caer 5E **29**
Coedriglan Dr. CF5: Ely 5C **92**
Coed Trecastle CF72: Tyle 5B **64**
Coed-y-Brain Ct. CF83: L'brad 1B **28**
Coed-y-Brain Rd. CF83: L'brad 1B **28**
Coed y Brenin CF37: P'prdd 1A **24**
Coed-y-Caerau La. NP18: Cat A, Kem I 5G **23**
Coed-y-Canddo Rd. NP4: New I 4F **7**
Coed y Capel CF62: Barry 6E **105**
COED-Y-CEARAU 3H **23**
Coed-y-Dafarn CF14: L'vne 3C **72**
Coed y Dyffryn CF38: Chu V 3E **43**
Coed-y-Felin CF62: Barry 2E **117**
Coed-y-Gloriau CF23: Pent 6D **72**
Coed-y-Gores CF23: L'dyrn 1E **87**
(not continuous)
Coedygric Rd. NP4: Grif 5E **7**
Coed-y-Lan Rd. CF37: Glync 2D **14**
Coed-y-Llinos CF83: Caer 6A **28**
Coed-y-Llyn CF15: Rad 1E **83**
CF23: Cyn 3B **86**
Coed y Pandy CF83: B'ws 3F **29**
Coed-y-Pica CF83: Abert 3E **27**
Coed-yr-Eos CF83: Caer 6A **28**
Coed yr Esgob CF72: L'sant 1E **65**
Coed-yr-Odyn CF62: Barry 4D **116**
Coed yr Ynn CF14: R'ina 5E **71**
Coed y Wenallt CF14: R'ina 4D **70**
Coed-y-Wennol CF83: Caer 1A **46**
COGAN 6H **101**
Cogan Ct. CF64: L'dgh 5G **101**
Cogan Hill CF64: P'rth 5G **101**
Cogan Pill Rd. CF64: L'dgh 4F **101**
(not continuous)
Cogan Spur CF11: Card 5G **101**
Cogan Station (Rail) 5G **101**
Cogan Ter. CF24: Card 2A **96**
Coggins Cl. CF83: Caer 2H **45**
Cog Rd. CF64: Sul 2G **119**
Coigne Ter. CF63: Barry 2B **118**
Coity Cl. CF3: St M 6E **75**
Colborne Wlk. CF11: Card 4F **95**
Colbourne Rd. CF38: Bed 5A **42**
Colchester Av. CF23: Pen L 6D **86**
Colchester Ct. CF23: Pen L 6D **86**
Colchester Est. CF23: Pen L 6E **87**
COLCOT 5F **105**
Colcot Leisure Cen. 6F **105**
Colcot Rd. CF62: Barry 5F **105**
Cold Bath Rd. NP18: C'ln 5H **21**
Coldbrook Rd. E. CF63: Barry 6C **106**
Coldbrook Rd. W. CF63: Barry 6B **106**

Cold Knap Way CF62: Barry 5E **117**
(not continuous)
COLDRA 2D **38**
Coldra, The NP18: Newp 2C **38**
Coldra Rd. NP20: Newp 6A **36**
Coldra Woods Dr. NP18: Chris 1C **38**
Cold Store, The NP44: C'brn 4A **12**
Coldstores Rd. CF10: Card 2E **103**
Coldstream Cl. NP44: C'iog 6G **9**
Coldstream Ter. CF11: Card 4A **4** (4H **95**)
Cole Ct. CF83: Caer 5F **29**
Coleford Dr. CF3: St M 1D **88**
Coleford Path NP44: St D 2E **11**
Coleg Glan Hafren
City Cen. Campus 2F **5** (3B **96**)
Coleridge Av. CF64: P'rth 1D **108**
Coleridge Cres. CF62: Barry 5G **105**
Coleridge Gdns. CF83: Mac 3C **30**
Coleridge Grn. NP44: St D 3E **11**
Coleridge Rd. CF11: Card 2F **101**
NP19: Newp 4G **37**
Colhugh Cl. CF61: Llan M 3B **110**
Colhugh Pk. CF61: Llan M 4B **110**
Colhugh St. CF61: Llan M 3B **110**
Colin Way CF5: Ely 3A **94**
Collard Cres. CF62: Barry 6H **105**
College Cl. CF14: Whit 3D **84**
CF37: R'fln 4F 25
(off Chapel St.)
College Cres. NP18: C'ln 5H **21**
College Flds. Cl. CF62: Barry 2G **117**
College Gdns. CF61: Llan M 3B **110**
College Glade NP18: C'ln 3G **21**
College Pl. CF62: Barry 3G **117**
College Rd. CF10: Card 1B **4** (2H **95**)
CF14: Llan N, Whit 5C **84**
CF14: Whit 3D **84**
CF62: Barry 2F **117**
(not continuous)
NP4: P'garn 2C **6**
NP18: C'ln 4H **21**
College St. CF61: Llan M 3B **110**
College Ter. CF61: Llan M 3B **110**
NP4: P'nydd 1A **6**
College Way CF37: R'fln 4F **25**
Collier St. NP19: Newp 3D **36**
Colliery Rd. CF83: B'ws, Tret 2G **29**
Collingwood Av. NP19: Newp 5G **37**
Collingwood Cl. NP16: Bul 5G **63**
NP19: Newp 5G **37**
Collingwood Cres. NP19: Newp 5G **37**
Collingwood Rd. NP19: Newp 5G **37**
Collins Cl. NP20: Newp 1G **53**
Collins Ter. CF37: T'rest 3E **25**
Collivaud Pl. CF24: Card 5D **96**
Collwyn St. CF39: Coed 3A **40**
Colne St. NP19: Newp 4D **36**
Colston Av. NP19: Newp 6F **37**
Colston Ct. NP19: Newp 6G **37**
Colston Pl. NP19: Newp 6G **37**
Colts Foot Cl. NP20: Newp 4A **36**
Columbus Cl. CF62: Barry 5A **106**
Columbus Ho. NP18: L'stne 6E **23**
Columbus Wlk. CF10: Card 6F **5** (5B **96**)
Colum Dr. CF10: Card 1H **95**
Colum Hall CF10: Card 1H **95**
Column St. CF64: Sul 1E **119**
Colum Pl. CF10: Card 1H **95**
Colum Rd. CF10: Card 1H **95**
Colum Ter. CF10: Card 2H **95**
Colwill Rd. CF14: Llan N 5D **84**
Colwinstone Cl. CF14: Llan N 4C **84**
Colwinstone St. CF14: Llan N 4C **84**
Colwyn Rd. CF3: Rum 3H **87**
Comet St. CF24: Card 3H **5** (3C **96**)
Comfrey Cl. CF3: St M 5E **75**
NP20: Newp 3A **36**
Commercial La. NP11: Ris 6E **17**
Commercial Rd. CF63: Barry 1A **118**
CF83: Mac 2F **31**
(Dranllwyn La.)
CF83: Mac 3H **31**
(Royal Oak)
NP20: Newp 6C **36**
Commercial St. CF38: Bed 4A **42**
CF61: Llan M 3B **110**

Commercial St. CF72: L'sant 2F **65**
NP4: Grif 6E **7**
NP4: P'pool 2C **6**
NP11: Ris 6D **16**
NP20: Newp 4C **36**
(not continuous)
NP44: C'brn 3G **11**
NP44: Pnwd 6E **9**
Commercial St. Cvn. Site
NP11: Ris 1E **33**
Commercial Wharf NP20: Newp 1E **55**
Common, The CF14: Whit 3D **84**
Common App. CF38: Bed 5A **42**
Common Rd. CF37: P'prdd 6D **14**
(not continuous)
COMMON-Y-COED 1E **59**
Compass Rd. CF10: Card 2D **102**
Compton Cl. NP10: Roger 3D **34**
Compton St. CF11: Card 5G **95**
Congress Theatre
Cwmbran *1G 11*
(off Gwent Sq.)
Conifer Cl. NP18: C'ln 5E **21**
Conifer Ct. CF5: F'wtr 1F **93**
Coniston Cl. NP19: Newp 1E **37**
Connaught Rd. CF24: Card 1C **96**
Constable Dr. NP19: Newp 1F **37**
Constables Cl. NP20: Newp 1D **54**
Constance St. NP19: Newp 2D **36**
Constant Cl. CF11: Card 3A **102**
Constant Row NP11: Ris 5E **17**
Constellation St. CF24: Card 3H **5** (3C **96**)
Constitution Hill CF71: C'bri 4C **90**
Conway Cl. CF37: Glync 2C **14**
CF64: Din P 2A **108**
NP44: C'brn 1G **11**
Conway Ct. CF83: Caer 5H **27**
NP19: Newp 5G **37**
Conway Cres. CF38: Tont 1F **43**
Conway Cft. NP19: Newp 5G **37**
Conway Dr. CF62: Barry 1E **117**
Conway Gro. NP10: Duf 6F **53**
Conway Rd. CF11: Card 2F **95**
NP4: P'pool 2B **6**
NP19: Newp 4F **37**
Conway Sac NP19: Newp 5G **37**
Conway Ter. NP44: C'iog 6F **9**
Conybeare Rd. CF5: Card 2D **94**
CF64: Sul 1H **119**
Cook Rd. CF62: Barry 4A **106**
Coolgreany Cl. NP20: Malp 6A **20**
Coolgreany Cres. NP20: Malp 6A **20**
Coomassie St. NP20: Newp 2D **54**
Coopers Ct. CF10: Card 5D **4**
Coopers La. CF71: C'bri 3C **90**
Coopers Pl. CF83: Caer 2H **45**
Coopers Way CF72: C Inn 2H **65**
Coopers Yd. CF10: Card 6A **96**
Copleston Rd. CF14: Llan N 5C **84**
Copper Beech Cl. NP18: C'ln 5E **21**
Copperfield Ct. CF62: Barry 2G **117**
Copperfield Dr. CF14: Thorn 3H **71**
Copper St. CF24: Card 2H **5** (3D **96**)
Coppice, The CF38: Tont 1G **43**
CF72: Mis 5F **65**
Coppice Rd. CF23: Pontp 3H **73**
Coppins, The CF14: L'vne 2B **72**
NP20: Malp 4B **20**
Copse Wlk. CF23: Pontp 3G **73**
Copthorne Way CF5: Cul C 1C **98**
Cora St. CF63: Barry 2A **118**
Corbett Cres. CF83: Caer 2D **46**
Corbett Gro. CF83: Caer 2A **46**
Corbett Rd. CF10: Card 1B **4** (2H **95**)
CF64: P'rth 5F **101**
Corbetts La. CF83: Caer 3C **28**
Corelli St. NP19: Newp 3D **36**
Coriander Cl. NP20: Newp 3A **36**
Corinthian Cl. CF64: L'dgh 4F **101**
Cork Dr. CF23: Pontp 3G **73**
Cork Rd. NP20: Newp 2D **54**
Cormorant Cl. CF3: St M 5D **74**
Cormorant Way NP10: Duf 5H **53**
Cornbrook Rd. NP20: Bet 4F **19**
Cornelly Cl. CF14: Llan N 4C **84**
Cornelly St. CF14: Llan N 4C **84**

Cornerswell La. CF64: P'rth .2D **108**
Cornerswell Pl. CF64: P'rth .1C **108**
Cornerswell Rd. CF64: P'rth .2D **108**
Cornfield Cl. CF14: L'shn .4F **71**
Cornfield Ri. CF83: B'ws .3F **29**
Cornflower Cl. CF14: L'vne .1A **72**
NP10: Roger .3A **34**
Corn Glas CF63: Barry .5C **106**
Cornish Cl. CF11: Card .1A **102**
Corn Stairs Hill CF37: P'prdd .6D **14**
Corn St. NP20: Newp .4C **36**
Cornwall Ri. CF62: Barry .6H **105**
Cornwall Rd. CF62: Barry .1H **117**
NP19: Newp .3E **37**
Cornwall St. CF11: Card .6G **95**
Cornwood Cl. CF5: F'wtr .6F **83**
Coronation Pl. NP11: P'waun .1A **16**
Coronation Rd. CF14: Heath .3F **85**
Coronation St. CF63: Barry .3A **118**
CF83: Tret .3A **30**
NP11: Ris .6E **17**
Coronation Ter. CF37: P'prdd .4E **15**
CF64: P'rth .6A **102**
NP4: P'nydd .1A 6
(off Hanbury Rd.)
Corporation Rd. CF11: Card .6H **95**
NP19: Newp .4D **36**
Corris NP44: C'iog .5F **9**
Corsham Rd. CF23: Cyn .4C **86**
Corvette Ct. CF10: Card .6C **96**
Corwen Cres. CF14: Llan N .4C **84**
Cory Pk. NP44: L'tnam .1B **20**
Cory Pl. CF11: Card .3A **102**
CORYTON .6B **70**
Coryton Cl. CF14: Whit .6B **70**
Coryton Cres. CF14: Whit .6A **70**
Coryton Dr. CF14: Whit .6A **70**
Coryton Interchange CF15: Tong .5A **70**
Coryton Ri. CF14: Whit .6A **70**
Coryton Station (Rail) .1B **84**
Cory Way CF63: Barry .3A **118**
Cosheston Rd. CF5: F'wtr .5H **83**
COSMESTON .5E **109**
Cosmeston Dr. CF64: P'rth .6E **109**
Cosmeston Lakes Country Pk. .5C **108**
Cosmeston Lakes Country Pk. Vis. Cen. .6D **108**
Cosmeston St. CF24: Card .6H **85**
Cosslett Pl. CF11: Card .1A **102**
Cot Farm Circ. NP19: Newp .3D **38**
Cot Farm Cl. NP19: Newp .3D **38**
Cot Farm Gdns. NP19: Newp .3D **38**
Cot Farm Wlk. NP19: Newp .3D **38**
Cot Hill NP18: L'wrn .3E **39**
Cotman Cl. NP19: Newp .2G **37**
Cotswold Av. CF14: L'vne .2B **72**
Cotswold Cl. NP19: Newp .3A **38**
Cotswold Ri. CF63: Barry .1B **118**
Cotswold Way NP11: Ris .6G **17**
NP19: Newp .3A **38**
Cottage Cl. CF14: Thorn .3H **71**
Cottage Row CF5: Twyn .3D **98**
Cottesmore Way CF72: C Inn .3G **65**
Cottingham Dr. CF23: Pontp .4G **73**
Cottrell Rd. CF14: Whit .3D **84**
CF24: Card .1C **96**
Cottrell Sq. CF63: Barry .6A **106**
Coulson Cl. NP20: Newp .6C **36**
Countess Pl. CF64: P'rth .2D **108**
Countisbury Av. CF3: L'rmy .1A **88**
Country Vw. CF37: R'fln .5A **26**
COUNTY HOSPITAL .5E **7**
Court, The CF14: L'vne .1B **72**
CF24: Card .1D **96**
Court Cl. CF14: Whit .4E **85**
CF61: Llan M .2B **110**
CF71: A'thin .2G **91**
Court Cres. NP10: Bass .1D **52**
Courtenay Cl. CF3: Old M .6B **74**
Courtenay Rd. CF24: Card .3E **97**
CF63: Barry .1B **118**
Court Farm Cl. NP44: L'tnam .5A **12**
Court Farm Rd. NP44: L'tnam .5A **12**
Courtfield Cl. NP10: Roger .3A **34**
Court Gdns. NP10: Roger .3A **34**
Court Ho. NP26: Cald .5D **60**
Court Ho. Cl. NP26: Cald .5D **60**
Court Ho. St. CF37: P'prdd .1C **24**
Courtis Rd. CF5: Ely .4F **93**
Courtlands CF62: Barry .4E **117**
Courtlands, The NP44: G'mdw .2D **10**
Court Mdw. NP18: L'stne .1G **39**
Court Newton CF63: Barry .1A **118**
Courtney St. NP19: Newp .3D **36**
Court Rd. CF11: Card .6A **4** (5G **95**)
CF14: Whit .4E **85**
CF63: Barry .1B **118**
CF83: Caer .4B **28**
NP44: C'brn, Oakf .4H **11**
Court Rd. Ind. Est.
NP44: L'tnam .4H **11**
Court Vw. NP18: L'stne .1G **39**
Courtyard, The CF24: Card .3D **96**
NP10: Coedk .5F **53**
Courtybella Gdns. NP20: Newp .1C **54**
Courtybella Ter. NP20: Newp .1C **54**
Court-y-Bella Ter. NP20: Newp .1B **54**
Coveny St. CF24: Card .3E **97**
Coverack Rd. NP19: Newp .5D **36**
Covert Wlk. NP44: F'wtr .4D **10**
COWBRIDGE .3D **90**
Cowbridge By-Pass
CF71: C'bri, St H .2A **90**
Cowbridge Leisure Cen. .3C **90**
Cowbridge Physic Garden .3C **90**
Cowbridge Rd. CF61: Llan M .1B **110**
CF62: St Ath .4D **112**
CF72: T Grn .4D **64**
(not continuous)
CF72: Taly .3A **78**
Cowbridge Rd. E. CF5: Card .3B **94**
CF10: Card .4A **4** (4G **95**)
CF11: Card .4A **4** (4G **95**)
Cowbridge Rd. W. CF5: Cul C, Ely .6E **93**
Cowbridge St. CF63: Barry .6B **106**
Cowleaze NP26: Magor .4D **58**
Cowper Cl. CF64: P'rth .1D **108**
NP20: Newp .1G **53**
Cowper Pl. CF24: Card .1G **5** (2C **96**)
Cowshed La. NP10: Bass .1C **52**
Cowslip Cl. CF23: Pontp .4G **73**
Cowslip Dr. CF64: P'rth .6G **101**
Coychurch Ri. CF63: Barry .5A **106**
Craddock St. CF11: Card .5A **4** (4G **95**)
Cradoc Rd. CF14: Whit .3E **85**
Cragside Cl. CF3: St M .1D **88**
Craig Castell CF15: Rad .1F **83**
Craig-Ceiliog La. NP10: Roger .3C **18**
NP20: H'lys .3C **18**
NP44: H'lys .3C **18**
Craiglee Dr. CF10: Card .6F **5** (5B **96**)
Craigmuir Rd. CF24: Card .2F **97**
Craig Rd.
NP44: G'mdw, Thorn, Up Cwm .1C **10**
CRAIGYFEDW .2F **27**
Craig-yr-Allt CF14: R'ina .4D **70**
Craig yr Haul Av. *CF3: Cas .2G 75*
(off Craig yr Haul Dr.)
Craig yr Haul Ct. CF3: Cas .2G **75**
Craig yr Haul Dr. CF3: Cas .2G **75**
Cranbourne Way CF23: Pontp .4E **73**
Cranbrook St. CF24: Card .1E **5** (2B **96**)
Crane St. NP4: P'pool .3C **6**
Cranleigh Ri. CF3: Rum .3G **87**
Cranmer Ct. CF5: L'dff .1C **94**
Cranwell Cl. CF5: L'dff .5A **84**
Craven Wlk. CF64: P'rth .5E **109**
Crawford Cl. CF38: Bed .5B **42**
Crawford Dr. CF23: Pontp .4G **73**
Crawford St. NP19: Newp .3D **36**
Crawford Trad. Est.
NP19: Newp .2D **36**
Crawley Cl. CF14: Thorn .2G **71**
Crawshay Ct. CF61: Llan M .2D **110**
Crawshay Dr. CF61: Bov .3C **110**
Crawshay St. CF10: Card .5A **96**
Crediton Rd. CF3: L'rmy .1A **88**
CREIGIAU .6E **67**
Crescent, The CF5: F'wtr .2H **93**
CF5: L'dff .1D **94**
CF62: Barry .2D **116**
CF83: B'ws .3G **29**
Crescent, The CF83: Caer .6A **28**
CF83: Mac .3F **31**
NP44: C'brn .4F **11**
Crescent Cl. CF71: C'bri .5D **90**
Crescent Ct. NP19: Newp .3F **37**
Crescent Rd. CF83: Caer .6C **28**
NP11: Ris .4C **16**
NP19: Newp .3F **37**
Cressfield Dr. CF23: Pontp .4H **73**
Cresswell Cl. CF3: St M .5E **75**
Cresswell Ct. CF62: Barry .5H **105**
Cresswell Wlk. NP44: St D .2E **11**
Cressy Rd. CF23: Pen L .6C **86**
Cresta Gro. CF5: Ely .4D **92**
Criccieth Cl. NP10: Duf .6G **53**
Criccieth Ct. CF64: Din P .1B **108**
Criccieth Rd. CF3: Rum .3A **88**
CRICK .1E **61**
Crickhowell Rd. CF3: Rum, St M .1C **88**
Crickhowell Wlk. CF3: St M .6D **74**
Crick Rd. NP26: Cri, Pskwt .1E **61**
NP26: Pskwt .5G **61**
CRINDAU .1B **36**
Crindau Ind. Est. NP20: Newp .1C **36**
Crindau Rd. NP20: Newp .1B **36**
Crockett's Pl. CF37: P'prdd .5A **14**
Crockherbtown La. CF10: Card .3D **4** (3A **96**)
Crocus Cl. NP10: Roger .3H **33**
Croescadarn Cl. CF23: Pent .4G **73**
Croescadarn Rd. CF23: Pent .4F **73**
CF23: Pontp .3F **73**
(not continuous)
Croescade La. CF38: Llan F .3C **42**
Croescade Rd. CF38: Llan F .4B **42**
Croesllanfro Gdns. NP10: Roger .2C **34**
Croeswen NP44: Oakf .5H **11**
CROESYCEILIOG .1A **12**
Croesyceiliog By-Pass NP44: C'iog .5H **9**
CROES-Y-MWYALCH .2A **20**
Croffta CF64: Din P .3G **107**
Crofft-y-Genau Rd. CF5: St F .3C **82**
Crofta CF14: L'vne .4B **72**
Croft Gdns. CF64: Sul .2G **119**
Croft John CF62: P'ark .1D **114**
Crofton Mede NP44: F'wtr .4D **10**
Crofts Cnr. NP44: G'mdw .2D **10**
Croft St. CF24: Card .1G **5** (2C **96**)
CF71: C'bri .4D **90**
Croft Ter. CF71: C'bri .4D **90**
Cromwell Pl. NP44: C'brn .6E **9**
Cromwell Rd. CF14: Heath .3F **85**
NP11: Ris .3B **16**
NP16: Bul .5E **63**
NP19: Newp .5F **37**
Cromwell Rd. Bungs. NP11: Ris .3B **16**
Crossbrook St. CF37: P'prdd .6C **14**
Cross Common Rd. CF64: Din P .3H **107**
Crossfield Rd. CF62: Barry .3E **117**
Crosshill CF62: Barry .6E **117**
CROSS INN .3G **65**
Cross Inn Rd. CF72: L'sant .2F **65**
CROSSKEYS .3A **16**
Cross Keys, The *CF61: Llan M .3B 110*
(off Colhugh St.)
Crosskeys RUFC .2A **16**
Crosskeys Station (Rail) .3A **16**
Cross La. NP20: Newp .5C **36**
Cross Pl. CF14: Card .6G **85**
Cross Roads CF38: Bed .4H **41**
Cross St. CF15: Tong .4G **69**
CF37: C'fydd .2F **15**
CF37: P'prdd .5D **14**
CF63: Barry .2A **118**
CF83: Abert .2E **27**
CF83: B'ws .3G **29**
NP18: C'ln .5A **22**
Crossway NP26: Rog .6A **60**
CROSSWAY GREEN .1D **62**
Crossways Cl.
NP26: Undy .5F **59**
Crossways Pk. CF83: Caer .4E **29**
Crossways Rd. CF5: Ely .4G **93**
Crossways St. CF63: Barry .2A **118**
Crossway St. CF37: P'prdd .5D **14**
Crosswells Way CF5: Ely .4E **93**
Crouch Cl. NP20: Bet .6F **19**

Crown Arc. *NP20: Newp* . . . *4C* ***36***
(off Market St.)
Crown Cl. NP18: C'ln . . . 5A **22**
NP44: Pnwd . . . 5D **8**
Crown Hill CF38: Llan F . . . 5C **42**
Crown Hill Dr. CF38: Llan F . . . 5C **42**
Crown La. NP19: Newp . . . 4E **37**
Crown Ri. NP44: Llanf . . . 3B **12**
Crown Rd. NP44: Llanf . . . 5B **12**
Crown St. NP19: Newp . . . 3E **37**
Crown Wlk. CF83: Mac . . . 2H **31**
Crown Way CF14: Card . . . 6G **85**
Croyde Av. CF3: L'rmy . . . 1A **88**
Croydon Cl. NP19: Newp . . . 1E **37**
Croydon Ct. NP19: Newp . . . 1E **37**
Crumlin Dr. CF3: St M . . . 6D **74**
Crumlin Rd. NP4: P'seg, P'nydd, P'pool . . . 4A **6**
Crumlin St. NP4: P'pool . . . 3B **6**
Crundale Cres. CF14: L'shn . . . 5H **71**
Crwys Cres. CF37: Up Bo . . . 5A **26**
Crwys La. CF63: Barry . . . 5B **106**
Crwys M. CF24: Card . . . 1A **96**
Crwys Pl. CF24: Card . . . 1B **96**
Crwys Rd. CF24: Card . . . 6A **86**
Crynant Cl. CF62: St Ath . . . 2D **112**
Crystal Av. CF23: Heath . . . 1A **86**
Crystal Ct. CF11: Card . . . 6H **95**
Crystal Glen CF14: L'shn . . . 1H **85**
Crystal Ri. CF14: Heath . . . 1H **85**
Crystal Wood Dr. CF72: Mis . . . 5E **65**
Crystal Wood Rd. CF14: Heath . . . 1H **85**
Cube, The *CF11: Card* . . . *4F* ***95***
(off Cowbridge Rd. E.)
Cuckoofield Cl. CF15: Morg . . . 5E **69**
Cudd y Coed CF63: Barry . . . 5C **106**
Cules Ter. CF15: Taff W . . . 6D **44**
Culver Cl. CF64: P'rth . . . 4C **108**
CULVERHOUSE CROSS . . . 1E **99**
Cumberland Rd. NP19: Newp . . . 1E **37**
Cumberland St. CF5: Card . . . 4E **95**
Cumnock Pl. CF24: Card . . . 4H **5** (4D **96**)
Cumnock Ter. CF24: Card . . . 4H **5** (4D **96**)
Cumrae St. CF24: Card . . . 4H **5** (4D **96**)
Cunningham Cl. CF23: Cyn . . . 3A **86**
Cunningham Rd. NP19: Newp . . . 2C **38**
Curie Cl. NP20: Malp . . . 4A **20**
Curlew Av. NP26: Cald . . . 6D **60**
Curlew Cl. CF14: Whit . . . 1C **84**
NP19: Newp . . . 2C **56**
Curlew Cres. CF62: St Ath . . . 3F **111**
Curll Av. CF14: Card . . . 4G **85**
Curran Emb. CF10: Card . . . 6A **96**
Curran Rd. CF10: Card . . . 5A **96**
Curzon Ct. NP19: Newp . . . 5B **38**
Custom Ho. Pl. CF64: P'rth . . . 5B **102**
Custom Ho. St. CF10: Card . . . 6D **4** (5A **96**)
Cutter Cl. NP19: Newp . . . 6F **21**
Cwarrau Mawr Farm La. CF83: Caer . . . 2A **28**
Cwlwm Cariad CF63: Barry . . . 4B **106**
Cwm Barry Way CF62: Barry . . . 3E **117**
CWMBRAN . . . 1G **11**
Cwmbran Dr. NP44: C'brn, Oakf, Pnwd . . . 1G **11**
Cwmbran FC . . . 4H **11**
Cwmbran Retail Pk. NP44: C'brn . . . 2F **11**
Cwmbran Stadium . . . 4H **11**
Cwmbran Station (Rail) . . . 1H **11**
CWMBRÂN . . . 1G **11**
CWMCARN . . . 1A **16**
Cwmcarn Cl. CF3: St M . . . 6D **74**
Cwmcarn Forest Dr.
NP11: C'crn, P'waun . . . 1A **16**
NP11: C'crn, Ris . . . 1C **16**
Cwm-Cidy Cotts. CF62: Barry . . . 3C **116**
Cwm-Cidy La. CF62: Barry . . . 3C **116**
Cwm Cwddy Dr. NP10: Bass, R'drn . . . 6A **34**
Cwm Cwddy La. NP10: Bass . . . 1A **52**
Cwmdare St. CF24: Card . . . 6H **85**
Cwm Dr. CF64: Din P . . . 1G **107**
Cwm Dylan Cl. NP10: Bass . . . 1A **52**
Cwm Farm Cl. NP4: P'pool . . . 4C **6**
Cwm Fedw CF83: Mac . . . 1G **31**
CWM FIELDS . . . 4C **6**
Cwm Gwynlais CF15: Tong . . . 5H **69**
Cwm La. NP10: Roger . . . 2D **34**
Cwm-Nant Flds. NP44: C'brn . . . 3F **11**
Cwmnant Vs. NP44: C'brn . . . 3F **11**
Cwm Nofydd CF14: R'ina . . . 5D **70**
Cwmnofydd La. CF83: Mac . . . 3E **31**
Cwm Parc CF62: Barry . . . 2E **117**
Cwmsor Cl. NP4: New I . . . 5H **7**
CWM TALWG . . . 1E **117**
Cwm-y-Nant NP11: Ris . . . 1E **33**
Cwmynyscoy Rd. NP4: P'pool . . . 5C **6**
Cwrdy Cl. NP4: Grif . . . 1D **8**
Cwrdy La. NP4: Grif, P'rheol . . . 1C **8**
Cwrdy Rd. NP4: Grif . . . 1D **8**
Cwrdy Wlk. NP4: Grif . . . 1D **8**
Cwrt Aethen CF63: Barry . . . 4B **106**
Cwrt Bala CF3: Rum . . . 2C **88**
Cwrt Bleddyn NP44: Two L . . . 4F **11**
Cwrt Bleddyn La. NP44: C'brn . . . 4F **11**
Cwrt Boston CF24: Card . . . 6G **87**
Cwrt Brynteg CF15: Rad . . . 2G **83**
Cwrt Camlas NP10: Roger . . . 4E **35**
Cwrt Cefn CF14: L'vne . . . 3A **72**
Cwrt Coed Fardre CF38: Llan F . . . 4B **42**
Cwrt Coed-y-Brenin
CF38: Chu V . . . 3E **43**
Cwrt Coles CF24: Card . . . 6G **87**
Cwrt Deri CF14: R'ina . . . 5D **70**
Cwrt Dowlas NP44: C'brn, Oakf . . . 6G **11**
NP44: T Coch . . . 5G **11**
Cwrt Draw Llyn CF83: Caer . . . 3B **46**
Cwrt Dyfed CF63: Barry . . . 5C **106**
Cwrt Edward CF62: Barry . . . 3G **117**
Cwrt Eglwys Newydd CF14: Whit . . . 2C **84**
Cwrt Eirlys CF63: Barry . . . 4A **106**
Cwrt Faenor CF38: Bed . . . 6H **41**
Cwrt Glas CF14: L'shn . . . 5G **71**
Cwrtglas NP44: C'iog . . . 1A **12**
Cwrt Glyndwr CF37: T'rest . . . 3D **24**
Cwrt Golwg Sianel NP11: Ris . . . 6F **17**
Cwrt Griffin CF83: Rud . . . 1C **48**
Cwrt Gwenllian CF63: Barry . . . 1D **118**
Cwrt Heledd CF24: Card . . . 6B **86**
Cwrt Illtyd *CF72: C Inn* . . . *3G* ***65***
(off Main Rd.)
Cwrt Isaf CF38: E Isaf . . . 6D **42**
Cwrt Leubren CF63: Barry . . . 4A **106**
Cwrt Llandough CF64: L'dgh . . . 5F **101**
Cwrt Llanfabon CF83: Caer . . . 4B **28**
Cwrt Llechau CF72: L'harry . . . 4C **78**
Cwrt Morgan NP26: C'ent . . . 1C **60**
Cwrt Nant y Felin CF83: Caer . . . 2H **45**
Cwrt Newton Pool CF62: Rho . . . 6F **115**
Cwrt Pegasus CF5: L'dff . . . 1C **94**
Cwrt Pencoedtre CF62: Barry . . . 5A **106**
Cwrt Penhill CF11: Card . . . 2E **95**
Cwrt Pensarn CF3: Rum . . . 2C **88**
Cwrt Pentre Bach CF3: St M . . . 5E **75**
Cwrt Pentwyn CF38: Llan F . . . 4B **42**
Cwrt Roberts CF5: Ely . . . 6E **93**
Cwrt St Cyres CF64: P'rth . . . 1C **108**
Cwrt Severn NP26: Cald . . . 6B **60**
Cwrt Syr Dafydd CF61: Llan M . . . 2B **110**
Cwrt-ty-Fferm CF83: L'brad . . . 1B **28**
Cwrt ty Mawr CF64: P'rth . . . 3C **108**
CF83: Caer . . . 1F **47**
Cwrt ty-Mynydd CF15: Rad . . . 1F **83**
Cwrt-y-Cadno CF5: Ely . . . 4D **92**
CF61: Llan M . . . 2C **110**
Cwrt y Castell CF83: Caer . . . 6D **28**
Cwrt y Ffoundri CF37: T'rest . . . 2E **25**
Cwrt y Gth. CF38: Bed . . . 6A **42**
Cwrt-y-Goedwig CF38: Llan F . . . 4B **42**
Cwrt y Melin *CF11: Card* . . . *4F* ***95***
(off Leckwith Pl.)
Cwrt y Parc CF14: L'shn . . . 6G **71**
Cwrt-yr-Ala Av. CF5: Ely . . . 6F **93**
Cwrt-yr-Ala Rd. CF5: Ely, Mic P . . . 6F **93**
Cwrt yr Ardal CF3: Rum . . . 2C **88**
Cwrt yr Efail CF38: Chu V . . . 3F **43**
Cwrt-yr-Lolo CF62: F'ton . . . 1C **112**
Cwrt-yr-Ysgol NP11: Ris . . . 4D **16**
Cwrt-y-Vil Rd. CF64: P'rth . . . 2E **109**
Cwrt-y-Vil Rd. (Lwr.) CF64: P'rth . . . 3E **109**
Cwrt y Waun CF38: Bed . . . 6A **42**
Cwrt Ywen CF72: L'harry . . . 5C **78**
Cyfarthfa St. CF24: Card . . . 2C **96**
Cymmer St. CF11: Card . . . 6H **95**
Cymric Bldgs. CF10: Card . . . 1C **102**
Cymric Cl. CF5: Ely . . . 4H **93**
Cynan Cl. CF38: Bed . . . 5A **42**
CF63: Barry . . . 5B **106**
CYNCOED . . . 1C **86**
Cyncoed Av. CF23: Cyn . . . 1C **86**
Cyncoed Cres. CF23: Cyn . . . 1D **86**
Cyncoed Flats CF23: Cyn . . . 3C **86**
Cyncoed Gdns. CF23: Pen L . . . 4C **86**
Cyncoed Pl. CF23: Cyn . . . 1C **86**
Cyncoed Ri. CF23: Cyn . . . 1C **86**
Cyncoed Rd. CF23: Cyn . . . 5C **72**
CF23: Cyn, Pen L . . . 4C **86**
Cynon Vw. CF37: C'fydd . . . 4F **15**
Cyntwell Av. CF5: Ely . . . 6F **93**
Cyntwell Cres. CF5: Ely . . . 6F **93**
Cyntwell Pl. CF5: Ely . . . 5F **93**
Cypress Cl. NP18: C'ln . . . 5E **21**
Cypress Dr. CF3: St M . . . 5D **74**
Cypress Pl. CF5: F'wtr . . . 6H **83**
Cypress St. CF37: R'fln . . . 4G **25**
Cyrch-y-Gwas Rd. CF37: T'rest . . . 2E **25**
Cyril Cres. CF24: Card . . . 2D **96**
Cyril St. CF63: Barry . . . 2B **118**
NP19: Newp . . . 5D **36**

D

Daffodil Ct. NP44: Ty C . . . 3B **10**
Daffodil La. NP10: Roger . . . 2H **33**
Dafydd Pl. CF63: Barry . . . 5A **106**
Daisy St. CF5: Card . . . 3D **94**
Daisy Vw. NP4: P'pool . . . 4D **6**
Dalcross St. CF24: Card . . . 6B **86**
Dale Av. CF14: Heath . . . 2F **85**
Dale Ct. CF62: Barry . . . 5H **105**
Dale Path NP44: F'wtr . . . 3D **10**
Dale Rd. NP19: Newp . . . 3B **38**
Dalmuir Rd. CF24: Card . . . 2F **97**
Dalton St. CF24: Card . . . 1A **96**
Damson Pl. CF23: Pontp . . . 2H **73**
Dan Caerlan CF72: L'sant . . . 1G **65**
Dancarga Dr. NP26: Cald . . . 5C **60**
Dancing Cl. NP26: Undy . . . 3D **58**
Dancing Hill NP26: Undy . . . 4D **58**
Danes Cl. NP16: Chep . . . 2D **62**
Danescourt Station (Rail) . . . 5A **84**
Danescourt Way CF5: L'dff . . . 5H **83**
Danes Hill NP16: Sed . . . 3H **63**
Daniel Hopkin Cl. CF61: Llan M . . . 4B **110**
Daniell Cl. CF64: Sul . . . 2G **119**
Daniel Pl. NP20: Newp . . . 6C **36**
Daniel St. CF24: Card . . . 6A **86**
CF63: Barry . . . 6A **106**
NP20: Newp . . . 6C **36**
Dannog y Coed CF63: Barry . . . 4B **106**
Dan-y-Bank Cotts. CF15: Tong . . . 4F **69**
Danybryn CF72: Bryns . . . 1B **78**
Dan-y-Bryn Av. CF15: Rad . . . 1E **83**
Dan-y-Bryn Cl. CF15: Rad . . . 1E **83**
Danybryn Vs. CF37: T'rest . . . 2D **24**
Danycoed CF83: Caer . . . 2D **46**
Dan-y-Coedcae Rd. CF37: P'prdd . . . 2B **24**
Dan-y-Coed Cl. CF23: Cyn . . . 1B **86**
Dan-y-Coed Ri. CF23: Cyn . . . 1B **86**
Dan-y-Coed Rd. CF23: Cyn . . . 6B **72**
Dan-y-Der CF83: B'ws . . . 2E **29**
Dan-y-Felin CF72: L'sant . . . 2E **65**
DANYGRAIG . . . 5D **16**
Dan y Graig NP11: Ris . . . 5D **16**
Danygraig CF83: Mac . . . 3B **30**
NP44: C'iog . . . 4G **9**
Dan-y-Graig CF14: R'ina . . . 5B **70**
CF83: Abert . . . 2E **27**
Dan y Graig Bungs. NP11: Ris . . . 6C **16**
Danygraig Cres. CF72: T Grn . . . 2E **65**
Danygraig Dr. CF72: T Grn . . . 2E **65**
Dan y Graig Hgts. CF72: T Grn . . . 2E **65**
Dan-y-Graig Rd. NP11: Ris . . . 5D **16**
Danygraig St. CF37: P'prdd . . . 2B **24**
Dan-y-Graig Ter. CF83: Abert . . . 2E **27**
Danylan Rd. CF37: P'prdd . . . 6A **14**
Dan-y-Meio CF83: Abert . . . 2D **26**
Dan y Myndd CF14: Thorn . . . 2E **71**
Dan-yr-Allt Cl. CF37: R'fln . . . 4H **25**
Dan yr Ardd CF83: Caer . . . 2A **46**
Dan-yr-Heol CF23: Cyn . . . 1A **86**

Darby Cl. NP10: Roger 3D **34**
Darby Rd. CF24: Card 5G **97**
Darent Cl. NP20: Bet 6E **19**
Darent Rd. NP20: Bet 6E **19**
Darent Wlk. NP20: Bet 6E **19**
Darlington Ct. NP19: Newp 1D **36**
Darran Rd. NP11: Ris, Cros K 2D **16**
Darran St. CF24: Card 1H **95**
Darren Cl. CF71: C'bri 3A **90**
CF83: Caer 4F **29**
Darren Ddu Rd. CF37: P'prdd, Y'bwl 1A **14**
Darren Hill CF71: C'bri 3B **90**
Darren Pk. CF37: P'prdd 4D **14**
Darren Vw. Ct. CF37: P'prdd 4E **15**
Dartington Dr. CF23: Pontp 4E **73**
Dart Rd. NP20: Bet 6G **19**
Darwin Dr. NP20: Malp 5A **20**
Darwyn Las CF83: B'ws 2E **29**
David Cl. NP20: Newp 2C **54**
David Davies Rd. CF63: Barry 3B **118**
David Lloyd Leisure
Cardiff 5F **87**
David Morgan Apartments
CF10: Card 5D **4**
David's Ct. CF72: P'clun 5D **64**
David St. CF10: Card 4E **5** (4B **96**)
CF63: Barry 5C **106**
David Wlk. *NP10: Roger 5D **34***
(off Ebenezer Dr.)
Davies Dr. CF83: Caer 3B **28**
Davies Pl. CF5: F'wtr 2B **94**
Davies Sq. *NP20: Newp 6C **36***
(off Charlotte Dr.)
Davies St. CF63: Barry 1A **118**
Daviot Ct. CF24: Card 6B **86**
Daviot St. CF24: Card 6B **86**
Davis Cl. NP4: P'pool 2B **6**
Davis Ct. *NP16: Chep 1E **63***
(off Bridge St.)
Davis's Ter. CF14: Whit 2D **84**
Davis St. CF24: Card 4G **5** (4C **96**)
Davnic Cl. CF63: Barry 1B **118**
Davy Cl. NP20: Malp 4A **20**
Dawan Cl. CF62: Barry 2E **117**
Dawson Cl. NP19: Newp 3D **38**
Dean Ct. NP44: H'lys 5B **10**
Deanery Gdns. NP20: Newp 5B **36**
Dean Ho. CF24: Card 2D **96**
Deans Cl. CF5: L'dff 1D **94**
CF37: R'fln 3F **25**
Deans Gdns. NP16: Chep 1D **62**
Deans Hill NP16: Chep 2D **62**
Dean St. NP19: Newp 3D **36**
De-Barri St. CF37: R'fln 5F **25**
De Bawdrip Rd. CF24: Card 1F **97**
De Braose Cl. CF5: L'dff 4H **83**
De Burgh Pl. CF11: Card 4A **4** (4G **95**)
De Burgh St. CF11: Card 4A **4** (4G **95**)
De Clare Ct. CF61: Bov 3D **110**
CF83: Caer 4C **28**
De Clare Dr. CF15: Rad 2H **83**
Decoypool La. NP18: Nash 4E **57**
De Croche Pl. CF11: Card 5G **95**
Deemuir Rd. CF24: Card 2F **97**
Deemuir Sq. CF24: Card 1F **97**
Deepdale Cl. CF23: Pen L 4B **86**
Deepdene Cl. CF5: Ely 4D **92**
Deepfield Cl. CF5: Ely 4D **92**
DEEPWEIR 6E **61**
Deepweir NP26: Cald 6E **61**
Deepweir Dr. NP26: Cald 5E **61**
Deepweir Gdns. NP26: Cald 6E **61**
Deepwood Cl. CF5: Ely 4D **92**
Deerbrook NP44: G'mdw 3D **10**
Deere Cl. CF5: Ely 5F **93**
Deere Pl. CF5: Ely 5F **93**
Deere Rd. CF5: Ely 5E **93**
CF38: Llan F 5C **42**
Deer Pk. La. NP10: Bass 6E **35**
Deganwy Cl. CF14: L'shn 4G **71**
DEGAR 6A **78**
De Havilland Rd. CF24: Card 2G **97**
Dehewydd La. CF38: Llan F 4D **42**
Delfryn CF72: Mis 6E **65**
Delius Cl. NP10: Roger 3C **34**
NP19: Newp 4A **38**
Dell, The CF3: Old M 5B **74**
CF38: Tont 6F **25**
Dell Vw. NP16: Chep 2E **63**
Delphinium Rd. NP10: Roger 2H **33**
Delta St. CF11: Card 4F **95**
Denbigh Cl. CF38: Tont 1F **43**
Denbigh Ct. CF64: P'rth 2D **108**
CF83: Caer 5G **27**
Denbigh Dr. CF61: Bov 3E **111**
NP16: Bul 5G **63**
Denbigh Rd. CF64: Din P 1A **108**
NP19: Newp 1E **37**
Denbigh St. CF11: Card 2F **95**
Denbigh Way CF62: Barry 6H **105**
Dene Ct. NP4: P'nydd 1A **6**
Denison Way CF5: Ely 4D **92**
Denmark Dr. NP16: Sed 3H **63**
Denny Vw. NP26: Cald 6E **61**
Den Roche Pl. CF10: Card 3E **5** (3B **96**)
DENSCOMBE 1B **46**
Denstone Ct. CF23: Pen L 4C **86**
Dental Dr. CF14: Heath 4G **85**
Denton Rd. CF5: Card 4F **95**
Dents Cl. NP19: Newp 4B **38**
Dents Hill NP19: Newp 4B **38**
Denys Cl. CF64: Din P 1H **107**
Derby Gro. NP19: Newp 1H **55**
Deri Cl. CF23: Pen L 6E **87**
Dering Rd. CF23: Pontp 4H **73**
Deri Rd. CF23: Pen L 1D **96**
Derwen Ct. CF23: Cyn 6C **72**
Derwendeg Av. CF37: Glync 2D **14**
Derwen Rd. CF23: Cyn 5C **72**
CF72: P'clun 6D **64**
Derwent Cl. CF14: Thorn 3G **71**
Derwent Ct. NP20: Bet 6E **19**
Deryn Ct. CF23: Pent 5F **73**
Despenser Av. CF72: L'sant 3F **65**
Despenser Gdns. CF11: Card 5A **4** (4H **95**)
Despenser Pl. CF11: Card 5A **4** (4H **95**)
Despenser Rd. CF64: Sul 2G **119**
Despenser St. CF11: Card 5A **4** (4H **95**)
Dessmuir Rd. CF24: Card 2F **97**
Devon Av. CF63: Barry 1H **117**
Devon Ct. NP18: C'ln 4G **21**
Devon Pl. CF11: Card 6G **95**
NP20: Newp 4B **36**
Devon St. CF11: Card 6G **95**
Dewberry Gro. NP10: Roger 1H **33**
Dew Cres. CF5: Ely 5A **94**
Dewi Ct. CF5: L'dff 1C **94**
Dewinton Ter. CF83: L'brad 1B **28**
DEWI SANT HOSPITAL 1C **24**
Dewi St. CF37: P'prdd 4E **15**
Dewsland Pk. Rd. NP20: Newp 5B **36**
Dewston Cl. NP26: Cald 5B **60**
Dewston Gdns. NP26: Cald 5B **60**
Dewstow Rd. NP26: C'ent, Cald 3A **60**
Dewstow St. NP19: Newp 5F **37**
Diamond Cl. CF83: Caer 5B **28**
Diamond St. CF24: Card 3D **96**
(not continuous)
Diana La. CF24: Card 6B **86**
Diana St. CF24: Card 6B **86**
Dibdin Cl. NP19: Newp 4D **38**
Dickens Av. CF3: L'rmy 6H **73**
Dickens Ct. CF83: Mac 3C **30**
Dickens Dr. NP20: Newp 1G **53**
(not continuous)
Digby Cl. CF5: L'dff 5A **84**
Digby St. CF63: Barry 2A **118**
Dilmands Rd. CF61: Llan M 3A **110**
Dinas Path NP44: F'wtr 3D **10**
Dinas Pl. CF11: Card 6H **95**
DINAS POWYS 2G **107**
Dinas Powys Castle 1G **107**
Dinas Powys Station (Rail) 3G **107**
Dinas Rd. CF64: P'rth 3C **108**
Dinas St. CF11: Card 6B **4** (5H **95**)
Dinch Hill NP26: Undy 4D **58**
Dingle, The CF64: P'rth 2F **109**
Dingle Cl. CF62: Barry 5D **116**
Dingle La. CF64: P'rth 1E **109**
NP44: Pnwd 5C **8**
Dingle Rd. CF64: P'rth 1E **109**
NP4: P'pool 4D **6**
Dingle Road Station (Rail) 1E **109**
Discovery Pk. NP20: Newp 3B **36**
Distillery Rd. La. *CF37: P'prdd 5A **14***
(off Margaret St.)
District Shop. Cen. CF3: St M 6C **74**
CF14: Thorn 3G **71**
Ditchling Ct. CF64: P'rth 3E **109**
Diwedd Camlas NP10: Roger 4E **35**
Dixon Pl. NP11: Ris 5E **17**
Dobbins Rd. CF63: Barry 5D **106**
Dochdwy Rd. CF64: L'dgh 5F **101**
Dock Rd. CF62: Barry 5H **117**
Dock St. CF64: P'rth 6H **101**
Docks Way NP20: Newp 3G **53**
Dock Vw. Rd. CF63: Barry 3H **117**
Dockwell Ter. NP18: L'wrn 5F **39**
Doddington Pl. CF37: P'prdd 5E **15**
Doe Cl. CF23: Pen L 6E **87**
Dogfield St. CF24: Card 6A **86**
Doglan Rd. CF62: T'gan 2F **115**
Dogo St. CF11: Card 2F **95**
Dol Fran CF83: Caer 5F **29**
Dolgellau Av. CF38: Tont 1F **43**
Dolgoch Cl. CF3: Rum 2B **88**
Dol Gwartheg CF64: P'rth 3C **108**
Doloman Theatre 5C **36**
Dolphin Ct. *NP20: Newp 6C **36***
(off Commercial Rd.)
Dolphin St. NP20: Newp 6D **36**
(not continuous)
Dolwen Rd. CF14: Llan N 5C **84**
Dolyfelin CF83: B'ws 2E **29**
Dol-y-Felin CF15: Cre 6D **66**
Dol-y-Felin St. CF83: Caer 6C **28**
Dol-y-Llan CF72: Mis 5F **65**
Dol-y-Pandy CF83: B'ws 2E **29**
Dol-y-Paun CF83: Caer 1A **46**
Dol-yr-Eos CF83: Caer 5E **29**
Dombey Cl. CF14: Thorn 3H **71**
Dominions Arc. CF10: Card 3D **4** (3A **96**)
Dominions Way CF24: Card 1E **97**
Dominions Way Ind. Est. CF24: Card 1E **97**
Donald St. CF24: Card 6B **86**
Don Cl. NP20: Bet 6F **19**
Doniford Cl. CF64: Sul 1H **119**
Donnington Rd. CF64: Sul 1E **119**
Dorallt Cl. NP44: H'lys 4A **10**
Dorallt Way NP44: H'lys 5A **10**
Dorchester Av. CF23: Pen L 5D **86**
Dorleigh Ct. NP44: Thorn 6B **8**
Dorothy Av. CF62: Barry 5G **105**
Dorothy Cl. CF62: Barry 5G **105**
Dorothy St. CF37: P'prdd 5D **14**
Dorset Av. CF63: Barry 1H **117**
Dorset Cl. NP19: Newp 1H **55**
Dorset Cres. NP19: Newp 1H **55**
Dorset St. CF11: Card 6G **95**
Dorstone Wlk. NP44: L'rfn 2A **12**
Dos Rd. NP20: Newp 2B **36**
Douglas Cl. CF5: L'dff 5A **84**
Dovedale Cl. CF23: Pen L 4B **86**
Dovedale St. CF63: Barry 1B **118**
Doverscourt Ho. CF11: Card 4A **102**
Dovey Cl. CF3: Rum 2B **88**
CF62: Barry 1E **117**
Dowlais Arc. *CF10: Card 1C **102***
(off W. Bute St.)
Dowlais Rd. CF24: Card 5D **96**
Dowland Cl. NP19: Newp 4B **38**
Dowland Rd. CF64: P'rth 4C **108**
Downfield Cl. CF64: L'dgh 5G **101**
Downing St. NP19: Newp 6G **37**
Downlands Way CF3: Rum 5G **87**
DOWNS 1B **98**
Down's Vw. CF71: A'thin 2F **91**
Down's Vw. Cl. CF71: A'thin 2F **91**
Downton Grange CF3: Rum 5A **88**
Downton Ri. CF3: Rum 5H **87**
Downton Rd. CF3: Rum 5H **87**
Doyle Av. CF5: F'wtr 1A **94**
Doyle Ct. CF5: F'wtr 1A **94**
DRAETHEN 6A **32**
Dragonfly Dr. CF62: Rho 2E **115**
Drake Cl. CF62: St Ath 2D **112**
NP19: Newp 3C **38**
Drake Wlk. CF10: Card 6F **5** (5B **96**)

Drangway CF61: Llan M 3B **110**
Dranllwyn Cl. CF83: Mac 2F **31**
Dranllwyn La. CF83: Mac 2F **31**
Drawlings Cl. CF3: Old M 5B **74**
Dray Ct. CF10: Card 5D **4** (4A **96**)
Drayton Ct. NP44: St D 2E **11**
Drinkwater Cl. NP20: Newp 1H **53**
Drinkwater Gdns.
NP20: Newp 1H **53**
Drinkwater Ri. NP20: Newp 1H **53**
Drinkwater Vw. NP20: Newp 1H **53**
Drive, The CF5: F'wtr 2H **93**
CF64: Din P 2A **108**
CF72: Mis 1F **79**
DROPE 5B **92**
Drope Rd. CF5: Ely 5C **92**
Drope Ter. CF5: St G 5C **92**
Dros Col CF72: L'harry 5A **78**
Dros-y-Mor CF64: P'rth 3F **109**
Dros-y-Morfa CF3: Rum 5A **88**
Drovers M. NP20: Newp 6C **36**
Drovers Way CF15: Rad 2F **83**
Druids Cl. CF83: Caer 1A **46**
Druids Grn. CF71: C'bri 3D **90**
Druidstone Rd. CF3: Old M 4C **74**
Drum Tower Vw. CF83: Caer 1H **45**
Drury Cl. CF14: Thorn 3G **71**
Dr William Price Bus. Cen.
CF37: T'rest 3E **25**
Drybrook Cl. CF3: St M 1D **88**
NP44: C'brn 2H **11**
Dryburgh Av. CF14: Heath 2F **85**
Dryden Cl. CF3: L'rmy 6H **73**
Dryden Rd. CF64: P'rth 1D **108**
Dryden Ter. CF62: Barry 5H **105**
Drylla CF64: Din P 3G **107**
Drysgol Rd. CF15: Rad 1F **83**
Ducansby Ho. CF11: Card 4A **102**
Duckpool Rd. NP19: Newp 3E **37**
Dudley Ct. CF10: Card 2B **102**
Dudley Pl. CF62: Barry 3F **117**
Dudley St. CF10: Card 2B **102**
NP19: Newp 5E **37**
DUFFRYN 4G **53**
Duffryn Av. CF23: Cyn 2B **86**
Duffryn Bach Ter. CF38: Chu V 4F **43**
Duffryn Cl. CF23: Cyn 1A **86**
NP10: Bass 6C **34**
Duffryn Dr. NP10: Duf 4G **53**
Duffryn Est. NP10: Duf 3G **53**
Duffryn Ffwd CF15: N'grw 4F **45**
Duffryn La. CF5: St N 6A **98**
NP10: Coedk 6E **53**
Duffryn Rd. CF23: Cyn 1C **86**
CF37: R'fln 4F **25**
Duffryn St. CF10: Card 5F **5** (4B **96**)
Duffryn Ter. *CF38: Chu V* *3F 43*
(off Main Rd.)
Duffryn Way NP10: Duf 5G **53**
Dugdale Wlk. CF11: Card 4F **95**
Duke St. CF10: Card 4C **4** (4A **96**)
CF37: T'rest 3D **24**
NP20: Newp 6D **36**
Duke St. Arc. CF10: Card 4C **4** (4A **96**)
Dulverton Av. CF3: L'rmy 6A **74**
Dulverton Dr. CF64: Sul 2H **119**
Dulwich Gdns. CF5: Card 2D **94**
Dumballs Rd. CF10: Card 5A **96**
Dumfries Pl. CF10: Card 2E **5** (3B **96**)
NP20: Newp 5C **36**
Dummer Cl. CF3: St M 1D **88**
Dunbar Cl. CF23: Pontp 4G **73**
Duncan Cl. CF3: St M 1B **88**
Dungarvan Dr. CF23: Pontp 4G **73**
Dunkery Cl. CF3: L'rmy 2H **87**
Dunleavy Dr. CF11: Card 3G **101**
Dunlin Av. NP26: Cald 6C **60**
Dunlin Ct. CF63: Barry 3H **117**
Dunnet Gdns. NP4: New I 6H **7**
Dunn Sq. *NP20: Newp* *6C 36*
(off Francis Dr.)
Dunraven Cl. CF64: Din P 2A **108**
Dunraven Ct. CF83: Caer 5G **27**
Dunraven Cres. CF72: T Grn 3C **64**
Dunraven Dr. NP10: Duf 6F **53**
Dunraven Ho. CF10: Card 4B **4**
Dunraven Rd. CF11: Card 5F **95**
NP44: L'rfn 3B **12**
Dunraven St. CF62: Barry 4E **117**
Dunsmuir Rd. CF24: Card 3F **97**
Dunstable Rd. NP19: Newp 4C **38**
Dunster Dr. CF64: Sul 2G **119**
Dunster Rd. CF3: L'rmy 1B **88**
Durand Rd. NP26: Cald 6C **60**
Durham La. NP19: Newp 2D **36**
(not continuous)
Durham Rd. NP19: Newp 2D **36**
Durham St. CF11: Card 6H **95**
Durleigh Cl. CF3: L'rmy 6A **74**
Durlston Cl. CF14: Llan N 4B **84**
Durrel St. CF61: Llan M 3B **110**
Duxford Cl. CF5: L'dff 5H **83**
Dyfan Rd. CF63: Barry 1A **118**
Dyfed CF64: P'rth 6C **102**
Dyfed Dr. CF83: Caer 4B **28**
DYFFRYN 1D **104**
Dyffryn Av. CF37: R'fln 3G **25**
Dyffryn Cres. CF37: R'fln 3G **25**
Dyffryn Gdns. 1D **104**
Dyffryn Gdns. CF37: R'fln 3G **25**
Dyffryn La. NP10: Coedk 5D **52**
Dyffryn Pl. CF62: Barry 6F **105**
Dyffryn Rd. CF37: R'fln 4G **25**
Dyfnallt Rd. CF63: Barry 5A **106**
Dyfrig Cl. CF5: Ely 3B **94**
Dyfrig Ct. CF61: Llan M 2D **110**
Dyfrig Rd. CF5: Ely 3B **94**
Dyfrig St. CF11: Card 2G **95**
CF62: Barry 5A **118**
Dyhewydd Isaf CF38: Llan F 4D **42**
Dylan Av. CF38: Bed 6A **42**
Dylan Cl. CF64: L'dgh 5G **101**
Dylan Cres. CF63: Barry 5B **106**
Dylan Dr. CF83: Caer 4C **28**
Dylan Pl. CF24: Card 1G **5** (2C **96**)
Dynea CF37: R'fln 5A **26**
Dynea Cvn. Site CF37: R'fln 4H **25**
Dynea Cl. CF37: R'fln 4H **25**
Dynea Rd. CF37: R'fln, Up Bo 3H **25**
Dynevor Cl. NP44: L'rfn 2B **12**
Dynevor Rd. CF23: Pen L 4D **86**
Dyserth Rd. CF64: P'rth 2D **108**

E

Eagle Cl. NP26: Cald 6D **60**
Eagle La. CF71: C'bri 3C **90**
Eagle Rd. CF62: St Ath 3F **111**
Eagleswell Rd. CF61: Bov 2D **110**
Eagle Ter. CF62: St Ath 3G **111**
Earl Cres. CF62: Barry 5H **117**
Earl Cunningham Ct. CF10: Card 6G **5**
Earle Pl. CF5: Card 4F **95**
Earl La. CF11: Card 2H **101**
Earl Rd. CF64: P'rth 2D **108**
Earl's Ct. Pl. CF23: Pen L 6D **86**
Earl's Ct. Rd. CF23: Pen L 5D **86**
Earlsmede NP44: G'mdw 2D **10**
Earl St. CF11: Card 2H **101**
Earlswood Rd. CF14: L'shn 6G **71**
EAST ABERTHAW 6H **113**
East Av. CF83: B'ws 3G **29**
CF83: Caer 5B **28**
NP4: Grif 2E **9**
E. Bank Rd. NP19: Newp 3E **55**
E. Bay Cl. CF10: Card 5G **5** (4C **96**)
E. Bay Link Rd. CF24: Card 6F **97**
Eastbourne Ct. CF63: Barry 5C **106**
EASTBROOK 1H **107**
Eastbrook Cl. CF64: Din P 1H **107**
Eastbrook Rd. CF64: P'rth 6F **101**
Eastbrook Station (Rail) 1A **108**
E. Bute St. CF10: Card 1C **102**
E. Dock Rd. NP20: Newp 6D **36**
(not continuous)
Eastern Av. CF3: Old M 6G **73**
CF14: Card, Cyn, Llan N 5F **85**
CF23: L'dyrn, Pen L 5D **86**
CF23: Pent 6G **73**
Eastern Bus. Pk., The CF3: Old M 5C **74**
Eastern Cl. CF3: Old M 5B **74**
Eastern Leisure Cen. 3H **87**
Eastfield Cl. NP18: C'ln 3G **21**
Eastfield Ct. CF72: L'sant 3G **65**
Eastfield Dr. NP18: C'ln 3G **21**
Eastfield M. NP18: C'ln 3G **21**
Eastfield Rd. NP18: C'ln 3G **21**
Eastfield Vw. NP18: C'ln 3G **21**
Eastfield Way NP18: C'ln 3G **21**
Eastgate CF71: C'bri 3D **90**
Eastgate Bus. Pk. CF3: Rum 6A **88**
Eastgate Cres. NP26: C'ent 1B **60**
Eastgate M. *CF71: C'bri* *4D 90*
(off Eastgate)
East Gro. CF24: Card 2G **5** (3B **96**)
East Gro. La. CF24: Card 2G **5** (3C **96**)
East Gro. Rd. NP19: Newp 4H **37**
E. Lynne Gdns. NP18: C'ln 4A **22**
E. Market St. NP20: Newp 6D **36**
(not continuous)
Eastmoor Rd. NP19: Newp 6A **38**
E. Moors Bus. Pk. CF24: Card 6H **5** (5D **96**)
E. Moors Rd. CF10: Card 4C **96**
CF24: Card 5H **5** (4C **96**)
East Ri. CF14: L'shn 5A **72**
East Rd. CF64: Sul 1F **119**
NP44: Oakf 5H **11**
East Roedin NP44: Coed E 5E **11**
East St. CF37: P'prdd 5D **14**
CF61: Llan M 3B **110**
CF62: Barry 3F **117**
NP20: Newp 4B **36**
E. Tyndall St. CF24: Card 5H **5** (4D **96**)
E. Usk Rd. NP19: Newp 3C **36**
East Vw. CF83: Caer 1D **46**
NP4: Grif 1E **9**
NP4: P'pool 3B **6**
East Vw. Ter. CF62: Barry 4F **117**
EAST VILLAGE 4C **90**
East Wlk. CF62: Barry 1G **117**
Eastway Rd. NP20: Newp 2D **54**
Ebbw Cl. CF62: St Ath 2C **112**
Ebbw Ct. NP11: Cros K 3A **16**
Ebbw Rd. NP26: Cald 4C **60**
Ebbw St. NP11: Ris 5D **16**
Ebenezer Dr. NP10: Roger 5C **34**
Ebenezer St. CF37: R'fln 3F **25**
Ebenezer Ter. NP20: Newp 5C **36**
Ebley Gdns. NP26: Cald 6E **61**
Ebwy Ct. CF5: Ely 5H **93**
Eckley Rd. CF64: Sul 2G **119**
Eclipse St. CF24: Card 3H **5** (3C **96**)
Eddystone Cl. CF11: Card 6G **95**
Edgcort NP44: F'wtr 4D **10**
Edgehill NP44: Llanf 4B **12**
Edgehill Av. CF14: L'shn 4E **71**
Edinburgh Cl. NP44: G'mdw 2C **10**
Edinburgh Ct. CF11: Card 4G **95**
Edington Av. CF14: Card 5H **85**
Edison Ridge NP20: Malp 4A **20**
Edith Rd. CF64: Din P 2H **107**
Edlogan Sq. NP44: C'iog 5G **9**
Edlogan Way NP44: C'iog, C'brn 1H **11**
Edmond Rd. NP16: Sed 2H **63**
Edmonds Ct. CF24: Card 6B **86**
Edmonton Ct. *NP4: P'pool* *2C 6*
(off Forge La.)
Edmund Pl. CF63: Barry 1D **118**
Edney Vw. NP10: Duf 4H **53**
Edward VII Av. NP20: Newp 5H **35**
Edward VII Cres. NP20: Newp 4A **36**
Edward VII La. NP20: Newp 4H **35**
Edward Clarke Cl. CF5: L'dff 5A **84**
Edward England Wharf
CF10: Card 6F **5** (5B **96**)
Edward German Cres. NP19: Newp 4C **38**
Edward Ho. CF11: Card 5A **4**
Edwardian Way CF72: Mis 6F **65**
Edward La. NP20: Newp 5B **36**
(not continuous)
Edward Nicholl Ct. CF23: Pen L 5D **86**
Edward St. CF10: Card 3E **5** (3B **96**)
CF63: Barry 6B **106**
NP4: Grif 6E **7**
NP4: P'pool 2B **6**
Edward Ter. CF83: Abert 1E **27**
Edward Thomas Cl. CF83: Rud 5B **30**

Edwin Ind. Est. NP20: Newp 2B **36**
Edwin St. NP10: Roger 5C **34**
NP20: Newp 2C **36**
EFAIL ISAF 6E **43**
Efail Isaf Rd. CF15: P'rch 2G **67**
Egerton M. CF5: Card 3E **95**
Egerton St. CF5: Card 3E **95**
Egham St. CF5: Card 3E **95**
Eglwys Av. CF37: R'fln 4G **25**
EGLWYS-BREWIS 2A **112**
Eglwysilan Rd. CF15: Gro-w 2B **26**
CF37: P'prdd, R'fln 5G **15**
CF83: Abert, N'grw 2B **26**
Eglwysilan Way CF83: Abert 2D **26**
EGLWYS Y DRINDOD 2B **38**
Egremont Rd. CF23: Pen L 4B **86**
Egypt St. CF37: T'rest 1D **24**
Eider Cl. CF3: St M 5C **74**
Eifion Cl. CF63: Barry 5A **106**
Eisteddfod Wlk. NP19: Newp 3B **38**
Eithinen Ber CF63: Barry 4B **106**
Elaine Cl. CF14: Thorn 3G **71**
Elaine Cres. NP19: Newp 2F **37**
Elan Cl. CF62: Barry 1E **117**
NP20: Bet 6G **19**
Elan Rd. CF14: L'shn 5A **72**
Elan Wlk. NP44: St D 3E **11**
Elan Way NP26: Cald 4D **60**
Elderberry Rd. CF5: F'wtr 6F **83**
Elder Cl. NP18: C'ln 5F **21**
Elder Wood Cl. CF23: Pen L 4E **87**
Eldon Ct. CF11: Card 4G **95**
Eleanor Pl. CF10: Card 2B **102**
Electra Ho. CF10: Card 1D **102**
Eleven St. CF64: Sul 1E **119**
Elfed Av. CF64: P'rth 2C **108**
Elfed Grn. CF5: F'wtr 6A **84**
Elfed Way CF63: Barry 5B **106**
Elford Rd. CF5: Ely 4G **93**
Elgar Av. NP19: Newp 4A **38**
Elgar Circ. NP19: Newp 4B **38**
Elgar Cl. NP19: Newp 4B **38**
Elgar Cres. CF3: L'rmy 6B **74**
Elgar Rd. CF64: P'rth 4D **108**
Elizabethan Ct. CF64: P'rth 5G **101**
Elizabeth Av. CF62: Barry 5G **105**
Elled Rd. NP4: P'nydd, P'pool 1A **6**
Ellen St. CF10: Card 5F **5** (4B **96**)
Ellesmere Ct. CF3: St M 1B **88**
Ellipse, The NP4: Grif 2D **8**
Ellis CF72: Y'erdy 6C **40**
Ellis Fisher Ct. CF62: Barry 3G **117**
Ellwood Cl. CF3: St M 1D **88**
Ellwood Path NP44: St D 2D **10**
Elm Av. NP26: Undy 5E **59**
Elm Cl. CF64: Sul 3A **120**
Elmdale NP16: Chep 1E **63**
Elm Dr. NP11: Ris 5E **17**
Elmfield Cl. CF3: St M 1C **88**
Elm Gro. CF62: E Bre 2B **112**
CF63: Barry 5C **106**
CF83: Caer 4E **29**
NP4: Seba 2E **9**
NP20: Malp 5B **20**
Elmgrove CF83: Tret 3H **29**
Elmgrove Cl. CF37: Glync 2C **14**
Elm Gro. La. CF64: Din P 2G **107**
Elm Gro. Pl. CF64: Din P 2H **107**
Elm Gro. Rd. CF64: Din P 2G **107**
Elmgrove Rd. CF14: Whit 3A **84**
Elm Ho. CF14: Whit 1A **84**
Elm Rd. CF72: L'harry 5A **78**
NP26: Cald 4B **60**
Elms, The NP26: Undy 4F **59**
Elms Hill NP26: Undy 4F **59**
Elms Pk. CF72: Mis 1F **79**
Elm St. CF24: Card 1H **5** (2C **96**)
CF37: R'fln 4G **25**
Elm St. La. CF24: Card 1H **5** (2C **96**)
Elmwood Ct. CF24: Card 1H **5** (2C **96**)
Elworthy Cl. CF64: Sul 2H **119**
Elwyn St. CF39: Coed 3A **40**
ELY 4H **93**
Ely Brewery Workshops *CF5: Ely* *3B* ***94***
(off Wroughton Pl.)
Ely Bri. Ind. Est. CF5: Ely 2A **94**
Ely Distribution Cen. CF5: Ely 5A **94**
Ely Rd. CF5: F'wtr, L'dff 2B **94**
Elysia St. NP19: Newp 2D **36**
Ely St. CF72: P'clun 5D **64**
Ely Valley Ind. Est. CF72: P'clun 5C **64**
Ely Valley Rd. CF39: Coed 2A **40**
CF72: T Grn, Y'erdy 4A **40**
Emanuel Cl. CF83: Caer 2H **45**
Emblem Cl. CF5: Ely 5A **94**
Emerald St. CF24: Card 3D **96**
Emerson Dr. CF5: Ely 1F **99**
Emlyn Dr. CF83: Caer 5C **28**
Emlyn Sq. NP20: Newp 5C **36**
Emlyn St. NP20: Newp 5C **36**
Emlyn Wlk. NP20: Newp 5C **36**
Empire Ho. CF10: Card 1B **102**
Empire Way CF11: Card 5A **102**
Emsworth Ct. CF23: Cyn 1C **86**
Enbourne Dr. CF23: Pontp 4F **73**
Endyngs NP44: F'wtr 4D **10**
ENERGLYN 4B **28**
Energlyn Cl. CF83: Caer 5B **28**
Energlyn Ct. *CF83: Caer* *5B* ***28***
(off Energlyn Cl.)
Energlyn Cres. CF83: Caer 4B **28**
Energlyn Row CF83: Caer 3B **28**
Energlyn Ter. CF83: Caer 4A **28**
Enfield Dr. CF62: Barry 6E **105**
Ennerdale Cl. CF23: Pen L 5B **86**
Ennerdale Ct. NP19: Newp 1F **37**
Enterprise Pk. Ind. Est. NP20: Newp 6D **36**
Enterprise Way NP20: Newp 6D **36**
Enville Cl. NP20: Newp 5G **35**
Enville Rd. NP20: Newp 5G **35**
Eppynt Cl. NP11: Ris 5G **17**
Epsom Cl. CF5: Ely 4B **94**
Epstein Cl. CF5: L'dff 5H **83**
Eric Coates Cl. NP19: Newp 5B **38**
Eric Coates Wlk. *NP19: Newp* *5B* ***38***
(off Eric Coates Cl.)
Erris Ct. CF37: P'prdd 4D **14**
Erskine Ct. CF24: Card 2E **97**
Erw Fach CF38: Llan F 2D **42**
Erw Hir CF5: St F 2C **82**
CF72: L'sant 2F **65**
Erw Las CF14: Whit 3C **84**
Erw'r Delyn Cl. CF64: P'rth 1B **108**
Erw Wen CF14: R'ina 5D **70**
Erw Wen Cotts. CF15: P'rch 4A **68**
Eschol Cl. NP19: Newp 6H **37**
Eschol Ct. NP19: Newp 6H **37**
Esgid Mair CF63: Barry 4C **106**
Eskdale Cl. CF23: Pen L 4B **86**
Esperanto Way NP19: Newp 2E **55**
Esplanade CF64: P'rth 2F **109**
Esplanade Bldgs. CF62: Barry 5G **117**
Esporta Health & Fitness
Cwmbran 6F **9**
Essex Ct. NP18: C'ln 4G **21**
Essex St. NP19: Newp 5E **37**
Essich St. CF24: Card 6C **86**
Estate Rd. NP4: P'nydd 1A **6**
Estuary Rd. NP19: Newp 2A **56**
Estuary Vw. NP26: Cald 6E **61**
Ethel St. CF5: Card 3D **94**
Eton Ct. CF14: Heath 1G **85**
Eton Pl. CF5: Card 4F **95**
Eton Rd. NP19: Newp 4D **36**
Eton St. CF62: Barry 4E **117**
Eugene Cl. CF3: St M 5E **75**
Eurgan Cl. CF61: Llan M 4B **110**
Europark NP26: Red 6A **58**
Eurwg Cres. CF3: Old M 5B **74**
Evans Bus. Cen. CF83: Caer 2A **46**
Evansfield Rd. CF14: Llan N 4B **84**
Evans Sq. CF37: P'prdd 4E **15**
Evans St. CF62: Barry 2H **117**
NP20: Newp 3C **36**
Evelian Ct. CF14: Whit 4F **85**
Evelyn St. CF63: Barry 2A **118**
Evenlode Av. CF64: P'rth 3D **108**
Evenwood Cl. CF23: Pontp 4F **73**
Evenwood Ct. CF5: Ely 3G **93**
Everard St. CF63: Barry 1B **118**
Everard Way CF23: Cyn 3B **86**
Everest Av. CF14: L'shn 4H **71**
Everest Wlk. CF14: L'shn 4H **71**
Everswell Av. CF5: F'wtr 2H **93**
Everswell Rd. CF5: F'wtr 2H **93**
Evesham Ct. NP20: Newp 2A **36**
Eve's Well Ct. NP19: Newp 4E **37**
Eveswell La. NP19: Newp 4F **37**
Eveswell Pk. Rd. NP19: Newp 3F **37**
Eveswell St. NP19: Newp 4F **37**
Evtol Ind. Est. *NP20: Newp* *1D* ***54***
(off Portland St.)
Ewbank Cl. CF63: Barry 5C **106**
Ewenny Cl. CF63: Barry 5A **106**
Ewenny Rd. CF14: L'shn 6A **72**
Excalibur Dr. CF14: Thorn 3F **71**
Excelsior Cl. NP19: Newp 5E **37**
Excelsior Ind. Est. CF14: Card 5E **85**
Excelsior Rd. CF14: Card 5E **85**
Exchange Ct. NP11: Ris 4D **16**
Exchange Rd. NP11: Ris 4D **16**
Exe Rd. NP20: Bet 5F **19**
Exeter Cl. NP44: G'mdw 2C **10**
Exeter Rd. NP19: Newp 3E **37**
Exeter St. NP19: Newp 4E **37**
Exford Cres. CF3: L'rmy 2G **87**
Exmouth Pl. NP16: Chep 1F **63**
Eyre St. CF24: Card 3E **97**
Ezel Ct. CF10: Card 1B **102**

F

Faber Way CF11: Card 6F **95**
Factory Cotts. NP11: Ris 6F **17**
Factory La. CF37: P'prdd 1B **24**
Factory Rd. CF71: L'thian 5B **90**
NP20: Newp 3B **36**
Fairacre Cl. CF14: Thorn 3G **71**
Fairbrook Cl. CF14: R'ina 5D **70**
Fairfax Rd. CF14: Heath 1F **85**
NP19: Newp 5G **37**
Fairfield NP4: P'pool 2A **6**
Fairfield Av. CF5: Card 3C **94**
Fairfield Bus. Pk. CF15: Gwae G 3F **69**
Fairfield Cl. CF5: Card 2B **94**
CF37: R'fln 5G **25**
CF61: Llan M 3C **110**
NP18: C'ln 4F **21**
NP26: Cald 5B **60**
Fairfield Cres. CF61: Llan M 3C **110**
Fairfield Ind. Est. CF15: Gwae G 3E **69**
Fairfield La. CF37: R'fln 5G **25**
Fairfield Ri. CF61: Llan M 2C **110**
Fairfield Rd. CF64: P'rth 1D **108**
NP16: Bul 4E **63**
NP18: C'ln 4F **21**
Fairford St. CF63: Barry 6B **106**
Fairhaven Cl. CF3: St M 5E **75**
Fairhill NP44: F'wtr, G'mdw 3D **10**
Fairhill Dr. CF38: Tont 2G **43**
Fairhill Wlk. NP44: Coed E 3C **10**
NP44: F'wtr 3D **10**
(not continuous)
Fairland Cl. CF72: L'sant 2G **65**
Fairleigh CF64: Mic P 4B **100**
Fairleigh Ct. CF11: Card 1F **95**
Fairleigh Rd. CF11: Card 1F **95**
Fairmead Ct. CF5: F'wtr 2H **93**
Fair Mdw. CF15: P'rch 4A **68**
Fairmound Pl. CF38: Tont 2G **43**
Fairoak Av. NP19: Newp 3E **37**
Fairoak Ct. CF23: Pen L 5B **86**
NP19: Newp 3E **37**
Fair Oak Gro. NP10: Bass 1B **52**
Fairoak La. NP44: C'iog 1A **12**
Fairoak M. CF24: Card 5A **86**
NP19: Newp 3E **37**
Fairoak Rd. CF23: Card 5B **86**
CF24: Card 6A **86**
Fairoaks CF64: Din P 2H **107**
Fairoak Ter. NP19: Newp 4E **37**
Fairthorn Cl. CF14: Thorn 2G **71**
Fair Vw. NP16: Bul 3D **62**
Fairview CF38: Bed 5A **42**
Fairview Av. NP11: Ris 5E **17**
Fair Vw. Cl. CF72: P'clun 6D **64**
Fairview Cl. CF3: St M 5E **75**

Fairview Ct. CF23: Pent 6D **72**
NP4: P'nydd 1A **6**
FAIRWATER
CF5 **6H 83**
NP44 **4D 10**
Fairwater Av. CF5: F'wtr 2B **94**
Fairwater Cl. CF3: Mic F 6E **51**
NP44: F'wtr 3D **10**
Fairwater Grn. CF5: F'wtr 2H **93**
Fairwater Gro. E. CF5: L'dff 1B **94**
Fairwater Gro. W. CF5: L'dff 1B **94**
Fairwater Leisure Cen.
Fairwater, Ty Gwyn Way 3C 10
Fairwater, Waterhall Rd. 5G 83
Fairwater Rd. CF5: F'wtr 1H **93**
CF5: L'dff 1B **94**
Fairwater Sports & Social Club 4D 10
Fairwater Sq. Shops NP44: F'wtr 3C **10**
Fairwater Station (Rail) **1A 94**
Fairwater Way NP44: F'wtr 4D **10**
Fairwater Workshops CF5: F'wtr 2A **94**
Fairway, The CF23: Cyn 5C **72**
NP4: New I 5H **7**
Fairway Cl. NP10: Roger 2C **34**
Fairway Dr. CF83: Caer 3B **28**
Fairways Cres. CF5: F'wtr 2G **93**
Fairways Vw. CF72: T Grn 2C **64**
Fairwood Cl. CF5: F'wtr 6A **84**
Fairwood Rd. CF5: F'wtr 6A **84**
Falcon Cl. NP26: Cald 6D **60**
Falcon Dr. CF10: Card 1D **102**
Falcon Gro. CF64: P'rth 6E **109**
Falcon Rd. CF63: Barry 6D **106**
Falconwood Dr. CF5: Ely 5D **92**
Falfield Cl. CF14: L'vne 3A **72**
Fallowfield Dr. NP19: Newp 6A **38**
Fallowfields NP44: F'wtr 4D **10**
Fan Heulog CF37: Glync 1D **14**
Fanheulog CF72: T Grn 3D **64**
Fanny St. CF24: Card 1A **96**
Faraday Cl. NP20: Malp 5H **19**
Fardre Ct. CF38: Chu V 1E **43**
Fardre Cres. CF38: Chu V 2F **43**
Farlays NP44: Coed E 4C **10**
Farlow Wlk. NP44: St D 3E **11**
Farm Cl. CF83: Abert 2E **27**
Farm Dr. CF23: Cyn 3B **86**
Farm Hill NP4: Trev 1B **6**
Farmhouse Way CF5: Ely 6F **93**
Farm La. NP19: Newp 2E **37**
NP44: C'brn 1H **11**
Farmleigh CF3: Rum 4H **87**
Farm Rd. CF83: Caer 6E **29**
NP4: P'pool 4C **6**
Farmville Rd. CF24: Card 3E **97**
Farmwood Cl. NP19: Newp 4H **37**
Farnaby Cl. NP19: Newp 4B **38**
Farriers Ga. NP10: Bass 1D **52**
Farthings, The CF23: Pent 4F **73**
Faulkner Rd. NP20: Newp 4B **36**
Fedw Wood NP16: Chep 2C **62**
Feering St. NP19: Newp 5E **37**
Felbridge Cl. CF10: Card 5C **96**
Felbrigg Cres. CF23: Pontp 4E **73**
Felin Fach CF14: Whit 4D **84**
Felinfach CF83: B'ws 2G **29**
Felin Wen CF14: R'ina 6E **71**
Felnex Ind. Est. NP19: Newp 3E **55**
Felsted Cl. CF23: Pontp 4F **73**
Fennel Cl. CF3: St M 5E **75**
CF64: P'rth 6G **101**
Fenner Brockway Cl. NP19: Newp 2B **38**
Fenviolet Cl. CF3: St M 1F **89**
Fernbank NP44: F'wtr 3D **10**
Fern Cl. CF37: R'fln 4H **25**
Fern Ct. NP16: Bul 5F **63**
Ferndale St. CF11: Card 6H **95**
Fern Dr. CF62: Barry 2F **117**
Ferney Cres. NP26: Cald 5A **60**
Ferneycross NP26: Cald 5B **60**
FERNLEA **4D 16**
Fernlea NP11: Ris 4E **17**
Fernleigh Rd. NP26: Cald 5B **60**
Fern Pl. CF5: F'wtr 1H **93**
Fern Ri. NP20: Malp 4B **20**
Fernside NP19: Newp 6H **37**

Fern St. CF5: Card 3D **94**
Ferntree Dr. CF3: St M 6C **74**
Ferny Ct. CF23: Pen L 5D **86**
Ferrier Av. CF5: F'wtr 1H **93**
Ferriers Ct. CF24: Card 2D **96**
Ferry Ct. CF11: Card 4A **102**
Ferry La. CF64: P'rth 6B **102**
Ferry Rd. CF11: Card 2H **101**
(not continuous)
Ferry Rd. Interchange CF11: Card 4H **101**
Ferry Way NP16: B'ly 6H **63**
Fescue Pl. CF5: Ely 4E **93**
Festiniog Rd. CF14: Llan N 5C **84**
Festival Cres. NP4: New I 5H **7**
Fetty Pl. NP44: Two L 4F **11**
Fferm-y-Graig *CF62: St Ath 5D 112*
(off Rock Rd.)
FFONT-Y-GARI **5C 114**
Fford Camlas NP10: Roger 4E **35**
Ffordd Bleddyn CF15: Taff W 1E **69**
Ffordd Bodlyn CF23: Cyn 4C **86**
Ffordd Brynhyfryd CF3: Old M 5C **74**
Ffordd Catraeth CF37: C'fydd 4F **15**
Ffordd Cefn-yr-Hendy CF72: Mis 5E **65**
Ffordd Celyn CF14: Whit 3D **84**
Ffordd Cwellyn CF23: Pen L 4B **86**
Ffordd Cwm Cidi CF62: Barry 3D **116**
Ffordd Daniel Lewis CF3: St M 2D **88**
Ffordd Deg CF83: Caer 2D **46**
Ffordd Dinefwr CF15: Cre 6D **66**
Ffordd Elin CF63: Barry 6D **106**
Ffordd Erw CF83: Caer 3A **46**
Ffordd Eynon Evans CF83: Caer 3H **27**
Ffordd Ffagan CF3: St M 5E **75**
Ffordd Garthorne CF10: Card 6C **96**
Ffordd Gerdinan CF38: Tont 1G **43**
Ffordd Glas-y-Dorlan CF38: Llan F 6B **42**
Ffordd Gower Davies CF37: Y'bwl 1A **14**
Ffordd Gwern CF5: St F 2C **82**
Ffordd Gwynfth CF63: Barry 5C **106**
Ffordd Gwynno CF38: Llan F 6B **42**
Ffordd Helygen CF72: L'harry 5C **78**
Ffordd James McGhan CF11: Card 2H **101**
Ffordd Kanetone CF11: Card 4D **94**
Ffordd Las CF15: Rad 1E **83**
CF83: Abert 1E **27**
Ffordd Mograig CF14: L'shn 6F **71**
Ffordd Morgannwg CF14: Whit 1A **84**
Ffordd Ottoway CF24: Card 4H **5** (4C **96**)
Ffordd Pengam CF24: Card 1G **97**
Ffordd Penrhos CF83: Caer 6H **27**
Ffordd Radcliffe CF10: Card 1B **102**
Ffordd Sealand CF62: Barry 3G **117**
Ffordd Taliesin CF37: C'fydd 3F **15**
Ffordd Talygarn CF72: P'clun 6D **64**
Ffordd Traws Cwm CF83: Caer 2A **46**
(Clos Enfys)
CF83: Caer 2H **45**
(Emanuel Cl.)
Ffordd Trecastell CF72: L'harry 4C **78**
Ffordd Treforgan CF15: Morg 5E **69**
Ffordd Tryweryn CF37: C'fydd 4F **15**
Ffordd ty Unnos CF14: Heath 1F **85**
Ffordd Windsor CF83: Abert 1D **26**
Ffordd-y-Barcer CF5: Ely 4D **92**
Ffordd y Bedol CF37: Glync 1D **14**
Ffordd y Berllan CF15: Morg 6E **69**
Ffordd y Brenin CF10: Card 3C **4** (3A **96**)
Ffordd-y-Capel CF38: E Isaf 6F **43**
Ffordd-y-Gollen CF38: Tont 1F **43**
Ffordd y Maes CF83: Caer 1H **45**
Ffordd y Mileniwm CF62: Barry 4G **117**
CF63: Barry 3H **117**
Ffordd yr Afon CF15: Gwae G 2E **69**
Ffordd-yr-Ywen CF38: Tont 1G **43**
Fforest Dr. CF62: Barry 3D **116**
Fforest Glade NP19: Newp 3F **37**
Fforest Rd. CF72: L'harry 6B **78**
Fforest Uchaf Farm & Pit Pony Sanctuary
4D 24
Fforest Vw. CF62: Barry 3D **116**
Ffos-y-Fran NP10: Bass 1B **52**
Ffos-y-Fran Cl. NP10: Bass 1B **52**
FFWL-Y-MWN **3B 114**
Ffwrwm Arts & Craft Cen. *6A 22*
(off High St.)

Ffwrwm Rd. CF83: Mac 2F **31**
Ffynnonbwla Rd. CF15: Gro-w 4C **26**
CF37: Up Bo 4C **26**
FFYNNON TAF **2E 69**
Fidlas Av. CF14: L'shn 6A **72**
Fidlas Rd. CF14: Cyn, L'shn 5H **71**
Fieldfare Dr. CF3: St M 1E **89**
Fielding Cl. CF3: L'rmy 6H **73**
Fieldings *NP44: F'wtr 4D 10*
(off Fairwater Way)
Fields Av. NP44: Pnwd 5D **8**
Fields Pk. Av. NP20: Newp 4H **35**
Fields Pk. Ct. NP20: Newp 4A **36**
Fields Pk. Cres. NP20: Newp 4A **36**
Fields Pk. Gdns. NP20: Newp 4H **35**
Fields Pk. La. NP20: Newp 4H **35**
Fields Pk. Rd. CF11: Card 1E **95**
NP20: Newp 5H **35**
Fields Pk. Ter. NP11: Cros K 2A **16**
Fields Rd. NP11: Ris 1F **33**
NP20: Newp 4A **36**
NP44: Oakf 4G **11**
Field Ter. CF15: P'rch 4A **68**
Field Vw. CF63: Barry 6A **106**
Fieldview Cl. CF64: P'rth 6G **101**
Field Vw. Rd. CF63: Barry 6A **106**
NP44: C'iog 6G **9**
Field Way CF14: Heath 1G **85**
Fifth St. NP19: Newp 4G **55**
Filey Rd. NP19: Newp 2D **36**
Finchley Rd. CF5: F'wtr 2A **94**
Finnimore Ct. CF14: Llan N 4B **84**
Firbank Av. NP19: Newp 3G **37**
Firbank Cres. NP19: Newp 3G **37**
Firbanks Way CF72: T Grn 2C **64**
Firs, The NP20: Malp 5C **20**
Firs Av. CF5: F'wtr 1F **93**
Firs Rd. NP26: Cald 4B **60**
First Av. CF83: Caer 6A **28**
Firstbrook Cl. CF23: Pen L 6E **87**
First St. NP19: Newp 3G **55**
Firtree Cl. CF5: F'wtr 1G **93**
NP18: C'ln 5E **21**
Firwood Cl. CF14: Whit 3B **84**
Fisher Cl. NP19: Newp 2D **38**
Fisher Hill Way CF15: Rad 2H **83**
Fishermans Wlk.
NP16: Bul 5F **63**
Fishguard Cl. CF14: L'shn 6A **72**
Fishguard Rd. CF14: L'shn 6H **71**
Fish La. *CF37: P'prdd 6C 14*
(off Bridge St.)
CF37: P'prdd 1C **24**
(Taff St.)
Fishpond Rd. CF3: L'rmy 1H **87**
Fitness First
Cardiff East 1G 97
Cardiff West 5G 93
Llanishen 6F 71
Newport 4D 36
Fitzalan Ct. CF24: Card 3F **5** (3B **96**)
Fitzalan Pl. CF24: Card 3G **5** (3B **96**)
Fitzalan Rd. CF24: Card 3F **5** (3B **96**)
(not continuous)
Fitzhamon Av. CF61: Llan M 4B **110**
Fitzhamon Emb. CF11: Card 5B **4** (4H **95**)
Fitzhamon La. CF11: Card 5B **4** (4H **95**)
Fitzosborn Cl. NP16: Chep 3D **62**
Fitzroy St. CF24: Card 1A **96**
(not continuous)
Fitzwalter Rd. NP26: Cald 6C **60**
Fitzwilliam Cl. CF72: C Inn 3G **65**
Five Ho's. NP4: Up R 5B **6**
FIVE LOCKS **5C 8**
Five Locks Cl. NP44: Pnwd 4D **8**
Five Locks Rd. NP44: Pnwd 5D **8**
Five Oaks La. NP44: C'iog 6G **9**
Flanders Mdw. CF61: Llan M 4B **110**
Flanders Rd. CF61: Llan M 4B **110**
Flatholm Ho. CF11: Card 4A **102**
Flavius Cl. NP18: C'ln 4F **21**
Flax Ct. CF64: P'rth 6G **101**
Flaxland Av. CF14: Card 4G **85**
Fleet Way CF11: Card 1G **101**
Fleetwood Cl. NP19: Newp 5F **37**
Fleming Cl. NP20: Malp 5A **20**

FLEMINGSTON . . . 1D **112**
Flemingston Rd. CF62: St Ath . . . 2C **112**
Fleming Wlk. CF38: Chu V . . . 3D **42**
Flindo Cres. CF11: Card . . . 4D **94**
Flint Av. CF61: Bov . . . 2D **110**
Flint Cl. NP19: Newp . . . 2G **37**
Flint Ct. *NP18: C'ln . . . 4G 21*
(off Roman Way)
Flint St. CF14: Card . . . 6G **85**
Flora St. CF24: Card . . . 1A **96**
Florence Av. CF62: Barry . . . 5G **105**
Florence Gro. CF83: Caer . . . 1C **46**
Florence Pl. NP4: Grif . . . 1E **9**
Florence St. CF24: Card . . . 2E **97**
Florentia St. CF24: Card . . . 6A **86**
Flush Mdw. CF61: Llan M . . . 4B **110**
Foel Vw. Cl. CF38: Llan F . . . 4B **42**
Folly La. NP4: P'pool, Trev . . . 1C **6**
(not continuous)
Folly Rd. NP4: Trev . . . 1C **6**
Folly Vw. NP4: P'garn . . . 2D **6**
FONMON . . . 3B **114**
Fonmon Castle . . . 2B **114**
Fonmon Cres. CF5: Ely . . . 4H **93**
Fonmon Pk. Rd. CF62: Rho . . . 5B **114**
Fonmon Rd. CF62: Rho . . . 4B **114**
Fonthill Pl. CF11: Card . . . 1F **101**
Fontigary Rd. CF3: Rum . . . 4A **88**
FONT-Y-GARY . . . 5C **114**
Fontygary Rd. CF62: Rho . . . 6C **114**
Ford Rd. CF37: P'prdd . . . 6A **14**
CF37: T'rest . . . 1B **44**
Ford St. NP20: Newp . . . 4B **36**
Fordwell CF5: L'dff . . . 6C **84**
Foreland Rd. CF14: Whit . . . 2C **84**
Foreshore Rd. CF10: Card . . . 6F **97**
Forest Cl. NP19: Newp . . . 3F **37**
NP44: Coed E . . . 5D **10**
Forest Ct. CF11: Card . . . 2F **95**
CF37: T'rest . . . 2E **25**
Forester Way CF23: Pontp . . . 3G **73**
Forest Farm Conservation Cen. . . . 1H **83**
Forest Farm Country Pk. . . . 6H **69**
Forest Farm Ind. Est. CF14: Whit . . . 1G **83**
Forest Farm Rd. CF14: Whit . . . 1H **83**
Forest Glade CF14: Whit . . . 1A **84**
Forest Gro. CF37: T'rest . . . 4E **25**
Forest Hills Dr. CF72: T Grn . . . 3C **64**
Forest Leisure Sedbury . . . 2G **63**
Forest Oak Cl. CF23: Cyn . . . 4C **72**
Forest Rd. CF15: Taff W . . . 1F **69**
CF37: T'rest . . . 3E **25**
CF38: Bed . . . 5A **42**
Forest Vw. CF5: F'wtr . . . 2G **93**
CF72: T Grn . . . 3E **65**
NP44: H'lys . . . 5A **10**
Forest Vw. Bus. Pk. CF72: L'sant . . . 5E **41**
Forest Wlk. CF72: T Grn . . . 3C **64**
Forge Cl. NP18: C'ln . . . 4H **21**
FORGE HAMMER . . . 1F **11**
Forge Hammer Ind. Est.
NP44: C'brn . . . 1F **11**
Forge La. NP4: P'pool . . . 2C **6**
NP10: Bass . . . 1D **52**
Forge M. NP10: Bass . . . 6D **34**
Forge Pl. CF5: Ely . . . 5F **93**
Forge Rd. CF83: Mac . . . 2G **31**
NP10: Bass, Coedk . . . 1D **52**
Forge Row *NP4: P'nydd . . . 1A 6*
(off Hanbury Rd.)
Forgeside NP44: C'brn . . . 1G **11**
Forgeside Cl. CF24: Card . . . 5D **96**
Forio Ho. *CF10: Card . . . 1C 102*
(off Ffordd Garthorne)
Forrest Rd. CF5: Card . . . 3D **94**
CF64: P'rth . . . 4E **109**
Forrest St. CF11: Card . . . 1H **101**
Forsythia Cl. NP11: Ris . . . 6G **17**
Forsythia Dr. CF23: Pent . . . 6D **72**
Fortlee *NP20: Newp . . . 6G 35*
(off Gaer Rd.)
Fortran Rd. CF3: St M . . . 5F **75**
Fort Rd. CF64: Lave . . . 1D **120**
Fort St. CF24: Card . . . 2E **97**
Fort Vw. NP10: Bass . . . 6C **34**
Fosse Cl. NP19: Newp . . . 1A **56**
Fosse La. NP18: C'ln . . . 5H **21**
Fosse Rd. NP19: Newp . . . 6A **38**
Foster Dr. CF23: Pen L . . . 6E **87**
Foster St. CF63: Barry . . . 1B **118**
Fothergill St. CF37: T'rest . . . 2E **25**
Foundry Cl. CF5: Card . . . 4F **95**
Foundry Pl. CF37: P'prdd . . . 5D **14**
Foundry Rd. CF37: P'prdd . . . 6A **14**
NP11: Ris . . . 6E **17**
Fountain La. CF3: St M . . . 5F **75**
Fountain Rd. NP4: P'pool . . . 4E **7**
Fountain Way NP16: Bul . . . 6F **63**
Four Acre CF61: Llan M . . . 2C **110**
Fouracres Cl. CF63: Barry . . . 6C **106**
Four Elms Ct. CF24: Card . . . 2H **5** (3C **96**)
Four Elms Rd. CF24: Card . . . 1H **5** (2D **96**)
FOURTEEN LOCKS . . . 3D **34**
Fourteen Locks Canal Cen. . . . 3D **34**
Fourth St. NP19: Newp . . . 3G **55**
Fowler St. NP4: P'pool . . . 1A **6**
Foxberry Cl. CF23: Pontp . . . 4H **73**
Foxglove Cl. CF5: Ely . . . 5F **93**
Foxglove Ri. CF64: P'rth . . . 6F **101**
FOX HILL . . . 4G **33**
Fox La. CF24: Card . . . 2D **96**
Fox Russell Cl. CF14: Llan N . . . 4C **84**
Fox St. CF24: Card . . . 2E **97**
Foxwood Cl. NP10: Bass . . . 6B **34**
Foxwood Ct. NP10: Bass . . . 6B **34**
FRAMPTON . . . 1C **110**
Frampton La. CF61: Llan M . . . 2D **110**
Francis Cl. *NP20: Newp . . . 6C 36*
(off Francis St.)
Francis Dr. NP20: Newp . . . 6C **36**
Francis Rd. CF62: Barry . . . 4A **106**
Francis St. CF37: R'fln . . . 5G **25**
CF83: Abert . . . 2D **26**
NP11: Ris . . . 6E **17**
NP20: Newp . . . 6C **36**
Francis Ter. CF37: P'prdd . . . 4E **15**
Franklen Rd. CF14: Whit . . . 3E **85**
Franklen St. CF11: Card . . . 6H **95**
Frank Rd. CF5: Ely . . . 3G **93**
Frank St. NP19: Newp . . . 3C **36**
Fraternal Pde. *CF37: P'prdd . . . 6C 14*
(off Taff St.)
Fred Edwards Cl. NP19: Newp . . . 4D **38**
Frederick M. NP20: Newp . . . 6D **36**
Frederick St. CF10: Card . . . 4E **5** (4A **96**)
(Hills St.)
CF10: Card . . . 3D **4** (3A **96**)
(St David's Link)
NP20: Newp . . . 1D **54**
Fremington Pl. CF3: L'rmy . . . 2A **88**
Freshmoor Rd. CF24: Card . . . 4E **97**
Freshwater Rd. NP19: Newp . . . 2B **56**
Frewer Av. CF5: F'wtr . . . 6H **83**
Friars Ct. NP20: Newp . . . 6B **36**
Friars Cres. NP20: Newp . . . 5B **36**
Friars Fld. NP20: Newp . . . 6B **36**
Friars Gdn. NP44: L'rfn . . . 4B **12**
Friars Rd. CF62: Barry . . . 5G **117**
(Paget Rd.)
CF62: Barry . . . 5H **117**
(Redbrink Cres.)
NP20: Newp . . . 6B **36**
Friars St. NP20: Newp . . . 5C **36**
Friary, The CF10: Card . . . 3D **4** (3A **96**)
Frigate Rd. CF10: Card . . . 2D **102**
Frobisher Rd. NP19: Newp . . . 6H **37**
Frome Wlk. NP20: Bet . . . 5E **19**
Fronheulog CF37: P'prdd . . . 5A **14**
Fron Ter. CF37: P'prdd . . . 5D **14**
Fryatt St. CF63: Barry . . . 3A **118**
Fryth Wood NP16: Chep . . . 2C **62**
Fulmar Cl. CF3: St M . . . 5D **74**
CF64: P'rth . . . 6E **109**
Furnace St. CF64: Sul . . . 1E **119**
Furness Cl. CF5: Ely . . . 5E **93**
Fuscia Way NP10: Roger . . . 3H **33**

G

GABALFA . . . 6E **85**
Gabalfa Av. CF14: Llan N . . . 5C **84**
Gabalfa Interchange CF14: Whit . . . 4F **85**
Gabalfa Rd. CF14: Llan N . . . 5C **84**
Gabalfa Workshops CF14: Card . . . 5E **85**
Gables, The CF64: Din P . . . 3G **107**
NP16: Chep . . . 1F **63**
Gadlys Rd. E. CF62: Barry . . . 2G **117**
Gadlys Rd. W. CF62: Barry . . . 3F **117**
Gaen St. CF62: Barry . . . 3E **117**
GAER . . . 2H **53**
Gaer La. NP20: Newp . . . 6A **36**
Gaer Pk. Av. NP20: Newp . . . 1G **53**
Gaer Pk. Dr. NP20: Newp . . . 1G **53**
Gaer Pk. Hill NP20: Newp . . . 6G **35**
Gaer Pk. La. NP20: Newp . . . 6G **35**
Gaer Pk. Pde. NP20: Newp . . . 1G **53**
Gaer Pk. Rd. NP20: Newp . . . 1G **53**
Gaer Rd. NP20: Newp . . . 6G **35**
(not continuous)
Gaer St. NP20: Newp . . . 1A **54**
Gaer Va. NP20: Newp . . . 2H **53**
Gaerwen Cl. CF14: L'shn . . . 5F **71**
Gainsborough Cl. NP44: L'tnam . . . 5A **12**
Gainsborough Ct. CF64: P'rth . . . 6H **101**
Gainsborough Dr. NP19: Newp . . . 1F **37**
Gainsborough Rd. CF64: P'rth . . . 6H **101**
Gala Bingo
Cardiff . . . 5E **85**
Galahad Cl. CF14: Thorn . . . 4E **71**
Galaxy Globe Cinema . . . 1C **96**
Galdames Pl. CF24: Card . . . 5D **96**
Gallagher Retail Pk. CF83: Caer . . . 3E **29**
Gallamuir Rd. CF24: Card . . . 2F **97**
Galleon Way CF10: Card . . . 6C **96**
Galston St. CF24: Card . . . 3H **5** (3D **96**)
Garden City Way NP16: Chep . . . 2E **63**
Gardenia Cl. CF23: Pent . . . 6D **72**
Gardens, The NP26: Magor . . . 4C **58**
Garden Suburbs NP11: P'waun . . . 1A **16**
Gardens Vw. Cl. NP11: P'waun . . . 1A **16**
Garden Village CF83: Caer . . . 5D **28**
Gardner Cl. CF37: Glync . . . 2D **14**
Garesfield St. CF24: Card . . . 4H **5** (4C **96**)
Gareth Cl. CF14: Thorn . . . 3F **71**
Garrick Dr. CF14: Thorn . . . 3G **71**
GARTH . . . 6B **34**
Garthalan Dr. NP26: Cald . . . 6B **60**
Garth Av. CF37: Glync . . . 2C **14**
Garth Cl. CF15: Morg . . . 5F **69**
CF83: Rud . . . 6B **30**
NP10: Bass . . . 6C **34**
Garth Est. CF83: Abert . . . 2C **26**
Garthfields Cotts. NP10: Bass . . . 6B **34**
Garth Hill CF15: Gwae G, P'rch . . . 3H **67**
NP10: Bass . . . 6B **34**
Garth La. CF83: Rud . . . 6B **30**
Garth Lwyd CF83: Caer . . . 4F **29**
Garth Maelwg CF72: T Grn . . . 3D **64**
Garth Olwg CF15: Gwae G . . . 6D **44**
GARTH PLACE . . . 6B **30**
Garth Pl. CF14: Llan N . . . 5F **85**
Garth Ri. CF5: St F . . . 2C **82**
Garth Rd. NP44: T Coch . . . 4F **11**
Garth St. CF10: Card . . . 5F **5** (4B **96**)
CF15: Taff W . . . 2E **69**
CF39: Coed . . . 3A **40**
Garth Ter. NP10: Bass . . . 1B **52**
Garth Vw. CF15: N'grw . . . 3E **45**
CF15: Taff W . . . 6D **44**
CF38: Bed . . . 5A **42**
CF38: Chu V . . . 3F 43
(off Main Rd.)
CF83: B'ws . . . 2F **29**
Garth Vs. CF83: Abert . . . 2D **26**
Garvey Cl. NP16: Bul . . . 6F **63**
Garw, The NP44: C'iog . . . 6H **9**
Garw Row NP44: C'iog . . . 6H **9**
Garw Wood Dr. NP44: C'iog . . . 5G **9**
Gaskell Cl. CF61: Bov . . . 3E **111**
Gaskell St. NP19: Newp . . . 6F **37**
Gaspard Pl. CF62: Barry . . . 5E **117**
Gas Rd. CF37: P'prdd . . . 6C **14**
Gateholm Cl. CF62: Barry . . . 5H **105**
Gateside Cl. CF23: Pontp . . . 3G **73**
Gateway, The CF14: Heath . . . 4G **85**
GATLAS . . . 1A **22**
Gatlas La. NP18: C'ln, P'hir . . . 5H **13**

Gaudi Wlk. NP10: Roger 3C **34**
Gaulden Gro. CF23: Pontp 4E **73**
Gawain Cl. CF14: Thorn 3F **71**
Gaynors *NP44: F'wtr* *4D* ***10***
(off Pace Rd.)
Gelli Av. NP11: Ris 6E **17**
Gelli Cl. NP11: Ris 5E **17**
Gelli Cres. NP11: Ris 5E **17**
Gelli Dawel CF83: Caer 5B **28**
Gellidawel Rd. CF37: R'fln 3G **25**
Gelli Deg CF14: R'ina 5D **70**
CF37: R'fln 5H **25**
CF83: Caer 4B **28**
Gellideg Rd. CF37: P'prdd 1A **24**
Gelli Est. CF72: L'harry 5B **78**
Gelli Fawr Ct. NP44: H'lys 5B **10**
Gelli Frongoch CF23: Pontp 4F **73**
Gelligaer Gdns. CF24: Card 6H **85**
Gelligaer La. CF14: Card 6H **85**
Gelligaer St. CF24: Card 6H **85**
Gelli Hirion CF37: R'fln 5A **26**
Gelli Hirion Ind. Est. CF37: R'fln 5A **26**
Gelli'r Felin CF83: Caer 5B **28**
Gelli Rd. CF72: L'harry 5B **78**
Gelli Ter. CF83: Sen 1E **27**
Gelli-Unig Pl. NP11: P'waun 1A **16**
Gelli-Unig Rd. NP11: P'waun 1A **16**
Gelli-Unig Ter. NP11: P'waun 1A **16**
Gelliwastad Gro. CF37: P'prdd 6C **14**
Gelliwastad Rd. CF37: P'prdd 6C **14**
Gelliwasted Ct. *CF37: P'prdd* *6C* ***14***
(off Library Rd.)
Gelliwion Rd. CF37: P'prdd 2A **24**
Gelliwion Woods CF37: P'prdd 1A **24**
Gelynis Ter. CF15: Morg 5F **69**
Gelynis Ter. Nth. CF15: Morg 5F **69**
Gelynog Ct. CF38: Bed 3H **41**
Gelyn-y-Cler CF63: Barry 4B **106**
General Rees Sq. NP44: C'brn 1G **11**
Geoffrey Ashe Ct. CF71: C'bri 4E **91**
George Cl. CF15: Gwae G 2E **69**
George Lansbury Dr. NP19: Newp 2C **38**
Georges Row CF64: Din P 1A **108**
George St. CF10: Card 1C **102**
CF63: Barry 2A **118**
CF72: L'sant 2F **65**
NP4: P'nydd 1A **6**
NP4: P'pool 2B **6**
(not continuous)
NP19: Newp 6C **36**
NP20: Newp 6C **36**
NP44: Pnwd 1G **11**
GEORGE THOMAS HOSPICE
(TY GEORGE THOMAS) **1A 84**
Georgetown CF15: Gwae G 2D **68**
Georgian Cl. CF61: Llan M 2D **110**
Georgian Way CF14: L'shn 5H **71**
CF72: Mis 6F **65**
Geraint Cl. CF14: Thorn 3F **71**
Geraint Pl. CF63: Barry 6A **106**
Geraint's Cl. CF71: C'bri 4B **90**
Geraint's Way CF71: C'bri 3B **90**
Gerbera Dr. NP10: Roger 2H **33**
Gerddi Margaret CF62: Barry 3G **117**
Gerddi Taf CF5: L'dff 4A **84**
Gerddi ty Celyn CF14: Whit 6B **70**
Gernant CF14: R'ina 6E **71**
Gerrard Ct. CF11: Card 4F **95**
Gerry Galvin Ct. CF24: Card 2E **97**
Ger y Afon CF37: Glync 1D **14**
Gibbet's Hill CF71: C'bri 2B **90**
Gibbon Cl. NP19: Newp 5A **38**
GIBBONSDOWN **6A 106**
Gibbonsdown Cl. CF63: Barry 5A **106**
Gibbonsdown Ri. CF63: Barry 6A **106**
Gibbs Rd. NP19: Newp 4G **37**
Gibraltar Way NP16: B'ly 6H **63**
Gibson Cl. CF14: L'shn 1H **85**
Gifford Cl. NP44: Two L 4F **11**
Gilbert Cl. NP19: Newp 5B **38**
Gilbert La. E. CF63: Barry 4C **106**
Gilbert La. W. CF63: Barry 4B **106**
Gilbert Pl. CF14: Llan N 5E **85**
Gilbert St. CF63: Barry 1A **118**
Gildas Cl. CF61: Llan M 2B **110**
GILESTON **6D 112**
Gileston Rd. CF11: Card 2F **95**
CF62: Gile, St Ath 5D **112**
Gileston Wlk. NP44: St D 3E **11**
Gilian Rd. CF5: L'dff 6B **84**
Gilwern Cres. CF14: L'shn 4G **71**
Gilwern Farm Cl. NP18: P'hir 6F **13**
Gilwern Pl. CF14: L'shn 4G **71**
NP44: Pnwd 6D **8**
Glade, The CF14: L'shn 4A **72**
Glade Cl. NP44: Coed E 5C **10**
Glades, The CF64: P'rth 2F **109**
Gladeside Cl. CF14: Thorn 2G **71**
Gladstone Bri. CF62: Barry 3G **117**
Gladstone Ct. CF62: Barry 2H **117**
Gladstone Pl. NP4: Seba 3E **9**
Gladstone Rd. CF62: Barry 3G **117**
CF63: Barry 3G **117**
Gladstone St. NP11: Cros K 3A **16**
Gladys St. CF24: Card 1A **96**
Glamorgan Cl. CF61: Bov 2D **110**
Glamorgan County Cricket Ground
1A 4 (2G 95)
Glamorgan M. CF5: Card 3E **95**
Glamorganshire Canal Nature Reserve
6H 69
Glamorgan St. CF5: Card 3E **95**
CF62: Barry 4E **117**
Glamorgan St. M. CF5: Card 3E **95**
Glamorgan Va. Retail Pk. CF72: T Grn 3F **65**
Glamorgan Wanderers RUFC
(Memorial Ground) **4E 93**
Glan Creigiau CF72: Groes F 6C **66**
Glandovey Gro. CF3: Rum 1C **88**
Glandwr Pl. CF14: Whit 3D **84**
Glan Ely Cl. CF5: F'wtr 2G **93**
Glanfa Dafydd CF63: Barry 3A **118**
Glanfelin Flats CF37: R'fln 5G **25**
Glan Ffrwd CF83: Caer 3H **27**
Glan Hafren CF62: Barry 5D **116**
Glanmor Ct. NP19: Newp 4H **37**
Glanmor Cres. CF62: Barry 2F **117**
NP19: Newp 4H **37**
Glanmor Pk. Av. NP19: Newp 4H **37**
Glanmuir Rd. CF24: Card 1G **97**
Glan Nant Cl. CF83: Caer 2C **46**
Glan Rhyd CF83: Caer 5B **28**
NP44: Coed E 5C **10**
Glanrhyd CF14: R'ina 6E **71**
Glan Rhymni CF24: Card 6G **87**
Glantorvaen Rd. NP4: P'pool 3C **6**
Glanwern Av. NP19: Newp 3A **38**
Glanwern Cl. NP19: Newp 3A **38**
Glanwern Dr. NP19: Newp 3A **38**
Glanwern Gro. NP19: Newp 3A **38**
Glanwern Ho. NP4: P'pool 3B **6**
Glanwern Ri. NP19: Newp 3A **38**
Glanwern Ter. NP4: P'pool 3B **6**
Glan-y-Dwr CF63: Barry 3H **117**
Glan-y-Ffordd CF15: Taff W 5E **45**
GLAN-Y-LLYN **6E 45**
Glan y Llyn CF23: Cyn 3B **86**
Glan-y-llyn Ind. Est. CF15: Taff W 6E **45**
Glan y Mor CF61: Bov 3E **111**
Glan-y-Mor CF62: Barry 5D **116**
CF63: Barry 3H **117**
Glan-y-Mor Rd. CF3: Rum 2C **88**
Glan y Nant CF37: R'fln 5A **26**
Glanynant NP44: Two L 4F **11**
Glan-y-Nant Cl. NP44: T Coch 4F **11**
Glan-y-Nant Rd. CF14: Whit 2D **84**
Glan-y-Nant Ter. CF14: Whit 2D **84**
Glan yr Afon CF72: P'clun 6D **64**
Glanyrafon CF15: Gwae G 1D **68**
Glan-yr-Afon CF83: Mac 3F **31**
Glan-yr-Ely CF72: Y'erdy 6C **40**
Glas, The CF11: Card 2F **95**
Glas Canol CF14: Whit 4D **84**
Glascoed Rd. NP4: New I 5H **7**
Glas Cwm CF37: Glync 1D **14**
Glas Efail CF14: R'ina 6F **71**
Glas Heulog CF14: Whit 3D **84**
GLASLLWCH **5E 35**
Glasllwch Cres. NP10: Newp 5E **35**
NP20: Newp 5E **35**
Glasllwch La. NP20: Newp 6E **35**
Glasllwch Vw. NP20: Newp 6E **35**
Glaslyn Cl. CF62: Barry 2E **117**
Glaslyn Ct. NP44: C'iog 6F **9**
Glass Av. CF24: Card 6E **97**
Glass Works Cotts. NP20: Newp 1C **36**
Glastonbury Cl. NP20: Newp 3C **36**
Glastonbury Rd. CF64: Sul 1H **119**
Glastonbury Ter. CF3: L'rmy 2H **87**
Glas y Llwyn CF63: Barry 4C **106**
Glas-y-Pant CF14: Whit 1B **84**
Glebe Gdns. NP10: Bass 1D **52**
Glebeland Pl. CF62: St Ath 5C **112**
Glebelands Stadium **1D 36**
Glebe Pl. CF14: L'shn 5H **71**
Glebe Rd. CF83: Tret 3A **30**
Glebe St. CF63: Barry 6A **106**
CF64: P'rth 6A **102**
CF83: B'ws 3G **29**
NP19: Newp 4E **37**
Glen, The NP18: L'stne 6H **23**
Glen Affric Cl. CF62: Barry 1F **117**
Glenbrook Cl. CF63: Barry 5D **106**
Glenbrook Dr. CF63: Barry 5D **106**
Glencoe St. CF63: Barry 1A **118**
Glencourt NP4: Seba 2E **9**
Glendale Av. CF14: L'shn 4G **71**
Glendower Ct. CF14: Whit 2B **84**
Glenfields Est. CF83: Caer 6A **28**
Glengariff Ct. NP4: Grif 1D **8**
Glen Mavis Way CF62: Barry 1F **117**
Glenmount Way CF14: Thorn 3F **71**
Glenrise Cl. CF3: St M 6E **75**
Glenroy NP4: Up R 6A **6**
Glenroy St. CF24: Card 1B **96**
GLENSIDE **4A 16**
Glenside NP44: Pnwd 5D **8**
Glenside Ct. CF23: Pen L 5C **86**
Glen Usk Vw. NP18: C'ln 3G **21**
Glen Vw. CF14: L'shn 1H **85**
NP16: Math 6B **62**
NP44: C'brn 1F **11**
Glenwood CF23: L'dyrn 1D **86**
Globe Cen., The CF24: Card 1C **96**
Glos Gwyn-y-Mor CF3: St M 1D **88**
Glossop Rd. CF24: Card 2H **5** (3C **96**)
Glossop Ter. CF24: Card 3H **5** (3C **96**)
Gloster Pl. NP19: Newp 3D **36**
Gloster's Pde. NP4: New I 6H **7**
Gloster St. NP19: Newp 3D **36**
Gloucester Cl. CF62: Barry 1H **117**
NP44: L'rfn 2B **12**
Gloucester Ct. *NP18: C'ln* *4G* ***21***
(off Caradoc Cl.)
Gloucester St. CF11: Card 5A **4** (4G **95**)
Glynbridge Cl. CF62: Barry 4H **105**
GLYNCOCH **2D 14**
Glyncoch Ter. CF37: Glync 2E **15**
Glyn Coed Rd. CF23: Pent 6E **73**
Glyn Collen CF23: Pent 6G **73**
Glyn Derw CF83: Caer 5C **28**
Glyndwr Av. CF62: St Ath 5C **112**
Glyn-Dwr Av. CF37: R'fln 3F **25**
Glyndwr Rd. CF5: Ely 3F **93**
CF62: Barry 2G **117**
CF64: P'rth 2C **108**
NP44: C'brn 1H **11**
Glyn Eiddew CF23: Pent 5F **73**
Glyn Glas CF14: Thorn 5D **46**
Glynne St. CF11: Card 3F **95**
Glynrhondda St. CF24: Card 1D **4** (2A **96**)
Glyn Rhosyn CF23: Pent 5D **72**
Glyn Rhymni CF3: Rum 5A **88**
Glyn Simon Cl. CF5: L'dff 4A **84**
Glynstell Cl. CF11: Card 1F **101**
GLYNTAFF **2F 25**
Glyntaff Cl. CF37: R'fln 3G **25**
Glyntaff Crematorium CF37: Glynt 2F **25**
Glyntaff Housing Est. CF37: R'fln 3G **25**
Glyntaff Rd. CF37: Glynt 1F **25**
Glyntirion NP44: Two L 4F **11**
Glyn Vw. *NP4: P'pool* *4A* ***6***
(off Crumlin Rd.)
Glyn y Gog CF62: Rho 6F **115**
Godfrey Rd. NP20: Newp 4A **36**
NP44: Pnwd 6D **8**
Godwin Cl. CF5: L'dff 3H **83**
Goetre Fawr CF15: Rad 2H **83**

Golate Ct. CF10: Card .5C **4**
Golate St. CF10: Card .5C **4** (4A **96**)
Gold Cliff Ct. NP44: C'brn .2H **11**
Goldcliff Rd. NP18: Gold, Nash .6B **56**
Goldcrest Dr. CF23: Pent .6D **72**
Goldcroft Comn. NP18: C'ln .5H **21**
Goldcroft Ct. NP18: C'ln .5H **21**
Golden Mile Vw. NP20: Newp .1E **53**
Goldfinch Cl. NP26: Cald .6C **60**
(not continuous)
Goldsland Pl. CF62: Barry .2E **117**
Goldsmith Cl. CF3: L'rmy .6H **73**
NP20: Newp .1G **53**
Gold St. CF24: Card .2H **5** (3C **96**)
Gold Tops NP20: Newp .4B **36**
Golf Rd. NP4: New I .5G **7**
Golwg y Coed CF83: Caer .4H **27**
Golwg-yr-Eglwys CF83: B'ws .3F **29**
Golygfa'r Eglwys CF37: P'prdd .6A **14**
GOLYNOS .6A **18**
Goodrich Av. CF83: Caer .1E **47**
Goodrich Ct. NP44: L'rfn .3B **12**
Goodrich Cres. NP20: Newp .2B **36**
Goodrich Gro. NP10: Duf .6G **53**
Goodrich La. NP20: Newp .2B **36**
Goodrich St. CF83: Caer .1D **46**
Goodwick Cl. CF62: Barry .5H **105**
Goodwick Rd. CF3: Rum .4A **88**
Goodwood Cl. CF5: Ely .5D **92**
Goossens Cl. NP19: Newp .3D **38**
Gordings NP44: G'mdw .2D **10**
Gordon Hall CF24: Card .1F **5** (2B **96**)
Gordon Rd. CF24: Card .1E **5** (2B **96**)
Gordon St. NP19: Newp .4E **37**
Gore St. NP19: Newp .2D **36**
Gorsedd Circle .3B **4**
Gorsedd Gdns. Rd. CF10: Card .2D **4** (3A **96**)
Gorse Pl. CF5: F'wtr .1G **93**
Goscombe Dr. CF64: P'rth .6H **101**
Gospel Ct. CF38: Bed .4A **42**
Gough Rd. CF5: Ely .4G **93**
Gould Cl. CF3: Old M .6B **74**
Govilon Pl. NP44: Pnwd .6D **8**
Gowan Ct. CF14: Thorn .2F **71**
Gower Ct. CF62: Barry .2F **117**
Gower Davies Ct. CF37: Y'bwl .1A **14**
Gower Grn. NP44: C'iog .5G **9**
Gower St. CF24: Card .6A **86**
Goya Cl. NP19: Newp .2G **37**
Gradon Cl. CF63: Barry .1C **118**
Grafton Cl. CF23: Pen L .4D **86**
Grafton Dr. CF72: C Inn .3G **65**
Grafton La. NP19: Newp .4D **36**
Grafton Rd. NP19: Newp .4C **36**
Grafton Ter. CF14: R'ina .1E **85**
Graham Bell Cl. NP20: Malp .3H **19**
Graham Cl. CF23: Pen L .5E **87**
Graham Ct. CF83: Caer .6E **29**
Grahamstown Gro. NP16: Sed .2G **63**
Grahamstown Rd. NP16: Sed .2H **63**
Graham St. NP20: Newp .5B **36**
Graham Wlk. CF11: Card .4F **95**
GRAIG .2B **24**
Graig Av. CF37: P'prdd .2B **24**
Graig Cl. NP10: Bass .6C **34**
Graig Fach CF37: Glynt .2F **25**
Graig Hir CF15: Rad .6F **69**
Graig-Llwyn Rd. CF14: L'vne, Pontp .1C **72**
Graig Lwyd CF15: Rad .6F **69**
Graig Pk. Av. NP20: Malp .5A **20**
Graig Pk. Circ. NP20: Malp .6A **20**
Graig Pk. Hill NP20: Malp .6B **20**
Graig Pk. La. NP20: Malp .6B **20**
Graig Pk. Pde. NP20: Malp .6B **20**
Graig Pk. Rd. NP20: Malp .6A **20**
Graig Pk. Vs. NP20: Malp .6A **20**
Graig Rd. CF14: L'vne .6A **48**
Graigside CF15: N'grw .5E **45**
Graig St. CF37: P'prdd .1C **24**
Graig Ter. CF37: P'prdd .1C **24**
Graig Vw. CF14: L'vne .2B **72**
CF15: N'grw .3F **45**
CF83: Mac .2H **31**
NP11: Ris .6D **16**
NP44: Up Cwm .5B **8**
Graig Wen CF15: Morg .5F **69**
Graigwen Cres. CF83: Abert .2F **27**
(not continuous)
Graigwen Parc CF37: P'prdd .4A **14**
Graigwen Pl. CF37: P'prdd .6B **14**
Graigwen Rd. CF37: P'prdd .4A **14**
Graig Wood Cl. NP20: Malp .6A **20**
Graig-y-Fedw CF83: Abert .2F **27**
Graig y Fforest CF37: T'rest .4E **25**
CF38: Tont, T'rest .4E **25**
GRAIG-Y-RHACCA .3C **30**
Graig-y-Rhacca CF83: Mac .2D **30**
Graig-yr-Helfa Rd. CF37: P'prdd, R'fln .1E **25**
Graig yr Hesg Pl. CF37: P'prdd .4D **14**
Graig yr Hesg Rd. CF37: P'prdd .4D **14**
Graig-yr-Wylan CF83: Caer .1A **46**
Grand, The CF10: Card .4B **4**
Grand Av. CF5: Ely .5E **93**
Grange, The CF3: M'fld .5A **76**
CF5: L'dff .1C **94**
CF64: P'rth .2D **108**
CF83: Caer .6B **28**
Grange Av. CF5: Wen .5E **99**
Grange Cl. CF5: Wen .4E **99**
CF83: Caer .6B **28**
Grange Ct. NP4: P'nydd .1A **6**
NP20: Newp .5A **36**
Grange Gdns. CF11: Card .1H **101**
CF61: Llan M .2C **110**
Grange Ind. Est. NP44: C'brn .3H **11**
Grange La. NP44: C'brn .1G **11**
Grangemoor Ct. CF11: Card .4G **101**
Grange Path NP44: Llanf .4B **12**
Grange Pl. CF11: Card .1A **102**
Grange Rd. NP26: Undy .3D **58**
NP44: C'brn .1H **11**
(not continuous)
GRANGETOWN .1H **101**
Grangetown Link CF11: Card .2F **101**
Grangetown Station (Rail) .1G **101**
Grangewood Cl. CF23: Pontp .4H **73**
Grannary, The *CF10: Card* .*6B* ***96***
(off Margretian Pl.)
Granston Ho. NP44: F'wtr .3D **10**
Granston Sq. NP44: F'wtr .3D **10**
Grantham Cl. CF5: L'dff .5A **84**
Grant's Cl. CF15: Tong .5G **69**
Grant's Fld. CF5: St N .1A **98**
Granville Av. CF5: Card .2C **94**
Granville Cl. NP10: Roger .5E **35**
Granville La. NP20: Newp .5D **36**
Granville Sq. NP20: Newp .5D **36**
Granville St. NP20: Newp .5D **36**
Granville Ter. NP16: Tut .1F **63**
Grasmere Av. CF23: Cyn .4A **86**
Grasmere Way NP16: Bul .6G **63**
Grassmere Cl. CF64: L'dgh .5G **101**
Gray Hill Vw. NP26: Pskwt .5F **61**
Graylands, The CF14: R'ina .1E **85**
Gray La. CF11: Card .3F **95**
Grays Gdns. CF83: Mac .3C **30**
(not continuous)
Gray St. CF11: Card .3F **95**
(not continuous)
Grays Wlk. CF71: C'bri .3D **90**
Gt. Brynhill La. CF62: Barry .4F **105**
Gt. Burnet Cl. CF3: St M .1F **89**
Greater Gwent Crematorium
NP44: C'iog .4H **9**
Great Ho. Mdws. CF61: Llan M .2B **110**
Great Oaks Pk. NP10: Roger .2B **34**
Great Oaks Vw. NP10: Roger .3B **34**
Gt. Ormes Ho. CF11: Card .4A **102**
Gt. Thomas Cl. CF62: Rho .5D **114**
Gt. Western Ct. CF5: Card .4E **95**
Gt. Western La. CF10: Card .5D **4** (4A **96**)
Greave Cl. CF5: Wen .4E **99**
Greek Chu. St. CF10: Card .5B **96**
Green, The CF11: Leck .2D **100**
CF15: Rad .2G **83**
CF61: Llan M .5C **110**
Green Acre CF15: Cre .6E **67**
NP44: Two L .4F **11**
Greenacre Dr. CF23: Pontp .3H **73**
CF83: B'ws .2F **29**
Greenacre Gdns. CF83: Tret .3H **29**
Greenacres CF63: Barry .6D **106**
Greenacres Pk. NP18: Nash .4D **56**
Green Av. NP26: Cald .5C **60**
Greenbanks Dr. CF62: Barry .1F **117**
Greenbay Rd. CF24: Card .3G **97**
Greenclose Rd. CF14: Whit .3E **85**
Green Ct. NP26: Cald .5B **60**
Greencourt NP44: C'iog .5G **9**
Greencroft Av. CF5: Ely .3B **94**
Greendale Pl. CF15: Tong .5H **69**
Greene Cl. NP19: Newp .4D **38**
Green Farm Cl. CF5: Ely .5E **93**
Green Farm La. CF5: Ely .6E **93**
Green Farm Rd. CF5: Ely .5E **93**
Greenfield NP18: C'ln .4F **21**
NP26: Cald .5C **60**
Greenfield Av. CF11: Card .2E **95**
CF14: Whit .2E **85**
CF37: Glync .2C **14**
CF64: Din P .1G **107**
Greenfield Cl. NP44: Pnwd .5D **8**
Greenfield Pl. CF83: Abert .2C **26**
Greenfield Rd. CF14: Whit .2E **85**
CF62: Barry .6F **105**
NP10: Roger .5D **34**
Greenfield Stones NP10: Roger .5D **34**
Greenfield Way CF71: L'thian .4B **90**
Greenforge Way NP44: C'brn .2E **11**
Greenhaven Ri. CF64: L'dgh .5G **101**
Greenhill Cl. NP4: Seba .2E **9**
Greenhill Ct. CF3: Rum .5B **88**
Greenhill Rd. NP4: Grif, Seba .1E **9**
NP44: C'brn .1F **11**
Greenland Cres. CF5: F'wtr .1G **93**
Greenland Rd. NP4: Trev .1B **6**
Greenlands Rd. CF72: L'sant .2G **65**
Green La. CF3: Pet W, St M .6G **75**
CF61: Llan M .3A **110**
CF63: Barry .5C **106**
CF64: Din P .5G **107**
CF72: T Grn .*3E* ***65***
(off Green Pk.)
NP10: Coedk, St Bri W .1F **77**
NP26: Cald .5C **60**
Green Lawns CF62: Barry .6A **106**
Greenlawns CF23: Pen L .5C **86**
GREENMEADOW .2C **10**
Greenmeadow CF83: Mac .4D **30**
Greenmeadow Av. NP19: Newp .6A **38**
Greenmeadow Cl. CF37: Glync .2D **14**
CF64: Din P .3H **107**
NP44: C'brn .3F **11**
Greenmeadow Community Farm .1D **10**
Greenmeadow Ct. CF72: L'sant .3G **65**
Greenmeadow Dr. CF15: Tong .4H **69**
NP11: Cros K .3B **16**
Greenmeadow Rd. NP19: Newp .6A **38**
Greenmeadows CF3: Rum .2C **88**
Greenmeadow Sq. *NP44: C'brn* .*3F* ***11***
(off Greenmeadow Way)
Greenmeadow Way
NP44: C'brn, G'mdw .2E **11**
Green Moor La. NP26: Magor .4B **58**
(not continuous)
Greenock Rd. CF3: Rum .1B **88**
Green Pk. CF72: P'clun .4B **64**
CF72: T Grn .3E **65**
Green Pl. CF15: Rad .2F **83**
Green Row CF83: Mac .3F **31**
Greenside CF71: C'bri .4D **90**
Green St. CF11: Card .4A **4** (4H **95**)
NP16: Chep .3E **63**
Greenway CF83: B'ws .3E **29**
Greenway Av. CF3: Rum .4A **88**
Greenway Cl. CF64: L'dgh .4E **101**
NP4: Grif .1D **8**
Greenway Ct. CF3: Rum .4A **88**
CF63: Barry .5D **106**
Greenway Dr. NP4: Grif .1D **8**
Greenway Rd. CF3: Rum, St M .4A **88**
Greenways, The NP26: Magor .4C **58**
Greenway Wlk. NP4: Grif .1D **8**
Greenway Workshops CF83: B'ws .3F **29**
Greenwich Rd. CF5: Card .2D **94**
NP20: Newp .2A **54**
Green Willows NP44: Oakf .5H **11**
Greenwood Av. NP44: Pnwd, Up Cwm .5B **8**

Greenwood Cl. CF23: Pontp . . . 3H **73**
Greenwood Ct. CF83: Caer . . . 6E **29**
Greenwood Dr. CF38: Llan F . . . 4B **42**
NP44: H'lys . . . 5A **10**
Greenwood La. CF5: St F . . . 2E **93**
Greenwood Rd. CF5: L'dff . . . 6B **84**
Greenwood St. CF63: Barry . . . 3H **117**
Grenadier Dr. NP18: L'stne . . . 1G **39**
Grenville Rd. CF23: Pen L . . . 1D **96**
Grenville Ter. NP26: Rog . . . 6A **60**
Gresford Cl. CF3: St M . . . 1B **88**
Greyfriars Pl. CF10: Card . . . 3D **4** (3A **96**)
Greyfriars Rd. CF10: Card . . . 3D **4** (3A **96**)
Greyhound La. CF72: L'sant . . . 2F **65**
Grey's Dr. CF61: Bov . . . 3D **110**
Greys Rd. NP4: P'pool . . . 5C **6**
Grey Waters NP44: L'rfn . . . 2A **12**
Griffin, The NP10: Bass . . . 1C **52**
Griffin Cl. CF62: Barry . . . 5E **105**
Griffin Ct. *NP4: P'pool . . . 2B **6***
(off Osborne Rd.)
Griffin St. NP20: Newp . . . 4C **36**
GRIFFITHSTOWN . . . **6E 7**
Griffithstown Railway Mus. . . . **1E 9**
Grimson Cl. CF64: Sul . . . 2H **119**
Grindle Wlk. NP10: Roger . . . 3C **34**
Grisedale Cl. CF23: Pen L . . . 5B **86**
Groes Cl. NP10: Roger . . . 2C **34**
GROES-FAEN . . . **1C 80**
Groes Lon CF14: R'ina . . . 5D **70**
Groes Rd. NP10: Roger . . . 3C **34**
(Great Oaks Vw.)
NP10: Roger . . . 2C **34**
(Groes Cl.)
GROES-WEN . . . **1F 45**
Groeswen CF61: Llan M . . . 2B **110**
Groeswen Dr. CF83: Caer . . . 5H **27**
Groeswen Riding Stables . . . **1A 30**
Groeswen Rd. CF15: Gro-w . . . 1E **45**
CF83: Caer . . . 1E **45**
Gron Ffordd CF14: R'ina . . . 4D **70**
Grongaer Ter. CF37: P'prdd . . . 1B **24**
Grosmont Pl. NP44: C'iog . . . 5G **9**
Grosmont Rd. NP4: New I . . . 5H **7**
Grosmont Way NP10: Duf . . . 6F **53**
Grosvenor Pl. NP4: Seba . . . 2E **9**
Grosvenor Rd. NP10: Bass . . . 6B **34**
Grosvenor St. CF5: Card . . . 4D **94**
Grouse St. CF24: Card . . . 1H **5** (2C **96**)
Grove, The CF3: Rum . . . 4A **88**
CF37: Glync . . . 1D **14**
CF62: Barry . . . 4E **117**
*NP20: Newp . . . 6C **36***
(off Clytha Sq.)
Grove Est. CF83: Tret . . . 2A **30**
NP4: P'nydd . . . 1A **6**
Grove Gdns. NP26: Cald . . . 5D **60**
Groveland Rd. CF14: Heath . . . 3F **85**
Grove La. CF62: Barry . . . 5E **117**
NP20: Newp . . . 6C **36**
Grove Pk. NP44: Pnwd . . . 5E **9**
Grove Pk. Av. NP44: Pnwd . . . 5E **9**
Grove Pk. Dr. NP20: Malp . . . 5B **20**
Grove Pk. Rdbt. NP20: Newp . . . 6C **20**
Grove Pl. CF14: Heath . . . 2F **85**
CF64: P'rth . . . 1E **109**
NP4: Grif . . . 1E **9**
*NP44: Pnwd . . . 5E **9***
(off Grove Pk.)
Grove Pl. La. CF64: P'rth . . . 1E **109**
Grove Rd. NP4: P'nydd . . . 1A **6**
NP11: Ris . . . 4C **16**
Grovers Cl. CF37: Glync . . . 1D **14**
Grovers Rd. CF37: Glync . . . 1D **14**
Grover St. CF37: P'prdd . . . 1B **24**
Groves Rd. NP20: Newp . . . 5E **35**
Grove Ter. CF64: P'rth . . . 1E **109**
NP4: P'nydd . . . 1A **6**
Grove Way CF3: Rum . . . 4H **87**
Gruffyd Dr. CF83: Caer . . . 4C **28**
Guardian Ind. Est. CF24: Card . . . 2F **97**
Guenever Cl. CF14: Thorn . . . 3E **71**
Guest Rd. CF24: Card . . . 5H **5** (4C **96**)
(Ocean Way)
CF24: Card . . . 5D **96**
(Regents Trade Pk.)
Guildford Cres. CF10: Card . . . 4F **5** (4B **96**)
Guildford St. CF10: Card . . . 4F **5** (4B **96**)
Guildhall Pl. CF10: Card . . . 5C **4** (4A **96**)
Gulf Ind. Area CF11: Card . . . 1G **101**
Guthrie St. CF63: Barry . . . 2A **118**
Guy's Rd. CF63: Barry . . . 1B **118**
Gwaelod y Foel CF38: Llan F . . . 3D **42**
GWAELOD-Y-GARTH . . . **1D 68**
Gwaelod y Garth Ind. Est.
CF15: Gwae G . . . 3F **69**
Gwaelod-y-Garth Rd. CF37: T'rest . . . 1A **44**
Gwalch y Penwaig CF62: Barry . . . 5H **117**
Gwalia Gro. CF37: R'fln . . . 3F **25**
Gwaun Cl. CF14: Whit . . . 3A **84**
Gwaun Hyfryd CF83: Caer . . . 5F **29**
Gwaun Illtuds CF61: Llan M . . . 2C **110**
Gwaunmiskin Rd. CF38: Bed . . . 4H **41**
Gwaun Newydd CF83: Caer . . . 5F **29**
Gwaun Rd. CF37: R'fln . . . 3F **25**
Gwaun-ruperra Cl. CF72: L'sant . . . 1F **65**
Gwaunruperra Rd. CF72: L'sant . . . 1F **65**
Gwaun y Cwrt CF83: Caer . . . 2H **45**
Gwaun-y-Groes *CF72: C Inn . . . 3H **65***
(off Main Rd.)
Gwbert Cl. CF3: Rum . . . 2C **88**
Gwendoline Pl. CF24: Card . . . 4D **96**
Gwendoline Rd. NP11: Ris . . . 6D **16**
Gwendoline St. CF24: Card . . . 4D **96**
GWENFÔ . . . **5E 99**
Gwenfo Dr. CF5: Wen . . . 4E **99**
Gwenllian St. CF63: Barry . . . 1D **118**
Gwenllian Ter. CF37: T'rest . . . 5F **25**
Gwennol y Mor CF62: Barry . . . 5H **117**
Gwennyth St. CF24: Card . . . 6A **86**
Gwenog Ct. CF62: Barry . . . 2E **117**
Gwent CF64: P'rth . . . 6C **102**
Gwentlands Cl. NP16: Bul . . . 3E **63**
Gwent Rd. CF5: Ely . . . 5F **93**
CF37: T'rest . . . 2C **44**
Gwent Sq. NP44: C'brn . . . 1G **11**
Gwent St. NP4: P'pool . . . 3B **6**
Gwern Hafren CF11: Card . . . 2F **95**
Gwern Heulog CF39: T'fail . . . 1A **40**
Gwern Rhuddi Rd. CF23: Cyn . . . 5C **72**
(not continuous)
Gwili Rd. CF37: Up Bo . . . 6B **26**
Gwilym Pl. CF63: Barry . . . 5A **106**
Gwilym St. CF37: R'fln . . . 5F **25**
Gwladys Pl. NP18: C'ln . . . 4G **21**
GWNDY . . . **4F 59**
Gwy Ct. NP16: Chep . . . 1F **63**
Gwyfryn Ter. CF38: Llan F . . . 4D **42**
Gwynant Cres. CF23: Cyn . . . 2B **86**
Gwyn Dr. CF83: Caer . . . 5C **28**
Gwyndy Rd. NP26: Undy . . . 4E **59**
Gwyn James Ct. CF64: P'rth . . . 6G **101**
Gwynllyw NP44: Pnwd . . . 5C **8**
Gwyn St. CF37: T'rest . . . 4E **25**
Gyfeillon Rd. CF37: Treh . . . 5A **14**
Gypsy La. CF15: Gro-w . . . 6G **27**

H

Habershon St. CF24: Card . . . 4E **97**
Hackerford Rd. CF23: Cyn . . . 5C **72**
Haden St. NP4: P'pool . . . 3B **6**
Hadfield Cl. CF11: Card . . . 6E **95**
Hadfield Rd. CF11: Card . . . 6E **95**
Hadley Ho. CF64: P'rth . . . 4D **108**
Hadrian Cl. NP18: C'ln . . . 4G **21**
Hafan Heulog CF37: Glync . . . 1D **14**
Hafan-Werdd CF83: Caer . . . 4F **29**
Hafod CF72: Y'erdy . . . 6C **40**
Hafod Cl. NP18: P'hir . . . 1F **21**
Hafod Ct. Rd. NP44: Thorn . . . 6A **8**
Hafod Cwrt NP20: Newp . . . 6A **36**
Hafod Gdns. NP18: P'hir . . . 1F **21**
Hafod La. CF37: Treh . . . 5A **14**
Hafod M. NP18: P'hir . . . 1F **21**
Hafod Rd. NP18: P'hir . . . 1F **21**
Hafod St. CF11: Card . . . 6B **4** (5H **95**)
Hafod-y-Bryn NP11: Ris . . . 6E **17**
Hafren Ct. CF11: Card . . . 2F **95**
Hafren Rd. CF62: Barry . . . 2G **117**
NP44: Thorn . . . 1C **10**
Haig Pl. CF5: Ely . . . 6E **93**
Hailey Ct. CF14: Llan N . . . 4B **84**
Haines Cl. CF83: Caer . . . 2A **46**
Haisbro Av. NP19: Newp . . . 1E **37**
Haldane Ct. CF83: Caer . . . 6F **29**
Haldane Pl. NP20: Malp . . . 5A **20**
Haldens, The NP44: F'wtr . . . 4D **10**
Hale Wood NP16: Chep . . . 2C **62**
Half Acre La. NP18: W'son . . . 6H **57**
Halifax Cl. CF24: Card . . . 2G **97**
Halle Cl. NP19: Newp . . . 4E **39**
Halley Ct. CF62: Rho . . . 6E **115**
Halliard Ct. CF10: Card . . . 6C **96**
Halls Rd. NP11: P'waun, Cros K . . . 1A **16**
Halls Rd. Ter. NP11: Cros K . . . 2A **16**
Halsbury Rd. CF5: Card . . . 2D **94**
Halstead St. NP19: Newp . . . 5E **37**
Halt, The CF64: Sul . . . 2G **119**
Halton Cl. CF64: P'rth . . . 5E **109**
Hamadryad Rd. CF10: Card . . . 2A **102**
Hamilton Ct. CF5: Card . . . 3E **95**
Hamilton St. CF11: Card . . . 3G **95**
NP19: Newp . . . 6F **37**
Ham La. E. CF61: Llan M . . . 4C **110**
Ham La. Sth CF61: Llan M . . . 4B **110**
Ham Mnr. CF61: Llan M . . . 4C **110**
Ham Mnr. Cvn. Pk. CF61: Llan M . . . 5C **110**
Ham M. CF61: Llan M . . . 5C **110**
Hammond Dr. NP19: Newp . . . 5F **37**
Hammond Way CF23: Pen L . . . 6E **87**
Hampden Ct. NP19: Newp . . . 6G **37**
Hampden Rd. NP19: Newp . . . 6G **37**
Hampshire Av. NP19: Newp . . . 1H **55**
Hampshire Cl. NP19: Newp . . . 1H **55**
Hampshire Cres. NP19: Newp . . . 1H **55**
Hampstead Wlk. CF5: Ely . . . 5D **92**
Hampton Ct. Rd. CF23: Pen L . . . 5D **86**
Hampton Cres. E. CF23: Cyn . . . 4D **72**
Hampton Cres. W. CF23: Cyn . . . 4C **72**
Hampton Rd. CF14: Heath . . . 3F **85**
Hanbury Cl. CF14: Whit . . . 2A **84**
NP18: C'ln . . . 6A **22**
NP44: C'brn . . . 1G **11**
Hanbury Gdns. NP4: P'nydd . . . 1A **6**
Hanbury Rd. NP4: P'nydd . . . 1A **6**
NP4: P'pool . . . 3C **6**
Handel Cl. CF64: P'rth . . . 4D **108**
NP19: Newp . . . 4D **38**
Hand Farm Rd. NP4: New I . . . 4F **7**
Handley Rd. CF24: Card . . . 2G **97**
Handsworth St. NP19: Newp . . . 5F **37**
Hanfield Pk. NP44: C'iog . . . 1A **12**
Hanley Path NP44: St D . . . 3E **11**
Hannah Cl. CF14: L'shn . . . 1H **85**
Hannah St. CF10: Card . . . 6B **96**
CF63: Barry . . . 1A **118**
Hanover Cl. NP16: Chep . . . 1D **62**
Hanover Ct. CF14: Whit . . . 1B **84**
CF63: Barry . . . 6D **106**
NP16: Tut . . . 2G **63**
Hanover St. CF5: Card . . . 4E **95**
CF62: Barry . . . 2H **117**
Hansom Pl. CF11: Card . . . 6G **95**
Harbour Dr. CF10: Card . . . 2C **102**
Harbour Rd. CF62: Barry . . . 4F **117**
Harbour Vw. Rd. CF64: P'rth . . . 6A **102**
Harding Av. NP20: Malp . . . 4A **20**
Harding Cl. CF61: Bov . . . 3E **111**
HARDWICK . . . **3E 63**
Hardwick Av. NP16: Chep . . . 3E **63**
Hardwicke Ct. CF5: L'dff . . . 1C **94**
Hardwick Hill NP16: Chep . . . 3D **62**
Hardwick Hill La. NP16: Chep . . . 3E **63**
Hardwick Ter. NP16: Chep . . . 2E **63**
(not continuous)
Hardy Cl. CF62: Barry . . . 5A **106**
NP20: Newp . . . 2G **53**
Hardy Ct. NP4: P'nydd . . . 1A **6**
Hardy Pl. CF24: Card . . . 1G **5** (2C **96**)
Harefield Cl. CF23: Pontp . . . 4H **73**
Harford Cl. CF14: Whit . . . 2A **84**
Hargreaves Dr. NP20: Malp . . . 4A **20**
Harlech Cl. CF64: Din P . . . 2A **108**
NP44: C'iog . . . 5G **9**
Harlech Ct. CF14: Whit . . . 1C **84**
CF83: Caer . . . 5H **27**

Harlech Dr. CF64: Din P . . . 1A **108**
NP10: R'drn . . . 6A **34**
Harlech Gdns. CF62: Barry . . . 5F **105**
Harlech Ho. CF15: Rad . . . 1G **83**
Harlech Retail Pk.
NP20: Newp . . . 1A **54**
Harlech Rd. CF3: Rum . . . 4A **88**
Harlequin Ct. NP20: Newp . . . 3B **36**
Harlequin Dr. NP20: Newp . . . 3B **36**
Harlequin Rdbt. NP20: Newp . . . 3C **36**
Harlequins Ct. CF24: Card . . . 1E **97**
Harold St. CF24: Card . . . 2E **97**
NP44: Pnwd . . . 6E **9**
Harold Wlk. *NP10: Roger . . . 5D 34*
(off Ebenezer Dr.)
Harpur St. CF10: Card . . . 5A **96**
Harriet St. CF24: Card . . . 1A **96**
CF64: P'rth . . . 6H **101**
Harrington Ct. CF5: Ely . . . 6F **93**
Harris Av. CF3: Rum . . . 3A **88**
Harrismith Rd. CF23: Pen L . . . 6C **86**
Harrison Dr. CF3: St M . . . 2D **88**
Harrison Way CF11: Card . . . 3H **101**
Harrogate Rd. NP19: Newp . . . 1E **37**
Harrowby La. CF10: Card . . . 2B **102**
Harrowby Pl. CF10: Card . . . 2B **102**
Harrowby St. CF10: Card . . . 1B **102**
Harrow Cl. NP18: C'ln . . . 3F **21**
Harrow Rd. NP19: Newp . . . 4D **36**
Hart Gdns. *NP20: Newp . . . 6C 36*
(off Alma St.)
Hartland Ho. CF11: Card . . . 4A **102**
Hartland Rd. CF3: L'rmy . . . 2G **87**
Hartley Pl. CF11: Card . . . 6F **95**
Hart Pl. CF24: Card . . . 1F **97**
Hartridge Farm Rd.
NP18: Newp . . . 5C **38**
Hartshorn Ct. CF83: Caer . . . 6F **29**
Harvard Rd. CF83: Abert . . . 2D **26**
Harvey Cl. NP20: Malp . . . 5A **20**
Harvey Pl. CF5: Card . . . 3E **95**
Harvey St. CF63: Barry . . . 1B **118**
(not continuous)
Hassocks Lea NP44: F'wtr . . . 4D **10**
Hastings Av. CF64: P'rth . . . 1C **108**
Hastings Cl. CF64: P'rth . . . 1C **108**
Hastings Cres. CF3: Old M . . . 5B **74**
Hastings Pl. CF64: P'rth . . . 1C **108**
Hathaway Pl. CF63: Barry . . . 5C **106**
Hathaway St. NP19: Newp . . . 5F **37**
Hatherleigh NP19: Newp . . . 4H **37**
Hatherleigh Rd. CF3: Rum . . . 3G **87**
Haul Fryn CF14: R'ina . . . 5B **70**
Havannah St. CF10: Card . . . 2B **102**
Havant Cl. CF62: Rho . . . 6E **115**
Havelock Pl. CF11: Card . . . 6H **95**
Havelock St. CF10: Card . . . 5C **4** (4A **96**)
NP20: Newp . . . 5B **36**
Havenwood Dr. CF14: Thorn . . . 2G **71**
Haverford Way CF5: Ely . . . 5H **93**
Hawarden Grn. NP44: L'rfn . . . 3B **12**
Hawarden Rd. NP19: Newp . . . 4G **37**
(not continuous)
Hawfinch Cl. CF23: Pent . . . 6D **72**
Hawke Cl. NP19: Newp . . . 2C **38**
Hawker Cl. CF24: Card . . . 2G **97**
Hawkes Ridge NP44: Ty C . . . 3B **10**
Hawkins Cres. NP19: Newp . . . 2C **38**
Hawks Moor Cl. NP10: Roger . . . 3D **34**
Hawksworth Gro. NP19: Newp . . . 5H **37**
Hawkwood Cl. CF5: F'wtr . . . 6F **83**
Hawse La.
NP10: Coedk, St Bri W . . . 3D **76**
HAWTHORN . . . **5G 25**
Hawthorn Av. CF64: P'rth . . . 2C **108**
Hawthorn Cl. CF64: Din P . . . 3H **107**
NP16: Bul . . . 6E **63**
NP18: Under . . . 3H **39**
Hawthorn Cres. CF37: R'fln . . . 5H **25**
Hawthorne Av. NP19: Newp . . . 5G **37**
Hawthorne Cl. NP26: Undy . . . 3D **58**
Hawthorne Fosse NP19: Newp . . . 5H **37**
Hawthorne Sq. NP19: Newp . . . 5G **37**
Hawthorn Gdns. NP18: C'ln . . . 4A **22**
Hawthorn Leisure Cen. . . . **5G 25**
Hawthorn Pl. NP11: P'waun . . . 1A **16**
Hawthorn Rd. CF37: R'fln . . . 5H **25**
CF62: Barry . . . 3E **117**
CF72: L'harry . . . 5B **78**
NP4: Seba . . . 2D **8**
Hawthorn Rd. E. CF14: Llan N . . . 4B **84**
Hawthorn Rd. W. CF14: Llan N . . . 4B **84**
Hawthorns, The CF23: Pent . . . 6E **73**
NP18: C'ln . . . 4A **22**
NP44: Up Cwm . . . 5B **8**
Haxby Ct. CF10: Card . . . 5C **96**
Hayes, The CF10: Card . . . 4D **4** (4A **96**)
Hayes Bri. Rd. CF10: Card . . . 5D **4** (4A **96**)
HAYES GATE . . . **6A 62**
Hayes La. CF64: Sul . . . 3D **118**
Hayes Rd. CF64: Barry, Sul . . . 3D **118**
Hayley Stadium . . . **2C 56**
Hayling Cl. NP19: Newp . . . 2F **37**
Haynes Ct. NP20: Newp . . . 1D **54**
Hayswayn NP44: F'wtr . . . 4D **10**
Hazel Av. NP26: Cald . . . 4B **60**
Hazel Cl. NP4: New I . . . 4H **7**
Hazeldene CF72: L'harry . . . 5A **78**
Hazeldene Av. CF24: Card . . . 5A **86**
Hazel Gro. CF64: Din P . . . 3H **107**
CF83: Caer . . . 4E **29**
CF83: Tret . . . 2H **29**
Hazelhurst Ct. CF14: Llan N . . . 4B **84**
Hazelhurst Rd. CF14: Llan N . . . 4B **84**
Hazell Dr. NP10: Coedk . . . 5D **52**
Hazel Pl. CF5: F'wtr . . . 6H **83**
Hazel Rd. CF64: P'rth . . . 3D **108**
Hazel Tree Cl. CF15: Rad . . . 1E **83**
Hazel Wlk. NP18: C'ln . . . 5F **21**
NP44: C'iog . . . 5G **9**
Hazelwood Dr. CF3: St M . . . 6C **74**
Hazledene Cl. CF63: Barry . . . 6A **106**
Hazlitt Cl. CF3: L'rmy . . . 5H **73**
NP20: Newp . . . 2G **53**
Headland, The NP16: Bul . . . 6G **63**
Hearte Cl. CF62: Rho . . . 5E **115**
HEATH . . . **2A 86**
Heath Av. CF64: P'rth . . . 6F **101**
Heathbrook CF14: L'shn . . . 6A **72**
Heathcliffe Cl. CF3: Old M . . . 5B **74**
Heath Cl. NP19: Newp . . . 1A **56**
Heath Cres. CF37: P'prdd . . . 6B **14**
Heather Av. CF5: Ely . . . 3B **94**
Heather Cl. NP16: Bul . . . 5F **63**
Heather Ct. NP44: Ty C . . . 4B **10**
Heather Rd. NP19: Newp . . . 1E **37**
Heathers, The CF62: Barry . . . 2F **117**
Heather Vw. Rd. CF37: P'prdd . . . 5E **15**
Heather Way CF5: F'wtr . . . 1H **93**
Heathfield Dr. CF62: Barry . . . 6G **105**
Heathfield Pl. CF14: Card . . . 5G **85**
Heathfield Rd. CF14: Card . . . 5G **85**
Heath Halt Ct. CF23: Heath . . . 2A **86**
Heath Halt Rd. CF23: Cyn, Heath . . . 2A **86**
Heath High Level Station (Rail) . . . **2A 86**
Heathland Vs. CF37: T'rest . . . 2E **25**
Heath Low Level Station (Rail) . . . **2A 86**
Heath Mead CF14: Heath . . . 3A **86**
HEATH PARK . . . **3F 85**
Heath Pk. Av. CF14: Heath . . . 2H **85**
Heath Pk. Ct. CF14: Heath . . . 3A **86**
Heath Pk. Cres. CF14: Heath . . . 3A **86**
Heath Pk. Dr. CF14: Heath . . . 2A **86**
Heath Pk. La. CF14: Heath . . . 2A **86**
(Heath Halt Rd.)
CF14: Heath . . . 4F **85**
(St George's Rd.)
Heath Pk. Way CF14: Heath . . . 3G **85**
Heath Sports Cen. . . . **3H 85**
Heath St. CF11: Card . . . 4G **95**
Heath Ter. CF37: P'prdd . . . 6B **14**
Heath Way CF14: Heath . . . 2G **85**
Heathwood Ct. CF14: Heath . . . 2G **85**
Heathwood Gro. CF14: Heath . . . 3A **86**
Heathwood Rd. CF14: Heath . . . 3F **85**
CF14: L'shn . . . 1A **86**
Hebbles La. CF63: Barry . . . 6C **106**
Heddfan Nth. CF23: Pent . . . 6F **73**
Heddfan Sth. CF23: Pent . . . 6F **73**
Hedel Rd. CF11: Card . . . 3C **94**
Heidenheim Dr. NP20: Newp . . . 2B **36**
Helen Pl. CF24: Card . . . 2D **96**
Helen St. CF24: Card . . . 2D **96**
Helford Sq. NP20: Bet . . . 5F **19**
Hellas Dr. CF62: Barry . . . 5E **105**
Helpstone Ter. NP4: P'pool . . . 2A **6**
Hemingway Rd. CF10: Card . . . 1C **102**
Hendre CF83: Caer . . . 2A **28**
Hendre Cl. CF5: L'dff . . . 1C **94**
Hendre Ct. NP44: H'lys . . . 5B **10**
Hendredenny Dr. CF83: Caer . . . 5G **27**
HENDREDENNY PARK . . . **5H 27**
Hendre Farm Ct. NP19: Newp . . . 3D **38**
Hendre Farm Dr. NP19: Newp . . . 3D **38**
Hendre Farm Gdns. NP19: Newp . . . 4C **38**
Hendre Gdns. CF5: L'dff . . . 1C **94**
Hendre Rd. CF3: Rum, St M . . . 1B **88**
CF83: Abert . . . 2C **26**
Hendrick Dr. NP16: Sed . . . 2G **63**
HENDY . . . **6F 65**
Hendy St. CF23: Card . . . 6B **86**
Henfron CF83: Caer . . . 3A **28**
Hengoed Cl. CF5: Ely . . . 5G **93**
Henke Ct. CF10: Card . . . 6C **96**
HENLLYS . . . **5B 10**
Henllys La. NP10: Roger . . . 5C **18**
NP20: Bet . . . 5C **18**
NP44: H'lys . . . 5A **10**
Henllys Rd. CF23: Cyn . . . 1B **86**
HENLLYS VALE . . . **2D 18**
Henllys Village Rd. NP44: H'lys . . . 5B **10**
Henllys Way NP44: C'brn . . . 4G **11**
NP44: Coed E, C'brn, F'wtr, H'lys . . . 5B **10**
Henry Morgan Cl. NP10: Duf . . . 5H **53**
Henry St. CF10: Card . . . 6B **96**
CF37: P'prdd . . . 5A **14**
CF63: Barry . . . 1D **118**
Henry Wood Cl. NP19: Newp . . . 5A **38**
Henry Wood Wlk. NP19: Newp . . . 5A **38**
HENSOL . . . **5G 79**
Hensol Cl. NP10: Roger . . . 3D **34**
NP44: L'rfn . . . 2A **12**
Hensol Rd. CF72: Hens, P'clun . . . 1E **79**
(not continuous)
Hensol Vs. CF72: Hens . . . 4G **79**
Henson St. NP19: Newp . . . 5F **37**
Henwysg Cl. CF37: P'prdd . . . 5A **14**
Heol Aer CF14: R'ina . . . 5E **71**
Heol Amlwch CF14: Llan N . . . 4D **84**
Heol Aneurin CF83: Caer . . . 3H **27**
Heol Ap Pryce CF38: Bed . . . 5A **42**
Heol Aradur CF5: L'dff . . . 4H **83**
Heol Barri CF83: Caer . . . 4B **28**
Heol Berllan CF83: Caer . . . 4D **28**
Heol Berry CF15: Gwae G . . . 2D **68**
Heol Beulah CF83: L'brad . . . 1B **28**
Heol Beuno NP4: New I . . . 4G **7**
Heol Billingsley CF15: N'grw . . . 3C **44**
Heol Blakemore CF14: Whit . . . 2B **84**
Heol Booker CF14: Whit . . . 2A **84**
Heol Briwnant CF14: R'ina . . . 4D **70**
Heol Broadland CF62: Barry . . . 3G **117**
Heol Brofiscin CF72: Groes F . . . 6B **66**
Heol Bro Wen CF83: Caer . . . 5D **28**
Heol Bryn Glas CF38: Llan F . . . 4D **42**
Heol Bryngias CF14: R'ina . . . 5C **70**
Heol Bryn Heulog CF38: Llan F . . . 3D **42**
Heol Brynhyfryd CF38: Llan F . . . 4B **42**
Heol Brynmor John CF38: Chu V . . . 2D **42**
Heol Cae Bach CF83: Caer . . . 3D **28**
Heol Cae Celynnen CF83: Caer . . . 3D **28**
Heol Cae Fan Heulog CF83: Caer . . . 4D **28**
Heol Cae Gwyn CF83: Caer . . . 2A **46**
Heol Cae Maen CF83: Caer . . . 4D **28**
Heol Cae Rhys CF14: R'ina . . . 1E **85**
Heol Caerlan CF38: Bed . . . 5H **41**
Heol Camddwr CF23: Pontp . . . 4H **73**
Heol Carnau CF5: Ely . . . 6H **93**
Heol Carne CF14: Whit . . . 3E **85**
Heol Cattwg CF14: Whit . . . 4D **84**
Heol Cawrdaf CF38: Bed . . . 5A **42**
Heol Cefn Onn CF14: L'vne . . . 2A **72**
Heol Cefn-yr Hendy CF72: Mis . . . 6E **65**
Heol Ceiniog CF63: Barry . . . 3H **117**
Heol Celyn CF38: Chu V, Tont . . . 2F **43**
Heol Celynen CF37: Glync . . . 1D **14**
Heol Celynnen CF72: L'harry . . . 5C **78**
Heol Chappell CF14: Whit . . . 2B **84**

Heol Chudleigh CF3: St M 2D **88**
Heol Cilffrydd CF63: Barry 3A **118**
Heol Clwyddau CF38: Bed 6A **42**
Heol Clyd CF83: Caer 4H **27**
Heol Coed Cae CF14: Whit 3D **84**
Heol Collen CF5: Cul C 1E **99**
Heol Coroniad CF38: Bed 4A **42**
Heol Corswigen CF63: Barry 5B **106**
Heol Creigiau CF15: Cre 4D **66**
CF38: E Isaf 6D **42**
Heol Crochendy CF15: N'grw 2C **44**
Heol Cwarrel Clark CF83: Caer 2H **27**
Heol Cwm Ifor CF83: Caer 3H **27**
Heol Dafydd CF72: P'clun 6C **64**
Heol Danyrodyn CF15: P'rch 4A **68**
Heol Dderwen CF38: Tont 1G **43**
Heol Ddeusant CF38: Bed 5H **41**
Heol Ddu CF72: L'sant 2C **40**
Heol Deg CF38: Tont 2F **43**
Heol Deiniol NP4: New I 4G **7**
Heol Dennant CF5: F'wtr 1A **94**
Heol Derlwyn CF14: R'ina 5D **70**
Heol Derwen NP4: New I 4G **7**
Heol Deva CF5: Ely 6G **93**
Heol Dewi Sant CF14: Heath 1F **85**
CF62: Barry 2G **117**
Heol Dolwen CF14: Whit 3E **85**
Heol Don CF14: Whit 2B **84**
Heol Dowlais CF38: E Isaf 6D **42**
Heol Draenen Wen CF5: Cul C 1E **99**
Heol Draw CF38: Chu V 2E **43**
Heol Dyfed CF14: Heath 2F **85**
CF38: Bed 6H **41**
Heol Dyfodwg CF72: L'sant 1F **65**
Heol Dyhewydd CF38: Llan F 4B **42**
Heol Ebwy CF5: Ely 5H **93**
Heol Edwards CF15: N'grw 3E **45**
Heol Eglwys CF5: Ely 5A **94**
Heol Erwin CF14: R'ina 4E **71**
Heol Erw-y-Rhos CF83: Caer 4D **28**
Heole Rye Mor CF62: Barry 6H **117**
Heol Esgyn CF23: Cyn 1A **86**
Heol Fach CF15: N'grw 3E **45**
CF83: Caer 5A **28**
Heol Faenor CF38: Bed 6H **41**
Heol Fair CF5: L'dff 1C **94**
Heol Fawr CF83: Caer 3H **27**
Heol Fer CF83: Caer 3A **28**
Heol Ffrwd Philip CF38: E Isaf 6F **43**
Heol Ffynnon Wen CF14: R'ina 5B **70**
Heol Fioled CF63: Barry 4B **106**
Heol Gabriel CF14: Whit 4D **84**
Heol Gam CF15: P'rch 4H **67**
Heol Ganol CF83: Caer 6B **28**
Heol Gelynog CF38: Bed 5A **42**
Heol Ger-y-Felin CF61: Llan M 2C **110**
Heol Glandulais CF23: Pontp 4F **73**
Heol Glan Elai CF72: P'clun 1C **78**
Heol Glan Rheidol CF10: Card 1B **102**
Heol Glaslyn CF23: Pontp 4H **73**
NP26: Cald 3D **60**
Heol Gledyr CF83: Caer 1C **46**
Heol Glyn CF83: Caer 4B **28**
Heol Goch CF15: Gwae G, P'rch 4A **68**
Heol Graig Wen CF83: Caer 4H **27**
Heol Groeswen CF37: Up Bo 6B **26**
Heol Gronfa CF37: C'fydd 3F **15**
Heol Gwaun Rhos CF83: Caer 4D **28**
Heol Gwendoline CF62: Barry 3G **117**
Heol Gwent CF14: Heath 2F **85**
Heol Gwerthyd CF63: Barry 4A **106**
Heol Gwilym CF5: F'wtr 6H **83**
Heol Gwrgan CF14: Whit 2D **84**
CF38: Bed 5H **41**
Heol Gwyndaf CF14: L'shn 6H **71**
Heol Gwynedd CF14: Heath 2F **85**
Heol Gwynno CF72: L'sant 1F **65**
Heol Gylfinir CF62: Barry 5H **117**
Heol Harlech CF5: L'dff 1C **94**
Heol Hendre CF14: R'ina 5E **71**
Heol Hendy CF72: P'clun 6E **65**
Heol Hensol CF38: Bed 5A **42**
Heol Hir CF14: L'shn, Thorn 3H **71**
CF14: Thorn 6G **47**
(not continuous)
Heol Homfray CF5: Ely 6E **93**

Heol Ida CF38: Bed 4A **42**
Heol Iestyn CF14: Whit 2D **84**
Heol Ifor CF14: Whit 2E **85**
Heol Ifor Bach CF14: R'ina 4D **70**
Heol Illtyd CF72: L'sant 1F **65**
Heol Isaf CF14: R'ina 4D **70**
CF15: Rad 6F **69**
CF38: Llan F 6B **42**
NP4: New I 4G **7**
Heol Isaf Hendy CF72: Mis 6E **65**
Heol Iscoed CF14: R'ina 5E **71**
CF38: E Isaf 6E **43**
Heol Johnson CF72: T Grn 3D **64**
Heol Las CF72: L'sant 1E **65**
CF83: Caer 2A **28**
Heol Letton *CF10: Card* *6B* ***96***
(off Letton Rd.)
Heol Leubren CF63: Barry 4A **106**
Heol Lewis CF14: R'ina 4E **71**
CF83: Caer 4F **29**
Heol Llangan CF14: R'ina 1D **84**
Heol Llanishen Fach CF14: R'ina 5D **70**
Heol Llinos CF14: Thorn 1G **71**
Heol Lodwig CF38: Chu V 3E **43**
Heol Mabon CF14: R'ina 5D **70**
Heol Maddoc NP4: New I 4G **7**
Heol Madoc CF14: Whit 3E **85**
Heol Maerdy CF83: Caer 5F **29**
Heol Maes Eirwg CF3: St M 1D **88**
Heol Mathew CF14: Whit 2B **84**
Heol Merioneth CF61: Bov 3E **111**
Heol Merlin CF14: L'shn 6H **71**
Heol Miaren CF63: Barry 5C **106**
Heol Miles CF72: T Grn 3D **64**
Heol Miskin CF72: Mis, P'clun 5D **64**
Heol Moor CF62: Barry 3D **116**
Heol Muston CF5: Ely 3H **93**
Heol Mwyrdy CF38: Bed 5H **41**
Heol Mynydd CF37: C'fydd 3F **15**
CF38: Chu V 2G **43**
Heol Mynydd Bychan CF14: Heath 1F **85**
Heol Nant CF37: C'fydd 3F **15**
CF38: Tont, Chu V 2F **43**
Heol Nant Castan CF14: R'ina 4D **70**
Heol Nest CF14: Whit 2D **84**
Heol Neuadd Cogan CF64: P'rth 4C **108**
Heol Newydd CF3: Rum 3B **88**
NP44: Up Cwm 5C **8**
Heol Padarn NP4: New I 4G **7**
Heol Pal CF62: Barry 5H **117**
Heol Pant Gwyn CF72: L'harry 5A **78**
Heol Pantycelyn CF14: Whit 1B **84**
CF62: Barry 3F **117**
Heol Pantyderi CF5: Ely 5G **93**
Heol Pant-y-Gored CF15: Cre, P'rch 6E **67**
Heol Pant-y-Rhyn CF14: Whit 6B **70**
Heol Pardoe CF15: N'grw 2D **44**
Heol Peartree CF62: Rho 6G **115**
Heol Pencarreg CF14: Llan N 5D **84**
Heol Penlan CF14: Whit 3A **84**
Heol Penllwyn CF15: P'rch 4H **67**
Heol Penmaen *CF72: L'sant* *2F* ***65***
(off Castle St.)
Heol Pennar CF5: Ely 5H **93**
Heol Pentre'r Cwrt CF61: Llan M 2B **110**
Heol Pentre'r Felin CF61: Llan M 2C **110**
Heol Pentwyn CF14: Whit 6B **70**
Heol-Pen-y-Bryn CF83: Caer 6A **46**
Heol Penyfai CF14: Whit 3E **85**
Heol Pen-y-Foel CF37: Glync 1D **14**
Heol Pen-y-Parc CF37: Glync 1D **14**
CF72: L'sant 2F **65**
Heol Peredur CF14: Thorn 3F **71**
Heol Pilipala CF62: Rho 6F **115**
Heol Pontprennau CF23: Pontp 4F **73**
(not continuous)
Heol Pont-y-Cwcw NP10: St Bri W 6A **54**
Heol Powis CF14: Heath 2F **85**
Heol Poyston CF5: Ely 6G **93**
Heol Pwllypant CF83: Caer 4B **28**
Heol Pwllyplaca CF3: St M 1D **88**
Heol Rhayader CF14: Whit 3A **84**
Heol Rhos CF83: Caer 6H **27**
Heol Rhosyn CF38: Llan F 6B **42**
Heol Robart *CF72: P'clun* *6D* ***64***
(off Ffordd Talygarn)

Heol St Denys CF14: L'vne 2A **72**
Heol Salem CF38: Chu V, Tont 2F **43**
Heol Seddon CF5: L'dff 5H **83**
Heol Serth CF83: Caer 3H **27**
Heol Seward CF38: Bed 6H **41**
Heol Sirhwi CF62: Barry 1E **117**
Heol Solva CF5: Ely 5A **94**
Heol Staughton *CF10: Card* *6B* ***96***
(off Dumballs Rd.)
Heol Sticil-y-Beddau
CF72: L'sant 2F **65**
Heol Stradling CF14: Whit 2D **84**
Heol Syr Lewis CF15: Morg 5F **69**
Heol Teifi NP26: Cald 4D **60**
Heol Teilo NP4: New I 4G **7**
Heol Terrell CF11: Card 4D **94**
Heol Thomas CF83: Caer 1B **46**
Heol Tir Bach CF83: Caer 3H **27**
Heol Tir Coch CF38: E Isaf 6E **43**
Heol Tir Gibbon CF83: Caer 4A **28**
Heol Towy NP26: Cald 3D **60**
Heol Trecastell CF83: Caer 1B **46**
Heol Tredwen CF10: Card 1B **102**
Heol Treferig CF38: Bed 5A **42**
Heol Trefgarne CF5: Ely 6G **93**
Heol Tre Forys CF64: P'rth 3C **108**
Heol Trelai CF5: Ely 6F **93**
(not continuous)
Heol Trenewydd CF5: Ely 6G **93**
Heol Trostre CF3: St M 2D **88**
Heol ty Crwn CF83: Caer 4D **28**
Heol Tyddyn CF83: Caer 2H **45**
Heol ty Ffynnon CF23: Pontp 4F **73**
Heol ty Maen CF37: Up Bo 1B **44**
Heol ty Merchant CF83: Caer 4D **28**
Heol Ty'n-y-Cae CF14: R'ina 1D **84**
Heol Ty'n y Coed CF14: R'ina 5E **71**
Heol Uchaf CF14: R'ina 4D **70**
Heol Undeb CF38: Bed 5H **41**
Heol Urban CF5: L'dff 5A **84**
Heol Waun Fawr CF83: Caer 2A **46**
Heol Waun Waelod CF83: Caer 3B **46**
Heol Waun y Nant CF14: Whit 4D **84**
Heol Wen CF14: R'ina 6D **70**
Heol Wernlas CF14: Whit 3E **85**
Heol y Barcud CF14: Thorn 1G **71**
Heol y Beddau CF83: Caer 1B **46**
Heol-y-Beddau CF38: Bed 4A **42**
Heol-y-Beilia CF72: L'sant 2F **65**
Heol-y-Berllan CF5: Ely 5G **93**
Heol y Berth CF83: Caer 3A **46**
Heol-y-Bont CF14: R'ina 6E **71**
Heol y Brenin CF64: P'rth 3C **108**
Heol-y-Bryn CF14: R'ina 6C **70**
CF15: P'rch 4H **67**
CF37: R'fln 3H **25**
CF62: Barry 5D **116**
CF72: P'clun 6E **65**
Heol-y-Bwnsi CF15: Gro-w 6B **26**
CF37: Up Bo 6B **26**
Heol-y-Cadno CF14: Thorn 2F **71**
Heol-y-Carnau CF83: Caer 4D **28**
Heol-y-Carw CF14: Thorn 2G **71**
Heol-y-Castell CF5: Ely 6G **93**
Heol-y-Cawl CF64: Din P 2G **107**
Heol y Clun CF38: Bed 5H **41**
Heol y Coed CF38: Bed 5H **41**
Heol-y-Coed CF14: R'ina 5C **70**
CF15: N'grw 3E **45**
CF61: Llan M 4C **110**
CF72: P'clun 5D **64**
Heol y Cwm CF15: Morg 6D **68**
Heol-y-Cwm CF83: Caer 2B **46**
Heol-y-Dderwen CF15: N'grw 3F **45**
Heol-y-Ddol CF83: Caer 4D **28**
Heol-y-Delyn CF14: L'vne 3B **72**
Heol-y-Deri CF14: R'ina 5D **70**
CF37: P'prdd 5A **14**
Heol-y-Dreflan CF83: Caer 4D **28**
Heol y Dryw CF62: Rho 6F **115**
Heol-y-Fedwen CF38: Tont 1G **43**
Heol-y-Felin CF5: Ely 3A **94**
CF14: R'ina 5D **70**
CF61: Llan M 4C **110**
CF72: P'clun 6C **64**
CF83: Caer 6B **28**

Heol-y-Fforest CF15: Tong 3H **69**
CF83: Caer 3H **69**
Heol-y-Ffynnon CF38: E Isaf 5F **43**
Heol-y-Foel CF38: Llan F 3D **42**
Heol-y-Forlan CF14: Whit 1C **84**
Heol-y-Frenhines CF64: Din P 3G **107**
Heol-y-Fro CF38: Chu V 2E **43**
CF61: Llan M 2C **110**
Heol-y-Gaer CF5: Ely 6G **93**
CF62: Barry 5D **116**
Heol y Gamlas CF15: N'grw 2C **44**
Heol y Gth. CF83: Rud 6B **30**
Heol y Goedwig CF38: Chu V 3E **43**
Heol-y-Gogledd CF83: Caer 3A **28**
Heol-y-Gors CF14: Whit 4E **85**
CF15: N'grw 3F **45**
CF83: Caer 4D **28**
Heol-y-Graig CF72: L'sant 2F **65**
Heol y Gyfraith CF72: T Grn 3E **65**
Heol y Llongau CF63: Barry 3H **117**
Heol-y-Maes CF38: Llan F 4D **42**
Heol-y-Nant CF14: R'ina 1D **84**
CF15: Gwae G 2D **68**
CF63: Barry 6A **106**
CF83: Caer 6B **28**
Heol Ynys Ddu CF83: Caer 2A **46**
Heol-y-Parc CF14: Pontp 1G **73**
CF15: P'rch 6H **67**
CF38: E Isaf 5F **43**
CF83: Caer 6B **28**
Heol-y-Pavin CF5: L'dff 6C **84**
Heol y Pentir CF62: Rho 6E **115**
Heol-y-Pentre CF15: P'rch 4A **68**
Heol-y-Pia CF83: Caer 6A **28**
Heol-y-Pistyll CF72: L'sant 2F **65**
Heol y Porthladd CF63: Barry 3H **117**
Heol y Pwca NP44: Pnwd 5C **8**
Heol y Pwll CF15: N'grw 3D **44**
Heol-yr-Efail CF14: R'ina 6E **71**
Heol-yr-Haul CF72: Groes F 6C **66**
Heol y Rhosog CF3: Rum 5B **88**
Heol yr Odyn CF5: Ely 6F **93**
CF15: N'grw 3D **44**
Heol-yr-Onen CF83: Caer 6B **28**
Heol yr Orsaf CF72: P'clun 6C **64**
Heol-yr-Ynys CF15: Gwae G, Tong 3F **69**
Heol-yr-Ysbyty CF83: Caer 2A **46**
Heol yr Ysgol CF83: Tret 3A **30**
Heol-y-Sarn CF72: L'sant 1F **65**
Heol Ysgawen CF72: L'harry 5C **78**
Heol Ysgubor CF83: Caer 2A **46**
Heol y Twyn CF72: T Grn 3A **64**
Heol-y-Waun CF14: Whit 4D **84**
Heol-y-Wenallt CF14: Thorn 1C **70**
Heol y Wern CF14: R'ina 5E **71**
Heol-y-Wern CF83: Caer 4D **28**
Herbert Av. NP11: Ris, Roger 1G **33**
Herbert Cl. CF3: M'fld 5A **76**
Herbert Dr. CF83: Caer 4B **28**
Herbert March Cl. CF5: L'dff 4H **83**
Herbert Rd. NP19: Newp 3D **36**
NP26: Cald 4C **60**
Herbert St. CF10: Card 6E **5** (5B **96**)
CF14: Card 6G **85**
CF63: Barry 6A **106**
NP20: Newp 6C **36**
Herbert Ter. CF64: P'rth 1E **109**
Herbert Wlk. NP20: Newp 6C **36**
Hereford Ct. NP18: C'ln 4G **21**
Hereford St. CF11: Card 5G **95**
NP19: Newp 4D **36**
Heritage Ct. NP44: L'tnam 6B **12**
Heritage Dr. CF5: Ely 1G **99**
CF62: Barry 2F **117**
Heritage Pk. CF3: St M 5D **74**
Hermon Hill CF15: Tong 4G **69**
Herne Pl. CF11: Card 4D **94**
Heron Rd. CF3: Rum 4A **88**
NP26: Cald 6D **60**
Heronston Cl. NP26: Undy 4F **59**
Herons Way CF83: Caer 2A **46**
Heron Way NP10: Duf 4H **53**
Herrick Pl. CF83: Mac 2D **30**
Hertford Pl. NP19: Newp 3F **37**
Heston Cl. NP26: Pskwt 5H **61**
Hewell Ct. CF11: Card 1H **101**
Hewell St. CF11: Card 1H **101**
CF64: P'rth 6H **101**
Hibiscus Ct. CF38: Llan F 6C **42**
Hickman Rd. CF64: P'rth 1E **109**
Hickory Ct. CF24: Card 4H **5** (4D **96**)
Highbank CF23: Pontp 3H **73**
High Banks NP19: Newp 1E **37**
High Beech La. NP16: Bul 4D **62**
NP16: Chep 4D **62**
(not continuous)
Highbridge Cl. CF64: Sul 2A **120**
Highbury Pl. CF5: Ely 5F **93**
Highbury Rd. CF5: Ely 4G **93**
High Cl. NP44: Llanf 4B **12**
High Cnr. CF15: P'rch 4A **68**
Highcroft Rd. NP20: Newp 3A **36**
High Cft. Wlk. CF3: L'rmy 2H **87**
HIGH CROSS 5D **34**
High Cross Cl. NP10: Roger 5D **34**
High Cross Dr. NP10: Roger 4D **34**
High Cross La. NP10: Roger 6E **35**
(not continuous)
Highcross Rd. NP10: Newp, Roger 4D **34**
Highdale Cl. CF72: L'sant 3G **65**
HIGHER END 4C **112**
Highfield NP26: C'ent 1B **60**
Highfield Cl. CF38: Tont 2G **43**
CF62: Barry 4E **117**
CF64: Din P 1A **108**
NP11: Ris 5D **16**
NP18: C'ln 3F **21**
NP44: Llanf 5B **12**
Highfield Ct. NP10: Bass 6C **34**
Highfield Gdns. NP10: Bass 6B **34**
Highfield La. NP10: Bass 6B **34**
Highfield Rd. CF14: Heath 3A **86**
CF23: Cyn 3A **86**
CF62: Barry 6F **105**
NP10: Bass 6C **34**
NP18: C'ln 4F **21**
NP20: Newp 6G **35**
Highfields CF5: L'dff 5B **84**
Highfield Ter. CF37: P'prdd 6B **14**
High Fld. Way NP18: C'ln 3F **21**
Highland Gro. NP44: Pnwd 5E **9**
Highlands CF3: Rum 5G **87**
Highlight La. CF62: Barry 5D **104**
(not continuous)
High Mdw. CF61: Llan M 4B **110**
Highmead Rd. CF5: Ely 4H **93**
High St. CF5: L'dff 1C **94**
CF10: Card 4C **4** (4A **96**)
CF37: P'prdd 1C **24**
CF61: Llan M 2B **110**
CF62: Barry 3F **117**
CF64: P'rth 1E **109**
CF71: C'bri 3C **90**
CF72: Bryns 1B **78**
CF72: L'sant 2F **65**
(not continuous)
CF83: Abert 1E **27**
CF83: Tret 2A **30**
NP4: Grif 6E **7**
NP4: P'pool 3B **6**
NP11: Cros K 2A **16**
NP16: Chep 2E **63**
NP18: C'ln 5H **21**
NP20: Newp 4C **36**
High St. Arc. CF10: Card 4C **4** (4A **96**)
High Trees NP11: Ris 5F **17**
High Vw. NP16: Chep 2E **63**
High Vw. Rd. CF64: P'rth 6H **101**
High Vw. Way CF37: Glync 2D **14**
Highwalls Av. CF64: Din P 1F **107**
Highwalls End CF64: Din P 1G **107**
Highwalls Rd. CF64: Din P 2G **107**
High Way, The NP4: New I, P'pool 4F **7**
Highway, The NP44: C'iog 5H **9**
NP44: Oakf 4H **11**
Hilda St. CF37: T'rest 4E **25**
CF62: Barry 3G **117**
Hiles Rd. CF5: Ely 4G **93**
Hilla Rd. NP20: Newp 5A **36**
Hillary Cl. CF14: L'shn 4H **71**
Hillary Ri. CF63: Barry 1B **118**
NP11: P'waun 1A **16**
Hill Barn Vw. NP26: Pskwt 5H **61**
(not continuous)
Hill Cl. NP4: P'pool 3A **6**
Hillcot Cl. CF14: L'vne 3A **72**
Hillcrest NP4: New I 5H **7**
NP18: C'ln 3F **21**
Hillcrest Cl. CF14: Thorn 2H **71**
Hillcrest Rd. NP4: New I 4F **7**
Hill Dr. CF38: Llan F 4D **42**
Hillfort Cl. CF5: Ely 6H **93**
Hill Gro. NP4: P'pool 2B **6**
Hillhead CF61: Llan M 3B **110**
Hillrise CF23: L'dyrn 2D **86**
Hillside CF83: Caer 2D **46**
NP11: Ris 6E **17**
(not continuous)
Hillside Av. CF83: Abert 2C **26**
Hillside Cl. CF63: Barry 1C **118**
Hillside Ct. CF23: Pen L 5C **86**
CF38: Llan F 5C **42**
NP44: Pnwd 6D **8**
Hillside Cres. NP10: Roger 5D **34**
Hillside Dr. CF71: C'bri 4D **90**
NP4: P'pool 5C **6**
Hillside Pk. Est. CF15: Taff W 6E **45**
Hillside Rd. NP4: Grif 6D **6**
Hillside Ter. CF37: P'prdd 5C **14**
CF83: B'ws 3G **29**
Hillside Vw. CF37: P'prdd 5B **14**
Hillsnook Rd. CF5: Ely 4G **93**
Hills St. CF10: Card 4D **4** (4A **96**)
Hill St. CF63: Barry 1B **118**
CF64: P'rth 6B **102**
NP4: Grif 6E **7**
NP4: P'nydd 1A **6**
NP11: Ris 6E **17**
NP20: Newp 5C **36**
NP44: C'brn 4G **11**
Hill Ter. CF5: Twyn 3D **98**
CF64: P'rth 6H **101**
Hill Top NP44: C'brn 3F **11**
Hilltop CF3: Old M 1B **88**
NP16: Chep 3D **62**
Hilltop Av. CF37: C'fydd 4F **15**
Hilltop Cres. CF37: P'prdd 6E **15**
Hilltop Grn. NP44: Pnwd 6C **8**
Hill Vw. CF5: F'wtr 1G **93**
(not continuous)
CF38: Bed 5A **42**
Hillview NP20: Newp 6H **35**
Hillview Cres. NP19: Newp 6H **37**
Hilton Pl. CF14: Llan N 4B **84**
Hinchsliff Av. CF62: Barry 5F **105**
Hind Cl. CF24: Card 2H **97**
Hinter Path *NP44: F'wtr 4D 10*
(off Jule Rd.)
Hinton St. CF24: Card 4E **97**
Hiraethog Rd. CF37: Up Bo 6B **26**
Hirst Cres. CF5: F'wtr 6H **83**
Hirwain St. CF24: Card 1H **95**
Hitchen Hollow NP16: B'ly 6H **63**
HMP Cardiff CF24: Card 4F **5** (4B **96**)
Hobart Cl. NP20: Newp 5G **35**
Hocker Hill St. NP16: Chep 1E **63**
Hodges Cl. NP26: Pskwt 5H **61**
Hodges Row CF10: Card 6B **96**
Hodges Sq. CF10: Card 6B **96**
Hodges Ter. NP44: C'brn 2F **11**
Hogarth Cl. NP19: Newp 2F **37**
NP44: L'tnam 5A **12**
Holbein Rd. NP19: Newp 2G **37**
Holden Rd. CF11: Card 1F **101**
Holdings La. CF5: Cap L 2H **81**
Holgate Cl. CF5: L'dff 3H **83**
Holland Cl. NP10: Roger 2C **34**
Holland Way CF63: Barry 6A **106**
Hollies, The CF3: M'fld 5A **76**
CF72: Bryns 1C **78**
Hollington Dr. CF23: Pontp 4G **73**
Hollins Cl. NP16: Chep 1F **63**
HOLLYBUSH 5E **11**
Hollybush Av. NP20: Malp 5A **20**
Hollybush Cl. CF38: Chu V 2G **43**
NP20: Malp 5A **20**
NP44: C'brn 4E **11**
Hollybush Est. CF14: Whit 1A **84**

Hollybush Hgts. CF23: Pent 6D **72**
Hollybush Ri. CF23: Cyn 1D **86**
Hollybush Rd. CF23: Cyn 1C **86**
CF23: Pent 1E **87**
Hollybush Ter. CF38: Chu V 2G **43**
NP4: P'nydd 1A **6**
Hollybush Vw. NP44: H'bush 5F **11**
Hollybush Vs. CF38: Chu V, Tont 2F **43**
Hollybush Wlk. NP10: Bass 6C **34**
Hollybush Way NP44: H'bush, T Coch 5D **10**
Holly Cl. NP16: Bul 5E **63**
Holly Ct. *CF62: Barry 4E **117***
(off St Nicholas Cl.)
Hollycroft Cl. CF5: Ely 3A **94**
Holly Gro. CF14: L'vne 1A **72**
Hollyhock Cl. NP10: Roger 3A **34**
Holly La. CF37: P'prdd 5E **15**
Holly Lodge Cl. NP44: C'iog 5H **9**
Holly Lodge Gdns. NP44: C'iog 5H **9**
Holly Lodge Grn. NP44: C'iog 5H **9**
Holly Lodge Rd. NP44: C'iog 5G **9**
Holly Rd. CF5: F'wtr 1H **93**
CF72: L'harry 5B **78**
NP11: Ris 5E **17**
Hollyrood Cl. CF62: Barry 5E **105**
Holly St. CF37: R'fln 4G **25**
Holly Ter. CF14: Llan N 5C **84**
Holmdale NP44: G'mdw 3D **10**
Holmesdale Ct. CF11: Card 2H **101**
Holmesdale St. CF11: Card 2H **101**
Holmeside CF14: L'vne 2A **72**
Holmes St. CF63: Barry 1B **118**
Holmsdale Pl. CF64: P'rth 2F **109**
Holmsview Cl. CF3: Rum 3A **88**
Holmview Ct. CF3: Rum 2A **88**
Holm View Leisure Cen. **5H 105**
Holmwood Cl. CF23: Cyn 3C **86**
Holst Cl. NP19: Newp 3E **39**
Holton Rd. CF63: Barry 3H **117**
Holyhead Ct. CF83: Caer 5G **27**
Holyoake Ter. NP4: P'nydd 1A **6**
Holywell Rd. CF38: Tont 1G **43**
Home Farm Cl. NP18: C'ln 5F **21**
Home Farm Cres. NP18: C'ln 5F **21**
Home Farm Grn. NP18: C'ln 5F **21**
Homelands Rd. CF14: Heath 1E **85**
Homeside Ho. CF64: P'rth 1F **109**
Honddu Cl. NP26: Cald 4C **60**
Honeysuckle Cl. CF5: F'wtr 1G **93**
NP10: Roger 6D **34**
Honiton Rd. CF3: L'rmy 6A **74**
Hood Rd. CF62: Barry 4G **117**
NP19: Newp 2D **38**
Hope Ct. CF10: Card 1G **95**
Hopefield NP20: Newp 2B **36**
Hopefield Ct. *NP20: Newp 2B **36***
(off Hopefield)
Hope St. CF10: Card 6E **5** (5B **96**)
Hope Ter. CF24: Card 3D **96**
Hopewell Cl. NP16: Bul 6G **63**
Hop Garden, The NP16: Bul 6F **63**
HOPKINSTOWN **6A 14**
Hopkinstown Rd. CF37: P'prdd 5A **14**
Hopkins Wlk. NP19: Newp 4D **38**
Hopyard Mdw. CF71: C'bri 3B **90**
Horace Ter. CF83: L'brad 1B **28**
Horle Cl. CF11: Card 1A **102**
Hornbeam Cl. CF3: St M 6E **75**
NP18: C'ln 5E **21**
Hornbeam Wlk. NP10: Bass 6B **34**
Hornchurch Cl. CF5: L'dff 6A **84**
Horrocks Cl. NP20: Malp 3A **20**
Horton Way CF64: Sul 1E **119**
Horwood Cl. CF24: Card 2E **97**
Hoskin Ind. Est. CF10: Card 1B **102**
Hoskins St. NP20: Newp 2C **36**
Hospital Rd. CF37: P'prdd 6E **15**
NP4: C'avn, P'nydd 1A **6**
Hotham Cl. CF23: Pontp 4G **73**
Houlston Ct. CF24: Card 2F **97**
Housman Cl. CF3: L'rmy 5A **74**
Hove Av. NP19: Newp 2G **37**
Howard Cl. NP19: Newp 3C **38**
Howard Ct. CF10: Card 6G **5**
CF62: Barry 3E **117**
Howard Dr. CF83: Caer 4C **28**
Howard Gdns. CF24: Card 3G **5** (3C **96**)
Howardian Cl. CF23: Pen L 6E **87**
Howardian Nature Reserve **4F 87**
Howard Pl. CF24: Card 2G **5** (3C **96**)
Howard St. CF24: Card 4D **96**
Howard Ter. CF24: Card 3G **5** (3C **96**)
Howe Circ. NP19: Newp 2C **38**
Howell Rd. CF5: Ely 4G **93**
Howell's Cres. CF5: L'dff 1D **94**
Howells Row *NP16: Chep 1F **63***
(off Bridge St.)
Howell St. CF37: C'fydd 2F **15**
Hubert Ri. NP10: Roger 5D **34**
Hubert Rd. NP19: Newp 2E **37**
Hughes Cres. NP16: Chep 3E **63**
Hughs Cl. CF5: L'dff 4A **84**
Hugon Cl. CF23: Pen L 6E **87**
Humber Cl. NP20: Bet 6G **19**
Humber Rd. NP20: Bet 6F **19**
Hunt Cl. CF14: L'shn 4H **71**
Hunter Cl. NP10: Roger 3C **34**
Hunters Ridge CF23: Cyn 3B **86**
NP26: Undy 4E **59**
Hunter St. CF10: Card 2B **102**
CF63: Barry 1B **118**
Huntfield Rd. NP16: Chep 1D **62**
Huntingdon Cl. NP44: G'mdw 2C **10**
Huntington Dr. CF23: Pontp 4F **73**
Hunt Pl. CF63: Barry 1B **118**
Huntsmead Cl. CF14: Thorn 2G **71**
Hurford Cres. CF37: P'prdd 6B **14**
Hurford Pl. CF23: Cyn 5C **72**
Hurford St. CF37: P'prdd 1A **24**
Hurman St. CF10: Card 1B **102**
Huron Cres. CF23: Cyn 3B **86**
Huxley Grn. NP20: Malp 5A **20**
Hydrangea Cl. CF23: Pent 6D **72**
NP10: Roger 6D **34**
Hyssop Cl. CF23: Pontp 4D **72**
Hywel Cres. CF63: Barry 6A **106**

I

Idencroft Cl. CF23: Pontp 4G **73**
Iestynian Av. CF11: Card 2F **95**
Iestyn St. CF11: Card 2F **95**
Ifor Hael Rd. NP10: Roger 3B **34**
Ifor Jones Ct. CF23: L'dyrn 2D **86**
Ifton Av. NP26: Rog 6A **60**
Ifton Ind. Pk. NP26: Rog 5A **60**
Ifton La. NP26: Rog 5A **60**
Ifton Pl. NP19: Newp 6G **37**
Ifton Quarry Ind. Est. NP26: Rog 5A **60**
Ifton Rd. NP26: Rog 5A **60**
Ifton St. NP19: Newp 6G **37**
Ifton Ter. NP26: Rog 6A **60**
Ilan Av. CF37: R'fln 3F **25**
Ilan Rd. CF83: Abert 2D **26**
Ilchester Rd. CF3: L'rmy 1A **88**
Ilex Cl. CF14: L'shn 5H **71**
Ilfracombe Cres. CF3: L'rmy 2A **88**
Illtyd Av. CF61: Llan M 3B **110**
Illtyd Rd. CF5: Ely 3F **93**
Illtyd St. CF37: P'prdd 2B **24**
Ilminster Cl. CF63: Barry 1B **118**
Ilminster St. CF63: Barry 1B **118**
Ilton Rd. CF23: Pen L 6D **86**
Imperial Bldgs. Row *CF5: L'dff 1C **94***
(off Heol Fair)
Imperial Ho. NP10: Coedk 5F **53**
Imperial Pk. Ind. Est. NP10: Coedk 5F **53**
Imperial Way NP10: Coedk, Duf 5F **53**
Inchmarnock St. CF24: Card 4D **96**
Incline La. NP44: H'lys 4B **10**
Indoor Bowls Cen.
Newport **1D 36**
Inglefield Av. CF14: Card 5H **85**
Ingles *NP44: F'wtr 4D **10***
(off Henllys Way)
Inner Loop Rd. NP16: B'ly 4H **63**
Insole Cl. CF5: L'dff 1B **94**
Insole Gdns. CF5: L'dff 1C **94**
Insole Gro. E. CF5: L'dff 1B **94**
Insole Gro. W. CF5: L'dff 1B **94**
Insole Pl. CF5: L'dff 2C **94**
Insole Ter. CF72: L'sant 2F **65**
Instow Pl. CF3: L'rmy 1B **88**
International Dr. CF11: Card 4H **101**
Inverness Pl. CF24: Card 6B **86**
Iolo Pl. CF63: Barry 6B **106**
Ipswich Rd. CF23: Pen L 6E **87**
Ireland Cl. CF3: St M 2E **89**
Ireton Cl. CF23: Pontp 4G **73**
Iris Rd. NP10: Roger 3H **33**
Iron Bri. Rd. CF15: Tong 5G **69**
Iron St. CF24: Card 3D **96**
Irving Pl. CF62: Barry 2G **117**
Isaf Rd. NP11: Ris 6F **17**
Isca Cl. NP44: C'brn 1H **11**
Isca Ct. NP18: C'ln 4H **21**
Isca M. NP18: C'ln 5A **22**
Isca Rd. NP18: C'ln 6A **22**
Isca (Roman Fortress) **6H 21**
Island Rd. CF62: Barry 3F **117**
Island Vw. Cvn. Pk. CF64: S'dge 3A **120**
Islwyn Ct. NP11: Ris 6F **17**
Islwyn Dr. CF83: Caer 5C **28**
Islwyn Way CF63: Barry 5A **106**
Islwyn Workshops NP11: Ris 1E **33**
Is-y-Coed CF5: Wen 5D **98**
Itchen Cl. NP20: Bet 4F **19**
Itchen Rd. NP20: Bet 4F **19**
Itton Rd. NP16: Chep 1C **62**
Ivor John Wlk. NP18: C'ln 3G **21**
Ivor Pk. CF72: Bryns 1C **78**
Ivor St. CF24: Card 4G **5** (4C **96**)
CF62: Barry 5H **117**
NP20: Newp 5C **36**
Ivydale CF14: L'vne 2A **72**
Ivy Rd. NP20: Newp 5A **36**
Ivy St. CF5: Card 3D **94**
CF64: P'rth 1E **109**
Ivy Ter. CF37: P'prdd 5A **14**

J

Jackson Cl. CF62: Rho 5E **115**
Jackson Ct. NP19: Newp 3E **37**
Jackson Pl. NP19: Newp 3E **37**
Jackson Rd. CF5: Ely 4F **93**
Jack's Pill Ind. Est. NP20: Newp 6D **36**
Jacrow Sq. CF5: Ely 5G **93**
Jade Cl. CF14: L'vne 1A **72**
Jamaica Circ. NP10: Duf 4F **53**
Jamaica Cl. NP10: Duf 4F **53**
Jamaica Gdns. NP10: Duf 4G **53**
Jamaica Gro. NP10: Duf 4G **53**
Jamaica Wlk. NP10: Duf 4G **53**
James Ct. CF3: St M 1D **88**
CF23: Cyn 2B **86**
James Pl. CF37: T'rest 2E **25**
James Stephens Way NP16: Bul 6F **63**
James St. CF10: Card 1B **102**
CF37: T'rest 2E **25**
CF63: Barry 1D **118**
CF83: Tret 2A **30**
NP4: P'garn 2C **6**
NP10: Roger 5C **34**
NP20: Newp 1D **54**
James Ter. *CF72: C Inn 3G **65***
(off Main Rd.)
Jane Austen Cl. NP20: Newp 2G **53**
Jane Cl. NP10: Duf 6H **53**
Janet St. CF24: Card 3D **96**
CF37: R'fln 4F **25**
Japonica Cl. NP20: Malp 4B **20**
Jasmine Cl. NP10: Roger 2H **33**
Jasmine Dr. CF3: St M 6E **75**
Jasper Cl. CF5: L'dff 5A **84**
Jaycroft Cl. CF23: Pontp 4G **73**
Jeans Cl. NP20: Malp 4A **20**
Jeddo Cl. NP20: Newp 1C **54**
Jeddo St. NP20: Newp 1C **54**
Jeffrey St. NP19: Newp 4E **37**
Jellicoe Cl. NP19: Newp 2D **38**
Jellicoe Ct. CF10: Card 6G **5** (5C **96**)
Jellicoe Gdns. CF23: Cyn 2A **86**
Jenkins St. CF37: P'prdd 6A **14**
NP19: Newp 6F **37**
Jenkin St. CF63: Barry 6B **106**

Jenkinsville *CF64: P'rth* 1F **109**
(off Clive Pl.)
Jenkins Way CF3: St M 2D **88**
Jenner Rd. CF62: Barry 3F **117**
Jenner St. CF63: Barry 1C **118**
Jenner Wlk. CF38: Chu V 2E **43**
Jerries La. CF83: B'ws 2F **29**
Jerusalem Cl. NP4: New I 6H **7**
Jerusalem La. NP4: Glas, New I 6H **7**
Jervis Wlk. NP19: Newp 3C **38**
Jesmond Dene CF15: Taff W 1F **69**
Jessop Cl. NP10: Roger 3D **34**
Jessop Rd. NP10: Roger 3D **34**
Jestyn Cl. CF5: Ely 5C **92**
CF64: Din P 1H **107**
Jevan Cl. CF5: L'dff 4H **83**
Jewell La. NP20: Bryng 1B **36**
Jewel St. CF63: Barry 2A **118**
Jim Crow Sq. NP44: C'iog 1B **12**
Jim Driscoll Way CF11: Card 2A **102**
Jindabyne Ct. CF3: Old M 3D **74**
JJB Sports Health Club
Newport 2B **54**
John Baker Cl. NP44: L'tnam 5H **11**
John Batchelor Way CF64: P'rth 5A **102**
John Bull Cl. NP19: Newp 3C **38**
John Fielding Gdns. NP44: L'tnam 6B **12**
John Fld. Wlk. *NP19: Newp* *5B* ***38***
(off Ringland Circ.)
John Frost Sq. NP20: Newp 5C **36**
John Ireland Cl. NP19: Newp 4B **38**
John Morgan Cl. CF5: L'dff 4A **84**
John Pl. CF37: T'rest 3E **25**
John Rastrick Ri. NP16: Bul 6F **63**
Johns La. CF14: Llan N 5C **84**
Johnston Cl. NP10: Roger 3C **34**
Johnston Rd. CF14: L'shn 4F **71**
John St. CF10: Card 6E **5** (5B **96**)
CF37: T'rest 3E **25**
CF63: Barry 1D **118**
CF64: P'rth 6B **102**
NP4: P'pool 3C **6**
NP20: Newp 6D **36**
Jolyons Ct. NP26: Cald 5D **60**
Jonathans Ter. *CF37: C'fydd* *2F* ***15***
(off Brynderwen Rd.)
Jones Ct. CF10: Card 4C **4** (4A **96**)
Jones Pl. CF37: P'prdd 5E **15**
Jones Point Ho. CF11: Card 4A **102**
Jones St. CF37: C'fydd 1F **15**
NP20: Newp 5B **36**
Jonquil Cl. CF3: St M 6E **75**
Joseph Parry Cl. CF64: L'dgh 5G **101**
Jovian Villa *NP18: C'ln* *4F* ***21***
(off Roman Way)
Joyce Cl. NP20: Newp 1G **53**
Jubilee Gdns. CF14: Heath 1G **85**
CF63: Barry 6D **106**
Jubilee La. CF64: P'rth 1F **109**
Jubilee St. CF11: Card 6A **4** (5G **95**)
Jubilee Ter. NP4: P'pool 1A **6**
Jubilee Trad. Est. CF24: Card 4D **96**
Jubilee Way NP26: Cald 5C **60**
Judkin Ct. CF10: Card 1B **102**
Jule Rd. NP44: F'wtr 4D **10**
Julius Cl. NP18: C'ln 4F **21**
Junction Cottage Mus. 4E **7**
Junction Ind. Est. CF72: P'clun 6C **64**
Junction Rd. NP19: Newp 3D **36**
Junction Ter. CF15: Rad 2G **83**
Juniper Cres. NP44: H'lys 5C **10**
Juno Villa *NP18: C'ln* *4G* ***21***
(off Flavius Cl.)
Justin Cl. CF23: Cyn 3C **86**

K

Kames Pl. CF24: Card 4H **5** (4C **96**)
Kane Cl. CF14: L'shn 6H **71**
Kathleen St. CF62: Barry 3E **117**
Kear Ct. *NP20: Newp* *5C* ***36***
(off Commercial St.)
Kear St. NP20: Newp 5C **36**
Keats Cl. NP20: Newp 1G **53**
NP44: C'brn 3F **11**
Keats Rd. NP26: Cald 5B **60**
Keats Way CF62: Barry 5G **105**
Keble Ct. CF83: Mac 2D **30**
Keene Av. NP10: Roger 6E **35**
Keene St. NP19: Newp 5F **37**
Keen Rd. CF24: Card 5H **5** (4D **96**)
(not continuous)
Keepers Gdns. CF64: L'dgh 4E **101**
Kelly Rd. NP19: Newp 2G **37**
Kelston Cl. CF14: Whit 2B **84**
Kelston Pl. CF14: Whit 2B **84**
Kelston Rd. CF14: Whit 2B **84**
Kelvedon St. NP19: Newp 5E **37**
Kelvin Cl. NP20: Malp 5H **19**
Kelvin Rd. CF23: Card 6B **86**
Kember Cl. CF3: St M 1E **89**
Kemeys Fawr Cl.
NP4: Seba 2D **8**
Kemeys Rd. CF62: Rho 5E **115**
Kemys Pl. CF14: Llan N 4E **85**
Kemys St. NP4: Grif 1E **9**
Kemys Wlk. NP44: Two L 4F **11**
Kendall Sq. NP16: Chep 1F **63**
Kendrick Rd. CF62: Barry 2H **117**
Kenfig Pl. NP44: L'rfn 2A **12**
Kenfig Rd. CF14: Whit 4F **85**
Kenilworth Ho. CF10: Card 4B **4**
Kenilworth Pl. NP44: C'brn 3E **11**
Kenilworth Rd. CF63: Barry 6B **106**
NP19: Newp 4G **37**
Kenley Cl. CF5: L'dff 6A **84**
Kenmare M. CF23: Pontp 3F **73**
Kenmuir Rd. CF24: Card 2F **97**
Kennedy Cl. CF38: Bed 4A **42**
Kennedy Ri. CF62: Barry 2E **117**
Kennerleigh Rd. CF3: Rum 3G **87**
Kenneth Treasure Ct. CF3: Old M 6B **74**
Kennilworth Ct. CF5: F'wtr 2B **94**
Kennington Cl. CF14: Thorn 3G **71**
Kensington Av. CF5: Card 3C **94**
Kensington Gdns. NP19: Newp 3F **37**
Kensington Gro. NP19: Newp 4F **37**
Kensington Pk. NP26: Magor 4B **58**
Kensington Pl. NP19: Newp 4F **37**
Kenson Cl. CF62: Rho 6C **114**
Kenson Hill CF62: P'ark 1C **114**
Kent Cl. NP10: Roger 2C **34**
Kent Ct. *NP18: C'ln* *4G* ***21***
(off Roman Way)
Kent Grn. CF62: Barry 1G **117**
Kent St. CF11: Card 1H **101**
Kenwood Rd. CF5: Ely 4F **93**
Kenwyn Ter. CF37: P'prdd 4D **14**
Kenyon Rd. CF24: Card 2G **97**
Keppoch St. CF24: Card 1B **96**
Kerrigan Cl. CF5: F'wtr 6H **83**
Kerrycroy St. CF24: Card 4D **96**
Kestell Dr. CF11: Card 3A **102**
Kestrel Cl. CF23: Pent 6D **72**
NP26: Cald 6C **60**
Kestrel Way CF64: P'rth 5E **109**
NP10: Duf 4G **53**
Keswick Av. CF23: Cyn 4A **86**
Keteringham Cl. CF64: Sul 2G **119**
Kewstoke Av. CF3: L'rmy 2H **87**
Kewstoke Cl. CF3: L'rmy 2H **87**
Kewstoke Pl. CF3: L'rmy 2H **87**
Keyes Av. CF23: Cyn 2A **86**
Keyes Ct. CF10: Card 6G **5**
Keynsham Av. NP20: Newp 6C **36**
Keynsham Rd. CF14: Heath 3E **85**
Keyston Rd. CF5: F'wtr 5H **83**
Kidwelly Cl. NP10: Duf 6G **53**
NP44: L'rfn 3A **12**
(not continuous)
Kidwelly Ct. CF83: Caer 5H **27**
Kidwelly Rd. NP44: L'rfn 3A **12**
Kidz Playground 6A **26**
Kier Hardie Cres. NP19: Newp 3B **38**
Kier Hardie Dr. NP19: Newp 2B **38**
Kilcattan St. CF24: Card 4D **96**
Kilcredaun Ho. CF11: Card 3A **102**
Kilgetty Cl. CF5: Ely 5G **93**
Kilgetty Ct. CF5: F'wtr 1F **93**
Kiln Way NP26: Undy 4E **59**
Kimberley Rd. CF23: Pen L 6C **86**
Kimberley Ter. CF14: L'shn 5H **71**
NP20: Malp 1A **36**
Kincraig St. CF24: Card 1B **96**
King Alfreds Rd. NP16: Sed 3G **63**
Kingarth St. CF24: Card 4H **5** (4D **96**)
King Edward VII Av. CF10: Card 1B **4** (2H **95**)
King Edward Av. CF83: Caer 1D **46**
Kingfisher Cl. CF3: St M 6D **74**
NP26: Cald 6D **60**
Kingfisher Pl. NP10: Duf 3G **53**
Kingfisher Sq. CF62: St Ath 3F **111**
King George V Dr. E. CF14: Heath 4H **85**
(not continuous)
King George V Dr. Nth. CF14: Heath 2G **85**
King George V Dr. W. CF14: Heath 4G **85**
King Harold's Vw. NP26: Pskwt 5G **61**
King La. NP20: Newp 6C **36**
Kings Acre NP20: Newp 4H **35**
Kingsacre CF38: Llan F 5C **42**
Kings Av. CF15: Rad 2G **83**
Kings Cl. CF83: Abert 2E **27**
Kings Ct. CF64: Din P 3H **107**
Kingsdale Ct. NP20: Newp 6A **36**
Kingshill Ct. NP20: Newp 5B **36**
Kingsland Cres. CF63: Barry 2A **118**
Kingsland Rd. CF5: Card 3D **94**
CF14: Whit 3B **84**
Kingsland Ter. CF37: T'rest 2E **25**
Kingsland Wlk. NP44: St D 2D **10**
Kingslea *NP44: F'wtr* *4D* ***10***
(off Jule Rd.)
Kingsley Cl. CF64: Sul 2H **119**
Kingsmark La. NP16: Chep 1C **62**
Kings M. CF11: Card 3G **95**
Kingsmill La. NP20: Newp 5B **36**
Kingsmill Ter. NP20: Newp 5B **36**
Kings Pde. NP20: Newp 6D **36**
(not continuous)
Kings Ride CF64: Din P 2F **107**
Kings Rd. CF11: Card 2F **95**
CF15: Rad 2G **83**
Kings Sq. CF63: Barry 2A **118**
Kingston Rd. CF11: Card 4F **95**
NP19: Newp 4E **37**
King St. CF15: Taff W 2E **69**
CF37: T'rest 3E **25**
CF64: P'rth 6A **102**
CF83: Abert 2E **27**
NP4: P'pool 2B **6**
NP20: Newp 5C **36**
Kingsvale *NP20: Newp* *5C* ***36***
(off King St.)
Kingsway CF10: Card 3C **4** (3A **96**)
NP20: Newp 4C **36**
(not continuous)
Kingsway Cen. NP20: Newp 5C **36**
Kingswood CF37: P'prdd 1A **24**
King Wood Cl. CF23: Pen L 4E **87**
Kinnock Ct. NP44: C'iog 5G **9**
Kinsale Cl. CF23: Pontp 3G **73**
Kipling Cl. CF3: L'rmy 6H **73**
CF64: P'rth 6H **101**
Kipling Hill NP20: Newp 1G **53**
Kipling Rd. NP26: Cald 5B **60**
Kirby Daniel Ct. NP20: Newp 6C **36**
Kirby La. NP20: Newp 6C **36**
Kirkby Ct. CF10: Card 5C **96**
Kirkhouse St. CF37: P'prdd 1B **24**
Kirkwall Ct. CF24: Card 2F **97**
Kirrlach Cl. NP26: Cald 5B **60**
Kirton Cl. CF5: L'dff 6A **84**
Kitchener Rd. CF11: Card 4F **95**
Kitty Hawk Dr. NP19: Newp 6G **37**
KNAP, THE 6E **117**
Knap Car Ter. CF62: Barry 5D **116**
Knight Cl. *NP20: Newp* *6C* ***36***
(off Francis Dr.)
Knighton Ct. CF24: Card 3H **5** (3D **96**)
NP18: C'ln 5H **21**
Knights Wlk. CF83: Caer 1H **45**
Knightswell Cl. CF5: Ely 1E **99**
Knightswell Rd. CF5: Ely 6E **93**
Knole Cl. CF23: Pontp 4G **73**
KNOLLBURY 3D **58**
Knowbury Av. CF64: P'rth 5F **109**
Knox Rd. CF24: Card 3F **5** (3B **96**)

Kyle Av. CF14: Whit 2D **84**
Kyle Cres. CF14: Whit 2E **85**
Kymin Rd. CF64: P'rth 1F **109**
Kymin Ter. CF64: P'rth 1F **109**
Kyveilog St. CF11: Card 2F **95**

L

Laburnum Bush La. NP19: Newp 6A **38**
Laburnum Cl. CF62: Barry 6H **105**
NP10: Roger 2A **34**
NP26: Undy 3E **59**
Laburnum Ct. *CF37: R'fln 4H 25*
(off Poplar Rd.)
Laburnum Dr. NP4: New I 4H **7**
NP19: Newp 5H **37**
NP44: H'lys 5C **10**
Laburnum Gro. NP26: Pskwt 5H **61**
Laburnum Pl. CF5: F'wtr 1H **93**
Laburnum Ter. CF37: R'fln 4H **25**
NP26: Pskwt 5H **61**
Laburnum Way CF64: Din P 3H **107**
CF64: P'rth 2C **108**
NP16: Bul 4E **63**
Ladybench NP44: Coed E 4D **10**
Ladyhill Grn. NP19: Newp 5A **38**
Ladyhill Rd. NP19: Newp 5A **38**
Lady Isle Ho. CF11: Card 3A **102**
Lady Margaret Ct. CF23: Pen L 6D **86**
NP16: Bul 6F **63**
Lady Margaret Ter. CF24: Card 4D **96**
Lady Mary Rd. CF23: Pen L 5B **86**
Ladysmith Rd. CF23: Pen L 6D **86**
Ladywell NP44: Pnwd 6E **9**
Lake Hill Dr. CF71: C'bri 4D **90**
Lakelands Ct. *CF23: Cyn 1A 86*
(off Rhyd-y-Penau Rd.)
Lake Rd. NP19: Newp 2A **56**
Lake Rd. E. CF23: Cyn 2B **86**
Lake Rd. Nth. CF23: Cyn 2A **86**
Lake Rd. W. CF23: Cyn 2A **86**
Lakeside CF62: Barry 5E **117**
Lakeside Cl. NP44: L'tnam 1A **20**
Lakeside Dr. CF23: Cyn 2B **86**
NP10: Coedk 5D **52**
Lakeview NP44: L'tnam 1A **20**
Lake Vw. Cl. CF23: Cyn 3B **86**
Lakin Dr. CF62: Barry 5E **105**
Laleston Cl. CF5: Ely 5G **93**
CF63: Barry 5A **106**
Lamb Cl. NP20: Newp 2G **53**
Lambert Cl. NP20: Newp 2B **36**
Lamberton St. CF24: Card 4D **96**
Lambert St. NP20: Newp 2B **36**
Lamb La. NP18: P'hir 6E **13**
Lambourne Cres. CF14: L'shn 6G **71**
NP20: Bet 6F **19**
Lambourne Wlk. NP20: Bet 6F **19**
Lambourne Way NP20: Bet 5F **19**
Lamby Ind. Pk. CF3: Rum 6B **88**
Lamby Way CF3: Rum 1G **97**
CF24: Card 1G **97**
Lamby Way Workshops CF3: Rum 5A **88**
Lancaster Dr. CF38: Llan F 4D **42**
Lancaster Rd. NP4: New I 1G **9**
Lancaster Way NP16: Chep 2D **62**
Lancers Way NP10: Duf 4H **53**
Lan Cl. CF37: P'prdd 5B **14**
Landau Cl. NP26: Undy 4E **59**
Landings, The CF64: P'rth 6H **101**
Landmark Pl. CF10: Card 4E **5**
Landraw Ct. CF37: P'prdd 6A **14**
Landraw Rd. CF37: P'prdd 6A **14**
Landseer Cl. NP19: Newp 2G **37**
Landwade Cl. CF5: F'wtr 2G **93**
Lane, The CF5: St N 1B **98**
Lanelay Cl. CF72: T Grn 3C **64**
Lanelay Ct. CF72: T Grn 3C **64**
Lanelay Cres. CF37: P'prdd 6B **14**
Lanelay Ind. Est. CF72: T Grn 4C **64**
Lanelay Pk. CF72: T Grn 3C **64**
Lanelay Rd. CF72: T Grn 3C **64**
Lanelay Ter. CF37: P'prdd 6B **14**
Lanes, The CF61: Llan M 3B **110**
Langdale Cl. CF23: Pen L 5C **86**
Langditch La. NP19: Newp 6B **38**
Langham Way CF11: Card 6G **95**
Langland Rd. CF3: Rum 4A **88**
Langlands Rd. CF63: Barry 5C **106**
Langland Way NP19: Newp 2G **55**
Langley Cl. NP26: Magor 3C **58**
Langport Av. CF3: L'rmy 1B **88**
LANGSTONE 1G **39**
Langstone Bus. Village
NP18: L'stne 1E **39**
Langstone Cotts. NP18: L'stne 1E **39**
Langstone Ct. NP44: C'brn 4E **11**
Langstone Ct. Rd. NP18: L'stne 3F **39**
Langstone La. NP18: L'stne, L'wrn 4F **39**
LANGSTONE PARK 1F **39**
Lanhydrock Cl. CF3: St M 1D **88**
Lanpark Rd. CF37: P'prdd 5C **14**
Lansbury Cl. CF83: Caer 4B **28**
LANSBURY PARK 5F **29**
Lansdale Dr. CF38: Tont 2G **43**
Lansdowne NP4: Seba 2E **9**
Lansdowne Av. CF14: R'ina 1E **85**
Lansdowne Av. E. CF11: Card 4D **94**
Lansdowne Av. W. CF11: Card 4D **94**
Lansdowne Gdns. NP44: L'tnam 2A **20**
Lansdowne Rd. CF5: Card 3D **94**
NP18: C'ln 5H **21**
NP20: Newp 1H **53**
Lantrisant Ind. Est. CF72: L'sant 5D **40**
Lanwern Rd. CF37: P'prdd 1B **24**
Lanwood Rd. CF37: P'prdd 5B **14**
Lapwing Av. NP26: Cald 6D **60**
Lapwing Cl. CF64: P'rth 6E **109**
Larch Cl. NP4: New I 5G **7**
Larch Ct. CF15: Tong 4H **69**
NP20: Malp 4A **20**
Larch Dr. CF72: C Inn 3H **65**
Larch Gro. CF14: L'vne 2B **72**
CF83: Caer 4E **29**
NP18: Under 3H **39**
NP20: Malp 4A **20**
Larch Ho. CF14: Whit 1A **84**
Larchwood CF5: Wen 5D **98**
Larkfield Av. NP16: Bul 3E **63**
Larkfield Cl. NP18: C'ln 3F **21**
Larkfield Gro. NP16: Chep 3D **62**
Larkfield Pk. NP16: Chep 3D **62**
Larkhill Cl. NP16: Bul 3E **63**
Larkwood Av. CF64: P'rth 3E **109**
Lascelles Dr. CF23: Pontp 4H **73**
Latch Sq. *NP20: Newp 6C 36*
(off Alma St.)
Latteys Cl. CF14: Heath 2F **85**
Laugharne Av. CF3: Rum 4A **88**
Laugharne Ct. CF62: Barry 6H **105**
Laugharne Rd. CF3: Rum 4A **88**
Launcelot Cres. CF14: Thorn 3F **71**
Laundry Rd. CF37: P'prdd 6B **14**
Laural Wlk. NP44: Pnwd 5C **8**
Laura St. CF37: T'rest 1D **24**
CF63: Barry 6D **106**
Laureate Cl. CF3: L'rmy 6H **73**
Laurel Av. CF37: R'fln 5H **25**
Laurel Cl. NP26: Undy 3E **59**
Laurel Ct. CF5: F'wtr 1H **93**
CF62: Barry 4E 117
(off St Nicholas Cl.)
CF83: B'ws 3G **29**
Laurel Cres. NP20: Malp 5B **20**
NP26: Undy 4F **59**
(not continuous)
Laureldene CF72: L'harry 5A **78**
Laurel Dr. NP10: Bass 6D **34**
Laurel Grn. NP44: Up Cwm 5B **8**
Laurel Rd. NP10: Bass 6B **34**
Laurels, The CF14: L'vne 2A **72**
Laurels Bus. Pk., The CF3: Rum 5B **88**
Lauriston Cl. CF5: Ely 1G **99**
Lauriston Pk. CF5: Ely 1G **99**
Lavender Gro. CF5: F'wtr 1G **93**
Lavender Way NP10: Roger 2H **33**
LAVERNOCK 1D **120**
Lavernock Point Nature Reserve 3D **120**
Lavernock Rd. CF64: P'rth, Sul 3D **108**
CF64: Sul 2B **120**
Lavery Cl. NP19: Newp 2G **37**
Lawns, The NP26: Magor 4C **58**
Lawn Ter. CF37: T'rest 2E **25**
LAWRENCE HILL 3H **37**
Lawrence Hill NP19: Newp 4H **37**
(not continuous)
Lawrence Hill Av. NP19: Newp 4H **37**
Lawrence St. CF83: Caer 6D **28**
Lawrenny Av. CF11: Card 5D **94**
Laybourne Cl. NP44: Pnwd 1G **11**
Laytonia Av. CF14: Card 5G **85**
Leach Rd. NP20: Bet 4E **19**
Lea Cl. NP20: Bet 5F **19**
NP26: Undy 3D **58**
Leacroft Pl. CF23: Pontp 4E **73**
Leadon Ct. NP44: Thorn 1C **10**
Lead St. CF24: Card 3D **96**
Leamington Rd. CF14: R'ina 1D **84**
Leas, The NP44: Pnwd 6C **8**
LECKWITH 2D **100**
Leckwith Av. CF11: Card 4E **95**
Leckwith Cl. CF11: Card 5F **95**
Leckwith Ct. CF5: Ely 5G **93**
Leckwith Ind. Est. CF11: Card 1F **101**
Leckwith M. CF11: Card 4E **95**
Leckwith Pl. CF11: Card 4F **95**
Leckwith Rd. CF11: Card 4F **95**
CF11: Leck 2D **100**
CF64: Din P 2D **100**
CF64: L'dgh 4E **101**
Leckwith Rd. Interchange CF11: Card 6E **95**
Leckwith Stadium 5F **95**
LECWYDD 2D **100**
Ledbrooke Cl. NP44: C'brn 4E **11**
Ledbury Dr. NP20: Newp 3C **36**
LEECHPOOL 3H **61**
Leechpool NP26: Pskwt 2H **61**
Lee Cl. CF23: L'dyrn 3D **86**
CF64: Din P 1H **107**
Lee Ct. CF14: R'ina 4E **71**
Lee Rd. CF63: Barry 1A **118**
Lee St. CF37: P'prdd 6B **14**
Lee Way NP19: Newp 1A **56**
Leeway Ct. NP19: Newp 2A **56**
Lee Way Ind. Est. NP19: Newp 3A **56**
Leicester Dr. NP44: G'mdw 2C **10**
Leicester Rd. NP19: Newp 3E **37**
Leigh Cl. CF61: Bov 3D **110**
Leigh Rd. NP4: Trev 1B **6**
Leighton Ct. NP44: St D 3E **11**
Lennard St. NP19: Newp 5E **37**
Lennox Grn. CF63: Barry 1D **118**
Leoline Cl. CF71: C'bri 3B **90**
Leon Av. CF15: Taff W 2E **69**
Le Pouliguen Way CF61: Llan M 3C **110**
Leslie Grn. Ct. NP10: Duf 3H **53**
Leslie Ter. NP10: Roger 5D **34**
Letterston Rd. CF3: Rum 3A **88**
Letton Rd. CF10: Card 6B **96**
Lettons Way CF64: Din P 1G **107**
Letty St. CF24: Card 1A **96**
Leven Cl. CF23: Cyn 2B **86**
Lewis Cl. NP20: Newp 6C **36**
Lewis Dr. CF83: Caer 4B **28**
Lewis Rd. CF24: Card 4D **96**
CF64: L'dgh 4E **101**
Lewis St. CF11: Card 4G **95**
CF37: P'prdd 1C **24**
CF37: T'rest 2E **25**
CF38: Chu V 3E **43**
CF62: Barry 3E **117**
CF72: P'clun 5D **64**
CF83: Mac 2G **31**
Lewis Ter. CF37: P'prdd 5C **14**
CF83: L'brad 1B 28
(off De Winton Ter.)
NP4: P'nydd 1A **6**
Lewis Vw. NP10: Roger 4D **34**
Lewis Way NP16: Bul 6F **63**
Lewis Wood NP4: P'nydd 1A **6**
Leydene Cl. NP11: Ris 4D **16**
Leyshon Cl. CF15: Taff W 6D **44**
Leyshon St. CF37: P'prdd 2B **24**
Libeneth Rd. NP19: Newp 5G **37**
Library Cl. CF37: R'fln 4G **25**
Library Rd. CF37: P'prdd 6C **14**
Library St. CF5: Card 3F **95**

Liddell Cl. CF23: Pontp .4H **73**
Liddicoat Ct. CF63: Barry .1C **118**
Lidmore Rd. CF62: Barry .2E **117**
Lighthouse Pk. NP10: St Bri W .5H **77**
Lighthouse Rd. NP10: Duf, St Bri W .3H **53**
Lilac Cl. CF5: F'wtr .6G **83**
Lilac Dr. CF38: Llan F .5C **42**
Lilac Gro. NP10: Roger .2H **33**
Lilburne Cl. CF23: Pontp .4G **73**
Lilburne Dr. NP19: Newp .5F **37**
Lili Mai CF63: Barry .4B **106**
Lilleshall St. NP19: Newp .5E **37**
Lily St. CF24: Card .2C **96**
Lily Way NP10: Roger .3A **34**
Limebourne Ct. CF14: Whit .4C **84**
Lime Cl. CF15: Rad .3G **83**
NP20: Newp .1C **54**
Lime Cres. NP19: Newp .5H **37**
Lime Gro. CF5: F'wtr .6F **83**
CF62: E Bre .2B **112**
Limes, The CF71: C'bri .3D **90**
NP26: Undy .4D **58**
Limes Ct. CF71: C'bri .4D **90**
Limeslade Cl. CF5: F'wtr .2B **94**
Lime St. CF37: R'fln .4G **25**
Limetree Cl. CF38: Chu V .3F **43**
Limewood Cl. CF3: St M .6C **74**
Lincoln Cl. NP19: Newp .3F **37**
Lincoln Ct. CF23: L'dyrn .2D **86**
NP18: C'ln .4G 21
(off Caradoc Cl.)
Lincoln St. CF5: Card .3D **94**
Lindbergh Cl. NP19: Newp .6G **37**
Linden Av. CF23: Pen L .6C **86**
Linden Cl. NP16: Bul .5E **63**
Linden Ct. CF72: L'harry .5A **78**
Linden Gro. CF3: Rum .3H **87**
CF83: Caer .4E **29**
Linden Rd. NP19: Newp .4G **37**
Lindway Ct. CF5: Card .2D **94**
Lingholm Cl. CF3: St M .6D **74**
Link Rd. NP4: New I .5G **7**
Links Bus. Pk., The CF3: St M .5F **75**
Linley Cl. NP19: Newp .3E **39**
Linnet Cl. CF23: Pent .6D **72**
Linnet Rd. NP26: Cald .6C **60**
Linton St. NP20: Newp .1D **54**
Lionel Rd. CF5: Card .3D **94**
Lionel Ter. CF37: R'fln .4F **25**
Liscombe St. NP19: Newp .5G **37**
Liscum Way CF62: Barry .6E **105**
Lisnagarvey Ct. CF14: R'ina .5B **70**
Lister Cl. CF38: Chu V .2D **42**
Lister Grn. NP20: Malp .5A **20**
LISVANE .2B 72
Lisvane & Thornhill Station (Rail) .2H 71
Lisvane Rd. CF14: L'vne, L'shn .4A **72**
Lisvane St. CF24: Card .6H **85**
LISWERRY .6A 38
Liswerry Cl. NP44: L'rfn .3B **12**
(not continuous)
Liswerry Dr. NP44: L'rfn .2B **12**
Liswerry Pk. Dr. NP19: Newp .5A **38**
Liswerry Rd. NP19: Newp .6H **37**
(not continuous)
Litchfield Ct. CF11: Card .6B **4** (5H **95**)
Lit. Brynhill La. CF62: Barry .5F **105**
Littlecroft Av. CF5: Ely .3B **94**
Littledene NP44: G'mdw .2D **10**
Lit. Dock St. CF64: P'rth .6H **101**
Lit. Frederick St. CF10: Card .4E **5**
Little Mill CF14: Whit .4C **84**
Lit. Moors Hill CF63: Barry .1C **118**
Little Orchard CF5: L'dff .6B **84**
CF64: Din P .2A **108**
Littleton St. CF11: Card .4G **95**
Livale Cl. NP20: Bet .5G **19**
Livale Ct. NP20: Bet .5G **19**
Livale Rd. NP20: Bet .5G **19**
Livale Wlk. NP20: Bet .5G **19**
Liverpool St. NP19: Newp .3E **37**
Livingstone Pl. NP19: Newp .4E **37**
Livingstone Way CF62: St Ath .2D **112**
(not continuous)
LivingWell Health Club
Cardiff .3C **4** (3A **96**)

Livorno Ho. *CF10: Card .6C 96*
(off Ffordd Garthorne)
Llanarth Cl. CF83: Mac .2H **31**
Llanarth Sq. NP11: Ris .6E **17**
Llanarth St. CF83: Mac .3H **31**
NP20: Newp .5C **36**
Llanbedr Rd. CF5: F'wtr .2A **94**
Llanberis Cl. CF38: Tont .1E **43**
NP10: R'drn .6A **34**
LLANBERTHERY .1H 113
Llanbleddian Ct. CF24: Card .2A **96**
Llanbleddian Gdns. CF24: Card .1D **4** (2A **96**)
LLANBLETHIAN .5C 90
Llanblethian Castle (remains of) .4B **90**
LLANBRADACH .1B 28
Llanbradach Station (Rail) .1B 28
Llanbradach St. CF11: Card .6H **95**
CF37: P'prdd .6B **14**
LLANBYDDERI .1H 113
LLANCADLE .4H 113
Llancaiach Rd. CF14: Whit .3D **84**
LLANCATAL .4H 113
LLANDAFF .1B 94
Llandaff Cathedral .6D **84**
Llandaff Chase CF5: L'dff .6B **84**
Llandaff Cl. CF64: P'rth .3E **109**
Llandaff Ct. CF5: L'dff .1C **94**
Llandaff (for Whitchurch) Station (Rail) .3B 84
Llandaff Grn. NP44: C'brn .1G **11**
LLANDAFF NORTH .4B 84
Llandaff Pl. CF5: L'dff .2E **95**
Llandaff Rd. CF11: Card .2E **95**
Llandaff Sq. CF3: Old M .6B **74**
Llandaff St. NP20: Newp .6A **36**
Llandegefedd Way NP4: New I .6G **7**
Llandegfedd Cl. CF14: Thorn .2H **71**
NP10: Roger .2D **34**
LLANDEGVETH .1H 13
Llandegveth Cl. NP44: C'iog .5H **9**
Llandennis Av. CF23: Cyn .1B **86**
Llandennis Ct. CF23: Cyn .1C **86**
Llandennis Grn. CF23: Cyn .1B **86**
Llandennis Rd. CF23: Cyn .1A **86**
Llandenny Rd. NP26: Magor .5B **58**
Llandenny Wlk. NP44: C'brn .2G **11**
Llanderfel Ct. NP44: Thorn .1C **10**
Llandetty Rd. CF5: F'wtr .2A **94**
LLANDEVENNY .5A 58
Llandilo Cl. CF64: Din P .2A **108**
Llandinam Cres. CF14: Llan N .6D **84**
Llandinam Rd. CF62: Barry .2G **117**
LLANDOCH .4F 101
LLANDOCHE .6D 90
Llandogo Rd. CF3: St M .6D **74**
LLANDOUCHAU .4F 101
LLANDOUGH
CF64 .4F 101
CF71 .6D 90
Llandough Hill CF64: L'dgh .4F **101**
LLANDOUGH HOSPITAL
(YSBYTY LLANDOCHAU) .5F **101**
Llandough St. CF24: Card .2A **96**
Llandough Trad. Est. CF11: Card .3F **101**
Llandovery Cl. CF5: Ely .5G **93**
Llandowlais St. NP44: C'brn, Oakf .4G **11**
Llandow Rd. CF5: Ely .5H **93**
Llandraw Woods CF37: P'prdd .6A **14**
Llandudno Rd. CF3: Rum .3A **88**
Llandyfrig Cl. CF64: Din P .2A **108**
LLANEDERN .2E 87
Llanederyn Dr. CF23: L'dyrn .1E **87**
LLANEDEYRN .2E 87
Llanedeyrn Cl. CF23: Pen L .4D **86**
Llanedeyrn Interchange CF23: L'dyrn .4F **87**
Llanedeyrn Rd. CF23: Pen L .5D **86**
Llanerch Cl. NP4: P'pool .2A **6**
Llanerch Goed CF38: Llan F .2D **42**
Llanerch Path NP44: F'wtr .3D **10**
Llanerch Vineyard .3G **79**
Llanewrwg Way CF3: St M .6C **74**
Llanfabon Ct. CF37: C'fydd .3F **15**
Llanfabon Dr. CF83: B'ws, Tret .2H **29**
LLAN-FAES .1E 111
Llanfair Rd. CF11: Card .2E **95**
CF37: P'prdd .1B **24**

Llanfedw Cl. CF83: Caer .4G **29**
LLANFIHANGEL NEAR ROGIET .3H 59
LLANFIHANGEL-Y-FEDW .5E 51
LLANFIHANGEL-Y-PWLL .4C 100
LLANFLEIDDAN .5C 90
LLANFRECHFA .5D 12
LLANFRECHFA GRANGE HOSPITAL .3C **12**
Llanfrechfa Way NP44: C'brn, L'rfn .3H **11**
Llangattock Ct. NP44: C'iog .6H **9**
Llangattock Rd. CF5: F'wtr .2A **94**
Llangefni Pl. CF14: L'shn .4G **71**
Llangorse Dr. NP10: Roger .2D **34**
Llangorse Path NP44: L'rfn .4A **12**
Llangorse Rd. CF23: Cyn .6C **72**
NP44: L'rfn .3A **12**
Llangranog Pl. CF14: L'shn .4F **71**
Llangranog Rd. CF14: L'shn .4F **71**
Llangwm Pl. CF3: Rum .3A **88**
Llangybi Cl. CF5: Ely .6D **92**
Llangynidr Rd. CF5: F'wtr .2A **94**
LLANHARRY .5A 78
Llanharry Rd. CF72: L'harry, P'clun .4C **78**
LLANHENNOCK .1C 22
LLANHENWG FAWR .1C 22
Llanidloes Rd. CF14: Llan N .5D **84**
LLANILLTUD FAERDREF .5D 42
LLANILLTUD FAWR .3B 110
Llanina Gro. CF3: Rum .2C **88**
LLANISHEN .4F 71
Llanishen Ct. CF14: L'shn .5H **71**
Llanishen Leisure Cen. .5G **71**
Llanishen Sailing Cen. .4B **72**
Llanishen Station (Rail) .4A 72
Llanishen St. CF14: Card .5H **85**
LLANISIEN .4F 71
LLANMAES .1E 111
Llanmaes Rd. CF61: Llan M .3C **110**
Llanmaes St. CF11: Card .1H **101**
Llanmead Gdns. CF62: Rho .5D **114**
Llanmihangel Ri. CF71: L'thian .5B **90**
Llanmihangel Rd. CF71: L'thian .6A **90**
Llanmorlais Rd. CF14: Llan N .6E **85**
Llanon NP44: C'iog .5F **9**
Llanon Rd. CF14: L'shn .4G **71**
Llanover Cl. NP20: Malp .6A **20**
Llanover Hall Arts Cen. .3E **95**
Llanover Rd. CF5: Ely .6D **92**
CF37: P'prdd .5D **14**
Llanover St. CF37: P'prdd .6D **14**
CF63: Barry .1B **118**
Llanquian Cl. CF71: C'bri .4D **90**
Llanquian Rd. CF71: A'thin .2F **91**
LLANRHYMNI .1A 88
LLANRUMNEY .1A 88
Llanrumney Av. CF3: L'rmy .3H **87**
LLANSANFFRAID-AR-ELAI .6H 81
LLANSANFFRAID GWYNLLWG .4G 77
Llansannor Dr. CF10: Card .6G **5** (5B **96**)
Llanstephan Rd. CF3: Rum .4A **88**
LLANTARNAM .6B 12
Llantarnam By-Pass NP44: L'tnam .2B **20**
Llantarnam Cl. NP44: C'brn .3H **11**
(not continuous)
Llantarnam Dr. CF15: Rad .2F **83**
Llantarnam Gdns. NP44: L'tnam .6B **12**
Llantarnam Grange Arts Cen. .1H **11**
Llantarnam Ind. Est. NP44: L'tnam .6A **12**
Llantarnam Ind. Pk. NP44: L'tnam .6H **11**
Llantarnam Leisure Cen. .6A **12**
Llantarnam Pk. Way NP44: L'tnam .6H **11**
Llantarnam Rd. CF14: Card .5F **85**
NP44: C'brn, Oakf .3H **11**
Llanthewy Cl. NP44: C'iog .6H **9**
Llanthewy Rd. NP20: Newp .5A **36**
Llanthony Cl. NP26: Cald .4D **60**
LLANTRISANT .2F 65
Llantrisant Bus. Pk. CF72: L'sant .4E **41**
Llantrisant Castle .2F **65**
Llantrisant Leisure Cen. .2F **65**
Llantrisant Ri. CF5: L'dff .5B **84**
Llantrisant Rd. CF5: Cap L .2E **81**
CF5: F'wtr, St F .3C **82**
CF5: L'dff, Rad .5H **83**
CF37: Pen c, P'prdd .5A **24**
CF38: Bed .4H **41**
CF38: Bed, Llan F .1A **66**

Llantrisant Rd. CF72: C Inn 2H **65**
CF72: Groes F 6H **65**
CF72: P'clun 6D **64**
Llantrisant St. CF24: Card 1H **95**
Llantrithyd Rd. CF71: St H 6H **91**
LLANTWIT FARDRE 5D **42**
Llantwit Fardre Leisure Cen. 2F **43**
Llantwit Fardre Sports Club 2F **43**
Llantwit Gdns. Cl. CF62: St Ath 4D **112**
LLANTWIT MAJOR 3B **110**
Llantwit Major Leisure Cen. 4D **110**
Llantwit Major Rd. CF61: Llan M 1B **110**
CF71: C'bri, L'thian 4A **90**
Llantwit Major Station (Rail) 3C **110**
Llantwit Rd. CF37: T'rest, Tont 3E **25**
CF62: Bov 4F **111**
(not continuous)
CF62: St Ath 5A **112**
Llantwit St. CF24: Card 1E **5** (2B **96**)
Llant Witt St. CF63: Barry 2A **118**
Llanvair Rd. NP19: Newp 3D **36**
LLANVIHANGEL PONTYMOEL 2G **7**
LLANWERN 4F **39**
Llanwern Rd. CF5: Ely 5G **93**
NP19: Newp 2C **38**
NP26: Red 6A **58**
Llanwern St. NP19: Newp 4E **37**
Llanwern Works NP19: Newp 1C **56**
Llanwonno Cl. CF37: P'prdd 5A **14**
(not continuous)
Llanwonno Rd. CF37: P'prdd 5A **14**
LLANYRAFON 3A **12**
Llanyrafon Farm Mus. 3A **12**
Llanyrafon Mill 3A **12**
Llan-yr-Avon Sq. NP44: L'rfn 3A **12**
Llan-yr-Avon Way NP44: L'rfn 3A **12**
Llest Ter. CF38: Llan F 5C **42**
Llety'r Eos *CF62: Rho* *6F* ***115***
(off Bryn y Gloyn)
Llew a Dor Ct. *NP18: C'ln* *5A* ***22***
(off Tram Rd.)
Llewellin St. NP19: Newp 4G **37**
Llewellyn Av. CF5: Ely 3F **93**
Llewellyn Dr. CF83: Caer 5C **28**
Llewellyn Gro. NP20: Malp 4A **20**
Llewellyn St. CF63: Barry 1A **118**
Llewellyn Wlk. NP20: Malp 4A **20**
NP44: C'brn 2G **11**
Llewelyn Goch CF5: St F 2C **82**
Llewelyn St. CF37: P'prdd 5A **14**
Lloft Deri CF14: R'ina 6E **71**
Lloyd Av. CF5: L'dff 2B **94**
CF62: Barry 1G **117**
Lloyd George Av. CF10: Card 6E **5** (5B **96**)
Lloyd Pl. CF3: St M 1E **89**
Lloyd St. NP19: Newp 6G **37**
Llwyd Coed CF14: R'ina 4B **70**
Llwyd-y-Berth CF83: Caer 1A **46**
Llwyn Bryn Melyn CF15: Rad 1E **83**
Llwyn Castan CF23: Pent 6E **73**
Llwyn Celyn NP44: Two L 4F **11**
Llwyncrwn Rd. CF38: Bed 5H **41**
Llwyn David CF62: Barry 3G **117**
Llwyn Deri Cl. NP10: Bass 1A **52**
Llwynderi Rd. NP20: Newp 5A **36**
Llwynderw Rd. CF14: Whit 4F **85**
Llwyn Drysgol CF15: Rad 1E **83**
Llwyn Eithan CF83: Caer 4F **29**
LLWYNELIDDON 5C **98**
Llwynfedw Gdns. CF14: Heath 2F **85**
(not continuous)
Llwynfedw Rd. CF14: Heath 2E **85**
Llwynfen Rd. CF72: P'clun 6D **64**
Llwyn Grug CF14: R'ina 5E **71**
Llwyn Gwyn CF72: L'harry 5A **78**
Llwynmadoc St. CF37: P'prdd 6B **14**
Llwyn Mallt CF15: Tong 5H **69**
Llwyn On NP18: P'hir 1G **21**
Llwynon NP11: Ris 5E **17**
Llwyn-on Cl. CF83: Caer 5B **28**
Llwyn Onn CF14: R'ina 5B **70**
CF72: Tyle 5C **64**
NP44: C'iog 1B **12**
Llwyn-on St. CF83: Caer 5B **28**
Llwyn Passat CF64: P'rth 6A **102**
Llwynpennau Cotts. CF72: Groes F 1B **80**
Llwyn Rhosyn CF14: R'ina 5E **71**
Llwyn-y-Grant Pl. CF23: Pen L 5D **86**
Llwyn-y-Grant Rd. CF23: Pen L 5D **86**
Llwyn-y-Grant Ter. CF23: Pen L 5D **86**
Llwyn-y-Pia Rd. CF14: L'vne 2B **72**
Llyn Berwyn Cl. NP10: Roger 3D **34**
Llyn Celyn Cl. NP10: Roger 2D **34**
Llyn Cl. CF23: Cyn 2B **86**
Llyn Pandy CF83: B'ws 3F **29**
Llys Cambria CF83: L'brad 1B **28**
Llys Caradog CF15: Cre 6D **66**
Llys Catwg CF72: T Grn 3E **65**
Llys Celyn *CF38: Tont* *2G* ***43***
(off Cedar Cres.)
Llys Coed CF37: Glync 1D **14**
Llys Coed Derw CF38: Llan F 3D **42**
Llys Corrwg CF37: R'fln 4H **25**
Llys Deri CF72: L'harry 5A **78**
Llys Derwen CF37: Glync 1D **14**
CF72: L'sant 3F **65**
Llys Dewi CF15: Cre 6E **67**
CF61: Llan M 2B **110**
Llys Dwynwen CF61: Llan M 1B **110**
Llys Dyfodwg CF15: Cre 1E **81**
Llys Dyfrig CF15: Cre 1D **80**
Llys Fach CF38: Chu V 3F **43**
LLYS-FAEN 2B **72**
Llys Gth. CF38: Llan F, Chu V 2D **42**
Llys Gwent CF63: Barry 5C **106**
Llys Gwynno CF15: Cre 1D **80**
Llys Gwyrdd NP44: H'lys 6C **10**
Llys Hafn CF15: Taff W 2E **69**
Llys Hanner Erw CF83: Caer 4D **28**
Llys Illtyd CF15: Cre 6D **66**
Llys Joseph CF72: L'harry 4A **78**
Llys Llywelyn CF38: Llan F 3D **42**
Llys Maelwg CF72: T Grn 3E **65**
Llys Nant Pandy CF83: Caer 5C **28**
Llys Nant yr Aber CF83: Caer 5B **28**
Llys Pegasus CF14: L'shn 5G **71**
Llys Pum Cyfair CF14: Llan N 5E **85**
Llys Steffan CF61: Llan M 1B **110**
Llys Tal-y-Bont Rd. CF14: Card 6G **85**
Llys Teilo CF15: Cre 1E **81**
CF61: Llan M 2B **110**
CF72: T Grn 3E **65**
Llys Tripp CF15: Gwae G 2E **69**
Llys Tudful CF15: Cre 6E **67**
Llys ty Gwyn CF37: P'prdd 5E **15**
Llyswen CF83: Mac 2F **31**
Llyswen Rd. CF23: Cyn 1B **86**
Llyswen Wlk. NP44: L'rfn 4A **12**
Llys-y-Celyn CF83: Caer 4E **29**
Llys y Coed CF62: Barry 3E **117**
Llys-y-Fedwen CF83: Caer 5E **29**
Llys y Fran CF38: Chu V 3E **43**
Llys y Gored Ddu CF10: Card 1G **95**
Llywelyn Rd. NP44: C'brn 1G **11**
Llywn y Gog CF62: Rho 6F **115**
Lobelia Cl. NP10: Roger 3A **34**
Lochaber St. CF24: Card 6C **86**
Locke Gro. CF3: St M 1E **89**
Locke St. NP20: Newp 4B **36**
Lock Keepers Ct. CF10: Card 1H **95**
Locks Rd. CF10: Card 3C **102**
Lock Ter. CF37: P'prdd 5D **14**
Lodden Cl. NP20: Bet 5G **19**
Lodge Av. NP18: C'ln 4G **21**
Lodge Cl. CF14: L'vne 1A **72**
Lodge Hill NP18: C'ln 4F **21**
NP18: L'wrn 4F **39**
Lodge Rd. NP18: C'ln 5E **21**
Lodge Way NP26: Pskwt 5F **61**
Lodge Wood NP4: New I, P'pool 4E **7**
Lodwick Ri. CF3: St M 2E **89**
Loftus St. CF5: Card 3D **94**
Lombard St. CF62: Barry 2H **117**
Lomond Cres. CF23: Cyn 2C **86**
Loncae Porth CF14: R'ina 4E **71**
Lon Cefn Mably CF62: Rho 6D **114**
Lon Cwrt Ynyston CF11: Leck 1E **101**
London St. NP19: Newp 4E **37**
Lon Elai CF72: P'clun 5D **64**
Lon Fach CF14: R'ina 6D **70**
CF83: Caer 1B **46**
Lon Fawr CF83: Caer 1B **46**
Lon Fferm Felin CF62: Barry 3D **116**
Long Acre NP44: F'wtr 4D **10**
Longacre Cl. CF63: Barry 5D **106**
CF72: L'sant 3G **65**
Lon Ganol CF14: R'ina 6D **70**
Longbridge NP18: P'hir 1F **21**
Longbridge Ct. *NP11: Ris* *4D* ***16***
(off St Mary St.)
Longcroft Rd. NP26: Cald 5C **60**
Longcross Ct. CF24: Card 2G **5** (3C **96**)
Longcross St. CF24: Card 2H **5** (3C **96**)
Longditch Rd. NP19: Newp 2B **56**
Longfellow Cl. NP26: Cald 5B **60**
Longfellow Ct. NP26: Cald 6B **60**
Longfellow Gdns. CF83: Mac 2C **30**
Longfellow Pl. NP26: Cald 6B **60**
Longfellow Rd. NP26: Cald 5B **60**
Long Hollow NP44: C'brn 1G **11**
Longhouse Cl. CF14: L'vne 3A **72**
Longhouse Gro. NP44: H'lys 5B **10**
Longleat Cl. CF14: L'vne 3B **72**
Long Mdw. Ct. CF71: C'bri 3D **90**
Longmeadow Ct. NP19: Newp 6A **38**
Long Mdw. Dr. CF62: Barry 6H **105**
Longmeadow Dr. CF64: Din P 3H **107**
Longreach Cl. CF5: Ely 5D **92**
Long Row *CF37: T'rest* *3E* ***25***
(off Park St.)
NP4: P'pool 5B **6**
Longships Rd. CF10: Card 1F **103**
Longspears Av. CF14: Card 4G **85**
Longtown Gro. NP10: Duf 6G **53**
Longueil Cl. CF10: Card 6C **96**
Longwood Dr. CF14: Whit 6G **69**
Lon Hafren CF83: Caer 2B **46**
Lon Helyg NP44: C'iog 1B **12**
Lon Helygen CF37: Glync 1D **14**
Lon Heulog CF37: R'fln 5G **25**
Lon Isa CF14: R'ina 6D **70**
Lon Isaf CF83: Caer 1B **46**
Lon Lindys CF62: Rho 6E **115**
Lon Madoc CF14: Whit 3E **85**
Lon Nant NP44: Pon'run 6F **9**
Lon-od-Nant CF61: Llan M 4C **110**
Lon Owain CF5: Ely 6F **93**
Lon Penllyn CF14: R'ina 1D **84**
Lon Robin Goch CF83: Caer 6A **28**
Lonsdale Rd. CF23: Pen L 4E **87**
Lon Stephens CF15: Taff W 2F **69**
Lon Ty'n-y-cae CF14: R'ina 1E **85**
Lon Ucha CF14: R'ina 6D **70**
Lon Uchaf CF83: Caer 1B **46**
Lon Werdd CF5: Ely 4E **93**
Lon Werdd Cl. CF5: Ely 4E **93**
Lon-y-Barri CF83: Caer 4B **28**
(not continuous)
Lon y Cadno CF38: Chu V 4E **43**
Lon-y-Castell CF5: Ely 6G **93**
Lon-y-Celyn CF14: Whit 1B **84**
Lon-y-Dail CF14: R'ina 6D **70**
Lon-y-Dderwen CF14: R'ina 6D **70**
Lon-y-Ddraenen CF83: Caer 1B **46**
Lon-y-Deri CF14: R'ina 6D **70**
CF83: Caer 1B **46**
Lon-y-Ffin CF5: Ely 4E **93**
Lon-y-Fran CF83: Caer 6A **28**
Lon-y-Fro CF15: P'rch 5A **68**
Lon-y-Garwa CF83: Caer 3B **46**
Lon y Goch CF15: P'rch 1A **82**
Lon-y-Gors CF83: Caer 1A **46**
Lon-y-Groes CF14: Heath 3F **85**
Lon-y-Llyn CF83: Caer 1B **46**
Lon-y-Mynydd CF14: R'ina 6E **71**
Lon y Nant CF14: R'ina 6E **71**
Lon-y-Parc CF14: Whit 2D **84**
Lon-yr-Awel CF72: P'clun 5E **65**
Lon-yr-Efail CF5: Ely 6F **93**
Lon-y-Rhedyn CF83: Caer 1A **46**
(not continuous)
Lon-y-Rheydyn CF83: Caer 1B **46**
Lon-y-Rhyd CF14: R'ina 6D **70**
Lon yr Odyn CF83: Caer 5E **29**
Lon yr Ysgol CF83: B'ws 3F **29**
Lon-Ysgubor CF14: R'ina 5D **70**
Lon y Tresglen CF83: Caer 6A **28**
Lon y Twyn CF83: Caer 1D **46**

Lon-y-Waun CF83: Caer 1A **46**
Lon-y-Wern CF83: Caer 1B **46**
Lon-y-Winci CF14: R'ina 5D **70**
Loop Rd. NP16: B'ly 4H **63**
Lord Eldon Dr. NP16: Bul 6F **63**
Lord St. CF64: P'rth 6B **102**
NP19: Newp 3D **36**
Lothian Cres. CF23: Pen L 4D **86**
Loudoun Ho. CF10: Card 6B **96**
Loudoun Sq. CF10: Card 6B **96**
Lougher Cl. CF5: F'wtr 2A **94**
Lougher Pl. CF62: St Ath 5C **112**
Louisa Pl. CF10: Card 1B **102**
Lovage Cl. CF23: Pontp 5E **73**
Love La. CF10: Card 4E **5** (4B **96**)
CF71: L'thian 4C **90**
Loveluck Ct. CF61: Llan M 3B **110**
Lowben Dr. CF15: Morg 5F **69**
Lowdon Ter. CF62: Barry 2G **117**
Lower Acre CF5: Ely 6F **93**
Lwr. Alma Ter. CF37: T'rest 1D **24**
Lwr. Bridge St. NP4: P'pool 3C **6**
Lwr. Cathedral Rd. CF11: Card 4A **4** (4H **95**)
Lwr. Church St. NP16: Chep 1F **63**
Lowerdale Dr. CF72: L'sant 3G **65**
Lwr. Dock St. NP20: Newp 5C **36**
Lwr. Farm Ct. CF62: Rho 5E **115**
Lwr. Glyn Gwyn St. CF83: Tret 3A **30**
Lwr. Guthrie St. CF63: Barry 2A **118**
Lwr. Holmes St. CF63: Barry 1C **118**
LOWER MACHEN 4B **32**
Lwr. Mill Fold NP4: P'pool 4E **7**
Lwr. Morel St. CF63: Barry 2A **118**
LOWER NEW INN 6G **7**
LOWER OCHRWYTH 1E **33**
Lwr. Park Gdns. NP4: P'garn 2C **6**
Lwr. Park Ter. NP4: P'pool 3C **6**
LOWER PENARTH 4D **108**
LOWER PORTKERRY 5H **115**
Lwr. Pyke St. CF63: Barry 2A **118**
Lwr. Rhymney Valley Relief Rd.
CF83: Caer, L'brad 2B **28**
Lwr. Taff Vw. CF37: P'prdd 4E **15**
Lwr. Wyndham Ter. NP11: Ris 6F **17**
Lowfield Dr. CF14: Thorn 3F **71**
Lowland Dr. CF38: Tont 2G **43**
LOWLANDS 5D **8**
Lowlands Cres. NP44: Pnwd 5D **8**
Lowlands Rd. NP44: Pnwd 5E **9**
Lowndes Cl. NP10: Bass 6B **34**
Lowther Ct. CF24: Card 1E **5** (2B **96**)
Lowther Rd. CF24: Card 1E **5** (2B **96**)
Lucas Cl. CF63: Barry 5C **106**
Lucas St. CF24: Card 6A **86**
NP20: Newp 3B **36**
Lucerne Dr. CF14: Thorn 3F **71**
Lucknow St. CF11: Card 6G **95**
Ludlow Cl. CF11: Card 1A **102**
NP19: Newp 5F **37**
NP44: L'rfn 4B **12**
(not continuous)
Ludlow La. CF64: P'rth 1E **109**
Ludlow St. CF11: Card 1H **101**
CF64: P'rth 1E **109**
CF83: Caer 1C **46**
Lulworth Rd. NP18: C'ln 6A **22**
Lundy Cl. CF14: L'shn 5G **71**
Lundy Dr. NP19: Newp 3F **37**
Lupin Gro. NP10: Roger 3A **34**
Lwynpia Cotts. CF15: Morg 5F **69**
Lydford Cl. CF14: R'ina 1D **84**
Lydstep Cres. CF14: Llan N 6D **84**
Lydstep Flats CF14: Llan N 5D **84**
Lydstep Rd. CF62: Barry 6H **105**
Lydwood Cl. CF83: Mac 2G **31**
Lynch Blosse Cl. CF5: L'dff 5A **84**
Lyncroft NP44: G'mdw 2D **10**
Lyncroft Cl. CF3: Old M 5B **74**
Lyndhurst Av. NP20: Newp 1H **53**
Lyndhurst St. CF11: Card 4F **95**
Lyndon Way NP10: Roger 4D **34**
Lyne Rd. NP11: Ris 6E **17**
NP20: Newp 2C **36**
Lynmouth Cres. CF3: Rum 4G **87**
Lynmouth Dr. CF64: Sul 3G **119**
Lyn Pac Trad. Est. NP44: Pnwd 5E **9**
Lynton Cl. CF3: L'rmy 3H **87**
CF64: Sul 2H **119**
Lynton Ct. CF10: Card 1B **102**
Lynton Pl. CF3: L'rmy 3G **87**
Lynton Ter. CF3: L'rmy 3G **87**
Lynwood Ct. CF24: Card 1H **5** (2C **96**)
Lyon Cl. CF11: Card 2F **101**
Lyric Way CF14: Thorn 3G **71**
Lysander Ct. CF24: Card 2G **97**
Lytham Gro. CF3: St M 5E **75**

M

Maberly Cl. CF14: L'shn 6A **72**
Macaulay Av. CF3: L'rmy 6H **73**
Macauley Gdns. NP20: Newp 2G **53**
McCale Av. CF5: F'wtr 2A **94**
McCarthy's Ct. NP20: Newp 5C **36**
Macdonald Cl. CF5: Ely 5E **93**
Macdonald Pl. CF5: Ely 5E **93**
Macdonald Rd. CF5: Ely 5E **93**
MACHEN 2F **31**
Machen Cl. CF3: St M 6D **74**
NP11: Ris 6F **17**
Machen Pl. CF11: Card 5A **4** (4G **95**)
Machen St. CF11: Card 6G **95**
CF64: P'rth 1D **108**
NP11: Ris 5D **16**
Mackintosh Pl. CF24: Card 6B **86**
Mackintosh Rd. CF37: P'prdd 6D **14**
Mackintosh Sports Club 1C **96**
McLay Ct. CF5: F'wtr 2A **94**
McQuade Pl. CF62: Barry 5G **117**
Madoc Cl. CF64: Din P 2A **108**
Madocke Rd. NP16: Sed 3G **63**
Madoc Rd. CF24: Card 3F **97**
Madoc St. CF37: P'prdd 1C **24**
Maelfa CF23: L'dyrn 3E **87**
Maelog Cl. CF72: P'clun 5D **64**
Maelog Pl. CF14: Card 6G **85**
Maelog Rd. CF14: Whit 3E **85**
Maendy Pl. NP44: Pnwd 5C **8**
Maendy Rd. CF37: Pen c 3B **24**
CF38: Up Chu 3B **24**
CF71: Maen 1F **91**
Maendy Sq. NP44: Pnwd 6C **8**
Maendy Way
NP44: C'brn, Pnwd, Up Cwm 5C **8**
Maendy Wood Ri. NP44: Pnwd 6C **8**
Maerdy Cl. NP20: Newp 2H **53**
Maerdy La. CF14: L'vne 3C **72**
MAERUN 4A **76**
MAES AWYR RHYNGWLADOL CAERDYDD 3F **115**
Maes Briallu CF83: Caer 5F **29**
Maes Brith y Garn CF23: Pontp 4F **73**
Maes Cadwgan CF15: Cre 6E **67**
Maes Cefn Mabley CF72: L'sant 1F **65**
Maes Coed Rd. CF37: P'prdd 1B **24**
Maesderwen Cres. NP4: P'pool 4D **6**
Maesderwen Ri. NP4: Grif 4D **6**
Maesderwen Rd. NP4: P'pool 4D **6**
Maes Ganol CF37: R'fln 5A **26**
MAES-GLAS 3H **53**
Maes Glas CF14: Whit 4C **84**
CF37: Glync 1D **14**
CF62: Barry 3E **117**
CF83: Caer 1E **47**
Maesglas Av. NP20: Newp 2H **53**
Maesglas Cl. NP20: Newp 3H **53**
Maesglas Cres. NP20: Newp 2H **53**
(not continuous)
Maesglas Gro. NP20: Newp 3H **53**
Maesglas Ind. Est. NP20: Newp 2A **54**
Maesglas Retail Pk. NP20: Newp 2C **54**
(Docks Way)
NP20: Newp 2B **54**
(Port Rd.)
Maesglas Rd. NP20: Newp 2H **53**
(not continuous)
Maesglas St. NP20: Newp 3H **53**
Maes Gwyn CF83: Caer 1D **46**
Maesgwyn NP44: Pnwd 5D **8**
Maes Hir CF83: Caer 4B **28**
Maes Ifor CF15: Taff W 6E **45**
Maes Illtuds CF61: Llan M 2C **110**
Maes Lindys CF62: Rho 6F **115**
Maes Lloi CF71: A'thin 2F **91**
Maes Maelwg CF38: Bed 5H **41**
Maesmawr Rd. CF38: Tont 2A **44**
Maes Sarn CF72: L'sant 1F **65**
Maes Slowes Leyes CF62: Rho 6F **115**
Maesteg Cres. CF38: Tont 2G **43**
Maesteg Gdns. CF38: Tont 2G **43**
Maesteg Gro. CF38: Tont 2G **43**
Maes Trane CF38: Bed 5A **42**
Maes Trisant CF72: T Grn 3E **65**
(not continuous)
Maes Uchaf CF37: R'fln 5A **26**
Maes Watford CF83: Caer 3B **46**
Maes y Briallu CF15: Morg 6E **69**
Maes y Bryn CF15: Rad 6F **69**
CF23: Pontp 5G **73**
Maes-y-Bryn Rd. CF23: Pontp 1G **73**
Maes-y-Celyn NP4: Grif 5D **6**
MAESYCOED 1A **24**
Maes-y-Coed CF62: Barry 5D **116**
Maesycoed Rd. CF37: P'prdd 6B **14**
Maes-y-Coed Rd. CF14: Heath 1F **85**
Maes y Cored CF14: Whit 1A **84**
Maes-y-Crochan CF3: St M 6F **75**
Maes y Crofft CF15: Morg 6E **69**
Maes-y-Cwm-St CF63: Barry 2H **117**
Maes-y-Dderwen CF15: Cre 1E **81**
Maes-y-Deri CF14: R'ina 6D **70**
CF37: P'prdd 5A **14**
Maes y Draenog CF15: Tong 3H **69**
Maes-y-Drudwen CF83: Caer 1A **46**
Maes y Felin CF37: R'fln 5A **26**
Maes-y-Felin CF14: R'ina 1D **84**
CF83: Caer 6D **28**
Maesyfelin Cres. CF72: P'clun 6C **64**
Maes y Fioled CF15: Morg 6E **69**
Maes y Gad CF5: St F 2D **92**
Maes-y-Gollen CF15: Cre 6E **67**
Maes y Grug CF38: Chu V 2E **43**
Maes y Gwair CF15: Morg 6D **68**
Maes y Gwenyn CF62: Rho 6G **115**
Maes y Llech CF15: Rad 2H **83**
Maes-y-Nant CF15: Cre 6D **66**
Maes y Pandy CF83: B'ws 2E **29**
Maes y Parc CF14: R'ina 1D **84**
Maes-yr-Afon CF72: P'clun 1C **78**
CF83: Caer 4F **29**
Maes yr Annedd CF5: Card 2D **94**
Maes yr Awel CF15: Rad 1F **83**
CF37: R'fln 5A **26**
Maes yr Eglwys CF38: Up Chu 1E **43**
Maes yr Haf CF14: R'ina 5B **70**
Maes yr Hafod CF15: Cre 6E **67**
Maes yr Haul Cotts. *CF72: C Inn* *3G 65*
(off Taff Cotts.)
Maes yr Haul Crossing CF72: C Inn 3G **65**
Maes yr Hedydd CF23: Pontp 3F **73**
Maes-y-Rhedyn CF15: Cre 1E **81**
CF72: T Grn 3D **64**
Maes y Rhiw Ct. NP44: G'mdw 2C **10**
Maes yr Odyn CF15: Morg 6E **69**
Maes-yr-Onnen CF15: Cre 1E **81**
Maes yr Orchis CF15: Morg 6E **69**
Maes-yr-Ysgol CF62: Barry 2G **117**
Maes-y-Sarn CF15: P'rch 4H **67**
Maes-y-Siglen CF83: Caer 6A **28**
Maes y Wennol CF23: Pontp 4F **73**
Maes-y-Wennol CF72: Mis 5F **65**
Mafeking Rd. CF23: Pen L 6C **86**
Magellan Cl. CF62: Barry 5A **106**
Magna Porta Gdns. NP44: L'tnam 1B **20**
Magnolia Cl. CF23: Pent 6D **72**
NP16: Bul 5F **63**
NP20: Malp 4B **20**
Magnolia Way CF38: Llan F 5C **42**
MAGOR 4D **58**
Magor Rd. NP18: L'stne 6H **23**
NP26: Wilc 2A **58**
MAGOR SERVICE AREA 2C **58**
Magor St. NP19: Newp 6F **37**
Magpie Rd. CF62: St Ath 3F **111**
Magretion Pl. CF10: Card 6B **96**
MAGWYR 4D **58**
Maia Ho. CF10: Card 1D **102**

Maillard's Haven CF64: P'rth 4F **109**
Main Av. CF23: Pen L 6E **87**
CF37: T'rest 1B **44**
MAINDEE 4E **37**
Maindee Pde. NP19: Newp 3E **37**
Maindee Swimming Pool 4E **37**
Maindee Ter. NP44: Pnwd 6D **8**
MAINDY 5F **85**
Maindy Ct. CF38: Chu V 2E **43**
Maindy M. CF24: Card 1A **96**
Maindy Pool & Cycle Track 6G **85**
Maindy Rd. CF24: Card 6G **85**
Main Rd. CF15: Gwae G, Taff W 6D **44**
CF38: Chu V, Tont 3E **43**
CF72: C Inn 3G **65**
CF72: Groes F 6B **66**
NP26: Pskwt 5G **61**
NP26: Undy 4D **58**
Main St. CF63: Barry 6B **106**
Maitland Pl. CF11: Card 5G **95**
Maitland St. CF14: Card 5G **85**
Major Cl. NP44: Ty C 3B **10**
Major Rd. CF5: Card 4F **95**
Malcolm Sargent Cl. NP19: Newp 5B **38**
Maldwyn St. CF11: Card 2F **95**
Malefant St. CF24: Card 6A **86**
Mall, The NP44: C'brn 2H **11**
Mallard Av. NP26: Cald 6C **60**
Mallard Cl. CF3: St M 6C **74**
Mallards Reach CF3: M'fld 4G **75**
Mallard Way CF64: P'rth 6E **109**
NP10: Duf 5G **53**
Mallory Cl. CF62: St Ath 2D **112**
Malmesbury Cl. NP20: Newp 3C **36**
Malmesmead Rd. CF3: L'rmy 6A **74**
MALPAS 4A **20**
Malpas Cl. CF3: St M 6D **74**
Malpas Junc. NP20: Newp 2A **36**
Malpas La. NP20: Bryng 1B **36**
Malpas Rd. NP20: Malp, Newp 3A **20**
(not continuous)
Malpas St. NP44: C'brn 3G **11**
Malpas Vs. NP20: Malp 4A **20**
Malthouse, The CF10: Card 5D **4**
Malthouse Av. CF23: Pontp 3G **73**
Malthouse La. NP4: P'pool 2B **6**
Malthouse Rd. NP18: C'ln 2E **21**
NP44: L'tnam 2A **20**
Maltings, The CF23: Pent 4F **73**
CF24: Card 4E **97**
NP20: Newp 1E **55**
Malus Av. CF38: Llan F 6C **42**
Malvern Cl. NP11: Ris 6H **17**
NP19: Newp 1G **37**
Malvern Dr. CF14: L'shn 6F **71**
Malvern Rd. NP19: Newp 4D **36**
Malvern Ter. NP11: Ris 6E **17**
Manchester St.
NP19: Newp 3D **36**
Mandeville Pl. CF11: Card 4G **95**
Mandeville St. CF11: Card 4G **95**
Manitoba Cl. CF23: Cyn 2C **86**
Manley Rd. NP20: Newp 5A **36**
Manod Rd. CF14: Llan N 5C **84**
Manor, The NP44: L'tnam 2A **20**
Manorbier Cl. CF38: Tont 1F **43**
CF64: Din P 2A **108**
Manorbier Ct. CF62: Barry 5H **105**
Manorbier Cres. CF3: Rum 3A **88**
Manorbier Dr. NP44: L'rfn 2A **12**
Manor Chase CF38: Bed 6A **42**
NP26: Undy 4F **59**
Manor Cl. CF14: Whit 2D **84**
NP11: Ris 6F **17**
Manor Cotts. CF72: Taly 2C **78**
Manor Ct. CF38: Chu V 2E **43**
NP11: Ris 5F **17**
NP26: Rog 6A **60**
Manor Ga. NP44: G'mdw 2D **10**
Manor Hill CF72: Mis 6F **65**
Manor Pk. CF61: Llan M 4C **110**
NP10: Duf 5H **53**
Manor Ri. CF14: Whit 3E **85**
Manor Rd. NP11: Ris 6F **17**
Manor Sq. CF61: Llan M 5C **110**
Manor St. CF14: Card 5H **85**
Manor Way CF14: Heath, Whit 2E **85**
NP11: Ris 6F **17**
NP16: Chep *2E* ***63***
(off Dell Vw.)
NP26: Pskwt 5G **61**
Manor Wood NP16: Chep 2C **62**
Mansell Av. CF5: Ely 5D **92**
Mansel St. NP19: Newp 4G **37**
Mansfield St. CF11: Card 4G **95**
Manston Cl. CF5: L'dff 6A **84**
Maple Av. NP11: Ris 5F **17**
NP16: Bul 4D **62**
Maple Cl. CF62: Barry 6A **106**
CF72: L'harry 5A **78**
NP18: Under 3H **39**
NP26: Cald 4C **60**
Maple Cres. NP4: Grif 2D **8**
Maple Gdns. NP11: Ris 1G **33**
Maple Rd. CF5: F'wtr 6F **83**
CF64: P'rth 2C **108**
NP4: Grif 1D **8**
Maple Rd. Sth. NP4: Grif 2D **8**
Maple St. CF37: R'fln 4G **25**
Maple Tree Cl. CF15: Rad 1E **83**
Maplewood Av. CF14: Llan N 4B **84**
Marchwood Cl. CF3: Rum 2A **88**
Marconi Av. CF64: P'rth 5H **101**
Marconi Cl. NP20: Malp 5H **19**
Marcross Rd. CF5: Ely 5E **93**
Mardy CF72: Y'erdy 6C **40**
Mardy Cl. CF83: Caer 6E **29**
Mardy Ct. CF11: Card 6A **4** (5H **95**)
Mardy Cres. CF83: Caer 6E **29**
Mardy Rd. CF3: Rum 6B **88**
(Lamby Ind. Pk.)
CF3: Rum 5A **88**
(New Rd.)
Mardy St. CF11: Card 6A **4** (5H **95**)
(not continuous)
Margam Cl. CF62: St Ath 2C **112**
Margam Rd. CF14: Card 5F **85**
Margaret Av. CF62: Barry 4H **105**
NP19: Newp 2D **36**
Margaret St. CF37: P'prdd 5A **14**
Margretts Way NP26: Cald 4C **60**
Marguerites Way CF5: Ely 4E **93**
Maria Ct. CF10: Card 6B **96**
Maria St. CF10: Card 5B **96**
MARIE CURIE HOSPICE 2F **109**
Marigold Cl. NP10: Roger 3H **33**
Marina Ct. NP19: Newp 6E **21**
Marine Dr. CF62: Barry 5C **116**
Marine Pde. CF64: P'rth 3F **109**
Mariner's Hgts. CF64: P'rth 6B **102**
Mariners Reach NP16: Bul 6G **63**
Mariners Way CF62: Rho 6D **114**
Mariner Way NP19: Newp 2E **55**
Marine Ter. NP26: Sud 6H **61**
Marion Ct. CF14: L'shn 4A **72**
Marion Pl. NP20: Newp 1D **54**
Marion St. CF24: Card 3E **97**
NP20: Newp 1C **54**
Marionville Gdns. CF5: F'wtr 1A **94**
Maritime Ct. CF83: B'ws 3E **29**
Maritime Ind. Est. CF37: P'prdd 2A **24**
Maritime St. CF37: P'prdd 1B **24**
Maritime Ter. CF37: P'prdd 1B **24**
Market, The CF37: P'prdd 6C **14**
Market Arc. *NP4: P'pool* *3C* ***6***
(off Crane St.)
NP20: Newp 4C **36**
Market Hall, The *NP4: P'pool* *3C* ***6***
(off Market St.)
Market Pl. CF5: Card 3F **95**
Market Rd. CF5: Card 3E **95**
Market St. CF15: Tong 4G **69**
CF37: P'prdd 6C **14**
CF62: Barry 4F **117**
CF83: Caer 1D **46**
NP4: P'pool 3C **6**
NP20: Newp 4C **36**
Mark St. CF11: Card 4A **4** (4H **95**)
Marland Ho. CF10: Card 6C **4** (4A **96**)
Marlborough Cl. CF38: Llan F 5D **42**
CF63: Barry 6C **106**
Marlborough Ho. CF10: Card 4B **4** (4H **95**)
Marlborough Rd. CF23: Pen L 6C **86**
NP19: Newp 4D **36**
NP44: G'mdw 2C **10**
Marlborough Ter. CF10: Card 1G **95**
Marl Ct. CF11: Card 2H **101**
NP44: Thorn 6B **8**
Marle Cl. CF23: Pent 5F **73**
Marloes Cl. CF62: Barry 6H **105**
Marloes Path NP44: G'mdw 2D **10**
Marloes Rd. CF5: Ely 4F **93**
Marlow Cl. NP10: Roger 3D **34**
Marlowe Gdns. NP20: Newp 2G **53**
Marquis Cl. CF62: Barry 5A **118**
Marryat Wlk. NP20: Newp 2G **53**
Marshall Cl. CF5: L'dff 5A **84**
Marsham Ct. CF15: Rad 2G **83**
MARSHFIELD 4A **76**
Marshfield Rd. CF3: Cas, M'fld 2G **75**
Marshfield St. NP19: Newp 6F **37**
Marsh Rd. NP16: Bul 5F **63**
Marston Ct. NP20: Newp 2A **36**
Marston Path NP44: St D 3E **11**
Marten Rd. NP16: Bul 4E **63**
Martindale Rd. NP4: Grif 1E **9**
Martin Rd. CF24: Card 5G **97**
Martins, The NP16: Tut 1G **63**
Martins Rd. NP26: C'ent 1B **60**
Mary Ann St. CF10: Card 5E **5** (4B **96**)
Maryland Rd. NP11: Ris 6E **17**
Maryport Rd. CF23: Pen L 5B **86**
Mary Price Ct. *CF24: Card* *4E* ***97***
(off Aberystwyth St.)
Marysfield Cl. CF3: M'fld 5A **76**
Mary St. CF14: Llan N 5B **84**
CF37: C'fydd 2F **15**
CF83: Tret 3A **30**
Masefield Rd. CF64: P'rth 1C **108**
NP26: Cald 6B **60**
Masefield Va. NP20: Newp 1G **53**
Masefield Way CF37: R'fln 3G **25**
Mathern Cres. NP16: Math 6B **62**
Mathern Rd. NP16: Bul, Math 6C **62**
Mathern Way NP16: Bul 4E **63**
Mathew Wlk. CF5: L'dff 5H **83**
Mathias Cl. CF23: Pen L 6E **87**
Matthew Rd. CF62: Rho 5C **114**
Matthewson Cl. CF14: Llan N 5E **85**
Matthew Ter. CF64: Din P 6F **101**
NP4: P'nydd *1A* ***6***
(off Chapel Rd.)
Matthysens Way CF3: St M 2D **88**
Maugham Cl. NP20: Newp 2H **53**
Maughan La. CF64: P'rth 6B **102**
Maughan Ter. CF64: P'rth 6B **102**
Maureen Av. CF5: Ely 3H **93**
Mavis Gro. CF14: Heath 1E **85**
MAVRID WOODBURY 1F **81**
Maxton Ct. CF83: Caer 6E **29**
Maxwell Rd. CF3: Rum 3H **87**
Mayfair CF5: Cul C 1E **99**
Mayfair Dr. CF14: Thorn 2G **71**
Mayfield Av. CF5: Card 3C **94**
Mayfield Pl. CF72: L'sant 3G **65**
Mayfield Rd. CF37: P'prdd 5B **14**
Mayflower Av. CF14: L'shn 4F **71**
Mayflower Way CF62: Rho 5E **115**
Mayhill Cl. CF14: Thorn 2H **71**
Maynard Ct. CF5: L'dff 1C **94**
Maynes NP44: F'wtr 4D **10**
May St. CF24: Card 6A **86**
(not continuous)
NP19: Newp 4E **37**
Mead La. NP44: C'brn 1G **11**
Meadow, The NP26: Magor 4C **58**
Meadowbank Ct. CF5: F'wtr 5H **83**
Meadow Brook CF38: Chu V 3F **43**
Meadowbrook Av. NP44: Pnwd 5D **8**
Meadow Cl. CF23: Cyn 5D **72**
NP4: Seba 3E **9**
NP11: Cros K 3B **16**
Meadow Cres. CF38: Tont 2G **43**
CF83: Caer 1D **46**
NP11: Ris 1G **33**
Meadow Cft. CF62: Rho 5F **115**
Meadowfield Way CF15: Morg 6E **69**
Meadowgate Cl. CF14: Whit 6B **70**

Meadow Hill CF38: Chu V 3D **42**
Meadowland Dr. NP10: Roger 2G **33**
Meadow La. CF64: P'rth 4D **108**
NP44: C'iog 6H **9**
Meadowlark Cl. CF3: St M 6C **74**
Meadow Ri. NP26: Undy 3D **58**
(not continuous)
Meadows, The CF3: M'fld 4G **75**
CF39: T'fail 1A **40**
NP11: Ris 3B **16**
Meadowside CF64: P'rth 2B **108**
NP44: G'mdw 2B **10**
Meadows Rd. NP19: Newp 4A **56**
Meadow St. CF11: Card 2E **95**
CF37: T'rest 3E **25**
Meadowsweet Dr. CF3: St M 1E **89**
Meadow Va. CF63: Barry 5C **106**
Meadow Vw. CF63: Barry 5D **106**
CF83: B'ws 2E **29**
Meadow Vw. Ct. CF64: Sul 2G **119**
Meadow Wlk. NP16: Chep 2D **62**
Meadow Way CF83: Caer 2H **45**
Meads Cl. NP19: Newp 1A **56**
Meads Ct. NP16: Bul 4E **63**
Meadvale Rd. CF3: St M 1B **88**
Mecca Bingo
Cwmbran **2G 11**
Medart Pl. NP11: Cros K 3B **16**
Medart St. NP11: Cros K 3B **16**
Medieval Village **6D 108**
Medlock Cl. NP20: Bet 5G **19**
Medlock Cres. NP20: Bet 4F **19**
Medlock Wlk. NP20: Bet 4G **19**
Medway Cl. NP20: Bet 4F **19**
Medway Ct. NP20: Bet 4F **19**
Medway Rd. NP20: Bet 5E **19**
Megabowl
Cardiff **6F 87**
Newport **1B 56**
Megan Ct. CF5: Ely 3A **94**
Meggitt Rd. CF62: Barry 5G **105**
Meirion Cl. CF63: Barry 5B **106**
Meirion Pl. CF24: Card 3F **97**
Meirwen Dr. CF5: Ely 1E **99**
Melbourne Ct. CF14: Whit 1D **84**
NP44: C'brn 2F **11**
Melbourne La. CF14: L'shn 5H **71**
Melbourne Rd. CF14: L'shn 5H **71**
Melbourne Way NP20: Newp 6F **35**
Melfort Gdns. NP20: Newp 6H **35**
Melfort Rd. NP20: Newp 6H **35**
Meliden La. CF64: P'rth 2D **108**
Meliden Rd. CF64: P'rth 2D **108**
Melin Corrwg Bus. Parc
CF37: R'fln 6A **26**
Melin Dwr NP10: Drae 6A **32**
Melingriffith Dr. CF14: Whit 2A **84**
Melin Gwlan CF83: Caer 5B **28**
Mellon St. NP20: Newp 5C **36**
Mellyn Mair Bus. Cen. CF3: Rum 5A **88**
Melrose Av. CF23: Pen L 6D **86**
Melrose Cl. CF3: Old M 5D **74**
Melrose Ct. CF11: Card 2E **95**
Melrose Gdns. CF23: Pen L 6D **86**
Melrose St. CF63: Barry 1B **118**
Melville Av. CF3: Old M 5C **74**
Melville Cl. CF62: Barry 4G **105**
Melville Ter. CF83: Caer 5D **28**
Melyn y Gors CF63: Barry 5C **106**
Menai Cl. CF38: Tont 1E **43**
Menai Way CF3: Rum 1B **88**
MENDALGIEF **2C 54**
Mendalgief Retail Pk. NP20: Newp 2B **54**
Mendalgief Rd. NP20: Newp 1B **54**
Mendip Cl. NP11: Ris 6H **17**
NP19: Newp 3A **38**
Mendip Rd. CF3: L'rmy 2G **87**
Mendip Vw. CF63: Barry 1C **118**
Meon Cl. NP20: Bet 5H **19**
Merchants Hill NP4: P'nydd, P'pool 1A **6**
Merchants Hill Cl. NP4: P'nydd 1A **6**
Merches Gdns. CF11: Card 6B **4** (5H **95**)
Merches Pl. CF11: Card 5H **95**
Mercian Way NP16: Sed 3G **63**
Mercia Rd. CF24: Card 3F **97**
Meredith Cl. NP20: Newp 1H **53**
Meredith Rd. CF24: Card 3F **97**
Mere Path NP44: G'mdw 2D **10**
Merevale CF64: Din P 2F **107**
Merganser Ct. CF63: Barry 2H **117**
Meridian Ct. CF14: Card 5G **85**
Merioneth Ho. CF64: P'rth 3D **108**
Merioneth Pl. CF62: Barry 6H **105**
Merlin Cl. CF14: Thorn 3G **71**
CF37: P'prdd *6B 14*
(off Pwll-Gwaun Rd.)
CF64: P'rth 5E **109**
Merlin Cres. NP19: Newp 2F **37**
Merlin Pl. CF63: Barry 6A **106**
Mermaid Quay CF10: Card 2C **102**
Merrett Ct. CF24: Card 2G **97**
Merriotts Pl. NP19: Newp 4E **37**
Mersey Wlk. NP20: Bet 6E **19**
MERTHYR DYFAN **5H 105**
Merthyr Dyfan Ct. CF62: Barry 4H **105**
Merthyr Dyfan Rd. CF62: Barry 6H **105**
(not continuous)
Merthyr Dylan Rd.
CF62: Barry 5H **105**
Merthyr Rd. CF14: Heath 3F **85**
CF14: Whit 3D **84**
CF15: Tong 4G **69**
CF37: P'prdd 6D **14**
Merthyr St. CF24: Card 1H **95**
CF63: Barry 2H **117**
CF72: P'clun 5D **64**
Mervinian Cl. CF10: Card 6G **5** (5C **96**)
Mervyn Rd. CF14: Whit 3D **84**
CF24: Card 3F **97**
Mervyn St. CF37: R'fln 4F **25**
Messina Ho. CF10: Card 6F **5** (5B **96**)
Metal St. CF24: Card 2H **5** (3D **96**)
Meteor St. CF24: Card 3H **5** (3C **96**)
Methodist La. CF61: Llan M 3B **110**
Methuen Rd. NP19: Newp 4D **36**
Metroplex Cinema **4B 36**
Mews, The CF11: Card 1A **102**
CF72: L'sant 2F **65**
NP11: C'crn 1A **16**
NP20: Newp 4H **35**
Meyrick Rd. CF5: Ely 5E **93**
Meyricks NP44: Coed E 5D **10**
Michael Ct. *NP4: P'pool* *2B 6*
(off Michael Way)
Michaelmas Cl. NP10: Roger 3A **34**
Michaelston Cl. CF63: Barry 5B **106**
Michaelston Ct. CF5: Ely 5D **92**
MICHAELSTON-LE-PIT **4C 100**
Michaelston Rd. CF5: Cul C, Ely, St F 6D **92**
MICHAELSTON-SUPER-ELY **4D 92**
MICHAELSTON-Y-FEDW **5E 51**
Michael Way NP4: P'pool 2B **6**
Michelston Ct. CF5: Ely 5G **93**
Middlegate Ct. CF71: C'bri 3D **90**
Middlegate Wlk. CF71: C'bri 3D **90**
Middle St. CF37: P'prdd 5D **14**
NP16: Chep 2E **63**
Middleton Dr. CF23: Pontp 4E **73**
Middle Way NP16: Bul 5F **63**
Midway Pk. CF37: Up Bo 6B **26**
Milburn Cl. CF62: Rho 6D **114**
Mildred Cl. CF38: Bed 4A **42**
Mildred St. CF38: Bed 4A **42**
Mile Rd. CF64: P'rth 4C **108**
Miles Ct. CF15: Gwae G 2E **69**
Milestone Cl. CF14: Heath 1F **85**
Milford Cl. CF38: Tont 1F **43**
Millands Pk. CF61: L'maes 2F **111**
Millbrook Cl. CF64: Din P 1H **107**
Millbrook Ct. NP26: Undy 4D **58**
Millbrook Hgts. CF64: Din P 1H **107**
Millbrook Pk. CF14: L'vne 2A **72**
Millbrook Rd. CF64: Din P 1H **107**
Mill Cl. CF14: L'shn 4A **72**
CF64: Din P 2G **107**
CF83: Caer 5B **28**
Mill Comn. NP26: Undy 4D **58**
Mill Ct. CF14: L'vne 3A **72**
Millennium Ct. CF24: Card 2D **96**
Millennium Plaza **5B 4 (4H 95)**
Millennium Vw. CF11: Card 6B **4** (5H **95**)
Millers Ride NP44: L'rfn 2A **12**
Millfield CF14: L'vne 2A **72**
CF72: P'clun 6C **64**
Millfield Cl. CF3: St M 1C **88**
Millfield Dr. CF71: C'bri 3D **90**
Millfield Pk. NP26: Undy 3D **58**
Millgate CF14: L'shn 4A **72**
Mill Heath NP20: Bet 4G **19**
Millheath Dr. CF14: L'vne, L'shn 4A **72**
Mill Ho. Ct. NP44: Coed E 5E **11**
Millicent St. CF10: Card 5E **5** (4B **96**)
Mill La. CF3: Cas 1G **75**
CF3: Old M 5H **73**
(not continuous)
CF5: L'dff 1D **94**
CF10: Card 6D **4** (5A **96**)
NP16: Chep 2F **63**
NP26: Cald 6C **60**
NP44: L'rfn 3B **12**
Mill-Lay La. CF61: Llan M 5B **110**
Mill Pde. NP20: Newp 2D **54**
(not continuous)
Mill Pk. CF71: C'bri 4C **90**
Mill Pl. CF5: Ely 3A **94**
CF14: L'vne 2B **72**
Millrace Cl. CF14: L'vne 3A **72**
Mill Reen NP26: Undy 4D **58**
Mill Rd. CF5: Ely 3A **94**
CF14: L'vne, L'shn 3A **72**
CF15: Tong 4G **69**
CF64: Din P 2G **107**
CF83: Caer 5C **28**
NP4: P'nydd 1A **6**
Mills Ct. CF62: Rho 6E **115**
Mill St. CF37: P'prdd 6B **14**
(not continuous)
NP11: Ris 6F **17**
NP18: C'ln 5H **21**
NP20: Newp 4B **36**
Mill Ter. NP11: Ris 6F **17**
Millwood CF14: L'vne 3A **72**
Millwood Ri. CF62: Barry 3E **117**
Milman St. NP20: Newp 2C **54**
Milner St. NP19: Newp 6F **37**
Milton Cl. CF38: Bed 5A **42**
CF61: Llan M 4D **110**
NP44: C'brn 3F **11**
Milton Ct. NP19: Newp 3D **38**
Milton Hill NP18: L'wrn 4F **39**
Milton Pl. CF5: F'wtr 1A **94**
CF83: Mac 2C **30**
Milton Rd. CF62: Barry 5G **105**
CF64: P'rth 1D **108**
NP19: Newp 4F **37**
Milton St. CF24: Card 1G **5** (2C **96**)
Milverton Rd. CF3: L'rmy 6A **74**
Milward Rd. CF63: Barry 1B **118**
Minafon CF14: R'ina 4D **70**
Minavon CF14: Whit 2D **84**
Minehead Av. CF64: Sul 2G **119**
Minehead Rd. CF3: L'rmy 1A **88**
Minister St. CF24: Card 1H **95**
Minny St. CF24: Card 1A **96**
(not continuous)
Minories *NP44: F'wtr* *4D 10*
(off Rede Rd.)
Minori Ho. *CF10: Card* *6C 96*
(off Ffordd Garthorne)
Minsmere Cl. CF3: St M 6F **75**
Minster Cl. CF63: Barry 5B **106**
Minster Rd. CF23: Pen L 1E **97**
Min-y-Coed CF15: Rad 6F **69**
Min-y-Mor CF62: Barry 5D **116**
Min-y-Nant CF14: R'ina 6D **70**
Min yr Afon CF83: Mac 2G **31**
MISKIN **1F 79**
Miskin Ct. CF38: Bed 5A **42**
NP26: Undy 4F **59**
Miskin Cres. CF72: Mis 6F **65**
Miskin Grn. NP44: L'rfn 2A **12**
Miskin St. CF24: Card 1E **5** (2A **96**)
CF62: Barry 4F **117**
Mission Ct. NP20: Newp 5D **36**
Mitchell Cl. CF3: St M 2E **89**
NP44: Llanf 4B **12**
Mitchell Ter. CF37: P'prdd, T'rest 1D **24**
NP4: P'nydd 1A **6**

Miterdale Cl. CF23: Pen L 4B **86**
Mithras Way NP18: C'ln 3G **21**
Mitre Ct. CF5: L'dff 6C **84**
Mitre Pl. CF5: L'dff 6C **84**
Moat, The CF3: Rum 5F **87**
Model Cotts. NP16: Math 6C **62**
Model House Craft & Design Cen. *2F 65*
(off Bull Ring)
Moel Fryn CF83: Caer 4H **27**
Moira Pl. CF24: Card 3G **5** (3C **96**)
Moira St. CF24: Card 3H **5** (3C **96**)
Moira Ter. CF24: Card 4G **5** (3C **96**)
Mole Cl. NP20: Bet 5E **19**
Molescombe NP44: F'wtr 4D **10**
Mona Cl. NP44: Pnwd 6F **9**
Mona Pl. CF24: Card 2F **97**
Monet Cres. NP19: Newp 2G **37**
Monico, The CF14: Heath 1E **85**
Monks Cl. NP26: Cald 4C **60**
Monk's Ditch NP18: Nash 3F **57**
Monkstone Cl. CF64: P'rth 4C **108**
Monkstone Ct. CF3: Rum 3H **87**
Monkstone Ri. CF3: Rum 2A **88**
Monkton Cl. CF5: F'wtr 2G **93**
Monmouth Cl. CF38: Tont 1F **43**
NP4: New I 6G **7**
Monmouth Ct. CF83: Caer 5H **27**
NP20: Newp 6H **35**
Monmouth Cres. Cl. NP4: New I 1G **9**
Monmouth Dr. NP19: Newp 1G **37**
Monmouth Ho. CF64: P'rth 3D **108**
NP44: C'brn 2G **11**
Monmouth St. CF11: Card 6A **4** (5H **95**)
Monmouth Wlk. NP44: C'brn 2G **11**
Monmouth Way CF61: Bov 2D **110**
CF62: Barry 1H **117**
Monnow Ct. NP44: Thorn 1C **10**
Monnow Wlk. NP20: Bet 5E **19**
Monnow Way NP20: Bet 5E **19**
Mons Cl. NP20: Newp 3A **36**
Montgomery Rd. CF62: Barry 3F **117**
NP20: Malp 3A **20**
Montgomery St. CF24: Card 6C **86**
Monthermer Rd. CF24: Card 6A **86**
Montreal Cl. NP20: Newp 6F **35**
Montresor Ct. NP44: L'tnam 6B **12**
Moorby Ct. CF10: Card 5C **96**
Moordale Rd. CF11: Card 1A **102**
Moore Cl. CF5: Ely 4F **93**
Moore Cres. NP19: Newp 3D **38**
Moore Rd. CF5: Ely 4F **93**
Moorhead Cl. CF24: Card 4D **96**
Moorings, The CF64: P'rth 6A **102**
NP4: P'pool 4E **7**
NP19: Newp 1E **37**
Moor King Cl. CF3: St M 1F **89**
Moorland Av. NP19: Newp 6A **38**
Moorland Cres. CF38: Bed 4A **42**
Moorland Gdns. NP19: Newp 6A **38**
Moorland Hgts. CF37: P'prdd 1E **25**
Moorland Pk. NP19: Newp 6A **38**
Moorland Pl. CF24: Card 3F **97**
Moorland Rd. CF24: Card 2E **97**
(not continuous)
Moorlands, The CF24: Card 2E **97**
Moorlands Vw. NP26: Cald 6E **61**
Moors La. CF11: Card 4C **94**
CF24: Card 4D **96**
Moor St. NP16: Chep 2E **63**
Morden La. NP19: Newp 2E **37**
Morden Rd. NP19: Newp 2E **37**
Morel Ct. CF11: Card 3H **101**
Morel St. CF63: Barry 1A **118**
Moreton St. NP4: P'pool 3B **6**
Morfa Cotts. CF61: Llan M 1A **110**
Morfa Cres. CF3: Rum 2C **88**
Morfa La. CF5: Wen 5E **99**
CF61: Llan M 1A **110**
Morgan Arc. CF10: Card 5D **4** (4A **96**)
Morgan Jones Flats CF83: Caer 6C **28**
MORGANSTOWN 5F **69**
Morgan St. CF10: Card 5F **5** (4B **96**)
CF37: P'prdd 6C **14**
CF63: Barry 2B **118**
CF83: Caer 5C **28**
NP19: Newp 3D **36**
Morgan Way NP10: Duf 5G **53**
Morgraig Av. NP10: Coedk, Duf 6G **53**
Moriah Hill NP11: Ris 5E **17**
Morien Cres. CF37: R'fln 3F **25**
Morlais Ct. CF83: Caer 5H **27**
Morlais St. CF23: Card 6B **86**
CF63: Barry 1C **118**
Morley Cl. NP19: Newp 4B **38**
Morningside Wlk. CF62: Barry 4H **105**
MORNINGTON MEADOWS 4G **29**
Morris Av. CF14: L'shn 4F **71**
Morris Finer Cl. CF5: Ely 4A **94**
Morris St. NP19: Newp 5D **36**
MORRISTOWN 2C **108**
Mortimer Rd. CF11: Card 2F **95**
Mortimer Way CF62: Fon 6H **113**
Morton Ct. CF14: Heath 3A **86**
Morton Way NP20: Newp 1H **53**
Moseley Ter. NP44: Pon'run 4E **9**
Moss Rd. NP44: G'mdw 2D **10**
Mostyn Rd. CF5: Ely 5E **93**
Mostyn Sq. CF14: L'shn 6F **71**
Mound Rd. CF37: P'prdd 1A **24**
Mount, The CF5: L'dff 2E **95**
CF14: L'vne 1B **72**
CF64: Din P 2G **107**
NP16: Chep 1D **62**
Mountain La. NP4: Grif 6D **6**
Mountain Rd. CF15: P'rch 3H **67**
CF83: B'ws 1F **29**
CF83: Caer 1D **46**
NP4: P'rheol 5A **8**
NP10: Roger 4G **17**
NP11: Ris 4G **17**
NP44: Up Cwm 5A **8**
Mountain Vw. CF37: R'fln 3F **25**
CF83: Abert 2F **27**
CF83: Caer 3C **28**
CF83: Mac 2F **31**
NP4: P'nydd 1A 6
(off Mountain Vw. Rd.)
Mountain Vw. Rd.
NP4: P'nydd 1A **6**
Mount Ballan NP26: Pskwt 2E **61**
Mountbatten Cl. CF23: Cyn 2A **86**
NP19: Newp 2D **38**
Mountbatten Rd. CF62: Barry 4A **106**
Mount Bax NP19: Newp 4A **38**
Mountford Cl. NP10: Roger 2C **34**
Mountjoy Av. CF64: P'rth 1C **108**
Mountjoy Cl. CF64: P'rth 1D **108**
Mountjoy Cres. CF64: P'rth 1D **108**
Mountjoy La. CF64: P'rth 2C **108**
Mountjoy Pl. CF64: P'rth 1C **108**
NP20: Newp 6C **36**
Mountjoy Rd. NP20: Newp 6C **36**
Mountjoy St. NP20: Newp 6C **36**
MOUNTON 3A **62**
Mounton Cl. NP16: Chep 3D **62**
Mounton Dr. NP16: Chep 3D **62**
Mounton Rd. NP16: Chep 3B **62**
MOUNT PLEASANT 1A **6**
Mt. Pleasant CF63: Barry 1B **118**
NP16: Chep 2E **63**
NP20: Malp 4A **20**
Mt. Pleasant Av. CF3: L'rmy 1A **88**
Mt. Pleasant Cl. NP44: Pnwd 6D **8**
Mt. Pleasant La. CF3: L'rmy 1A **88**
Mt. Pleasant Rd. NP4: P'nydd 1A **6**
NP11: Ris 5E **17**
NP44: Pnwd 5D **8**
Mt. Pleasant Ter. NP11: P'waun 1A **16**
Mount Rd. CF64: Din P 2G **107**
NP4: Trev 1D **6**
NP11: Ris 5E **17**
Mountside NP11: Ris 6H **17**
Mt. Stuart Sq. CF10: Card 1B **102**
Mount Way NP16: Chep 1D **62**
(not continuous)
Moxon Rd. NP20: Malp 6A **20**
Moxon St. CF63: Barry 1C **118**
Moyle Gro. NP18: P'hir 1F **21**
Moy Rd. CF15: Taff W 1E **69**
CF24: Card 1B **96**
Moy Rd. Ind. Est. CF15: Taff W 1E **69**
Muirton Rd. CF24: Card 3F **97**
Mulberry Cl. CF38: Llan F 6C **42**
NP10: Roger 2A **34**
Mulberry Ct. *CF62: Barry 4E 117*
(off St Nicholas Ct.)
Mulberry Dr. CF23: Pontp 2G **73**
Mulcaster Av. NP19: Newp 1H **55**
Mullins Av. CF3: Rum 2B **88**
Mundy Pl. CF24: Card 1A **96**
Muni Arts Cen. 6C **14**
Munnings Dr. NP19: Newp 2G **37**
Munro Pl. CF62: Barry 1G **117**
MURCH 3H **107**
Murch Cres. CF64: Din P 2A **108**
Murch Rd. CF64: Din P 2H **107**
Mur Gwyn CF14: R'ina 5E **71**
Murlande Way CF62: Rho 6F **115**
Murrayfield Rd. CF14: Heath 2F **85**
Murray Wlk. CF11: Card 4F **95**
Murrel Cl. CF5: Ely 6E **93**
Murrells Cl. CF38: Llan F 5D **42**
Museum Av. CF10: Card 1C **4** (2A **96**)
Museum Ct. NP4: Grif 1E **9**
Museum Pl. CF10: Card 1D **4** (2A **96**)
Museum St. NP18: C'ln 5H **21**
MWYNDY 5G **65**
Mwyndy Ter. CF72: Mwy 5G **65**
Mylo Griffiths Cl. CF5: L'dff 4A **84**
MYNACHDY 4F **85**
Mynachdy Rd. CF14: Card 5F **85**
CF14: Llan N 5E **85**
Mynydd Ct. NP4: P'pool 5C **6**
Mynydd Maen Rd.
NP44: Pnwd, Up Cwm 5C **8**
Mynydd Vw. NP4: P'pool 5B **6**
Myra Hess Cl. NP19: Newp 3D **38**
Myrtle Cl. CF64: P'rth 2C **108**
NP10: Roger 6D **34**
Myrtle Cotts. NP18: C'ln 5A **22**
Myrtle Dr. NP10: Roger 5D **34**
Myrtle Gro. CF63: Barry 6C **106**
NP19: Newp 4H **37**
Myrtle Pl. NP16: Chep 1F **63**
Myrtles, The NP16: Tut 1G **63**

N

Nailsea Ct. CF64: Sul 2H **119**
Nant Celyn Cl. NP44: Pnwd 5C **8**
Nant Coch Dr. NP20: Newp 5G **35**
Nant Coch Ri. NP20: Newp 5G **35**
Nant Ddu CF83: Caer 1C **46**
Nant Dyfed CF38: Bed 6H **41**
Nant-Fawr Cl. CF23: Cyn 1B **86**
Nant Fawr Ct. CF23: Cyn 1A **86**
Nant-Fawr Cres. CF23: Cyn 1B **86**
Nant-Fawr Rd. CF23: Cyn 1B **86**
NANTGARW 4D **44**
Nantgarw China Works Mus. 3E **45**
Nantgarw Rd. CF83: Caer 2H **45**
(not continuous)
Nant Isaf CF5: Wen 4E **99**
Nantsor Rd. NP18: L'veth 2H **13**
Nant Talwg Way CF62: Barry 2D **116**
Nant Walla CF14: R'ina 5E **71**
Nant y Coed CF37: P'prdd 5A **14**
Nant-y-Dall Av. CF37: R'fln 5F **25**
Nant-y-Dowlais CF5: Ely 5C **92**
Nant-y-Drope CF5: Ely 5D **92**
Nant-y-Fedw CF14: Heath 3F **85**
Nant y Felin CF38: E Isaf 6E **43**
Nant y Ffynnon CF5: Cap L 3B **82**
Nant y Garn NP11: Ris 3C **16**
Nant y Gth. CF15: Gwae G 2D **68**
Nant y Gwladys CF5: St F 2C **82**
Nant-y-Hwyad CF83: Caer 6A **28**
Nant-y-Milwr Cl. NP44: H'lys 6B **10**
Nant-y-Moor Cl. NP10: Coedk 5C **52**
Nant-y-Mynydd CF37: Glync 1D **14**
Nant-y-Pepra CF5: Ely 5D **92**
Nant-y-Plac CF5: Ely 5D **92**
Nant-yr-Adar CF61: Llan M 4C **110**
Nant-yr-Arthur CF5: Ely 5D **92**
Nant-yr-Ely CF5: Ely 5C **92**
Nant-y-Rhos CF5: Ely 5D **92**
Nant y Wedal CF14: Card 5A **86**

Napier St. CF83: Mac . . . 2F **31**
Narberth Cl. NP10: Duf . . . 6G **53**
Narberth Ct. CF62: Barry . . . 6H **105**
CF83: Caer . . . 5G **27**
Narberth Cres. NP44: L'rfn . . . 2B **12**
Narberth Rd. CF5: Ely . . . 5H **93**
Narcissus Gro. NP10: Roger . . . 3A **34**
Naseby Cl. CF23: Pontp . . . 4F **73**
NASH . . . 6A **56**
Nash Cl. NP10: Roger . . . 3D **34**
Nash Dr. NP19: Newp . . . 1H **55**
Nash Gro. NP19: Newp . . . 6H **37**
(not continuous)
Nash Mead NP19: Newp . . . 3A **56**
Nash Rd. NP18: Nash . . . 4B **56**
NP19: Newp . . . 6H **37**
Nasturtium Way CF23: Pontp . . . 4D **72**
National Assembly for Wales, The . . . 1C **102**
National Cricket Cen. . . . 2G **95**
National Indoor Athletic Stadium . . . 3D **86**
National Mus. . . . 1D **4** (2A **96**)
Navigation Rd. NP11: Ris . . . 4D **16**
Navigation St. CF83: Tret . . . 2A **30**
Neale St. CF62: Barry . . . 1G **117**
Neath Ct. NP44: Thorn . . . 1C **10**
Neath St. CF24: Card . . . 4E **97**
Neddern Ct. NP26: Cald . . . 4C **60**
Neddern Way NP26: Cald . . . 3C **60**
Neerings NP44: Coed E . . . 3C **10**
Neilson Cl. CF24: Card . . . 4D **96**
Nelson Ct. CF10: Card . . . 6G **5** (5C **96**)
Nelson Dr. NP19: Newp . . . 3C **38**
Nelson Ho. *CF10: Card* . . . *6B* ***96***
(off Loudoun Sq.)
Nelson Rd. CF62: Barry . . . 5A **106**
Nelson St. NP16: Chep . . . 2E **63**
(not continuous)
Neptune Ct. CF24: Card . . . 5D **96**
Nesta Rd. CF5: Card . . . 3D **94**
Neston Rd. NP19: Newp . . . 3B **38**
Nethercourt NP44: G'mdw . . . 2D **10**
Netherwent Vw. NP26: Magor . . . 3C **58**
Nettlefold Rd. CF24: Card . . . 5D **96**
Neuadda Cl. NP10: Bass . . . 1B **52**
Nevern Wlk. NP44: L'rfn . . . 3B **12**
Neville Pk. NP10: St Bri W . . . 4G **77**
Neville Pl. CF11: Card . . . 5A **4** (4G **95**)
Neville St. CF11: Card . . . 4A **4** (4G **95**)
Nevin Cres. CF3: Rum . . . 3A **88**
Newbarn Path NP44: Llanf . . . 4B **12**
Newborough Av. CF14: L'shn . . . 5G **71**
Newbridge Ct. CF37: P'prdd . . . 5D **14**
Newbridge Rd. CF72: L'sant . . . 1F **65**
Newby Ct. CF10: Card . . . 5B **96**
Newchurch Ct. NP44: St D . . . 2E **11**
New Cotts. NP19: Newp . . . 3C **36**
Newent Rd. CF3: St M . . . 1D **88**
New Forest Vw. CF71: C'bri . . . 4E **91**
Newfoundland Rd. CF14: Card . . . 5G **85**
Newgale Cl. CF62: Barry . . . 5H **105**
Newgale Pl. CF5: Ely . . . 5H **93**
Newgale Row NP44: C'brn . . . 2H **11**
New George St. CF10: Card . . . 2C **102**
New Ho. Ct. CF63: Barry . . . 6B **106**
Newhouse Farm Ind. Est.
NP16: Math . . . 6F **63**
New Ho's. CF37: Pen c . . . 5A **24**
NEW INN . . . 5G **7**
New Inn Cen. CF37: P'prdd . . . 6C **14**
Newlands Ct. CF14: L'shn . . . 4A **72**
Newlands Rd. CF3: Rum . . . 4D **88**
Newlands St. CF62: Barry . . . 2H **117**
Newman Cl. NP19: Newp . . . 4D **38**
Newman Rd. NP4: Trev . . . 1B **6**
New Mill Cnr. CF72: Mis . . . 1F **79**
Newmill Gdns. CF72: Mis . . . 5F **65**
Newminster Rd. CF23: Pen L . . . 1E **97**
Newnham Pl. NP44: C'brn . . . 2G **11**
New Pk. Rd. NP11: Ris . . . 4B **16**
New Pk. Ter. CF37: T'rest . . . 2E **25**
New Pastures NP20: Newp . . . 1A **54**
NEWPORT . . . 4C **36**
Newport Arc. *NP20: Newp* . . . *4B* ***36***
(off High St.)
Newport Athletic Club Ground . . . 4C **36**
Newport Castle . . . 4C **36**
Newport County FC . . . 1H **55**
Newport Gwent Dragons RUFC . . . 4D **36**
Newport Ind. Est. NP19: Newp . . . 2B **56**
Newport International Sports Village . . . 2H **55**
Newport Leisure Cen. . . . 5C **36**
Newport Mus. & Art Gallery . . . 5C **36**
Newport Provisions Market . . . 4B **36**
Newport Retail Pk. NP19: Newp . . . 1B **56**
Newport Rd. CF3: Cas . . . 2G **75**
CF3: L'rmy, Rum . . . 5G **87**
CF3: St M . . . 4E **75**
CF23: Pen L . . . 1E **97**
CF24: Card . . . 3F **5** (3B **96**)
(not continuous)
CF83: B'ws, Mac, Tret . . . 4F **29**
NP4: New I . . . 2G **9**
NP11: Ris . . . 1F **33**
NP16: Chep, Pwllm . . . 6A **62**
NP26: Cald . . . 5B **60**
NP26: Wilc . . . 3B **58**
NP44: C'iog . . . 5H **9**
NP44: L'tnam . . . 3A **20**
Newport Rd. La. CF24: Card . . . 3G **5** (3C **96**)
Newport Stadium . . . 2H **55**
Newport Station (Rail) . . . 4B **36**
Newport St. CF11: Card . . . 1A **102**
Newport Tennis Cen. . . . 2G **55**
Newport Wasps Speedway . . . 2C **56**
New Quay Rd. NP19: Newp . . . 3E **55**
New Rd. CF3: Rum . . . 5G **87**
CF37: Y'bwl . . . 1A **14**
NP4: Grif, New I . . . 6E **7**
NP18: C'ln . . . 6A **22**
NP26: Cald . . . 5B **60**
New Row CF83: Mac . . . 3F **31**
NP44: H'lys . . . 4A **10**
New Ruperra St. NP20: Newp . . . 6C **36**
New St. CF83: Caer . . . 3B **28**
NP20: Newp . . . 1D **54**
NP44: Pnwd . . . 6E **9**
New Theatre . . . 2D **4** (3A **96**)
NEWTON . . . 6D **88**
Newton Ct. CF24: Card . . . 4G **5** (4C **96**)
NEWTON GREEN . . . 6B **62**
Newton Ind. Est. NP11: Cros K . . . 4A **16**
Newton Rd. CF3: Rum . . . 4C **88**
(not continuous)
CF11: Card . . . 5F **95**
Newton St. CF63: Barry . . . 1B **118**
Newton Way NP20: Malp . . . 5H **19**
Newton Wynd NP44: F'wtr . . . 4D **10**
NEWTOWN . . . 5D **42**
Newtown Ind. Est. CF38: Llan F . . . 4D **42**
Newydd Ct. CF15: Tong . . . 5G **69**
New Zealand Rd. CF14: Card . . . 6G **85**
(not continuous)
Neyland Cl. CF38: Tont . . . 1F **43**
Neyland Ct. CF62: Barry . . . 5H **105**
Neyland Path NP44: F'wtr . . . 3D **10**
Neyland Pl. CF5: Ely . . . 5H **93**
Niagara St. CF37: T'rest . . . 1D **24**
Nicholas Ct. CF15: Rad . . . 2H **83**
Nicholas St. NP4: P'pool . . . 3C **6**
Nicholl Ct. CF61: Bov . . . 3D **110**
Nicholson Webb Cl. CF5: L'dff . . . 4H **83**
Nidd Cl. NP20: Bet . . . 6E **19**
Nidd Wlk. *NP20: Bet* . . . *6E* ***19***
(off Ogmore Cres.)
Nightingale Cl. NP26: Cald . . . 6D **60**
Nightingale Ct. NP10: Duf . . . 4G **53**
Nightingale Gdns. CF38: Chu V . . . 2D **42**
Nightingale Pl. CF64: Din P . . . 2A **108**
Nightingale's Bush CF37: P'prdd . . . 1E **25**
Nightingale Ter. NP4: P'nydd . . . 1A **6**
Nile Rd. CF37: T'rest . . . 1D **24**
Ninian Pk. . . . 5F **95**
Ninian Pk. Rd. CF11: Card . . . 5A **4** (4F **95**)
Ninian Park Station (Rail) . . . 5F **95**
Ninian Rd. CF23: Card . . . 5B **86**
Nolton Pl. NP44: C'brn . . . 4E **11**
Nora St. CF24: Card . . . 2D **96**
Norbury Av. CF5: F'wtr . . . 2A **94**
Norbury Ct. CF5: F'wtr . . . 2A **94**
Norbury Rd. CF5: F'wtr . . . 2A **94**
Nordale Ri. CF63: Barry . . . 1C **118**
Nordale Rd. CF61: Llan M . . . 3D **110**
Norfolk Cl. NP44: G'mdw . . . 2C **10**
Norfolk Ct. CF15: Rad . . . 6F **69**
Norfolk Rd. NP19: Newp . . . 3F **37**
Norfolk St. CF5: Card . . . 3D **94**
Norman Ct. NP26: Cald . . . 5C **60**
Normandy Way NP16: Chep . . . 1D **62**
Norman Rd. CF14: Whit . . . 3D **84**
Norman St. CF24: Card . . . 1B **96**
NP18: C'ln . . . 5H **21**
Norman Ter. NP18: C'ln . . . 5H **21**
Norman Way NP26: Pskwt . . . 6F **61**
Norrell Cl. CF11: Card . . . 4D **94**
Norris Cl. CF64: P'rth . . . 6F **101**
Norseman Cl. CF62: Rho . . . 5C **114**
Norse Way NP16: Sed . . . 3H **63**
Northam Av. CF3: L'rmy . . . 2G **87**
Nth. Church St. CF10: Card . . . 5B **96**
Northcliffe CF64: P'rth . . . 6B **102**
Northcliffe Dr. CF64: P'rth . . . 6B **102**
Nth. Clive St. CF11: Card . . . 6G **95**
Northcote La. CF24: Card . . . 2B **96**
Northcote St. CF24: Card . . . 2B **96**
Northcote Ter. CF63: Barry . . . 1C **118**
North Ct. NP4: P'nydd . . . 1A **6**
Nth. Edward St. CF10: Card . . . 3E **5** (3B **96**)
Northern Av. CF14: Heath, Whit . . . 2D **84**
CF14: Whit . . . 5A **70**
Northfield Cl. NP18: C'ln . . . 3F **21**
Northfield Rd. NP18: C'ln . . . 3G **21**
Nth. Lake Dr. NP10: Coedk . . . 6E **53**
Northlands CF3: Rum . . . 5H **87**
Nth. Luton Pl. CF24: Card . . . 4H **5** (4C **96**)
Nth. Morgan St. CF11: Card . . . 4G **95**
North Pk. Rd. CF24: Card . . . 3E **97**
Nth. Pentwyn Link Rd.
CF23: Pontp, St M . . . 5H **73**
North Ri. CF14: L'shn . . . 4A **72**
North Rd. CF10: Card . . . 1H **95**
CF14: Card, Heath . . . 1B **4** (4F **85**)
CF64: Sul . . . 1E **119**
CF71: C'bri . . . 3C **90**
NP4: P'pool . . . 3B **6**
NP11: C'crn, P'waun . . . 1A **16**
NP44: C'iog . . . 6G **9**
North St. CF11: Card . . . 6H **95**
CF37: P'prdd . . . 5D **14**
NP20: Newp . . . 4B **36**
Northumberland Rd. NP19: Newp . . . 3F **37**
Northumberland St. CF5: Card . . . 4E **95**
North Vw. CF15: Taff W . . . 1F **69**
North Vw. Ter. CF83: Caer . . . 6D **28**
NORTHVILLE . . . 1H **11**
North Wlk. CF62: Barry . . . 1F **117**
NP44: C'brn . . . 1G **11**
Norton Av. CF14: Heath . . . 3F **85**
Norwegian Church Arts Cen. . . . 2C **102**
Norwich Rd. CF23: Pen L . . . 6F **87**
Norwood CF14: Thorn . . . 3H **71**
Norwood Ct. CF24: Card . . . 1H **5** (2C **96**)
Norwood Cres. CF63: Barry . . . 6C **106**
Nottage Rd. CF5: Ely . . . 5G **93**
Nottingham St. CF5: Card . . . 3D **94**
Novello Wlk. NP19: Newp . . . 4C **38**
Nuns Cres. CF37: P'prdd . . . 5B **14**
Nurseries, The NP18: L'stne . . . 1H **39**
Nursery Cotts. CF64: Din P . . . 3F **107**
Nursery Ri. CF83: B'ws . . . 2E **29**
NURSTON . . . 4C **114**
Nurston Cl. CF62: Rho . . . 5C **114**
Nut Wlk. CF61: Llan M . . . 5C **110**
Nyth-y-Dryw CF62: Rho . . . 6E **115**
Nyth y Eos *CF62: Rho* . . . *6G* ***115***
(off Bryn y Gloyn)

O

Oak Bluff NP16: Pwllm . . . 4C **62**
Oak Cl. CF72: T Grn . . . 3E **65**
NP16: Bul . . . 5E **63**
NP26: Undy . . . 4D **58**
Oak Ct. CF15: Tong . . . 3H **69**
CF24: Card . . . 2C **96**
CF64: P'rth . . . 3C **108**
NP4: P'nydd . . . 1A **6**
Oakdale Cl. NP18: C'ln . . . 5F **21**

Oakdale Path NP44: St D 3E **11**
Oakdale Pl. NP4: P'nydd 1A **6**
Oakdene Cl. CF23: Cyn 3C **86**
OAKFIELD 5H **11**
Oakfield NP18: C'ln 4F **21**
Oakfield Av. NP16: Chep 1D **62**
Oakfield Cres. CF38: Tont 2H **43**
Oakfield Gdns. CF83: Mac 3H **31**
NP20: Newp 5A **36**
Oakfield M. CF24: Card 2D **96**
NP44: Oakf 4H **11**
Oakfield Rd. CF62: Barry 6F **105**
NP20: Newp 5H **35**
NP44: Oakf 4H **11**
Oakfields CF3: M'fld 4H **75**
Oakfield St. CF24: Card 2C **96**
Oakford Cl. CF23: Pent 4E **73**
Oak Gro. CF62: E Bre 2B **112**
Oak Ho. CF14: Whit 6A **70**
Oakland Cres. CF37: C'fydd 3F **15**
Oaklands CF64: Din P 1G **107**
CF72: Mis 5F **65**
NP18: P'hir 1E **21**
Oaklands Cl. CF3: St M 6C **74**
Oaklands Pk. NP26: Pskwt 5G **61**
Oaklands Pk. Dr. NP10: R'drn 6A **34**
Oaklands Rd. NP4: Seba 2D **8**
NP19: Newp 4F **37**
Oaklands Vw. NP44: G'mdw 2C **10**
Oakland Ter. CF37: C'fydd 3F **15**
NP44: T Coch 5G **11**
Oak La. CF83: Mac 3H **31**
Oakleafe Dr. CF23: Pent 5E **73**
Oakleigh Ct. NP44: H'lys 5B **10**
Oakley Cl. NP26: Cald 4B **60**
Oakley Pl. CF11: Card 1H **101**
Oakley St. NP19: Newp 6F **37**
Oakley Way NP26: Cald 4B **60**
Oakmead Cl. CF23: Pontp 4E **73**
Oakmeadow Ct. CF3: St M 6D **74**
Oakmeadow Dr. CF3: St M 1D **88**
Oakridge E. CF14: Thorn 2H **71**
Oakridge W. CF14: Thorn 3G **71**
Oak Rd. CF72: L'harry 5A **78**
NP10: Roger 3B **34**
Oaks, The CF14: L'vne 3B **72**
CF38: Llan F 3D **42**
CF83: Mac 3H **31**
NP44: C'iog 6H **9**
Oaks Cl. NP20: Newp 1A **54**
Oaksford NP44: Coed E 3C **10**
Oak St. CF37: R'fln 3G **25**
NP19: Newp 1D **36**
NP44: C'brn 3G **11**
Oak St. Cl. CF37: R'fln 3G **25**
Oak Ter. NP11: Cros K 2A **16**
Oak Tree Cl. CF15: Rad 1E **83**
NP4: New I 4G **7**
Oak Tree Ct. CF23: Pontp 2G **73**
NP19: Newp 4H **37**
NP44: Oakf 4G **11**
Oak Tree Dr. NP10: Roger 2H **33**
Oakway CF5: F'wtr 2G **93**
Oak Wood Av. CF23: Pen L 5E **87**
Oakwood Cl. CF64: L'dgh 5G **101**
Oakwood St. CF37: T'rest 4E **25**
Oban St. CF63: Barry 1B **118**
Ocean Bldgs. *CF10: Card 1C 102*
(off Bute Cres.)
Ocean Rd. CF24: Card 5E **97**
Ocean Way CF24: Card 5H **5** (4D **96**)
Ochr y Coed CF11: Card 5A **4** (4H **95**)
CF14: Thorn 2H **71**
Octagon, The NP16: Bul 5F **63**
Octavius Cl. NP10: Duf 6G **53**
Odeon Cinema
Cardiff 1C **102**
Odet Ct. CF14: Whit 6A **70**
O'Donnell Rd. CF63: Barry 6A **106**
Odyn's Fee CF62: Rho 5C **114**
Offas Cl. NP16: Sed 3G **63**
Offway NP44: Coed E 5E **11**
Ogmore Ct. CF83: Caer 5H **27**
Ogmore Cres. NP20: Bet 6E **19**
Ogmore Pl. CF63: Barry 5A **106**
NP44: L'rfn 3B **12**
Ogmore Rd. CF5: Ely 5G **93**
Ogwen Dr. CF23: Cyn 1B **86**
Okehampton Av. CF3: L'rmy 5A **74**
Old Bakery Ct. CF15: P'rch 4A **68**
Old Barn NP19: Newp 1F **37**
Old Barn Ct. NP26: Undy 4F **59**
Old Barn Est. NP19: Newp 1F **37**
Old Barry Rd. CF64: P'rth 5G **101**
Old Brewery Quarter, The
CF10: Card 5D **4**
Oldbridge Ct. NP44: Thorn 6A **8**
Old Bulwark Rd. NP16: Bul 3E **63**
Oldbury Rd. NP44: C'brn 3G **11**
Old Cardiff Rd. NP20: Newp 2H **53**
Old Castle Cl. NP10: Duf 6G **53**
Old Chepstow Rd.
NP18: L'stne 1G **39**
Old Church Rd. CF14: Whit 2C **84**
Old Clipper Rd. CF10: Card 1E **103**
(not continuous)
Old Estate Yd. NP4: P'pool 4E **7**
Old Farm La. CF15: Cre 6E **67**
Old Farm M. CF64: Din P 2G **107**
Old Farm Shop. Cen., The
NP16: Bul 6F **63**
Old Field Rd. CF15: Tong 5A **70**
OLD FURNACE 4A **6**
Old Furnace Rd. CF83: Caer 5A **28**
Old Garden Ct. CF15: Rad 1F **83**
Old Green Ct. CF3: M'fld 5A **76**
Old Green Rdbt. NP20: Newp 4C **36**
Old Hall Cl. NP10: Duf 4H **53**
Old Hill CF3: Old M 1B **88**
NP18: Chris 1A **38**
Old Hill, The NP16: Tut 1F **63**
Old Hill Cres. NP18: Chris 2B **38**
Old Langstone Ct. Rd.
NP18: L'stne 1F **39**
Old Library, The 4D **4**
Old Malt Ho. CF64: Din P 2G **107**
Old Market CF5: Wen 5E **99**
Old Mill Dr. CF5: St F 2C **82**
Old Mill Rd. CF14: L'vne 3A **72**
Oldmill Rd. CF63: Barry 1C **118**
Old Nantgarw Rd. CF15: N'grw 3E **45**
Old Newport Rd. CF3: Old M 5D **74**
Old Oak Cl. NP16: Bul 5F **63**
Old Parish Rd. CF37: Y'bwl 1A **14**
Old Park Ter. CF37: T'rest 2E **25**
OLD PENYGARN 1C **6**
Old Pill Farm Ind. Est.
NP26: Cald 6E **61**
Old Port Rd. CF5: Cul C 2D **98**
Old Roman Rd.
NP18: Cat A, L'stne 5G **23**
Old Row NP26: Sud 6H **61**
NP44: H'lys 4A **10**
OLD ST MELLONS 5B **74**
Old School Ct. NP11: Cros K 2A **16**
Old School Pl. NP4: P'nydd 1A **6**
Old School Rd. CF5: Ely 4A **94**
Old Shirenewton Rd.
NP26: Cri 1E **61**
Old Station Yd. CF83: B'ws 2F **29**
Old Stone La. NP26: Undy 4E **59**
Old Vicarage Cl. CF14: L'shn 5H **71**
Old Village Rd. CF62: Barry 4E **117**
Oldwell Ct. CF23: Pen L 6C **86**
Old Well La. NP26: Undy 5F **59**
O'Leary Dr. CF11: Card 3H **101**
Oliphant Circ. NP20: Malp 4H **19**
Oliver Rd. NP19: Newp 5G **37**
Oliver St. CF37: P'prdd 6A **14**
Oliver Ter. CF37: T'rest 3E **25**
Ollivant Cl. CF5: L'dff 4H **83**
Olway Cl. NP44: L'rfn 4A **12**
(not continuous)
Olympian Dr. CF11: Card 4H **101**
Olympic Gymnastic Training Cen. 3D **86**
Ombersley La. NP20: Newp 5H **35**
Ombersley Rd. NP20: Newp 5H **35**
O'Neal Av. NP19: Newp 3G **55**
Ontario Way CF23: Cyn 2C **86**
Open Hearth Cl. NP4: Grif 1E **9**
Orange Gro. CF5: F'wtr 6G **83**
Orangery Wlk. NP10: Duf 4H **53**
Orbit St. CF24: Card 2H **5** (3C **96**)
Orchard, The CF71: A'thin 2F **91**
NP18: P'hir 1F **21**
Orchard Av. NP16: Bul 5E **63**
Orchard Castle CF14: Thorn 3F **71**
Orchard Cl. CF3: M'fld 5H **75**
CF5: Wen 4E **99**
CF61: Bov 4F **111**
NP10: Bass 6B **34**
NP26: Cald 6C **60**
Orchard Ct. CF14: L'vne 1H **71**
NP19: Newp 2D **36**
Orchard Cres. CF64: Din P 2H **107**
Orchard Dr. CF14: Whit 2C **84**
CF37: Glync 2C **14**
CF61: Llan M 5C **110**
CF62: Barry 1H **117**
Orchard Farm Cl. NP16: Sed 3H **63**
Orchard Gdns. NP16: Chep 1F **63**
NP19: Newp 2E **37**
NP26: Pskwt 5G **61**
Orchard Gro. CF15: Morg 5F **69**
Orchard La. NP19: Newp 2E **37**
NP44: C'brn 6E **9**
Orchard Lodge CF61: Bov 3E **111**
Orchard M. NP19: Newp 2D **36**
Orchard Pk. CF3: St M 6B **74**
Orchard Pk. Cl. CF3: St M 6C **74**
Orchard Pl. CF11: Card 3F **95**
NP44: C'brn 3F **11**
Orchard Ri. CF64: P'rth 1C **108**
NP16: Pwllm 5B **62**
Orchard Rd. NP18: C'ln 3G **21**
Orchards, The CF14: L'shn 5H **71**
Orchard St. NP19: Newp 2D **36**
Orchard Way CF62: Gile 6D **112**
Orchid Cl. CF3: St M 1E **89**
Orchid Ct. NP44: Ty C 4C **10**
Orchid Dr. NP26: Cald 6E **61**
Orchid Mdw. NP16: Pwllm 5B **62**
Ordell St. CF24: Card 3D **96**
Oregano Cl. CF3: St M 5E **75**
Oriel Ho. CF24: Card 4H **5** (4C **96**)
Oriel Rd. NP19: Newp 4E **37**
Orion Ct. CF24: Card 3H **5** (3C **96**)
Ormerod Rd. NP16: Sed 3H **63**
Ormonde Cl. CF23: Pen L 4E **87**
Osborne Cl. NP19: Newp 4E **37**
Osborne Rd. NP4: P'nydd, P'pool 1B **6**
Osborne Sq. CF11: Card 6G **95**
Osprey Cl. CF3: St M 5C **74**
CF64: P'rth 6E **109**
Osprey Ct. CF63: Barry 3H **117**
Osprey Dr. NP26: Cald 6D **60**
Oswald Rd. NP20: Newp 1C **54**
(not continuous)
Oswestry Cl. CF3: Rum 4A **88**
Othery Pl. CF3: L'rmy 5A **74**
Otter Cl. NP20: Bet 5E **19**
Outfall La. NP10: St Bri W 5F **77**
Overstone Ct. CF10: Card 6A **96**
Ovington Ter. CF5: Card 2D **94**
Owain Cl. CF23: Cyn 3C **86**
CF64: P'rth 2C **108**
Owain Ct. CF62: St Ath 5D **112**
Owen Cl. NP18: C'ln 3G **21**
Owens Cl. CF62: Barry 2G **117**
Owen's Ct. CF14: Whit 3F **85**
Owen St. CF37: R'fln 5G **25**
Oxford Arc. CF10: Card 5D **4** (4A **96**)
Oxford Cl. NP18: C'ln 3F **21**
Oxford La. CF24: Card 2G **5** (3C **96**)
Oxford St. CF15: N'grw 3C **44**
CF24: Card 1G **5** (2C **96**)
CF37: T'rest 3E **25**
CF62: Barry 4E **117**
NP4: Grif 6E **7**
NP16: Chep 2E **63**
NP19: Newp 4E **37**
Oxtens NP44: Coed E 5D **10**
Oxwich Cl. CF5: F'wtr 2B **94**
Oxwich Gro. NP10: Duf 6F **53**
Oxwich Rd. NP19: Newp 2F **55**
Oyster Bend CF64: Sul 3H **119**
Oystermouth M. NP10: Duf 6G **53**
Oystermouth Way NP10: Duf 6G **53**

P

Pace Cl. CF5: L'dff 5H **83**
Pace Rd. NP44: F'wtr 4D **10**
Pacific Bus. Pk. CF24: Card 5F **97**
Pacific Rd. CF24: Card 4F **97**
Padarn Cl. CF23: Cyn 2B **86**
Padarn Pl. NP44: Pnwd 6E **9**
Paddock, The CF14: L'vne 2A **72**
CF23: Pen L 5C **86**
CF71: C'bri 4E **91**
NP16: Bul 4D **62**
Paddock Cl. NP44: Pnwd 6D **8**
Paddock Pl. CF63: Barry 6B **106**
Paddock Ri. NP44: L'rfn 4B **12**
Paddocks, The CF38: Up Chu 2D **42**
(not continuous)
CF64: P'rth 4E **109**
CF72: Groes F 1C **80**
NP18: C'ln 4F **21**
NP18: L'stne 1H **39**
NP26: Undy 4F **59**
NP44: L'rfn 4B **12**
Paddocks Cres. CF72: Bryns 1B **78**
Page Dr. CF24: Card 6G **87**
Paget La. CF11: Card 6H **95**
Paget Pl. CF64: P'rth 6B **102**
Paget Rd. CF62: Barry 5G **117**
(not continuous)
CF64: P'rth 6A **102**
Paget St. CF11: Card 6H **95**
Paget Ter. CF64: P'rth 6B **102**
Palace Av. CF5: L'dff 1D **94**
Palace Ct. CF23: Cyn 1C **86**
Palace Rd. CF5: L'dff 1D **94**
Palalwyf Av. CF72: P'clun 6D **64**
Pallot Way CF24: Card 1F **97**
Palm Cl. NP4: New I 4H **7**
Palmers Dr. CF5: Ely 4A **94**
Palmerston Rd. CF63: Barry 1D **118**
Palmerston Workshops CF63: Barry 6D **106**
PALMERSTOWN **6D 106**
Palmer St. CF63: Barry 5D **106**
Palmers Vale Bus. Cen. CF63: Barry 6D **106**
Palm Sq. NP19: Newp 5G **37**
Palmyra Pl. NP20: Newp 5C **36**
Pandy NP44: G'mdw 2E **11**
Pandy La. CF83: Mac 2G **31**
Pandy-Mawr Rd. CF83: B'ws 1D **28**
Pandy Pk. 2A **16**
Pandy Rd. CF83: B'ws, L'brad 2C **28**
Pandy Vw. NP11: Cros K 2A **16**
Pant Bach CF15: P'rch 5A **68**
Pantbach Av. CF14: Heath 3F **85**
Pantbach Pl. CF14: Heath 3E **85**
Pantbach Rd. CF14: Heath, R'ina 1E **85**
Pant Du Rd. CF37: C'fydd 1F **15**
PANTEG **6H 7**
Panteg CF15: P'rch 5A **68**
Panteg Cl. CF5: Ely 6D **92**
PANTEG HOSPICE ***5E 7***
(within County Hospital)
Panteg Ind. Est. NP4: Grif 1E **9**
Panteg Way NP4: New I 6F **7**
Pant Glas CF23: Pent 6G **73**
Pantglas CF15: P'rch 5A **68**
Pant-Glas Ct. NP10: Bass 1B **52**
Pant Glas Ind. Est. CF83: B'ws 4H **29**
Pant Glas Rd. NP44: L'tnam 1F **19**
Pantglas Vs. CF83: Tret 3H **29**
Pant Gwyn Cl. NP44: H'lys 5B **10**
Pantgwynlais CF15: Tong 4H **69**
Pant La. *NP20: Bryng* *1B 36*
(off Pant Rd.)
Pant Llygodfa CF83: Caer 2A **46**
PANTMAWR **5B 70**
Pantmawr Ct. CF14: R'ina 5B **70**
Pantmawr Rd. CF14: R'ina 6B **70**
CF14: Whit 6B **70**
Pant Pl. CF15: Gwae G 6D **44**
Pant Rd. NP20: Bryng 1B **36**
Pant Tawel La. CF15: Rad 1D **82**
Pant-y-Celyn CF62: St Ath 5C **112**
Pantycelyn Dr. CF83: Caer 4B **28**
Pantycelyn Rd. CF64: L'dgh 5F **101**
Pant y Dderwen CF72: P'clun 4C **64**
Pant-y-Deri Cl. CF5: Ely 5G **93**
PANTYGRAIG-WEN **5A 14**
Pantygraigwen Rd. CF37: P'prdd 5A **14**
Pant-yr-Eos NP44: Pnwd 1F **11**
Pant-yr-Heol Cl. NP44: H'lys 6B **10**
Pant yr Wyn CF23: Pen L 5B **86**
Paper Mill Rd. CF11: Card 3C **94**
Parade, The CF14: Whit 3B **84**
CF24: Card 2F **5** (3B **96**)
CF37: P'prdd 5D **14**
CF38: Chu V 3E **43**
CF62: Barry 5E **117**
CF64: Din P 2A **108**
NP44: C'brn 2G **11**
Parc Av. CF83: Caer 4E **29**
NP44: Pnwd 5D **8**
Parc Castell-y-Mynach
CF15: Cre 5E **67**
(not continuous)
Parc Cefn Onn Country Pk. **6H 47**
Parc Cenedlaethol Bannau Brycheiniog **1F 7**
Parc Clwyd CF63: Barry 5C **106**
Parc Hafod CF14: Whit 1B **84**
Parc Ifor Hen CF72: Mis 6G **65**
Parc Manwerthu Parcnewydd
CF72: T Grn 3E **65**
Parc Nant Celyn CF38: E Isaf 4G **43**
Parc Nantgarw CF15: N'grw 3D **44**
Parc Newydd CF72: T Grn 3E **65**
Parc Newydd Shop. Cen.
CF72: T Grn 3E **65**
Parc Pontypandy CF83: Caer 3D **28**
Parc-ty-Glas CF14: L'shn 5G **71**
Parc ty Glas Ind. Est. CF14: L'shn 6G **71**
Parc y Brain Rd. NP10: Roger 1D **34**
Parc-y-Bryn CF15: Cre 5D **66**
CF38: Llan F 3D **42**
Parc-y-Coed CF15: Cre 6E **67**
Parc-y-Felin CF15: Cre 6D **66**
Parc-y-Felin St. CF83: Caer 5D **28**
Parc-y-Fro CF15: Cre 5E **67**
Parc-y-Nant CF15: N'grw 4E **45**
Pardoe Cres. CF62: Barry 1G **117**
Pardoe Thomas Cl. *NP20: Newp* *6C 36*
(off Francis St.)
Parfitt St. NP19: Newp 6H **37**
Parfitt Ter. NP44: Pnwd 6D **8**
Parish Gdns. CF3: Rum 5H **87**
Parish Rd. CF38: Bed 4A **42**
Park Av. CF5: Cul C 1E **99**
CF14: Whit 1B **84**
CF62: Barry 5F **117**
CF83: B'ws 3G **29**
NP10: Roger 3B **34**
NP20: Newp 2G **53**
Park Cl. CF37: T'rest 3D **24**
NP20: Newp 2G **53**
NP44: H'lys 5B **10**
Park Ct. CF62: Barry 4E **117**
NP4: P'garn 2C **6**
NP26: Undy 4F **59**
Park Cres. CF14: Whit 1B **84**
CF37: T'rest 2E **25**
CF62: Barry 4E **117**
CF72: P'clun 6C **64**
NP4: P'garn 2D **6**
NP20: Newp 2G **53**
Parkdale Vw. CF72: L'sant 3G **65**
Park Dr. NP20: Newp 2H **53**
Park End NP18: L'stne 6G **23**
Park End Ct. CF23: Cyn 1A **86**
NP18: L'stne 1G **39**
Park End La. CF23: Cyn 1A **86**
Parker Pl. CF5: Ely 5F **93**
Parker Rd. CF5: Ely 5F **93**
Parke's La. NP4: P'pool 4A **6**
Parkfield Ho. CF14: Card 6G **85**
Parkfield Pl. CF14: Card 6G **85**
NP20: Newp 4A **36**
Park Gdns. NP4: P'garn 2C **6**
NP20: Newp 2G **53**
Park Gro. CF10: Card 1E **5** (2B **96**)
Park Ho. Flats NP4: P'pool 2C **6**
Parklands NP16: Math 6B **62**
NP18: W'son 5G **57**
Parklands Cl. NP10: Roger 6E **35**
NP44: Pnwd 6E **9**
Parklands Ind. Est.
CF24: Card 6H **5** (5C **96**)
Parkland Wlk. CF62: Barry 3E **117**
Park La. CF10: Card 1D **4** (2A **96**)
CF14: Whit 1B **84**
CF15: Taff W 1D **68**
CF72: Groes F 6B **66**
CF83: Caer 1C **46**
Parklawn Cl. NP44: Pnwd 5E **9**
Park Pl. CF10: Card 2A **96**
CF37: C'fydd 1F **15**
NP11: Cros K 2A **16**
NP11: Ris 6E **17**
Park Prospect CF37: P'prdd 5B **14**
Park Rd. CF14: Whit 1B **84**
CF15: Rad 1F **83**
CF62: Barry 4D **116**
CF64: Din P 1G **107**
CF64: P'rth 2F **109**
NP4: P'garn, P'pool 2C **6**
(not continuous)
NP11: Ris 6D **16**
NP26: Cald 5B **60**
Park Rd. Ind. Est. NP11: Ris 6E **17**
Parkside NP44: C'brn 3G **11**
Parkside Ct. NP4: P'nydd 1A **6**
Park Side La. CF37: P'prdd 6C **14**
Park Sq. NP20: Newp 5C **36**
Parkstone Av. CF3: Old M 5C **74**
Park St. CF10: Card 5C **4** (4A **96**)
CF37: T'rest 2E **25**
NP4: Grif 6E **7**
NP11: Cros K 2A **16**
Park Ter. NP4: P'nydd 1A **6**
Park Vw. CF10: Card 3D **4** (3A **96**)
CF72: L'sant 2F **65**
NP4: P'pool 4D **6**
NP10: Bass 6E **35**
NP11: Cros K 2A **16**
NP16: Chep 1C **62**
NP16: Sed 2H **63**
NP44: Pnwd 5E **9**
Park Vw. Ct. CF14: Whit 1C **84**
CF64: P'rth 5G **101**
Park Vw. Gdns. NP10: Bass 6D **34**
Park Vw. Ter. NP4: P'nydd 1A **6**
Parkwall Rd. CF14: Pontp 3F **73**
Parkway CF3: Rum 5B **88**
Parkway Sth. CF3: Rum 5C **88**
Park Wood Cl. NP18: C'ln 4E **21**
Park Wood Dr. NP10: Bass 1A **52**
Parracombe Cl. CF3: L'rmy 6A **74**
Parracombe Cres. CF3: L'rmy 1H **87**
Parret Cl. NP20: Bet 5H **19**
Parret Rd. NP20: Bet 5H **19**
Parret Wlk. NP20: Bet 5H **19**
Parry Dr. NP19: Newp 4A **38**
Parry St. CF5: Card 3E **95**
Partridge La. CF24: Card 1H **5** (2C **96**)
Partridge Rd. CF24: Card 1H **5** (2C **96**)
CF62: St Ath 3G **111**
Partridge Way NP10: Duf 3G **53**
(not continuous)
Pascal Cl. CF3: St M 5F **75**
Pascall Ct. CF24: Card 1G **5**
Pasteur Gro. CF38: Chu V 2D **42**
Pastures, The CF62: Barry 6G **105**
NP44: L'rfn 2B **12**
Patch, The CF72: L'harry 4A **78**
Patchway Cres. CF3: Rum 3G **87**
Patmore Cl. CF15: Gwae G 1D **68**
Patreane Way CF5: Cul C 6D **92**
Patterdale Cl. CF23: Pen L 5B **86**
Patti Cl. NP19: Newp 3D **38**
Pauls End Ct. NP20: Newp 5C **36**
Pavaland Cl. CF3: St M 1D **88**
Pavia Ct. CF37: P'prdd 6C **14**
Pavillion Ind. Est.
NP4: P'nydd 1B **6**
Paxton Wlk. NP10: Roger 2C **34**
Peach Pl. CF5: F'wtr 1H **93**
Pearce Cl. CF3: St M 2E **89**
Pearce Ct. CF63: Barry 5A **106**
Pearl Pl. CF24: Card 3D **96**

Pearl St. CF24: Card 3D **96**
(not continuous)
Pearson Cres. CF37: Glync 2C **14**
Pearson St. CF24: Card 1G **5** (2C **96**)
Pear Tree Cl. NP18: C'ln 5E **21**
Pear Tree Cotts. NP19: Newp 6H **37**
Pear Tree La. NP19: Newp 6H **37**
Peckham Cl. CF5: L'dff 4H **83**
Pedair Erw Rd. CF14: Heath 2F **85**
Pellett St. CF10: Card 5F **5** (4B **96**)
Pembrey Path NP44: St D 2E **11**
Pembridge Dr. CF64: P'rth 6H **101**
Pembroke Cl. CF38: Tont 1F **43**
CF64: Din P 2A **108**
NP26: Undy 4F **59**
Pembroke Ct. CF83: Caer 5G **27**
NP26: Undy 4F **59**
Pembroke Cres. CF72: Y'erdy 6C **40**
Pembroke Gro. NP19: Newp 1G **55**
Pembroke M. CF5: Card 3D **94**
Pembroke Pl. CF61: Bov 3D **110**
CF62: Barry 1H **117**
NP44: L'rfn 2B **12**
Pembroke Rd. CF5: Card 3E **95**
NP16: Bul 5E **63**
Pembroke Ter. CF64: P'rth 6B **102**
Penally Rd. CF5: Ely 5A **94**
PENARTH **1E 109**
Penarth Ct. NP44: L'rfn 4B **12**
(not continuous)
PENARTH HEAD **6B 102**
Penarth Head La. CF64: P'rth 1F **109**
Penarth Leisure Cen. **6G 101**
Penarth Pier **2G 109**
Penarth Portway CF64: P'rth 6A **102**
Penarth Rd. CF10: Card 6D **4** (5A **96**)
CF11: Card 3F **101**
CF64: L'dgh 3F **101**
Penarth Rd. Retail Pk. CF11: Card 4F **101**
Penarth Station (Rail) **2E 109**
Penbedw NP44: C'iog 1B **12**
Penbryn Coch CF72: L'harry 4B **78**
Pen Bryn Hendy CF72: Mis 6E **65**
Penbury Ct. CF15: Morg 5F **69**
Pencader Rd. CF5: Ely 3A **94**
Pencarn Av. NP10: Coedk 5E **53**
Pencarn La. NP10: Coedk, Duf 5E **53**
(not continuous)
Pencarn Way NP10: Coedk, Duf 4E **53**
Pencerrig St. CF37: P'prdd 6B **14**
Pencisely Av. CF5: L'dff 2C **94**
Pencisely Cres. CF5: L'dff 2C **94**
Pencisely Ri. CF5: L'dff 2C **94**
Pencisely Rd. CF5: L'dff 2C **94**
Penclawdd CF83: Caer 4F **29**
Pencoed Av. CF37: P'prdd 6E **15**
Pencoed Pl. NP44: C'iog 5F **9**
Pencoedtre Rd. CF63: Barry 4A **106**
(not continuous)
Penda Pl. NP16: Sed 2H **63**
Pendine Cl. CF62: Barry 5H **105**
Pendine Rd. CF5: Ely 4A **94**
Pendine Wlk. NP44: F'wtr 3E **11**
Pendoylan Cl. CF63: Barry 5B **106**
Pendoylan Ct. CF5: Ely 3A **94**
Pendoylan Rd. CF72: Groes F 1A **80**
Pendoylan Wlk. NP44: C'brn 3E **11**
Pendragon Cl. CF14: Thorn 3F **71**
Pendraw Pl. CF23: Cyn 1B **86**
Pendwyallt Rd. CF14: Whit 6A **70**
Pendyris St. CF11: Card 6A **4** (5H **95**)
Penedre CF5: L'dff 6C **84**
Penffordd CF15: P'rch 5A **68**
Penford Ct. CF24: Card 1G **5**
PENGAM **1F 97**
Pengam Ind. Est. CF24: Card 3H **97**
Pengam Rd. CF24: Card 1F **97**
Pengwern Rd. CF5: Ely 3A **94**
Pen Hendy CF72: Mis 6E **65**
Penheol Ely Rd. CF37: P'prdd 5E **15**
Penhevad St. CF11: Card 1H **101**
Penhill Cl. CF5: L'dff 2E **95**
Penhill Ct. CF5: Card 2E **95**
Penhill Rd. CF11: Card 2E **95**
Penhow M. NP10: Duf 6G **53**
Penkin Cl. NP19: Newp 5B **38**
Penkin Hill NP19: Newp 4B **38**
Penlan Ri. CF64: L'dgh 5F **101**
Penlan Rd. CF64: L'dgh 4F **101**
Pen Lasgan CF3: Rum 1D **88**
Penlline Ct. CF14: Whit 2C **84**
Penlline Rd. CF14: Whit 2C **84**
Penlline St. CF24: Card 1F **5**
Penllwyn La. CF83: Mac 2D **30**
Penllwyn Wlk. CF83: Mac 2C **30**
Penllyn Av. NP20: Newp 5H **35**
NP44: Pnwd 5E **9**
Penllyn Castle **1A 90**
Penllyn La. NP20: Newp 5H **35**
Penllyn Rd. CF5: Card 4F **95**
Penmaen Wlk. CF5: Ely 6D **92**
Penmaes CF15: P'rch 5A **68**
Penmaes Rd. NP44: G'mdw 2B **10**
PEN-MARC **1D 114**
PENMARK **1D 114**
Penmark Castle (ruins) **1D 114**
Penmark Grn. CF5: Ely 4E **93**
Penmark Rd. CF5: Ely 5E **93**
Pennant Cres. CF23: Cyn 1C **86**
Pennant Ho. *CF37: P'prdd 6C 14*
(off Church St.)
Pennard Cl. NP10: Duf 6G **53**
Pennard Pl. CF14: Llan N 4F **85**
Pennine Cl. CF14: L'shn 6G **71**
NP11: Ris 6H **17**
Pennsylvania CF23: L'dyrn 2D **86**
(not continuous)
Penny Cres. NP20: Malp 4H **19**
Pennyfarthing La. NP26: Undy 4D **58**
Pennyfields NP44: G'mdw 2D **10**
Penny La. CF71: C'bri 3D **90**
Pennyroyal Cl. CF3: St M 5E **75**
PENRHIW **5E 17**
Penrhiw La. CF83: Mac 1G **31**
Penrhiw Rd. CF37: P'prdd 2B **24**
NP11: Ris 5E **17**
Penrhos CF15: Rad 6E **69**
Penrhos Cres. CF3: Rum 3A **88**
Penrhyn Cl. CF3: Rum 2C **88**
Penrice Grn. NP44: L'rfn 3B **12**
Pensarn Rd. CF3: Rum 2C **88**
Pensarn Way NP44: H'lys 5B **10**
Pensidan Vw. NP10: Bass 1B **52**
Penstone Ct. CF10: Card 1B **102**
Penterry Pk. NP16: Chep 2D **62**
Pentir y De CF62: Rho 6G **115**
Pentland Cl. CF14: L'shn 6F **71**
NP11: Ris 6H **17**
Pent Lee CF23: Pent 6E **73**
Pentonville NP20: Newp 4B **36**
PENTREBACH **1E 25**
Pentrebach Rd. CF37: P'prdd, R'fln 1E **25**
PENTREBANE **1G 93**
Pentrebane Rd. CF5: F'wtr, St F 6D **82**
Pentrebane St. CF11: Card 1H **101**
CF83: Caer 1C **46**
Pentre Cl. NP44: Coed E 5D **10**
Pentre Gdns. CF11: Card 5H **95**
Pentre La. NP44: Bet, H'lys, Oakf 2C **18**
Pentrepiod Rd. NP4: Abers, P'nydd 1A **6**
Pentre Pl. CF11: Card 6H **95**
Pentre-Poeth Cl. NP10: Bass 1A **52**
Pentre-Poeth Rd. NP10: Bass, R'drn 2G **51**
Pentre St. CF11: Card 6H **95**
Pentre Tai Rd. NP10: R'drn 3H **33**
PENTWYN **6F 73**
Pentwyn CF15: Rad 1E **83**
CF83: Caer 3A **28**
Pentwyn Bus. Cen. CF23: Pent 5F **73**
Pentwyn Cl. NP16: Pwllm 4B **62**
Pentwyn Ct. CF14: Whit 1C **84**
Pentwyn Dr. CF23: Pent 1E **87**
Pentwyngwyn Rd. CF83: Rud 5B **30**
Pentwyn Interchange CF23: Pent 1G **87**
Pentwyn Isaf CF83: Caer 3B **28**
Pen-Twyn La. NP20: Bet 4G **19**
Pentwyn Leisure Cen. **1F 87**
Pentwyn Rd. CF23: Pent 4D **72**
Pentwyn Ter. CF3: M'fld 5A **76**
PENTYRCH **5H 67**
Pentyrch St. CF24: Card 1H **95**
Penuel La. CF37: P'prdd 6C **14**
Penuel Rd. CF15: P'rch 5H **67**
Pen-y-Bryn CF37: Glync 2D **14**
CF62: Barry 5D **116**
CF63: Barry 6D **106**
CF83: Caer 3H **27**
NP4: P'garn 2D **6**
Pen-y-Bryn Cl. NP20: Bet 5G **19**
Pen-y-Bryn Pl. CF14: Card 5G **85**
Pen-y-Bryn Rd. CF14: Card 5G **85**
CF23: Cyn 6C **72**
Pen-y-Bryn Way CF14: Card 5G **85**
Pen-y-Cae CF83: Caer 4F **29**
Pen-y-Cefn CF14: Thorn 3F **71**
PEN Y COEDCAE **3B 24**
Penycoedcae Rd. CF38: Bed 4H **41**
Pen-y-Cwm CF15: P'rch 4A **68**
Pen-y-Darren Cl. CF37: P'prdd 5C **14**
Penydarren Dr. CF14: Whit 2A **84**
Pen-y-dre CF14: R'ina, Whit 1C **84**
CF83: Caer 2A **28**
Penyffordd CF83: Caer 5B **28**
PENYGARN **2D 6**
Penygarn Rd. CF5: Ely 3H **93**
NP4: P'garn 1C **6**
PENYGAWSI **3F 65**
Penyglog Rd. NP18: L'veth 1G **13**
Penygraig CF14: R'ina 4D **70**
Pen-y-Graig Ter. NP4: P'pool 4C **6**
Pen y Groes CF72: Groes F 6B **66**
Pen-y-Groes CF83: Caer 3A **28**
Pen-y-Groes Av. CF14: R'ina 6F **71**
Pen-y-Groes Gro. NP10: Bass 1A **52**
Pen-y-Groes Rd. CF14: R'ina 6E **71**
PEN-Y-LAN **4C 86**
Penylan Cl. NP4: New I 5H **7**
NP10: Bass 6C **34**
Penylan Ct. CF23: Pen L 4C **86**
NP44: Coed E 5D **10**
Pen-y-Lan Oval CF23: Pen L 4C **86**
Pen-y-Lan Pl. CF23: Pen L 6C **86**
Penylan Rd. CF37: P'prdd 1B **24**
NP19: Newp 4G **37**
NP44: Coed E 4C **10**
Pen-y-Lan Rd. CF23: Card, Pen L 6C **86**
CF71: A'thin, C'bri 2F **91**
NP10: Bass 4A **52**
Pen-y-Lan Ter. CF23: Pen L 5D **86**
Pen-y-Llan La. NP4: P'pool 1H **7**
Pen-y-Mynydd CF37: Glync 1D **14**
Penyoedcae Rd. CF37: Pen c 4H **41**
Penyparc NP44: Pnwd 5D **8**
Pen-y-Parc CF38: Bed 4H **41**
Pen-y-Peel Rd. CF5: Card 3E **95**
Pen-yr-Allt CF83: Caer 3B **46**
Pen-yr-Eglwys CF38: Chu V, Llan F 3D **42**
PENYRHEOL
CF83 . . . . **4A 28**
NP4 . . . . **6C 6**
Penyrheol Rd. NP4: P'rheol 5C **6**
Pen yr Ysgol CF37: T'rest 2D **24**
Pen-y-Turnpike Rd.
CF64: Din P, Mic P 3D **100**
Penyturnpike Vw. CF64: P'rth 1B **108**
Penywain La. NP4: P'pool 3A **6**
Pen-y-Wain La. CF24: Card 6A **86**
Pen-y-Wain Pl. CF24: Card 6B **86**
Penywain Rd. NP4: P'pool 2A **6**
Pen-y-Wain Rd. CF24: Card 6B **86**
Penywain St. NP4: P'pool 2B **6**
Penywain Ter. NP4: P'pool 2B **6**
Penywaun CF38: E Isaf 6F **43**
Pen-y-Waun CF15: P'rch 4H **67**
CF64: Din P 2H **107**
Pen-y-Waun Cl. NP44: C'brn 3F **11**
Penywaun Rd. NP44: F'wtr 4E **11**
(not continuous)
Pen-y-Waun Rd. NP44: St D 3F **11**
(not continuous)
Peppermint Dr. CF23: Pontp 4D **72**
Pepys Cres. CF3: L'rmy 1H **87**
Pepys Gro. NP20: Newp 1G **53**
Percival Cl. CF14: Thorn 3F **71**
Perclose CF64: Din P 2H **107**
Percoed La. NP10: Coedk, St Bri W 2D **76**
(not continuous)
Percy Smith Rd. CF61: Bov 3E **111**

Percy St. CF10: Card .5A **96**
Peregrine Ct. NP26: Undy .4E **59**
Perrots Cl. CF5: F'wtr .1A **94**
Perry Ct. NP44: Thorn .1C **10**
Persondy La. CF5: Ely .4D **92**
Perthy Cl. NP44: Coed E .5D **10**
Peterston Rd. CF72: Groes F .1C **80**
Peterswell Rd. CF62: Barry .2E **117**
Petherton M. CF5: L'dff .6B **84**
Petherton Pl. CF3: L'rmy .1A **88**
Pethybridge Rd. CF5: Ely .3F **93**
Petrel Cl. CF64: P'rth .5E **109**
Pettingale Rd. NP44: C'iog .5H **9**
Petunia Wlk. NP10: Roger .2H **33**
Philadelphia Cl. CF63: Barry .6D **106**
Philanthropic Cotts. *NP44: H'lys .5B **10***
(off Doralit Way)
Philip Cl. CF14: Heath .1F **85**
Philippa Freeth Ct. CF63: Barry .3A **118**
Philip St. CF11: Card .4F **95**
Phillip Ct. NP19: Newp .4E **37**
Phillips Grn. NP10: Roger .5D **34**
Phillip St. CF37: P'prdd .2B **24**
NP11: Ris .5D **16**
NP19: Newp .4E **37**
Philog, The CF14: Whit .3E **85**
Philog Ct. CF14: Whit .3E **85**
Phoenix Dr. NP16: Bul .6G **63**
Phoenix Est. CF14: Heath .1F **85**
Phoenix Way CF14: Heath .2F **85**
Phyllis St. CF62: Barry .5G **117**
Piccadilly CF71: L'thian .5B **90**
Piccadilly Sq. CF83: Caer .6D **28**
Picked La. NP18: Nash .4H **55**
PICKETSTON .1A **112**
Picketston Cl. CF62: E Bre .2A **112**
Pickwick Cl. CF14: Thorn .3H **71**
Picton Ct. CF61: Llan M .2C **110**
Picton Pl. CF11: Card .4F **95**
Picton Rd. CF62: Rho .5E **115**
Picton St. NP4: Grif .6E **7**
Picton Wlk. CF11: Card .4F **95**
NP10: Duf .6G **53**
NP44: F'wtr .3D **10**
Picwic Grn. *NP44: G'mdw .3D **10***
(off Byways)
Piercefield Av. NP16: Chep .1C **62**
Piercefield Pl. CF24: Card .1H **5** (2D **96**)
Pierhead St. CF10: Card .1C **102**
Pierhead Vw. CF64: P'rth .5H **101**
Pilgrim Cl. CF15: Rad .2F **83**
PILL, THE .6F **61**
Pill Farm Ind. Est. NP26: Cald .6F **61**
PILLGWENLLY .6C **36**
Pillgwenlly Millennium Cen. .1C **54**
Pillmawr Circ. NP20: Malp .5B **20**
Pillmawr Rd. NP18: C'ln .5B **20**
NP20: Malp .5B **20**
Pill Row NP26: Cald .5E **61**
Pill St. CF64: P'rth .6G **101**
Pill Way NP26: Pskwt .5F **61**
Pilton Pl. CF14: Card .5F **85**
Pilton Va. NP20: Malp .4B **20**
Pine Cl. NP11: Ris .5E **17**
Pine Ct. CF15: Tong .4H **69**
CF38: Llan F .6C **42**
CF72: T Grn .2C **64**
Pinecrest Dr. CF14: Thorn .2H **71**
Pine Gdns. NP4: P'pool .3A **6**
Pine Gro. NP10: Duf .3H **53**
Pinehurst Rd. CF5: F'wtr .1G **93**
Pines, The CF14: Whit .2C **84**
Pine Tree Cl. CF15: Rad .6E **69**
Pine Tree Rd. NP4: New I .5G **7**
Pinewood Av. CF37: R'fln .4H **25**
Pinewood Cl. CF64: L'dgh .5G **101**
NP20: Malp .5B **20**
Pine Wood Cres. CF23: Pen L .4E **87**
Pinewood Hill CF72: T Grn .3C **64**
Pinewood Sq. CF62: E Bre .2B **112**
Pinewood Vw. CF37: Glync .1C **14**
Pinnell Pl. *NP20: Newp .6C **36***
(off Coulson Cl.)
Pioden For CF62: Barry .6H **117**
Piper Cl. CF5: L'dff .5H **83**
NP19: Newp .1G **37**

Pipkin Cl. CF23: Pontp .4F **73**
Pitman La. CF11: Card .3G **95**
Pitman St. CF11: Card .3G **95**
Pitmedden Cl. CF3: St M .6D **74**
Place de Cormeilles NP16: Chep .2E **63**
Plane St. CF37: R'fln .4G **25**
Plane Tree Cl. NP18: C'ln .5F **21**
Planet St. CF24: Card .3H **5** (3C **96**)
Plantagenet St. CF11: Card .5A **4** (4H **95**)
Plantation, The NP26: Undy .4D **58**
Plantation Dr. NP44: C'iog .1B **12**
Plas Bryn CF5: F'wtr .6G **83**
Plas Bryn Gomer NP44: C'iog .5G **9**
Plas Cae Llwyd CF83: L'brad .1B **28**
Plas Carmel CF37: P'prdd .6B **14**
Plas Cleddau CF62: Barry .2E **117**
Plas Craig NP44: C'brn .1H **11**
Plas Cwrt NP44: Oakf .5H **11**
Plas Derwen NP44: C'iog .1B **12**
Plas Ebbw NP44: C'brn .1G **11**
Plas Essyllt CF64: Din P .3H **107**
Plas Glen Rosa CF64: P'rth .6A **102**
Plas Grug CF83: Caer .2B **46**
Plas Gwernen CF63: Barry .5B **106**
Plas Gwyn CF5: L'dff .6C **84**
Plas Gwynt M. CF11: Card .2A **4** (3G **95**)
Plas Islwyn NP44: C'brn .1G **11**
Plasmawr Rd. CF5: F'wtr .6H **83**
Plas Melin CF14: Whit .3B **84**
Plas Nant CF83: Abert .2E **27**
Plas Newydd CF14: Whit .3C **84**
Plasnewydd Pl. CF24: Card .1C **96**
Plasnewydd Rd. CF24: Card .1G **5** (1B **96**)
(not continuous)
Plasnewydd Sq. CF24: Card .1B **96**
Plas Pamir CF64: P'rth .5B **102**
Plas Phillips CF83: Caer .6B **28**
Plas St Andresse CF64: P'rth .5B **102**
Plas St Pol de Leon
CF64: P'rth .6B **102**
Plassey Sq. CF64: P'rth .6A **102**
Plassey St. CF64: P'rth .6H **101**
Plas Taliesin CF64: P'rth .5B **102**
Plas Thomas CF83: Caer .1B **46**
Plas Treoda CF14: Whit .3D **84**
Plas Trosnant NP44: C'brn .6E **9**
Plasturton Av. CF11: Card .2F **95**
Plasturton Gdns. CF11: Card .3G **95**
Plasturton Pl. CF11: Card .3G **95**
Plas Twyn NP44: C'brn .6F **9**
Plas ty-Coch NP44: Oakf .5H **11**
Plas y Biswail CF3: St M .1D **88**
Plas y Coed CF23: Cyn .4B **86**
Plas-y-Delyn CF14: L'vne .2B **72**
Plas-y-Fedwen CF37: Glync .1D **14**
Plas-y-Llan CF14: Whit .2C **84**
Plas y Mynach CF15: Rad .3G **83**
Plas yr Eglwys *CF37: P'prdd .5D **14***
(off Dorothy St.)
Plas-yr-Odyn CF72: L'harry .4C **78**
Playford Cres. NP19: Newp .3D **38**
Pleasant Pl. CF83: Caer .4A **28**
Pleasant Vw. CF37: P'prdd .5D **14**
CF38: Bed .5A **42**
CF62: Barry .5F **105**
*NP4: P'nydd .1A **6***
(off Hanbury Rd.)
Plover Cl. NP19: Newp .2C **56**
Plover Cres. NP26: Cald .6D **60**
Plover Way CF64: P'rth .5E **109**
Plum Tree La. NP26: Cald .6C **60**
Plymouth Dr. CF15: Rad .2G **83**
Plymouth Rd. CF37: P'prdd .6A **14**
CF62: Barry .5G **117**
CF64: P'rth .2F **109**
Plymouth Wood Cl. CF5: Ely .3H **93**
Plymouth Wood Cres. CF5: Ely .3G **93**
Plymouth Wood Rd. CF5: Ely .3H **93**
Plym Wlk. NP20: Bet .5G **19**
Poets Cl. CF37: R'fln .3G **25**
Poets Fld. Rd. CF62: Barry .5G **105**
Pollard Cl. NP18: C'ln .5E **21**
Polo Ground Ind. Est. NP4: New I .6F **7**
(Pontyfelin Av.)
NP4: New I .5F **7**
(Sth. Pontypool Ind. Pk.)

Pomeroy St. CF10: Card .2B **102**
Pommergelli Rd. CF14: Llan N .3B **84**
Pontalun Cl. CF63: Barry .5A **106**
Pont Ap Hywell NP4: P'pool .2C **6**
PONTCANNA .2F **95**
Pontcanna Ct. CF5: L'dff .1E **95**
Pontcanna Pl. CF11: Card .2F **95**
Pontcanna St. CF11: Card .2F **95**
Pontfaen CF23: Pent .5D **72**
Pontfaen Rd. NP19: Newp .6A **38**
PONTHIR .1F **21**
Ponthir Rd. NP18: C'ln, P'hir .2G **21**
PONTNEWYDD .6E **9**
Pontnewydd Wlk. NP44: C'brn .6E **9**
PONTNEWYNYDD .1A **6**
Pontnewynydd Ind. Est. NP4: P'nydd .1A **6**
Pontnewynydd Small Bus. Cen.
NP4: P'nydd .1A **6**
Pont-Pentre Cvn. Pk. *CF37: Up Bo .6A **26***
(off Crwys Cres.)
PONTPRENNAU .4F **73**
PONTRHYDYRUN .5G **9**
Pontrhydyrun Rd. NP44: Pon'run .4E **9**
Pontrilas Cl. CF5: Ely .6D **92**
Pontshonnorton Rd.
CF37: P'prdd, C'fydd .4E **15**
PONT SIÔN NORTON .4E **15**
PONTYCLUN .6D **64**
Pontyclun Station (Rail) .6C **64**
PONT-Y-FELIN .1G **9**
Pontyfelin Av. NP4: New I .6F **7**
Pontyfelin Ind. Est. NP4: New I .1F **9**
Pont-y-Felin La. NP4: New I .1G **9**
Pont-y-Felin Rd. NP4: New I .6F **7**
Pontygwindy Ind. Est. CF83: Caer .3C **28**
Pontygwindy Rd. CF83: Caer .3C **28**
Pontymason Cl. NP10: Roger .2A **34**
Pontymason Ct. NP10: Roger .2A **34**
Pontymason La. NP10: Roger .6H **17**
NP11: Ris, Roger .6H **17**
Pontymason Ri. NP10: Roger .2A **34**
PONTYMISTER .6D **16**
Pontymister Ind. Est. NP11: Ris .1E **33**
PONTYMOEL .4D **6**
Pontypandy Ind. Est. CF83: Caer .3C **28**
Pontypandy La. CF83: Caer .4C **28**
Ponty Pandy Vw. CF83: Caer .4C **28**
PONTYPOOL .2C **6**
Pontypool Active Living Cen. .3D **6**
Pontypool & New Inn Station (Rail) .4G **7**
Pontypool Nth. Ind. Est. NP4: P'nydd .1A **6**
Pontypool Pk. .3D **6**
Pontypool RFC .3D **6**
Pontypool Ski & Leisure Cen. .2D **6**
Pontypool Western By-Pass
NP4: P'nydd, P'pool .1B **6**
PONTYPRIDD .1C **24**
PONTYPRIDD COTTAGE HOSPITAL (Y BWTHYN)
.6E **15**
Pontypridd Cricket Club .1D **24**
Pontypridd Mus. .6C **14**
Pontypridd Rd. CF62: Barry .2D **116**
Pontypridd RUFC (Sardis Road Ground)
.1D **24**
Pontypridd Rugby Football Ground .*6B 14*
(off Sardis Rd.)
Pontypridd Station (Rail) .1C **24**
Pontypridd St. CF63: Barry .1B **118**
PONTYPWL .2C **6**
PONTYWAUN .1A **16**
Pool La. NP19: Newp .2E **37**
(not continuous)
Poplar Av. NP4: New I .4G **7**
Poplar Cl. CF5: F'wtr .6G **83**
NP26: Rog .6A **60**
Poplar Ct. CF62: Barry .6A **106**
NP18: C'ln .4F **21**
Poplar Ho. CF14: Whit .1A **84**
Poplar Rd. CF5: F'wtr .6G **83**
CF37: R'fln .4G **25**
CF83: Caer .1E **47**
NP19: Newp .4H **37**
NP44: C'iog .6G **9**
Poplars, The CF72: L'harry .5B **78**
NP11: Ris .4B **16**
NP16: Chep .1E **63**

Poplar Ter. *NP4: P'nydd* *1A 6*
(off Charlesville)
Poppyfield Cl. CF3: St M 1C **88**
Poppy Pl. NP10: Roger 2H **33**
Porcher Av. CF37: Glync 2C **14**
Porlock Dr. CF64: Sul 2H **119**
Porlock Rd. CF3: L'rmy 6B **74**
Porset Cl. CF83: Caer 6E **29**
Porset Dr. CF83: Caer 6D **28**
Porset Pk. CF83: Caer 5E **29**
Porset Row CF83: Caer 4F **29**
Portfield Cres. CF14: L'shn 6H **71**
Porthamal Gdns. CF14: R'ina 1E **85**
Porthamal Rd. CF14: R'ina 1E **85**
Porthcawl Rd. CF5: Ely 5G **93**
PORTHCERI **5A 116**
PORTHKERRY **5A 116**
Porthkerry Country Pk. **4B 116**
Porthkerry Pl. CF14: Card 5F **85**
Porthkerry Rd. CF62: Barry 4F **117**
CF62: Rho 4G **115**
Porth Mawr Rd. NP44: C'brn 1G **11**
Porth-y-Castell CF62: Barry 4C **116**
Porth-y-Green Cl. CF71: L'thian 4C **90**
PORTH YSGEWIN **5G 61**
Portland Cl. CF64: P'rth 3F **109**
Portland Pl. CF14: L'vne 3B **72**
Portland St. NP20: Newp 1D **54**
Portland Way NP20: Newp 1D **54**
Port Madoc Rd. CF3: Rum 2C **88**
Portmanmoor Rd. CF24: Card 4E **97**
(not continuous)
Portmanmoor Rd. Ind. Est. CF24: Card . . . 5E **97**
Portmanmoor Rd. La. CF24: Card 4E **97**
Port M. CF62: Barry 3M **105**
Portreeve Cl. CF72: L'sant 3F **65**
Port Rd. CF5: Cul C, Wen 1D **98**
CF62: Barry 6F **105**
(Highlight La.)
CF62: Barry 5F **105**
(Hinchsliff Av.)
CF62: Barry 4H **105**
(Port M.)
CF62: E Abe 5A **114**
CF62: Rho 4G **115**
CF63: Barry 4H **105**
NP20: Newp 2B **54**
Port Rd. E. CF62: Barry 5F **105**
Port Rd. W. CF62: Barry 1D **116**
PORTSKEWETT **5G 61**
Portskewett St. NP19: Newp 6F **37**
Port Wall 2E **63**
Portwall Rd. NP16: Chep 2E **63**
Postern *NP44: F'wtr* *4E 11*
(off Henllys Way)
Post Office Row CF15: Gwae G 6D **44**
NP26: Sud 6H **61**
Post Office Ter. NP18: P'hir 1F **21**
Potters Cft. NP16: B'ly 6H **63**
Potter St. NP20: Newp 1D **54**
Pottery Rd. NP20: Newp 1D **54**
Pottery Ter. NP20: Newp 1C **54**
Pound Fld. CF61: Llan M 3B **110**
Pound Hill NP10: Bass, Coedk 4A **52**
Pound La. CF5: Wen 5D **98**
NP26: C'ent 1A **60**
Powderham Dr. CF11: Card 5F **95**
Powell Duffryn Way CF62: Barry 4F **117**
(not continuous)
Powell's Pl. NP20: Newp 5C **36**
Powerleague Cardiff **2D 84**
Power St. NP20: Newp 3B **36**
Powis Cl. NP10: Duf 6F **53**
Powis Vw. CF63: Barry 6C **106**
Powys Cl. CF64: Din P 1A **108**
Powys Dr. CF64: Din P 1H **107**
Powys Gdns. CF64: Din P 1A **108**
Powys Pl. CF37: R'fln 3F **25**
CF64: Din P 1A **108**
Powys Rd. CF37: T'rest 2B **44**
CF64: P'rth 3D **108**
Precinct, The CF38: Chu V 2G **43**
CF61: Llan M 3B **110**
Prendergast Pl. CF5: Ely 6H **93**
Prennau Ho. CF23: Pontp 3G **73**
Presceli Cl. NP11: Ris 5G **17**
Prescoch La. NP4: P'pool 5D **6**
Prestatyn Rd. CF3: Rum 2B **88**
Presteigne Av. CF38: Tont 1F **43**
Presteigne Wlk. NP44: C'brn 3E **11**
Preston Av. NP20: Newp 5H **35**
Preston Cl. CF72: L'sant 1F **65**
NP16: Bul 6F **63**
Preswylfa St. CF5: Card 2D **94**
Price Av. CF63: Barry 6B **106**
Price Cl. NP20: Newp 1C **54**
Priestley Cl. NP20: Newp 2H **53**
Priest Rd. CF24: Card 2D **96**
Primrose Cl. CF3: Rum 5H **87**
CF71: C'bri 4E **91**
Primrose Ct. NP44: Ty C 4B **10**
Primrose Hill CF71: C'bri 4E **91**
Primrose Way NP10: Roger 2H **33**
Prince Charles Ct. CF64: P'rth 6A **102**
Prince Edward Ho. CF64: P'rth 6A **102**
Prince Leopold St. CF24: Card 3H **5** (3D **96**)
Prince Llewellyn Ho. CF64: P'rth 6A **102**
Prince of Wales Dr. CF5: St F 2C **82**
Prince Rhodry Ho. CF64: P'rth 6A **102**
Princes Av. CF24: Card 2D **96**
CF83: Caer 2D **46**
Princes Ct. CF24: Card 2F **5** (3B **96**)
Princes Ri. CF83: Caer 2D **46**
Princess St. CF37: T'rest 2D **24**
Princes St. CF24: Card 2D **96**
CF62: Barry 3F **117**
Prince St. NP4: P'pool 2B **6**
NP19: Newp 3D **36**
Prince's Wlk. NP4: New I 5H **7**
Priority Bus. Cen. CF10: Card 6A **96**
(not continuous)
Priority Bus. Pk. CF63: Barry 6E **107**
Priory, The NP16: Chep 2F **63**
Priory Cl. CF37: P'prdd 4B **14**
NP16: Chep 1D **62**
NP18: C'ln 4E **21**
NP26: Cald 4C **60**
Priory Ct. NP26: Magor 5D **58**
Priory Cres. NP18: L'stne 1F **39**
Priory Dr. NP18: L'stne 1E **39**
Priory Gdns. CF63: Barry 5B **106**
NP18: L'stne 6F **23**
NP26: Magor 5C **58**
Priory Gro. NP18: L'stne 1F **39**
Priory (remains of) . . . . **3B 4 (3H 95)**
Priory St. NP11: Ris 6E **17**
Priory Vw. NP18: L'stne 1F **39**
Priory Way NP18: L'stne 6F **23**
Pritchard Cl. CF5: L'dff 5A **84**
Pritchard Ct. CF5: L'dff 1C **94**
Probert Pl. NP19: Newp 4E **37**
Proctor Cl. CF62: Barry 2E **117**
Promenade CF62: Barry 6E **117**
(Lakeside)
CF62: Barry 6G **117**
(Paget Rd.)
Prospect Cres. NP26: Cald 5D **60**
Prospect Dr. CF5: L'dff 1B **94**
Prospect Pl. NP4: New I 6G **7**
NP44: C'brn 3F **11**
Prospect St. NP20: Newp 2B **36**
Prosser La. NP20: Newp 5H **35**
Providence Pl. CF14: Whit 6B **70**
Prysg Field Roman Barracks ***5H 21***
(in Roman Legionary Mus.)
Pugsley St. NP20: Newp 3C **36**
Pum Erw Rd. CF14: Heath 2F **85**
Pump St. NP20: Newp 4B **36**
Purbeck St. CF5: Card 3E **95**
Purcell Rd. CF3: L'rmy 6B **74**
CF64: P'rth 4D **108**
Purcell Sq. NP19: Newp 4A **38**
Purdey Cl. CF62: Barry 6E **105**
Pwhelli Ct. CF3: Rum 3A **88**
PWLL-GWAUN **6B 14**
Pwll-Gwaun Rd. CF37: P'prdd 6B **14**
Pwllhelyg CF15: Tong 5H **69**
Pwll Mawr Av. CF3: Rum 4A **88**
Pwll-Mawr Ct. CF3: Rum 5A **88**
Pwllmelin La. CF5: L'dff 1B **94**
Pwllmelin Rd. CF5: F'wtr, L'dff 6H **83**
PWLLMEURIG **5B 62**
PWLLMEYRIC **5B 62**
Pwllmeyric Cl. NP16: Pwllm 5B **62**
Pwll-Pen Ct. NP18: L'wrn 5D **38**
PWLLYPANT **3C 28**
PYE CORNER **4B 56**
Pye Cnr. NP10: Roger 6E **35**
Pyke St. CF63: Barry 1A **118**
Pyle Rd. CF5: Ely 5G **93**
Pyra Ct. *CF62: Barry* *4E 117*
(off St Nicholas Cl.)
Pytchley Cl. CF72: C Inn 3G **65**

Q

QED Centre, The CF37: T'rest 2B **44**
Quail Ct. CF24: Card 1H **5** (2C **96**)
Quantock Cl. NP11: Ris 6G **17**
Quantock Dr. NP19: Newp 3A **38**
Quarella St. CF63: Barry 1B **118**
Quarry Cl. CF5: F'wtr 1G **93**
Quarry Cres. CF5: F'wtr 2G **93**
Quarry Dale CF3: Rum 5H **87**
Quarry Hill Cl. CF37: P'prdd 6A **14**
Quarry La. CF15: N'grw 4E **45**
Quarry Ri. NP26: Undy 3D **58**
Quarry Rd. CF37: P'prdd 6A **14**
Quarry St. CF15: N'grw 3D **44**
Quasar Cen. ***5H 117***
(off Station App. Rd.)
Quay St. CF10: Card 4C **4** (4A **96**)
Quebec Cl. NP20: Newp 6F **35**
Queen Anne Sq. CF10: Card 1B **4** (2H **95**)
Queen Charlotte Dr. CF15: Cre 1F **81**
Queens Arc. CF10: Card 3D **4** (4A **96**)
Queensberry Rd. CF23: Pen L 4D **86**
Queen's Cl. NP20: Newp 3B **36**
Queen's Cft. NP20: Newp 3B **36**
Queens Dr. CF5: Cul C 1E **99**
CF38: Llan F 5D **42**
Queens Gdns. NP26: Magor 4C **58**
Queen's Hill NP20: Newp 3B **36**
Queen's Hill Cres. NP20: Newp 3B **36**
Queens Rd. CF64: P'rth 6A **102**
NP16: Bul 4E **63**
Queens Rd. Sth. CF10: Card 4D **102**
Queen St. CF10: Card 3D **4** (3A **96**)
CF15: Tong 4G **69**
CF37: T'rest 2E **25**
CF62: Barry 3F **117**
NP4: Grif 6E **7**
NP4: P'pool 2B **6**
NP20: Newp 6C **36**
Queens Way CF63: Barry 4A **118**
NP19: L'wrn, Newp 2B **56**
Queensway CF15: N'grw 4E **45**
NP20: Newp 4B **36**
Queensway Mdws. NP19: Newp 1A **56**
Queensway Mdws. Ind. Est.
NP19: Newp 2A **56**
Queenwood CF23: Pen L 4E **87**
Queenwood Cl. CF23: Pen L 4C **86**
Quentin St. CF14: Card 5G **85**
Quilter Cl. NP19: Newp 5B **38**

R

Rachel Cl. CF5: L'dff 4H **83**
Rachel Sq. NP10: Duf 5G **53**
Radnor Ct. CF5: Card 3E **95**
Radnor Dr. CF38: Tont 1F **43**
Radnor Grn. CF62: Barry 6H **105**
Radnor Ho. CF64: P'rth 3D **108**
Radnor Rd. CF5: Card 3E **95**
CF61: Bov 3E **111**
NP19: Newp 3E **37**
Radnor Way NP44: C'brn 3G **11**
RADUR **2G 83**
RADYR **2G 83**
RADYR COURT **4A 84**
Radyr Ct. Cl. CF5: L'dff 5B **84**
Radyr Ct. Ri. CF5: L'dff 5B **84**
Radyr Ct. Rd. CF5: L'dff 4H **83**
(not continuous)

Radyr Ct. Shop. Pct. CF5: L'dff 4H **83**
Radyr Farm Rd. CF15: Rad 3G **83**
Radyr Golf Course 2E **83**
Radyr Pl. CF14: Llan N 5F **85**
Radyr Rd. CF14: Llan N 4B **84**
Radyr Station (Rail) 2G **83**
Radyr Wood Nature Reserve 2G **83**
RAF St Athan Track 2D **112**
Raglan Cl. CF3: St M 6E **75**
CF64: Din P 2A **108**
Raglan Ct. CF83: Caer 5H **27**
NP20: Newp 6C **36**
NP44: C'iog .5F **9**
Raglande Ct. CF61: Llan M 4C **110**
Raglan Ho. CF10: Card 4B **4**
Raglan M. NP10: Duf 6G **53**
Raglan St. NP11: Ris 4C **16**
Raglan Way NP16: Bul 5F **63**
Ragnall Cl. CF14: Thorn 2G **71**
Railway Cres. CF24: Card 3D **96**
Railway St. CF14: Card 6G **85**
CF24: Card .3D **96**
NP11: Ris 4D **16**
NP20: Newp 4B **36**
Railway Ter. CF11: Card 4F **95**
CF15: Tong .4G **69**
CF38: Llan F 4D **42**
CF64: Din P 1A **108**
CF64: P'rth .1E **109**
CF72: P'clun 6D **64**
CF83: Caer .1D **46**
NP4: Seba 3E **9**
Railway Vw. NP26: Cald 6E **61**
Raisdale Gdns. CF64: P'rth 3F **109**
Raisdale Rd. CF64: P'rth 3E **109**
Raldan Cl. CF63: Barry 5B **106**
Raleigh Wlk. CF10: Card 6F **5** (5B **96**)
Ralph St. CF37: P'prdd 5D **14**
Rambler Cl. CF14: Thorn 2H **71**
Ramp, The NP26: Undy 5E **59**
Ramsey Cl. NP19: Newp 2F **37**
Ramsey Rd. CF62: Barry 5H **105**
Ramsey Wlk. NP19: Newp 2F **37**
NP44: Pnwd .6C **8**
Ramsons Way CF5: Ely 4E **93**
Rankine Cl. NP20: Malp 5H **19**
Rannoch Dr. CF23: Cyn 2C **86**
Raphael Cl. NP19: Newp 2G **37**
Ravensbrook CF15: Morg 5E **69**
Ravenscourt CF24: Card 1B **96**
NP44: G'mdw 2D **10**
Ravens Ct. Cl. CF23: Pen L 5D **86**
Ravenshoe Rd. CF63: Barry 6D **106**
Ravenswood CF11: Card 5H **101**
Ravenswood Ct. NP11: Ris 4C **16**
Raven Way CF64: P'rth 6E **109**
Rawden M. CF11: Card 4A **4** (4G **95**)
Rawden Pl. CF11: Card 4A **4** (4G **95**)
Raymond Ter. CF37: T'rest 3E **25**
Readers La. CF62: Rho 5E **115**
Readers Way CF62: Rho 5D **114**
Reardon Smith Ct. CF5: F'wtr 1H **93**
Rectory Cl. CF5: Wen 6E **99**
CF15: Rad 2G **83**
CF83: Caer .2C **46**
Rectory Ct. CF61: L'maes 1D **110**
CF64: P'rth .1F **109**
Rectory Dr. CF62: St Ath 4D **112**
Rectory Gdns. CF83: Mac 2G **31**
NP26: Undy .4F **59**
Rectory Rd. CF5: Card 3E **95**
CF62: St Ath 4D **112**
CF63: Barry .1B **118**
CF64: P'rth .1F **109**
CF83: B'ws 2G **29**
CF83: Caer .1C **46**
Rectory Rd. La. CF64: P'rth 1F **109**
Redberth Cl. CF62: Barry 6H **105**
Redbrink Ct. CF5: Ely 3G **93**
Redbrink Cres. CF62: Barry 5H **117**
Redbrook Av. CF83: Tret 3A **30**
Redbrook Ct. CF83: Caer 2C **46**
Redbrook La. CF83: Mac 3B **30**
Redbrook Rd. NP20: Newp 4G **35**
Redbrook Way NP44: C'brn 2H **11**
Redcliffe Av. CF5: Card 3C **94**

Reddings, The NP16: Bul 5F **63**
Red Dragon Cen., The 1C **102**
Rede Rd. NP44: F'wtr 4D **10**
Redgate Ter. CF72: Groes F 6C **66**
Red Ho. Cl. CF5: Ely 3G **93**
Red Ho. Cres. CF5: Ely 4G **93**
Red Ho. Pl. CF5: Ely 3H **93**
Red Ho. Rd. CF5: Ely 3G **93**
Redlands, The NP19: Newp 5A **38**
Redlands Av. CF64: P'rth 1C **108**
Redlands Ho. CF64: P'rth 1C **108**
Redlands Rd. CF64: P'rth 6F **101**
Redland St. NP20: Newp 2B **36**
Redlaver St. CF11: Card 6H **95**
Redmeadow Cres. NP26: Cald 6E **61**
Redvers St. NP19: Newp 5F **37**
Redwell Ct. CF23: Pen L 5C **86**
Redwick Ct. NP44: C'brn 3H **11**
Redwick Rd. NP26: Magor 5C **58**
Redwood Cl. CF3: St M 6C **74**
CF61: Bov 4E **111**
NP16: Bul 5E **63**
NP18: C'ln 5E **21**
Redwood Ct. CF14: L'shn 5H **71**
Redwood Dr. CF38: Llan F 5C **42**
Reene Ct. NP19: Newp 6G **37**
Rees Cl. NP20: Malp 4A **20**
Rees Ct. CF61: Bov 3D **110**
Rees Ter. *CF37: T'rest* . . . . *.3E 25*
(off Meadow St.)
Reevesland Ind. Est. NP19: Newp 3G **55**
Regency Cl. CF61: Llan M 2C **110**
Regent Av. CF5: Cul C 1E **99**
Regent Ct. CF37: P'prdd 6A **14**
Regent Gdns. CF14: Whit 1C **84**
Regents Trade Pk. CF24: Card 5D **96**
Regent St. CF62: Barry 2H **117**
(not continuous)
Regent Way NP16: Chep 2E **63**
Reginald Ter. NP10: Roger 5D **34**
Regina Ter. CF5: Card 2D **94**
Regus Ho. CF23: Pontp 3G **73**
Reigate Cl. CF14: Thorn 2G **71**
Relf Rd. CF3: Rum 3A **88**
Rembrandt Way NP19: Newp 1F **37**
Rennie St. CF11: Card 4G **95**
Renoir Rd. NP19: Newp 2G **37**
Reresby Ct. CF10: Card 1B **102**
Reservoir Cl. NP10: Roger 5D **34**
Residention Cvn. Pk. CF38: Bed 3A **42**
Restway Ct. CF5: L'dff 4A **84**
Restways Cl. CF5: L'dff 5H **83**
Restway Wall NP16: Chep 2E **63**
Retford Ct. CF14: Whit 3E **85**
Retreat, The CF23: Pen L 5D **86**
NP26: Cald 6C **60**
Reynolds Cl. NP19: Newp 2F **37**
Rheidol Cl. CF14: L'shn 5A **72**
Rheidol Dr. CF62: Barry 1D **116**
Rhigoes St. CF24: Card 6H **85**
Rhigos Gdns. CF24: Card 6H **85**
RHISGA 4D **16**
RHIWBEINA 6E **71**
RHIWBINA 6E **71**
Rhiwbina Garden Village CF14: R'ina 6D **70**
Rhiwbina Hill CF14: R'ina, Tong 3B **70**
CF83: Caer 6A **46**
Rhiwbina Station (Rail) 1D **84**
RHIWDERIN 6A **34**
RHIWDERYN 6A **34**
Rhiwderyn Cl. CF5: Ely 6D **92**
Rhiw Fach CF83: Caer 4A **28**
Rhiw Felin CF37: R'fln 3G **25**
Rhiwlas CF14: Thorn 3E **71**
Rhiw Melin NP44: Up Cwm 5B **8**
Rhiwr Ddar CF15: Taff W 6E **45**
Rhiwr Ddar Ho. CF15: Taff W 1E **69**
RHIWSAESON 3C **66**
Rhiwsaeson Rd. CF72: R'son 3H **65**
Rhoda Fa'r Mor CF62: Rho 6G **115**
Rhoddfa'r Gwagenni CF63: Barry 3H **117**
Rhodfa Felin CF62: Barry 3E **117**
Rhodfa Marics CF72: Y'erdy 1D **64**
Rhodfar Orsaf CF38: Chu V 3F **43**
Rhodfa Sweldon CF62: Barry 3G **117**
Rhododendron Cl. CF23: Pent 6D **72**

Rhodri Pl. NP44: L'rfn 3B **12**
Rhondda Rd. CF37: P'prdd 6B **14**
RHOOSE 5F **115**
Rhoose Rd. CF62: Rho 5F **115**
Rhoose Station (Rail) 6E **115**
Rhos, The CF83: Caer 5E **29**
Rhos Ddu CF64: P'rth 3C **108**
Rhos Helyg CF83: Caer 5F **29**
Rhos Llan CF14: R'ina 6E **71**
Rhos Llantwit CF83: Caer 5E **29**
Rhossilli Av. CF3: Rum 3A **88**
Rhossilli Rd. CF3: Rum 3A **88**
Rhos St. CF83: Caer 4C **28**
Rhuddlan Cl. NP10: R'drn 6A **34**
Rhuddlan Ct. CF83: Caer 4G **27**
Rhuddlan Way CF64: Din P 1A **108**
Rhydhelig Av. CF14: Heath 3F **85**
Rhydlafar Dr. CF5: St F 3C **82**
RHYDRI 1C **48**
RHYDYFELIN 4G **25**
Rhyd-y-Gwern Cl. CF83: Caer 4F **29**
Rhyd y Gwern Isaf CF83: Mac 2G **31**
Rhyd-y-Gwern La. CF83: Mac 3F **31**
Rhyd y Nant CF72: P'clun 6D **64**
RHYDYPENAU 6H **71**
Rhyd-y-Penau Cl. CF14: L'shn 1A **86**
Rhyd-y-Penau Rd. CF23: Cyn 1A **86**
Rhyd-yr-Helyg CF15: N'grw 3D **44**
Rhyl Rd. CF3: Rum 3A **88**
Rhymney Ct. NP44: Thorn 1C **10**
Rhymney Ho. CF23: Pontp 3G **73**
Rhymney River Bri. Rd. CF23: Pen L 6F **87**
Rhymney River Sailing & Angling Club
. . . . .2H **97**
Rhymney St. CF24: Card 1B **96**
Rhymney Ter. CF24: Card 1A **96**
CF83: Caer 1C **46**
RHYMNI 5A **88**
Rialto Ct. CF14: Whit 2D **84**
Ribble Sq. NP20: Bet 5G **19**
Ribble Wlk. NP20: Bet 5G **19**
Richard Apartments *CF24: Card* . . . . *.2B 96*
(off Richmond Rd.)
Richard Lewis Cl. CF5: L'dff 5A **84**
Richards Ct. CF24: Card 2D **96**
Richards Pl. CF24: Card 2D **96**
Richards Ter. CF24: Card 2D **96**
CF37: P'prdd 5D **14**
Richard St. CF24: Card 1A **96**
CF37: C'fydd .2F **15**
CF62: Barry .2H **117**
Richmond Cl. CF83: L'brad 1B **28**
NP44: Pnwd 6E **9**
Richmond Ct. CF24: Card 1F **5** (2B **96**)
Richmond Cres. CF24: Card 1F **5** (2B **96**)
Richmond Pl. NP44: Pnwd 6E **9**
Richmond Rd. CF24: Card 1F **5** (1B **96**)
NP4: Seba 3E **9**
NP19: Newp .2E **37**
NP44: Pnwd 5E **9**
Richmond St. NP44: Pnwd 6E **9**
Rich's Rd. CF14: Heath 3F **85**
Rickards St. CF37: P'prdd 1C **24**
Rickards Ter. CF37: P'prdd 1C **24**
RIDGEWAY 4H **35**
Ridgeway CF14: L'vne 2A **72**
CF83: Mac 3B **30**
NP20: Newp .5F **35**
Ridgeway Av. NP20: Newp 4G **35**
Ridgeway Cl. CF37: P'prdd 5B **14**
NP20: Newp .4H **35**
Ridgeway Ct. NP20: Newp 4G **35**
Ridgeway Cres. NP20: Newp 5G **35**
Ridgeway Dr. NP20: Newp 5G **35**
Ridgeway Gdns. NP20: Newp 4H **35**
Ridgeway Gro. NP20: Newp 5G **35**
Ridgeway Hill NP20: Newp 4H **35**
Ridgeway Pk. Rd. NP20: Newp 4G **35**
Ridgeway Pl. CF38: Tont 2G **43**
NP20: Newp .4G **35**
Ridgeway Reach NP20: Newp 4H **35**
Ridgeway Ri. NP20: Newp 4H **35**
Ridgeway Rd. CF3: L'rmy, Rum 3G **87**
CF62: Barry .5F **105**
Ridgeway Vw. NP20: Newp 4H **35**
Ridgeway Vs. NP20: Newp 4H **35**

Ridgeway Wlk. NP20: Newp 4H **35**
Ridings, The CF38: Tont 2G **43**
Rifleman St. NP11: Ris 5D **16**
Riflemans Way NP16: Chep 2E **63**
Rimini Ho. CF10: Card 6C **96**
Rinastone Ct. CF5: L'dff 1B **94**
RINGLAND 3D **38**
Ringland Cen. NP19: Newp 3D **38**
Ringland Circ. NP19: Newp 4B **38**
Ringland Way NP18: Newp 5B **38**
Ringside Bus. Cen. CF3: Rum 5B **88**
Ringwood Av. NP19: Newp 3A **38**
Ringwood Cres. CF62: St Ath 1D **112**
Ringwood Hill NP19: Newp 4A **38**
Ringwood Pl. NP19: Newp 4B **38**
RISCA 4D **16**
Risca & Pontymister Station (Rail) 6E **17**
Risca Cl. CF3: St M 6D **74**
RISCA DAY HOSPITAL 4C **16**
Risca Leisure Cen. 6H **17**
Risca Rd. NP10: Roger 1H **33**
NP11: Cros K 2A **16**
NP20: Newp 5F **35**
Rise, The CF14: L'shn 4A **72**
CF37: Up Bo 6A **26**
CF38: Tont 1F **43**
CF62: Barry 1H **117**
NP44: Pnwd 6C **8**
Rivendell Ct. NP19: Newp 6F **37**
Riverdale CF5: Ely 3H **93**
Riverfront, The 4C **36**
River Glade CF15: Gwae G, Taff W 1D **68**
Rivermead Way NP10: Roger 2H **33**
Riversdale CF5: L'dff 5B **84**
River's Edge CF72: P'clun 6C **64**
RIVERSIDE 5A **4** (4G **95**)
Riverside NP4: P'pool 1B **6**
*NP16: Chep 1F **63***
(off The Back)
NP19: Newp 3C **36**
Riverside Ct. NP4: P'pool 2C **6**
Riverside Ind. Pk. CF37: T'rest 2B **44**
Riverside Pk. CF83: B'ws 2E **29**
Riverside Pl. CF63: Barry 1D **118**
Riverside St. CF15: Taff W 6D **44**
Riverside Ter. CF5: Ely 3B **94**
CF83: Mac 3F **31**
Riversmead NP44: L'rfn 3A **12**
River St. CF37: T'rest 2E **25**
River Vw. CF14: Llan N 5C **84**
(College Rd.)
CF14: Llan N 6D **84**
(Lydstep Cres.)
CF64: P'rth 5H **101**
NP16: Chep 2E **63**
(School Hill)
NP16: Chep 1F **63**
(The Back)
River Vw. Ct. CF5: L'dff 5B **84**
River Wlk. CF61: Llan M 3B **110**
CF64: P'rth 5H **101**
CF71: C'bri 4C **90**
Road D NP10: Roger 4B **34**
Roald Dahl Plass 1C **102**
Roam Rd. CF72: L'sant 2F **65**
ROATH 1C **96**
Roath Ct. CF24: Card 1D **96**
NP44: L'rfn 2A **12**
Roath Ct. Pl. CF24: Card 1D **96**
Roath Ct. Rd. CF24: Card 1C **96**
Roath Dock Rd. CF10: Card 1D **102**
ROATH PARK 4B **86**
Robbins La. NP20: Newp 5C **36**
Robert Pl. NP20: Newp 1C **54**
Roberts Cl. CF62: St Ath 4D **112**
NP10: Roger 2C **34**
Robertson Way NP20: Malp 3A **20**
Robert St. CF5: Ely 3B **94**
CF24: Card 6A **86**
CF63: Barry 2B **118**
Robin Cl. CF23: Pent 6D **72**
Robin Hill CF64: Din P 3H **107**
Robins La. CF63: Barry 6B **106**
Robinswood Cl. CF64: P'rth 3E **109**
Robinswood Cres. CF64: P'rth 3E **109**
Rochdale Ter. NP4: P'nydd 1A **6**
Roche Cres. CF5: F'wtr 6G **83**
Rochester Rd. NP19: Newp 4F **37**
Rock Cotts. CF37: P'prdd 5A **14**
Rockfield Cres. NP26: Undy 4F **59**
Rockfield Gro. NP26: Undy 3F **59**
Rockfield Ho. NP4: P'pool 2B **6**
Rockfield La. NP26: Undy 3F **59**
Rockfield Ri. NP26: Undy 4F **59**
Rockfield St. NP19: Newp 2D **36**
Rockfield Vw. NP26: Undy 3E **59**
Rockfield Way NP26: Undy 3F **59**
Rockhill Rd. NP4: P'pool 3D **6**
Rockingstone Ter. CF37: P'prdd 1E **25**
Rock Rd. CF62: St Ath 5D **112**
Rockrose Way CF64: P'rth 6G **101**
Rock Villa La. NP16: Tut 1F **63**
Rockwood Rd. CF15: Taff W 1F **69**
NP16: Chep 3E **63**
Roden Ct. CF24: Card 1H **5**
Roding Cl. NP20: Bet 6F **19**
Rodney Parade 4D **36**
Rodney Pde. NP19: Newp 4C **36**
Rodney Rd. NP19: Newp 4C **36**
Rogart Ter. CF37: P'prdd 3D **14**
Rogersmoor Cl. CF64: P'rth 3E **109**
ROGERSTONE 4C **34**
Rogerstone Cl. CF3: St M 6D **74**
Rogerstone Station (Rail) 2A **34**
ROGIET 6A **60**
Rogiet Rd. NP26: Cald 5A **60**
Roland St. CF10: Card 6F **5** (5B **96**)
Rolls Cl. NP44: F'wtr 3C **10**
Rolls St. CF11: Card 4F **95**
Rolls Wlk. NP10: Roger 3C **34**
Roma CF11: Card 4G **101**
Roma Ho. CF10: Card 5B **96**
Roman Amphitheatre 6H **21**
Roman Cl. CF5: Ely 6H **93**
Roman Gates NP18: C'ln 5H **21**
Roman Legionary Mus. 5H **21**
Roman Reach NP18: C'ln 5E **21**
Roman Way NP18: C'ln 4F **21**
Romanwell Rd. CF62: Barry 5G **117**
Romilly Av. CF62: Barry 4E **117**
Romilly Bldgs. CF63: Barry 3B **118**
Romilly Ct. CF62: Barry 4F **117**
Romilly Cres. CF11: Card 3F **95**
Romilly Pk. Rd. CF62: Barry 5D **116**
Romilly Pl. CF5: Card 3E **95**
Romilly Rd. CF5: Card 3E **95**
CF62: Barry 4F **117**
(not continuous)
CF62: Rho 6E **115**
Romilly Rd. W. CF5: Card 2D **94**
Romney Cl. NP19: Newp 2G **37**
Romney Wlk. CF64: P'rth 6H **101**
Rompney Ter. CF3: Rum 5H **87**
Romsley Ct. NP44: St D 3E **11**
Ronald Pl. CF5: Ely 3H **93**
Ronald Rd. NP19: Newp 3E **37**
Rook Cl. CF62: St Ath 4F **111**
Rookery Cl. CF64: Sul 2G **119**
Rookery Wood CF64: Sul 2G **119**
Rookwood Av. CF5: L'dff 6B **84**
Rookwood Cl. CF5: L'dff 6B **84**
ROOKWOOD HOSPITAL 6B **84**
Rookwood St. CF11: Card 6G **95**
Roper Cl. CF5: L'dff 5H **83**
Rosamund Cl. NP10: Duf 6H **53**
Rosary, The NP4: P'garn 1C **6**
NP16: Chep 1D **62**
Roseberry Pl. CF64: P'rth 2D **108**
Roseberry St. NP4: Grif 6E **7**
Rose Cotts. CF37: P'prdd 6B **14**
Rose Ct. NP44: Ty C 3B **10**
Rosecroft Dr. NP18: L'stne 1G **39**
Rosedale Cl. CF5: F'wtr 1G **93**
Rosegarden, The
NP20: Newp 4H **35**
Rose Gdns. NP44: C'iog 1B **12**
Rosemary La. NP4: P'pool 2C **6**
Rosemary St. CF10: Card 5F **5** (4C **96**)
Rosemead NP44: G'mdw 2B **10**
Rosemont Av. NP11: Ris 5E **17**
Rosemount Pl. CF14: Heath 4F **85**
Rosendale Ct. NP19: Newp 4F **37**
Rose St. CF24: Card 2C **96**
NP20: Newp 3B **36**
Rose Ter. *NP4: P'nydd 1A **6***
(off Chapel Rd.)
Rose Wlk. NP10: Roger 2H **33**
Rosewood Cl. CF14: L'vne 2A **72**
Ross Cl. CF37: Pen c 3B **24**
Rosser St. CF37: P'prdd 1B **24**
NP4: P'pool 2A **6**
Rosset Cl. CF3: St M 1C **88**
Rossetti Cl. CF5: L'dff 4A **84**
Ross La. NP20: Newp 2B **36**
Rosslyn Rd. NP19: Newp 4F **37**
Ross St. NP20: Bryng 1B **36**
Rother Cl. NP20: Bet 4F **19**
Rothesay Rd. NP19: Newp 4F **37**
Rothsay Ho. CF10: Card 6B **96**
Rougemont Gro. NP16: Bul 6F **63**
Roundabout Ct. CF83: B'ws 3D **28**
Roundel Cl. CF14: Thorn 1H **71**
Round Wood CF23: L'dyrn 2E **87**
Round Wood Cl. CF23: Pen L 4E **87**
Routs Vw. NP18: L'wrn 4F **39**
Rover Way CF10: Card 1F **103**
CF24: Card, Pen L 1F **97**
Row, The NP10: Drae 6A **32**
Rowan Cl. CF37: Pen c 3B **24**
CF64: P'rth 4E **109**
NP26: Undy 3E **59**
Rowan Ct. CF5: L'dff 1C **94**
CF62: Barry 4E **117**
CF72: L'harry 5A **78**
Rowan Cres. NP4: Grif 1D **8**
Rowan Dr. NP16: Bul 5E **63**
Rowan Gdns. CF38: Chu V 4E **43**
Rowan Gro. *CF62: E Bre 2B **112***
(off Sycamore Av.)
Rowan Rd. NP11: Ris 5F **17**
Rowan Tree La. CF72: Mis 5F **65**
Rowan Way CF14: L'vne 2B **72**
NP20: Malp 4B **20**
Rowena Ct. CF5: F'wtr 1G **93**
Rowland Dr. CF83: Caer 2A **46**
Rowsby Ct. CF23: Pontp 4F **73**
Roxburgh Gdn. Ct. CF64: P'rth 2F **109**
Roxby Ct. CF10: Card 6F **5** (5B **96**)
Royal Arc. CF10: Card 5D **4** (4A **96**)
Royal Bldgs. CF64: P'rth 2E **109**
Royal Cl. CF64: P'rth 6A **102**
ROYAL GLAMORGAN HOSPITAL 6D **40**
ROYAL GWENT HOSPITAL 6B **36**
Royal Oak CF83: Mac 3H **31**
Royal Oak Cl. CF83: Mac 2H **31**
Royal Oak Dr. NP18: Newp 2C **38**
Royal Oak Grn. NP44: C'iog 1B **12**
Royal Oak Hill NP18: Chris, Newp 1C **38**
Royal Stuart La. CF10: Card 2B **102**
Royce Wlk. NP10: Roger 3C **34**
Royde Cl. CF5: Ely 5C **92**
Roy Jenkins Hall CF24: Card 6A **86**
Royston Cres. NP19: Newp 5H **37**
Rubens Cl. NP19: Newp 2F **37**
Ruby St. CF24: Card 3D **96**
RUDRY 1C **48**
Rudry Cl. CF83: Caer 4G **29**
Rudry Rd. CF14: L'vne 2C **72**
CF83: Caer 4F **29**
CF83: Rud 2C **72**
Rudry St. CF11: Card 6G **95**
CF64: P'rth 1D **108**
NP19: Newp 3C **36**
Ruffett's Cl. NP16: Chep 2D **62**
Rugby Rd. NP19: Newp 4D **36**
RUMNEY 5A **88**
Rumney Wlk. NP44: L'rfn 2B **12**
Run, The CF83: Mac 2F **31**
Runcorn Cl. CF3: Old M 5B **74**
CF63: Barry 6D **106**
Runway Rd. CF24: Card 2G **97**
Ruperra Castle 2A **50**
Ruperra Cl. CF3: Old M 4B **74**
NP10: Bass 6D **34**
Ruperra La. NP20: Newp 6C **36**
Ruperra St. CF72: L'sant 1F **65**
NP20: Newp 6C **36**
Rupert Brooke Dr. NP20: Newp 1H **53**

Rushbrook NP44: G'mdw . . . 2D **10**
Rushbrook Cl. CF14: Whit . . . 3A **84**
Rush Wall NP26: Red . . . 6A **58**
Ruskin Av. NP10: Roger . . . 2C **34**
Ruskin Cl. CF3: L'rmy . . . 6H **73**
NP44: F'wtr . . . 3C **10**
Ruskin Ri. NP20: Newp . . . 1G **53**
Russel Cl. NP4: New I . . . 5H **7**
Russell Cl. NP10: Bass . . . 6B **34**
Russell Dr. NP20: Malp . . . 4A **20**
Russell Dr. Gdns. NP20: Malp . . . 5A **20**
Russell St. CF24: Card . . . 1F **5** (2B **96**)
NP44: Pnwd . . . 6E **9**
Russet Cl. NP18: L'stne . . . 1G **39**
Ruthen Ter. CF62: Barry . . . 2F **117**
Rutherford Hill NP20: Malp . . . 4A **20**
Ruthin Gdns. CF24: Card . . . 1D **4** (2A **96**)
Ruthin Way CF38: Tont . . . 1F **43**
Ruth Rd. NP4: New I . . . 4F **7**
Rutland Cl. CF62: Barry . . . 5E **105**
Rutland Pl. NP20: Newp . . . 6C **36**
Rutland St. CF11: Card . . . 5G **95**
Ryder St. CF11: Card . . . 3G **95**

S

Sable Cl. CF14: L'vne . . . 1A **72**
Sachville Av. CF14: Card . . . 5G **85**
Saffron Ct. NP44: Ty C . . . 4B **10**
Saffron Dr. CF3: St M . . . 5E **75**
SAIN FFAGAN . . . **2E 93**
SAIN HILARI . . . **6H 91**
SAIN SIORYS . . . **3A 92**
St Agatha Rd. CF14: Heath . . . 3G **85**
St Agnes Ct. CF24: Card . . . 2E **97**
St Agnes Rd. CF14: Heath . . . 3F **85**
St Aidan Cres. CF14: Heath . . . 3F **85**
St Aidens Ri. CF63: Barry . . . 1C **118**
St Alban's Av. CF14: Heath . . . 3F **85**
St Ambrose Cl. CF64: Din P . . . 3G **107**
St Ambrose Rd. CF14: Heath . . . 3G **85**
SAINT ANDRAS . . . **1C 106**
St Andrew's Av. NP16: Bul . . . 3E **63**
St Andrews Cl. CF38: Llan F . . . 5D **42**
NP44: Pon'run . . . 4F **9**
St Andrews Ct. CF37: P'prdd . . . 1C **24**
St Andrew's Cres. CF10: Card . . . 2E **5** (3B **96**)
St Andrew's La. CF10: Card . . . 2E **5** (3B **96**)
ST ANDREWS MAJOR . . . **1C 106**
St Andrew's Pl. CF10: Card . . . 2D **4** (3A **96**)
St Andrews Rd. CF5: Wen . . . 6E **99**
CF37: Pen c . . . 3B **24**
CF62: Barry . . . 1G **117**
CF64: Din P, St And . . . 6E **99**
St Angela Rd. CF14: Heath . . . 3G **85**
St Anne's Av. CF64: P'rth . . . 3D **108**
St Anne's Cl. NP10: Roger . . . 5D **34**
NP44: C'brn . . . 6E **9**
St Annes Ct. CF72: Taly . . . 2B **78**
St Annes Cres. NP19: Newp . . . 2E **37**
NP26: Undy . . . 4F **59**
St Annes Dr. CF38: Llan F . . . 5D **42**
St Annes Gdns. CF83: Abert . . . 2E **27**
ST ANNE'S HOSPICE . . . 4B 20
St Ann's Ct. CF62: Barry . . . 5A **106**
St Ann St. NP16: Chep . . . 1F **63**
St Anthony Rd. CF14: Heath . . . 3G **85**
St Anthony's Cl. NP4: Grif . . . 1D **8**
St Arvans Cres. CF3: St M . . . 6D **74**
St Arvans Rd. NP44: C'brn . . . 2H **11**
St Asaph Cl. CF14: Heath . . . 1G **85**
St Asaph's Way CF83: Caer . . . 2C **46**
SAIN TATHAN . . . **5D 112**
ST ATHAN . . . **5D 112**
St Athan Rd. CF62: F'ton . . . 1A **112**
CF71: C'bri, L'thian . . . 5D **90**
St Athan's Ct. CF83: Caer . . . 1B **46**
St Augustine Rd. CF14: Heath . . . 3G **85**
NP4: Grif . . . 1D **8**
St Augustine's Cres. CF64: P'rth . . . 6B **102**
St Augustine's Path CF64: P'rth . . . 6B **102**
St Augustine's Pl. CF64: P'rth . . . 6B **102**
St Augustines Rd. CF64: P'rth . . . 6B **102**
St Baruch Cl. CF64: Din P . . . 3G **107**
St Baruchs Ct. CF62: Barry . . . 5H **117**
St Basil's Cres. NP10: Bass . . . 6C **34**
St Benedict Ct. NP10: Bass . . . 1C **52**
St Benedict Cres. CF14: Heath . . . 3G **85**
St Benedicts Cl. NP4: Grif . . . 1D **8**
St Bleddians Cl. CF71: C'bri . . . 3B **90**
St Brannocks Cl. CF62: Barry . . . 2E **117**
St Briavels M. *NP10: Duf . . . 6G 53*
(off White Av.)
St Brides Cl. NP26: Magor . . . 3C **58**
NP44: L'rfn . . . 3A **12**
St Brides Ct. CF5: Ely . . . 5G **93**
St Brides Cres. NP20: Newp . . . 3H **53**
St Brides Gdns. NP20: Newp . . . 3H **53**
St Brides Mnr. CF38: Llan F . . . 6D **42**
St Brides Pl. CF5: St Bri E . . . 1A **92**
St Brides Rd. CF5: St Bri E, St F . . . 6H **81**
NP26: Magor . . . 2C **58**
ST BRIDES-SUPER-ELY . . . **6H 81**
St Bride's Way CF63: Barry . . . 5A **106**
ST BRIDE'S WENTLOOGE . . . **4G 77**
St Brigid Rd. CF14: Heath . . . 1G **85**
St Brioc Rd. CF14: Heath . . . 1G **85**
St Cadoc Rd. CF14: Heath . . . 2G **85**
St Cadocs Av. CF64: Din P . . . 3G **107**
St Cadoc's Cl. NP18: C'ln . . . 4G **21**
ST CADOC'S HOSPITAL . . . 5G 21
St Cadoc's Ri. CF63: Barry . . . 5D **106**
St Cadoc's Rd. NP4: Trev . . . 1D **6**
St Canna Cl. CF5: Card . . . 3E **95**
St Catherines Cl. CF83: B'ws . . . 3F **29**
St Catherine's Ct. CF62: Barry . . . 5H **105**
NP11: Cros K . . . 3A **16**
St Catherines M. CF11: Card . . . 2F **95**
St Catherine's Pk. CF24: Card . . . 1F **97**
St Cecilia Ct. NP20: Newp . . . 4A **36**
St Cenydd Cl. CF83: Caer . . . 5A **28**
St Cenydd Leisure Cen. . . . 5H 27
St Cenydd Rd. CF14: Heath . . . 1H **85**
CF83: Caer . . . 5A **28**
St Christophers Cl. CF83: B'ws . . . 3F **29**
St Christopher's Dr. CF83: Caer . . . 1B **46**
St Clair Ct. *CF10: Card . . . 1C 102*
(off W. Bute St.)
St Clears Cl. CF83: Caer . . . 1C **46**
St Clements Ct. CF23: Pent . . . 5E **73**
St Curig's Cl. CF62: Rho . . . 6E **115**
St Cuthberts Ct. CF10: Card . . . 1B **102**
St Cyres Cl. CF64: P'rth . . . 1C **108**
St Cyres Rd. CF64: P'rth . . . 2C **108**
St Davids Av. CF38: Chu V . . . 3E **43**
CF61: Llan M . . . 4C **110**
CF64: Din P . . . 1H **107**
St David's Cen. CF10: Card . . . 4D **4** (4A **96**)
St David's Cl. CF37: T'rest . . . 3C **44**
NP4: P'garn . . . 2C **6**
NP16: Bul . . . 3E **63**
St Davids Ct. CF3: M'fld . . . 4A **76**
NP26: Magor . . . 4C **58**
St Davids Cres. CF5: Ely . . . 4H **93**
CF62: St Ath . . . 4D 112
(off Cowbridge Rd.)
CF64: P'rth . . . 2B **108**
NP20: Newp . . . 2G **53**
St David's Dr. CF83: Mac . . . 3B **30**
St David's Hall . . . 4D 4 (4A 96)
St David's Hgts. CF72: Mis . . . 5E **65**
ST DAVIDS HOSPITAL . . . 3G 95
St David's Link CF10: Card . . . 4E **5** (4B **96**)
St Davids Mans. *CF11: Card . . . 4G 95*
(off Cowbridge Rd. E.)
St Davids Pl. CF72: L'sant . . . 1G **65**
St Davids Rd. CF14: Whit . . . 3C **84**
CF72: Mis . . . 1F **79**
NP44: C'brn, Pnwd . . . 6F **9**
St David's Way CF10: Card . . . 4D **4** (4A **96**)
CF83: Caer . . . 2B **46**
St Denis Rd. CF14: Heath . . . 2H **85**
ST DIALS . . . **2E 11**
St Dials Ct. NP44: C'brn . . . 3G **11**
St Dials Rd. NP44: C'brn, G'mdw . . . 2D **10**
(not continuous)
St Dogmaels Av. CF14: L'shn . . . 6H **71**
St Dominics Retreat NP4: P'pool . . . 3B **6**
St Donats Cl. CF64: Din P . . . 2H **107**
St Donats Ct. CF5: Ely . . . 5G **93**
CF83: Caer . . . 1B **46**
St Donats Pl. NP44: L'rfn . . . 3B **12**
St Donats Rd. CF11: Card . . . 5F **95**
St Dubricius Gdns. NP26: Undy . . . 4F **59**
St Dyfrig Cl. CF64: Din P . . . 3H **107**
St Dyfrig Rd. CF64: P'rth . . . 3C **108**
St Edeyrns Cl. CF23: Cyn . . . 1D **86**
St Edeyrn's Rd. CF23: Cyn . . . 1C **86**
St Edward St. NP20: Newp . . . 5B **36**
St Edwen Gdns. CF14: Heath . . . 2G **85**
St Ewens Rd. NP16: Bul . . . 4E **63**
ST FAGANS . . . **2E 93**
St Fagans Av. CF62: Barry . . . 1G **117**
St Fagans Castle . . . 2D 92
St Fagans Cl. CF5: F'wtr . . . 2A **94**
St Fagans Ct. CF5: Ely . . . 5D **92**
St Fagans Dr. CF5: St F . . . 1E **93**
St Fagans: National History Mus. . . . 2D 92
St Fagans Ri. CF5: F'wtr . . . 1G **93**
St Fagans Rd. CF5: F'wtr . . . 2G **93**
St Fagans St. CF11: Card . . . 1H **101**
CF83: Caer . . . 1C **46**
St Francis Ct. CF24: Card . . . 4F **97**
St Francis Rd. CF14: Whit . . . 2C **84**
St Garmon Rd. CF64: P'rth . . . 3C **108**
St George Rd. NP16: Bul . . . 3E **63**
ST GEORGE'S . . . **3A 92**
St George's Cres.
NP19: Newp . . . 2F **37**
St George's Rd. CF14: Heath . . . 4F **85**
St Georges Way NP16: B'ly . . . 6H **63**
St Germans M. CF24: Card . . . 3D **96**
St Gildas Rd. CF14: Heath . . . 2G **85**
St Govan's Cl. CF62: Barry . . . 5H **105**
St Gowan Av. CF14: Heath . . . 2G **85**
St Gwynnos Cl. CF64: Din P . . . 2G **107**
St Helen's Ct. CF83: Caer . . . 1B **46**
St Helen's Rd. CF14: Heath . . . 3F **85**
ST HILARY . . . **6H 91**
St Hilary Ct. CF5: Ely . . . 5H **93**
St Hilda's Rd. NP4: Grif . . . 1E **9**
St Ilan's Way CF83: Caer . . . 2C **46**
St Illtud's Church . . . 3A 110
St Illtyd Cl. CF64: Din P . . . 2H **107**
St Illtyd Rd. CF38: Chu V, Up Chu . . . 1E **43**
St Ina Rd. CF14: Heath . . . 2G **85**
St Isan Rd. CF14: Heath . . . 2G **85**
St James Cl. CF83: Caer . . . 4G **29**
St James Ct. CF64: P'rth . . . 3C **108**
St James Cres. CF62: Barry . . . 2D **116**
St James' Fld. NP4: P'pool . . . 3C **6**
St James Mans. CF10: Card . . . 1B **102**
CF14: L'vne . . . 2A **72**
St James M. *CF11: Card . . . 2F 95*
(off Severn Gro.)
St Johns Cl. CF71: C'bri . . . 4D **90**
NP4: P'pool . . . 2A **6**
St Johns Ct. *CF62: Barry . . . 5H 117*
(off Friars Rd.)
NP10: Roger . . . 3B **34**
St John's Cres. CF5: Card . . . 4F **95**
CF14: Whit . . . 1C **84**
NP4: P'pool . . . 2A **6**
NP10: Roger . . . 3B **34**
St Johns Gdns. NP16: Chep . . . 1D **62**
St John's Hill CF62: St Ath . . . 4D **112**
St John's M. *CF5: Card . . . 4F 95*
(off St John's Cres.)
St John's Pl. CF14: Whit . . . 1C **84**
CF62: Rho . . . 5C **114**
St John's Rd. NP19: Newp . . . 4F **37**
St John St. CF10: Card . . . 4C **4** (4A **96**)
St John's Vw. CF62: St Ath . . . 4C **112**
St Joseph Pl. NP44: L'tnam . . . 1B **20**
St Josephs Cl. NP26: Undy . . . 4F **59**
St Joseph's Ct. CF14: Card . . . 5H **85**
ST JOSEPH'S HOSPITAL . . . 3B 20
St Julian Cl. CF63: Barry . . . 6C **106**
ST JULIANS . . . **2F 37**
St Julian's Av. NP19: Newp . . . 2E **37**
St Julians Ct. CF83: Caer . . . 1B **46**
NP19: Newp . . . 2E **37**
St Julian's Rd. NP19: Newp . . . 2E **37**
St Julian St. NP20: Newp . . . 5B **36**
St Kingsmark Av. NP16: Chep . . . 1D **62**
St Lawrence La. NP16: Chep . . . 3C **62**
St Lawrence Pk. NP16: Chep . . . 2C **62**

St Lawrence Rd. NP16: Chep 1C **62**
(not continuous)
St Luke's Av. CF37: R'fln 5G **25**
CF64: P'rth 3C **108**
St Lukes Rd. NP4: P'nydd 1A **6**
St Lythan Cl. CF64: Din P 3G **107**
St Lythan Ct. CF5: Ely 5G **93**
ST LYTHANS 5C **98**
St Lythans Burial Chamber 6A **98**
ST LYTHANS DOWN 3C **98**
St Lythan's Rd. CF62: Barry 2E **117**
St Malo Rd. CF14: Heath 1G **85**
St Margarets Cl. CF14: Whit 1C **84**
CF83: Tret 3H **29**
St Margaret's Cres. CF23: Pen L 1D **96**
St Margaret's Pk. CF5: Ely 3A **94**
St Margaret's Pl. CF14: Whit 1C **84**
St Margaret's Rd. CF14: Whit 2C **84**
CF83: Caer 1B **46**
St Mark's Av. CF14: Card 4G **85**
St Mark's Cres. NP20: Newp 4A **36**
St Marks Gdns. CF14: Card 4G **85**
St Mark's Rd. CF64: P'rth 3D **108**
ST MARTINS 1C **46**
St Martin's Cl. CF64: P'rth 3C **108**
St Martins Ct. NP20: Newp 6H **35**
St Martin's Cres. CF14: L'shn 6H **71**
CF83: Caer 2C **46**
St Martin's Rd. CF83: Caer 2B **46**
St Mary's Av. CF63: Barry 2A **118**
St Marys Cl. CF5: Ely 6H **93**
CF37: Glynt 2F **25**
NP4: Grif 6D **6**
St Marys Ct. CF5: Ely 1G **99**
NP11: Ris 4D **16**
NP20: Newp 5B **36**
St Mary's Pl. NP26: Pskwt 5G **61**
(not continuous)
St Mary's Rd. CF14: Whit 1C **84**
NP44: C'iog 6G **9**
St Mary St. CF10: Card 4C **4** (4A **96**)
CF83: B'ws 3F **29**
NP4: Grif 6D **6**
NP11: Ris 4C **16**
NP16: Chep 2E **63**
NP20: Newp 5B **36**
St Mary's Well Bay Rd.
CF64: S'dge 4B **120**
St Matthew's Rd. NP4: P'pool 4D **6**
St Maur Gdns. NP16: Chep 1D **62**
ST MELLONS 1D **88**
St Mellons Bus. Pk. CF3: St M 5F **75**
St Mellons Cl. NP26: Undy 4E **59**
St Mellons Ct. CF83: Caer 1B **46**
St Mellons Interchange
CF3: Old M 4C **74**
St Mellons Rd. CF3: M'fld 6G **75**
CF14: L'vne 2C **72**
CF14: Pontp 3F **73**
CF23: Pontp 3F **73**
St Michael Gro. NP44: L'tnam 6B **12**
St Michael's Av. CF37: T'rest 2D **24**
St Michaels Cl. CF15: Tong 4G **69**
CF38: Bed 5H **41**
CF62: St Ath 4D **112**
CF64: Mic P 4C **100**
St Michaels Ct. NP20: Newp 1D **54**
St Michaels Gdns. CF62: Barry 5G **105**
St Michaels M. NP20: Newp 1D **54**
St Michael's Rd. CF5: L'dff 2C **94**
St Michael St. NP20: Newp 1D **54**
St Nicholas Cl. CF62: Barry 4E **117**
CF64: Din P 2G **107**
St Nicholas Ct. CF5: Ely 5G **93**
CF23: Pent 5E **73**
CF83: Caer 1B **46**
St Nicholas Rd. CF62: Barry 4E **117**
St Oswalds Cl. NP4: Seba 2E **9**
St Oswald's Rd. CF63: Barry 6C **106**
St Osyth Ct. CF62: Barry 5E **117**
St Paul's Av. CF62: Barry 3G **117**
CF64: P'rth 3D **108**
St Pauls Cl. CF64: Din P 3G **107**
St Peters Cl. NP44: F'wtr 3D **10**
St Peter's Rd. CF64: P'rth 3C **108**
St Peters St. CF24: Card 1F **5** (2B **96**)
St Philip Evans Cl. CF23: L'dyrn 1E **87**
St Phillip's Flats *NP19: Newp* *5F* ***37***
(off Cromwell Rd.)
St Pierre Cl. CF3: St M 5E **75**
St Quentins Cl. CF71: L'thian 4C **90**
St Quentins Hill CF71: L'thian 4B **90**
St Siors Meade CF62: Rho 5D **114**
St Stephen's Cl. NP26: C'ent 1B **60**
St Stephens Ct. NP26: Undy 4F **59**
St Stephens Mans.
CF10: Card 1B **102**
St Stephens Pl. NP26: Undy 4F **59**
St Stephens Rd. NP20: Newp 1D **54**
St Tanwg Rd. CF14: Heath 2G **85**
St Tathan's Pl. NP26: C'ent 1B **60**
St Tecla Rd. NP16: Bul 4E **63**
St Teilo Av. CF62: Barry 1G **117**
St Teilo Cl. CF64: Din P 2H **107**
St Teilo Ct. NP26: Undy 4F **59**
St Teilos Ct. CF23: Pen L 1D **96**
St Teilo's Way CF83: Caer 2B **46**
St Tewdric Rd. NP16: Bul 3E **63**
St Tewdrics Pl. NP16: Math 6B **62**
St Thomas Cl. CF14: Heath 2E **85**
St Vincent Rd. NP19: Newp 4C **36**
St Vincents Ct. NP19: Newp 4C **36**
St Winifred's Cl. CF64: Din P 3G **107**
ST WOOLOS 6G **35**
St Woolos Cathedral 5B **36**
St Woolos Grn. NP44: C'brn 1G **11**
ST WOOLOS HOSPITAL 6B **36**
St Woolos Pl. NP20: Newp 5B **36**
St Woolos Rd. NP20: Newp 5B **36**
St Y Nyll La. CF5: Cap L, St Bri E 3H **81**
Salem La. CF38: Chu V 2F **43**
Salem Row CF15: Gwae G 6D **44**
Salem Ter. CF15: Gwae G 6D **44**
Salisbury Av. CF64: P'rth 2D **108**
Salisbury Cl. CF64: P'rth 2D **108**
NP20: Newp 3C **36**
Salisbury Ct. CF64: P'rth 2D **108**
NP44: C'brn 2E **11**
Salisbury Rd. CF24: Card 1E **5** (2B **96**)
CF62: Barry 4E **117**
Salisbury St. NP11: Cros K 3A **16**
Sally, The NP4: P'pool 3A **6**
Salmon Cl. CF23: Pen L 6E **87**
Salop Pl. CF64: P'rth 6A **102**
Salop St. CF64: P'rth 6A **102**
CF83: Caer 1D **46**
Salvia Cl. CF3: St M 6E **75**
Samson St. CF61: Llan M 2B **110**
Samuel Rodgers Cres.
NP16: Bul 6F **63**
Samuels Cres. CF14: Whit 2A **84**
Sanatorium Rd. CF11: Card 4C **94**
Sanctuary, The CF5: Ely 6E **93**
Sanctuary Ct. CF5: Ely 1E **99**
Sandalwood Ct. NP19: Newp 4D **36**
Sandbrook Rd. CF3: St M 1E **89**
Sanderling Dr. CF3: St M 6C **74**
Sandon Rd. CF24: Card 4F **5** (3B **96**)
Sandon St. CF24: Card 4F **5** (4B **96**)
Sandown Ct. CF5: Ely 4A **94**
Sandpiper Cl. CF3: St M 5D **74**
Sandpiper Way NP10: Duf 5G **53**
Sandringham Cl. CF62: Barry 5E **105**
Sandringham Rd. CF23: Pen L 6C **86**
Sandwell Ct. CF64: L'dgh 5F **101**
Sandwick Ct. CF23: Cyn 6C **72**
Sandybrook Cl. NP44: C'brn 4E **11**
Sandy La. CF3: Cas 3G **75**
NP10: Duf 3H **53**
NP26: C'ent, Cald 2C **60**
Sanquahar St. CF24: Card 5H **5** (4C **96**)
Sansom St. NP11: Ris 4D **16**
Sapele Dr. CF24: Card 5H **5** (4D **96**)
Sapphire St. CF24: Card 2D **96**
Sardis Rd. CF37: P'prdd 1B **24**
(not continuous)
Sarn Pl. NP11: Ris 4D **16**
Saron St. CF37: T'rest 2E **25**
Saundersfoot Cl. CF5: Ely 6H **93**
Saunders Rd. CF10: Card 6D **4** (5A **96**)
Sawtells Ter. NP4: P'nydd 1A **6**
Saxon Pl. NP16: Sed 3G **63**
Scala Cinema
Pontypool 2C **6**
Scarborough Rd. CF37: P'prdd 5E **15**
NP19: Newp 1D **36**
Scard St. NP20: Newp 5B **36**
School Cl. NP4: P'pool 3B **6**
NP18: P'hir 1E **21**
School Ct. NP44: C'brn 3G **11**
School Cres. NP4: Seba 2E **9**
Schooler Av. NP10: Duf 5H **53**
School Hill NP16: Chep 2E **63**
School Hill Trad. Est. NP16: Chep 2E **63**
School La. CF15: Gwae G 1D **68**
CF37: R'fln 6H **25**
NP4: P'pool 2B **6**
NP20: Newp 4C **36**
School Rd. CF72: Mis 1F **79**
NP4: P'nydd 1A **6**
School St. CF10: Card 6E **5** (5B **96**)
CF72: L'sant 2F **65**
CF72: P'clun 5D **64**
CF83: L'brad 1B **28**
School Ter. *NP4: P'nydd* *1A* ***6***
(off Old School Pl.)
NP10: Roger 4B **34**
School Vw. NP4: P'pool 4D **6**
Schooner Circ. NP10: Duf 5H **53**
Schooner Cl. NP10: Duf 5H **53**
Schooner Wlk. *NP10: Duf* *5A* ***54***
(off Morgan Way)
Schooner Way CF10: Card 6G **5** (5C **96**)
Scotney Way CF23: Pontp 4G **73**
Scott Cl. CF62: St Ath 2D **112**
NP20: Newp 2G **53**
Scott Ct. CF23: Cyn 4B **86**
Scott Rd. CF10: Card 5C **4** (4A **96**)
Scott Wlk. NP10: Roger 2C **34**
Seabank CF64: P'rth 2F **109**
Seabreeze Av. NP19: Newp 5E **37**
Seabreeze Cres. NP19: Newp 6E **37**
Seabreeze Dr. NP19: Newp 6E **37**
Seager Dr. CF11: Card 3H **101**
Sealawns CF62: Barry 6E **117**
Sealock Warehouse *CF10: Card* *2B* ***102***
(off Burt St.)
Sea Point *CF62: Barry* *6E* ***117***
(off Sealawns)
Seasons Cl. NP26: Magor 4C **58**
Seaton's Pl. CF37: P'prdd 6B **14**
Seaton St. CF37: P'prdd 6A **14**
Sea Vw. NP26: Sud 6H **61**
Seaview Cotts. CF3: Old M 6B **74**
Seaview Ct. CF64: P'rth 1F **109**
Seaview Ind. Est. CF24: Card 4E **97**
Seaview Pl. CF61: Llan M 3B **110**
Sea Vw. Ter. CF5: Twyn 3C **98**
CF63: Barry 6C **106**
Seawall Rd. CF24: Card 4F **97**
Seawall Rd. Ind. Est. CF24: Card 3G **97**
SEBASTOPOL 2E **9**
Second Av. CF23: Pen L 6E **87**
CF83: Caer 6A **28**
Second St. NP19: Newp 3G **55**
SEDBURY 2H **63**
Sedbury Bus. Pk. NP16: Sed 1G **63**
Sedbury La. NP16: Tut, Sed 1G **63**
(not continuous)
Sedgemoor Ct. NP20: Newp 3A **36**
Sedgemoor Rd. CF3: L'rmy 6A **74**
Sefton Ct. *CF15: Rad* *1F* ***83***
(off Maes yr Awel)
Selby Cl. NP44: Llanf 3B **12**
Selwyn Morris Ct. CF24: Card 4E **97**
Senghennydd Ct. CF24: Card 1E **5** (3B **96**)
Senghennydd Hall CF24: Card 1E **5**
Senghennydd Pl. CF24: Card 1E **5** (2B **96**)
Senghennydd Rd. CF24: Card 1D **4** (2A **96**)
Senlan Ind. Est. CF23: Pen L 6G **87**
Senni Cl. CF62: Barry 1E **117**
Sentinel Ct. CF5: F'wtr 2B **94**
Serpentine Rd. NP20: Newp 4B **36**
Sevenoaks Rd. CF5: Ely 4F **93**
Sevenoaks St. CF11: Card 1H **101**
Seven Stiles Av. NP19: Newp 1B **56**
Severn Av. CF62: Barry 2E **117**
NP16: Tut 1G **63**

Severn Bri. Ind. Est. NP26: Pskwt 6F **61**
Severn Bri. Pk. Homes NP16: B'ly 5H **63**
Severn Cl. NP11: Ris 6F **17**
Severn Ct. CF11: Card 3F **95**
Severn Cres. NP16: Chep 3E **63**
Severn Gro. CF11: Card 2F **95**
Severn Rd. CF11: Card 3F **95**
CF37: T'rest 1A **44**
Severn Sq. CF11: Card 3F **95**
Severn Ter. NP20: Newp 5B **36**
Severn Tunnel Junction Station (Rail) 6A **60**
Severn Vw. NP16: Chep 2D **62**
NP26: Cald 5B **60**
NP44: Up Cwm 5B **8**
Sevins *NP44: F'wtr 4E* ***11***
(off Henllys Way)
Seymour St. CF24: Card 3E **97**
Seys Cl. CF71: C'bri 3B **90**
Seys Ct. CF61: Llan M 2D **110**
Sgubor Goch CF72: L'harry 4C **78**
Shackleton Cl. CF62: St Ath 2D **112**
Shadow Wood Dr. CF72: Mis 5E **65**
Shaftesbury Cl. CF14: Thorn 2G **71**
Shaftesbury St. NP20: Newp 3C **36**
Shaftesbury Wlk. *NP20: Newp 3C* ***36***
(off Shaftesbury St.)
Shakespeare Av. CF64: P'rth 1C **108**
Shakespeare Cl. NP26: Cald 5B **60**
Shakespeare Ct. CF24: Card 1G **5** (2C **96**)
Shakespeare Cres. NP20: Newp 1G **53**
Shakespeare Dr. CF61: Llan M 3D **110**
NP26: Cald 6B **60**
Shakespeare Ri. CF37: R'fln 3G **25**
Shakespeare Rd. CF62: Barry 5H **105**
NP44: St D 3E **11**
Shakespeare St. CF24: Card 1G **5** (2C **96**)
Shamrock Rd. CF5: F'wtr 1G **93**
Shannon Cl. NP20: Bet 5H **19**
Sharpe Cl. CF23: Pen L 6E **87**
Sharps Way NP16: Bul 5F **63**
Shaw Cl. CF3: L'rmy 6H **73**
Shaw Gro. NP20: Newp 1G **53**
Shawley Ct. NP44: St D 3E **11**
Sheaf La. NP19: Newp 3D **36**
Shea Gdns. *NP20: Newp 6C* ***36***
(off Francis Dr.)
Shearman Pl. CF11: Card 3A **102**
Shears Rd. CF5: F'wtr 2B **94**
Shearwater Cl. CF64: P'rth 6E **109**
Sheerwater Cl. CF3: St M 6C **74**
Shelburn Cl. CF11: Card 5G **95**
Shelley Cl. NP26: Cald 5B **60**
Shelley Ct. CF83: Mac 2C **30**
Shelley Cres. CF62: Barry 5G **105**
CF64: P'rth 1D **108**
Shelley Grn. NP44: St D 3E **11**
Shelley Rd. NP19: Newp 4F **37**
Shelley Wlk. CF24: Card 1G **5** (2C **96**)
CF37: R'fln 3G **25**
Shephers Hill Cvn. Site NP4: P'pool 5B **6**
Sheppard St. CF37: P'prdd 6B **14**
Sherborne Av. CF23: Cyn 6C **72**
Sherbourne Cl. CF62: Barry 5D **104**
Sherbourne Ct. NP4: Seba 2E **9**
Sherbourne Rd. NP4: Seba 2E **9**
Sheridan Cl. CF3: L'rmy 6H **73**
NP20: Newp 1G **53**
Sherman Theatre 1D 4 (2A 96)
Sherwood Ct. CF5: F'wtr 6H **83**
Shetland Cl. NP19: Newp 2F **37**
Shetland Wlk. NP19: Newp 2F **37**
Shields Cl. CF23: Pontp 4H **73**
Ship La. *CF10: Card 1C* ***102***
(off W. Bute St.)
Shirenewton Cvn. Pk. CF3: Rum 5E **89**
Shires, The CF3: M'fld 4H **75**
(not continuous)
Shirley Cl. CF63: Barry 5D **106**
Shirley Rd. CF23: Card 5A **86**
Short Path *NP44: F'wtr 4D* ***10***
(off Jule Rd.)
Showcase Cinema
Cardiff 3D 44
Showle Acre CF62: Rho 5D **114**
Shrewsbury Cl. NP20: Newp 3C **36**
Sickert Cl. NP19: Newp 3G **37**
Sidings, The *CF37: T'rest 3E* ***25***
(off Park St.)
Sidney St. NP20: Newp 5B **36**
Sienna Ho. CF10: Card 5B **96**
SILI 3H 119
Siloam Hill CF83: Mac 2F **31**
SILSTWN 6D 112
Silure Way NP18: L'stne 1F **39**
Silurian Pl. CF10: Card 6B **96**
(not continuous)
Silver Birch Cl. CF14: Whit 4D **84**
NP18: C'ln 5E **21**
Silver Fir Sq. NP10: Roger 6D **34**
Silverhill Cl. CF37: C'fydd 3F **15**
Silver Jubilee Cotts. CF5: Ely 4H **93**
Silverstone Cl. CF3: Old M 5B **74**
Silver St. CF24: Card 2H **5** (3D **96**)
NP11: P'waun 1A **16**
Silverton Dr. CF72: C Inn 3G **65**
Simpson Cl. NP20: Malp 4A **20**
Sims Sq. NP19: Newp 4B **38**
Sinclair Dr. CF23: Pen L 6E **87**
Sindercombe Cl. CF23: Pontp 4F **73**
Singleton Rd. CF24: Card 4E **97**
Sion St. CF37: P'prdd 6C **14**
Siop-y-Coed CF38: Tont 1G **43**
Sir Alfred Owen Way CF83: Caer 3C **28**
Sir Charles Cres. NP10: Duf 5H **53**
Sir Charles Sq. *NP10: Duf 5G* ***53***
(off Sir Charles Cres.)
Sirhowy Ct. NP44: Thorn 1D **10**
Sirius Ho. CF10: Card 1D **102**
Sir Ivor Pl. CF64: Din P 3H **107**
Sir Stafford Cl. CF83: Caer 4E **29**
Sixth St. NP19: Newp 4H **55**
Skaithmuir Rd. CF24: Card 2F **97**
Skelmuir Rd. CF24: Card 2F **97**
Skenfrith M. NP10: Duf 6G **53**
Skewfields NP4: Grif 5E **7**
Skibereen Cl. CF23: Pontp 4G **73**
Skillion Bus. Cen. NP19: Newp 2F **55**
(not continuous)
Skinner La. NP20: Newp 4C **36**
Skinner Row NP19: Newp 5A **38**
Skinner St. NP20: Newp 4C **36**
Skomer Ct. CF11: Card 5H **95**
Skomer Island Way CF83: Caer 1H **45**
Skomer Rd. CF62: Barry 5H **105**
Slade Cl. CF64: Sul 1H **119**
CF71: C'bri 3D **90**
Slade Rd. CF62: Barry 6H **105**
Slade St. NP19: Newp 6F **37**
Slade Wood Ho. CF62: Barry 5A **106**
Slipway, The CF64: P'rth 6A **102**
Sloper Rd. CF11: Card 5F **95**
Sluvad Rd. NP4: New I 6H **7**
Smallbrook Cl. NP44: C'brn 2H **11**
Small Mdw. Ct. CF83: Caer 5D **28**
Smeaton Cl. CF62: Rho 6C **114**
Smeaton St. CF11: Card 4G **95**
Smithies Av. CF64: Sul 3H **119**
Smith Rd. CF14: L'shn 6F **71**
Smooth Stones NP16: Moun 3A **62**
Sneyd St. CF11: Card 2F **95**
Snipe St. CF24: Card 2C **96**
Snowden Ct. CF83: Caer 6E **29**
Snowden Rd. CF5: Ely 4F **93**
Snowdon Cl. NP11: Ris 5F **17**
Snowdon Ct. NP44: C'iog 6G **9**
Snowdrop La. NP10: Roger 2H **33**
Soane Cl. NP10: Roger 2C **34**
SOAR 2H 67
Soar Cl. NP44: C'iog 5H **9**
Soarel Cl. CF3: St M 2D **88**
Soberton Av. CF14: Card 5H **85**
Soho St. NP19: Newp 4E **37**
(not continuous)
Solent Rd. CF63: Barry 5C **106**
Solva Av. CF14: L'shn 5A **72**
Solva Cl. CF62: Barry 6H **105**
Somerset Ct. CF3: L'rmy 6A **74**
Somerset Ind. Est. NP44: C'brn 1H **11**
Somerset Rd. CF62: Barry 1H **117**
NP19: Newp 2E **37**
NP44: C'brn, Pnwd 1H **11**
Somerset Rd. E. CF63: Barry 1H **117**
Somerset St. CF11: Card 5G **95**
Somerset Vw. CF64: Sul 3H **119**
Somerset Way NP16: Bul 6F **63**
SOMERTON 6H 37
Somerton Ct. NP19: Newp 6G **37**
Somerton Cres. NP19: Newp 4H **37**
Somerton La. NP19: Newp 5G **37**
Somerton Pk. NP19: Newp 5G **37**
Somerton Pl. NP19: Newp 4H **37**
Somerton Rd. NP19: Newp 5G **37**
Sophia Cl. CF11: Card 2A **4** (3G **95**)
Sophia Gdns. 2A 4 (3G 95)
Sophia Wlk. CF11: Card 2G **95**
Sorrel Dr. NP20: Newp 4A **36**
Sorrento Ho. CF10: Card 6F **5** (5B **96**)
Soudrey Way CF10: Card 1B **102**
South Av. NP4: Seba 3D **8**
Southbourne Ct. CF62: Barry 5H **117**
Southbrook Vw. NP26: Pskwt 6F **61**
Sth. Clive St. CF11: Card 2H **101**
South Cl. NP44: Llanf 4B **12**
Southcourt Rd. CF23: Pen L 5D **86**
South Dr. CF72: L'sant 2G **65**
South East Wales Regional Swimming Pool 2G 55
Southern St. CF83: Caer 1D **46**
Southern Way CF23: Pen L 4F **87**
Southesk Pl. CF62: Barry 5E **117**
Southey St. CF24: Card 1H **5** (2C **96**)
CF62: Barry 2H **117**
Southgate CF71: C'bri 3C **90**
Southgate Av. CF72: L'sant 2F **65**
South Glade CF15: Gwae G 2E **69**
Southglade CF64: Sul 1H **119**
(not continuous)
Sth. Lake Dr. NP10: Coedk 5F **53**
Sth. Loudoun Pl. CF10: Card 6B **96**
Sth. Luton Pl. CF24: Card 4H **5** (4C **96**)
South Mkt. St. NP20: Newp 6D **36**
Southminster Rd. CF23: Pen L 1D **96**
Sth. Morgan Pl. CF11: Card 4G **95**
Sth. Pandy Rd. CF83: Caer 4C **28**
South Pk. Rd. CF24: Card 4F **97**
South Point CF10: Card 6F **97**
Sth. Pontypool Ind. Pk. NP4: New I 5F **7**
SOUTHRA 3G 107
Southra CF64: Din P 3G **107**
South Ri. CF14: L'shn 5A **72**
South Rd. CF64: Sul 2G **119**
NP44: Oakf 5H **11**
South St. CF37: P'prdd 6D **14**
NP4: Seba 2E **9**
South Vw. CF15: Taff W 1F **69**
CF62: Rho 6D **114**
NP4: P'pool 2B **6**
South Vw. Dr. CF3: Rum 2A **88**
SOUTHVILLE 3G 11
Southville Rd. NP20: Newp 5H **35**
South Wlk. CF62: Barry 1G **117**
NP44: C'brn 2G **11**
Sovereign Arc. NP20: Newp 5C **36**
Sovereign Gdns. CF72: Mis 5F **65**
SOWHILL 3B 6
Spartan Cl. NP18: L'stne 1G **39**
Speedwell Cl. CF23: Pontp 4H **73**
Speedwell Dr. CF62: Rho 6D **114**
Speke St. NP19: Newp 4E **37**
Spencer David Way CF3: St M 2D **88**
Spencer Dr. CF64: L'dgh 4F **101**
Spencer La. CF37: R'fln 5G **25**
Spencer Pl. CF37: R'fln 5G **25**
Spencer Rd. NP20: Newp 5A **36**
Spencer's Row CF5: L'dff 6C **84**
Spencer St. CF24: Card 6A **86**
CF62: Barry 2H **117**
Spillers & Bakers CF10: Card 6G **5**
Spinney, The CF14: L'vne 3B **72**
CF71: A'thin 2F **91**
NP20: Malp 5B **20**
Spinney Cvn. Pk., The CF64: S'dge 3B **120**
Spinney Cl. CF5: Ely 3G **93**
Spires Wlk. CF63: Barry 5B **106**
Spitzkop CF61: Llan M 3B **110**
SPLOTT 3E 97
Splott Ind. Est. *CF24: Card 4E* ***97***
(off Portmanmoor Rd.)

Splott Rd. CF24: Card 3D **96**
Splott Swimming Pool 3F **97**
Spooner Cl. NP10: Coedk 5D **52**
Springfield Cl. CF5: Wen 5E **99**
NP10: R'drn 6H **33**
NP44: C'iog 5G **9**
Springfield Ct. CF38: Chu V 2E **43**
Springfield Dr. NP19: Newp 3B **38**
Springfield Gdns. CF15: Morg 5F **69**
Springfield La. NP10: R'drn 6H **33**
Springfield Pl. CF11: Card 3F **95**
Springfield Ri. CF63: Barry 6A **106**
Springfield Rd. NP4: Seba 2D **8**
NP10: R'drn 6H **33**
NP11: Ris 1F **33**
Springfields CF3: Cas 3H **75**
Springfield Ter. CF37: R'fln 3F **25**
NP4: New I 5G **7**
Spring Gdns. NP20: Newp 1C **54**
Spring Gdns. Pl. CF24: Card 2E **97**
Spring Gdns. Ter. CF24: Card 2E **97**
Spring Gro. CF14: Thorn 3H **71**
NP44: G'mdw 2C **10**
Springhurst Cl. CF14: Whit 6B **70**
Spring La. NP20: Newp 5A **36**
NP44: C'iog 6G **9**
Spring Mdw. Bus. Pk. CF3: Rum 5A **88**
Springmeadow Rd. CF3: Rum 5A **88**
Spring St. CF63: Barry 1C **118**
NP20: Newp 2B **36**
Spring Ter. NP4: Grif 1D **8**
Springvale NP44: C'brn 1E **11**
Springvale Ind. Est. NP44: C'brn 1E **11**
Springvale Way NP44: C'brn 1F **11**
Springwood CF23: L'dyrn 2D **86**
Spruce Cl. CF24: Card 5H **5** (4D **96**)
Spytty La. NP19: Newp 1G **55**
Spytty Rd. NP19: Newp 1G **55**
Square, The CF38: Bed 4H **41**
CF62: St Ath 4D **112**
CF64: Din P 2G **107**
CF83: Abert 2D **26**
CF83: B'ws 3G **29**
NP26: Magor 4C **58**
Squires Cl. NP10: Roger 3D **34**
Squires Ct. CF38: Bed 6A **42**
Squires Ga. NP10: Roger 3C **34**
Stacey Ct. CF24: Card 1D **96**
Stacey Rd. CF24: Card 2D **96**
CF64: Din P 2G **107**
Stadium Cl. CF11: Card 2G **101**
Stafford M. CF11: Card 5H **95**
Stafford Rd. CF11: Card 6A **4** (5G **95**)
NP4: Grif, P'pool 5E **7**
NP19: Newp 2D **36**
NP26: Cald 6C **60**
Stag La. *CF61: Llan M* *3B* ***110***
(off Durrel St.)
Staines St. CF5: Card 2D **94**
Stallcourt Av. CF23: Pen L 1D **96**
CF61: Llan M 4B **110**
Stallcourt Cl. CF23: Pen L 6E **87**
CF71: L'thian 4B **90**
Stamford Ct. NP20: Newp 3A **36**
Standard St. CF83: Tret 3A **30**
Stanford Rd. NP19: Newp 4B **38**
Stanier Ct. CF24: Card 3D **96**
Stanley Dr. CF83: Caer 4B **28**
Stanley Pl. NP44: Pnwd 6E **9**
Stanley Rd. NP20: Newp 4B **36**
Stanton Way CF64: P'rth 5E **109**
Stanway Pl. CF5: Ely 4F **93**
Stanway Rd. CF5: Ely 4F **93**
Stanwell Cres. CF64: P'rth 6B **102**
Stanwell Rd. CF64: P'rth 1F **109**
Starbuck St. CF83: Rud 6B **30**
Star La. CF5: Cap L 1H **81**
NP4: Trev 1B **6**
Starling Rd. CF62: St Ath 3F **111**
Star Recreation Community Cen. 3E **97**
Star St. CF24: Card 2H **5** (3D **96**)
NP44: C'brn 3G **11**
Star Trad. Est. NP18: P'hir 2G **21**
Star Vs. NP18: P'hir 2G **21**
Station App. CF64: P'rth 2E **109**
CF72: P'clun 5D **64**
Station App. NP10: Bass 6D **34**
NP18: C'ln 5H **21**
Station App. Rd. CF62: Barry 5G **117**
Station Cl. NP26: Cald 6B **60**
Station Farm NP44: C'iog 6F **9**
Station Ind. Est. NP16: Chep 2F **63**
Station Pl. NP11: Ris 5D **16**
Station Rd. CF14: Llan N 4B **84**
CF14: L'shn 5H **71**
CF15: Cre 6E **67**
CF15: Rad 2G **83**
CF38: Chu V, E Isaf 3F **43**
CF61: Llan M 3B **110**
CF62: Rho 6E **115**
CF64: Din P 2G **107**
CF64: P'rth 2E **109**
NP4: Grif 6E **7**
NP11: Ris 6D **16**
NP16: Chep 2E **63**
NP18: C'ln 4H **21**
NP18: L'wrn 6F **39**
NP18: P'hir 1E **21**
NP26: Cald 6B **60**
NP26: Pskwt 5H **61**
NP44: Pnwd 6E **9**
Station Rd. E. CF5: Wen 4E **99**
Station Rd. W. CF5: Wen 5E **99**
Station St. CF63: Barry 2A **118**
CF83: Mac 2G **31**
NP20: Newp 4B **36**
Station Ter. CF5: Ely 3B **94**
CF10: Card 3F **5** (3B **96**)
CF38: Llan F 4D **42**
CF64: P'rth 2E **109**
CF72: L'harry 4C **78**
CF72: P'clun 6D **64**
CF83: Caer 1D **46**
(Bartlett St.)
CF83: Caer 5A **28**
(St Cenydd Rd.)
NP44: Pnwd 6E **9**
Steepfield NP44: C'iog 5G **9**
Steep St. CF64: P'rth 6A **102**
NP16: Chep 2E **63**
Steer Cres. NP19: Newp 2G **37**
Steffani Ct. CF10: Card 6B **96**
Stella Cl. CF14: Thorn 2H **71**
Stella Maris Cl. CF15: Rad 2F **83**
Stelvio Pk. Av. NP20: Newp 6H **35**
Stelvio Pk. Cl. NP20: Newp 6H **35**
Stelvio Pk. Ct. NP20: Newp 6H **35**
Stelvio Pk. Cres. NP20: Newp 6H **35**
Stelvio Pk. Dr. NP20: Newp 6H **35**
Stelvio Pk. Gdns. NP20: Newp 6H **35**
Stelvio Pk. Gro. NP20: Newp 6H **35**
Stelvio Pk. Ri. NP20: Newp 6H **35**
Stelvio Pk. Vw. NP20: Newp 6H **35**
Stenhousemuir Pl. CF24: Card 2F **97**
Stephenson Ct. CF24: Card 2H **5** (3C **96**)
Stephenson Ind. Est. NP19: Newp 2F **55**
Stephenson St. CF11: Card 4G **95**
NP19: Newp 2D **54**
Sterling Cl. CF24: Card 2G **97**
Sterndale Bennett Rd. NP19: Newp 4C **38**
Stevelee NP44: Coed E 4E **11**
Stevenson Cl. NP10: Roger 3C **34**
Stevenson Ct. NP10: Roger 3C **34**
Stevenson St. Ind. Est. NP19: Newp 3E **55**
Steven Wlk. *NP10: Roger* *5D* ***34***
(off Ebenezer Dr.)
Stewart Rd. CF62: Rho 6E **115**
Steynton Path NP44: F'wtr, G'mdw 3E **11**
Stiels NP44: Coed E 5D **10**
Stirling Dr. CF72: Y'erdy 5C **40**
Stirling Rd. CF5: Ely 5E **93**
CF62: Barry 6E **105**
Stirling Rd. Shop. Cen.
CF62: Barry 6E **105**
Stockland St. CF11: Card 1H **101**
CF83: Caer 1C **46**
Stockton Cl. NP19: Newp 6E **21**
Stockton Rd. NP19: Newp 2D **36**
Stockwood Cl. NP18: L'stne 6F **23**
Stockwood Vw. NP18: L'stne 1F **39**
Stokes Ct. NP18: P'hir 1F **21**
Stokes Dr. NP18: P'hir 1F **21**
Stonebridge Pk. NP44: C'iog 6F **9**
Stonechat Cl. CF3: St M 1E **89**
Stone Cotts. NP26: Sud 6H **61**
Stoneleigh Ct. CF11: Card 2F **95**
Stonewell Ct. CF23: Pen L 5C **86**
Stone Yd., The CF11: Card 4F **95**
Storehouse Row *CF15: N'grw* *4D* ***44***
(off Tyla Gwyn)
Storrar Pl. CF24: Card 1G **97**
Storrar Rd. CF24: Card 1G **97**
Stour Ct. NP44: Thorn 1C **10**
Stowepath NP44: L'rfn 3B **12**
Stow Hill CF37: T'rest 2D **24**
NP20: Newp 5A **36**
STOW PARK 6A **36**
Stow Pk. Av. NP20: Newp 5A **36**
Stow Pk. Circ. NP20: Newp 6A **36**
Stow Pk. Cres. NP20: Newp 5A **36**
Stow Pk. Dr. NP20: Newp 6A **36**
Stow Pk. Gdns. NP20: Newp 6A **36**
Stow Pas. NP20: Newp 5B **36**
Stradling Cl. CF62: Barry 1D **116**
CF64: Sul 2G **119**
CF71: C'bri 3B **90**
Stradling Pl. CF61: Llan M 4C **110**
Stradmore Cl. CF15: Taff W 6E **45**
Straits La. NP18: Nash 6B **56**
Strand, The *CF61: Llan M* *3B* ***110***
(off East St.)
NP44: C'brn 1G **11**
Stratford Grn. CF63: Barry 5C **106**
Stratford Ho. NP20: Newp 6G **35**
Strathnairn St. CF24: Card 1B **96**
Strathy Rd. CF3: St M 6E **75**
Striguil Rd. NP16: Bul 4E **63**
Strongbow Rd. NP16: Bul 4E **63**
Stryd Silurian CF72: L'harry 5C **78**
Stryd y Berllan CF72: L'harry 5A **78**
Stryd-y-Gollen CF72: L'harry 5A **78**
Stuart Av. NP16: Chep 1D **62**
Stuart Cl. CF11: Card 3F **101**
Stuart Crystal ***1F 63***
(off Bridge St.)
Stuart Pl. CF10: Card 2C **102**
Stuart St. CF10: Card 2B **102**
(not continuous)
CF72: P'clun 6C **64**
Stuart Ter. *CF72: T Grn* *3D* ***64***
(off Cowbridge Rd.)
Sturminster Rd. CF23: Pen L 1E **97**
Stuttgarter Strasse CF10: Card 2E **5** (3B **96**)
Subway Rd. CF63: Barry 3A **118**
SUDBROOK 6H **61**
Sudbrook Rd. NP26: Pskwt, Sud 5G **61**
Sudbury Wlk. NP20: Newp 2C **36**
Sudcroft St. CF11: Card 5E **95**
Sufflex Est. NP11: Ris 1F **33**
Suffolk Ho. CF5: Card 2E **95**
Sullivan Circ. NP19: Newp 5B **38**
Sullivan Cl. CF3: L'rmy 6B **74**
CF64: P'rth 4D **108**
SULLY 3H **119**
Sully Moors Rd. CF64: Sul 6F **107**
Sully Pl. CF64: P'rth 2E **109**
Sully Rd. CF64: P'rth, Sul 1A **120**
Sully Ter. CF64: P'rth 3E **109**
Sully Ter. La. CF64: P'rth 3E **109**
Sully Vw. CF63: Barry 6E **107**
Summerau Ct. CF5: L'dff 2E **95**
Summer Dale Cl. CF38: Chu V 2F **43**
Summerfield Av. CF14: Card 5H **85**
Summerfield Dr. CF72: L'sant 3G **65**
Summerfield La. CF83: Mac 3C **30**
Summerfield Pl. CF14: Heath 2F **85**
SUMMER HILL 3E **37**
Summerhill Av. NP19: Newp 3E **37**
Summerhill Cl. CF3: St M 6E **75**
Summerhill Ho. NP19: Newp 3E **37**
Summerhouse La. NP16: Bul 6F **63**
Summerland Cl. CF64: L'dgh 5F **101**
Summerland Cres. CF64: L'dgh 5F **101**
Summerwood Cl. CF5: F'wtr 1F **93**
Sumner Cl. CF5: L'dff 5A **84**
Sunbeam Cl. NP19: Newp 5E **37**
Sundew Cl. CF5: L'dff 5H **83**
CF64: P'rth 6G **101**

Sunlea Cres. NP4: New I, P'pool 3F **7**
Sunningdale CF83: Caer 1A **46**
Sunningdale Cl. CF23: Cyn 3B **86**
Sunningdale Ct. NP19: Newp 3A **38**
Sunny Bank *CF72: L'sant 2F 65*
(off Heol-y-Beilia)
Sunnybank CF64: Din P 1A **108**
CF83: Abert 2F **27**
NP10: Bass 1B **52**
NP44: H'lys 5B **10**
Sunnybank Cl. CF14: Whit 4F **85**
Sunnybank Ct. NP4: Grif 6E **7**
Sunnybank Rd. NP4: Grif 6D **6**
Sunny Bank Ter. CF83: Mac 2F **31**
Sunnybank Way NP4: Grif 1D **8**
Sunnybrook Ct. CF5: F'wtr 6H **83**
Sunnycroft NP26: Pskwt 5H **61**
Sunnycroft Cl. CF64: Din P 2H **107**
Sunnycroft La. CF64: Din P 2H **107**
Sunnycroft Ri. CF64: Din P 2H **107**
Sunny Pl. NP18: P'hir 6E **13**
Sunny Side *CF37: P'prdd 5B 14*
(off Graigwen Rd.)
Sun St. CF24: Card 2H **5** (3D **96**)
Supakart **1A 56**
Suran-y-Gog CF63: Barry 4B **106**
Surrey Pl. NP19: Newp 2E **37**
Surrey St. CF5: Card 3D **94**
Sussex Cl. NP19: Newp 1G **55**
Sussex St. CF11: Card 6A **4** (5H **95**)
Sutherland Cres.
NP19: Newp 2G **37**
Sutton Gro. CF23: Pontp 4D **72**
Sutton Rd. NP19: Newp 2D **36**
Swalec Stadium **1A 4 (2G 95)**
Swallow Dr. NP26: Cald 6D **60**
Swallowhurst Cl. CF5: Ely 5D **92**
Swallow Way NP10: Duf 3G **53**
Swanage Cl. CF3: St M 6E **75**
SWANBRIDGE **3B 120**
Swanbridge Ct. CF83: B'ws 3E **29**
(not continuous)
Swanbridge Gro. CF64: Sul 2A **120**
Swanbridge Rd. CF64: Sul 1A **120**
Swan Cl. NP26: Cald 6D **60**
Swansea St. CF24: Card 4E **97**
Swan St. CF72: L'sant 2F **65**
Sward Cl. NP10: Roger 2C **34**
Sweldon Cl. CF5: Ely 6F **93**
Swift Bus. Cen., The
CF24: Card 4D **96**
Swift Cl. CF3: L'rmy 6H **73**
Swinburne Cl. NP19: Newp 4G **37**
Swinton St. CF24: Card 2E **97**
Swn-y-Mor CF62: Barry 5C **116**
Swn-y-Nant CF38: Chu V 2E **43**
Sword Hill CF83: Caer 1H **45**
Sycamore Av. CF62: E Bre 2B **112**
NP16: Bul 5E **63**
NP19: Newp 5G **37**
NP26: Cald 4B **60**
Sycamore Cl. CF64: Din P 3H **107**
CF64: L'dgh 5G **101**
CF72: Mis 6F **65**
Sycamore Ct. NP44: H'lys 5B **10**
Sycamore Cres. CF62: Barry 6A **106**
NP11: Ris 6F **17**
Sycamore Ho. CF14: Whit 1A **84**
Sycamore Pl. CF5: F'wtr 1H **93**
NP44: Up Cwm 6B **8**
(not continuous)
Sycamore Rd. CF72: L'harry 5A **78**
NP4: Grif 2D **8**
Sycamore Rd. Sth. NP4: Grif 2D **8**
Sycamore St. CF15: Taff W 1E **69**
CF37: R'fln 4G **25**
Sycamore Ter. NP26: Magor 4D **58**
Sycamore Tree Cl. CF15: Rad 1E **83**
Sylvan Cl. CF5: F'wtr 6A **84**
NP20: Malp 4B **20**
Symondscliff Way
NP26: Pskwt 6F **61**
Syon Pk. Cl. CF3: St M 6E **75**
Syr David's Av. CF5: Card 2D **94**
Syr David's Ct. CF5: Card 2D **94**
System St. CF24: Card 2H **5** (3C **96**)

T

Tabor St. CF15: Taff W 1E **69**
Tacoma Sq. CF10: Card 2C **102**
Taf Cl. CF62: Barry 1E **117**
Taff Bus. Cen. CF37: T'rest 6A **26**
Taff Cotts. CF72: C Inn 3G **65**
Taff Ct. NP44: Thorn 6A **8**
Taff Emb. CF11: Card 6H **95**
Taff Gorge Countryside Cen. **2H 69**
Taff Rd. NP26: Cald 4D **60**
Taffs Fall Rd. CF37: T'rest 1B **44**
Taffs Mead Emb. CF11: Card 6B **4** (5H **95**)
Taffs Mead Rd. CF37: T'rest 1A **44**
Taff St. CF10: Card 5F **5** (4B **96**)
CF15: Tong 4G **69**
CF37: P'prdd 1C **24**
TAFF'S WELL **2E 69**
Taff's Well Station (Rail) **2E 69**
Taff Ter. CF11: Card 1A **102**
CF15: Rad 2G **83**
Taff Va. Flats CF37: P'prdd 1C **24**
Taff Va. Shop. Cen. CF37: P'prdd 6C **14**
Taff Valley Quad Bike & Activity Cen. **4B 26**
Tafwy's Wlk. CF83: Caer 6C **28**
Tai Cae Bryn CF15: Gro-w 6G **27**
Tai Derwen CF3: Cefn M 5B **50**
Tai Duffryn CF15: N'grw 4E **45**
Tair Erw Rd. CF14: Heath 3F **85**
Tair Gwaun CF64: P'rth 4C **108**
Talbot Cl. CF72: T Grn 2E **65**
TALBOT GREEN **3D 64**
Talbot La. NP20: Newp 5C **36**
Talbot Pl. CF11: Card 3G **95**
Talbot Rd. CF72: T Grn, L'sant 3E **65**
Talbot Sq. CF72: T Grn 3D **64**
Talbot St. CF11: Card 3G **95**
Talgarth Cl. NP44: C'brn 3G **11**
Taliesin NP44: C'brn 1G **11**
Taliesin Cl. NP10: Roger 3D **34**
Taliesin Ct. CF10: Card 1B **102**
Taliesin Dr. NP10: Roger 3D **34**
Tallard's Pl. NP16: Sed 2G **63**
Tallis Cl. NP19: Newp 4C **38**
Talworth St. CF24: Card 1G **5** (2C **96**)
Talybont Cl. CF62: St Ath 2D **112**
Talybont Ct. CF14: Card 1G **95**
Talybont Nth. CF14: Card 6F **85**
Talybont Rd. CF5: Ely 4H **93**
Tal-y-Bryn CF64: P'rth 3C **108**
Talyfan Cl. CF71: C'bri 4D **90**
TALYGARN **2C 78**
Talygarn Cl. CF72: Taly 2B **78**
Talygarn Ct. CF72: Taly 2C **78**
Talygarn Dr. CF72: Bryns 1B **78**
Talygarn M. CF72: Taly 2C **78**
Tal-y-Garn St. CF14: Card 5H **85**
TALYGARN UNIT ***5E 7***
(within County Hospital)
Tamar Cl. NP20: Bet 5G **19**
Tanglewood Cl. CF14: L'vne 3A **72**
Tangmere Dr. CF5: L'dff 5H **83**
Tan Ho. Dr. NP18: C'ln 5A **22**
Tansy Cl. CF14: Thorn 2F **71**
Tantallus Cl. NP19: Newp 6E **37**
Tantallus Cres. NP19: Newp 6E **37**
Tantallus Way NP19: Newp 6E **37**
Tanybryn NP11: Ris 1G **33**
Tan-y-Bryn CF38: Bed 4A **42**
CF83: Sen 1E **27**
Tan-y-Fron CF62: Barry 4D **116**
Tan-yr-Allt CF72: C Inn 3G **65**
Tapley Cl. CF5: Ely 6H **93**
Tarragon Way CF23: Pontp 4E **73**
Tarrws Cl. CF5: Wen 4E **99**
Tarwick Dr. CF3: St M 6C **74**
Tasker Sq. CF14: L'shn 6F **71**
Tatem Dr. CF5: F'wtr 2F **93**
Tatham Rd. CF14: L'shn 6F **71**
Tathan Cres. CF62: St Ath 4D **112**
Tatton Rd. NP19: Newp 3B **56**
Taunton Av. CF3: L'rmy 2H **87**
Taunton Cres. CF3: L'rmy 2A **88**
Taverner Trad. Est. NP18: C'ln 4H **21**
Tavern-y-Coed CF38: Tont 6F **25**
Tavistock St. CF24: Card 1F **5** (2B **96**)
Taylor St. NP11: Ris 4D **16**
Taymuir Rd. CF24: Card 1F **97**
Teal Cl. NP26: Undy 4E **59**
Tealham Dr. CF3: St M 6F **75**
Teal St. CF24: Card 1H **5** (2C **96**)
Teamans Row CF15: Morg 5F **69**
Team Sport Karting **6A 96**
Teasel Av. CF64: P'rth 6G **101**
Techniquest **2B 102**
Tedder Cl. CF14: L'shn 6H **71**
Tees Cl. NP20: Bet 5H **19**
Tegfan CF11: Card 3F **95**
CF72: P'clun 1C **78**
CF83: Caer 6A **28**
Tegfan Cl. CF14: L'shn 5G **71**
Tegfan Ct. NP44: H'lys 5B **10**
TEGFAN DAY HOSPITAL **2A 84**
Teifi Dr. CF62: Barry 2E **117**
Teifi Pl. CF5: Ely 4H **93**
Teilo St. CF11: Card 2F **95**
Telelkebir Rd. CF37: P'prdd 5A **14**
Telford Cl. NP10: Roger 3D **34**
Telford St. CF11: Card 4G **95**
NP19: Newp 5E **37**
Temperance Ct. CF15: P'rch 4H **67**
Temperance Hill
NP11: Ris 4D **16**
Temperance Pl. CF37: P'prdd 6C **14**
Temperance Rd. CF15: P'rch 4H **67**
Tempest Dr. NP16: Chep 2D **62**
Tempest Way NP16: Chep 2D **62**
Templar Pk. Ind. Est.
CF24: Card 6H **5** (5C **96**)
Temple Ct. CF11: Card 3A **4** (3G **95**)
Temple St. NP20: Newp 1C **54**
Templeton Av. CF14: L'shn 4F **71**
Templeton Cl. CF14: L'shn 4G **71**
Tenby Cl. CF64: Din P 2A **108**
NP10: Duf 6G **53**
NP44: L'rfn 2A **12**
Tenby Ct. CF83: Caer 5H **27**
Tenby La. NP16: Bul 6F **63**
Tenison Rd. NP4: Trev 1D **6**
Tennyson Av. NP18: L'wrn 5E **39**
Tennyson Cl. CF37: R'fln 3G **25**
NP26: Cald 5B **60**
Tennyson Rd. CF62: Barry 5G **105**
CF64: P'rth 1C **108**
NP19: Newp 4G **37**
NP26: Cald 5B **60**
Tennyson Way CF61: Llan M 4D **110**
Tensing Cl. CF14: L'shn 4H **71**
Tensing Ter. CF63: Barry 1B **118**
Tern Cl. CF3: St M 5D **74**
Tern Ct. NP44: Thorn 6A **8**
Terrace, The CF15: Cre 5E **67**
NP26: Sud 6H **61**
Terra Nova Way CF64: P'rth 5H **101**
Tetbury Cl. NP20: Newp 2C **36**
Tewdric Ct. NP44: C'iog 6H **9**
Tewdrig Cl. CF61: Llan M 4B **110**
Tewends NP44: F'wtr 4D **10**
Tewkesbury Pl. CF24: Card 5A **86**
Tewkesbury St. CF24: Card 6A **86**
Tewkesbury Wlk. *NP20: Newp 3C 36*
(off Shaftesbury St.)
Teynes NP44: Coed E 4D **10**
Thackeray Cres. CF3: L'rmy 6H **73**
Thames Cl. NP20: Bet 6G **19**
Tharsis Cl. CF24: Card 4G **5** (4C **96**)
Thaw Cl. CF62: Rho 6C **114**
The ....
Names prefixed with 'The' for example 'The Acorns' are indexed under the main name such as 'Acorns, The'
Theatre Royal Cinema **3G 117**
Theobald Rd. CF5: Card 4E **95**
Theodora St. CF24: Card 2E **97**
Thesiger Ct. CF24: Card 1A **96**
Thesiger St. CF24: Card 1A **96**
Third Av. CF83: Caer 6A **28**
Third St. NP19: Newp 3G **55**
Thirlmere Pl. NP19: Newp 1F **37**
Thistle Cl. CF62: Barry 1F **117**
Thistle Ct. NP44: Ty C 3B **10**

Thistle Way CF5: L'dff 1C **94**
NP11: Ris 6F **17**
Thomas Davies Ct. CF3: Rum 4H **87**
Thomas Gro. NP10: Roger 5D **34**
Thomas St. CF11: Card 6H **95**
CF37: P'prdd 6C **14**
CF83: Abert, Caer 2E **27**
CF83: L'brad 1B **28**
CF83: Tret 3A **30**
NP16: Chep 2E **63**
Thomasville CF83: Caer 5A **28**
Thompson Av. CF5: Card 2C **94**
NP19: Newp 6H **37**
Thompson Cl. NP19: Newp 6A **38**
Thompson Pl. CF5: Card 2C **94**
Thompson St. CF37: P'prdd 6A **14**
CF63: Barry 2H **117**
Thorley Cl. CF23: Cyn 3B **86**
Thornaby Ct. CF10: Card 6F **5** (5B **96**)
Thornbury Cl. CF14: Heath 1E **85**
Thornbury Pk. NP10: Roger 5C **34**
(not continuous)
Thorncliff Ct. NP44: St D 3E **11**
Thorne Way CF5: Ely 6F **93**
Thorn Gro. CF64: P'rth 5F **109**
THORNHILL
CF14 3G **71**
CF83 5D **46**
NP44 1D **10**
Thornhill Cen. NP44: Thorn 1C **10**
Thornhill Cl. NP44: Up Cwm 5B **8**
Thornhill Ct. CF14: R'ina 5F **71**
Thornhill Crematorium & Cemetery
CF14: Thorn 3E **71**
Thornhill Gdns. NP10: Roger 2A **34**
Thornhill Rd. CF14: L'shn, R'ina, Thorn 4D **46**
CF14: Thorn 4D **46**
CF83: Caer, R'ina 4D **46**
NP44: Thorn, Up Cwm 1D **10**
Thornhill St. CF5: Card 3E **95**
Thornhill Way NP10: Roger 2A **34**
Thorn Tree Dr. NP16: Bul 6F **63**
Thornwell Rd. NP16: Bul 4E **63**
Thornwood Cl. CF14: Thorn 2G **71**
Three Arches Av. CF14: L'shn 6A **72**
Three Oaks Cl. CF83: B'ws 2E **29**
Threipland Dr. CF14: Heath 2F **85**
Thrush Cl. CF3: St M 6E **75**
Thurston Rd. CF37: P'prdd 5D **14**
Thurston St. CF5: Card 4E **95**
Tidal Sidings CF24: Card 5E **97**
Tide Flds. Rd. CF24: Card 4G **97**
Tidenham Ct. CF5: Ely 5H **93**
Tidenham Rd. CF5: Ely 5H **93**
Till Gro. NP18: C'ln 4F **21**
Tillsland NP44: Coed E 5E **11**
Timbers Sq. CF24: Card 1D **96**
Timothy Rees Cl. CF5: L'dff 4H **83**
Tin St. CF24: Card 3D **96**
Tintagel Cl. CF14: Thorn 4F **71**
Tintern Cl. CF62: St Ath 2C **112**
NP44: C'brn 3G **11**
Tintern St. CF5: Card 3E **95**
Tippet Cl. NP19: Newp 4C **38**
Tir-Afon Ct. CF72: P'clun 6D **64**
Tir Coed CF83: Caer 4A **28**
Tir Meibion La. CF72: L'sant 2F **65**
Tir-y-Cwm La. NP11: Ris 6D **16**
Tir-y-Cwm Rd. NP11: Ris 5D **16**
Tir-y-Graig CF38: Tont 1G **43**
Titan Rd. CF24: Card 5D **96**
Tiverton Dr. CF3: Rum 3G **87**
Toftingall Av. CF14: Heath 2F **85**
Toghill Dr. CF15: Taff W 2F **69**
Tollgate Cl. CF11: Card 2F **101**
CF83: Caer 4F **29**
Tolpath NP44: Coed E 4C **10**
Tom Mann Cl. NP19: Newp 2B **38**
Ton, The CF3: Old M 6B **74**
Tone Cl. NP20: Bet 5F **19**
Tone Rd. NP20: Bet 5F **19**
Tone Sq. NP20: Bet 5F **19**
TONGWYNLAIS 4G **69**
Ton Rd. NP44: C'brn 4E **11**
NP44: F'wtr 3C **10**
TON-TEG 2G **43**
Tonteg Cl. CF38: Tont 1G **43**
Tonteg Ind. Est. CF37: T'rest 6H **25**
Tonteg Rd. CF37: T'rest 6H **25**
CF38: Tont 1H **43**
Ton y Felin CF37: R'fln 3G **25**
Ton-y-Felin Rd. CF83: Caer 6D **28**
TONYREFAIL 2A **40**
Tonyrefail Rd. CF37: Pen c 5A **24**
Ton-yr-Ywen Av. CF14: Heath 2G **85**
Topaz St. CF24: Card 3D **96**
Torbay Ter. CF62: Rho 6E **115**
Tordoff Way CF62: Barry 1G **117**
Torfaen Bus. Cen. NP4: New I 5F **7**
TORFAEN COMMUNITY HOSPITAL (TALYGARN) *5E 7*
(within County Hospital)
Toronto Cl. NP20: Newp 6F **35**
Torrens Dr. CF23: Cyn 3B **86**
Torridge Rd. NP20: Bet 4E **19**
Torrington Rd. CF3: L'rmy 6A **74**
Tor Vw. CF83: B'ws 2E **29**
Tourist Info. Cen.
Barry Island 5G **117**
Caerleon 5H **21**
Caerphilly 1D **46**
Cardiff 4D **4** (4A **96**)
Chepstow 1E **63**
Magor Service Area 3C **58**
Newport 5C **36**
Penarth 2F **109**
Pontypridd 5C **14**
Tower Hill CF64: P'rth 2F **109**
Towers, The NP44: C'brn 2H **11**
Tower St. CF37: T'rest 2D **24**
Tower Way CF64: Sul 1E **119**
Town Hall Sq. CF71: C'bri 3D **90**
Town Mill Rd. CF71: C'bri 4C **90**
Town Wall CF10: Card 4D **4** (4A **96**)
Towyn Rd. CF3: Rum 3A **88**
Towyn Way CF38: Tont 1G **43**
Towy Rd. CF14: L'shn 6A **72**
Trade La. CF10: Card 6A **96**
Trade St. CF10: Card 5A **96**
Trafalgar Rd. CF23: Pen L 1D **96**
Trafalgar St. NP11: Ris 1E **33**
Traherne Dr. CF5: Ely 5D **92**
TRALLWNG 5D **14**
Tram La. NP18: C'ln 5A **22**
NP44: Llanf 6C **12**
Tramore Way CF23: Pontp 4G **73**
Tram Rd. NP18: C'ln 5A **22**
NP44: Up Cwm 5B **8**
Tramway Cl. NP44: F'wtr 4C **10**
TRANCH 3A **6**
Tranch Rd. NP4: P'pool 3A **6**
Trannon Ct. NP44: Thorn 1D **10**
Tranquil Pl. NP44: C'brn 4G **11**
Transporter Bridge 2D **54**
Tranters Ter. *NP44: Pnwd 5C 8*
(off Ty Pwca Rd.)
Trap Well CF83: Caer 4F **29**
Traston Av. NP19: Newp 2H **55**
Traston Cl. NP19: Newp 2H **55**
Traston La. NP19: Newp 2H **55**
Traston Rd. NP19: Newp 3F **55**
(not continuous)
Traws Mawr La. NP20: Bet, Oakf 4F **19**
NP44: L'tnam 4F **19**
Trebanog Cl. CF3: Rum 1C **88**
Trebanog Cres. CF3: Rum 2C **88**
Tre-Beferad CF61: Bov 4E **111**
TREBEFERED 4E **111**
Treberth Av. NP19: Newp 3C **38**
Treberth Cl. NP19: Newp 3C **38**
Treberth Ct. NP19: Newp 3C **38**
Treberth Cres. NP19: Newp 3B **38**
Treberth Dr. NP19: Newp 3C **38**
Treberth Est. NP19: Newp 3C **38**
Treberth Gdns. NP19: Newp 3C **38**
Treberth Gro. NP19: Newp 3C **38**
Treberth Ri. NP19: Newp 3C **38**
Treberth Vw. NP19: Newp 3B **38**
Treberth Way NP19: Newp 3C **38**
Treborth Rd. CF3: Rum 2C **88**
Trecastle Av. CF14: L'shn 4G **71**
TRECENYDD 6A **28**
Trecenydd Ind. Est. CF83: Caer 6A **28**
Trecinon Rd. CF3: Rum 2D **88**
Tredegar Ct. CF14: Whit 2B **84**
NP11: Cros K 4A **16**
NP20: Newp 1C **54**
Tredegar Dr. NP26: Undy 4F **59**
Tredegar Fort 1F **53**
Tredegar House 4F **53**
Tredegar House Country Pk. 4F **53**
Tredegar Ho. Dr. NP10: Duf 4F **53**
TREDEGAR PARK 2F **53**
Tredegar Pk. Vw. NP10: Roger 5E **35**
Tredegar St. CF10: Card 5E **5** (4B **96**)
NP10: R'drn 6A **34**
NP11: Cros K 3A **16**
NP11: Ris 5D **16**
NP20: Newp 6C **36**
Tredegar Ter. NP11: Cros K 3A **16**
NP11: Ris 6D **16**
Tredelerch Rd. CF3: Rum 5G **87**
TREDOGAN 3G **115**
Tredogan Rd. CF62: P'ark, Rho 1E **115**
Treetops NP26: Pskwt 5G **61**
Treetops Cl. CF5: F'wtr 6F **83**
Trefaser Cres. CF3: Rum 1C **88**
TREFFLEMIN 1D **112**
TREFOREST 2E **25**
Treforest Estate Station (Rail) 2B **44**
Treforest Ind. Est. CF37: T'rest 1C **44**
(Main Av.)
CF37: T'rest 6A **26**
(Severn Rd., not continuous)
Treforest Station (Rail) 3E **25**
TREFORGAN 5F **69**
Tregare St. NP19: Newp 3D **36**
Tregarn Rd. NP18: L'stne 6H **23**
Tregaron Rd. CF5: Ely 4F **93**
Tre Garth Cl. CF15: Cre 5D **66**
Tre Garth Ct. CF15: Cre 5D **66**
Tregwilym Cl. NP10: Roger 5D **34**
Tregwilym Ind. Est. NP10: Roger 6C **34**
Tregwilym Rd. NP10: Roger 4B **34**
(not continuous)
Tregwilym Wlk. NP10: Roger 5C **34**
Treharne Flats CF37: R'fln 4H **25**
Treharne Rd. CF63: Barry 6A **106**
Treharris St. CF24: Card 2B **96**
Tre-Herbert Rd. NP18: L'veth, P'hir 2G **13**
NP44: C'iog 4H **9**
NP44: C'iog, P'hir 1F **13**
Treherbert St. CF24: Card 1H **95**
Trelai Ct. CF5: Ely 6G **93**
Trelawney Av. CF3: Rum 4H **87**
Trelawney Cres. CF3: Rum 4H **87**
Trelech Cl. NP44: C'brn 3H **11**
TRELÁI 4H **93**
Trem Echni CF62: Rho 6F **115**
Trem Groeswen CF83: Caer 1H **45**
Trem Mapgoll CF63: Barry 4A **106**
TREMORFA 2F **97**
Tremorfa Ind. Est. CF24: Card 5F **97**
Trem Powys CF63: Barry 5C **106**
Trem Twynbarlwm NP44: Two L 4G **11**
Trem y Castell CF83: Caer 2H **45**
Trem-y-Coed CF63: Barry 4B **106**
Trem-y-Cwm CF38: Bed 5A **42**
Trem-y-Don CF62: Barry 5C **116**
Trem-y-Fforest CF72: L'harry 6B **78**
Trem-y-Garth CF72: L'harry 5C **78**
Trenchard Dr. CF14: L'shn 6H **71**
Trenewydd Rd. CF3: Rum 2C **88**
Trent Rd. NP20: Bet 5F **19**
Tre Oda Ct. CF14: Llan N 4D **84**
Treorchy St. CF24: Card 1H **95**
Treseder Way CF5: Ely 4A **94**
Tresigin Rd. CF3: Rum 1C **88**
Tresilian Cl. CF61: Llan M 4B **110**
Tresillian Ter. CF10: Card 6D **4** (5A **96**)
Tresillian Way CF10: Card 6D **4** (5A **96**)
Tresillian Way Ind. Est. CF10: Card 5A **96**
TRETHOMAS 3A **30**
Tretower Ct. NP44: L'rfn 2B **12**
Trevelyan Ct. CF61: Llan M 2D **110**
CF83: Caer 6E **29**
Trevethick St. CF11: Card 4G **95**
Trevine Path NP44: F'wtr 3E **11**

Trevithick Cl. NP20: Malp 4H **19** (not continuous)
Trewartha Ct. CF14: Whit 2D **84**
Triangle, The *CF62: Barry* *5H* ***117*** *(off Redbrink Cres.)*
Triassic Towers *5G* ***117*** ***(in Esplanade Bldgs.)***
Trident Ct. CF24: Card 6H **5** (4C **96**)
Tridwr Rd. CF83: Abert 2D **26**
Trinity Ct. CF24: Card 2F **5** (3B **96**)
CF62: Barry 3G **117**
NP11: Ris 5D **16**
NP20: Newp 1D **54**
Trinity La. NP18: C'ln 4F **21**
Trinity Pl. NP20: Newp 1D **54**
Trinity Rd. NP44: Pnwd 6D **8**
Trinity St. CF10: Card 4D **4** (4A **96**)
CF62: Barry 3F **117**
Trinity Vw. NP18: C'ln 4E **21**
Triscombe Dr. CF5: L'dff 6A **84**
Tristram Cl. CF14: Thorn 3F **71**
Troddi Cl. NP26: Cald 4C **60**
TROEDRHIW-TRWYN 5A 14
Troed-y-Bryn CF83: Caer 4A **28**
Troed-y-Garth CF15: P'rch 4H **67**
Troed y Rhiw CF14: R'ina 4C **70**
TROSNANT 4C 6
Trosnant St. NP4: P'pool 3C **6** (not continuous)
Trostrey NP44: H'bush 5E **11**
Trostrey Cl. NP4: New I 5H **7**
Trostrey St. NP19: Newp 3D **36**
Trotman Dickenson Pl. CF14: Card 6G **85**
TROWBRIDGE 2C 88
Trowbridge Grn. CF3: Rum 1C **88**
TROWBRIDGE MAWR 3C 88
Trowbridge Rd. CF3: Rum 2B **88**
Trussel Rd. NP44: C'brn 1G **11**
Tubular Cotts. NP16: Tut 1G **63**
Tudor Cl. CF5: F'wtr 2H **93**
CF64: P'rth 4E **109**
Tudor Ct. NP26: Undy 5F **59**
Tudor Cres. NP10: Roger 5D **34**
Tudor Dr. NP16: Chep 1C **62**
Tudor Gdns. CF83: Mac 3F **31**
Tudor La. CF11: Card 6A **4** (5H **95**)
Tudor M. CF72: Mis 6F **65**
Tudor Pl. CF61: Llan M 4C **110**
Tudor Rd. NP19: Newp 1E **37**
NP44: C'brn 2G **11**
Tudors, The CF23: Pen L 6C **86**
Tudor St. CF11: Card 6A **4** (4G **95**)
CF37: R'fln 5G **25**
Tudor Way CF38: Llan F 5C **42**
Tudor Woods NP44: L'rfn 3B **12**
Tulip Wlk. NP10: Roger 3H **33**
Tullock St. CF24: Card 6C **86**
Tummel Cl. CF23: Cyn 2C **86**
Tump La. NP26: Undy 4E **59**
Tunnel Ter. NP20: Newp 5B **36**
Turberville Pl. CF11: Card 3F **95**
Turberville Rd. NP44: C'brn 1H **11**
Turkey St. CF61: Llan M 2B **110**
Turner House Gallery 2F **109**
Turner Rd. CF5: Card 3D **94**
Turners End NP44: F'wtr 4D **10**
Turner St. NP19: Newp 3D **36**
Turnham Grn. CF23: Pen L 5E **87**
Turnpike Cl. CF64: Din P 1G **107**
NP4: P'pool 3F **7**
NP16: Chep 1C **62**
Turnpike End NP16: B'ly 6H **63**
Turnpike Rd. NP44: C'iog, Llanf 1B **12**
Turnstiles, The NP20: Newp 2C **36**
Tuscan Cl. CF64: L'dgh 4F **101**
TUTSHILL 1G 63
Tutshill Gdns. NP16: Tut 1G **63**
Tweedsmuir Rd. CF24: Card 2F **97**
Tweedy La. NP19: Newp 4F **37**
Twinings, The NP44: G'mdw 2D **10**
Twissell's Rd. NP4: P'pool 3A **6**
Twm Barlwm Cl. NP11: Ris 5G **17**
Twmbarlwm Ri. NP44: H'lys 4A **10**
Twm Barlwm Vw. NP44: Llanf 3B **12**
Twmpath Gdns. NP4: P'pool 3B **6**
Twmpath Rd. NP4: P'pool 3B **6**
TWO LOCKS 4G 11
Two-Locks Rd. NP44: Two L 4F **11**
Twyn, The CF83: Caer 1D **46**
Twyncarn Rd. NP11: C'crn, P'waun 1A **16**
TWYNCYN 2F 107
Twyncyn CF64: Din P 2F **107**
Twyn Oaks NP18: C'ln 4B **22**
TWYN Y CADNO 4G 33
Twyn-y-Fedwen Rd. CF14: Whit 4F **85**
TWYN-YR-ODYN 3D 98
Ty Box Cl. NP44: Pnwd 6D **8**
Ty Box Rd. NP44: Pnwd 6D **8** (not continuous)
Ty Bryncoch CF15: Taff W 1E **69**
Ty Camlas CF63: Barry 3H **117**
Ty-Canol Ct. NP44: F'wtr 4C **10**
Ty Canol La. CF83: Mac 2F **31**
Ty-Canol La. CF83: Tret 1A **30**
Ty-Canol Row NP44: F'wtr 4C **10**
Ty Canol Way NP44: H'lys 4B **10**
Ty-Canol Way NP44: G'mdw, Ty C 3B **10**
Ty-Cefn Rd. CF5: Ely 3H **93**
Ty Celyn M. CF14: Whit 6B **70**
Ty Cerrig CF23: Pent 5E **73**
Ty-Cerrig CF63: Barry 6B **106**
Ty Charlotte CF64: P'rth 5A **102**
TY-COCH 5G 11
Ty-Coch Cl. NP10: Bass 1B **52**
NP44: L'tnam 1A **20**
Ty Coch Ct. CF3: St M 1B **88**
Ty-Coch Distribution Cen. NP44: C'brn 5G **11**
Ty-Coch La. NP44: L'tnam 6H **11**
NP44: T Coch 5F **11**
Ty-Coch Rd. CF5: Ely 3G **93**
Ty-Coch Way NP44: C'brn, Oakf 4G **11**
Ty Coed NP44: Thorn 6B **8**
Ty Crwyn CF38: Chu V 3E **43**
Ty Dewi Sont CF64: P'rth 3C **108**
Tydfil Pl. CF23: Card 5B **86**
Tydfil Rd. CF83: B'ws 2F **29**
Tydfil St. CF63: Barry 1B **118**
Tydies NP44: Coed E 5D **10**
Ty Draw CF38: Chu V 2E **43**
Ty-Draw Pl. CF23: Pen L 6C **86**
Ty-Draw Rd. CF14: Pontp 4D **72**
CF23: Pen L 5B **86**
TY-DU 4C 34
Tydu Vw. NP10: Roger 4D **34**
Ty-Dyfan CF63: Barry 5A **106**
Ty Enfys CF23: Pent 5F **73**
Tyfica Cres. CF37: P'prdd 6C **14**
Tyfica Rd. CF37: P'prdd 6B **14**
Ty-Fry Av. CF3: Rum 4H **87**
Ty Fry Cl. CF3: Rum 3H **87**
Ty-Fry Gdns. CF3: Rum 3H **87**
Ty-Fry Rd. CF3: Rum 4H **87**
Ty Gambig CF62: Barry 6H **117**
Ty-Glas Av. CF14: L'shn 5G **71**
Ty-Glas Rd. CF14: L'shn 6F **71**
Ty-Glas Station (Rail) 1G 85
Ty Gwenfo CF63: Barry 1C **118**
Ty-Gwyn Av. CF23: Pen L 5C **86**
Ty-Gwyn Cres. CF23: Pen L 4C **86**
Ty Gwyn Rd. NP44: Coed E 3C **10**
NP44: G'mdw 2D **10**
Tygwyn Rd. CF37: P'prdd 6E **15**
Ty-Gwyn Rd. CF14: R'ina 6E **71**
CF23: Pen L 4C **86**
CF38: Chu V 2E **43**
Ty Gwyn Way NP44: F'wtr, G'mdw 2C **10**
TY HAFAN CHILDREN'S HOSPICE 3E **119**
Ty Isaf CF72: L'harry 5A **78**
Ty-Isaf CF83: Caer 4H **27**
NP11: Ris 1F **33**
Ty-Isaf Bungs. CF83: Caer 4H **27**
Ty-Isaf Cres. NP11: Ris 1F **33**
Ty-Isaf Pk. Av. NP11: Ris 1F **33**
Ty-Isaf Pk. Circ. NP11: Ris 1F **33**
Ty-Isaf Pk. Cres. NP11: Ris 1F **33**
Ty-Isaf Pk. Rd. NP11: Ris 1F **33**
Ty-Isaf Pk. Vs. NP11: Ris 1F **33**
Tylacoch CF72: L'harry 5B **78**
Tylagarw Ct. CF72: Tyle 5C **64**
Tylagarw Ter. CF72: Tyle 5B **64**
Tyla Glas CF83: Caer 3B **46**
Tyla Gwyn CF15: N'grw 3D **44**
Tyla La. CF3: Old M, St M 1E **75**
Tyla Rhosyr CF71: C'bri 3B **90**
Tyla Teg CF14: R'ina 5B **70**
Tylcha Fach Cl. CF39: T'fail 1A **40**
TYLE-GARW 5B 64
Tyle Garw CF72: Tyle 5B **64**
Tyle Ho. Cl. CF61: L'maes 1D **110**
Tyle'r Hendy CF72: Mis 6E **65**
Tyler St. CF24: Card 2E **97**
Tylers Way NP16: Sed 2H **63**
TYLLGOED 6H 83
Tyllwyd Rd. NP20: Newp 5H **35**
Ty-Mawr Av. CF3: Rum 5G **87**
Ty-Mawr Cl. CF3: Rum 5G **87**
Tymawr La. CF3: M'fld 5A **76**
Ty Mawr Parc CF37: P'prdd 5A **14**
Ty-Mawr Rd. CF3: Rum 4G **87**
CF14: Llan N, Whit 2A **84**
CF37: P'prdd 5A **14**
Tymawr Ter. CF37: P'prdd 5A **14**
Ty Mawr Uchaf CF37: Treh 5A **14**
Ty Mynydd NP44: C'brn 6E **9**
Tymynydd Cl. CF15: Rad 6F **69**
TYNANT 4A 42
Ty Nant CF83: Caer 5A **28**
Tynant CF14: Whit 3D **84**
Ty Nant Ct. CF15: Morg 4F **69**
Ty Nant Ddu NP4: P'pool 1B **6**
Tynant Rd. CF15: Cre 1D **80**
CF38: Bed 5A **42**
Ty-Nant Rd. CF15: Gwae G, Morg 4F **69**
Ty-Nant St. CF11: Card 6G **95**
Tyndall St. CF10: Card 6F **5** (5B **96**)
Tyndall St. Ind. Est.
CF10: Card 5F **5** (4B **96**)
Tyne Cl. NP20: Bet 6F **19**
Tyneside Rd. CF10: Card 1D **102**
Tynewydd CF14: Whit 3C **84**
Tynewydd Av. NP44: Pnwd 5E **9**
Ty-Newydd Ct. NP44: Pnwd 6E **9**
Tynewydd Dr. CF3: Cas 2G **75**
Tynewydd Farm Cl. NP44: Pnwd 5E **9**
Tynewydd Grn. NP44: Pnwd 5E **9**
Ty-Newydd Ho. NP44: Pnwd 6E **9**
Tynewydd Nth. Cl. NP44: Pnwd 5E **9**
Ty-Newydd Rd. CF62: Barry 1H **117**
NP44: Pnwd 6E **9**
Tynewydd Sth. Cl. NP44: Pnwd 5E **9**
Ty'n-y-Cae Gro. CF14: R'ina 1E **85**
Ty'n-y-Coedcae CF83: Mac 4D **30**
Ty'n-y-Coed La. CF24: Card 6B **86**
Ty'n-y-Coed Pl. CF24: Card 6B **86**
Tyn-y-Coed Rd. CF15: Cre, P'rch 3D **66**
Tyn-y-Cwm Rd. NP11: Ris 1G **33**
Tyn y Parc CF83: Abert 1D **26**
Tyn-y-Parc Rd. CF14: R'ina, Whit 2D **84**
Ty'n-y-Pwll Rd. CF14: Whit 2C **84**
Tyn y Waun Rd. CF83: Mac 2G **31**
Tynywern Ter. CF83: Tret 2A **30**
Ty Parc Cl. CF5: L'dff 4H **83**
Ty-Pica Dr. CF5: Wen 4E **99**
Ty Pont Haearn CF10: Card 5F **5**
Ty Pucca Cl. CF83: Mac 3G **31**
Ty Pwca Pl. NP44: Pnwd, Up Cwm 5C **8**
Ty Pwca Rd.
NP44: Pnwd, Up Cwm 5C **8**
TY RHIW 1F 69
Ty-Rhiw CF15: Taff W 1F **69**
Tyrhiw Est. CF15: Taff W 1F **69**
Ty'r Person CF38: Chu V 2E **43**
Tyr Sianel CF63: Barry 3H **117**
Ty'r Waun CF15: N'grw 3F **45**
Tyrwhitt Cres. CF23: Cyn 2A **86**
Tyr Winch Rd. CF3: Old M 6B **74**
Tyr-y-Sarn Rd. CF3: Rum 4H **87**
Ty'r Ysgol CF24: Card 4H **5**
TY-SIGN 5F 17
Ty-to-Maen Cl. CF3: Old M 5C **74**
Ty Trappa NP44: Pnwd 5C **8**
Ty Trappa Pl. NP44: Pnwd 5C **8**
Ty Tudor NP44: C'brn 2H **11**
Ty Twyn CF38: Chu V 2D **42**
Ty Uchaf CF64: P'rth 3C **108**
Ty Verlon Ind. Est. CF63: Barry 6E **107**
Ty-Wern Av. CF14: R'ina 1E **85**
Ty-Wern Rd. CF14: Heath, R'ina 1E **85**

U

Ullswater Av. CF23: Cyn . . . 4A **86**
Ullswater Ct. NP44: St D . . . 2E **11**
Underhill Dr. CF38: Tont . . . 2G **43**
UNDERWOOD . . . 3H **39**
Underwood CF83: Caer . . . 2D **46**
Underwood Ter. CF37: P'prdd . . . 5A **14**
CF83: Abert . . . 2F **27**
UNDY . . . 4F **59**
Union St. CF37: P'prdd . . . 1C **24**
Universal St. CF11: Card . . . 5H **95**
University Ct. CF23: Pen L . . . 4C **86**
UNIVERSITY DENTAL HOSPITAL . . . 4G **85**
UNIVERSITY HOSPITAL OF WALES (YSBYTY ATHROFAOL CYMRU) . . . 4H **85**
University of Cardiff
Bute Building . . . 1B **4 (2H 95)**
Glamorgan Building . . . 2C **4 (3A 96)**
Museum Av. . . . 1C **4 (2A 96)**
North Rd. . . . 1B **4 (2H 95)**
The Parade . . . 2F **5 (3B 96)**
University of Glamorgan
Adamsdown . . . 4F **5 (4B 96)**
Trefforest . . . 3D **24**
University of Wales . . . 2C **4 (3A 96)**
University of Wales Institute, Cardiff
Colchester Avenue Campus . . . 6E **87**
Cyncoed Campus . . . 3C **86**
Howard Gdns. Campus . . . 3G **5 (3C 96)**
Llandaff Campus . . . 6D **84**
University of Wales, Newport
Allt-yr-yn Campus . . . 4A **36**
Caerleon Campus . . . 4G **21**
University of Wales, Newport Sports Cen. . . . 4G **21**
University Pl. CF24: Card . . . 3E **97**
Uphill Cl. CF64: Sul . . . 1H **119**
Uphill Rd. CF3: L'rmy . . . 2H **87**
Upland Dr. NP4: Trev . . . 1B **6**
UPLANDS, THE . . . 3B **34**
Uplands, The CF15: Rad . . . 1F **83**
NP10: Roger . . . 3B **34**
Uplands Ct. NP10: Roger . . . 3B **34**
NP19: Newp . . . 3F **37**
Uplands Cres. CF64: L'dgh . . . 5G **101**
Uplands Rd. CF3: Rum . . . 5G **87**
Uplands Ter. NP44: C'brn . . . 2E **11**
Up. Alma Ter. CF37: T'rest . . . 1D **24**
UPPER BOAT . . . 6B **26**
Up. Boat Ind. Pk. CF37: Up Bo . . . 6A **26**
Up. Bridge St. NP4: P'pool . . . 3C **6**
Up. Church St. CF37: P'prdd . . . 6C **14**
NP16: Chep . . . 1E **63**
UPPER CHURCH VILLAGE . . . 2E **43**
Uppercliff Cl. CF64: P'rth . . . 6B **102**
Uppercliff Dr. CF64: P'rth . . . 1G **109**
Up. Clifton St. CF24: Card . . . 1H **5 (2D 96)**
Up. Cosmeston Farm
CF64: P'rth . . . 6E **109**
UPPER CWMBRAN . . . 5B **8**
Up. Cwmbran Rd.
NP44: Up Cwm . . . 5A **8**
Up. Dock St. NP20: Newp . . . 4C **36**
Up. Francis St. CF83: Abert . . . 2D **26**
Up. Glyn Gwyn St. CF83: Tret . . . 2A **30**
Up. Kincraig St. CF24: Card . . . 1C **96**
Upper Mdw. CF5: Ely . . . 6F **93**
Up. Nelson St. NP16: Chep . . . 2E **63**
UPPER OCHRWYTH . . . 2D **32**
Up. Park Ter. NP4: P'pool . . . 3C **6**
Up. Power St. NP20: Newp . . . 3B **36**
UPPER RACE . . . 5A **6**
Up. Tennyson Rd. NP19: Newp . . . 4F **37**
Up. Trosnant St. NP4: P'pool . . . 3C **6**
Up. Tyn-y-Parc Ter. CF14: R'ina . . . 1D **84**
Up. Vaughan St. CF37: P'prdd . . . 6B **14**
Upton La. NP20: Newp . . . 5H **35**
Upton Pl. CF38: Bed . . . 5A **42**
Upton Rd. NP20: Newp . . . 5H **35**
Usk Cl. NP26: Cald . . . 3D **60**
Usk Ct. NP44: Thorn . . . 1D **10**
Uskley Ct. CF3: St M . . . 1C **88**
Usk Rd. CF14: L'shn . . . 5A **72**
NP4: Lit M, New I, P'pool . . . 4E **7**
Usk Rd. NP16: Chep, Pwllm . . . 1A **62**
NP18: C'ln . . . 5H **21**
Uskside NP18: C'ln . . . 6A **22**
Usk St. NP19: Newp . . . 3D **36**
Usk Va. Cl. NP18: C'ln . . . 4H **21**
Uskvale Ct. NP4: P'pool . . . 3F **7**
Usk Va. Dr. NP18: C'ln . . . 4H **21**
Usk Va. M. NP18: C'ln . . . 4H **21**
Uskvale Vw. NP18: C'ln . . . 6A **22**
Usk Vw. NP19: Newp . . . 1G **37**
Usk Way CF62: Barry . . . 1E **117**
NP20: Newp . . . 5C **36**
Usk Way Ind. Est.
NP20: Newp . . . 6D **36**
UWIC Inter Cardiff FC . . . 3D **86**

V

Vachell Ct. CF61: Bov . . . 3D **110**
Vachell Rd. CF5: Ely . . . 4G **93**
Vaindre Cl. CF3: St M . . . 5E **75**
Vaindre Dr. CF3: St M . . . 5E **75**
Vaindre La. CF3: St M . . . 5E **75**
(Clos Elphan)
CF3: St M . . . 5D **74**
(Heritage Pk.)
Valarian Cl. CF3: St M . . . 1F **89**
Vale Ct. CF64: Din P . . . 2H **107**
CF71: C'bri . . . 4E **91**
Vale Ent. Cen. CF64: Sul . . . 2F **119**
Vale Gdns. CF37: P'prdd . . . 5B **14**
Valegate Bus. Pk. CF5: Cul C . . . 1D **98**
Valegate Retail Pk. CF5: Cul C . . . 1C **98**
Vale Hotel, Golf & Spa Resort . . . 6E **79**
Valentine La. NP16: Bul . . . 6F **63**
Vale of Glamorgan Health and Racquets Club . . . 6F **79**
Vale of Glamorgan Steam Railway and Heritage Cen. . . . 5H **117**
Vale Rd. CF24: Card . . . 2E **97**
Vale St. CF62: Barry . . . 3E **117**
Vale Touring Cvn. Pk. CF62: P'ark . . . 3H **115**
Vale Vw. CF62: Barry . . . 5F **105**
NP11: Ris . . . 5E **17**
NP19: Newp . . . 2G **37**
NP44: H'lys . . . 5B **10**
Vale Vw. Cl. CF64: L'dgh . . . 5F **101**
Vale Vw. Cres. CF64: L'dgh . . . 5F **101**
Valley Ent. CF83: B'ws . . . 3F **29**
Valley Vw. CF3: Rum . . . 3B **88**
VAN . . . 1E **47**
Vanbrugh Cl. NP10: Roger . . . 3D **34**
Vanbrugh Gdns. NP20: Newp . . . 2G **53**
Vancouver Dr. NP20: Newp . . . 6F **35**
Van Dyke Cl. NP19: Newp . . . 2F **37**
Vanfield Cl. CF83: Caer . . . 1E **47**
Vanguard Way CF24: Card . . . 5D **96**
Van Ind. Est. CF83: Caer . . . 1E **47**
Van Rd. CF83: Caer . . . 1D **46**
Van St. CF11: Card . . . 6G **95**
Van Ter. CF83: Caer . . . 1F **47**
Vaughan Av. CF5: L'dff . . . 1B **94**
Vaughan Ct. NP10: Coedk . . . 4E **53**
Vaughan St. CF37: P'prdd . . . 6B **14**
Vaughan Williams Dr.
NP19: Newp . . . 4A **38**
Vauxhall La. NP16: Chep . . . 2D **62**
Vauxhall Rd. NP16: Chep . . . 3D **62**
Vega Ho. CF10: Card . . . 1D **102**
Velindre Ct. CF14: Whit . . . 2B **84**
VELINDRE HOSPITAL (YSBYTY FELINDRE) . . . 2B **84**
Velindre Pl. CF14: Whit . . . 2B **84**
Velindre Rd. CF14: Whit . . . 2A **84**
Vellacott Cl. CF10: Card . . . 5B **96**
Vendre Cl. CF3: St M . . . 4E **75**
Venosa Trad. Est. CF83: Caer . . . 5D **28**
Ventnor Pl. CF14: Card . . . 5F **85**
Ventnor Rd. NP44: C'brn . . . 3G **11**
Venture Pk. NP19: Newp . . . 5E **37**
Venwood Cl. CF5: Wen . . . 5E **99**
Verallo Dr. CF11: Card . . . 4D **94**
Verbena Cl. CF3: St M . . . 5E **75**
Vere St. CF24: Card . . . 1G **5 (2C 96)**
CF63: Barry . . . 1C **118**
Veritys Ct. CF71: C'bri . . . 3C **90**
Verlands, The CF71: C'bri . . . 3B **90**
Verlands Cl. CF5: L'dff . . . 1C **94**
Verlon Cl. CF63: Barry . . . 6E **107**
Vermeer Cres. NP19: Newp . . . 2G **37**
Vernon Gro. NP26: C'ent . . . 1B **60**
Verona Ct. CF10: Card . . . 5B **96**
Verona Pl. CF63: Barry . . . 6C **106**
Veronica Cl. NP10: Roger . . . 6D **34**
Vervain Cl. CF5: Ely . . . 4E **93**
Viaduct Cl. NP10: Bass . . . 6D **34**
Viaduct Ct. NP4: P'pool . . . 4D **6**
Viaduct Rd. CF15: Gwae G . . . 3E **69**
CF63: Barry . . . 3B **118**
Viaduct Vw. NP10: Bass . . . 6D **34**
Viaduct Way NP10: Bass . . . 6D **34**
Viburnum Ri. CF38: Llan F . . . 6C **42**
Vicarage Cl. NP10: Bass . . . 1D **52**
Vicarage Ct. CF3: M'fld . . . 3H **75**
CF38: Chu V . . . 1F **43**
Vicarage Gdns. CF3: M'fld . . . 4H **75**
NP10: Roger . . . 3A **34**
NP26: C'ent . . . 1B **60**
Vicarage Hill NP20: Newp . . . 5B **36**
(not continuous)
Vicarage M. CF11: Card . . . 3F **95**
Victoria Av. CF5: Card . . . 3D **94**
CF64: P'rth . . . 2E **109**
NP19: Newp . . . 4E **37**
Victoria Bri. CF64: P'rth . . . 1E **109**
Victoria Cl. NP20: Newp . . . 5C **36**
Victoria Ct. NP19: Newp . . . 4E **37**
Victoria Cres. NP20: Newp . . . 5B **36**
Victoria Hall CF10: Card . . . 1H **95**
Victoria Ho. CF11: Card . . . 6A **4 (5H 95)**
Victoria La. NP19: Newp . . . 3F **37**
(not continuous)
Victoria M. CF14: Card . . . 5G **85**
Victoria Pk. Rd. CF63: Barry . . . 6B **106**
Victoria Pk. Rd. E. CF5: Card . . . 3D **94**
Victoria Pk. Rd. W.
CF5: Card . . . 2C **94**
Victoria Pl. CF10: Card . . . 4D **4 (4A 96)**
NP20: Newp . . . 5C **36**
Victoria Rd. CF14: Whit . . . 2C **84**
CF62: Barry . . . 4E **117**
CF64: P'rth . . . 3D **108**
NP4: P'pool . . . 4D **6**
NP16: Bul . . . 5F **63**
NP20: Newp . . . 5C **36**
Victoria Sq. CF64: P'rth . . . 2E **109**
Victoria St. NP4: Grif . . . 6E **7**
NP44: C'brn . . . 3G **11**
Victoria Wlk. NP20: Newp . . . 5C **36**
Victoria Way NP26: Undy . . . 4E **59**
Victoria Wharf CF11: Card . . . 5H **101**
Vigar Ter. NP11: Ris . . . 6E **17**
Viking Pl. CF10: Card . . . 1F **103**
Village Way CF15: Tong . . . 5A **70**
Villas, The NP26: Sud . . . 6H **61**
Vincent Cl. CF63: Barry . . . 5C **106**
Vincent Ct. CF5: Ely . . . 3A **94**
Vincent Rd. CF5: Ely . . . 3A **94**
Vine Cotts. *NP16: Chep* . . . *2E 63*
(off Portwall Rd.)
VINEGAR HILL . . . 4E **59**
Vinegar Hill NP26: Undy . . . 3E **59**
Vine Pl. NP19: Newp . . . 3E **37**
Violet Pl. CF14: Whit . . . 3F **85**
Violet Row CF24: Card . . . 1B **96**
Violet Wlk. NP10: Roger . . . 2G **33**
Virgil Ct. CF11: Card . . . 6G **95**
Virgil St. CF11: Card . . . 6G **95**
Virginia Cl. CF83: Caer . . . 5D **28**
Virginia Ter. CF83: Caer . . . 5C **28**
Virginia Vw. CF83: Caer . . . 5D **28**
Viscount Evan Dr. NP10: Duf . . . 4H **53**
Vishwell Rd. CF5: Card . . . 2D **94**
CF5: Wen . . . 6E **99**
Vista Ri. CF5: L'dff . . . 5H **83**
Vivian Rd. NP19: Newp . . . 5E **37**
Voss Pk. Cl. CF61: Llan M . . . 3D **110**
Voss Pk. Dr. CF61: Llan M . . . 3D **110**
Voysey Pl. CF5: F'wtr . . . 2G **93**
Vue Cinema
Cardiff . . . 6B **4 (5H 95)**

W

Wades, The *NP44: F'wtr* 4D **10**
(off Rede Rd.)
Waghausel Cl. NP26: Cald 5C **60**
Wagtail Cl. CF23: Pontp 2H **73**
Wagtail Rd. CF62: St Ath 3G **111**
Wain Cl. CF23: Pontp 4H **73**
WAINFELIN 2A **6**
Wainfelin Av. NP4: P'pool 2A **6**
Wainfelin Rd. NP4: P'pool 1B **6**
Wakehurst Pl. CF3: St M 6D **74**
Wakelin Cl. CF38: Chu V 3E **43**
Walden Grange Cl. NP19: Newp 4H **37**
Wales Millennium Cen. 1C **102**
Wales National Velodrome 1H **55**
Wales Sports Cen. for the Disabled 3C **86**
Walford Davies Dr. NP19: Newp 4A **38**
Walford Pl. CF11: Card 4F **95**
Walford St. NP20: Newp 2B **36**
Walk, The CF3: Rum 4G **87**
CF24: Card 2F **5** (3B **96**)
NP4: New I 5G **7**
Walkdens NP44: F'wtr 4D **10**
Walker Flats NP26: Sud 6H **61**
Walker Rd. CF24: Card 4E **97**
CF62: Barry 1G **117**
Walk Farm Dr. CF3: Cas 1G **75**
Wallis St. NP20: Newp 1D **54**
WALLSTON 4D **98**
Wallwern Wood NP16: Chep 1C **62**
Walmer Rd. NP19: Newp 4F **37**
Walnut Cl. CF72: Mis 5F **65**
Walnut Dr. NP18: C'ln 5E **21**
Walnut Gro. CF62: E Bre 2B **112**
NP26: Cri 1E **61**
Walnut Tree Cl. CF15: Rad 6E **69**
Walpole Cl. CF3: L'rmy 5A **74**
Walsall St. NP19: Newp 5E **37**
Walston Cl. CF5: Wen 4E **99**
Walston Rd. CF5: Wen 4D **98**
Walters Rd. CF37: P'prdd 2B **24**
Walton Cl. NP19: Newp 5A **38**
Walton Pl. CF11: Card 6F **95**
Waltwood Rd. NP18: Under 3H **39**
Walwyn Pl. CF3: St M 2D **88**
Wanderers Cres. CF5: Ely 5E **93**
Ward Cl. NP19: Newp 2G **37**
Ware Rd. CF83: Caer 2A **46**
Warlock Cl. NP19: Newp 3D **38**
Warlow Cl. CF62: St Ath 5D **112**
Warren Cl. CF37: R'fln 4G **25**
Warrendale *NP44: F'wtr* 4D **10**
(off Rede Rd.)
Warren Dr. CF83: Caer 2D **46**
Warren Evans Ct. CF14: Whit 3D **84**
Warren Slade NP16: Bul 5F **63**
Warwick Cl. NP4: New I 1G **9**
NP16: Bul 4D **62**
NP44: G'mdw 2C **10**
Warwick Ho. CF10: Card 4B **4**
Warwick La. NP19: Newp 4G **37**
Warwick Pl. CF11: Card 6H **95**
Warwick Rd. NP19: Newp 4G **37**
Warwick St. CF11: Card 6H **95**
Warwick Way CF62: Barry 1H **117**
Wasdale Cl. CF23: Pen L 5B **86**
Washford Av. CF3: L'rmy 6A **74**
Watchet Cl. CF3: L'rmy 2H **87**
Watch Ho. Pde. NP20: Newp 2C **54**
(not continuous)
Water Avens Cl. CF3: St M 1F **89**
Waterfall M. CF61: Llan M 4C **110**
Waterford Cl. CF11: Card 5G **95**
Waterhall Rd. CF5: F'wtr 6H **83**
Waterhouse Dr. CF11: Card 6F **95**
WATERLOO 4D **30**
Waterloo Cl. CF23: Pen L 6E **87**
Waterloo Ct. NP4: Seba 3E **9**
Waterloo Gdns. CF23: Pen L 1D **96**
Waterloo Pl. CF83: Mac 4D **30**
Waterloo Rd. CF23: Pen L 5D **86**
NP20: Newp 1A **54**
Waterloo Ter. Rd. CF83: Mac 4D **30**
Watermark CF11: Card 4A **102**

Waterside Bus. Pk. CF3: Rum 5H **87**
Waterside Cl. NP10: Roger 2C **34**
Waterside Ct. NP20: Newp 1C **36**
Waterside Wlk. W. NP10: Roger 3C **34**
Waters La. NP20: Newp 4B **36**
Waters Rd. NP16: Chep 3E **63**
Waterston Ct. CF14: Llan N 5D **84**
Waterston Rd. CF14: Llan N 5D **84**
Watery La. CF71: Wel 1G **91**
Watford Cl. CF83: Caer 2B **46**
WATFORD PARK 2B **46**
Watford Ri. CF83: Caer 2C **46**
Watford Rd. CF24: Card 1F **97**
CF83: Caer 3B **46**
Watkins La. NP20: Newp 5H **35**
Watkins Sq. CF14: L'shn 6F **71**
Watkins Wlk. *NP10: Roger* 5D **34**
(off Ebenezer Dr.)
Watkiss Way CF11: Card 4H **101**
Watson Rd. CF14: Llan N 5C **84**
Watson St. CF63: Barry 2A **118**
Watt Cl. NP20: Malp 4A **20**
Watton Cl. CF14: L'shn 5G **71**
Watts Cl. NP10: Roger 3D **34**
Waun Ddyfal CF14: Heath 1F **85**
Waun Erw CF83: Caer 4D **28**
Waun Fach CF23: Pent 6E **73**
Waunfach Flats CF83: Caer 5C **28**
Waunfach St. CF83: Caer 5C **28**
Waunfain CF83: Caer 3B **28**
Waunfawr Gdns. NP11: Cros K 4B **16**
Waunfawr Ho. NP11: Cros K 4A **16**
Waunfawr Pk. Rd. NP11: Cros K 3A **16**
Waunfawr Rd. NP11: Cros K 3A **16**
Waun-Fawr Rd. CF14: R'ina 1F **85**
Waunfawr Ter. NP11: Cros K 3A **16**
Waun Ganol CF64: P'rth 4C **108**
Waunganol St. CF83: Caer 5D **28**
Waun Gron CF61: Llan M 2C **110**
Waun-Gron Park Station (Rail) 2B **94**
Waun Gron Rd. CF5: L'dff 2B **94**
Waun Hir CF38: E Isaf 6F **43**
Waun Hywel Rd. NP44: Pnwd 5C **8**
Waun Lee Ct. CF23: Pent 5E **73**
Waun Rd. NP44: C'brn 4E **11**
Wauntreoda Rd. CF14: Whit 3E **85**
Waunwaelod Way CF83: Caer 5A **46**
Waunwern Pk. Cvn. Site NP4: P'pool 4A **6**
Waun-y-Groes Av. CF14: R'ina 6E **71**
Waun-y-Groes Rd. CF14: R'ina 6E **71**
Wavell Cl. CF14: L'shn 1H **85**
Wavell Dr. NP20: Malp 3A **20**
Waveney Cl. NP20: Bet 5E **19**
Waverley Cl. CF64: L'dgh 5G **101**
Waverley Sq. CF10: Card 2B **102**
Waycock Cross CF62: Barry 1C **116**
Waycock Rd. CF62: Barry 6C **104**
Wayfield Cres. NP44: C'brn 6E **9**
Weare Cl. NP20: Bet 5E **19**
Webley Cl. NP18: C'ln 3G **21**
Webley Gdns. NP18: C'ln 3G **21**
Wedal Rd. CF14: Card 5A **86**
Wedgewood Ct. CF83: Caer 6F **29**
Wedgewood Dr. NP26: Pskwt 5H **61**
Wedmore Rd. CF11: Card 6A **4** (5G **95**)
Wednesbury St. NP19: Newp 5E **37**
Weekes Cl. CF3: L'rmy 6B **74**
Welby La. CF5: Card 4F **95**
Welby Rd. CF5: Card 4F **95**
Welch Regiment Mus., The
(41st Regiment & 69th Regiment of Foot) 3C **4** (3A **96**)
Weldon Cl. NP44: C'iog 6H **9**
Welford St. CF62: Barry 4F **117**
Welland Circ. NP20: Bet 5E **19**
Welland Cres. NP20: Bet 5E **19**
Well Cl. NP16: Bul 6F **63**
Wellfield CF38: Bed 3A **42**
Wellfield Ct. CF3: M'fld 5H **75**
CF38: Chu V 1E **43**
CF63: Barry 4A **106**
Wellfield La. NP4: Seba 2D **8**
Wellfield M. CF38: Bed 3A **42**
Wellfield Pl. CF24: Card 1C **96**
Wellfield Rd. CF3: M'fld 5H **75**
CF24: Card 1C **96**

Wellington Dr. NP44: G'mdw 2C **10**
Wellington La. NP4: P'pool 3A **6**
Wellington Rd. NP20: Newp 6F **35**
Wellington St. CF11: Card 4F **95**
CF15: Tong 4G **69**
Wellright Rd. CF5: F'wtr 2H **93**
Wells Cl. NP20: Newp 2G **53**
Wellspring Ter. NP11: Ris 6E **17**
Wells St. CF11: Card 4G **95**
Wells St. La. *CF11: Card* 4G **95**
(off Wyndham Pl.)
Well Wlk. CF62: Barry 5E **117**
Wellwood CF23: L'dyrn 4E **87**
Well Wood Cl. CF23: Pen L 5E **87**
Wellwood Dr. CF64: Din P 3G **107**
Welsh Assembly Government Offices 1B **4** (2H **95**)
Welsh Hawking Cen. 6C **104**
Welsh Institute of Sport 1A **4** (3G **95**)
Welsh National Opera 1C **102**
(within Wales Millennium Cen.)
Welsh National Tennis Cen. 6H **5** (5D **96**)
Welsh St. NP16: Chep 1C **62**
Welwyn Rd. CF14: Whit 2E **85**
Wembley Rd. CF5: Card 4E **95**
Wenallt Ct. CF14: R'ina 5D **70**
Wenallt Mans. *CF14: Thorn* 1G **71**
(off Heol Llinos)
Wenallt Rd. CF14: R'ina 3C **70**
WENTLOOG 5A **88**
Wentloog Av. CF3: Pet W, Rum 6A **88**
Wentloog Cl. CF3: Rum 4H **87**
NP44: C'brn 2G **11**
Wentloog Corporate Pk.
CF3: Rum 3D **88**
Wentloog Ct. CF3: Rum 4H **87**
Wentloog Ri. CF3: Cas 2G **75**
Wentloog Rd. CF3: Rum 4H **87**
Wentsland Cres. NP4: P'pool 3A **6**
Wentsland Rd. NP4: P'pool 3A **6**
Wentwood Cl. NP44: Pnwd 5C **8**
Wentwood Pl. NP11: Ris 6G **17**
Wentwood Rd. NP18: C'ln 5E **21**
Wentwood Vw. NP26: Cald 3C **60**
Wentworth Cl. CF3: St M 5E **75**
NP10: Bass 6B **34**
Wentworth La. CF3: St M 5E **75**
WENVOE 5E **99**
Wenvoe Cl. CF5: Wen 5E **99**
Wenvoe Ct. CF5: Ely 5G **93**
Wenvoe Ter. CF62: Barry 3F **117**
Werfa St. CF23: Card 6B **86**
Wernddu Ct. CF83: Caer 1F **47**
Wern-ddu Row CF83: Caer 2G **47**
Wern Fach Ct. NP44: H'lys 5B **10**
Wern Fawr Cl. CF3: Old M 5C **74**
Wern Fawr La. CF3: Old M 5C **74**
Wern Gethin La. CF3: St M 1E **89**
Wern-Gethin La. CF3: Rum 2C **88**
CF3: St M 1D **88**
Wern Goch E. CF23: Pent 1E **87**
Wern-Goch Rd. CF23: Cyn 1C **86**
Wern Goch W. CF23: L'dyrn 1D **86**
Wern Hill NP4: P'pool 3B **6**
Wern Ind. Est. NP10: Roger 3C **34**
Wern Migna CF5: St F 2C **82**
Wern Rd. NP4: Seba 2E **9**
Wern School Cl. NP4: Seba 2E **9**
Wern Ter. NP4: P'pool 3B **6**
NP10: Roger 3B **34**
Wern Trad. Est. NP10: Roger 4C **34**
Wesley Av. CF62: Rho 5D **114**
Wesley Bldg. NP26: Cald 5C **60**
Wesley Cl. NP44: C'brn 3F **11**
Wesley Ct. CF3: L'rmy 2A **88**
CF64: Din P 2G **107**
Wesley Hill CF83: Mac 2E **31**
Wesley La. CF10: Card 4E **5** (4B **96**)
(not continuous)
Wesley Pl. NP11: Ris 6D **16**
NP20: Newp 5B **36**
Wesley Rd. CF83: Caer 2H **45**
Wesley St. CF61: Llan M 3B **110**
NP44: C'brn 3G **11**
Wessex Pl. CF62: Barry 5E **117**
Wessex St. CF5: Card 3D **94**

WEST ABERTHAW .6E **113**
West Acre CF61: L'maes .1D **110**
West Av. CF83: Caer .6A **28**
NP4: Grif .2D **8**
West Bank NP44: Llanf .3B **12**
Westbourne Ct. CF3: Rum .5A **88**
CF63: Barry .5C **106**
Westbourne Cres.
CF14: Whit .3A **84**
Westbourne Rd. CF14: Whit .3B **84**
CF64: P'rth .4E **109**
Westbury Cl. CF63: Barry .6B **106**
Westbury Ter. CF5: Card .2D **94**
W. Bute St. CF10: Card .1C **102**
W. Canal Wharf CF10: Card .6D **4** (5A **96**)
West Cl. CF10: Card .1B **102**
West End NP26: Magor .5C **58**
NP26: Undy .5E **59**
West End Gdns. NP26: Undy .4E **59**
West End Ter. CF61: Llan M .3A **110**
WEST-END TOWN .3A **110**
Western Av. CF5: F'wtr, L'dff .2B **94**
CF14: Card .1D **94**
NP16: Bul .5E **63**
NP20: Newp .5E **35**
Western Av. Ct. CF5: L'dff .2B **94**
Western Av. Nth. CF14: Llan N .6E **85**
Western Courtyard CF72: Taly .2C **78**
Western Dr. CF14: Llan N .6E **85**
CF83: Caer .2A **46**
Western Ind. Est. CF83: Caer .2A **46**
NP18: C'ln .3H **21**
Western Leisure Cen. .5H **93**
Western Ter. NP11: Cros K .2A **16**
Western Valley Rd. NP10: Roger .5D **34**
Westfield NP26: Cald .5B **60**
Westfield Av. CF14: Heath .2E **85**
NP20: Malp .5A **20**
NP26: Cald .5B **60**
Westfield Cl. NP18: C'ln .3F **21**
Westfield Ct. CF72: L'sant .3G **65**
Westfield Dr. CF64: P'rth .3C **108**
NP20: Malp .5A **20**
Westfield Gdns. NP20: Malp .5A **20**
Westfield Rd. CF14: Whit .3E **85**
CF37: Glync .2C **14**
NP18: C'ln .4F **21**
NP20: Newp .5A **36**
Westfield Way NP20: Malp .5A **20**
Westgate CF71: C'bri .3B **90**
Westgate Ct. NP18: C'ln .5H **21**
Westgate St. CF10: Card .4B **4** (4H **95**)
West Gro. CF5: Cul C .1D **98**
CF24: Card .2F **5** (3B **96**)
West Gro. Ct. CF24: Card .2F **5** (3B **96**)
Westhill Dr. CF72: L'sant .3G **65**
Westhill St. CF61: Llan M .3B **110**
Westland Cl. CF24: Card .2G **97**
West Lee CF11: Card .3A **4** (3G **95**)
W. Luton Pl. CF24: Card .4H **5** (4C **96**)
West Mkt. St. NP20: Newp .6C **36**
(not continuous)
Westminster Cres. CF23: Cyn .6C **72**
Westminster Dr. CF23: Cyn .5C **72**
CF64: Sul .2H **119**
Westmoor Cl. NP19: Newp .6A **38**
Westmoreland St. CF5: Card .4E **95**
W. Mound Cres. CF38: Tont .2G **43**
West Nash Rd. NP18: Nash .6B **56**
Weston Av. CF64: Sul .3H **119**
Westonbirt Cl. CF3: St M .1D **88**
Weston Ct. *CF38: Chu V .3F 43*
(off Station Rd.)
Weston Rd. CF3: L'rmy .2H **87**
Weston Sq. CF63: Barry .1B **118**
Weston St. CF63: Barry .1B **118**
W. Orchard Cres. CF5: Card .2C **94**
West Pk. La. NP20: Newp .5H **35**
West Pk. Rd. NP20: Newp .5H **35**
West Pl. NP4: P'pool .3C **6**
W. Point Ind. Est. CF11: Card .4G **101**
WEST PONTNEWYDD .6C **8**
WESTRA .2E **107**
Westra CF64: Din P .3D **106**
Westray Cl. NP19: Newp .2F **37**
West Ri. CF14: L'shn .5A **72**
West Rd. CF14: Llan N .4B **84**
CF64: Sul .1E **119**
West Roedin NP44: Coed E .5E **11**
West St. CF37: P'prdd .6D **14**
CF61: Llan M .3B **110**
NP20: Newp .4B **36**
West Ter. CF64: P'rth .1E **109**
West Vw. CF15: Taff W .1F **69**
NP44: C'brn .2E **11**
Westview Ter. CF83: Caer .4F **29**
WEST VILLAGE .3B **90**
Westville Rd. CF23: Pen L .6C **86**
NP20: Newp .5H **35**
Westville Wlk. CF23: Pen L .6C **86**
West Wlk. CF62: Barry .1F **117**
Westward Ri. CF62: Barry .5C **116**
Westway NP26: Rog .6A **60**
Westway Rd. NP20: Newp .2B **54**
Westwood Ct. CF64: P'rth .1E **109**
Wetlands Nature Reserve .2B **102**
Wexford Ct. CF23: Pontp .3G **73**
Wharfedale Rd. CF23: Pent .5F **73**
Wharf La. NP19: Newp .4E **37**
Wharf Rd. NP19: Newp .4E **37**
Wharf Rd. E. CF10: Card .6H **5** (5C **96**)
Wharton Cl. CF62: Rho .6C **114**
Wharton St. CF10: Card .4D **4** (4A **96**)
Wheate Cl., The CF62: Rho .5E **115**
Wheatley Rd. CF5: Ely .5G **93**
Wheatsheaf Ct. NP26: Magor .4D **58**
Wheeler St. NP20: Newp .2C **36**
Wheel La. NP10: St Bri W .3E **77**
Whinberry Way CF5: Ely .4E **93**
Whinchat Cl. CF3: St M .6E **75**
Whistler Cl. NP19: Newp .2F **37**
Whitaker Rd. CF24: Card .1G **97**
Whitby Pl. NP19: Newp .3D **36**
WHITCHURCH .3D **84**
WHITCHURCH HOSPITAL
(YSBYTY EGLWYS NEWYDD) .2B **84**
Whitchurch Pl. CF24: Card .6A **86**
Whitchurch Rd. CF14: Card .4G **85**
Whitchurch Station (Rail) .1C **84**
Whitcliffe Dr. CF64: P'rth .5F **109**
Whiteacre Cl. CF14: Thorn .3H **71**
White Ash Glade NP18: C'ln .5F **21**
White Av. NP10: Duf .6G **53**
White Barn Rd. CF14: L'shn .5F **71**
Whitebrook Way NP44: C'brn .3G **11**
Whitechapel Wlk. NP26: Undy .3E **59**
White Cosy Cnr. CF62: Barry .5G **117**
White Cross La. CF83: Caer .5H **27**
Whitefield Rd. CF14: Llan N .5C **84**
Whitehall Av. CF3: Rum .4G **87**
Whitehall Cl. CF5: Wen .4D **98**
White Hall Gdns. NP26: Undy .5F **59**
White Hall La. NP44: Llanf .3B **12**
Whitehall Pde. CF3: Rum .4H **87**
Whitehall Pl. CF3: Rum .4G **87**
Whitehall Rd. CF5: L'dff .6B **84**
White Hart Dr. CF83: Mac .2E **31**
White Hart La. NP18: C'ln .6A **22**
White Ho. CF62: Barry .6E **117**
Whitehouse Cl. NP44: C'iog .6G **9**
Whitehouse Rd. NP44: C'iog .6G **9**
White Oaks Dr. CF3: Old M .5C **74**
Whiterock Av. CF37: P'prdd .5B **14**
Whiterock Cl. CF37: P'prdd .5B **14**
Whiterock Dr. CF37: P'prdd .5B **14**
Whitesands Rd. CF14: L'shn .4F **71**
White St. CF83: Caer .1D **46**
Whitethorn CF3: M'fld .5A **76**
Whitewall NP26: Magor .5D **58**
White Water Cen. .5H **101**
Whiteways CF61: Llan M .2D **110**
Whitewell Dr. CF61: Llan M .4B **110**
Whitewell Rd. CF62: Barry .6F **105**
Whitland Cl. CF5: F'wtr .6H **83**
Whitland Cres. CF5: F'wtr .6A **84**
Whitmore Pk. Dr. CF62: Barry .6E **105**
Whitmuir Rd. CF24: Card .2F **97**
Whitstone Rd. NP19: Newp .3H **37**
Whittan Cl. CF62: Rho .6C **114**
Whittle Ct. NP20: Malp .4A **20**
Whittle Dr. NP20: Malp .4H **19**
Whittle Rd. CF11: Card .6E **95**
Whitworth Ct. CF11: Card .6A **4** (5H **95**)
Whitworth Sq. CF14: Whit .6A **70**
Wicken Cl. CF3: St M .6E **75**
Wicklow Cl. CF23: Pontp .4G **73**
Wick Rd. CF61: Llan M .2A **110**
Wick St. CF61: Llan M .2A **110**
Widecombe Dr. CF3: Rum .4G **87**
Wiesental Cl. NP26: Cald .4D **60**
Wigmore Cl. CF14: Thorn .3G **71**
WILCRICK .2A **58**
Wilcrick Pl. NP44: Pon'run .6F **9**
Wilde Ct. CF15: Rad .3H **83**
Wild Gdns. Rd. CF23: Cyn .2A **86**
Wilfred Brook Ho. CF11: Card .1H **101**
Wilfred St. CF63: Barry .2B **118**
Wilkinson Cl. CF24: Card .4D **96**
Wilkins Ter. CF83: Caer .3B **28**
Willenhall St. NP19: Newp .5E **37**
William Belcher Dr. CF3: St M .2E **89**
William Brown Cl. NP44: L'tnam .6A **12**
William Harris Bungs. CF83: Abert .2E **27**
William Lovett Gdns. NP20: Newp .5B **36**
William Morris Dr. NP19: Newp .3B **38**
William Nicholls Dr. CF3: Old M .5C **74**
Williams Cl. *NP20: Newp .6C 36*
(off Francis Dr.)
Williams Cres. CF62: Barry .2G **117**
Williams Pl. CF37: T'rest, Up Bo .6A **26**
(not continuous)
William St. CF11: Card .2F **95**
CF37: C'fydd .2F **15**
CF83: Abert .2E **27**
CF83: Tret .2A **30**
NP44: C'brn .6E **9**
Williams Way CF10: Card .6A **96**
(not continuous)
Willie Seager Cotts. CF23: Pen L .6D **86**
Willie Seager Memorial Homes
CF23: Pen L .6F **87**
Willins NP44: Coed E .5D **10**
Williton Rd. CF3: L'rmy .6A **74**
Willowbrook NP20: Bet .5F **19**
Willowbrook Dr. CF3: St M .6C **74**
Willowbrook Gdns. CF3: St M .6D **74**
Willowbrook Laboratory Units
CF3: St M .6D **74**
Willow Cl. CF38: Bed .6H **41**
CF64: P'rth .2C **108**
NP16: Bul .4E **63**
NP19: Newp .1H **55**
NP26: Cald .4C **60**
Willow Ct. CF24: Card .1H **5** (2C **96**)
Willow Cres. CF63: Barry .6A **106**
Willowdale Cl. CF5: F'wtr .1G **93**
Willowdale Rd. CF5: F'wtr .1F **93**
Willowdene Way CF3: St M .5E **75**
Willowfield Ct. CF23: Cyn .1C **86**
WILLOWFORD, THE .2C **44**
Willowford CF37: T'rest .3C **44**
Willowford, The CF37: T'rest .3C **44**
Willowford Rd. CF38: Tont .1A **44**
Willow Grn. NP18: C'ln .4F **21**
Willow Gro. CF3: St M .5E **75**
Willowherb Cl. CF3: St M .1F **89**
Willowmere CF64: L'dgh .4F **101**
Willow Rd. CF72: L'harry .5B **78**
Willows, The *CF62: St Ath .5D 112*
(off Gileston Rd.)
CF83: B'ws .2G **29**
NP26: Undy .4D **58**
Willows Av. CF24: Card .3F **97**
Willow St. CF37: R'fln .4G **25**
Willow Tree Cl. CF15: Rad .1D **82**
Willow Wlk. CF71: C'bri .3D **90**
NP10: Roger .2H **33**
Will Paynter Wlk. *NP19: Newp .2B 38*
(off Kier Hardie Dr.)
Wills Row NP10: Roger .4D **34**
Wilson Pl. CF5: Ely .5G **93**
Wilson Rd. CF5: Ely .4F **93**
NP19: Newp .2G **37**
Wilson St. CF24: Card .2E **97**
NP20: Newp .1D **54**
Wimborne Cres. CF64: Sul .2H **119**
Wimborne Ri. NP44: Pnwd .6C **8**
Wimbourne Cl. CF61: Llan M .4B **110**

Wimbourne Rd. CF63: Barry . . . 2C **118**
Winchester Av. CF23: Pen L . . . 5D **86**
Winchester Cl. CF62: Barry . . . 2F **117**
NP20: Newp . . . 2A **54**
Windermere Av. CF23: Cyn . . . 3A **86**
Windermere Ct. NP44: St D . . . 2E **11**
Windermere Sq. NP19: Newp . . . 1E **37**
Windflower Cl. CF3: St M . . . 6E **75**
Windhover Cl. CF3: St M . . . 1E **89**
Windlass Ct. CF10: Card . . . 6C **96**
Windmill Cl. CF14: Thorn . . . 3G **71**
CF61: Llan M . . . 2C **110**
Windmill Ind. Area CF64: Sul . . . 3D **118**
Windmill La. CF61: Llan M . . . 2C **110**
(not continuous)
CF71: L'thian . . . 4C **90**
Windmill Sq. *NP20: Newp . . . 6C* ***36***
(off Commercial Rd.)
Windrush Cl. NP20: Bet . . . 5G **19**
Windrush Pl. CF5: F'wtr . . . 1H **93**
Windsor Arc. CF64: P'rth . . . 1E **109**
Windsor Av. CF15: Rad . . . 1F **83**
Windsor Clive Dr. CF5: St F . . . 2C **82**
Windsor Cl. CF15: Rad . . . 1F **83**
CF61: Bov . . . 3D **110**
NP26: Magor . . . 4C **58**
Windsor Ct. CF15: Rad . . . 1F **83**
CF24: Card . . . 3G **5** (3C **96**)
CF64: P'rth . . . 2F **109**
CF72: P'clun . . . 6D **64**
Windsor Cres. CF15: Rad . . . 2G **83**
Windsor Dr. CF72: Mis . . . 6F **65**
NP26: Magor . . . 4C **58**
Windsor Esplanade CF10: Card . . . 2B **102**
Windsor Gdns. CF5: Ely . . . 3A **94**
CF38: Bed . . . 3A **42**
NP26: Magor . . . 4C **58**
Windsor Grn. CF5: Ely . . . 3A **94**
Windsor Gro. CF15: Rad . . . 1F **83**
Windsor Ho. CF10: Card . . . 4B **4** (4H **95**)
Windsor La. CF10: Card . . . 3E **5** (3B **96**)
CF64: P'rth . . . 6A **102**
Windsor Lofts *CF64: P'rth . . . 1F* ***109***
(off Ludlow La.)
Windsor M. CF24: Card . . . 4H **5** (4C **96**)
Windsor Pk. NP26: Magor . . . 4C **58**
Windsor Pl. CF10: Card . . . 2E **5** (3B **96**)
CF64: P'rth . . . 1E **109**
CF83: Abert . . . 2D **26**
NP10: Roger . . . 5D **34**
WINDSOR QUAY . . . 2A **102**
Windsor Rd. CF15: Rad . . . 2F **83**
CF24: Card . . . 4G **5** (4C **96**)
CF37: T'rest . . . 2E **25**
CF62: Barry . . . 4F **117**
CF64: P'rth . . . 5G **101**
NP4: Grif . . . 6E **7**
NP19: Newp . . . 5F **37**
NP44: F'wtr, G'mdw . . . 3D **10**
Windsor St. CF83: Caer . . . 1D **46**
Windsor Ter. CF10: Card . . . 2B **102**
CF64: P'rth . . . 1F **109**
NP20: Newp . . . 5B **36**
Windsor Ter. La. CF64: P'rth . . . 1F **109**
Windway Av. CF5: Card . . . 3C **94**
Windway Rd. CF5: Card . . . 2B **94**
Windyridge CF64: Din P . . . 3A **108**
Wine St. CF61: Llan M . . . 3B **110**
Wingate Dr. CF14: L'shn . . . 1H **85**
Wingate St. NP20: Newp . . . 2C **54**
Wingfield Av. CF38: Bed . . . 4H **41**
Wingfield Cl. CF37: P'prdd . . . 6E **15**
Wingfield Rd. CF14: Whit . . . 3B **84**
Winifred Av. CF62: Barry . . . 5G **105**
Winnipeg Dr. CF23: Cyn . . . 2C **86**
Winsford Rd. CF64: Sul . . . 3A **120**
Winston Av. CF5: Cul C . . . 1E **99**
Winston Rd. CF62: Barry . . . 5G **105**
Wintour Cl. NP16: Chep . . . 1D **62**
Wisley Pl. CF23: Pontp . . . 4E **73**
Wistaria Cl. NP20: Malp . . . 4B **20**
Wiston Path NP44: F'wtr . . . 3D **10**
Witham St. NP19: Newp . . . 5E **37**
Withy Cl. NP26: Magor . . . 4C **58**
Withycombe Rd. CF3: L'rmy . . . 5A **74**
Withy Wlk. NP26: Magor . . . 4C **58**
Witla Ct. Rd. CF3: Rum . . . 2A **88**
Wolfe Cl. CF63: Barry . . . 6C **106**
CF71: C'bri . . . 3B **90**
Wolfs Castle Av. CF14: L'shn . . . 4G **71**
Wolseley Cl. NP20: Newp . . . 2C **54**
Wolseley St. NP20: Newp . . . 2C **54**
Womanby St. CF10: Card . . . 4C **4** (4A **96**)
Woodbine Gdns. NP26: Magor . . . 4D **58**
Wood Cl. CF14: L'vne . . . 4B **72**
NP10: Roger . . . 2C **34**
NP44: Llanf . . . 4B **12**
Woodcock St. CF24: Card . . . 2C **96**
Wood Cotts. CF15: Taff W . . . 1F **69**
Wood Cres. NP10: Roger . . . 2C **34**
Woodfield Av. CF15: Rad . . . 3G **83**
Woodfield Cl. CF3: M'fld . . . 4A **76**
Woodfield Rd. CF72: T Grn . . . 3C **64**
NP4: New I . . . 5G **7**
Woodford Cl. CF5: L'dff . . . 6A **84**
Woodham Cl. CF62: Barry . . . 1F **117**
Woodham Pk. CF62: Barry . . . 1F **117**
Woodham Rd. CF63: Barry . . . 3A **118**
(not continuous)
Woodhouse CF62: Fon . . . 2B **114**
Woodland Ct. NP44: C'iog . . . 1A **12**
(not continuous)
Woodland Cres. CF15: Cre . . . 5E **67**
CF23: Cyn . . . 3C **86**
Woodland Dr. CF64: P'rth . . . 1E **109**
NP10: Bass . . . 6B **34**
NP10: Roger . . . 2A **34**
Woodland Flats CF83: L'brad . . . 1B **28**
Woodland Pk. Rd. NP19: Newp . . . 3F **37**
Woodland Pk. Vw. NP19: Newp . . . 3F **37**
Woodland Pl. CF24: Card . . . 1H **5** (2C **96**)
CF64: P'rth . . . 1E **109**
Woodland Rd. CF14: Whit . . . 3B **84**
CF38: Bed . . . 5A **42**
NP19: Newp . . . 3F **37**
NP44: C'iog . . . 6G **9**
Woodlands CF15: Morg . . . 4F **69**
Woodlands, The CF14: L'vne . . . 3B **72**
CF38: Llan F . . . 4B **42**
NP4: P'garn . . . 2D **6**
Woodlands Cl. CF71: C'bri . . . 3B **90**
Woodlands Ct. CF62: Barry . . . 2H **117**
Woodlands Dr. NP20: Malp . . . 3A **20**
Woodlands Pk. Dr. CF5: Ely . . . 6G **93**
Woodlands Rd. CF62: Barry . . . 2H **117**
CF63: Barry . . . 2H **117**
Woodland St. NP44: C'brn . . . 1E **11**
Woodlands Workshops
CF72: P'clun . . . 4C **64**
Woodland Ter. CF37: P'prdd . . . 1B **24**
(not continuous)
CF72: Tyle . . . 5B **64**
CF83: Abert . . . 2D **26**
Woodland Valley NP26: C'ent . . . 2C **60**
Woodland Vw. CF38: Chu V . . . 3D **42**
NP4: P'pool . . . 1B **6**
NP26: Cald . . . 4B **60**
NP26: Rog . . . 6A **60**
NP44: C'iog . . . 6G **9**
Woodlawn Way CF14: Thorn . . . 2G **71**
Woodley Ct. CF5: L'dff . . . 5H **83**
Wood Path NP44: C'iog . . . 5G **9**
Woodpecker Sq. CF62: St Ath . . . 3G **111**
Wood Rd. CF37: T'rest . . . 1D **24**
Woodruff Way CF14: Thorn . . . 2F **71**
Woodside CF5: Wen . . . 5E **99**
CF23: Pen L . . . 5C **86**
NP10: Duf . . . 4G **53**
Woodside Ct. CF14: L'shn . . . 4A **72**
Woodside Rd. NP44: C'brn . . . 1G **11**
Woodside Ter. NP44: C'brn . . . 1F **11**
Woodside Way NP44: C'brn . . . 1E **11**
Woodstock Cl. CF62: Barry . . . 2F **117**
NP26: Cald . . . 6C **60**
Woodstock Ct. NP26: Cald . . . 6C **60**
Woodstock Way NP26: Cald . . . 6C **60**
Wood St. CF10: Card . . . 6B **4** (5H **95**)
CF37: C'fydd . . . 2F **15**
CF64: P'rth . . . 1E **109**
Woodsy Cl. CF23: Pontp . . . 3G **73**
Woodvale Av. CF23: Cyn . . . 6C **72**
Woodview Ct. NP4: P'pool . . . 3B **6**
Wood Vw. Cres. NP11: Ris . . . 6E **17**
Wood Vw. Rd. NP11: Ris . . . 5E **17**
Woodview Ter. NP4: P'pool . . . 3B **6**
Woodville Ct. CF24: Card . . . 1A **96**
Woodville Rd. CF24: Card . . . 1A **96**
NP20: Newp . . . 5H **35**
Woodward Av. NP11: Cros K . . . 3A **16**
Woodward Rd. NP11: Cros K . . . 3A **16**
Woolacombe Av. CF3: L'rmy . . . 2A **88**
Woolaston Av. CF23: Cyn . . . 2B **86**
Woolmer Cl. CF5: L'dff . . . 5H **83**
Woolos Ct. NP20: Newp . . . 5B **36**
Woolpitch NP44: G'mdw . . . 2D **10**
Woolpitch Wood NP16: Chep . . . 2C **62**
Woosnham Cl. CF23: Pen L . . . 5E **87**
Worcester Cl. CF11: Card . . . 1H **101**
NP44: L'rfn . . . 2A **12**
Worcester Ct. CF11: Card . . . 2H **101**
Worcester Cres. NP19: Newp . . . 1F **37**
Worcester Path NP44: L'rfn . . . 2A **12**
Worcester St. CF11: Card . . . 1H **101**
Wordsworth Av. CF24: Card . . . 1H **5** (2C **96**)
CF64: P'rth . . . 1C **108**
Wordsworth Cl. CF61: Llan M . . . 3D **110**
NP26: Cald . . . 6B **60**
NP44: C'brn . . . 3F **11**
Wordsworth Gdns. CF37: R'fln . . . 3H **25**
Wordsworth Rd. NP19: Newp . . . 4F **37**
Working St. CF10: Card . . . 4D **4** (4A **96**)
Worle Av. CF3: L'rmy . . . 2H **87**
Worle Pl. CF3: L'rmy . . . 2H **87**
Worrells Pl. CF5: Ely . . . 1F **99**
Wren Cl. CF3: St M . . . 1E **89**
Wrenford Ct. *NP20: Newp . . . 5C* ***36***
(off Commercial St.)
Wren Rd. CF62: St Ath . . . 3G **111**
Wrexham Ct. CF3: Rum . . . 2C **88**
Wright Cl. NP19: Newp . . . 6H **37**
Wroughton Pl. CF5: Ely . . . 2A **94**
Wyebank Av. NP16: Tut . . . 1G **63**
Wyebank Cl. NP16: Tut . . . 2G **63**
Wyebank Cres. NP16: Tut . . . 2G **63**
Wyebank Dr. NP16: Tut . . . 1G **63**
Wyebank Pl. NP16: Tut . . . 2G **63**
Wyebank Ri. NP16: Tut . . . 2G **63**
Wyebank Rd. NP16: Tut . . . 2G **63**
Wyebank Vw. NP16: Tut . . . 2G **63**
Wyebank Way NP16: Tut . . . 2G **63**
Wye Cl. CF62: Barry . . . 1E **117**
Wye Ct. NP44: Thorn . . . 1D **10**
Wye Cres. NP16: Chep . . . 3E **63**
NP20: Bet . . . 5G **19**
Wye Dean Ct. NP16: Sed . . . 2H **63**
Wyelands Vw. NP16: Math . . . 6B **62**
Wye Valley Link Rd.
NP16: Chep, Math, Pwllm . . . 3D **62**
Wye Valley Wlk. NP16: Chep . . . 1D **62**
Wyeverne Ct. CF24: Card . . . 2A **96**
Wyeverne Rd. CF24: Card . . . 1A **96**
NP19: Newp . . . 4G **37**
Wyfan Pl. CF14: Card . . . 5F **85**
Wyncliffe Gdns. CF23: Pent . . . 5F **73**
Wyncliffe Rd. CF23: Pent . . . 5G **73**
Wyndham Arc. CF10: Card . . . 5D **4** (4A **96**)
Wyndham Cres. CF11: Card . . . 3F **95**
Wyndham Pl. CF11: Card . . . 4G **95**
Wyndham Rd. CF11: Card . . . 3F **95**
Wyndham St. CF11: Card . . . 4G **95**
(not continuous)
CF15: Tong . . . 4G **69**
CF63: Barry . . . 2H **117**
CF83: Mac . . . 2F **31**
NP20: Newp . . . 3C **36**
Wyndham Ter. CF14: L'shn . . . 5A **72**
NP11: Ris . . . 6F **17**
Wynd St. CF63: Barry . . . 1B **118**
Wynnstay Cl. CF11: Card . . . 6G **95**
Wyon Cl. CF5: L'dff . . . 4H **83**

Y

Yarrow Cl. CF5: Ely . . . 4E **93**
Y BONT-FAEN . . . 3D **90**
Y Cerigos CF62: Barry . . . 5D **116**
Y Cilgant CF83: Caer . . . 3A **28**

Y Clifordd CF83: Caer 5B **28**
Y Deri CF38: Llan F 5C **42**
Y Dolydd CF83: Caer 2B **46**
Yellow Row *NP4: P'pool* *4A* ***6***
(off Crumlin Rd.)
Yeo Cl. NP20: Bet 6F **19**
Yeo Rd. NP20: Bet 6G **19**
Yetts, The NP16: Sed 3H **63**
Yewberry Cl. NP20: Malp 5B **20**
Yewberry La. NP20: Malp, Newp 5B **20**
(not continuous)
Yew St. CF15: Taff W 1E **69**
Yew Tree Cl. NP26: Cald 6C **60**
Yewtree Cl. CF5: F'wtr 1G **93**
NP26: Undy 5E **59**
Yew Tree Ct. CF23: Pen L 5C **86**
CF62: Barry 4E **117**
Yewtree Gro. CF62: E Bre 2B **112**
Yew Tree La. NP18: C'ln 4H **21**
Yew Tree Ri. NP26: Rog 6A **60**
Yew Tree Ter. NP44: C'brn 3F **11**
NP44: C'iog 6G **9**
Yew Tree Wood NP16: Chep 2B **62**
Y Felin Ffrwd CF83: Caer 5A **28**
Y Goedwig CF14: R'ina 5C **70**
Y Groes CF14: R'ina 6D **70**
Y Nyll CF5: St Bri E 5H **81**
Ynysangharad Rd. CF37: P'prdd 6D **14**
Ynysangharad Swimming Pool **6C 14**
Ynys Bri. Ct. CF15: Gwae G 3F **69**
Ynysbryn Cl. CF72: T Grn 2E **65**
Ynys Cl. CF37: R'fln 3F **25**
Ynys Coed CF5: L'dff 1C **94**
Ynyscorrwg Rd. CF37: R'fln 5H **25**
Ynysddu CF72: P'clun 5C **64**
Ynysfach Yd. CF15: Tong 4F **69**
Ynys-Gyfelin Rd. CF37: P'prdd 5C **14**
Ynys Hir CF37: Glync 1D **14**
Ynys La. NP44: C'iog 6G **9**
Ynyslyn Rd. CF37: R'fln 5H **25**
YNYSMAERDY **6C 40**
Ynysmaerdy Ter. CF72: Y'erdy 6C **40**
Ynys Ter. CF37: R'fln 4F **25**
Ynys Wlk. NP26: Magor 6B **58**
YNYS Y BARRI **5G 117**
Ynysybwl Rd.
CF37: Y'bwl, P'prdd, Glync 1B **14**
Yorath Rd. CF14: Whit 2D **84**
York Cl. NP44: G'mdw 2C **10**
York Ct. CF10: Card 6G **5** (5C **96**)
CF15: Rad *1F* ***83***
(off Maes yr Awel)
York Dr. CF38: Llan F 5D **42**
York Pl. CF11: Card 2H **101**
CF62: Barry 4F **117**
NP11: Ris 4D **16**
NP20: Newp 5B **36**
York Rd. NP19: Newp 2E **37**
York St. CF5: Card 4E **95**
(not continuous)
Youghal Cl. CF23: Pontp 3G **73**
Youldon Ho. CF64: Din P 2H **107**
Y Parc CF72: Groes F 6B **66**
Yr Allt CF72: L'sant 2F **65**
Yr Arglawdd CF14: Heath 2H **85**
YR EGLWYS NEWYDD **3D 84**
Yr Graig CF72: L'sant 2E **65**
Y RHATH **1C 96**
Yr Hendre CF15: N'grw 3E **45**
Y Rhodfa CF63: Barry 3H **117**
Y RHWS **5F 115**
Yr Onnen CF72: L'harry 5C **78**
Ysgol Pl. NP44: Pnwd 5C **8**
Ysgubor Fach CF83: Mac 2F **31**
Ystradbarwig CF38: Llan F 5C **42**
Ystradbarwig Ter. CF38: Llan F 5C **42**
Ystrad Bldgs. *CF83: Tret* *3A* ***30***
(off Newport Rd.)
Ystrad Cl. CF3: St M 6E **75**
Ystrad St. CF11: Card 1A **102**

Z

Zinc St. CF24: Card 3D **96**
Zion Hill *NP4: P'nydd* *1A* ***6***
(off Pentrepiod Rd.)

Every possible care has been taken to ensure that, to the best of our knowledge, the information contained in this atlas is accurate at the date of publication. However, we cannot warrant that our work is entirely error free and whilst we would be grateful to learn of any inaccuracies, we do not accept any responsibility for loss or damage resulting from reliance on information contained within this publication.

The representation on the maps of a road, track or footpath is no evidence of the existence of a right of way.

The Grid on this map is the National Grid taken from Ordnance Survey® mapping with the permission of the Controller of Her Majesty's Stationery Office.

Copyright of Geographers' A-Z Map Company Ltd.

No reproduction by any method whatsoever of any part of this publication is permitted without the prior consent of the copyright owners.

SAFETY CAMERA INFORMATION

Safety camera locations are publicised by the Safer Roads Partnership who operate them in order to encourage drivers to comply with speed limits at these sites. It is the driver's absolute responsibility to be aware of and to adhere to speed limits at all times.

By showing this safety camera information it is the intention of Geographers' A-Z Map Company Ltd., to encourage safe driving and greater awareness of speed limits and vehicle speed. Data accurate at time of printing.

Printed and bound in the United Kingdom by Polestar Wheatons Ltd., Exeter

Cymerwyd pob gofal posibl i sicrhau, hyd eithaf ein gwybodaeth, fod y wybodaeth yn yr atlas hwn yn gywir adeg ei gyhoeddi. Fodd bynnag, ni allwn warantu bod ein gwaith yn gwbl ddi-frycheuyn ac er y byddai'n dda gennym glywed am unrhyw gamgymeriadau, nid ydym yn derbyn unrhym gyfrifoldeb am golled neu ddifrod sy'n digwydd yn sgîl dibynnu ar wybodaeth a gynhwysir yn y cyhoeddiad hwn.

Nid yw'r ffaith bod ffordd, trac neu lwybr wedi eu nodi ar y map yn brawf bod hawl tramwyo yn bodoli.

Y grid ar y map hwn yw'r Grid Cenedlaethol a gymerwyd oddi ar Fap yr Arolwg Ordnans® gyda chaniatâd Rheolwr Llyfrfa Ei Mawrhydi.

Hawlfraint Geographers' A-Z Map Co. Ltd.

Ni chaniateir atgynhyrchu, trwy unrhyw gyfrwng bynnag, unrhyw ran o'r cyhoeddiad hwn heb sicrhau caniatâd ymlaen llaw gan berchnogion yr hawlfraint.

GWYBODAETH CAMERA DIOGELWCH

Rhoddir cyhoeddusrwydd i leoliadau camerâu diogelwch gan y Bartneriaeth Ffyrdd Mwy Diogel sy'n eu gweithredu nhw, er mwyn annog gyrwyr i gydymffurfio â chyfyngiadau cyflymder yn y mannau hyn. Cyfrifoldeb llwyr y gyrrwr yw bod yn ymwybodol o gyfyngiadau cyflymder, a chadw atyn nhw, bob amser.

Drwy ddangos y wybodaeth am gamerâu diogelwch, bwriad Geographers' A-Z Map Company Ltd., yw annog gyrru diogel a gwell ymwybyddiaeth o gyfyngiadau cyflymder a chyflymder cerbydau. Roedd y data'n gywir pan aed i'r wasg.

Wedi'i argraffu a'i rwymo yn y Deyrnas Unedig gan Polestar Wheatons Ltd., Exeter